T0301427

NBER Macroeconomics Annual 2016

NBER Macroeconomics Annual 2016

Edited by
Martin Eichenbaum and Jonathan A. Parker

The University of Chicago Press
Chicago and London

NBER Macroeconomics Annual 2016, Number 31

Published annually by The University of Chicago Press.

Standing orders
To place a standing order for this book series, please address your request to The University of Chicago Press, Chicago Distribution Center, Attn. Standing Orders/Customer Service, 11030 S. Langley Avenue, Chicago, IL 60628. Telephone toll free in the U.S. and Canada: 1-800-621-2736; or 1-773-702-7000. Fax toll free in the U.S. and Canada: 1-800-621-8476; or 1-773-702-7212.

Single-copy orders
In the U.K. and Europe: Order from your local bookseller or direct from The University of Chicago Press, c/o John Wiley Ltd. Distribution Center, 1 Oldlands Way, Bognor Regis, West Sussex PO22 9SA, UK. Telephone 01243 779777 or Fax 01243 820250. E-mail: cs-books@wiley.co.uk

In the U.S., Canada, and the rest of the world: Order from your local bookseller or direct from The University of Chicago Press, Chicago Distribution Center, 11030 S. Langley Avenue, Chicago, IL 60628. Telephone toll free in the U.S. and Canada: 1-800-621-2736; or 1-773-702-7000. Fax toll free in the U.S. and Canada: 1-800-621-8476; or 1-773-702-7212.

Special orders
University of Chicago Press books may be purchased at quantity discounts for business or promotional use. For information, please write to Sales Department—Special Sales, The University of Chicago Press, 1427 E. 60th Street, Chicago, IL 60637 USA or telephone 1-773-702-7723.

This book was printed and bound in the United States of America.

ISSN: 0889-3365
ISBN-13: 978-0-226-49019-9 (hc.:alk.paper)
ISBN-13: 978-0-226-49036-6 (e-book)

10 9 8 7 6 5 4 3 2 1

Relation of the Directors to the Work and Publications of the NBER

1. The object of the NBER is to ascertain and present to the economics profession, and to the public more generally, important economic facts and their interpretation in a scientific manner without policy recommendations. The Board of Directors is charged with the responsibility of ensuring that the work of the NBER is carried on in strict conformity with this object.

2. The President shall establish an internal review process to ensure that book manuscripts proposed for publication DO NOT contain policy recommendations. This shall apply both to the proceedings of conferences and to manuscripts by a single author or by one or more co-authors but shall not apply to authors of comments at NBER conferences who are not NBER affiliates.

3. No book manuscript reporting research shall be published by the NBER until the President has sent to each member of the Board a notice that a manuscript is recommended for publication and that in the President's opinion it is suitable for publication in accordance with the above principles of the NBER. Such notification will include a table of contents and an abstract or summary of the manuscript's content, a list of contributors if applicable, and a response form for use by Directors who desire a copy of the manuscript for review. Each manuscript shall contain a summary drawing attention to the nature and treatment of the problem studied and the main conclusions reached.

4. No volume shall be published until forty-five days have elapsed from the above notification of intention to publish it. During this period a copy shall be sent to any Director requesting it, and if any Director objects to publication on the grounds that the manuscript contains policy recommendations, the objection will be presented to the author(s) or editor(s). In case of dispute, all members of the Board shall be notified,

and the President shall appoint an ad hoc committee of the Board to decide the matter; thirty days additional shall be granted for this purpose.

5. The President shall present annually to the Board a report describing the internal manuscript review process, any objections made by Directors before publication or by anyone after publication, any disputes about such matters, and how they were handled.

6. Publications of the NBER issued for informational purposes concerning the work of the Bureau, or issued to inform the public of the activities at the Bureau, including but not limited to the NBER Digest and Reporter, shall be consistent with the object stated in paragraph 1. They shall contain a specific disclaimer noting that they have not passed through the review procedures required in this resolution. The Executive Committee of the Board is charged with the review of all such publications from time to time.

7. NBER working papers and manuscripts distributed on the Bureau's web site are not deemed to be publications for the purpose of this resolution, but they shall be consistent with the object stated in paragraph 1. Working papers shall contain a specific disclaimer noting that they have not passed through the review procedures required in this resolution. The NBER's web site shall contain a similar disclaimer. The President shall establish an internal review process to ensure that the working papers and the web site do not contain policy recommendations, and shall report annually to the Board on this process and any concerns raised in connection with it.

8. Unless otherwise determined by the Board or exempted by the terms of paragraphs 6 and 7, a copy of this resolution shall be printed in each NBER publication as described in paragraph 2 above.

Contents

Editorial

Martin Eichenbaum, *Northwestern and NBER*
Jonathan A. Parker, *MIT and NBER*

The NBER's 31st Annual Conference on Macroeconomics brought together leading scholars to present, discuss, and debate six research papers on central issues in contemporary macroeconomics. We also lis-
tened to and questioned Lawrence Summers, former Treasury Secretary
of the United States, about the persistent slowdown in the growth rate
of output in advanced economies. Finally, we had a special panel ses-
sion on the economics of global commodities prices featuring James D.
Hamilton, Steven B. Kamin, and Steven H. Strongin. The panelists discussed the economics of oil and other commodity prices, including the
changing economic effect of prices on the US economy, how the slowdown of the Chinese economy and the rise of fracking have contributed
to recent price declines, and the implications of these factors for the
dynamics of oil prices in the future. At the previous year's 30th conference, we experimented with recording paper summaries and pre-
sentations by authors and making them available online through the
NBER Web pages. We have made such recordings a regular feature of
the *Macroeconomics Annual*, and we have expanded the available multimedia for the 31st conference to include the panel on commodity prices.
All recordings remain accessible on the NBER Web pages, and we hope
they make a useful complement to this volume.

This conference volume contains edited versions of the six papers
presented at the conference, each followed by two written discussions
by leading scholars and a summary of the debates that followed each
paper. A final chapter contains a paper by Lawrence Summers based on
his speech at the conference.

The first two of the six papers in this year's volume are rigorous and
data-driven analyses of the European financial crisis. The first paper,
"The Analytics of the Greek Crisis," by Pierre-Olivier Gourinchas,

Thomas Philippon, and Dimitri Vayanos analyzes the causes of the Greek Crisis of 2010 and the policy efforts that followed in its wake. Using a rich structural model, the authors find that Greece experienced a typical emerging-market sudden-stop crisis, but with the levels of debt exposure of an advanced economy. Tragically, Greece had few policy levers to soften the effects of the sudden stop. According to the estimates, financial assistance and alternative funding sources in 2009 and 2010 did help to mitigate the initial impact of the crisis. But those measures were insufficient to avoid one of the most extreme economic downturns on record. Both the presentation and the discussion focused on the key structural factors in the Greek economy that led to the crisis and the severity of the outcome.

The second paper on the European crisis, "Jump Starting the Euro-Area Recovery: Would a Rise in Core Fiscal Spending Help the Periphery?" is coauthored by Olivier Blanchard, Christopher J. Erceg, and Jesper Lindé. The authors' analysis implies that a fiscal expansion by the core euro-area economies would have a large and positive impact on periphery gross domestic product (GDP), assuming that policy rates remain low for a prolonged period. The state-of-the-art estimated DSGE model implies that an expansion of core government spending equal to 1% of euro-area GDP would boost periphery GDP by roughly 1% in a liquidity trap lasting three years, nearly half as large as the effect on core GDP. Consistent with the intuition based on a small-scale model, the estimated model implies that periphery GDP expands as domestic demand is "crowded in" by lower real interest rates, and as net exports are boosted by terms of trade depreciation and an expansion of domestic demand in the core economies.

Our third paper continues the theme of social scientific analyses of financial crises. "Macrofinancial History and the New Business Cycle Facts" by Òscar Jordá, Moritz Schularick, and Alan M. Taylor introduces a new set of stylized facts about economic growth and financial ratios as well as a new macrofinancial database for the study of financial booms and busts throughout history and around the world. In terms of new facts, the paper documents the increasing use of finance in the advanced economies over time, and how this trend accelerated in the second half of the twentieth century. Over time, as finance grew in importance, economies became more stable, but not less prone to financial crises. The paper documents many additional interesting patterns in the business cycle as well as how the patterns have changed over the long run. By taking a global, historical view of financial crises, the database enhances our ability to reject theories or policies based on overreliance on more spatially or temporally proximate crises, as well as allowing us to better predict, understand, and possibly avoid crises.

Our fourth and fifth papers deal with monetary policy and nominal rigidities, respectively. "Forward Guidance and Macroeconomic Outcomes since the Financial Crisis" by Jeffrey R. Campbell, Jonas D. M. Fisher, Alejandro Justiniano, and Leonardo Melosi studies one of the most hotly debated topics in recent US monetary policy, the efficacy of the Federal Reserve efforts to provide guidance about the future path of the funds rate, that is, forward guidance. The authors address this question using time series methods focused on identified forward guidance shocks and a state-of-the-art structural model. The analysis concludes that forward guidance was counterproductive until late 2011 when the Fed introduced "calendar-based" communications. Following that change, forward guidance boosted real activity and moved inflation closer to target.

Despite the long history of economic modelling and analysis of price stickiness, there is no consensus about how best to model price stickiness or how the conclusions of an analysis depend on the particular mathematical representation of price stickiness. The paper "Are State- and Time-Dependent Models Really Different?" by Fernando Alvarez, Franceso Lippi, and Juan Passadore addresses the questions of how to distinguish models of price setting and associated nominal frictions using data on price-setting behavior, and how sensitive the conclusions of any economic analysis are to the assumed model of price stickiness and the economic issues being addressed. The paper contrasts the two central approaches to modeling pricing frictions theoretically, and then, using these theoretical results, empirically.

State-dependent price setting has the feature that firms continuously monitor their prices and profits and adjust their actual price when it deviates sufficiently from an optimal price. Under time-dependent price setting, the timing of price adjustment depends on how much time has elapsed since the last price change and is independent of the evolution of the state of the firm. The paper shows that for small economic disturbances, the two modeling assumptions have quite similar economic implications, suggesting that results based on either type of model are robust to the particular price-setting friction assumed. This result, however, fails for large disturbances. The larger the shock, the more rapid is adjustment in a model with state dependence. The paper provides evidence from exchange rate pass-through into prices, testing whether pass-through is increasing in the size of exchange rate movements.

Our final paper by Paul Beaudry, Dana Galizia, and Franck Portier, "Is the Macroeconomy Locally Unstable and Why Should We Care?" is an ambitious effort that tackles a core issue in macroeconomics. Modern macroeconomic models almost always assume that, following shocks that induce a recession or boom, the economy will return over time to where it would have been in the absence of disturbances or at least return to its previous growth rate. Beaudry, Galizia, and Portier consider the possibility that the behavior of the economy is governed instead by nonlinear dynamics that lead it to cycle. Under these circumstances we would observe booms and busts even absent shocks. Whether this possibility is indeed the case cannot be determined by the analysis of linear models of the sort that are typically used to study the dynamics of the economy. The paper considers a class of simple nonlinear models that permit limit cycles, as well as local stability and global instability. The estimated models show that there is some evidence that the US economy is not locally stable. More robustly, whenever the estimated statistical models imply instability, the dynamics of the economy are not chaotic. Instead the model implies that the economy has limit cycles. This second result implies that even under this radically different view of economic dynamics, the current state of the economy contains useful information about its future state. Thus economic disturbances may not be the only causes of the business cycle. Booms can sometimes just die of old age.

The final chapter is a speech by Lawrence Summers, longtime NBER member, former US Treasury Secretary, and one of the authors in the inaugural issue of the *NBER Macroeconomics Annual*. In his talk, Larry began by reviewing the sluggish recent performance of the US economy, drawing focus to both the unusually sclerotic recovery and the repeated overestimation by markets and forecasters of the speed of the recovery, and increases in interest rates and inflation. The talk then turned to the limits of fiscal and monetary policy. Finally, Larry challenged the profession to step away from the set of models and methods that dominate academic discourse in macroeconomics and instead to pursue a more central role for elements that currently sit at the fringes, including multiple equilibria, hysteresis, and strong causal links from temporary economic disturbances to long-term economic growth. The published text of the talk provides an expanded look at the data and a set of challenges for research on macroeconomics going forward.

Finally, the authors and the editors would like to take this opportunity to thank Jim Poterba and the National Bureau of Economic Research for their continued support for the *NBER Macroeconomics Annual*
and the associated conference. We would also like to thank the NBER
conference staff, particularly Rob Shannon, for his continued excellent
organization and support. We would also like to thank the NBER Public
Information staff, and Charlie Radin in particular, for publicizing the
conference and producing the high-quality multimedia content. Financial assistance from the National Science Foundation is gratefully acknowledged. Arlene Wong and Daniel Green provided invaluable help
in preparing the summaries of the discussions. And last but far from
least, we are grateful to Helena Fitz-Patrick for her invaluable assistance in editing and publishing the volume.

Endnote

For acknowledgments, sources of research support, and disclosure of the authors' material financial relationships, if any, please see http://www.nber.org/chapters/c13763.ack.

Abstracts

1 The Analytics of the Greek Crisis
Pierre-Olivier Gourinchas, Thomas Philippon, and Dimitri Vayanos

We provide an empirical and theoretical analysis of the Greek crisis of 2010. We first benchmark the crisis against all episodes of sudden stops, sovereign debt crises, and lending booms/busts in emerging and advanced economies since 1980. The decline in Greece's output, especially investment, is deeper and more persistent than in almost any crisis on record over that period. We then propose a stylized macrofinance model to understand what happened. We find that a severe macroeconomic adjustment was inevitable given the size of the fiscal imbalance; yet, a sizable share of the crisis was also the consequence of the sudden stop that started in late 2009. Our model suggests that the size of the initial macro/financial imbalances can account for much of the depth of the crisis. When we simulate an emerging-market sudden stop with initial debt levels (government, private, and external) of an advanced economy, we obtain a Greek crisis. Finally, in recent years, the lack of recovery appears driven by elevated levels of nonperforming loans and strong price rigidities in product markets.

2 Jump Starting the Euro-Area Recovery: Would a Rise in Core Fiscal Spending Help the Periphery?
Olivier Blanchard, Christopher J. Erceg, and Jesper Lindé

We show that a fiscal expansion by the core economies of the euro area would have a large and positive impact on periphery GDP assuming that policy rates remain low for a prolonged period. Under our preferred model specification, an expansion of core government spending equal to 1% of euro-area GDP would boost periphery GDP by over 1% in a liquidity trap lasting three years, nearly half as large as the effect on core GDP. Accordingly, under a standard ad hoc loss function involving output and inflation gaps, increasing core spending would generate substantial welfare improvements, especially in the periphery. The benefits are considerably smaller under a utility-based welfare measure, reflecting in part that higher net exports play a material role in raising periphery GDP.

3   Macrofinancial History and the New Business Cycle Facts
Òscar Jordà, Moritz Schularick, and Alan M. Taylor

In advanced economies, a century-long, near-stable ratio of credit to GDP gave way to rapid financialization and surging leverage in the last forty years. This "financial hockey stick" coincides with shifts in foundational macroeconomic relationships beyond the widely noted return of macroeconomic fragility and crisis risk. Leverage is correlated with central business cycle moments, which we can document thanks to a decade-long international and historical data collection effort. More financialized economies exhibit somewhat less real volatility, but also lower growth, more tail risk, as well as tighter real-real and real-financial correlations. International real and financial cycles also cohere more strongly. The new stylized facts that we discover should prove fertile ground for the development of a new generation of macroeconomic models with a prominent role for financial factors.

4   Forward Guidance and Macroeconomic Outcomes since the Financial Crisis
Jeffrey R. Campbell, Jonas D. M. Fisher, Alejandro Justiniano, and Leonardo Melosi

This chapter studies the effects of FOMC forward guidance. We begin by using high-frequency identification and direct measures of FOMC private information to show that puzzling responses of private-sector forecasts to movements in federal funds futures rates on FOMC announcement days can be attributed entirely to Delphic forward guidance. However, a large fraction of futures rates' variability on announcement days remains unexplained, leaving open the possibility that the FOMC has successfully communicated Odyssean guidance. We then examine whether the FOMC used Odyssean guidance to improve macroeconomic outcomes since the financial crisis. To this end we use an estimated medium-scale New Keynesian model to perform a counterfactual experiment for the period 2009:Q1–2014:Q4, in which we assume the FOMC did not employ any Odyssean guidance and instead followed its reaction function from before the crisis as closely as possible while respecting the effective lower bound. We find that a purely rule-based policy would have delivered a shallower recession and kept inflation closer to target in the years immediately following the crisis than FOMC forward guidance did in practice. However, starting toward the end of 2011, after the Fed's introduction of "calendar-based" communications, the FOMC's Odyssean guidance appears to have boosted real activity and moved inflation closer to target. We show that our results do not reflect Del Negro, Giannoni, and Patterson's (2015) forward-guidance puzzle.

5   Are State- and Time-Dependent Models Really Different?
Fernando Alvarez, Francesco Lippi, and Juan Passadore

Yes, state- and time-dependent models are really different, but only for large monetary shocks. In particular, we show that in a broad class of models where shocks have continuous paths, the propagation of a monetary impulse is independent of the nature of the sticky price friction when shocks are *small*. The propagation of large shocks instead depends on the nature of the friction: the impulse response of inflation to monetary shocks is independent of the shock size in time-dependent models, while it is nonlinear in state-dependent models. We use data on exchange rate devaluations and inflation for a panel of countries from 1974 to 2014 to test for the presence of state-dependent decision rules. We present some evidence of a nonlinear effect of exchange rate changes on prices in a sample of flexible exchange rate countries with low inflation. We discuss the dimensions in which this finding is robust and the ones in which it is not.

6   Is the Macroeconomy Locally Unstable and Why Should We Care?
Paul Beaudry, Dana Galizia, and Franck Portier

In most modern macroeconomic models, the steady state (or balanced growth path) of the system is a local attractor, in the sense that, in the absence of shocks, the economy would converge to the steady state.

In this chapter, we examine whether the time-series behavior of macro-economic aggregates (especially labor market aggregates) is in fact supportive of this local-stability view of macroeconomic dynamics, or if it instead favors an alternative interpretation in which the macroeconomy may be better characterized as being locally unstable, with nonlinear deterministic forces capable of producing endogenous cyclical behavior. To do this, we extend a standard AR representation of the data to allow for smooth nonlinearities. Our main finding is that, even using a procedure that may have low power to detect local instability, the data provide intriguing support for the view that the macroeconomy may be locally unstable and involve limit-cycle forces. An interesting finding is that the degree of nonlinearity we detect in the data is small, but nevertheless enough to alter the description of macroeconomic behavior. We complete the chapter with a discussion of the extent to which these two different views about the inherent dynamics of the macroeconomy may matter for policy.

1

The Analytics of the Greek Crisis

Pierre-Olivier Gourinchas, *UC Berkeley, NBER, and CEPR*
Thomas Philippon, *NYU Stern and NBER*
Dimitri Vayanos, *London School of Economics, NBER, and CEPR*

I. Introduction and Motivation

The economic crisis that Greece has been experiencing from 2008 onward has been particularly severe. Real gross domestic product (GDP) per capita stood at approximately €22,600 in 2008, and dropped to €17,000 by 2014, a decline of 24.8%.[1] The unemployment rate was 7.8% in 2008, and rose to 26.6% in 2014. The entire Greek banking system became insolvent during the crisis, and a large-scale recapitalization took place in 2013. In 2012, Greece became the first Organisation for Economic Co-operation and Development (OECD) member country to default on its sovereign debt, and that default was the largest in world history. Greece received financial assistance from other Eurozone (EZ) countries and the International Monetary Fund (IMF), and the size of this bailout package was also the largest in history.

The implications of the Greek crisis extended well beyond Greece. The bailout package that Greece received was large partly because of fears of contagion to other countries in the EZ and to their banking systems. Moreover, at various stages during the crisis, the continued membership of Greece in the EZ was put in doubt. This tested the strength and the limits of the currency union, and of the European project more generally.

This paper provides an "interim" report on the Greek crisis ("interim" in the sense that the crisis is still unfolding). We proceed in three steps. First, we describe the main macroeconomic dynamics that Greece experienced before and during the crisis. Second, we put these dynamics in perspective by benchmarking the Greek crisis against all episodes of sudden stops, sovereign debt crises, and lending boom/busts in emerging and advanced economies since 1980. Third, we develop a dynamic stochastic general equilibrium (DSGE) model designed to capture many of the relevant features of the Greek crisis and help us identify its main drivers.

The global financial crisis that began in 2007 in the United States hit Greece through three interlinked shocks. The first shock was a *sovereign debt crisis*: investors began to perceive the debt of the Greek government as unsustainable, and were no longer willing to finance the government deficit. The second shock was a *banking crisis*: Greek banks had difficulty financing themselves in the interbank market, and their solvency was put in doubt because of projected losses to the value of their assets. The third shock was a *sudden stop*: foreign investors were no longer willing to lend to Greece as a whole (government, banks, and firms), and so the country could not finance its current account deficit.

To many observers, that last shock was a startling development. After all, the very existence of a common currency, and therefore of an automatic provision of liquidity against good collateral through its common central bank, was supposed to insulate member countries against a sudden reversal of private capital of the kind experienced routinely by emerging-market (EM) economies. Just like a sudden stop on California or Texas could not happen since Federal Reserve funding would substitute instantly and automatically for private capital, the common view was a sudden stop could not happen to Greece or Portugal since European Central Bank (ECB) funding would substitute instantly and automatically for private capital.[2] The belief that sudden stops were a thing of the past may have, in turn, contributed to the emergence of mounting internal and external imbalances, in Greece and elsewhere in the EZ (Blanchard and Giavazzi 2002). Yet, at the onset of the crisis, Greece and other EZ members did experience a *classic* sudden stop. The built-in defense mechanisms of the EZ were activated and the ECB provided much needed funding to the Greek economy. How much, then, did this sudden stop contribute to the subsequent meltdown and through what channels? And what was the contribution of other factors? These are among the questions that we seek to address in this paper.

The first main result that emerges from our macro-benchmarking exercise is that Greece's drop in output (a 25% decline in real GDP per capita between 2008 and 2013) was significantly more severe and protracted than during the average crisis. This applies to the sample of countries that experienced sudden stops, to the sample that experienced sovereign defaults, to the sample that experienced lending booms and busts, and even to the sample that experienced all three shocks combined (we call these episodes "trifectas"). The collapse in investment (75% decline between 2008 and 2013) was even more severe. Importantly, we find that the difference in output dynamics is not driven by the exchange-rate regime. Countries whose currency remains pegged experience a larger output drop, on average, than countries with floating rates. But unlike these countries, whose output rebounds after a few years, Greece's output continued to drop to a significantly lower level.

One possible explanation for the severity of Greece's crisis is the high level of debt—government, private, and external—at the onset of the crisis. Greece's government debt stood at 103.1% of output in 2007, its net foreign assets at –99.9% of output, and its private-sector debt at 92.4% of output. On the former two measures, Greece fared worse than Ireland, Italy, Portugal, and Spain, the four other major EZ countries hit by the crisis. Greece fared worse than those countries also on its government deficit and current-account deficit, which stood at 6.5% and 15.9% of output, respectively, in 2007. And debt levels in Greece were more than twice as large than the average of the emerging-market economies, which account for most of the crisis episodes in our sample.

To identify the role of debt, as well as of other factors such as the sudden stop of private capital in driving the severity of the Greek crisis, we turn to our DSGE model. The model is designed to capture in a simple and stylized manner the three types of shocks that hit Greece. It also captures a rich set of interdependencies between the shocks. The model features a government, two types of consumers, firms, and banks. The government can borrow, raise taxes, spend, and possibly default on its debt. Consumers differ in their subjective discount rate. Impatient consumers are those who borrow in equilibrium, subject to a debt limit. Firms can borrow and invest and face sticky wages and prices. Consumers and firms can borrow from banks and can default on their debts. The rates at which the government, consumers, and firms can borrow depend on the probability with which these entities can default and on the losses given default. In turn, the expected costs of default (probability times losses) depend on the ratio of debt to income.

In the model, a sovereign risk shock increases the government's funding costs. The government responds by increasing taxes and reducing expenditures, which exerts a contractionary effect on the economy. In turn, the decline in output increases the expected costs of default on private-sector loans, causing funding costs for consumers and firms to rise and investment to drop. Conversely, a sudden stop increases directly the rate at which consumers and firms can borrow, causing investment, consumption, and output to decline. The decline in fiscal revenues pushes up sovereign yields and has an adverse impact on public debt dynamics. Hence, in our model, sovereign risks and private-sector risks are intertwined and shocks to one sector of the economy can affect funding costs and default rates throughout all sectors.

We estimate the model using Bayesian methods and annual data on government revenue and spending, household debt, nonperforming loans in the private sector, borrowing rates for the government and the corporate sector, as well as price and wage inflation. The model features eight stochastic shocks in each year, identical to the number of variables that we use in the estimation. We find that the model does an excellent job of matching additional variables such as output, investment, and the current account (which the model was not asked to replicate). We then perform two tasks with the model. First, we decompose the movements in output, investment, and other key variables into the contribution of each type of shock. This helps us determine which shocks were the most important in driving the crisis dynamics. Second, we use the model to perform a number of "counterfactuals" to identify the role played by different aspects of the institutional environment. We examine, in particular, how the dynamics of output and investment would have been different if debt levels in Greece were set at the average of emerging-market economies, if banks' funding costs had not increased during the crisis as a possible effect of a European banking union, if the Greek government had followed a more virtuous fiscal path in the years preceding the crisis, and if prices and wages had been more flexible.

As in Agatha Christie's *Murder on the Orient Express*, our model indicates that many forces contributed to the "murder" of the Greek economy. Yet a few factors stand out. First and most importantly, given the size of the fiscal imbalances, a substantial fiscal correction was inevitable. According to our estimates, fiscal consolidation accounted for approximately 50% of the output drop from peak to trough. Much of the remainder is explained by the increase in funding costs for the private sector ("sudden stop" in our model) and the sovereign ("sovereign risk shock"). The combination of the two shocks accounted for an additional 40% of the output drop from peak to trough, with the sudden stop driving more than half of the effect.

Lastly, our estimates indicate that markup shocks in product markets and a surge in nonperforming loans contributed significantly to the lack of recovery in 2014 and 2015: in the absence of these shocks, output in 2014–15 would have recovered approximately 35% of its peak-to-trough drop. These findings indicate that the external dimension of the crisis may slowly be fading, and that the forces holding back the Greek economy are now largely domestic and microeconomic: the recovery will entail cleaning up nonperforming loans and facilitating the adjustment of prices relative to wages. The lack of a sufficient price adjustment may have been due to limited competition in goods and services markets, as well as to a rise in firms' costs stemming from factors such as the uncertainty about EZ exit and the taxation of key inputs.

The effects of the shocks described above were made larger by high leverage and low price flexibility. Our counterfactual exercises allow us to examine more directly the effects of these factors. We find that if the levels of government, private, and external debt in Greece had been comparable to those in the average of the emerging-market economies (so smaller by about half), the peak-to-trough decline in output would have been smaller by about a third, and the same conclusion holds if the prices and wages had been twice as flexible.

II.   The Greek Economy before and during the Crisis

This section describes the dynamics of key macroeconomic variables in Greece before and during the crisis. We focus on the behavior of output and investment, as well as on the accumulation of debt—government, private, and external. We also describe the three shocks through which the global financial crisis affected Greece (sudden stop, sovereign debt crisis, and banking crisis) as well as their interrelationships. This sets the stage for the empirical exercise in section III, and motivates some of the modeling choices and analysis in sections IV–VI.

A.   Pre-crisis

Output

Figure 1 plots GDP per capita in 2014 US dollars, adjusted for purchasing power parity (PPP) and in a log scale from 1980 onward. In this figure, as well as in subsequent figures and tables in this section, we compare Greece to the four other major Eurozone (EZ) countries that were hit by the EZ crisis: Ireland (IE), Italy (IT), Spain (ES), and Portugal (PT).

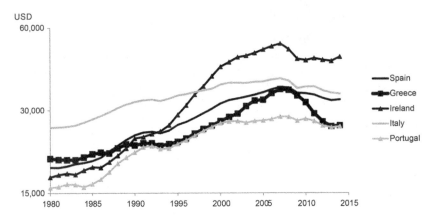

Fig. 1.   GDP per capita for Greece and other EZ crisis countries, 1980–2014

Source: The data come from the Conference Board Total Economy Database. The GDP is expressed in 2014 US dollars, is adjusted for PPP using 2011 weights, and is plotted in a log scale.

As of 1980, Greek GDP per capita was above that of Ireland, Portugal, and Spain. During the 1980s, Greece experienced relative stagnation and was overtaken by Ireland and Spain. Greece grew faster during the period 1996–2000 and especially from 2001, when it entered the Eurozone (EZ), until 2008. By 2008, Greece had almost caught up with Spain.

Motivated by figure 1, we divide the period 1996–2014 into three subperiods: the period 1996–2000, during which Greece experienced a boom in anticipation of EZ entry; the period 2001–2008, during which the boom continued with Greece inside the EZ; and the crisis period 2009–2014. In the tables constructed in the rest of this section, we report averages of macroeconomic variables for the three subperiods. In some of the tables we also compare with the year 1995, which we take as indicative of the Greek economy before the (actual or anticipated) effects of EZ entry.[3]

Investment

Table 1 reports the level of investment in Greece during the periods 1996–2000, 2001–2008, and 2009–2014, and compares with 1995. The table also decomposes investment into corporate, residential, and public and compares with Ireland, Italy, Portugal, and Spain. Greece experienced the second-largest increase in corporate investment from

Table 1

Investment in Greece and other EZ Crisis Countries, 1995–2014, as Percentage of GDP

	Total Investment				Corporate Investment				Residential Investment				Public Investment			
	95	96–00	01–08	09–14	95	96–00	01–08	09–14	95	96–00	01–08	09–14	95	96–00	01–08	09–14
ES	22.0	23.7	28.8	21.0	11.7	13.0	13.9	12.0	6.0	7.0	10.7	5.7	4.3	3.7	4.2	3.3
GR	**20.4**	**23.1**	**23.7**	**14.6**	**8.4**	**10.5**	**10.3**	**7.7**	**8.6**	**8.8**	**9.2**	**3.7**	**3.4**	**3.8**	**4.2**	**3.2**
IE	18.2	22.3	26.1	16.2	10.6	12.3	11.4	11.0	5.2	7.1	10.6	2.7	2.4	2.9	4.1	2.5
IT	19.0	19.4	21.1	18.6	11.3	11.8	12.9	10.8	5.1	4.8	5.3	5.1	2.6	2.8	2.9	2.7
PT	23.3	26.5	23.9	17.4	11.6	13.8	13.7	11.1	7.3	7.7	6.1	3.1	4.4	5.0	4.1	3.2

Source: The data come from AMECO. Investment is measured by the series "gross fixed capital formation: total economy," and does not include inventories. Residential investment is measured by "gross fixed capital formation: dwellings"; corporate investment by "gross fixed capital formation: private sector" minus residential investment; and public investment by "gross fixed capital formation: government."

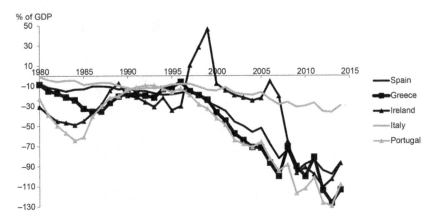

Fig. 2.   Net foreign assets in Greece and other EZ crisis countries, 1980–2014, as percentage of GDP.

Source: The data come from Lane and Milesi-Ferretti (2007).

1995 to 1996-2000, after Portugal. Corporate investment remained at that elevated level during 2001-2008. Thus, EZ entry and its anticipation was associated with a significant rise in corporate investment in Greece. That rise, however, occurred from a low base, and corporate investment remained significantly lower than in the other countries.

Unlike Ireland and Spain, Greece did not experience a significant increase in residential investment from 1995 to 1996–2008. Residential investment was already high in 1995, however, and the real estate boom in Ireland and Spain only meant that residential investment in those countries caught up with and exceeded somewhat that in Greece.

Net Foreign Assets

The fast growth of Greek GDP per capita during the period 1996–2008 was associated with an increase in external indebtedness. Figure 2 plots net foreign assets (NFA) from 1980 onward as percentage of GDP. The NFA for Greece were negative throughout that period. They were a relatively small fraction of GDP in absolute value until the mid-1990s, and they subsequently declined to a much more negative fraction. Greece's NFA position deteriorated at a comparable rate to Portugal's and Spain's, while Ireland experienced a more abrupt deterioration. The behavior of Greece's NFA from the mid-1990s onward is indicative of large current account deficits. Table 2 reports the level of the current

Table 2
The Current Account in Greece and other EZ Crisis Countries, 1995–2014, as Percentage of GDP

	Current Account Surplus				Net Exports				Net Current Transfers Plus Net Primary Incomes			
	95	96–00	01–08	09–14	95	96–00	01–08	09–14	95	96–00	01–08	09–14
ES	-1.2	-2.0	-6.7	-1.6	-1.0	-1.1	-4.1	0.8	-0.2	-0.9	-2.6	-2.4
GR	**-2.8**	**-5.7**	**-11.7**	**-7.3**	**-8.3**	**-9.1**	**-10.6**	**-5.9**	**5.5**	**3.4**	**-1.1**	**-1.4**
IE	2.6	1.2	-2.3	1.7	10.9	12.0	12.4	19.2	-8.3	-10.8	-14.7	-17.5
IT	2.0	1.5	-1.1	-1.0	3.7	2.8	0.1	0.4	-1.7	-1.3	-1.2	-1.4
PT	-3.4	-7.7	-9.8	-4.5	-6.4	-9.1	-8.5	-3.0	3.0	1.4	-1.3	-1.5

Source: The data come from AMECO. Net exports are measured by the series "net exports of goods and services"; net current transfers by "net current transfers from the rest of the world"; and net primary income by "net primary income from the rest of the world." The current account surplus is the sum of the three series.

account in Greece, Ireland, Italy, Portugal, and Spain during the periods 1996–2000, 2001–2008, and 2009–2014, and compares with 1995. The table decomposes the current account into (a) net exports and (b) the sum of net current transfers and net primary income.

Greece's current account deteriorated from 1995 to 1996–2000, and deteriorated further from 2001 to 2008. The deterioration from 1996–2000 to 2001–2008 was particularly severe: 6.0% of GDP, larger than in the other countries. From 2001 to 2008, Greece was running an average current account deficit of 11.7% of GDP, also larger than in the other countries.

The deterioration of Greece's current account from 1995 onward was primarily driven by a decline in net current transfers and net primary income. Net current transfers to Greece declined partly because of the drop in EU subsidies, especially after the 2005 EU enlargement, as funds were redirected to new entrants that were poorer than Greece. Net primary income also declined because workers' remittances became smaller as Greece became a net immigration country and because of growing interest payments on Greece's rising external debt. Greece's trade balance also deteriorated through that period, reaching –10.6% of GDP during the period 2001–2008.

The increase in Greece's current account deficit from 1995 to 1996–2000 was associated with an increase in corporate investment and, hence, in productive capacity. Indeed, the current account deficit increased by 2.9% of GDP, corporate investment increased by 2.1%, and public investment by 0.4%. The increase in the current account deficit from 1996–2000 to 2001–2008, however, was associated with an increase in consumption. Indeed, the current account deficit increased by 6.0% of GDP, total saving declined by 6.7%, and corporate investment dropped slightly. The decline in total saving from 1996–2000 to 2001–2008 was primarily driven by private saving, which declined by 4.3% of GDP.[4]

Government Debt

Figure 3 plots government debt from 1980 onward, as percentage of GDP. As of 1980, government debt in Greece was 21.4% of GDP, lower than in all other countries except for Spain. Debt rose sharply during the 1980s, and by 1993 it had reached 94.4% of GDP, a level larger than in all other countries except for Italy. A combination of fiscal tightening to meet the criteria for EZ entry, and sharply lower interest rates in anticipation of that entry, helped stabilize and even reduce slightly

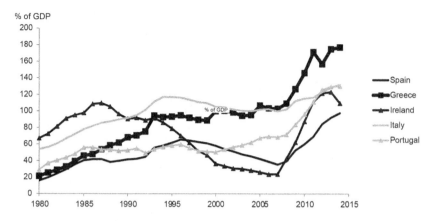

Fig. 3.   Government debt in Greece and other EZ crisis countries, 1980–2014, as percentage of GDP.

Source: The data come from AMECO, series "general government consolidated gross debt."

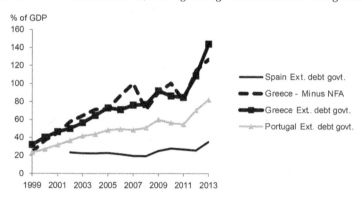

Fig. 4.   Gross government external debt for Greece, Portugal, and Spain, 1999–2013, as percentage of GDP.

Source: The data come from the ECB, series "gross external debt: government." The data are quarterly, and we report the average over each year.

the ratio of debt to GDP to 88.5% in 1999. Budget discipline became looser after EZ entry, and especially after 2007. As a consequence, debt to GDP increased—to 103.1% in 2007 and 126.8% in 2009—despite the fast growth in GDP during the period 2001–2008.

While debt to GDP increased only mildly from 1999 to 2007, there was a sharp increase in the amount of the debt held by foreign entities and a consequent decrease in the amount held domestically. That trend was due mainly to the decline in private saving. Figure 4 plots gross government external debt for Greece, and compares with the same se-

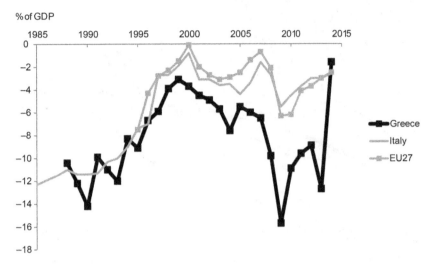

Fig. 5. Government deficit in Greece, Italy, and the EU average, 1985–2014, as percentage of GDP.

Source: The data come from the EC, series "surplus (net lending or net borrowing: general government)."

ries for Portugal and Spain, and with Greece's NFA.[5] Gross government external debt for Greece essentially coincides with the negative of NFA. By contrast, gross government external debt for Portugal and Spain is significantly lower than the negative of those countries' NFA (which are not plotted, but are similar to Greece's from figure 2). Figure 4 thus indicates that Greece's current account deficit essentially financed government borrowing.[6]

Figure 5 plots government deficit as percentage of GDP. The figure compares Greece to Italy, which was the most similar to Greece in terms of the size of its government debt until the crisis, and to the EU average. The figure shows that Greece's public finances improved in the run-up to EZ entry, but worsened steadily post-entry. The pre-entry improvement was similar to that in Italy and the EU average. Unlike in Greece, however, the latter series remained relatively stable post-entry and until the crisis.

Banks and Credit

From the mid-1990s until the crisis, Greece experienced a boom in private credit. An extensive program of financial liberalization that took

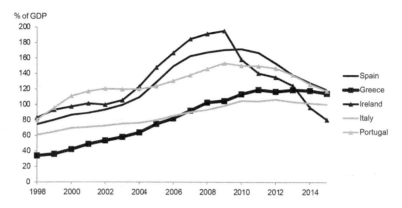

Fig. 6. Bank loans to the private sector excluding financial firms in Greece and other EZ crisis countries, 1998–2014, as percentage of GDP.
Source: The loans data come from the Bank of Greece (BoG) in the case of Greece and from the European Central Bank (ECB) for the other countries. The loan data are monthly and are sampled in December of each year.

place in the late 1980s and the 1990s paved the way for the credit boom. It was also fueled by easier access to foreign capital following EZ entry (and the anticipation of it). Figure 6 plots bank loans to the nonfinancial private sector for Greece, Ireland, Italy, Portugal, and Spain, as percentage of GDP.

Private-sector loans to GDP were significantly lower in Greece than in the other countries before EZ entry: they stood at 34.1% of GDP in 1998, compared to 60.8% in Italy, 74.6% in Spain, 80.31% in Portugal, and 82.8% in Ireland. Loans to GDP grew faster in Greece than in any other country, however, after EZ entry. As of 2008, they stood at 103.0%, a ratio smaller than Ireland's, Portugal's, and Spain's, but larger than Italy's.

To finance their increasing lending activity, Greek banks became more reliant on wholesale funding through the interbank market. Figure 7 plots gross external debt for Greek banks and compares with Italy, Portugal, and Spain. Gross external debt of banks consists mainly of interbank loans. Gross external debt of Greek banks increased from 12.3% of GDP in 1999 to 46.2% of GDP in 2008. As in the case of private-sector loans to GDP, the growth rate was higher than in the other countries, and the 2008 level was smaller than Portugal's and Spain's, but larger than Italy's.

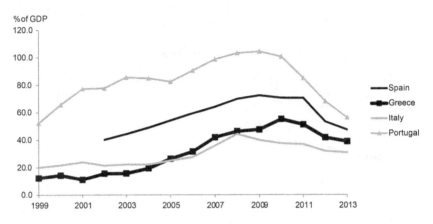

Fig. 7. Gross external debt of financial firms for Greece and other EZ crisis countries, 1999–2013, as percentage of GDP.

Source: The data come from the ECB, series "Gross External Debt: MFIs." The data are quarterly and we report the average over each year. We exclude the series for Ireland, which rises up to 425% of GDP, so that the series for the other countries can be seen more clearly.

B.   Crisis

The Three Shocks

The global financial crisis that began in 2007 found Greece in a highly vulnerable position. As of 2007, Greece's current account deficit had reached 15.9% of GDP, NFA stood at –99.9%, government deficit at 6.5%, and government debt at 103.1%. On all four measures, Greece fared worse than Ireland, Italy, Portugal, and Spain. Greece's banking system was also vulnerable. While the ratio of private-sector loans to GDP in Greece was lower than in Ireland, Portugal, and Spain, the exposure of Greek banks to their sovereign was larger than in those countries.

Greece was hit by three interdependent shocks during the crisis. The first shock was a *sovereign debt crisis*: investors began to perceive the debt of the Greek government as unsustainable, and were no longer willing to finance the government deficit. The second shock was a *banking crisis*: Greek banks had difficulty financing themselves, and their solvency was put in doubt because of projected losses to the value of their assets. The third shock was a *sudden stop*: foreign investors were no longer willing to lend to Greece as a whole (government, banks, and firms), and so the country could not finance its current account deficit, nor roll over its maturing gross liabilities.

The three shocks were interlinked. The banking crisis made the government's fiscal problems worse. This was because the government had to inject equity capital into the banks and had to provide them with guarantees so that they could borrow in the interbank market. Moreover, because banks had to curtail their lending, the economy slowed down and the government's tax revenues declined. These channels were at play starting from the fall of 2008, when Greek banks faced significant difficulties financing themselves in the interbank market. The Greek government passed a law in December 2008 that provided support to the banks in the form of guarantees and equity capital.

Conversely, the sovereign crisis made the banks' liquidity and solvency problems worse. This was because concerns about default risk by the Greek government reduced the value of the Greek banks' government-bond portfolio, and this put the banks' solvency in doubt. Moreover, the government had to engage in significant fiscal tightening, and the ensuing recession meant that firms and households had difficulty repaying their loans, adding to the banks' solvency problems. Finally, the guarantees given by the government to Greek banks diminished in value. That applied both to the guarantees intended to help the banks borrow in the interbank market and to the government-supplied deposit insurance. Hence, banks had more difficulties financing themselves and their liquidity problems worsened. These channels were at play beginning in September 2009, when investors began to perceive the debt of the Greek government as unsustainable.

Both the sovereign and the banking crises were closely linked to the sudden stop. Indeed, most of government debt was held by foreign investors: out of government debt equal to 103.1% of GDP in 2007, the debt held by foreign investors was 76.1% of GDP. Greek financial firms also had significant foreign debt: their gross external debt was 41.8% of GDP in 2007. Since the Greek government and Greek banks intermediated most of the flow of foreign capital to Greece, the withdrawal of foreign capital meant that both sectors' access to funds was seriously impaired.

Ireland, Italy, Portugal, and Spain were hit by some or all of the same shocks. The shocks' effects were more severe in the case of Greece, however, given the country's larger vulnerability.[7]

Assistance to the Sovereign and Sovereign Default

In May 2010, Greece agreed to follow an adjustment program financed and monitored by European institutions and the IMF. Under the terms of the agreement, Greece received a loan so as to avoid a default on its private creditors and reduce its government deficit more smoothly. In exchange, it had to engage in significant fiscal tightening and implement a battery of structural reforms. The agreed loan amount was 110 billion euros, or 44% of Greece's 2010 GDP. Out of that amount 80 billion came from other EZ countries, and the remaining 30 billion from the IMF. The first adjustment program was rolled over into a second, agreed to in February 2012. A third program began in August 2015.

In March 2012, Greece agreed to a debt restructuring with its private creditors. Under the terms of this private-sector involvement (PSI), privately held government debt with face value of 199.2 billion euros was replaced by debt with a face value of 92.1 billion. Greece was the only EZ country to default on its creditors.

Assistance to the Banks, Recapitalizations, and Capital Controls

In addition to the loans made to the Greek government under the adjustment programs, assistance was provided to Greece through ECB loans to its banking system. These loans were administered either directly from the ECB, with a low interest rate and stringent collateral requirements, or indirectly via the Bank of Greece (BoG) as emergency liquidity assistance (ELA), with a higher interest rate and less stringent collateral requirements. The ECB loans were necessary to address the liquidity problems of Greek banks. They rose from 48 billion euros in January 2010 to a maximum of 158 billion euros in February 2012, then dropped to a minimum of 45 billion euros in November 2014, and then rose again to a maximum of 122 billion in September 2015. The ECB loans were at their maxima around times when there was a high-perceived risk of Greece exiting the EZ (Grexit). The risk of Grexit was high around the double election of May and June 2012, and during the first half of 2015 after a new Greek government opposed to the adjustment programs had been elected in January 2015.

Greek banks went through a series of recapitalizations. Losses on the banks' government-bond portfolio reduced the capital of all banks and rendered most of the large ones insolvent. Some of the banks were resolved, and their deposits and some of the loans were transferred to the four largest banks. The latter were recapitalized. The resolution and recapitalization process was completed in July 2013, and involved 38.9 billion euros of public funds, which were loaned to Greece. An additional 3.1 billion euros were raised by private investors. That first, large-scale recapitalization was followed by a second in April and May 2014, when the banks raised 8.3 billion euros, solely from private investors. A third recapitalization took place in the fourth quarter of 2015. The total amount that was raised then was 13.7 billion euros, of which 8 billion euros was raised from private sources via new investment and debt-equity conversions. The second and third recapitalizations were made necessary because of increased projected losses on banks' loans to the private sector.

Macroeconomic Developments

We finally review the macroeconomic developments during the crisis period 2009–2014, following a roughly similar order as for the pre-crisis period. Greek GDP per capita declined sharply during the crisis, as shown in figure 1. The decline was 25.8% between 2008 and 2014. It was much sharper than in Ireland (6.1%), Italy (10.3%), Portugal (7.8%), and Spain (9.6%).

The decline in GDP was accompanied by a large decline in investment. The latter decline can be seen in table 1 by comparing the crisis period with the pre-crisis one. It can be seen more sharply by comparing investment in 2014 to that in 2008. Investment in 2014 was less than half of its 2008 value, having dropped by 12.2% of GDP. Both the relative and the absolute declines were larger than in Ireland, Italy, Portugal, and Spain. The level of investment in 2014 was also significantly lower than in the other countries.

During the crisis, Greece reduced and almost eliminated its current account deficit. That deficit stood at 2.2% of GDP in 2014, down from 16.5% in 2008. The adjustment occurred entirely through a drop in investment. Total saving did not change: government saving increased as a result of the fiscal tightening that took place during the crisis, but that effect was offset by a decline in private saving. Private saving in Greece declined between 2008 and 2014, while it increased in Ireland, Italy, Portugal, and Spain. Conversely, government saving increased in Greece during the same period, while it declined in the other countries. Thus, the austerity undergone by Greece during the crisis was more severe than in the other countries.

During the crisis, public debt to GDP followed explosive dynamics, rising from 103.1% in 2007 and 126.8% in 2009 to 177.1% in 2014. The increase resulted from the deficits run during the crisis and from the drop in GDP. The debt restructuring agreed to in 2012 countered these effects somewhat.[8] Greece eliminated its primary budget deficit in 2014—it ran a primary surplus of 0.4% in that year.

The ratio of private-sector loans to GDP declined slowly during the crisis. As figure 6 shows, it stood at almost the same level as Portugal's and Spain's in 2014, and above Ireland's and Italy's. The slow decline of private-sector loans to GDP in Greece is due to the sharp decline in GDP and the relatively slow pace of resolving nonperforming loans.

III.   Benchmarking the Greek Crisis

The previous section argued that Greece experienced three quasi-simultaneous and interlinked shocks: a sudden stop, with the abrupt withdrawal of private foreign capital starting in 2009; a sovereign debt crisis, with rapidly deteriorating fiscal accounts in 2008 and 2009, culminating in a sovereign default in 2012; and a banking crisis with the bursting of a boom in credit to the private nonfinancial sector in 2008 and 2009. This section provides a systematic comparison between Greece and other countries experiencing each type (and sometimes combinations) of similar shocks.

A.   The Incidence of Crisis

We begin by identifying episodes of sudden stops, sovereign defaults, and lending booms/busts.

Sudden Stops

Starting with the work of Dornbusch and Werner (1994), Calvo et al. (2006), Adalet and Eichengreen (2007), and many others, an abundant literature has explored the macroeconomic consequences of a sudden reversal in foreign lending. Calvo et al. (2006), in particular, compiled a list of 33 sudden stop episodes between 1980 and 2004 for a sample of 31 emerging markets. In the authors' classification, a sudden stop is identified by the combination of (a) a reversal in capital flows; (b) an increase in emerging-market bond spreads, capturing times of global stress on financial markets; and (c) a large drop in domestic output. Mendoza (2010) adopts a similar classification, while Korinek and Mendoza (2014) extend the Calvo et al. (2006) sample to 2012 and to advanced economies.[9] As in these earlier papers, we define the year t of a sudden stop episode as the year of a sharp reduction in foreign lending that coincides with a large decline in output.[10] With this criterion, we identify 49 sudden stop events, 36 for emerging-market economies, and 13 for advanced economies (see table 3).

Sovereign Defaults

We identify sovereign debt crisis as in Gourinchas and Obstfeld (2012). The year t of a sovereign debt crisis corresponds to the year identified with a default on domestic or external public debt, as tabulated by Reinhart and Rogoff (2009), Cantor and Packer (1995), Chambers (2011), Moody's (2009) and Sturzenegger and Zettelmeyer (2007).[11] Since 1980, we record 64 default episodes in emerging-market economies, and one in an advanced economy: Greece in 2012.

Lending Booms/Busts

Credit boom episodes are defined as in Gourinchas, Valdés, and Landerretche (2001), from the deviation of the ratio of credit to the nonfinancial sector to output from its trend.[12] A lending boom episode is recorded when this cyclical deviation exceeds a given boom threshold. The year t of the lending boom then coincides with the year in which the maximum (positive) deviation of credit to GDP occurs. Our calculations identify 114 lending boom episodes, 96 of which are in emerging-market economies.

Finally, we identify *"trifecta" episodes*: sovereign defaults that coincide with a lending boom and a sudden stop.[13] We find nine such crises for emerging markets, including well-known episodes such as Mexico in 1982, Chile and Uruguay in 1983, Indonesia and Russia in 1998, Ecuador in 1999, Argentina and Turkey in 2001, and Uruguay again in 2003. Again, Greece is the only advanced economy to have experienced a trifecta crisis in our sample.

Table 3 reports the incidence of each type of crisis for advanced and emerging-market economies. It illustrates the relative prevalence of sovereign defaults, lending booms, and trifecta crises among emerging economies. By contrast, sudden stops are roughly distributed in proportion to the number of countries in each group in our sample.

We compare each type of episode to the Greek crisis. For the purpose of this exercise, we consider that the Greek episode begins in 2010.[14]

Table 3
Crises Incidence in Advanced and Emerging Economies, 1980–2014

	Sudden Stop	Sovereign Default	Lending Boom	Trifecta	No. Countries
Advanced economies	13	1	18	1	22
Emerging markets	36	64	96	9	57
Total	49	65	114	10	79

Note: Details on how each type of episode is identified are in the appendix.

B. The Data

We construct a database of macrovariables for a large sample of advanced and emerging economies between 1980 and 2014.[15] The sample contains 22 advanced economies (including Greece) and 57 emerging-market economies, distributed across six broad regions. The list of emerging-market economies includes all countries classified as emerging according to leading outlets and are therefore reasonably well integrated into global bond markets.[16]

In the spirit of a large literature in international macroeconomics, we examine the behavior of key macroeconomic variables around the three types of shocks discussed above: sudden stops, sovereign debt crises, and lending boom/busts episodes, as well as trifecta crises.[17] Our event study considers the response of seven macroeconomic variables: output, consumption, investment, exports and imports of goods and services, the current account, credit to the nonfinancial sector, and public debt. The data is collected from the World Bank's Development Indicators, the IMF's International Financial Statistics, and Reinhart and Rogoff (2009) estimates of total (domestic and external) gross public debt for a large number of countries.[18] In addition to these macroeconomic variables, we use the Reinhart and Rogoff (2004) and Ilzetzki, Reinhart, and Rogoff (2010) de facto exchange rate regime classification and sort countries into "pegs" or "floats" based on the exchange rate regime in the year preceding the episode. Further, we split pegs into "de-peggers," that is, countries that abandon their peg within two years of the shock, and "strict peggers" who maintain their peg for at least two years. This will allow us to contrast the macroeconomic response of countries based on their post-shock exchange rate regime. This is an important consideration given the often-heard argument that the main constraint on the Greek economy is its lack of nominal exchange rate flexibility (e.g., see Krugman 2012).

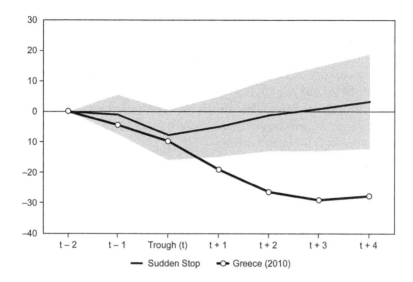

Fig. 8. The response of output to a sudden stop

Source: See the appendix for data sources.

Note: The figure reports real output per capita relative to period $t - 2$, in 100 log points for a typical sudden stop episode (with output collapse) and for Greece in the 2010 crisis.

C. *Findings*

Figure 8 reports the output response to a typical sudden stop across the 48 episodes (excluding Greece). It measures output per capita, relative to its pre-crisis level at $t - 2$, in 100 log points, so that a value of x indicates that output per capita is $e^{x/100}$ times pre-crisis output. The figure also includes point-wise, one-sided 10% confidence intervals (the grayed area), as well as the trajectory of Greek output (bullet points) during the 2010 episode. As expected, since our definition of sudden stops requires a large output drop, the mean response indicates a sharp decline in output, marginally significant, close to 10% below its peak in the year of the sudden stop, followed by a gradual recovery. By year $t + 2$, output has typically recovered to its pre-crisis level and continues to expand. Two facts are relevant here. First, Greece experienced a strikingly worse output decline. By 2013, that is, $t + 3$, Greek output per capita was 25% below its pre-crisis level ($e^{-0.29} = 0.75$), significantly below the average response and showing few signs of recovery. Second, unlike the typical sudden stop, Greece's output path was "back loaded." The initial recession in 2009 and 2010 ($t - 1$ and t) is similar to a typical sudden stop episode and milder than the subsequent decline in Greek output. By contrast, typical episodes are "front loaded" with a more pronounced "V" shape.[19] This is not surprising if we consider that Greece's sudden stop was of a particular nature. As discussed in the previous section, the sudden withdrawal of foreign lending was accommodated initially via ECB lending against collateral, and after 2010 via official assistance from the IMF and the European Union. Hence there was no sharp immediate downturn, as is typical when countries experience sudden loss of market access.

Claim 1. *The Greek crisis was significantly more severe, persistent, and back loaded than the typical sudden stop.*

Figure 9 reports a similar analysis for the consumption and investment ratios to output. As for output, each variable is expressed in 100 log points, relative to its value at $t - 2$, that is, at the beginning of the episode. Equivalently, this figure reports the growth differential between consumption or investment and output since $t - 2$. The top panel reports the consumption-to-output ratio. In a typical sudden stop, consumption mostly moves in line with output. Instead, Greek consumption grew modestly faster than output, although not significantly so. The bottom panel reports the investment-to-output ratio. Greek investment collapsed dramatically, much more so than in a typical sudden stop. By 2013, that is, $t + 3$, the investment-to-output ratio was less than half of its pre-crisis level ($e^{-0.76} = 0.47$), while a typical sudden stop sees a decline of 20% to 30%. Given the decline in output per capita documented in figure 8, real investment per capita collapsed by almost two-thirds between 2008 and 2013 ($0.75 \times 0.47 = 0.35$).

Claim 2. *The collapse in Greek aggregate investment in this crisis was unprecedented in its persistence and magnitude, in comparison to the typical sudden stop.*

A sudden withdrawal of foreign capital is only one of the shocks that Greece experienced since 2009, and one might be concerned that the previous comparison might be too unfavorable to Greece. For instance, like Greece in 2010, Argentina in 2001, Chile in 1983, or Indonesia in 1998, among others, experienced a simultaneous drying-up of foreign capital, a sovereign default, and a collapse in lending, that is, a trifecta shock. These episodes are among the worst documented economic crises in postwar history, often accompanied by a banking crisis, and unprecedented levels of economic hardship and political turmoil. In light of the economic and political dislocation associated with it, one would expect the Greek crisis to be on a comparable scale. To investi-

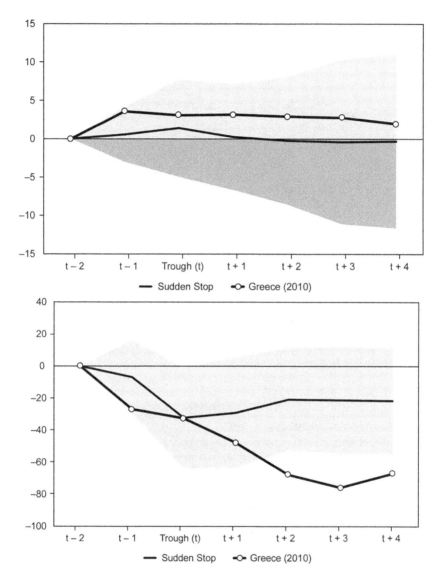

Fig. 9. The response of consumption and investment to a sudden stop

Source: See the appendix for data sources.

Note: The figure reports the consumption-output ratio (top panel) and the investment output ratio (bottom panel) relative to period $t-2$ in 100 log points for a typical sudden stop episode (with large output collapse) and for Greece in 2010.

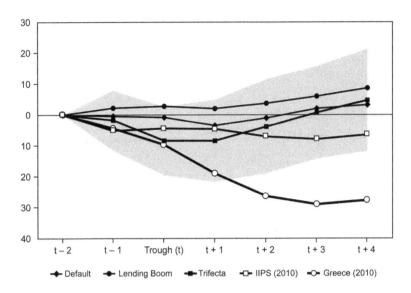

Fig. 10.   The response of output to various crises

Source: See the appendix for data sources.

Note: The figure reports the mean output per capita relative to period $t - 2$ in 100 log points for various episodes, and for Greece in 2010; 10% one-sided, point-wise confidence intervals for trifecta episodes.

gate this, figure 10 reports the average output response to each of the following shocks: a sovereign default, a lending boom/bust, as well as the trifecta shock that consists of these two shocks occurring during a sudden stop episode. As an additional point of comparison, the figure also includes the average output response for Ireland, Italy, Portugal, and Spain, that is, the other peripheral countries most affected by the Eurozone crisis (under the label IIPS). Finally, the graph also includes 10% point-wise, one-sided confidence intervals for the trifecta shocks.

The figure illustrates how much of an outlier the Greek crisis truly was. While output per capita initially declined in line with that of a trifecta crisis, by 2011 (i.e., $t + 1$) output had declined significantly more and kept falling. By contrast, in a typical trifecta crisis, output is back to its pre-crisis level by $t + 3$. The figure allows us to make a number of additional points. First, trifecta crises are more severe than a typical default crisis, although the differences are small and often insignificant. Second, following a lending boom, output keeps growing. This is because many lending booms in our sample are not always followed by an economic downturn or crisis, as noted also by Gourinchas et al.

(2001) and Ranciere, Tornell, and Westermann (2008). Lastly, the trajectory for the IIPS countries illustrates that, in these countries too, the crisis has been much more persistent then expected, with output still 7% below the pre-crisis level as of 2014 ($t + 4$).

Claim 3. *The collapse in Greek output per capita has been significantly more severe and more persistent than the typical trifecta crisis.*

Figure 11 makes the same point even more vividly. The panel on the left reports the output trajectory for *all* countries that experienced a sudden stop in our sample. The panel on the right presents similar results for all trifecta episodes. Both panels also report the Greek 2010 episode. As is clear from both figures, Greece's economic performance is cumulatively much worse than all episodes from the last 35 years, including crises such as Argentina in 2001 or Uruguay in 1983, with the single exception of the United Arab Emirates crisis of 2009.[20]

We next consider the role of the exchange rate regime. Our data set includes information on the de facto exchange rate regime from Reinhart and Rogoff (2004) and Ilzetzki et al. (2010). We use this data to construct an indicator of the exchange rate regime in the year of the shock and the preceding year (peg/float). We further subdivide pegs based on whether countries maintain their peg for at least two years after the crisis (strict peggers) or abandoned it (de-peggers).[21] Figure 12 contrasts the output response following an emerging market sudden stop for de-peggers, strict peggers, and floaters, together with that of Greece and of the IIPS countries. The figure also includes 10% point-wise, one-sided confidence intervals for strict peggers. Unsurprisingly, we find that strict peggers experience a worse adjustment than de-peggers, who in turn perform worse than floaters: by $t + 4$, output is still 4% below its pre-crisis level for strict peggers, while it is 3% (resp. 8%) above its trend for de-peggers (resp. floaters): a more flexible exchange rate regime is associated with a less severe and less persistent crisis. Greece's experience is very singular in that respect as well: its output loss is much larger and significantly more persistent than for countries that maintained their exchange rate. By contrast, the experience of the IIPS countries is more in line with that of strict peggers, albeit less severe in 2010 and 2011 (t and $t + 1$).

There are two ways to think about this result. One possible interpretation is that the severity of the Greek crisis cannot be attributed entirely to the strictures of the common currency, since it significantly underperformed other "strict fixers." This would direct our attention toward other features of the Greek economy than just the exchange rate

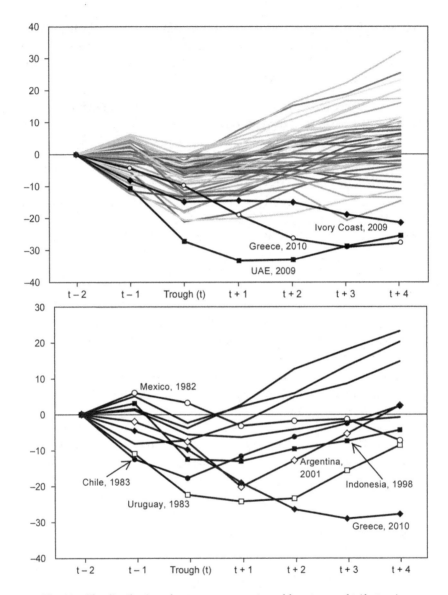

Fig. 11. The distribution of output responses to sudden stops and trifecta crises

Source: See the appendix for data sources.

Note: The figure reports output per capita relative to period $t-2$ in 100 log points for each sudden stop episode (top panel), and for each trifecta crises (bottom panel), together with Greece in 2010.

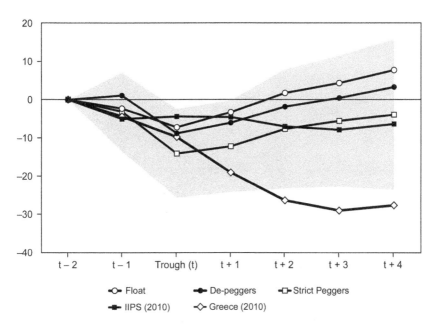

Fig. 12. The role of the exchange rate regime

Source: See the appendix for data sources.

Note: The figure reports output per capita relative to period $t - 2$ in 100 log points for emerging market sudden stops, by exchange rate regime, together with Greece in 2010; 10% one-sided, point-wise confidence intervals for strict peggers.

regime. This is not the only interpretation. Clearly, countries can and often choose their exchange rate regime in response to the economic environment. Therefore, the sample of strict fixers may consist precisely of countries who stand to lose relatively less from keeping the exchange rate pegged in the aftermath of a sudden stop. This could be the case in particular if these countries were experiencing a relatively modest decline in output. To investigate this question further, figure 13 reports the data for strict fixers alongside that for Estonia, Latvia, and Greece. Both Latvia and Estonia experienced severe recessions following their 2009 sudden stop episode. Estonia's output per capita declined by 19% between 2007 and 2009, while that of Latvia declined by 17% between 2007 and 2010. Nevertheless, both countries chose to maintain their peg to the euro and "doubled down" by subsequently adopting the common currency in January 2011 for Estonia and January 2014 for Latvia. Overall, both countries have an experience similar to that of the full sample of strict peggers. Yet, it could hardly be argued that the costs

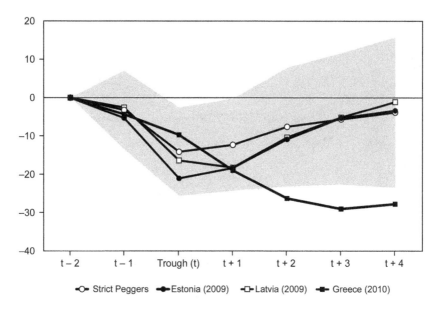

Fig. 13.   Output response for strict peggers

Source: See the appendix for data sources.

Note: The figure reports output per capita relative to period $t - 2$ in 100 log points for emerging market strict peggers, together with Estonia (2009), Latvia (2009), and Greece (2010); one-sided 10% point-wise confidence intervals for strict peggers.

of maintaining a fixed exchange rate were small for either country. Instead, their decision to carry forward and adopt the euro can be related to historical and geostrategic reasons, in particular the desire to anchor their country firmly in the West. Both countries, therefore, adopted the euro *despite* the large short-run costs associated with doing so: the comparison of their trajectory with Greece's is unlikely to suffer from a strong selection bias. It is therefore interesting that the experience of Greece appears significantly worse than either country.[22]

Claim 4.   *The Greek crisis was significantly more severe than the typical emerging market sudden stop, even for countries such as Latvia or Estonia that maintained a fixed exchange rate in the aftermath of a sudden stop with large output collapse.*

Figure 14 reports credit to the nonfinancial sector (left panel) and public debt (right panel), relative to output. The credit-to-output ratio is measured in deviation from a Hodrick-Prescott (HP) filter trend, while the debt-to-output ratio is measured relative to the country mean. Each

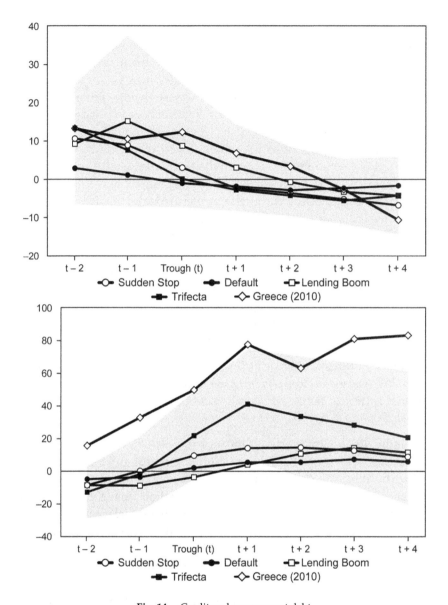

Fig. 14. Credit and government debt

Source: See the appendix for data sources.

Note: The left panel reports the ratio of credit to the nonfinancial sector to output, in deviation from a Hodrick-Prescott trend, in percent of GDP. The right panel reports the ratio of government debt to output, in deviation from a country mean, in percent of GDP. Both panels report the typical response over each type of episode, together with Greece in 2010; one-sided 10% point-wise confidence intervals for lending boom (top panel) and trifecta (bottom panel).

variable is expressed in percent of GDP. The left panel reports 10% one-sided, point-wise confidence bands for lending boom/bust episodes, while the right panel reports similar confidence bands for trifecta episodes, since these episodes witness the largest increase in public debt. Starting with the credit-to-output ratio, we see that the initial leverage was high, but not as high as in typical lending boom episodes, around 10% of GDP. The ratio of credit to GDP was gradually reduced, although at a more measured pace than in typical episodes. Overall, the contraction in credit to the economy is similar to what is observed in other countries. Confidence bands are quite large.

Turning to public debt, we observe an elevated level of public debt even before the crisis (18% of GDP above mean in 2008), increasing rapidly and remaining significantly more elevated than in other episodes. We can see on the graph the effect of the 2012 debt restructuring (in $t + 2$), reducing the debt-to-output ratio from 80% to 60% of GDP above its mean, but followed by a subsequent worsening, in part due to the collapse in economic activity in 2013 and 2014. Compared to trifecta or other episodes, levels of public debt remain extraordinarily high and it is clear from this figure that efforts to bring public debt back to sustainable levels have failed.

Claim 5. *Domestic leverage in Greece was similar to other lending boom/bust episodes and evolved similarly. By contrast, public debt to output remained extremely elevated. Efforts to reduce the public debt burden mostly failed, despite a substantial debt restructuring in 2012.*

Figure 15 reports the trade balance-to-output ratio as well as the consumer price index (CPI)-based multilateral real exchange rate compiled by the IMF. As for domestic credit and public debt, the trade balance-to-output ratio is measured in deviation from country means and expressed in percent of GDP. The multilateral real exchange rate is expressed in percentage deviation from its country mean. The figure also reports 10% point-wise, one-sided confidence intervals for sudden stop episodes. The left panel (trade balance) illustrates the gradual but large improvement of the Greek trade balance between 2008 and 2014, in excess of 10% of GDP, compared to the typical sudden stop episode. Unlike typical sudden stops, where loss of market access forces the trade balance and current account to improve overnight, the overall improvement in Greece was spread out gradually. The cumulated improvement in the trade balance in a typical sudden stop represents 6.2% of output, 5% of which occurs in the year of the sudden stop itself. As discussed in the previous section, financial assistance and access to the liquidity facilities

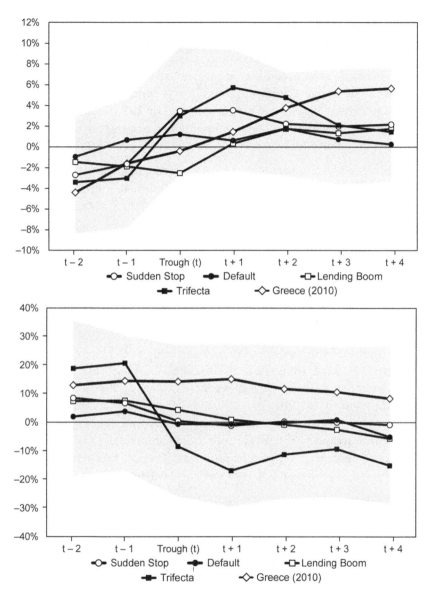

Fig. 15. Net exports and real exchange rate

Source: See the appendix for data sources.

Note: The top panel reports the ratio of net exports on goods and services to output, in deviation from country mean, in percent of GDP. The bottom panel reports the multilateral real exchange rate in percentage deviation from a country mean. Both panels report the typical response over each type of episode, together with Greece in 2010; one-sided, point-wise confidence intervals for trifecta episodes.

of the European Central Bank allowed Greece to spread out a massive and necessary adjustment in its trade balance. The right panel indicates that most of this adjustment occurred without major movements in the real exchange rate. Like other countries experiencing a sudden stop, Greece's real exchange rate was initially overappreciated by about 13%. Yet, while the real exchange rate depreciates by 10% in the aftermath of a typical sudden stop (and a massive 35% following a trifecta), Greece's real exchange rate only depreciated by 4.5% between 2008 and 2014.[23]

Claim 6. *The adjustment of external balances occurred more gradually, but was nevertheless very significant in size. The improvement in external accounts occurred despite any significant movement in the real exchange rate.*

IV. Model

This section presents a stylized model of a small open economy in a currency union with rich macrofinancial linkages. The model is designed to shed light on two sets of issues. First, we want a realistic enough model that allows us to understand which shocks were responsible for the performance of the Greek economy, both before and during the crisis. Second, we want to use the model to perform some simple counterfactual exercises. To achieve these objectives, the model needs to remain stylized. In particular, while we introduce many macrofinance features, we abstract from a full microfounded model of the banking sector that would put excessive constraints on the data. The model features eight exogenous stochastic processes. They are labeled ζs and each is assumed to follow an AR(1) process of the form:

$$\zeta_t^i = \rho^i \zeta_{t-1}^i + \sigma^i \varepsilon_t^i, \tag{1}$$

where the persistence and volatility parameters (ρ^i, σ^i) are estimated from the data, and the innovations ε_t^i are i.i.d. with mean zero and unit variance, and $i = \{dg, \text{spend}, ..\}$ is the name of the shock. We next specify the government, households, nonfinancial firms, and the financial sector.

A. Government

Budget Constraint

The government imposes a flat tax on income, spends G_t on goods and services, and makes social transfers T_t. Let $B_{\$,t-1}^g$ be the face value (in units of the common currency) of the debt issued at time $t - 1$ and due at time t. The nominal budget constraint of the government, conditional on not defaulting, is

$$\frac{B_{\$,t}^g}{R_t^g} + \tau_t P_{H,t} Y_t = P_{H,t}(G_t + T_t) + B_{\$,t-1}^g, \tag{2}$$

where $P_{H,t}$ is the price index of home goods (so $P_{H,t} Y_t$ is nominal GDP), τ_t is a time-varying tax rate, and R_t^g is the gross interest rate on sovereign debt. It will be convenient to work with real variables. We define real government debt $B_t^g \equiv B_{\$,t}^g / P_{H,t}$. We can then rewrite the budget constraint (conditional on not defaulting) as

$$\frac{B_t^g}{R_t^g} + \tau_t Y_t = G_t + T_t + \frac{B_{t-1}^g}{\Pi_t^H}, \tag{3}$$

where $\Pi_t^H \equiv P_{H,t} / P_{H,t-1}$ is the domestic (i.e., PPI) inflation rate from $t - 1$ to t. This formula makes clear that unexpected inflation at time t lowers the real debt burden. We use this convention for all other nominal assets.

Sovereign Default

Sovereign risk plays an important role in the Greek crisis.[24] We do not model an optimal default decision by the government. Instead, we introduce a default shock $\tilde{\varepsilon}_t^{dg}$ and assume that the default happens when $\tilde{\varepsilon}_t^{dg} < F(B_{t-1}^g / \Pi_t^H; Y_t)$. We assume that the function F is increasing in the real debt burden B_{t-1}^g / Π_t^H and decreasing in real GDP Y_t. For instance, F could simply be the ratio of debt to GDP. The expected default rate is $\mathbb{E}_t[\tilde{d}_{t+1}] = \Pr(\tilde{\varepsilon}_{t+1}^{dg} < F(B_t^g / \Pi_{t+1}^H; Y_{t+1}) | \mathcal{I}_t)$, where $\mathcal{I}_t$ is the information set of investors at time t. Notice that the distribution of $\tilde{\varepsilon}_{t+1}^{dg}$ can be time varying. What matters most in our model, however, are *expected* credit losses, which take into account the probability of default and expected loss given default. Upon default, government debt is reduced by some haircut and we let d_t^g denote expected credit losses. In our quantitative analysis, we adopt the following log-linear specification for expected credit losses at time $t + 1$:

$$d_t^g = \bar{d}_g \frac{B^g}{Y} (b_t^g - \mathbb{E}_t[y_{t+1}] - \mathbb{E}_t[\pi_{t+1}^h] + \zeta_t^{dg}), \tag{4}$$

where B^g / Y is the average debt-to-GDP ratio, $\bar{d}_g$ is a sensitivity parameter, and lowercase variables (e.g., b_t^g) represent log deviations from steady-state values. The sovereign risk shock ζ_t^{dg} follows an AR(1) as postulated in equation (1), with persistence ρ^{dg} and volatility σ^{dg}. Equation (4) states that expected default losses increase with the level of debt, decrease with the inflation rate since the latter reduces the real debt burden, and increase with the sovereign default shock ζ_t^{dg}. We will use data on sovereign yields to estimate the parameters $\{\bar{d}_g, \rho^{dg}, \sigma^{dg}\}$. The rate paid by the government on its debt is then (in log deviations)

$$r_t^g = r_t + d_t^g,$$

where r_t is the international interest rate.

Fiscal Policy

The government's spending policy and its social transfer policy are represented by the same rule

$$g_t = F_l g_{t-1} - F_n n_t - F_r r_t^g - F_b b_t^g + \zeta_t^{spend}, \tag{5}$$

where g_t is the log deviation of spending, and n_t, r_t^g, and b_t^g are log deviations of employment N_t, government credit risk spread R_t^g, and government debt B_t^g from their steady-state values, F_l, F_n, F_r, and F_b are fixed parameters, and ζ_t^{spend} is a spending shock that follows equation (1) with persistence ρ^{spend} and volatility σ^{spend}.[25] We have the same rule for transfers t_t. We allow spending itself to be autoregressive (with $F_l > 0$) to capture the fact that government programs are often scheduled for several years. This fiscal rule implies that the fiscal authorities respond to an increase in sovereign debt by tightening expenditures and reducing social transfers. The term F_n captures automatic stabilizers: as the economy deteriorates, fiscal transfers and spending tends to increase. This formulation allows government expenditures and transfers to change both because of macro and financial channels, and also because of spending shocks. Lastly, we specify the following process for the tax rate:

$$\tau_t = \bar{\tau} + \zeta_t^{tax},$$

where ζ_t^{tax} follows equation (1) with persistence ρ^{tax} and volatility σ^{tax} and $\bar{\tau}$ is calibrated to the steady state.

B.   Households

Household debt dynamics played an important role during the Great Recession, so we need to introduce borrowers and savers in the model.

Households are heterogeneous in their time preferences, as in Eggertsson and Krugman (2012) and Martin and Philippon (2014).[26] There are two types of households: a measure $1 - \chi$ of patient households indexed by $i = s$ (who will be *savers* in equilibrium), and a measure χ of impatient households indexed by $i = b$ (who will be *borrowers* in equilibrium). These households have identical preferences over goods and hours worked, but differ in their discount factors: we assume that $\beta_s > \beta_b$. Household i maximizes expected lifetime utility

$$\mathbb{E}_0 \sum_{t=0}^{\infty} \beta_i^t \left(\frac{(C_t^i)^{1-\gamma}}{1 - \gamma} - \frac{(N_t^i)^{1+\phi}}{1 + \varphi} \right),$$

where C_t^i is a bundle of home and foreign goods, defined in Gali and Monacelli (2008) by

$$C_t^i \equiv [(1 - \varpi)^{1/\epsilon_h} C_{H,t}^{i(\epsilon_h - 1)/\epsilon_h} + \varpi^{1/\epsilon_h} C_{F,t}^{i(\epsilon_h - 1)/\epsilon_h}]^{\epsilon_h/(\epsilon_h - 1)},$$

where ϵ_h is the elasticity of substitution between home and foreign goods and ϖ is the degree of openness of the economy. As usual, the home consumer price index (CPI) is

$$P_t \equiv [(1 - \varpi)P_{H,t}^{1-\epsilon_h} + \varpi P_{F,t}^{1-\epsilon_h}]^{1/(1-\epsilon_h)}.$$

Household Default

Households borrow at the rate R_t^h and can default on their debts. Let d_t^h be the credit loss rate on household loans. Default is a loss for the banks and a positive transfer to borrowers, similar to the financial shock described in Iacoviello (2015). The *borrowers'* budget constraint, following the same convention as with the government, is

$$P_t C_t^b = (1 - \tau_t)W_t N_t^b + \frac{P_{H,t}B_t^h}{R_t^h} - (1 - d_t^h)P_{H,t-1}B_{t-1}^h + P_{H,t}T_t^b. \tag{6}$$

where $(1 - \tau_t)W_t N_t^b$ denotes after-tax labor income, R_t^h the gross interest rate faced by borrowers, B_t^h is the real face value of the household debt issued at t and due at $t + 1$, and T_t^b the transfers received by borrowers. Borrowers are subject to the following borrowing limit:

$$B_t^h < \frac{\bar{B}_t^h}{\chi}.$$

In our notations, B_t^h is a *per capita* measure, while $\bar{B}_t^h$ denotes the aggregate lending capacity of the financial sector to households. We later derive this lending limit from the lender's problem, and we anticipate the result that only impatient households borrow in equilibrium. The credit loss rate is assumed to follow the process:

$$d_t^h = -\bar{d}_{hy}y_t + \bar{d}_{hb}b_t^h + \zeta_t^{dh}, \tag{7}$$

where ζ_t^{dh} follows equation (1) with persistence ρ^{dh} and volatility σ^{dh}. Equation (7) states that the credit loss rate on household loans increases with their debt level, decreases with output, and increases with a household default shock ζ^{dh}. We will use data on nonperforming loans to estimate $\{\bar{d}_{hy}, \bar{d}_{hb}, \rho_{dh}, \sigma_{dh}\}$. Note that d_t^h are *realized* credit losses at time t, unlike d_t^g, which is an *expected* loss that may or may not materialize at $t + 1$.

The *savers'* budget constraint is

$$P_t C_t^s = (1 - \tau_t)W_t N_t^s + \tilde{R}_t P_{H,t-1}S_{t-1} - P_{H,t}S_t + P_{H,t}T_t^s, \tag{8}$$

where $\tilde{R}_t$ is the nominal after-tax gross return on savings $P_{H,t-1}S_{t-1}$ at time t and T_t^s denotes real transfers to savers. This return is a complex object since savers are residual claimants: in equilibrium, they hold shares of firms and of banks, but also deposits, government bonds, and potentially foreign assets. Notice, however, that in equation (3) we have assumed a uniform tax rate on aggregate income, and this is what matters in the end. The savers' Euler equation is

$$\mathbb{E}_t\left[\beta\left(\frac{C_{t+1}^s}{C_t^s}\right)^{-\gamma}\frac{\tilde{R}_{t+1}}{\Pi_{t+1}}\right] = 1,$$

where $\Pi_{t+1} = P_{t+1} / P_t$ denotes the gross CPI inflation rate from t to $t + 1$. Finally, in the aggregate, we have

$$C_{H,t} = \chi C_{H,t}^b + (1 - \chi)C_{H,t}^s$$

$$C_t = \chi C_t^b + (1 - \chi)C_t^s.$$

Nominal Wage Rigidity

We assume a standard model of wage stickiness with a representative union setting wages à la Calvo. The wage equations are standard and satisfy:

$$\pi_t^w = \beta\mathbb{E}_t\pi_{t+1}^w - \lambda^w(w_t - \gamma c_t - \varphi n_t) + \zeta_t^w,$$

$$\pi_t = (1 - \varpi)\pi_t^h + \varpi\pi_t^f,$$

$$w_t = w_{t-1} + \pi_t^w - \pi_t^h,$$

where π_t^w denotes wage inflation, w_t is the real wage in terms of the CPI $(\ln(W_t / P_t))$, ζ_t^w is a wage-markup shock that follows equation (1) with persistence ρ^w and volatility σ^w; π_t denotes CPI inflation, π_t^h is home inflation, π_t^f is foreign inflation, and λ^w is derived from the Calvo wage-setting process. The first equation is a forward-looking wage Phillips curve. Wage inflation depends on expected future wage inflation, on the marginal rate of substitution between consumption and leisure, and on the wage-markup shock ζ^w.

C. Nonfinancial Firms

We separate firms into goods-producing and capital-producing firms in order to simplify the derivation of the price-setting equation on the one hand, and the investment/Q equation on the other hand.

Capital-Producing Firms

Capital firms convert consumption goods into capital through investment and rent this capital to goods-producing firms for a rental rate $Z_{k,t}$. The capital stock evolves according to

$$K_t = (1 - \delta)K_{t-1} + I_t, \qquad (9)$$

and real period profits (i.e., scaled by $P_{H,t}$) for these firms are given by

$$Div_t = Z_{k,t}K_{t-1} - I_t - \frac{\varphi_k}{2} K_{t-1}\left(\frac{I_t}{K_{t-1}} - \delta\right)^2,$$

where the last term captures adjustment costs to physical capital. Let R_t^k be the firm's funding cost. The real value of capital-producing firms is $V(K_{t-1})$ and satisfies the following Bellman equation

$$V(K_{t-1}) = \max_{I_t, K_t}\left\{Z_{k,t}K_{t-1} - I_t - \frac{\varphi_k}{2} K_{t-1}\left(\frac{I_t}{K_{t-1}} - \delta\right)^2 + \mathbb{E}_t\left[\frac{\Pi_{H,t+1}}{R_t^k} V(K_t)\right]\right\}$$

subject to equation (9).

   Let $x_t \equiv (K_t - K_{t-1}) / K_{t-1}$ be the net investment rate. Given our homotheticity assumptions, we guess and verify that the value function can be written as

$$V(K_{t-1}) = \mathcal{V}_t K_{t-1},$$

where

$$V_t = \max_{x_t} \left\{ Z_{k,t} - x_t - \delta - \frac{\varphi_k}{2} x_t^2 + (1 + x_t) \mathbb{E}_t \left[\frac{\Pi_{H,t+1}}{R_t^k} V_{t+1} \right] \right\}. \quad (10)$$

Define Tobin's Q as the end-of-period value of assets divided by the end-of-period replacement cost of capital

$$Q_t \equiv \mathbb{E}_t \left[\frac{\Pi_{H,t+1}}{R_t^k} V_{t+1} \right]. \quad (11)$$

Optimal investment yields the standard Q-equation:

$$x_t = \frac{Q_t - 1}{\varphi_k}. \quad (12)$$

Goods-Producing Firms

Goods-producing firms produce differentiated varieties of a domestic good using capital and labor. The production function for a producer of good j is

$$Y_t(j) = AK_t(j)^\alpha N_t(j)^{1-\alpha},$$

where A is aggregate total factor productivity (TFP). We focus here on the case where TFP is constant because the model is simpler to present and fits the data quite well. Goods-producing firms are subject to a financial friction that requires them to pay part of their operating costs in advance, before production is undertaken, as in Christiano, Eichenbaum, and Evans (2005) or Jermann and Quadrini (2012).[27] Let ψ_{sk} denote the fraction of input cost that needs to be financed by working capital loans. Profits are given by

$$\text{Profits}_t = \text{Revenues}_t - \text{Costs}_t[1 + \psi_{sk}(R_t^k - 1)].$$

Standard cost minimization yields an expression for the nominal marginal cost,

$$MC_t^\$ = \frac{[1 + \psi_{sk}(R_t^k - 1)]}{A} \left(\frac{P_{H,t} Z_{k,t}}{\alpha} \right)^\alpha \left(\frac{W_t}{1 - \alpha} \right)^{1-\alpha}.$$

Notice that the working-capital friction can be represented by an incremental marginal cost for the firm. This will be an important property, as it allows financial frictions to pass through to inflation. Differentiated goods producers solve a standard Calvo problem, given factor demands. Given real marginal cost $MC_t \equiv MC_t^\$ / P_{H,t}$, we can write the (log-linear) Phillips curve as

$$\pi_{h,t} = \lambda_p \mathrm{mc}_t + \beta \mathbb{E}_t \pi_{h,t+1} + \zeta_t^{\pi h},$$

where λ_p is derived from the Calvo price-setting process, β is the discount factor of savers, and the (log) real marginal cost is

$$\mathrm{mc}_t = \frac{\psi_{sk} R^k}{1 + \psi_{sk}(R^k - 1)} r_t^k + \alpha z_{k,t} + (1 - \alpha)(w_t + \varpi tot_t);$$

$\zeta_t^{\pi h}$ is an AR(1) price markup shock that satisfies equation (1) with persistence $\rho^{\pi h}$ and volatility $\sigma^{\pi h}$. Notice that marginal costs are deflated in terms of the price of home-produced goods, hence the terms-of-trade adjustment for the real wage, which reflects the term $P_t / P_{H,t}$. Finally, we have the usual static optimality condition for labor demand:

$$\frac{K_{t-1}}{N_t} = \frac{\alpha}{1 - \alpha} \frac{W_t}{P_{H,t} Z_{k,t}}.$$

D. Banks, Sudden Stop, and Funding Cost

A fully specified model of banking intermediation as in Gertler and Kiyotaki (2010) is beyond the scope of this paper. Moreover, the financial-sector data necessary to estimate the restrictions of such a model, such as the balance sheet of banks and its components, are not available (see Faria-e-Castro [2016] for a more ambitious estimation). There is, however, one fundamental insight from the models of banking intermediation that is theoretically straightforward and, as we show later, empirically relevant. At the heart of many banking models is a capital requirement of the type

$$V_t^{bank} \geq \kappa \left(\frac{B_t^k}{R_t^k} + \frac{B_t^h}{R_t^h} \right), \tag{13}$$

where V_t^{bank} is the franchise value of the banking sector and B_t^k and B_t^h denote the outstanding loans to the corporate nonfinancial and household sectors, respectively, both measured at the end of period t. This equation assumes that there is no capital requirement for sovereign exposure, as was the case in Europe at the time. Equation (13) says that bank equity V_t^{bank} must cover a fraction κ of the total credit exposure to firms and to households. The second important equation is the current account of the banking sector:

$$\Pi_{H,t+1} E_{t+1} = (1 - d_{t+1}^k) B_t^k + (1 - d_{t+1}^h) B_t^h - D_t. \tag{14}$$

Equation (14) states that nominal bank earnings $\Pi_{H,t+1}E_{t+1}$ consist of repayment from firms and households net of default losses, minus the repayment of banks' liabilities D_t. Finally, bank value solves a Bellman equation

$$V_t^{bank} = \max_{\{B_t\}, D_t} Div_t + \mathbb{E}_t\left[\frac{\Lambda_{t+1}}{\Pi_{t+1}}\Pi_{H,t+1}((1-\sigma)E_{t+1} + \sigma V_{t+1}^{bank})\right], \quad (15)$$

where σ is an exogenous exit rate, Λ_{t+1} is the pricing kernel of savers, and dividends Div_t are assumed to be a fixed fraction of earnings E_t. This captures the assumption that banks cannot raise equity very quickly, and it implies that capital losses lead to tighter lending constraints, as least in the short run.

Equations (13), (14), and (15) capture the fundamental credit channel in the economy. Credit losses reduce banks' earnings in equation (14), lower bank value in equation (15), and tighten capital requirement in equation (13). This leads to an increase in the economy's funding cost. All else equal, this channel is stronger the higher the bank leverage. We capture this idea in two steps. First, we model the banks' (log) funding cost r_t^d as

$$r_t^d = r_t + \zeta_t^r + \xi^d L \mathbb{E}_t[d_{t+1}^p],$$

where L is bank leverage (assets over equity capital) in steady state, ξ^d is a sensitivity parameter to be estimated, d_{t+1}^p measures losses on *private* credit portfolio (households and firms' loans), and ζ_t^r is a sudden stop shock that increases funding costs to banks; ζ^r satisfies equation (1) with persistence ρ^r and volatility σ^r. Since we only have data on total nonperforming loans, we will assume that loss rates on households' and firms' credit are identical: $d_t^h = d_t^k \equiv d_t^p$.

Second, we assume that banks' funding costs are passed on to banks' customers (with a constant margin that drops out in logs), therefore

$$r_t^k = r_t^d.$$

Note that in our notations above, r_t^k is the *funding cost* of firms, which enters directly the Q equations (10) and (11). For households, we had defined r_t^h as the interest rate on loans, gross of expected losses, that enters the budget constraint (6). If we were to quote an interest rate for corporate loans, it would be $r_t^d + \mathbb{E}_t[d_{t+1}^k]$, and the expected return would be r_t^d. With our assumptions, the sudden stop shock is an increase in the country's funding cost above and beyond what can be explained by domestic intermediation spreads.

E.   Equilibrium

All transactions with the rest of the world happen at rate R_t. Let NFA_t denote the net foreign assets of the country (in units of domestic goods). By definition, NFA evolves as

$$\frac{NFA_t}{R_t} = NFA_{t-1} - \mathbf{P}_t\mathbf{C}_t + P_{H,t}\left(Y_t - G_t - I_t - \frac{\varphi_k}{2}K_{t-1}\left(\frac{K_t}{K_{t-1}} - 1\right)^2\right).$$

As is common in the literature, we make a technical assumption to ensure stationarity of NFA.[28] We assume that there is a (small) price impact of NFA on the country's borrowing (or saving) rate

$$\frac{\partial \log R_t}{\partial \log NFA_t} = -\epsilon_r,$$

where ϵ_r is a small but strictly positive number. Clearing in the market for domestic goods requires

$$Y_t = C_{Ht} + \left(\frac{P_{Ht}}{\mathbf{P}_t^F}\right)^{-\epsilon_f}\mathbf{C}_t^F + G_t + I_t + \frac{\varphi_k}{2}K_{t-1}\left(\frac{K_t}{K_{t-1}} - 1\right)^2,$$

where $\mathbf{C}_t^F$ represents aggregate foreign consumption and $\mathbf{P}_t^F$ the foreign CPI; ϵ_f is the demand elasticity.

Household Debt

Banks lend to domestic households. We assume that borrowers are impatient enough to hit their borrowing limits, so

$$\chi B_t^h = \bar{B}_t^h.$$

The basic model does not pin down a unique borrowing rate R_t^h. As long as $R_t^h > R_t^d$, banks are willing to lend more. As long as $\beta_b\mathbb{E}_t[(R_t^h / \Pi_{t+1})u'(c_{t+1})] < u'(c_t)$ borrowers want to borrow more. In steady state, any $R^h \in (\beta_s^{-1}, \beta_b^{-1})$ is potentially an equilibrium.[29] This issue is present in and out of steady state. For the steady state, however, a reasonable assumption is that the lending spread is pinned down by free entry into banking. We will directly calibrate the steady-state spread $\Delta_t \equiv R_t^h / R_t$ using empirical studies of financial intermediation: Philippon (2012) shows that the spread is remarkably stable in the long run at $\Delta = 1.02$. Out of steady state, we expect both loan supply and loan demand to decrease in response to an increase in banks' funding cost, so we specify in log deviations from steady-state values

$$b_t^h = \psi_{bh}b_{t-1}^h - \xi^{bh}r_t^d + \zeta_t^{bh}, \tag{16}$$

where ζ_t^{bh} is an AR(1) shock that satisfies equation (1) with persistence ρ^{bh} and volatility σ^{bh}.

Interest Rates and Funding Costs in the Model

There are four interest rates in the model, so it is useful to summarize them here. First of all, there is the baseline interest rate r_t that enters the NFA and the Euler equation of savers. Above and beyond this rate there are spreads and expected losses, so that

$$r_t^d = r_t + \zeta_t^r + \xi^d \mathbb{LE}_t\left[d_{t+1}^p\right]$$

$$d_t^p = -\bar{d}_y y_t + \bar{d}_b b_{t-1} + \zeta_t^{def}$$

$$r_t^k = r_t^d$$

$$r_t^h = r_t^d + \mathbb{E}_t\left[d_{t+1}^p\right]$$

$$r_t^g = r_t + d_t^g$$

$$d_t^g = \bar{d}_g \frac{B^g}{Y}\left(b_t^g - \mathbb{E}_t\left[y_{t+1}\right] - \mathbb{E}_t\left[\pi_{t+1}^h\right] + \zeta_t^{dg}\right)$$

Notice our assumptions here. First, domestic savers do not earn higher expected returns when there is a sudden stop. They earn r, which remains essentially constant and equal to the rate in the Eurozone. Second, the banks are sensitive to the sudden stop and to credit losses. The sudden stop ζ_t^r enters the economy via the banks, which then pass it on to their customers. Nonperforming loans d_{t+1}^p hurt banks and increase the funding costs of all private agents. We only have data on total nonperforming loans, so we do not model separately firm and household defaults. We assume that they move together and we estimate only one equation for d_t^p. The shock ζ_t^{def} captures the evolution of NPLs that is not predicted by macroeconomic fundamentals.

Fourth, the government is not necessarily affected by the same sudden stop as the private sector. The shock ζ_t^{dg} raises the cost of funds for the government. It captures pessimism by investors about the creditworthiness of the government, whether or not this pessimism is borne out in equilibrium. There are many reasons why ζ_t^{dg} and ζ_t^r are different, but let us just mention two. First, as we discussed, the ECB provided funding to Greek banks both directly and indirectly via emergency liquidity assistance, insulating them from sovereign risk, in particular during the sovereign debt restructuring. Second, government debt is now largely held by official creditors, rather than domestic banks, attenuating the link between sovereign and banking risks.

Finally, while the two shocks ζ^r and ζ^{dg} are conceptually distinct, the model features important feedback loops between the sovereign and the banks. This "doom loop" has been extensively discussed in policy circles and analyzed in stylized models (see Brunnermeier et al. 2016; Farhi and Tirole 2016). The impact of banks on the sovereign is always present via general equilibrium effects and tax revenues. If banks experience a sudden stop, the economy contracts and credit risk, both private and sovereign, increases. Conversely, if sovereign risk increases, the worsening of economic outcomes increases default in the private sector, affecting bank values. Hence, our model features rich and complex interactions between the financial and public sectors.

V. Estimation

In this section, we describe the estimation of the model. We combine the Kalman Filter with Bayesian techniques, which allow us to recover estimates for the structural shocks that affected Greece during the first decade of the twenty-first century. These estimated shocks can then be used to conduct counterfactual exercises.

A. Data, Observables, and Calibration

The sample is annual, from 1999 to 2015. Figure 16 shows the eight series that we feed into the model, all measured in log deviations from steady state. For interest rates and inflation, we also take the difference from the Eurozone average series.

The model features as many shocks as observables, which are described in table 4.[30] In addition, we allow for measurement error to domestic inflation, wage inflation, and the measure of nonperforming loans since these variables are quite noisy and/or measured imprecisely. Specifically, we assume that we observe $\tilde{x}_t$, where

$$\tilde{x}_t = x_t + \varepsilon_t^{error}$$

and ε_t^{error} is a measurement error term.[31] For household debt, we take as a proxy the series for total credit to the private nonfinancial sector for Greece.

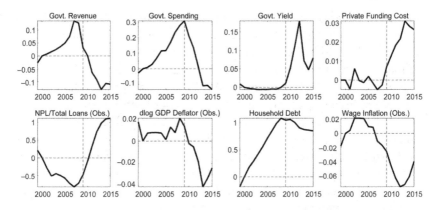

Fig. 16. Observables: Filtered data

Note: All series are in log deviations from steady state. Interest rates and inflation rates are also in deviation from the Eurozone average. The NPL, GDP deflator, and wages are assumed to be measured with errors.

Table 4
Observables and Shocks

Observable	Description	Shock	Shock Description
$G_t + T_t$	Government spending	ζ_t^{spend}	Govt. spending shock
$\tau_t Y_t$	Government revenues	ζ_t^{tax}	Tax rate shock
R_t^g	Greek government spread over EZ average	ζ_t^{dg}	Sovereign risk shock
R_t^k	SME spread over EZ average	ζ_t^{r}	Funding cost shock
$\exp(d_t^p)$	Nonperforming loans/total loans, $def = npl$	ζ^{def}	Private default shock
Π_t	Greece CPI – EZ CPI	$\zeta^{\pi h}$	PPI cost push shock
B_t^h	Household debt	ζ_t^{bh}	Household credit shock
Π_t^w	Greek wage inflation – EZ wage inflation	ζ^{w}	Wage inflation shock

Note: We use a combination of calibration and estimation. We calibrate parameters that affect steady-state variables. Most of the calibrated parameters take standard values for small open economies and are reported in tables A5, A6, and A7 in the appendix.

We estimate the remaining "dynamic" parameters using standard Bayesian estimation techniques following An and Schorfheide (2007).[32] We estimate a total of 25 parameters: the persistence and volatility of the eight structural shocks, the variance of the three measurement errors, as well as six other dynamic parameters: the elasticity of expected

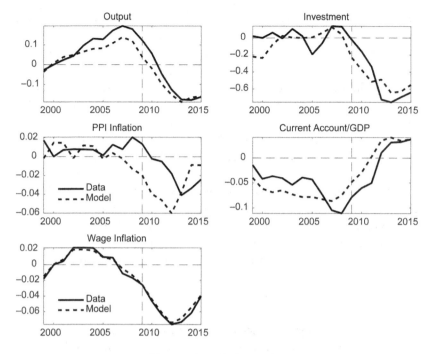

Fig. 17. Smoothed variables

Note: The figure reports the model estimated values of output, investment, inflation (price and wage), and next exports-to-GDP ratio. Both inflation series are part of the estimation, but are assumed to be measured with error.

sovereign default losses with respect to debt to GDP, the elasticities of private default with respect to GDP and debt, the persistence of the household credit equation, the elasticity of household credit with respect to the cost of funds, and the pass-through of future default to current lending rates. The estimation results, along with our choice of priors, are described in table A9 in the appendix.

B.   Results

Smoothed Variables

The smoothed shocks are reported in figure A2 in the appendix. We also use the Kalman Filter to extract the sequences implied by the model for the remaining endogenous variables. This provides a good way of gauging the fit of the model. We present the most important series in figure 17, where we plot the data and model-implied paths for GDP, corporate investment, PPI inflation, and current account-to-GDP ratio.

The main point to take away from figure 17 is that the model's predictions for output and investment are good, even though we did not use any data on output or investment in the estimation. This means that our fiscal and financial multipliers are consistent with the data. For domestic price inflation, whose measurement is imperfect, we plot the observed raw data series against the model-based series that filters out the noise.[33] For wage inflation, on the other hand, measurement errors appear small.

Figures 18–21 are the first main findings of the model. In each case, the black line is the smoothed value of the corresponding endogenous variable, in percent deviations from steady state. Each bar represents the contribution of a corresponding shock and its lagged values to the predicted value of the corresponding variable at each point in time.[34]

GDP

The GDP series in figure 18 shows how our model interprets the Greek crisis. Around 2000, credit demand is high and credit risk is low, so households borrow and consume. During that period, government spending increases more than predicted by our fiscal rule, as captured by the positive spending shocks. This is the same finding as in Martin and Philippon (2014). This massive fiscal expansion explains most of the output gap, which is around +15% in 2007. The recessionary shocks arrive in sequence. The model finds that the sudden stop starts in 2009 and remains very significant until 2013, depressing output by 5% to 10%. It is important to keep in mind that this is a decomposition with respect to shocks, not propagation mechanisms. For example, the sudden stop shock appears first in the funding cost of the private sector, but its effects propagate via several mechanisms: lower credit, lower demand, more private and sovereign default risk, and so forth. The effect of all of these mechanisms is aggregated into the bar corresponding to the sudden stop shock (right-slanted dashed line).

Role of Government Spending

It is important to understand how exactly the model interprets fiscal policy shocks. We feed in actual government spending in our calibration, and since the model implies significant fiscal multipliers (around

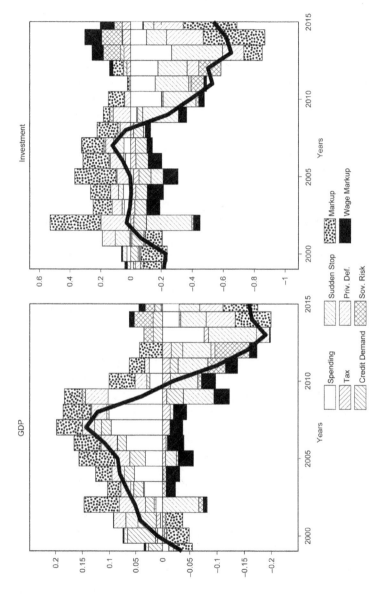

Fig. 18. Decomposition of GDP and investment

Note: The figure reports the decomposition of the predicted path for output (left panel) and investment (right panel) into the contribution of each of the eight shocks.

1.5), fiscal dynamics "accounts" for much of GDP dynamics. But that is not how the model computes the contribution of each shock. The model seeks to understand *why* government spending moves using the fiscal rule (5). Government default risk increases in 2011 and especially in 2012, the year of the sovereign default. From 2010 to 2012, there is no autonomous negative spending shock. In other words, the observed path of government spending can be explained by our fiscal rule, given the increase in funding costs.[35] In reality, spending was largely determined by official financing. Under the 2010 program, the Greek government received 110 billion euros. Another 130 billion euros became available as part of the 2012 program and debt restructuring. What the model says is that the size of the program (and the implied path of spending and taxes) was consistent with a fiscal rule such as equation (5).

Autonomous (negative) spending shocks emerge in 2013, and to a lesser extent in 2014, because sovereign spreads decrease and spending does not increase (or even decreases). This coincides with the implementation of the 2012 IMF and Eurogroup program.

Figure 19 reports the decomposition for government debt (left panel) and its yield (right panel). Both variables are part of the estimation. We see that the accumulation of government debt is mostly the consequence of past spending decisions. Fiscal expansions do not increase debt much in the short run because GDP and revenues increase. In the long run, however, they increase debt. The debt accumulation *after* the crisis in figure 19 is mostly due to spending shocks that happened *before* the crisis. The yield on sovereign debt is also mostly affected by the fiscal shock, and also by sovereign risk. We observe a sharp decline in sovereign risk following the 2012 debt restructuring.

Markups and Nonperforming Loans

Finally, starting in 2013, two important factors dragging down the Greek economy are the rise in nonperforming loans and the increase in price markups. As in Agatha Christie's *Murder on the Orient Express*, the boom and bust in Greek output per capita cannot be attributed to a single cause: over time, different shocks played a role. This decomposition also indicates that, by 2015, the external drags on the Greek economy due to the sudden stop and the sovereign debt crisis have subsided. What remains are mostly domestic factors: some fiscal austerity, mounting losses on private loans, and the relative lack of adjustment in Greek prices relative to wages.

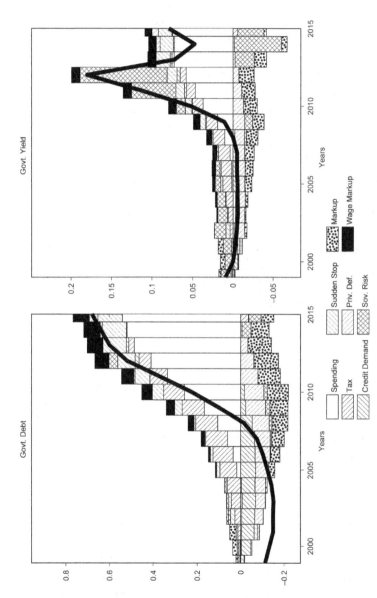

Fig. 19. Decomposition of government debt and yield

Note: The figure reports the decomposition of the predicted path for sovereign debt (left panel) and the yield on sovereign debt (right panel) into the contribution of each of the eight shocks.

Investment (figure 18, right panel) is mostly affected by the increase in funding costs due to the sudden stop in 2009–2013. In 2014 and 2015, investment remains subdued largely because of private-sector credit risk, fiscal austerity, and especially price markup shocks.

Figure 20 reports both expected private defaults (left panel) and the funding cost of the private sector (right panel). Both variables are also perfectly predicted by the model, by construction. Private credit losses were low early in the sample because of low private default risk and the strong stimulus coming from government spending. After 2007, private credit losses mount rapidly, mostly as a consequence of macrodynamics. The increase in funding costs due to the sudden stop, the collapse in credit demand, fiscal austerity, and the increase in private default risk all contribute to raise private credit losses. The right panel illustrates that the main driver of private sector cost of funds was the sudden stop.[36]

Figure 21 reports government spending (left panel) and revenues (right panel). Government spending is largely autonomous in the boom, a finding consistent with Martin and Philippon (2014). In the bust, it is explained by the funding constraint, and then by restrictions consistent with the IMF/Eurogroup program. Government revenues are dominated by macrodynamics. While tax shocks move from negative to positive, revenues decline overall due to the sudden stop and its effect on output and investment, the impact of spending cuts on output, and mounting nonperforming loans.

Finally, figure 22 decomposes domestic price (left panel) and wage inflation (right panel). Fiscal austerity, private sector default, and wage compression (negative wage markup shocks) contribute to deflationary price and wages forces. Yet wage adjustment is significantly larger than price adjustment, and the difference can largely be attributed to price markup shocks $\zeta^{\pi h}$.

C. Impulse Responses

We next explore the internal mechanics of the model by plotting some impulse response functions, estimated at the posterior mean of the parameters. Each impulse response reports the effect of a one standard deviation shock on the variables of the model, expressed in percent deviation from their steady state. We present here only a few impulse responses. Other figures are in the appendix.

Figure 23 shows the response to a transfer shock, ε_i^{spend}. Our model is not Ricardian. An increase in government spending raises the consumption

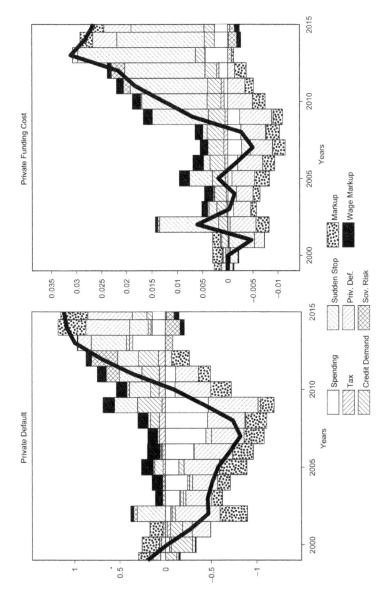

Fig. 20. Decomposition of private default and funding cost

Note: The figure reports the decomposition of the predicted path for household credit losses (left panel) and the borrowing rate (right panel) into the contribution of each of the eight shocks.

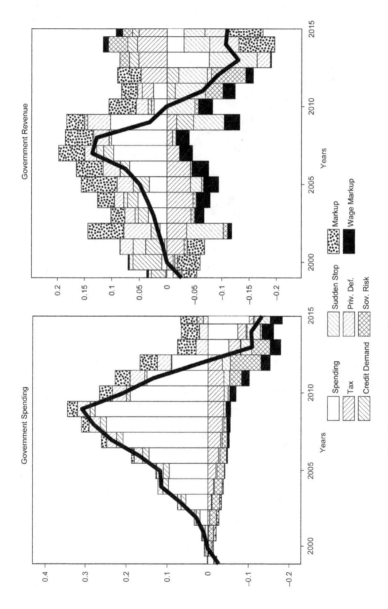

Fig. 21. Decomposition of government spending and revenues

Note: The figure reports the decomposition of the predicted path for government spending (left panel) and government revenues (right panel) into the contribution of each of the eight shocks.

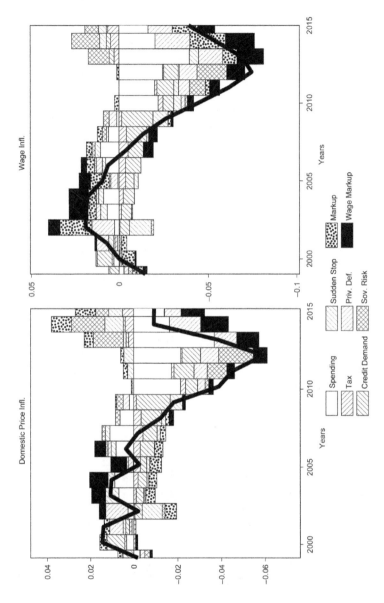

Fig. 22. Decomposition of domestic price and wage inflation

Note: The figure reports the decomposition of the predicted path for domestic price and wage inflation into the contribution of each of the eight shocks.

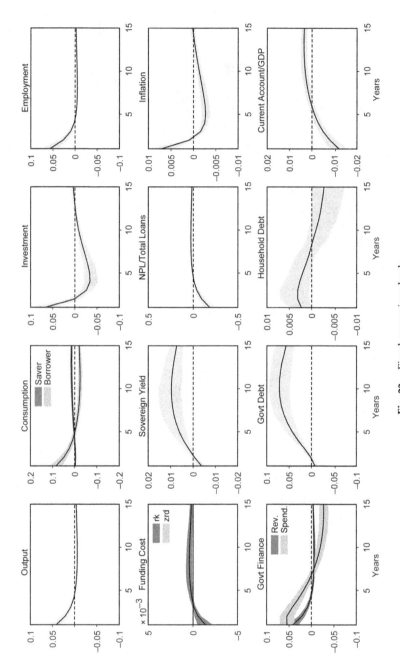

Fig. 23. Fiscal expansion shock

Note: The figure reports 90% Bayesian confidence bands.

of borrowers, as well as output, employment, investment, and inflation. As the economy expands, nonperforming loans decline. Over time, public debt gradually increases, which pushes up sovereign yields. The model thus features a significant but temporary effect of a fiscal expansion on output, and a long-lasting effect on the level of public debt.

Figure 24 shows the response to a sovereign risk shock, ε_t^{dg}. The fiscal rule forces a cut in spending that leads to a drop in output, employment, and inflation. The decline in output increases private credit risk, which feeds back into funding costs and curtails investment. Figure 24 (and figure A3 in the appendix, which looks at the response to a private default shock) illustrates the sovereign/bank interactions: as sovereign risk increases, the funding costs of the private sector are affected. Conversely, as private default risk increases, sovereign risk increases as well. In our model, these effects work via general equilibrium effects.

Finally, figure 25 shows the response to a sudden stop, ε^r. An increase in the country's funding cost causes corporate investment to decline. Impatient household debt declines as well, and so does borrower consumption. The decline in consumption and investment drives output, employment, and inflation down. The interest rate on government debt increases because the decline in economic activity heightens sovereign risks.

VI.   Counterfactuals

In this section, we run five counterfactual exercises. To understand our counterfactual exercises, let y_{it} denote the observation of variable i at date t, and let $\hat{x}_{it}$ denote the smoothed value for variable i at date t. Let $\hat{x}_i^T \equiv \{\hat{x}_{i,t}\}_{t=0}^T$ denote the estimated smoothed sequence for variable i in our sample period for $t = 0, \ldots, T$ and denote $\hat{x}^T$ the sequence of all smoothed variables: $\hat{x}^T \equiv \{\hat{x}_i^T\}$. Every estimated sequence can be written as a mapping $\Gamma(.)$ from the estimated parameters $\hat{\Theta}$ and the sequences of smoothed shocks, $\{\hat{\varepsilon}_k\}_{k=1}^K \equiv \{\hat{\varepsilon}_{k,t}\}_{k=1,t=0}^{K,T}$, where K is the number of shocks in our model:

$$\hat{x}^T = \Gamma(\hat{\Theta}, \{\hat{\varepsilon}_k^T\}_{k=1}^K).$$

A counterfactual exercise consists in postulating an alternate choice for $\hat{\Theta}$ and $\{\hat{\varepsilon}_k^T\}_{k=1}^K$, denoted $\tilde{\Theta}$ and $\{\tilde{\varepsilon}_k^T\}_{k=1}^K$ and then compute the counterfactual $\tilde{x}^T$ as:

$$\tilde{x}^T = \Gamma(\tilde{\Theta}, \{\tilde{\varepsilon}_k^T\}_{k=1}^K).$$

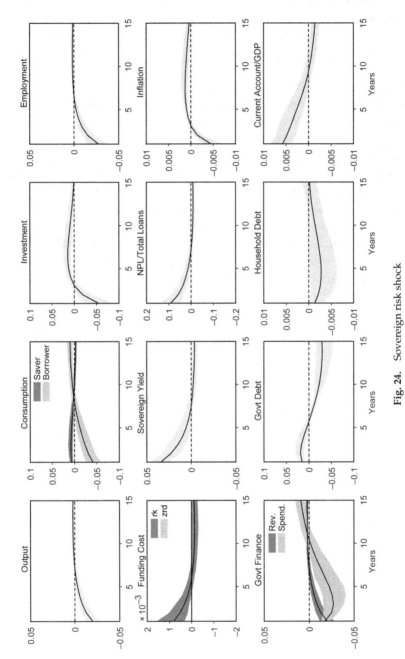

Fig. 24. Sovereign risk shock

Note: The figure reports 90% Bayesian confidence bands.

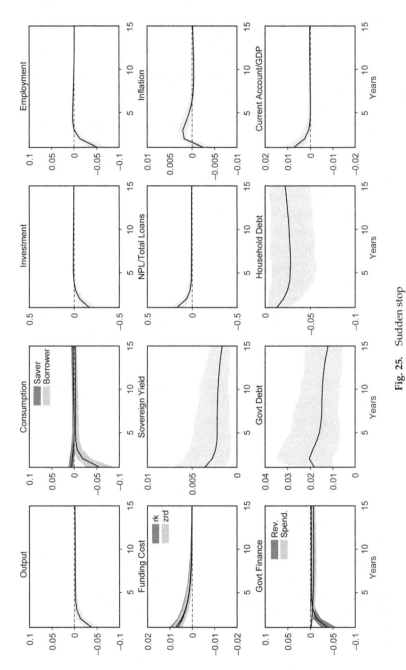

Fig. 25. Sudden stop

Note: The figure reports 90% Bayesian confidence bands.

57

Based on the empirical analysis of section III and the analytical results of section V, we begin with a "low leverage" counterfactual. In that exercise, we ask what would have happened, through the lens of our model, if Greece's external and internal leverage had been similar to that of emerging-market economies about to experience a sudden stop. This counterfactual is motivated by the evidence from section III that documents the severity and persistence of the Greek crisis when compared to many other—especially emerging-market economies—crises. In our second counterfactual we ask: What would Greece have looked like without a "sudden stop" for private capital? Setting $\varepsilon_t^r = 0$ for all t represents the situation that would have prevailed with a well-functioning European Banking Union.[37] The third counterfactual asks what would have happened if Greece had maintained fiscal discipline before 2007. In that counterfactual, we set $\varepsilon_t^{spend} = 0$ for all t. The fourth counterfactual explores the role of price markups and sets $\varepsilon_t^{\pi h} = 0$ for all t. This is an important exercise, since the analytical decomposition of section V indicates that price markup shocks are an important drag on output and investment in 2014 and 2015. Our last counterfactual considers the role of price and wage stickiness in the adjustment path of Greece. As discussed in section III, other countries such as Latvia or Estonia that maintained their peg in the face of a sudden stop and output collapse experienced a much faster recovery. We ask how much a lack of price flexibility may be responsible for this outcome. To do this, we reduce the calibrated price stickiness parameters λ_p and λ_w while keeping the sequence of shocks unchanged.

A. Low Leverage Economy

For our first counterfactual exercise, we calibrate the Greek economy to the level of government, private, and banking leverage observed in the typical emerging-market economy just prior to a sudden stop.

Table 5 compares the leverage of Greece to the leverage of other EMs that have experienced a sudden stop as described in section III. It is clear that leverage is much higher in Greece along all dimensions, and in particular with respect to sovereign debt. Typically, leverage in EMs prior to sudden stops is roughly half of that of Greece prior to the 2010 crisis. Accordingly, we reduce B^h / Y, B^g / Y, G / Y, T / Y, and bank leverage at the steady state by half. With these alternate parameters $\tilde{\Theta}$, and the same sequence of smoothed shocks $\{\hat{\varepsilon}_k^T\}_{k=1}^K$, we recompute the path of the endogenous variables, $\tilde{x}^T$.

Table 5
Leverage and Imbalances before Sudden Stop

	Greece	Typical EME	Min.	Max.
Credit/GDP	1.01	0.46	0.025	1.46
Sovereign debt/GDP	1.38	0.343	0.063	0.68
Current account/GDP	–0.083	–0.039	–0.10	+0.17

Note: Average from $t-6$ to $t-2$ where t is the year of the sudden stop. Credit refers to domestic credit to nonfinancial institutions.

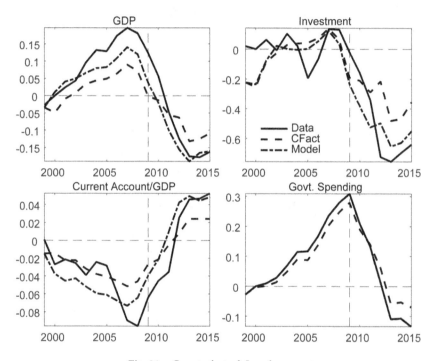

Fig. 26. Counterfactual: Low leverage
Note: The figure reports the counterfactual when we set the government, private and banking leverage to the value for EM economies prior to a sudden stop.

Figure 26 reports the path for the actual data (solid line), the smoothed original estimates (tightly dotted line) and the counterfactual (dotted line). In this counterfactual, Greece would have been much more constrained in the build-up phase of the crisis. The smaller size of its government sector would have prevented it from excessively stimulating its economy, reducing the output gap from +14.1% in 2007 in the smoothed estimates to +9.2% (top-left panel). Once the fiscal contraction, sudden stop, and sovereign risk materialize, we find that they would have had a substantially more muted impact on the economy. For instance, the peak-to-trough decline in output is now only 22% instead of 33%. The decline in investment is also more muted, around 64% instead of 77%. Hence, some of the excess drop in investment observed in figure 9 can be attributed to the exceptional leverage of the Greek economy relative to other emerging economies. Were it not for its elevated exposure levels, Greece would have experienced a more typical emerging market trifecta crisis. Similarly, limited external exposure would have reduced the build up in external deficits, to –6.7% of GDP instead of –8.6%, and consequently imposed a smaller turnaround in the current account (+8% instead of +12.7%).

B. No Sudden Stop Shocks

For our second counterfactual exercise, we keep our vector of estimated and calibrated parameters fixed, $\hat{\Theta}$, and we recompute $\tilde{x}^T$ based on a new sequence of smoothed shocks. This new sequence is identical to the one that we estimated, with the exception that we set the private sudden stop shock to zero, $\hat{\varepsilon}_t^r = 0$. Figure 27 reports the results with the same convention as the previous counterfactual.

The absence of a private sudden stop can be interpreted as the outcome in presence of a well-functioning banking union. With a European-level resolution and supervision authority, foreign and domestic creditors would have no incentive to run. The counterfactual reveals that a banking union would have had almost no impact on the path of output during the build up (figure 27, top-left panel). Recall that the path for output prior to 2007 was largely driven by high credit demand, as well as by the stimulative effect of expansionary fiscal policies. The eventual consolidation of fiscal accounts was unavoidable, with or without a private sudden stop. In other words, a banking union would not have insulated Greece from the consequences of its past unsustainable fiscal policies. However, the sudden stop did contribute to worsen the output response once the crisis got under way. By 2013, we find that output would have been higher by 9 percentage points in the absence of sudden stop, although the difference would have subsequently declined. Much of the effect of the sudden stop was on investment (top-right panel), which would have been higher by 33 percentage points otherwise in 2013.

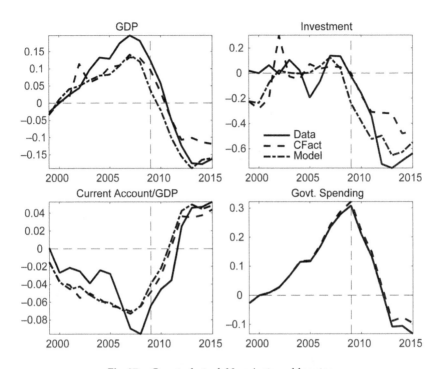

Fig. 27. Counterfactual: No private sudden stop

Note: The figure reports the counterfactual when we set the private sudden stop shock $\tilde{\varepsilon}_t^r = 0$.

C. Fiscal Discipline

As mentioned already many times, it is perhaps not entirely surprising that Greece would experience a serious downturn given the size of the needed fiscal consolidation. What would have happened if, instead, Greece had followed a virtuous fiscal path since 2000? We consider this counterfactual by setting $\tilde{\varepsilon}_t^{spend} = 0$, that is, assuming away both the fiscal excesses of the 2000–2007 period and the subsequent required fiscal consolidation. Figure 28 reports the results. Not surprisingly, the crisis would have been much more muted, especially for output, government spending, and net exports. Output (top-left panel) would have declined by around 16% instead of 33% between 2007 and 2013. Government spending (bottom-right panel) would have barely increased between 2000 and 2010, then declined a modest 8% instead of 34% relative to steady state. Finally, the current account would have started to improve as early as 2006.[38]

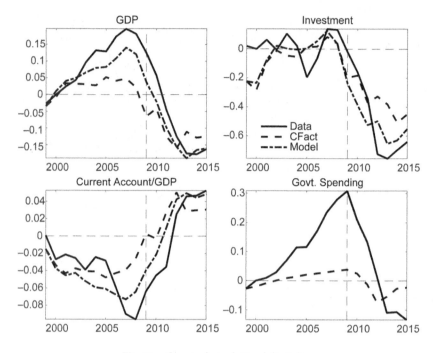

Fig. 28.   Counterfactual: Fiscal discipline

Note: The figure reports the counterfactual when we set the spending shocks $\tilde{\varepsilon}_t^{spend} = 0$.

D.   No Markup Shocks

Next, we consider the relative contribution of price markup shocks by studying the paths of the variables of the model while turning shocks to domestic inflation $\hat{\varepsilon}_t^{\pi h} = 0$.

Figure 29 reports the results. The figure suggests that price markup shocks play an important role in the analysis. Perhaps surprisingly, in the absence of price markup shocks Greece would have experienced no boom (top-left panel), but a bust of a similar magnitude. Most importantly, this counterfactual reveals that the increase in price markups has become a significant force hindering the recovery of the Greek economy: without markup shocks, investment would have recovered to 18% of its steady-state value (top-right panel) by 2015, while output would have rebounded by 11% of its steady-state value since the trough. Interestingly, lower markups would translate into stronger deflation, which would have adversely affected government debt dynamics, triggering further declines in government spending (bottom-right panel). We infer

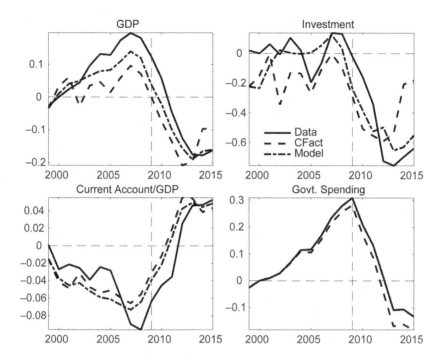

Fig. 29. Counterfactual: No domestic price markup shocks
Note: The figure reports the counterfactual when we set price markup shocks $\tilde{\varepsilon}_t^{\pi h} = 0$.

from this counterfactual analysis that price dynamics are crucial to the recovery of the Greek economy. Recall that in our model, marginal costs include a financial component due to working capital. The increase in price-marginal costs markups cannot, therefore, be attributed to an increase in financial frictions that raise the nonwage components of the marginal costs. Instead, our estimates indicate that lack of entry and competition in product markets, as well as a rise in firms' costs stemming from factors such as the uncertainty about EZ exit and higher taxes on key inputs, may be responsible for a very sluggish recovery.

E. Latvia: Low Price Stickiness

Our final counterfactual aims to explore the role of price and wage rigidities more closely. Ideally, one would like to analyze how the Greek economy would have performed had it left the euro and been able to depreciate its own currency. Yet this is not a counterfactual that we can easily analyze, at least without auxiliary assumptions. For instance, un-

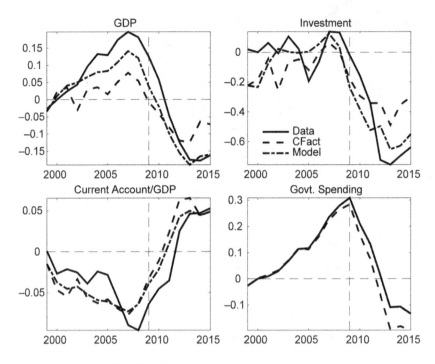

Fig. 30. Counterfactual: Low price stickiness

Note: The figure reports the counterfactual when we set wage and price stickiness λ_p and λ_w to half their calibrated values.

der a "Grexit" scenario, one needs to specify what would happen to euro-denominated liabilities. Instead, we ask the converse—and easier—question: What would have happened if prices had been more flexible in Greece? In the limit where prices are perfectly flexible, the nominal exchange rate regime becomes irrelevant. It is well known also that price and wage flexibility may work perversely, aggravating Fisherian debt-deflation dynamics either at the zero lower bound, or under a fixed exchange rate. Nevertheless, the evidence of Latvia and Estonia discussed in section III suggests that countries with more flexible wages and prices may experience shorter recessions. To investigate these questions, we keep the sequence of shocks fixed and reduce the calibrated price stickiness parameters, λ_p and λ_w, to half of their original values.

Figure 30 reports the results. The figure indicates that Greece would have avoided a significant share of the boom/bust cycle with a peak-to-trough decline in output of 20% instead of 33%. Similarly, investment would have declined by only 55% instead of 77%. The recovery in output would also have been sharper with output 8 percentage points above the baseline estimates in 2015. We conclude that faster price and wage adjustment would have dampened the boom/bust cycle and accelerated the recovery.

VII. Conclusion

In this paper we analyze the macroeconomic dynamics of Greece before and during the crisis that it has been experiencing since 2008. This is only an interim report since, six years down the road, the crisis is still playing out and the Greek economy is still very much on life support. Nevertheless, we believe that enough time has elapsed to make it possible to provide preliminary answers. We put Greek macroeconomic dynamics in perspective by comparing with crisis episodes in other countries, including sudden stops, sovereign defaults, lending booms and busts, and combinations of the above. We also interpret Greece's crisis dynamics through the lens of a DSGE model that incorporates key features of the crisis such as sovereign default and financial frictions. Using the model, we decompose the movements of macroeconomic variables such as output and investment into the contributions of different types of shocks, including fiscal shocks and shocks to the financial sector. We also perform counterfactuals to examine how factors such as debt levels, fiscal policy, and price rigidities may have contributed to the severity of the crisis.

Our main findings are as follows. First, Greece's drop in output was significantly more severe and protracted than in the average crisis episode. Second, the unusually large drop in output was accompanied by an unusually large drop in the investment-to-output ratio. Third, much of the discrepancy can be accounted for by the higher levels of debt—government, private, and foreign—that Greece entered the crisis with. Fourth, Greece's output drop at the early stages of the crisis appears to have been driven mainly by fiscal shocks and by the sudden stop (which raised funding costs). At the later stages of the crisis, however, the effects of these shocks appear to have subsided, and the shocks that account for protracted drop in output appear to be the slow resolution of nonperforming loans and price rigidities in product markets. Hence, the microdimension of the crisis may now have taken precedence over macroeconomic forces.

While our model captures a rich set of dynamics, it undoubtedly leaves aside many factors that may prove to be important when the final account will be written. One such factor is the uncertainty about EZ exit (Grexit). That uncertainty hampered investment and contributed to the liquidity problems of Greek banks. Retail deposits in Greek banks dropped by about 50% between 2009 and 2015, while they remained stable or even increased in Irish, Italian, Portuguese, and Spanish banks. Hence, uncertainty about EZ exit seems to have been much larger in Greece than in the other countries. Some of the effects of Grexit may be "relabeled" under other shocks in our model, such as the sudden stops, but introducing a more primitive shock may give a more accurate decomposition. Another factor that relates to the uncertainty is the political response to the crisis: domestic consensus on a strategy to exit the crisis was lacking in Greece, while it was present to a larger extent in other crisis-hit EZ countries such as Ireland and Portugal.

Appendix A

Empirical Appendix

List of Countries

The list of countries and regions is in table A1.

Definition and List of Episodes

We adopt the following definition of episodes:

1. Sudden Stop. Our sudden stop episodes are constructed by combining an output collapse filter and a capital flow reversal filter. To construct the output collapse filter, we first identify all cumulated episodes of real GDP decline (see the annual real GDP growth from International Financial Statistics). We define an "output collapse" as in Calvo et al. (2006), when the cumulated decline in output exceeds the within-group median (AE and EME). To construct the capital flow filter, we measure the changes in net capital flows as follows: (a) year-on-year change in the (opposite of the) current account relative to output, $\Delta_4(-CA_t / Y_t)$ as in Korinek and Mendoza (2013), where $\Delta_k x_t = x_t - x_{t-k}$; (b) year-on-year change in the (opposite of the) current account plus change in official reserves, relative to output: $\Delta_4((-CA_t + \Delta RES_t) / Y_t)$. This measure attempts to measure private capital flows; (c) year-on-year change in the cumulated change in the (opposite of the) current account + change in official reserves, relative to cumulated output, $\Delta_4((-\widetilde{CA}_t + \widetilde{\Delta RES}_t) / \tilde{Y}_t)$ where $\tilde{X}_t = \Sigma_{s=0}^3 X_{t-s}$. (see current account, official reserves, and output in US dollars from IFS). For each measure of net capital inflows, an episode is triggered when net capital inflows fall more than two standard deviations away from the mean (both mean and standard deviation are

Table A1
List of Countries

Region	Countries
Latin America (13)	Argentina, Brazil, Chile, Colombia, Dominican Republic, Ecuador, El Salvador, Jamaica, Mexico, Panama, Peru, Uruguay, and Venezuela
Asia (11)	China, Hong Kong, India, Indonesia, South Korea, Malaysia, Pakistan, Philippines, Singapore, Sri Lanka, and Thailand
Middle East and North Africa (10)	Egypt, Iraq, Israel, Jordan, Kuwait, Lebanon, Morocco, Oman, Tunisia, and United Arab Emirates
Central and Eastern European (15)	Bosnia, Bulgaria, Croatia, Czech Republic, Estonia, Hungary, Latvia, Lithuania, Macedonia, Poland, Romania, Serbia, Slovak Republic, Slovenia, and Turkey
South Saharan Africa (3)	Cote d'Ivoire, Nigeria, and South Africa
Commonwealth of Independent States (5)	Belarus, Georgia, Kazakhstan, Russian Federation, and Ukraine
Advanced Economies (22)	Australia, Austria, Belgium, Canada, Denmark, Finland, France, Germany, Greece, Iceland, Ireland, Italy, Japan, The Netherlands, New Zealand, Norway, Portugal, Spain, Sweden, Switzerland, United Kingdom, and the United States

Table A2
List of Sudden Stop Episodes with Output Collapse

Country	Years	Country	Years
		Advanced economies	
Canada	1982	Denmark	2009
Germany	2009	Iceland	2010
Japan	2009	Netherlands	2009
Spain	2010, 2013	Sweden	1993
Switzerland	2009	United Kingdom	1981
United States	2009		
		Emerging-market economies	
Argentina	1982, 1990, 2002	Bulgaria	2009
Chile	1983	Colombia	1999
Cote d'Ivoire	1984	Croatia	2014
Ecuador	1999	Estonia	2009
Hong Kong	1998	Hungary	2009
Indonesia	1998	Korea	1998
Lithuania	2009	Malaysia	1998
Mexico	1983, 1995	Philippines	1985
Romania	1999, 2010	Russia	1998, 2009
Slovak R.	2009	Slovenia	2009
Thailand	1998	Turkey	1994, 2001, 2009
U.A.E	2009	Ukraine	1999, 2009, 2014
Uruguay	1984		

Table A3
List of Sovereign Debt Crises

Country	Years	Country	Years
Argentina	1982, 1989, 2001*	Brazil	1983, 1986, 1990, 2002
Bulgaria	1990	Chile	1983*
Cote d'Ivoire	1983, 2000	Croatia	1993
Dominican R.	1982, 2005	Ecuador	1982, 1999*, 2008
Egypt	1984	El Salvador	1981
Indonesia	1998*, 2002	Iraq	1990
Jamaica	2010	Jordan	1989
Kuwait	1990	Mexico	1982*
Morocco	1983, 1986	Nigeria	1982, 2001, 2004
Pakistan	1981, 1999	Panama	1983, 1987
Peru	1980, 1984	Philippines	1983
Poland	1981	Romania	1981, 1986
Russia	1991, 1993, 1998*	Serbia	1983, 1992
South Africa	1985, 1989, 1993	Sri Lanka	1981, 1996
Turkey	1982, 2001*	Ukraine	1998, 2000
Uruguay	1983*, 1987, 1990, 2003*	Venezuela	1982, 1990, 1995, 1998, 2005

* Trifecta episodes.

country specific). Consecutive episodes less than eight quarters apart are merged into a single episode. Finally, a sudden stop occurs in year t when the trough of the output collapse (output collapse filter) overlaps with a sudden stop episode, according to any of the above definitions.

2. Sovereign Defaults. Sovereign defaults are defined as in Gourinchas and Obstfeld (2012), based on the tabulations of Reinhart and Rogoff (2009), Cantor and Packer (1995), and Chambers (2011). The year t of a sovereign debt crisis corresponds to the year identified with a default on domestic or external debt in these sources.

3. Lending Boom/Bust. We define a lending boom/bust episode as in Gourinchas et al. (2001), using the deviation of the ratio of credit to the nonfinancial sector to output from its trend (see bank credit to the nonfinancial sector from BIS and depository corporations survey, claims on the private sector from IFS). The trend is an HP filter with smoothing parameter $\lambda = 1000$. Define cy_t^T for the trend component of the credit-to-output ratio cy_t. A boom occurs whenever $cy_t > 1.14cy_t^T$ (boom threshold). The boom begins when $cy_t > 1.05cy_t^T$ (limit threshold) and ends when that limit threshold is crossed again. Episodes less than two years apart are combined. The year t of the lending boom is the year in which the maximum deviation from trend is achieved, within a given episode.

4. Trifecta. Trifecta crises are defined as a sovereign debt crisis that occurs during a sudden stop and a lending boom episode. These episodes are marked with a * in table A3.

Table A4
List of Lending Booms

Country	Years	Country	Years
	Advanced economies		
Australia	1980	Canada	1982
Denmark	2009	Finland	1989
Greece	1985	Iceland	1982, 2006
Ireland	1981, 2009	Norway	1988, 2007
Portugal	1984, 2001, 2009	Spain	1982, 2007
Sweden	1990		
	Emerging-market economies		
Argentina	1999, 2013	Belarus	2010
Bosnia	1997, 2008	Brazil	1995
Bulgaria	1991, 2008	Chile	1984, 2003
Colombia	1984, 1997, 2014	Croatia	1998
Czech R.	1997	Dominican R.	1989, 2003
Ecuador	1984, 1997	Egypt	1981, 2001
El Salvador	2000	Estonia	2009
Georgia	1997, 2008	Hong Kong	1983, 1997
Hungary	1990, 2009	Indonesia	1998
Iraq	2004	Israel	2002
Jamaica	1983, 1989, 2000, 2008	Jordan	2006
Kazakhstan	1993, 2007	Korea	1998
Kuwait	1988, 1998, 2009	Latvia	2010
Lebanon	2000	Lithuania	2008
Macedonia	2008	Malaysia	1997
Mexico	1981, 1994	Morocco	1981, 1997
Nigeria	1986, 2009	Oman	1998
Pakistan	1986, 2008	Panama	1981, 2001
Peru	1983, 1998	Philippines	1983, 1997, 2014
Poland	1992, 2009	Romania	1996, 2008
Russia	1995, 2009	Serbia	2000, 2010
Slovak R.	1999, 2008	Slovenia	1991, 2009
South Africa	2008	Sri Lanka	1983, 1995, 2006
Thailand	1997	Tunisia	1989
Turkey	1987, 1997	U.A.E	1988, 1998, 2009
Ukraine	2008	Uruguay	1982, 2002
Venezuela	2007, 2013		

Appendix B

Calibration

This appendix contains more details on the calibration. Table A6 contains the parameters that we choose to match steady-state targets for Greece. Table A7 contains the fiscal rule parameters that we calibrate rather than estimate.

The following table describes the steady state of the model for reference.

Table A5
Standard Parameters

Parameter	Description	Value
β	Discount factor	0.97
α	Capital share	1/3
ϵ_h	Elasticity between H and F	1
ϵ_f	Elasticity between exports	1
φ	Inverse labor supply elasticity	1
γ	Risk aversion	1
ϑ	Price stickiness	0.5
ε	Elasticity of substitution goods	6
ϑ_w	Wage stickiness	0.5
ε_w	Elasticity of substitution labor	6
ϵ_r	Elasticity of R to NFA	0.0001
φ_k	Adjustment cost	1
δ	Depreciation	0.07
FC	Fixed cost of production, 10% of Y	0.0955

Table A6
Internally Calibrated Parameters for Greece

Parameter	Description	Value
ϖ	Openness (Martin and Philippon 2014)	0.3
χ	Fraction of impatient (Martin and Philippon 2014)	0.65
Δ	Annual lending spread of 2%	1.02
$\bar{B}^h / Y$	Household debt to GDP of 50%	0.5
B^g / Y	Government debt to GDP of 120%	1.2
G / Y	Government consumption to GDP of 20%	0.2
T / Y	Public social expenditure to GDP of 20%	0.2
$\bar{d}^h$	Steady-state default rate for households	5.4%
$\bar{d}^k$	Steady-state default rate for corporates	5.4%
B^k / Y	Corporate debt to GDP of 50%	0.5
ψ_{sk}	Working capital constraint	1
τ	Tax rate, budget balance in SS	0.436
L	Leverage scaling	1

Table A7
Other Parameters

Parameter	Description	Value
F_b	Elasticity of govt. spending to public debt	0.05
F_n	Elasticity of govt. spending to employment	0.025
F_r	Elasticity of govt. spending to the int. rate	0.5
F_l	Persistence of govt. spending	0.75

Table A8
Steady-State Values

Variable	Description	Value
Y	Output	0.9548
$C = C^b = C^s$	Consumption	0.6315
N	Labor	0.7830
W	Wage rate	0.8767
$R = R^g$	SOE and sovereign rates	$1/\beta = 1.0309$
$G = T$	Government spending and transfers	0.1910
K	Capital	1.8897
Q	Investment Q	1
$R^k = R^h$	Corporate debt and household debt rates	1.1116
Z_k	Rental rate of capital	0.1816
R^{sk}	Working capital rate	1.02
B^g	Government debt	1.1457
B^h	Household debt	0.4774

We focus on a zero inflation steady state, and normalize all price levels to 1, so that there is no distinction between variables in euros, or real variables deflated by either the CPI or the PPI. We also assume, for simplicity, that NFA = 0 at the steady state, and that trade is balanced. This is straightforward to generalize by appropriately adapting the interest rate equation. Finally, we assume that steady-state transfers from the government to the borrower are such that both agents choose the same amount of labor and consumption.

Appendix C

Estimation

Our priors impose that most estimated parameters be in the [0,1] interval, with the exception of some of the elasticities for which we assume Gamma priors.

Figure A1 plots the priors with a thick line and the estimated posterior distributions with a thin line for the dynamic parameters, with the posterior mode with a black dashed line. Our default priors for shock persistence and variances are Beta distributions with mean 0.85 and variance 0.1, and mean 0.2 and variance 0.1, respectively. The only exceptions are the spending and household debt shocks, where we lower the persistence and raise the variance due to the presence of an autoregressive term in the structural equations for these variables.

Using the Kalman Smoother at the posterior mode, we can retrieve sequences for the structural shocks in the model, which are shown in fig-

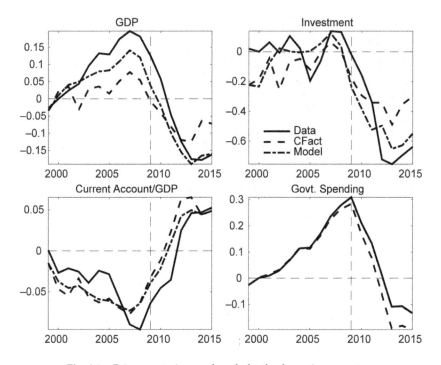

Fig. A1.   Priors, posteriors, and mode for the dynamic parameters

Note: The thin line is the posterior density, the thick line is the prior density, and the black dashed line is the posterior mode.

ure A2. These are obtained by applying the Kalman Smoother for the sequence of observables, with all parameters set at their posterior modes.

Impulse Responses

Figure A3 shows the impulse response to a private default shock, ε_t^{def}. The surge in private defaults increases the private-sector funding cost and reduces the spending of impatient households who are at their borrowing constraint. This adversely affects investment, output, and employment. As the economy enters a recession, sovereign yields increase. Government expenditures are the result of two offsetting forces: the recession increases spending (automatic stabilizers), but the increase in public debt triggers some automatic consolidation. The net effect is a mild decline in spending. Net exports improve as both competitiveness increases (lower domestic inflation) and domestic absorption declines.

Figure A4 shows the response of the economy to credit demand shock, ε_t^{bh}. Impatient households borrow to finance consumption. This

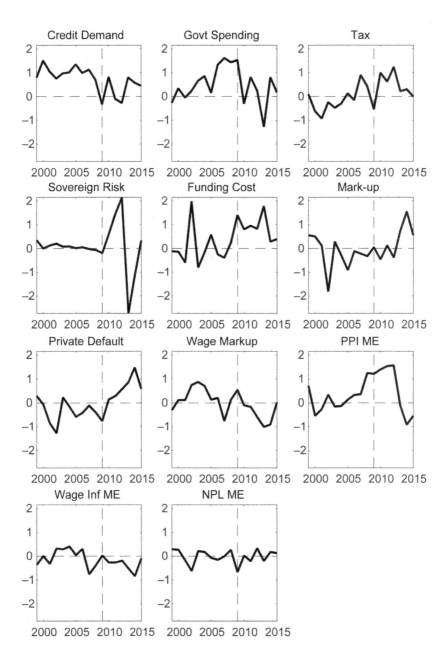

Fig. A2. Smoothed shocks

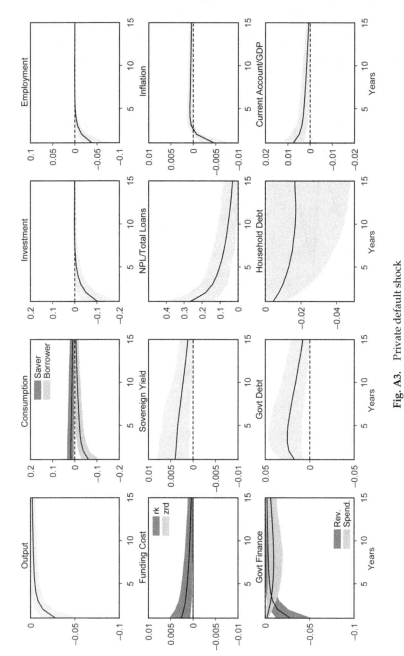

Fig. A3. Private default shock

Note: The figure reports 90% Bayesian confidence bands.

74

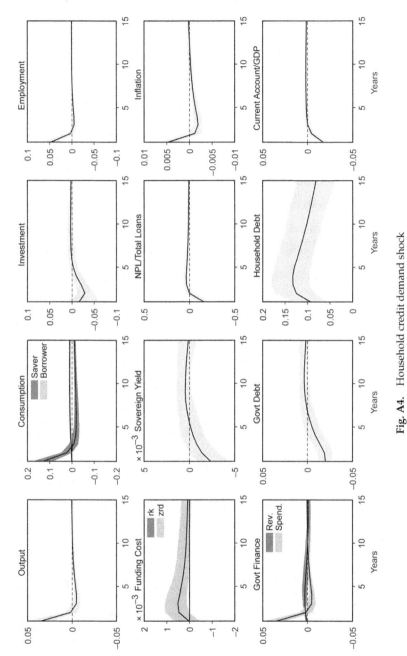

Fig. A4. Household credit demand shock

Note: The figure reports 90% Bayesian confidence bands.

75

initially stimulates output, employment, and inflation, but crowds out investment as credit risk increases, and therefore private-funding costs, leading to a subsequent output decline. The increase in absorption exceeds output, so the current account deteriorates.

Endnotes

We are grateful to Miguel Faria-e-Castro for outstanding research assistance. We thank Olivier Blanchard and Markus Brunnermeier, our discussants at the 31st NBER Macroeconomics Annual Conference, as well as Gikas Hardouvelis, Maurice Obstfeld, Jonathan Parker, and other participants at that conference, for very helpful comments. For acknowledgments, sources of research support, and disclosure of the authors' material financial relationships, if any, please see http://www.nber.org/chapters/c13780.ack.

1. The GDP per capita comes from Eurostat and is expressed in 2010 euros.

2. Ingram (1973) was among the first to articulate the view that sudden stops could not happen in a currency union, with the corollary that there was no need to monitor external imbalances. Against this view, Garber (1999) argued that the European payment system (target) at the core of the European Monetary Union could itself propagate a speculative attack.

3. An average during the period 1980–1995 would have been more informative of the state of the Greek economy before EZ entry. We use only the year 1995 because data before 1995 are not available or precise enough.

4. The fact that in the years immediately preceding and following EZ entry poorer members of the union—like Greece—would run large current account deficits was not a surprise. Rather, it is precisely what theory suggests should happen when countries catch up and converge, as argued by Blanchard and Giavazzi (2002) in an influential paper that examined the experience of Greece and Portugal. That paper also noted that Greece did not experience an investment boom following EZ entry and that the decline in saving was mostly driven by private saving.

5. Figure 4 starts in 1999 rather than 1980 because data before 1999 are not available. Subsequent figures also start later than 1980 for the same reason.

6. While figure 4 plots gross rather than net government external debt, gross external assets of the Greek government were negligible, as shown by Hyppolite (2016).

7. Ireland and Spain had significantly lower levels of public debt. Italy had much lower levels of net external debt. Portugal was in a position somewhat similar to Greece, although with smaller government debt and deficits.

8. The figures for Greek government debt during the crisis overstate the value of the debt, especially when Greece is compared to other high-debt countries such as Italy and Portugal. This is because Greek debt is computed in nominal terms, by adding the principal (face value) payments that are due in all future years, rather than by adding all principal and coupon payments after discounting them at appropriate market rates. This overstates the value of the debt because assistance loans by the EZ during the crisis came with long maturities and below-market interest rates. In particular, the average interest rate on Greek debt is smaller than for Italy and Portugal. For estimates of Greek debt in present-value terms see, for example, Schumacher and Weder di Mauro (2015).

9. Like Calvo et al. (2006), Korinek and Mendoza (2014) focus on "systemic" sudden stops that occur in times of turmoil on global bond markets.

10. The appendix provides additional details. In short, we identify large output drops when the peak-to-trough cumulated output decline in a recession exceeds the median cumulated output decline within group (advanced or emerging markets). A sudden stop occurs when this large output drop overlaps a capital flow reversal episode, defined as a year-on-year decline in net capital inflows that is more than two standard deviations away from the country mean.

11. See Gourinchas and Obstfeld (2012) for details.

12. See details in the appendix.

13. Technically, we record a trifecta episode when the sovereign default event t occurs during a lending boom episode and during a sudden stop episode.

14. Different dimensions of the Greek crisis unfolded at different times. According to our dating procedure, the lending boom peaked in 2008, the sovereign default occurred in 2012, and the collapse in output during the sudden stop episode occurred in 2013. Nevertheless, 2010 is a natural starting point since specific concerns about the Greek economy arose first in late 2009. The five-year spread between Greece and Germany was 120 bp in September 2009, but climbed to 277 bp by January 2010, before reaching 680 bp by April of that year.

15. We choose to begin in 1980 because of data availability and also because this period marks a phase of growing international financial integration, especially for emerging-market economies.

16. Our list includes all countries listed as emerging economies in either J.P. Morgan's EMBIG index, the FTSE's Group of Advanced or Secondary Emerging Markets, the MSCI-Barra classification of emerging or frontier economies and the Dow Jones list of emerging-market economies. We add to these countries Israel, Hong Kong, and Singapore, all countries that are now often included in the group of advanced economies but belong to the group of emerging-market economies for most of the sample. The list of countries in our sample is included in the appendix.

17. See Eichengreen, Rose, and Wyplosz (1995) and Kaminsky and Reinhart (1999) for seminal contributions.

18. Detailed sources for each variable are provided in the appendix.

19. By dating the Greek crisis in 2010 instead of later (see fn. 14), it may appear as if we mechanically make the Greek output collapse more protracted compared to other episodes where the output collapse may have started before $t - 2$. This is not a concern: the median duration of output collapses in our sample of sudden stops is 1.5 years for advanced economies and one year for emerging-market economies. Only two output collapses last for six years or longer: Bosnia between 2008 and 2014 (six years) and Ukraine between 1992 and 1999 (seven years). Hence our choice of 2010 as the crisis year for Greece does not affect the results.

20. The economy of the United Arab Emirates experienced a sudden stop episode in 2009 as a consequence of the burst of a real estate bubble, and the sharp decline in oil and natural gas prices in the immediate aftermath of the Global Financial Crisis. Real output per capita declined by 11%, 10.7%, and 16.4% in 2007, 2008, and 2009, respectively, culminating with the collapse of Dubai World in November 2009.

21. We classify countries into peggers and floaters based on the fine classification of Ilzetzki et al. (2010). Peggers have an index smaller than 9. The sample consists of 20 floats, 10 strict peggers, 15 de-peggers, and 2 others.

22. There are, of course, other differences between the Baltic countries and Greece and we want to acknowledge the limits of the comparison. For instance, price and wages adjusted more rapidly in Latvia than in Greece. Blanchard, Griffiths, and Bertrand (2013), in a case study of the Latvia boom, bust, and recovery, argue that internal devaluation worked fast in part due to nominal wage cuts, but also to rapid productivity increases that fueled a solid supply response. We explore in section VI what would have happened in Greece with more rapid price and wage adjustment.

23. As pointed out to us by M. Obstfeld, the fall in spending required by the unavoidable fiscal consolidation required a large real depreciation in order to maintain equilibrium on the market for nontraded goods. Absent an adjustment in the real exchange rate, the improvement in external balances must be associated with an output decline. See Corden and Neary (1982).

24. The literature on sovereign risk is large and we can only refer the reader to the classic contribution of Arellano (2008) and the recent survey by Águiar and Amador (2014).

25. The rate that enters equation (3) is not necessarily the same as the one in equation (5) because debt is long term and only a fraction is refinanced every period. During the crisis, Greek debt was refinanced by official creditors at low rates, in equation (3), while the secondary market rate was high. This secondary rate is the one that enters equation (5).

26. There are two types of models with heterogeneity: models where types are transient, as in Bewley models or Guerrieri and Lorenzoni (2011), and models where types are permanent, as in Campbell and Mankiw (1989), Mankiw (2000), Eggertsson and Krugman (2012), and Martin and Philippon (2014). Midrigan and Philippon (2010) propose a hybrid model that includes precautionary savings, but is simple enough to incorporate in a standard macro model.

27. The assumption that this loan is intraperiod is made for simplicity. The fact that the loan is made by the bank allows for financial shocks to pass through to the production sector, with the added advantages that (a) we do not need to keep track of an extra state variable, and (b) we avoid any complications arising from the interaction of two dynamic frictions: nominal rigidities and financial frictions. If debt were intertemporal, we would have to keep track of the joint distribution of prices and debt, as firms with different preset prices would produce different quantities and thus borrow different amounts. Intraperiod loans allow us to introduce a financial friction that is static from the firm's point of view.

28. See Schmitt-Grohe and Uribe (2003).

29. To see why, simply pick some $R^h \in (\beta_s^{-1}, \beta_b^{-1})$. Given this rate and the other parameters, there is a unique steady state for bank equity, bank size, and so forth. Hence, there is a unique value for B^h. Now, as long as interest payments do not violate the nonnegativity constraint on consumption (which never happens for reasonable values), then this level of B^h also satisfies the households' problem, since for them B^h is a constraint. This shows that any $R^h \in (\beta_s^{-1}, \beta_b^{-1})$ is potentially an equilibrium, corresponding to different values of B^h.

30. We treat the sovereign spread as a secondary market price that contains information about sovereign risk. On the other hand, it does not enter the government budget constraint since Greece did not refinance its stock of debt at that price. In the budget constraint we scale down the spread by a factor of 5 so that it is in line with the data.

31. In practice, as we will see, domestic inflation deviates most from the model in 2010. According to the Bank of Greece, that year saw a surge in inflation due to a significant rise in oil prices and an increase in indirect taxes, in particular VAT.

32. The "dynamic" parameters are those parameters that are not required to compute the steady state and that only affect the dynamics of the model, such as the pass-through elasticities and the persistence as well as the standard deviation of the exogenous shocks (ρ^i, σ^i).

33. As discussed earlier, the model implies that domestic inflation starts declining as early as 2008. In the data we observe a spike in domestic inflation in 2009 and 2010, most likely due to the impact of oil prices (not modeled) and changes in the VAT rate (not modeled).

34. Knowledge of the structural shocks and the structural matrices that describe the law of motion for the endogenous variables as functions of the states allows us to estimate the contribution of each shock to the observed behavior of each variable in the model. This can be done for any endogenous variable, observed or not. Note that the plotted contributions of the shocks do not need to add up to the value of the variable due to initial conditions estimated by the Kalman filter.

35. Remember that we do not assume that the Greek government actually borrowed at these rates. In equation (3) the cash flows are much more stable.

36. As in the case of sovereign yields, one may argue that the borrowing rate for small and medium enterprises may not have been allocative at that time. However, recall that Greek banks could obtain liquidity at the ECB and the Bank of Greece against eligible collateral. Hence, the supply of loanable funds to the private sector was presumably not vertical.

37. We also performed another counterfactual where we remove the sudden stop on public capital by setting $\varepsilon_t^{dg} = 0$. This corresponds to the situation that would have prevailed in the presence of a sovereign debt "backstop" in the form of ECB or bailout guaranties. These results are available upon request.

38. In our model, eliminating fiscal profligacy would not have eliminated the Greek crisis altogether because we are still keeping the sudden stop and sovereign risk shocks.

Our estimates of the benefit of fiscal discipline are only a lower bound. This is the main difference with Martin and Philippon (2014), who estimate the impact of sovereign debt on the sudden stop itself. Martin and Philippon (2014) find much larger benefits of fiscal discipline, but their estimation requires cross-sectional information from different countries and is not feasible here.

References

Adalet, Muge, and Barry Eichengreen. 2007. "Current Account Reversals: Always a Problem?" In *G7 Current Account Imbalances: Sustainability and Adjustment*, ed. Richard H. Clarida, 205–46. Chicago: University of Chicago Press.
Aguiar, Mark, and Manuel Amador. 2014. "Sovereign Debt." In *Handbook of International Economics*, vol. 4, ed. G. Gopinath, E. Helpman, and K. Rogoff, 647–84. Amsterdam: North Holland.
An, Sungbae, and Frank Schorfheide. 2007. "Bayesian Analysis of DSGE Models." *Econometric Reviews* 26 (2-4): 113–72.
Arellano, Cristina. 2008. "Default Risk and Income Fluctuations in Emerging Economies." *American Economic Review* 98 (3): 690–712.
Blanchard, Olivier J., and Francesco Giavazzi. 2002. "Current Account Deficits in the Euro Area: The End of the Feldstein Horioka Puzzle?" *Brookings Papers on Economic Activity* 33 (2): 147–210.
Blanchard, Olivier J., Mark Griffiths, and Bertrand Gruss. 2013. "Boom, Bust, Recovery: Forensics of the Latvia Crisis." *Brookings Papers on Economic Activity* 2013 (Fall): 325–71. http://www.jstor.org/stable/23723442.
Brunnermeier, Markus, Luis Garicano, Philip Lane, Marco Pagano, Ricardo Reis, Tano Santos, Macro Pagano, David Thesmar, Stijn Van Nieuwerburgh, and Dimitri Vayanos. 2016. "The Sovereign-Bank Diabolic Loop and ESBies." *American Economic Review, P&P* 106:508–12.
Calvo, Guillermo A., Alejandro Izquierdo, and Ernesto Talvi. 2006. "Phoenix Miracles in Emerging Markets: Recovering without Credit from Systemic Financial Crises." NBER Working Paper no. 12101, Cambridge, MA.
Campbell, J. Y., and N. G. Mankiw. 1989. "Consumption, Income and Interest Rates: Reinterpreting the Time Series Evidence." *NBER Macroeconomics Annual*, vol. 4, ed. J. A. Parker and M. Woodford, 185–246. Chicago: University of Chicago Press.
Cantor, Richard, and Frank Packer. 1995. "Sovereign Credit Ratings." *Current Issues in Economics and Finance* 1 (3): 1–6.
Chambers, John. 2011. "Sovereign Defaults and Rating Transition Data, 2010 Update." *Standard & Poor's Global Credit Portal*, February. https://www.standardandpoors.com/ja_JP/delegate/getPDF?articleId=1498474&type=COMMENTS&subType=.
Christiano, Lawrence J., Martin Eichenbaum, and Charles L. Evans. 2005. "Nominal Rigidities and the Dynamic Effects of a Shock to Monetary Policy." *Journal of Political Economy* 113 (1): 1–45.
Corden, Max W., and J. Peter Neary. 1982. "Booming Sector and De-Industrialisation in a Small Open Economy." *Economic Journal* 92 (368): 825–48.
Dornbusch, Rudiger, and Alejandro Werner. 1994. "Mexico: Stabilization, Reform, and No Growth." *Brookings Papers on Economic Activity* 1994 (1): 253–315.
Eggertsson, Gauti, and Paul Krugman. 2012. "Debt, Deleveraging, and the Liquidity Trap: A Fisher-Minsky-Koo Approach." *Quarterly Journal of Economics* 127 (3): 1469–513.

Eichengreen, Barry, Andrew Rose, and Charles Wyplosz. 1995. "Exchange Market Mayhem: The Antecedents and Aftermath of Speculative Attacks." *Economic Policy* 10 (21): 249–312.

Farhi, Emmanuel, and Jean Tirole. 2016. "Deadly Embrace: Sovereign and Financial Balance Sheets Doom Loops." NBER Working Paper no. 21843, Cambridge, MA.

Faria-e-Castro, Miguel. 2016. "Fiscal Policy and Financial Crises in a Monetary Union." Working Paper, New York University.

Gali, Jordi, and Tommaso Monacelli. 2008. "Optimal Monetary and Fiscal Policy in a Currency Union." *Journal of International Economics* 76:116–32.

Garber, Peter M. 1999. "The Target Mechanism: Will it Propagate or Stifle a Stage III Crisis?" *Carnegie-Rochester Conference Series on Public Policy* 51 (1): 195–220.

Gertler, Mark, and Nobuhiro Kiyotaki. 2010. "Financial Intermediation and Credit Policy in Business Cycle Analysis." In *Handbook of Monetary Economics*, vol. 3, ed. B. Friedman and M. Woodford, 547–99. Amsterdam: Elsevier.

Gourinchas, Pierre-Olivier, and Maurice Obstfeld. 2012. "Stories of the Twentieth Century for the Twenty-First." *American Economic Journal Macro* 4 (1): 226–65.

Gourinchas, Pierre-Olivier, Rodrigo O. Valdés, and Oscar Landerretche. 2001. "Lending Booms: Latin America and the World." *Economia* 1 (2): 47–99.

Guerrieri, Veronica, and Guido Lorenzoni. 2011. "Credit Crises, Precautionary Savings and the Liquidity Trap." NBER Working Paper no. 17583, Cambridge, MA.

Hyppolite, Paul-Adrien. 2016. "Towards a Theory on the Causes of the Greek Depression." *CES Open Forum Series 2016–2017*, Center for European Studies Harvard. https://ces.fas.harvard.edu/publications/towards-a-theory-on-the-causes-of-the-greek-depression.

Iacoviello, Matteo. 2015. "Financial Business Cycles." *Review of Economic Dynamics* 18 (1): 140–64.

Ilzetzki, Ethan, Carmen M. Reinhart, and Kenneth S. Rogoff. 2010. "Exchange Rate Arrangements Entering the 21st Century: Which Anchor Will Hold?" Unpublished manuscript, Harvard University.

Ingram, James C. 1973. *The Case for European Monetary Integration* (Essays in International Finance, no. 98). Princeton, NJ: Princeton University Press.

Jermann, Urban, and Vincenzo Quadrini. 2012. "Macroeconomic Effects of Financial Shocks." *American Economic Review* 102 (1): 238–71.

Kaminsky, Graciela L., and Carmen M. Reinhart. 1999. "The Twin Crises: The Causes of Banking and Balance of Payments Problems." *American Economic Review* 89 (3): 473–500.

Korinek, Anton, and Enrique G. Mendoza. 2013. "From Sudden Stops to Fisherian Deflation: Quantitative Theory and Policy Implications." NBER Working Paper no. 19362, Cambridge, MA.

Korinek, Anton, and Enriq. 2014. "From Sudden Stops to Fisherian Deflation: Quantitative Theory and Policy." *Annual Review of Economics* 6 (1). Annual Reviews: 299–332.

Krugman, Paul. 2012. "Revenge of the Optimum Currency Area." In *NBER Macroeconomics Annual 2012*, vol. 27, ed. D. Acemoglu, J. Parker, and M. Woodford, 439–48. Chicago: University of Chicago Press.

Lane, Philip R., and Gian Maria Milesi-Ferretti (2007), "The external wealth of nations mark II: Revised and extended estimates of foreign assets and liabilities, 1970–2004", *Journal of International Economics* 73:223–250.

Mankiw, N. Gregory. 2000. "The Savers-Spenders Theory of Fiscal Policy." *American Economic Review* 90 (2): 120–25.

Martin, Philippe, and Thomas Philippon. 2014. "Inspecting the Mechanism: Leverage and the Great Recession in the Eurozone." NBER Working Paper no. 20572, Cambridge, MA.

Mendoza, Enrique G. 2010. "Sudden Stops, Financial Crises, and Leverage." *American Economic Review* 100:1941–66.

Midrigan, Virgiliu, and Thomas Philippon. 2010. "Household Leverage and the Recession." NYU Working Paper no. 2451/31371, New York University.

Moody's. 2009. "Sovereign Default and Recovery Rates, 1983–2008." *Moody's Global Credit Policy*, March. https://www.moodys.com/sites/products/DefaultResearch/2007400000587968.pdf

Philippon, Thomas. 2012. "Has the Us Finance Industry Become Less Efficient? On the Theory and Measurement of Financial Intermediation." NBER Working Paper no. 18077, Cambridge, MA.

Ranciere, Romain, Aaron Tornell, and Frank Westermann. 2008. "Systemic Crises and Growth." *Quarterly Journal of Economics* 123 (1): 359–406.

Reinhart, Carmen M., and Kenneth S. Rogoff. 2004. "The Modern History of Exchange Rate Arrangements: A Reinterpretation." *Quarterly Journal of Economics* 119 (1): 1–48.

———. 2009. *This Time Is Different: Eight Centuries of Financial Folly*. Princeton, NJ: Princeton University Press.

Schmitt-Grohe, Stephanie, and Martin Uribe. 2003. "Closing Small Open Economy Models." *Journal of International Economics* 61:163–85.

Schumacher, Julian, and Beatrice Weder di Mauro. 2015. "Greek Debt Sustainability and Official Crisis Lending." *Brookings Papers on Economic Activity* Fall:279–305.

Sturzenegger, Federico, and Jeromin Zettelmeyer. 2007. *Debt Defaults and Lessons from a Decade of Crises*. Cambridge, MA: MIT Press.

Comment

Olivier Blanchard, *Peterson Institute of International Economics and NBER*

This is an extremely ambitious paper. The Greek drama is one of the most complex macroeconomic developments of the last 10 years. Before I read the paper, my tight prior was that DSGE models were not at a stage where they could handle the relevant complexity. After reading the paper, my posterior is substantially more favorable. In the right hands, DSGE models can shed light even on such complex developments and, while they may not deliver definitive answers, they can lead to a much more interesting discussion. I have learned a lot from the paper.

I have organized my discussion as follows. First, I go through the many mechanisms at work when a country confronts the end of a boom under fixed exchange rates (here, a common currency). My purpose is to show the many dimensions of the adjustment process. Then, I examine how close the DSGE model captures the relevant mechanisms, what the model tells us about Greece, and whether we should believe its conclusions.

The End of Booms under Fixed Exchange Rates

By the end of a boom, a country operating under fixed exchange rates typically suffers from three related imbalances. The first is overvaluation, the second is a large current account deficit, and the third is high debt. Debt may be private or public. Households may have borrowed too much to buy houses or simply to increase consumption; firms may have borrowed too much to finance investment; and the government may have gone on a spending spree, leading to large deficits and a large increase in public debt.

All three imbalances were very much present in Greece at the start of the crisis. Average output growth from 1996 to 2008 was a high 4%.

Average inflation (measured by the CPI) was also 4%, so 2% above the average euro inflation rate, leading to steady real appreciation. In 2008, the current account deficit was equal to 14% of GDP. The fiscal deficit was 14.5% of GDP, and public debt stood at 108% of GDP.

Booms Come to an End in Two Ways

First, They Can Die of Old Age. While the country can still borrow abroad, the factors behind the boom fade or reverse. The high real exchange rate implies low external demand, and internal demand slows down or even decreases. This may be because reality takes over and expectations of a bright future are revised downward, leading to lower demand. Or, the accelerator effect behind the housing boom or the increase in durable goods comes to an end. Or, the government embarks on fiscal consolidation. All of these lead to a slump and an increase in unemployment.

This starts a typically painful process of adjustment. Relative prices have to adjust, competitiveness has to be restored, and the current account deficit has to be reduced. Under fixed exchange rates, this has to happen through a decrease in domestic prices relative to those of competitor countries. Consider the steps in turn:

The best adjustment path, if it can be achieved, is to reestablish competitiveness through higher productivity growth. Thus, the frequent call for structural reforms by the European commission or the IMF. The political room for major structural reforms in the middle of a slump is, however, limited. De facto, most of the adjustment process has to happen through the adjustment of nominal wages.

Short of social pacts, which are nearly never seen, and short of a coordinated decrease in wages and prices, unemployment is what puts downward pressure on nominal wages; how strong the pressure is depends on the degree of nominal and real wage rigidities, reflected not only in the strength of the response of nominal wages to unemployment, but also the relevance of the zero lower bound on wage decreases.

The decrease in wages has then to pass through to prices. The pass-through depends on the market structure, for example, on whether exporting firms are price takers or price makers in foreign markets. One of the surprising features of adjustment within the Eurozone has been the limited pass-through from unit labor costs to prices. An interesting hypothesis is that firms, squeezed for profits because of the decrease in output, and more financially constrained because of tight credit supply, have decided to increase current profits at the expense of future profits. Whatever the reason, incomplete pass-through has slowed down the improvement in competitiveness and the improvement in external demand.

The improvement in relative prices then leads to an increase in external demand. Here again, many elements are at play. The size of the export sector is clearly crucial: the more closed the economy, the smaller the effect. The nature of exports is also essential: the elasticity of demand for tourism or for olive oil may be quite different from the elasticity of demand for cars.

Even if external demand improves, internal demand may be adversely affected by the adjustment process. Lower inflation—or even deflation in the current context—leads to higher real interest rates and thus lower spending. Deflation also increases the value of the debt. In the context of high debt to start with, this may slow or even derail the adjustment. The improvement in external demand may be more than offset by a decrease in internal demand.

Why did I go through all these steps? To make the point that, even if there had not been a sudden stop in Greece, there was a need for a large adjustment process, and that process would likely have been long and painful. Given that there was a sudden stop, we do not know what would have happened, but we can look at the case of Portugal. Portugal's boom ended in 2001, and, six years later, by the time the financial crisis started, little adjustment had taken place. Unemployment had increased from 4% in 2001 to 7.7% in 2007; average productivity growth over the period was less than 0.2%. Unit labor costs had further increased relative to the euro by 13%, and the current account deficit had further increased, from 5% to 10%. Many of the structural characteristics of Portugal are shared by Greece, among them a narrow export base and a slow adjustment of nominal wages. There is little reason to think that, absent the sudden stop, things would have turned out much better in Greece than they did in Portugal in the first half of the first decade of the twenty-first century.

The Other Way in Which Booms End Is with a Sudden Stop

Creditors start having doubts about the solvency of some of the debtors. They ask for large spreads, or they cut lending altogether. Not all sudden stops are the same. The nature of the debtor matters:

The sudden stop may affect the government. What combination of public debt and deficits trigger doubts is hard to predict: debt sustainability is a probabilistic concept, and probability is typically hard to assess. The possibility of self-fulfilling liquidity runs makes it even harder to predict whether and when investors will be reluctant to roll over debt and ask for higher spreads. When the doubts are triggered and spreads rise, what was a difficult fiscal situation becomes intractable. What happens next varies depending on restructuring and on outside help. If the country is on its own, wants to maintain parity, and does not want to restructure its debt, the outcome is an extreme fiscal consolidation, with its predictable adverse effects on output. If creditors agree to a debt restructuring, the pressure to adjust is smaller. And if the country gets into a program with the IMF or other official creditors, outside funds can help smooth the adjustment. In most cases, the outcome is likely to be a strong fiscal consolidation, with its attendant effects on output.

This discussion is clearly relevant for Greece. Worries about public debt sustainability led to an increase in interest rates, and by May 2010, the starting date of the first Troika program, the 10-year yield had reached 9%. By January 2012, the yield reached a peak of 35%. It would be wrong, however, to assume that the high rates on the secondary market were the main driver of fiscal policy. From May 2010 on, Greece had access to official financing at much lower rates, and rates on the secondary market were de facto irrelevant. What determined the adjustment of fiscal policy was the amount of financing provided by the program. While very large, namely 110 billion euros for the first program in 2010 and another 130 billion euros for the second program in 2012 (relative to a GDP of about 200 billion euros), it still required a very dramatic fiscal consolidation.

Debt restructuring was delayed, taking place only in 2012, leading to a haircut of about 50%, and reducing the debt by about 100 billion euros. One issue is how costly this delay was to Greece, and how much it worsened the adjustment. The answer depends very much on the cost of public debt overhang on private demand. This is another dimension of adjustment that is important, but poorly understood.

The Sudden Stop May Affect Banks. Here again, solvency and liquidity issues are likely to combine. The slump decreases the value of the assets. Worries about solvency lead depositors and other creditors to take out their funds. Again, the possibility of self-fulfilling liquidity runs introduces substantial uncertainty as to whether and when banks will survive. Even if they do, lower capital lead to a sharp contraction of credit. To the extent that banks hold sovereign bonds, and investors believe that the state will bail out the banks, "doom loops," interactions between doubts about public debt sustainability and doubts about bank solvency, can slow or derail the adjustment.

The decrease in liabilities of Greek banks was more of a slow stop than a sudden stop. Demand deposits did not decrease much until 2011, although deposits with maturity up to a year did. When currency risk became more acute, and demand deposits starting decreasing, it was more like a walk than like a run. Also, foreign banks did not withdraw funds to their Greek subsidiaries; indeed, they initially increased them. And when Greek banks needed to borrow, they were able to get funds first from the ECB, and then, when eligible collateral became scarce, from the Greek central bank through ELA. Just as for the government, the rates at which Greek banks could borrow were not the market rates, but rather the low rates charged by the ECB, and the slightly higher rates charged by the Greek central bank. Nevertheless, increasing non-performing loans due to slump, and the resulting decrease in capital, led to a sharp contraction in credit supply.

Finally, the sudden stop may come from doubts about the peg, or in the case of a common currency, the perception of a positive probability of exit and depreciation. Even if foreign creditors, official or private, continue to lend at low rates in terms of foreign currency, the implicit interest rate facing borrowers can increase substantially. National deposit insurance, which offers protection against losses in domestic currency, does not offer protection against a depreciation, so depositors have an incentive to run. Beyond interest rate effects, the option value of waiting increases and is likely to lead to lower investment. The adjustment process can again be derailed.

Whenever the adjustment leads to a large decline in output, the perceived probability that the country will give up the peg increases. Indeed, this has been the case in Greece. Both in 2012, and then again after the election of Tsipras in 2015, the perceived probability of Grexit increased. Anecdotal evidence (I do not know of formal empirical work on it) suggests that the effects on activity were substantial. Withdrawals of bank deposits accelerated. Investment decreased further. As the paper rightly emphasizes, perhaps the most striking number of the Greek crisis is the decrease in the ratio of investment to GDP, from a peak of 26% in 2007 to 9% in 2015.

Greece and the DSGE Model

I insisted intentionally on the complexity of the adjustment mechanism. The purpose of a model, even a DSGE model, is not, however, to capture all the intricate details, but the essential features of the mechanisms at work and to focus on a few central questions. In the case of Greece, I see three central questions:

1. From 2008 to 2015, output decreased by about 18%. What was the role of fiscal consolidation, a question that has been at the center of the main controversies?

2. What other factors played a role in explaining the decline in output?

3. Given the situation Greece was in at the start of the crisis, how bad did the adjustment have to be anyway?

Does the DSGE model presented in the paper convincingly answer these three questions? My answer is "not yet." But it yields a rich discussion and a structure to build on. Let me develop these arguments, starting with a discussion of the specification and estimation of the model.

There is no question that the specification of the model represents major progress. The model has the essential features needed to answer the questions above. It has two goods, domestic and foreign, so we can think about relative price adjustment. It has nominal rigidities, so the adjustment is slow. Rather than being a representative agent model, it has savers and borrowers, so one can think about financial intermediation. It has intermediation by banks. It allows for endogenous default risk, for the government, for banks, for firms, and for households. It has rich interactions between the different default risks, and captures various "doom loops": For example, higher default risk for firms leads to lower investment, which leads to lower output, which leads to higher default risk for the government. From a methodological viewpoint, it is an impressive achievement. Those who are religious about strict microfoundations may object to a number of shortcuts taken in formalizing the behavior of banks and the determination of the various spreads, but the shortcuts strike me as reasonable and a fully microbased treatment is probably beyond reach at this point.

The authors, however, face a major specification issue: their model is not a model of a country with a Troika program. Much of what happened in Greece from 2010 on has been determined by the two programs, rather than by decisions of the Greek government or the Greek banks. The authors make the choice of ignoring this aspect. This may well be the right choice in showing what a model with default risk can do, but it creates problems of interpretation when applied to Greece, problems that I will return to below.

They capture the stance of fiscal policy by a rule determining the deficit as a function of debt, of the cost of borrowing measured by the spread on Greek sovereign bonds, and of a fiscal shock. But, in fact, the stance of fiscal policy has been mostly determined by the amount of funding given by the Troika, and the interest rate at which the government has obtained this funding has been much lower than the rate on the secondary market for Greek government bonds. This makes the interpretation of "fiscal shocks," estimated as residuals from a nonexistent rule, rather difficult.

A related problem concerns banks. In the model, the rate at which banks can borrow depends on their default risk and on a funding shock (which the authors also call a sudden stop shock). The banks pass that cost on to their customers, so the rate at which banks can borrow determines the rate at which people and firms can borrow, adjusted for their own default risk. In the estimated model, much of the increase in the rate at which people and firms can borrow is interpreted as coming from an increase in the funding rate of banks. But, in fact, as we saw earlier, Greek banks have been able to borrow at low rates throughout, either from the ECB or from the Greek central bank. The implication is that the increase in spreads on lending to firms and households does not reflect a funding shock, but rather something else in the banking sector, probably the effects of losses on capital and in turn on credit supply. This makes the interpretation of the estimated funding shock difficult. It may capture the effect of a probability of euro exit, but in this case, it would affect other variables in the model, from the cost of borrowing by the government to investment.

Turning to calibration and estimation, I have the same negative reaction I have to similar calibrations and estimations in other DSGEs. It is again an impressive technological tour de force. But, it is nearly impossible for the reader (at least for this reader) to get a good sense of the plausibility of the estimated/calibrated parameters, and, by implication, of the estimated shocks. Getting a sense of the various choices, be it which parameters are calibrated and which ones are estimated, which variables are chosen to be used for the estimation of shocks and which are left aside, and how robust the results are to assumptions, is difficult. I understand that it would take a much longer paper (or a very long appendix) to discuss and defend the various choices, but it makes it difficult to assess the results. Some of the choices strike me as debatable. To take a few examples: It cannot be right to use the same Calvo specification for wages in every country (or maybe for any country). The best way to find out what the fiscal multipliers were in Greece since 2007 cannot be to estimate the full DSGE model. Some implications of the calibration seem implausible. The elasticity of investment with respect to interest rates seems too large: A 60 basis point increase in the rate appears to decrease investment by 8% and output by 3%. This plays an important role in the results. I believe that general equilibrium Bayesian estimation just asks too much of the data, and is too much of a black box. From both a communication viewpoint and from a robustness viewpoint, I believe that much of the needed evidence must be collected through careful partial equilibrium, equation by equation, estimation, before we can run DSGEs with enough comfort. (I think it can be done. Indeed, an IV approach to estimation was followed by one of the authors [Martin and Philippon 2015] in a related paper.)

Let me now go back to the three questions about Greece posed earlier. What does the model tell us?

Take the role of fiscal policy, both in the boom and in the bust. Figure 18 presents the decomposition of movements in output as a result of the underlying shocks. And, on the face of it, it yields a surprising conclusion. While much of the pre-crisis increase in output is attributed to positive fiscal spending shocks, relatively little of the fall in output since then is attributed to negative fiscal shocks. Why is this? The authors explain it well. Shocks are defined as deviations of spending from the (postulated) fiscal rule. And given that the rule makes spending depend on the rate on sovereign bonds, it implies that, even in the absence of fiscal shocks, the large increase in spreads would have implied a large fiscal consolidation. The logic is fine, but the conclusion is potentially misleading. If we defined the fiscal spending shocks instead as the change in the cyclically adjusted primary surplus imposed by the Troika programs, they would account for much more of the decline in output. (One other aspect of the decomposition also puzzles me. The buildup in debt from 2010 to today is attributed nearly fully to positive spending shocks, which took place before the crisis. I find the long lags difficult to believe.)

Take the role of other shocks. Particularly interesting is the role of markup shocks. As discussed earlier, one of the puzzling features of the adjustment has been the limited pass-through of wages to prices, slowing the competitiveness adjustment. Surprisingly (and with a slight tension between text and figure 18), markup shocks play a limited role in accounting for the decline in output. (The model allows for an effect of financial conditions on marginal cost through the use of working capital

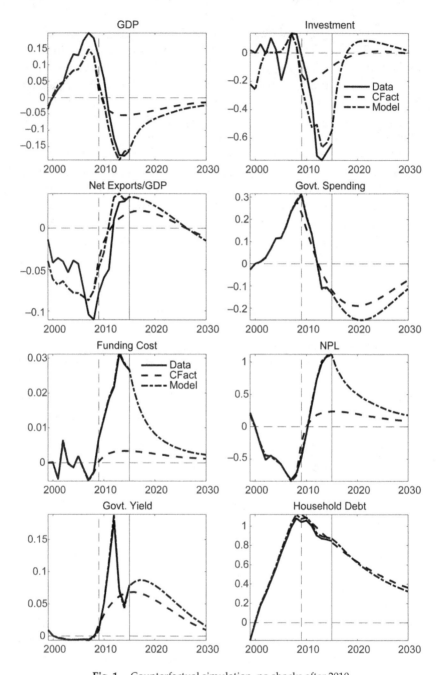

Fig. 1. Counterfactual simulation, no shocks after 2010

Note: Eight series: GDP, Investment, Net Exports/GDP, Govt. Spending, Funding Cost, NPL, Govt. Yield, and Household Debt.

in production. Higher spreads imply higher costs, and thus an increase in prices relative to wages. This is an interesting angle, but will need to be documented at more directly). However, negative markup shocks, that is, incomplete pass-through of increases in wages into prices, play a substantial role in the pre-crisis buildup in output. This is a new angle in the discussion and worth exploring further.

Finally, given where Greece was when the crisis started, how painful would the adjustment have been absent further shocks? I asked the authors to see what the model implied, by setting all the shocks equal to zero from 2010 on, so the dynamics from then on only depend on the state variables in 2009. They kindly did it, and the results are shown in the attached figure 1. The conclusion is that, despite the buildup of debt and the initial overvaluation, the contraction in output would have been substantially smaller. The mechanism behind the result, however, is suspicious. One would have expected that, in the absence of sovereign risk shocks and fiscal spending shocks the adjustment of government spending would be smaller, leading to a smaller output contraction. This, however, is not the main mechanism at play. Government spending without shocks is nearly the same as with shocks. The main difference is in the behavior of investment, which falls much less than in the presence of shocks. This in turn is due to turning off the funding cost shock, and the large elasticity of investment to the funding cost; as discussed earlier, I am skeptical about the interpretation of the funding cost shock, and the elasticity of investment, and thus skeptical about the conclusion.

Lest my comments appear too negative, let me repeat what I said at the start. The model developed in this paper is not at the stage where it will settle debates about what lies behind the Greek depression. But it has an extremely rich structure, which can be built on and lead to a much more interesting discussion of what has happened in Greece in the last 15 years.

Endnote

For acknowledgments, sources of research support, and disclosure of the author's material financial relationships, if any, please see http://www.nber.org/chapters/c13781.ack.

Reference

Philippe, Martin and Thomas Philippon. 2015. "Inspecting the Mechanism: Leverage and the Great Recession in the Eurozone." Unpublished manuscript, New York University, May.

Comment

Markus Brunnermeier, *Princeton University and NBER*

The euro crisis is a tragedy for Greece and its people. There are very few peace-time episodes during which a country's GDP declines by a quarter. This paper does a good job at summarizing the main macro time series and enriches the analysis by comparing it with other crisis episodes, as well as by estimating a formal DSGE model capturing important features of that crisis.

The main point of my discussion is that the analysis should also include uncertainty and, especially, political uncertainty in understanding this episode. Two absolutely crucial aspects of the crisis, the debate on the optimal speed of deleveraging and the desirability of a Grexit, were instrumental in driving uncertainty, and hence are key in understanding the depth and length of the crisis. Moreover, the combination of uncertainty with financial frictions helps explain the subsequent crisis dynamics, yet the presented DSGE model does not include a channel that helps link political uncertainty to the dynamics of the economy.

I first start my discussion by analyzing how an overly indebted and deficit-ridden economy should be delevered, ignoring political constraints. Stickiness—of wages, prices, and capital allocations—is the keyword here. Then I will add constraints back in and evaluate the Grexit option. I will argue that Grexit and its threat of economic and political contagion was strategically used to improve Greece's bargaining position, sometimes for ideological reasons. This strategy, however, led to a huge amount of uncertainty. My main critique for the DSGE then follows from that analysis: it ignores these important political uncertainty aspects and hence estimation and interpretation of the results have to be taken with a grain of salt.

Optimal Speed of Deleveraging

The paper nicely establishes that Greece built up unsustainable imbalances. Its debt level reached 120% of GDP. Its annual government budget deficit in 2009—before the outbreak of the Greek crisis—exceeded 15%. This path was clearly unsustainable, though market discipline failed in the run-up to the crisis. Indeed, financial markets financed these deficits at minimum spread over the German Bund.

Given the already high annual primary deficit in the boom phase, a fiscal stimulus would not have been able to solve Greece's dilemma. The economy had to be delevered and put on a more solid footing. The first main question to ask, then, concerns the optimal speed of delevering in a world in which financing is provided without any financial frictions and one faces no political constraints. That is, how fast can one bring the economy on a sustainable path if one assumes all financial funding constraints, political constraints, and even legacy debt away.

The adjustment path should be stretched if the capital stock of an economy cannot be easily adjusted. This is, for example, the case if the economy is specialized in industry sectors with long-run fixed investments that are difficult to reverse. Take shipping, for example, an important industry for Greece: ships cannot be easily reallocated to other activities. On the other hand, if the physical capital stock is very flexible, the adjustment can be pushed through more quickly, since it can be easily redeployed for alternative activities.

Price and wage stickiness also play an important role in considering the optimal speed of deleveraging. The higher their stickiness, the longer one should take to delever an economy. Interestingly, empirical data suggest that wages were relatively flexible, while prices seemed more rigid. This pattern holds across many countries in peripheral Europe and deserves further study, especially since the authors find in their shock decomposition that markup shocks may have played an important role in the lack of recovery.

In the real world, *financial frictions* impede countries' funding and make an orderly deleverage more difficult. Investors are reluctant to provide funding since they are afraid that the government might dilute their bonds, and governments cannot commit to implement growth-enhancing reforms that are unpopular in the short term. Hence, financiers and investors demand a premium. In theory, this was less of a concern in the case of Greece since other national governments in Europe could provide the funding—even if uncertainty remained high.

Hence, instead of facing a sudden stop like many other countries, the source of Greek funding switched to official European lending. This is a major difference in comparing Greece with other sudden stop episodes. Indeed, unlike for Ireland, whose crisis erupted earlier, various programs were set up for Greece. European funds were mobilized through various rescue packages. As a result of these funding arrangements, so far Greece did not manage to reach a primary surplus, which other countries with a sudden stop were forced to achieve.

Often a sudden stop not only brings funding difficulties to the government, but also to the local banking sector. Twin crises emerge and a diabolic loop between sovereign and banking risks make things worse (see Brunnermeier et al. 2016) Again, unlike a plain vanilla sudden stop, the Greek banking sector received considerable help from the ECB through Emergency Liquidity Assistance (ELA) and other support programs. Heightened Target 2 claims provided a lens about the extent of the funding support. Indeed, bank deposits proved very resilient. Unlike what traditional theory predicts, many depositors kept their money in the banks. Figure 1 shows that the bank deposits declined, but not to zero. A significant drop in bank deposits occurred when the newly elected Syriza government followed a more confrontational course, which stirred additional uncertainty in the first half of 2015.

Nevertheless, as the paper convincingly documents, the Greek economy suffered significantly more compared to other sudden stop countries. Especially the investment-to-GDP level literally collapsed. Yet, rather than a lack of funding ability, it was a rising climate of political uncertainty that inevitably contributed to this contraction. The vigorous debates about the optimal speed of deleveraging, with Greek authorities asking for slow deleveraging and the Troika requiring a faster one, created this uncertainty as policymakers were unable to settle on a stable path for deleveraging.

The optimal speed of deleveraging also depends on a country's degree of trade openness and on its exchange rate regime. Typically, exchange rate depreciation can help an open economy like Greece with its emphasis on shipping and tourism. However, within a currency union, a country's currency cannot be used to depress relative real wages via a currency devaluation. As the authors duly acknowledge by comparing the Greek case with that of countries that pegged their currencies, this creates slower deleveraging and, given frictions, is more painful for the economy.

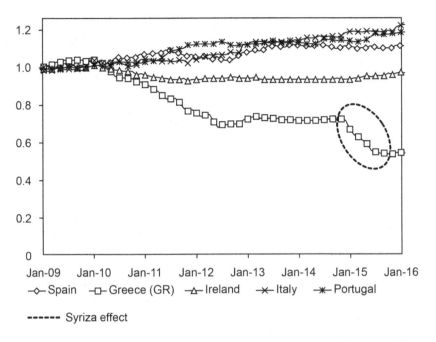

Fig. 1. Bank deposits across peripheral European countries in Spain (ES), Greece (GR), Ireland (IE), Italy (IT), and Portugal (PT).
Source: Earlier version of "The Analytics of the Greek Crisis."
Note: The initial levels are normalized to 1.

Of course, an exit from the European Monetary Union, a Grexit, would have allowed a devaluation. I will discuss the Grexit option and threats next.

The Grexit Option

The paper does not evaluate the impact of a looming Grexit and the uncertainty associated with it. At least twice Grexit was at the doorsteps: The first time in the summer of 2012, when many peripheral European countries suffered from high interest rates and a banking crisis. Economic contagion forces to other peripheral countries were very powerful at that time. This allowed Greece to extract some additional funding from its European partners. The second time was in the summer of 2015, when the newly elected Syriza government tried to shift the economic policy across all of Europe from a consolidation-based (austerity) approach to a Keynesian stimulus approach. A battle of ideas emerged between proponents of the Keynesian school, which contended that structural reforms are counterproductive when the economy hits the zero lower bound, and those of the German school, which asserted that structural reforms are overdue in Greece and for political reasons can only be pushed through in times of crisis. However, the Greek government made a strategic miscalculation. By then economic contagion was under control—thanks also to ECB's Quantitative Easing program—and political contagion worked against the Greek government. Political leaders in other countries were more concerned by the fact that if Greeks were to receive further concessions, political parties in analogous situations would ask for the same concessions (for details, see Brunnermeier, James, and Landau [2016]).

A Grexit would have been accompanied with significant debt restructuring. This would have solved the stock problem, but still left the flow problem of ongoing annual primary deficit (which by 2015 was much smaller). In addition, a Grexit would have led to a sharp devaluation of the new national currency, not only melting the stock of debt but also making industry, especially the tourist and shipping industries, more competitive. On the other hand, it would reduce the need to improve the institutional framework in Greece, for example, such as implementing a better legal structure, a more systematic land registry, and many supply reforms that can have a growth enhancing impact in the long run.

Both in 2012 and 2015, the possible Grexit was used as a threat to obtain concessions. Hence, political considerations played an important role. Brinkmanship and war of attrition games led policymakers to "kick the can down the road." Resolutions were delayed. Things became worse over time and the outcome became a negative sum game. Importantly, the gaming created immense uncertainty. Given this uncertainty, it is not surprising that investment came to an unprecedented halt. Recall that at the height of the Grexit 2015 debate, banks were shut and economic activity literally collapsed. I will discuss in the next section the analysis and the estimated DSGE model abstracts from these political uncertainty considerations.

Missing Politics and Uncertainty in the Model

After the authors have pinpointed the main stylized facts of the Greek crisis and compared them to other sudden stop crises, they design a DSGE model aimed at capturing the main aspects of the Greek episode.

In their model a small open economy interacts with a larger country within a currency union, without exchange rate adjustments to shocks. Wages are assumed to be sticky in order to trigger an output gap after shocks, in a New Keynesian fashion. Financial frictions are also present in the model, as firms are forced to borrow in order to finance their activities; patient lenders guarantee a source of funding. Tractability and data availability forces the authors to introduce financial intermediation in a reduced-form way. They assume that banks simply lever deposits at a given funding cost, and (competitively) redistribute funds to borrowers at the same rate. The funding cost depends on three factors: the real interest rate, an exogenous autoregressive shock, as well as expected losses on private credit portfolios, adjusted for leverage. This is sufficient to yield a credit supply channel to the economy and produce some diabolic loops, as higher funding costs eventually feed back. However, as discussed, the assumptions of (1) the exogeneity of the default processes, and particularly the absence of a political uncertainty shock, and (2) a reduced-form decision rule that neglects, in particular, volatility aspects have important potential implications. The assumption of a constant pass-through of banks' credit supply conditions to credit demand can be seen as problematic as well.

These omissions affect the estimation of the model, as well as the exercises that are done using it. Of course, my remarks will remain grounded on an intuitive level—Bayesian DSGE estimations have their own challenges and can be obscure. This makes it difficult to interpret the robustness of the findings, at least in the way they are presented here.

No parts of the model capture the political economy aspects of the crisis in an explicit way. Perhaps one could argue that it is too difficult, for now, to introduce the kind of war of attrition games with political economy forces I've been describing earlier. But this creates identification problems for the shocks currently introduced in the model. Too many of them have a potentially common "political" root that would need to be accounted for as such. Moreover, and worse, it is likely that the political economy shock itself is endogenous to economic conditions—at least to some extent—reflecting the evolution of the political economy game.

To be concrete, consider the probability of a Grexit. Certainly, through its effects on different risk premia, as well as future economic outcomes, the Grexit probability affects credit demand as well as supply. Investment decisions, funding costs (the sudden stop shock), sovereign risk, and so forth are all affected by the Grexit risk. Through these shock channels, the Grexit probability affects the accounting of the sources of the Greek slump. There is likely to be an endogenous feedback: when these shocks hit, the conditions of the political economy game change itself, as the players' outside options change. This seems particularly important in the case of government spending: fiscal rules. In reality, they are likely to be more endogenous than the one suggested in the paper, and were certainly heavily affected not only by Greek economic conditions but also the decision-making processes of the Troika (consisting of the IMF, the European Commission, and the European Central Bank).

This is not to say that the model does not provide a useful lens through which one can analyze the Greek crisis, an objective it certainly achieves. Yet caution must be taken before inferring from its results because it seems that political economy issues were extremely important in that particular episode. The "Syriza shock" is a particular example. It cannot be neglected when analyzing Greece's economy in the last two years.

Volatility Dynamics and Nonlinearities

The model attempts, as well as it can, to capture variables affecting banks' as well as fiscal authorities' decisions given current economic conditions. The model is, however, linearized. Hence, it cannot—beyond the exogenous shock rules—price in the rise in market volatility nor political uncertainty. Indeed, even if agents have precautionary motives, second-moment considerations drop out after log linearizations.

Indicators such as the volatility index VIX certainly priced uncertainty during the crisis. As far as the interpretation is concerned, it seems that the rise in risk premia in the presence of increased uncertainty was an important reason why banks increased lending costs. This is despite the fact that their effective borrowing costs objectively remained low. This rise in spread is at the source of the investment slump that the model has a hard time explaining. Of course, DSGE models that are solvable up to second moments and go beyond a local approximation around the steady state remain a nascent and evolving area of research.

The absence of a volatility channel also matters because my recent work with Yuliy Sannikov has shown that endogenous volatility can play an important role in explaining the length of a slump.[1] After an adverse shock, volatility rises endogenously, reinforcing the precautionary motive and leading to more cutbacks. Overall, it makes the amplification mechanism even more powerful. In addition, the fear of further (even more amplified) shocks can be a source of a prolong slump.

Given this persistence and amplification, one should find a way to clearly account the contribution of not only shocks, but also their transmission mechanisms. Indeed, in the recent literature that has managed to introduce nonlinearity in DSGE models of financial frictions, transmission mechanisms play an important amplifying role. Indeed, it could be that the credit supply/sudden stop shock, which as the authors note is curiously absent in explaining the absence of a strong recovery—at the expense of a markup shock—takes a much more prominent role once an amplification channel is added to the model.

Conclusion

I highly recommend reading this paper. It documents well the evolution of the main macrovariables prior and during the Greek malaise and contrasts it nicely with other sudden stop episodes. The paper does not directly address the important question of what the optimal speed of deleveraging an overly indebted country with a large primary deficit is. Second, political concerns should not be ignored. Brinkmanship, games of chicken, and so forth introduce additional uncertainty that played an important role in the Greek crisis. They affect the shock structure and hence should be part of any structural model.

Endnotes

For acknowledgments, sources of research support, and disclosure of the author's material financial relationships, if any, please see http://www.nber.org/chapters/c13782.ack.
1. See Brunnermeier and Sannikov (2014).

References

Brunnermeier, Markus K., Luis Garicano, Philip Lane, Marco Pagano, Ricardo Reis, Tano Santos, David Thesmar, Stijn Van Nieuwerburgh, and Dimitri Vayanos. 2016. "The Sovereign-Banking Diabolic Loop and ESBies." *American Economic Review Papers and Proceedings* 106 (5): 508–12.
Brunnermeier, Markus K., Harold James, and Jean-Pierre Landau. 2016. *The Euro and the Battle of Ideas.* Princeton, NJ: Princeton University Press.
Brunnermeier, Markus K., and Yuliy Sannikov. 2014. "A Macroeconomic Model with a Financial Sector." *American Economic Review* 104 (2): 379–421.

Discussion

Yannis Ioannides opened the discussion with a question about the ability of the model used in the paper to capture the very slow rate of recovery in economic activity. He noted that in these models, output usually recovers quite quickly following credit spread declines. However in many countries, including the United States and some of the euro periphery, we have seen a slow recovery in growth, despite credit spreads coming back down.

Presenter Thomas Philippon responded that they have not had time to look at this issue. He did clarify that the relevant borrowing costs used in the model for small and medium enterprises in Greece have not actually come down very much. He stressed that the model does quite well in terms of persistence, generating a long decrease in GDP, high debt, nonperforming loans, and credit spreads. Philippon noted that there is no investment puzzle in Greece, unlike the United States. Therefore, if credit spreads did come down, there would be a large boom in investment.

Pierre-Olivier Gourinchas added, in response to Olivier Blanchard's discussion, that the high interest rates fed into the model as funding costs actually seem to do a good job explaining investment. Those were much higher than the effective marginal borrowing costs. If the latter had been fed into the model, it would not have been able to match the investment behavior in the data. Blanchard commented that government borrowing costs were much lower in practice than yields on Greek debt to the bailout programs.

Jón Steinsson raised concerns that the counterfactual evolution of the Greek economy with lower leverage still appeared to be much worse than that of the crises used as the comparison group in the reduced-form section of the paper. Thus, he wondered if the model is really suggesting that high leverage can account for why the Greek crisis was so much worse than other historical episodes.

Gourinchas responded by confirming that the counterfactual output path for Greece is right on the confidence interval for the comparison group. He also noted that the level of leverage used in the low-leverage counterfactual was on the high end of potentially reasonable choices. The reason was that they chose to discipline themselves by using a leverage-level representative of other countries as they entered their sudden stop episodes. Like Greece, these countries had also increased their leverage in their run-ups. Gourinchas did concede, however, that the exercise is not able to completely account for the size of the Greek crisis. Philippon added that while they are not explaining all of the Greek episode, the counterfactual exercise still implies that GDP would have been 5 percentage points higher if the run-up in leverage had not occurred, which is an extremely large and significant amount.

Harald Uhlig suggested that the authors attempt to take seriously the measurement and accounting issues in the Greek data, which could partially account for the observed extreme aggregate output dynamics. For instance, if transfers, such as government jobs that required no work, had been labeled as government spending, then GDP in Greece could have mechanically risen and then subsequently declined in line with the transfers. If the transfers were financed by lump-sum taxation, then they would affect GDP, but not private consumption. Uhlig also stressed that the large shadow economy in Greece may have absorbed some of the drop in measured output in response to increased tax collection efforts.

Gourinchas agreed in principle with Uhlig's points, but noted that there is evidence that substantial portions of government-spending increases can be attributed to asset purchases, infrastructure, and the buildup of Greece's large military capacity.

Philippon noted that how one accounts for overpaying government workers matters in DSGE models. The correct way is to treat it as a transfer rather than government expenditure. On private consumption measurement, Philippon agreed that this is an issue, but he is not aware that the problem in Greece is much worse than in other countries.

Fernando Alvarez then asked a question regarding the composition of markup shocks in the model. Philippon conceded that the composition of markups was the most sensitive part of the DSGE estimation. He noted that while everyone had the idea, as in Blanchard's discussion, that the flexibility of wages and the comparative rigidity of retail prices could explain the output decline in Greece, this was not a robust outcome of the model estimation.

Ricardo Reis asked if the authors had examined how different the boom in Greece was from the booms that preceded sudden stop episodes in emerging-market economies. Gourinchas responded that while they have not yet performed a comparative analysis of boom periods, his sense is the boom was probably much bigger in Greece. Greece was allowed to build up much more leverage and exposure than emerging-market economies typically can before markets increase borrowing costs. That excessive leverage, he hypothesized, would certainly feed into output and lead to a larger boom. Philippon clarified that the boom and bust in Greece were almost symmetric—a positive output gap of 15% followed by a negative output gap of the same size.

Michael Klein noted two features of the Greek crisis that distinguish it from the crises episodes used in the comparison group—the inopportune timing on the heels of the global financial crisis and Greece's relatively low level of exports and the importance of shipping. He asked if the authors have a story for why these specific aspects of the Greek experience might have contributed to a slow recovery.

Gourinchas agreed that these details are important, but were not considered in the paper. He stressed that the problem with going to that level of detail was the need to fully understand these institutional features in Greece, as well as other countries, during their crises experiences. Building this into the model would require a lot of granular data that is not necessarily available.

2

Jump-Starting the Euro-Area Recovery: Would a Rise in Core Fiscal Spending Help the Periphery?

Olivier Blanchard, *Peterson Institute of International Economics and NBER*
Christopher J. Erceg, *Federal Reserve Board*
Jesper Lindé, *Sveriges Riksbank and Stockholm School of Economics*

I. Introduction

If the euro area were a fiscal union like the United States, there would be a strong case for fiscal expansion: the unemployment rate remains near double digits, inflation has run persistently too low, and monetary policy has limited scope to provide additional stimulus. However, the euro area is not a fiscal union, and fiscal expansion has to be carried out by member states. Given that the periphery economies most likely to benefit from domestic fiscal expansion are constrained from doing so because of concerns about high public debt and fiscal solvency, any sizable fiscal expansion has to come from the euro area's core economies.

In this paper, we analyze the effects of an expansion of fiscal spending in the euro area's core economies. Rather than limiting attention to the effects on the euro area as a whole, we focus on how the stimulative effects would be distributed between core and periphery: Would a core fiscal expansion have sizable positive "spillovers" to periphery output and inflation, or would the stimulus mostly be limited to those core economies opting to raise public spending? The answer is clearly critical to evaluating potential welfare benefits. Even if core fiscal expansion increased euro-area output and inflation, it may not be desirable if it caused core economies to overheat, while imparting little positive impetus to the periphery.

The fiscal consolidations that began in 2010 in Greece, Portugal, Ireland, and Spain offer some clues about the channels through which a prospective core fiscal expansion might play out. On the one hand, the deep fiscal cuts carried out from 2010 to 2013 had strong adverse effects on the periphery countries' domestic demand due, at least in part, to cur-

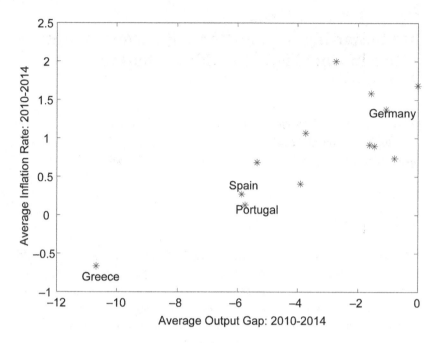

Fig. 1. Average output gaps and inflation rates in euro area: 2010–2014

rency union membership and the zero lower bound on monetary policy (Blanchard and Leigh 2014). On the other hand, the large negative output gaps in those countries led to a decrease in relative price levels and some improvement in external demand. In this vein, figure 1 illustrates the positive relationship between the average output gap and price inflation for euro-area economies in the aftermath of the financial crisis: the high degree of resource slack in countries such as Spain and Portugal, partly driven by massive fiscal consolidation, translated into lower average inflation than in Germany. The euro area's recent experience makes clear that the net result of fiscal consolidation, for both periphery and core countries, depends on the stance of monetary policy and the relevance of the zero lower bound on the size of the multipliers, on the effect of output gaps on inflation and by implication on relative prices, and on the effect of relative prices on imports and exports.

The same considerations are likely to play a key role in influencing the macroeconomic effects of a rise in core government spending, and suggest the importance of both aggregate (euro-wide) and compositional channels.

From an aggregate perspective, the effects are likely to depend on how strongly monetary policy reacts to the induced rise in euro-area output and inflation. Outside of a liquidity trap, the European Central Bank (ECB) would raise interest rates in real terms, which would dampen private demand in both the core and periphery; unless periphery net exports rose enough to compensate, periphery gross domestic product (GDP) would likely fall. In a liquidity trap, higher core spending boosts inflation in both the core and periphery and potentially reduces real interest rates enough to provide a significant boost both to periphery and core GDP. From a compositional perspective, while the demand stimulus is likely to affect primarily core countries, the increase in inflation in core relative to periphery countries leads to an increase in core relative prices and to some reallocation of demand toward periphery countries.

To gauge the strength of the various channels and make an assessment of the likely effects of a core fiscal expansion on core and periphery GDP, we use two variants of a New Keynesian model of a currency union. Our benchmark model is quite simple—extending Galí and Monacelli (2008) mainly by adding habit persistence in consumption to get more plausible dynamics—but is useful for pinpointing how the various aggregate and compositional channels shape the response of periphery output. Moreover, the simple structure facilitates showing how key features such as the Phillips curve slope affect both the aggregate multiplier and spillovers to the periphery. However, we also use a larger-scale dynamic stochastic general equilibrium (DSGE) model—which includes price and wage rigidities, endogenous investment, and allows for non-Ricardian consumption behavior—to derive quantitative assessments in a more empirically realistic setting. Following the general approach of Christiano, Eichenbaum, and Evans (2005) and Altig et al. (2011), we estimate key parameters in this model to match the empirical responses to both a euro-area monetary policy shock and government-spending shock.

We find that, outside of a liquidity trap, the effects of higher core government spending on periphery GDP tend to be small and even negative (assuming that the import content of core government spending is low). The small response of periphery GDP reflects that the central bank raises real interest rates, more than offsetting the stimulus arising from a depreciation of the periphery's terms of trade. These results concur with previous research by Wieland (1996) and Kollmann et al. (2014) indicating that fiscal spillovers tend to be negative under fixed exchange rates (assuming that the central bank responds according to a standard policy reaction function).

The spillovers to periphery GDP are markedly different in a liquidity trap: periphery GDP tends to rise, reflecting the weaker interest rate response. The size of the periphery GDP response to a core spending hike increases with the expected duration of the liquidity trap, with the import content of core government spending, and with the responsiveness of inflation. In a relatively short-lived trap lasting only a few quarters, the GDP stimulus to the periphery is small (unless a sizable fraction of core spending is imported), so that most of the expansionary effects of the fiscal stimulus is confined to the core. However, higher core spending can provide a potent source of stimulus to the periphery if monetary policy is expected to be constrained from raising interest rates for a prolonged period of a couple of years or more.

The larger-scale model implies that a rise in core government spending has effects on periphery GDP that are about half as large as on core GDP in a three-year liquidity trap; the aggregate euro-area multiplier of around 2 seems in line with both model-based analysis suggesting high multipliers in a liquidity trap, and empirical analysis (both of which are reviewed in the next section). The large spillovers to the periphery reflect a combination of factors: higher periphery net exports, lower real interest rates as periphery inflation rises, and Keynesian multiplier effects that boost domestic demand (captured by the hand-to-mouth consumers in our model). But it bears emphasizing that the sizable spillovers do not hinge on an implausibly large inflation response; though consistent with the empirical responses of inflation to monetary and spending shocks, our model implies an extremely flat Phillips curve relative to most existing estimates. The Keynesian multiplier effects do play an important role, which seems in line with the substantial *crowding in* of domestic demand in response to government spending shocks in our empirical vector autoregression (VAR), as well as with evidence from the literature on local multipliers (Nakamura and Steinsson 2014; Acconcia, Corsetti, and Simonelli 2014).

We also use the simple model to conduct normative analysis: one important upshot is the reminder that the output and inflation responses perhaps should not be the sole criteria for judging whether fiscal adjustment is desirable. We consider two alternative welfare metrics, including an ad hoc but standard criterion based on output and inflation gap variability in each region and a utility-based criterion that is based on a population-weighted average of the utility functions of households. Under either criterion, we show that the welfare benefits of core fiscal expansion are smaller than under fiscal union. This is intuitive, and simply reflects that a core-only spending hike delivers the most stimulus to where it is "needed least," insofar as resource slack is much smaller than in the periphery. Under fiscal union, more of the expansion could be targeted to the periphery, allowing comparatively large welfare gains.[1]

However, the alternative welfare criteria differ substantially in their assessment of whether a core fiscal expansion would improve welfare in the periphery economies. The ad hoc criterion indicates that an expansion of core spending can elicit large welfare gains in both the core and periphery by shrinking output gaps and increasing inflation closer to target. By contrast, the utility-based criterion cares about whether the fiscal stimulus boosts periphery consumption enough—and in a front-loaded manner—to justify the utility cost of the increased employment. Accordingly, the utility-based measure sees less benefit from core fiscal expansion than the simple ad hoc measure because net exports play a substantive role in reducing the periphery's output gap. In addition, the consumption rise in the periphery is very drawn out, so that much of it occurs when the economy has largely recovered. Our sense is that the utility-based analysis is useful for highlighting that a focus on reducing output and inflation gaps may be too narrow in assessing the merits of fiscal expansion. However, as we argue below, the utility-based measure probably understates the benefits of reducing the output gap and unemployment in economies facing high resource slack.

This paper is organized as follows. Section II provides an overview of the literature on fiscal multipliers and spillovers. Section III presents the simple benchmark model in log-linearized form, while section IV reports impulse responses to a core fiscal expansion with a focus on factors determining spillovers to the periphery. Section V considers both the positive and normative effects of alternative fiscal expansion packages against a reasonable baseline for the euro area. Section VI examines robustness in the larger-scale model, while section VII concludes.

II. Brief Overview of the Literature

From an aggregate perspective, the models we consider are closely related to those of an extensive literature examining fiscal policy in a liquidity trap. This literature shows that the spending multiplier is likely to be substantially larger than in normal times; for example, Eggertsson (2011), Christiano, Eichenbaum, and Rebelo (2011), and Woodford (2011). The higher multiplier reflects that the central bank does not raise nominal policy rates even though inflation rises, so that real interest rates fall and domestic demand is crowded in. These crowding-in effects can be large if inflation is responsive to resource slack. For example, Christiano, Eichenbaum, and Rebelo (2011) showed that the peak multiplier exceeds 2 in a long-lived liquidity trap under their preferred model specification.

A number of empirical papers have corroborated the implication of a large spending multiplier when monetary policy is constrained. Some of this analysis has focused on the Great Depression period, given that monetary policy was arguably unreactive to fiscal stimulus during most of that time. Almunia et al. (2010) found a spending multiplier of over 2 using a panel VAR for major industrial economies that is estimated over the interwar period and uses the same identifying assumptions as in Blanchard and Perotti (2002). Gordon and Krenn (2010) estimated a spending multiplier of slightly under 2 for the United States in a narrow window preceding the US entry into World War II. They argue that this is an ideal period for estimating the multiplier, given that government spending rose massively (by 13% of US GDP between 1940:Q2–1941:Q4), monetary policy was passive, resource slack still large, and tax rates were not (yet) adjusted up. They also document a substantial crowding in of private demand.

Blanchard and Leigh (2014) focused on the recent experience of fiscal consolidation in the euro area during the 2010–2012 period. While some analysis suggested that deep spending cuts would exert only a modest drag on output—or possibly even raise output through confidence channels (Alesina and Ardagna 2010)—Blanchard and Leigh showed that fiscal multipliers in euro-area countries turned out to be much larger than forecast ex ante, implying that fiscal cuts in the periphery had considerably more adverse effects than anticipated. Their estimates suggest a spending multiplier of around 1.5 for the euro area.

Both the theoretical and empirical literature has attempted to identify key factors influencing the size of the aggregate spending multiplier. In addition to the inflation response, the multiplier is larger in a longer-lived liquidity trap if the bulk of spending occurs when the zero bound constraint is still binding (see the papers by CER and Woodford mentioned above), or if the economy is in a deep recession with substantial excess capacity (Auerbach and Gorodnichenko 2012; Gordon and Krenn 2010). Moreover, as indicated by Uhlig (2010), Erceg and Lindé (2014), and Drautzberg and Uhlig (2015), the tax reaction function can be quite consequential: the spending multiplier can be significantly lower if tax rates are adjusted quickly and if distortionary tax rates account for most of the adjustment. In our analysis, we assume that fiscal stimulus can be implemented fairly quickly, and that taxes are either lump sum (as in the simple model of section III), or that tax rates at least adjust very slowly. The multipliers derived from our simulations would be lower under less favorable assumptions on these dimensions.

Several recent papers have analyzed fiscal spillovers in a liquidity trap in stylized open economy models. The qualitative analysis of Farhi and Werning (2012) shows that the pattern of spillovers flips sign—from negative in normal times when the currency union monetary authority raises interest rates—to positive in a liquidity trap. Other papers, including Cook and Devereux (2011) and Fujiwara and Ueda (2013), have focused on environments with flexible exchange rates and have shown that a country expanding fiscal spending is likely to cause its currency to depreciate, potentially generating negative spillovers to its trading partners.

As discussed in the introduction, an empirical implication of the models we consider is that fiscal expansion in core countries should boost periphery real net exports. This implication is consistent with Beetsma, Giuliodori, and Klaassen (2006), who used a panel VAR framework to show that expansionary fiscal shocks in European Union economies typically increase the net exports of their trading partners (and conversely for fiscal contractions).

We also draw on the literature estimating "local multipliers" to help assess the empirical plausibility of our model(s) for the differential effects of a rise in core government spending on core versus periphery output. This literature estimates how output is affected in a region that boosts government spending (e.g., a city or state) relative to other regions, and typically finds that relative output—that is, output in the region experiencing the spending hike—rises by considerably more than the increase in relative government spending (scaled by GDP). For example, Acconcia et al. (2014) estimated a local multiplier of 1.5–1.9 for municipalities in Italy using as an instrument sudden cuts in municipal public spending triggered by the removal of local city councils (following evidence of Mafia-related corruption), while Nakamura and Steinsson (2014) analyzed the effects of changes in defense expenditures concentrated in particular US states, and estimated a local multiplier of 1.5. Although our simple model in the next section constrains the local multiplier to be less than unity, we interpret the estimates of high local multipliers as suggestive of strong Keynesian multiplier channels, and hence build these features into the larger-scale model of section VI.

Finally, the Phillips curve slope plays a paramount role in influencing both the aggregate multiplier and in determining the size of compositional effects on trade. The extensive empirical literature estimating the Phillips curve slope—both for the industrial economies, and the euro area in particular—generally points to a low Phillips curve slope. This includes estimates based on DSGE models (Smets and Wouters 2003), as well as from single equation models as in Blanchard, Cerutti, and Summers (2015), with the latter highlighting a substantial fall in the Phillips curve slope in the early 1990s. Even so, it bears emphasizing that these estimates are generally consistent with a noticeable response of inflation to a sustained rise in fiscal spending, as we will show below. Moreover, a number of papers suggest that the low estimated slopes partly reflect various forms of misspecification—including, for example, not taking adequate account of how TFP shocks or financial conditions influence marginal cost (Christiano, Eichenbaum, and Trabandt 2015; Gilchrist et al. 2015)—and that the actual Phillips curve slope is considerably higher. Thus, although our own estimates in section VI imply a low Phillips curve slope, and we embed a low slope in the baseline calibration of our models, we also consider the implications of a higher slope.

III.   The Benchmark Open Economy Model

Our benchmark model is comprised of two countries that may differ in population size. Households are infinitely lived, derive utility from consumption and leisure, and make consumption decisions based on their permanent income. Monopolistically competitive firms are subject to Calvo-style pricing frictions, so that nominal prices adjust sluggishly. Similar to Galí and Monacelli (2008), our model assumes that financial markets are complete both domestically and internationally, and that producers set the same price in both the home and foreign market (producer currency pricing). We generalize the Galí and Monacelli model by allowing for habit persistence in consumption, and by assuming that some fraction of government consumption may be imported.

Given the symmetric structure across countries, we look at the home country: the same equations and calibration apply to the foreign country (aside from population size). Our formulation below highlights how the model can be decomposed into two parts. The first part, which determines the equilibrium for the currency union (CU) as a whole, is completely standard. The familiar three equations—the New Keynesian IS curve, the AS curve, and the policy reaction function—determine aggregate CU output, inflation, and policy rates, respectively; per usual, a core fiscal expansion boosts CU output and inflation. The second part involves characterizing the difference between the response of periphery and core variables. These differences depend exclusively on the terms of trade and exogenous shocks, including to fiscal policy. Importantly, monetary policy only affects the core and periphery through its effects on the CU as a whole, but does not influence the terms of trade, or the differences between the responses of periphery and core variables.[2]

Our discussion below focuses on the log-linearized equations of the model; a full description of the underlying model structure is provided in Appendix A.

A.   The Log-Linearized Benchmark Model

Consumption demand in each economy is determined by the consumption Euler equation condition, which for the home economy is given by:

$$\lambda_{ct} = \lambda_{ct+1|t} + i_t^{CU} - \pi_{ct+1|t'} \tag{1}$$

where i_t^{CU} is the policy rate of the central bank in the currency union (CU), π_{ct} is consumer price inflation in the home economy, and λ_{ct} is the marginal utility of consumption:

$$\lambda_{ct} = -\frac{1}{\hat{\sigma}}(c_t - \varkappa c_{t-1} - \nu v_t). \tag{2}$$

The marginal utility of consumption varies inversely with current consumption c_t, but rises with past consumption due to habit persistence. Taken together, these equations imply that consumption falls in response to higher real interest rates, with the sensitivity depending on intertemporal elasticity in substitution parameter $\hat{\sigma} = \sigma(1 - \varkappa - \nu)$. The preference shock v_t boosts consumption demand at any given interest rate.[3] Given that households are infinitely lived and taxes are lump sum, the manner in which changes in government spending are financed has no effect on consumption decisions.

Consumption demand in the CU as a whole is determined as a population-weighted average of the demand of the home and foreign economies (with weights ζ and ζ^*, respectively). Imposing the aggregate resource constraints that equate CU consumption c_t^{CU} to CU output y_t^{CU} less government spending g_t^{CU} (i.e., $c_y c_t^{CU} = y_t^{CU} - g_y g_t^{CU}$) and CPI infla-

tion in each country to CU inflation π_t^{CU} ($\zeta\pi_{Ct} + \zeta^*\pi_{Ct}^* = \pi_t^{CU}$), aggregate
demand in the CU may be expressed in terms of a familiar New Keynes-
ian IS curve:

$$x_t^{CU} = \frac{1}{1+\varkappa} x_{t+1|t}^{CU} + \frac{\varkappa}{1+\varkappa} x_{t-1}^{CU} - c_y \hat{\sigma}(i_t^{CU} - \pi_{t+1|t}^{CU} - r_t^{CU,pot}), \quad (3)$$

where c_y denotes the consumption-output ratio in steady state, and g_y is
the government-spending share. As seen in equation (3), the CU output
gap x_t^{CU} depends both on past and future output gaps, and inversely on
the difference between the real policy rate in the CU $i_t^{CU} - \pi_{t+1|t}^{CU}$ and its
potential or "natural" rate of $r_t^{CU,pot}$.[4]

On the aggregate supply side, the inflation rate of domestically produced goods in each country is determined by a New Keynesian Phillips curve. Thus, the home inflation rate π_{Dt} depends both on the current marginal cost of production mc_t and future expected inflation:

$$\pi_{Dt} = \beta\pi_{Dt+1|t} + \kappa_{mc}mc_t. \quad (4)$$

The subscript "D" on inflation is used to distinguish the inflation rate on
domestically produced goods π_{Dt} from the consumer price inflation rate
π_{Ct}. Given our assumption of monopolistically competitive producers
and Calvo-style staggered price contracts, the parameter κ_{mc} determining
the sensitivity of inflation to marginal cost mc_t depends on the mean price
contract duration $1/(1 - \xi_p)$ according to $\kappa_{mc} = [(1 - \xi_p)(1 - \beta\xi_p)]/\xi_p$. Thus,
longer-lived price contracts flatten the slope of the Phillips curve. Mar-
ginal cost in turn depends on the gap between the product real wage w_t^r
and the marginal product of labor mpl_t:

$$mc_t = w_t^r - mpl_t = [\chi n_t - \lambda_{ct} + \omega_c\tau_t] + \alpha n_t - (1 - \alpha)z_t. \quad (5)$$

The effects on marginal cost associated with fluctuations in the product
real wage are captured by the term in brackets. Because wages are fully
flexible, the product real wage rises in response to an increase in work
hours n_t (χ is the inverse Frisch elasticity), a fall in the marginal utility
of consumption λ_{ct} (reflecting a wealth effect), or to a depreciation of the
terms of trade τ_t. Marginal costs also rise in response to factors that reduce the marginal product of labor, including a rise in hours worked
(with sensitivity α), or decline in technology z_t.

Aggregate CU inflation is determined as a population-weighted average of equation (4):

$$\pi_t^{CU} = \beta\pi_{t+1|t}^{CU} + \kappa_{mc}mc_t^{CU}. \quad (6)$$

Using the production function to substitute for hours in terms of output, CU marginal cost can be expressed solely in terms of the CU output gap and its lag (with the latter reflecting the effect of habit persistence in consumption on labor supply). Thus, the New Keynesian Phillips curve for CU inflation is given by:

$$\pi_t^{CU} = \beta\pi_{t+1|t}^{CU} + \kappa_{mc}[\phi_x x_t^{CU} + \frac{1}{c_y\hat{\sigma}}(x_t^{CU} - \varkappa x_{t-1}^{CU})], \tag{7}$$

where the composite parameter $\phi_x = (\alpha + \chi)/(1 - a)$ captures the influence of diminishing returns and the disutility of working, and $1/c_y\hat{\sigma}$ the wealth effect on labor supply.

The currency union central bank is assumed to adhere to a Taylor-type policy rule subject to the zero lower bound (ZLB) of the form:

$$i_t^{CU} = \max(-i, \psi_\pi\pi_t^{CU} + \psi_x x_t^{CU}). \tag{8}$$

Thus, outside of a liquidity trap, the policy rate i_t^{CU} rises in response to an increase in the CU inflation rate π_t^{CU} or expansion in the CU output gap x_t^{CU}. Because the policy rate is measured as a deviation from the steady-state nominal interest rate i—the sum of the steady-state interest rate r and inflation rate π—the zero-bound constraint becomes binding only when the policy rate falls below $-i$. The CU output gap x_t^{CU} is the difference between currency union output y_t^{CU} and its potential level $y_t^{CU,pot}$, with both variables again simply population-weighted averages of the respective country variables.

Both the potential output measure $y_t^{CU,pot}$ relevant for the CU output gap ($x_t^{CU} = y_t^{CU} - y_t^{CU,pot}$) and the potential real rate $r_t^{CU,pot}$ depend only on population-weighted averages of the underlying shocks and lags of $y_t^{CU,pot}$ (due to habit persistence). For example, abstracting from habit persistence for expositional simplicity, CU potential output is given by:

$$y_t^{CU,pot} = \Theta(g_y g_t^{CU} + v(1 - g_y)v_t^{CU} + (1 - g_y)(1 + \chi)z_t^{CU}), \tag{9}$$

where $\Theta = 1/[\hat{\sigma}(1 - g_y)\phi_x + 1] < 1$, while the potential real interest rate may be expressed as:[5]

$$r_t^{CU,pot} = (1 - \rho)\left(\frac{(1 - \Theta)}{1 - g_y}g_y g_t^{CU} + vv_t^{CU} + (1 + \chi)z_t^{CU}\right), \tag{10}$$

where ρ is the (common) persistence coefficient of the exogenous shocks, g_t^{CU}, v_t^{CU} and z_t^{CU}. A rise in average CU government spending g_t^{CU} has the same positive effect on currency union potential output and the potential real interest rate $r_t^{CU,pot}$ irrespective of how it is distributed across the member states (as does the preference shock v_t^{CU} and technology shock z_t^{CU}). This result rests on our assumption of a symmetric structure across the home and foreign economy, aside from population size and home bias in trade.

Our formulation highlights how a core fiscal expansion can be thought of as partly operating through aggregate channels—boosting euro-area inflation, the output gap, and possibly the policy rate. Given the simple equation structure implied by the IS curve in equation (3), the Phillips curve in equation (7), and the CU policy rule in equation (8), the fiscal expansion has exactly the same effects on aggregate variables (including x_t^{CU}, π_t^{CU}, and i_t^{CU}) as in a similarly calibrated closed economy model. Of course, in addition to the aggregate impact, we are also interested in how the effects of core fiscal stimulus would be distributed between the periphery and core. Accordingly, we next solve for the differences in the responses between the home and foreign economy. This approach allows us to solve the model in a way that sheds light on the question of why the stimulus has a differential impact on each economy.

The resource constraint implies that home output y_{Dt} may be expressed as a weighted average of consumption c_t, government spending g_t, and "net exports" nx_t, which are the difference between exports m_t^* and imports m_t scaled by the trade share of GDP:

$$y_{Dt} = c_y c_t + g_y g_t + nx_t, \tag{11}$$

Net exports in turn depend on the percentage difference between exports and imports of each type of tradable good, including private consumption goods (i.e., $m_{ct}^* - m_{ct}$) and government goods/services ($m_{gt}^* - m_{gt}$):

$$nx_t = \omega_{cy}(m_{ct}^* - m_{ct}) + \omega_{gy}(m_{gt}^* - m_{gt}). \tag{12}$$

Each component is weighted by its respective GDP share (i.e., $\omega_{cy} = \omega_C \times C/Y$ and $\omega_{gy} = \omega_G \times G/Y$). Net exports of either type of tradable rise if home goods become relatively cheaper—that is, the home terms of trade τ_t depreciates—or if foreign demand rises relative to home demand. Thus:

$$m_{ct}^* - m_{ct} = c_t^* - c_t + \varepsilon_c \tau_t, \tag{13}$$

$$m_{gt}^* - m_{gt} = g_t^* - g_t + \varepsilon_g \tau_t. \tag{14}$$

The parameters ε_c and ε_g capture the sensitivity of each component of real net exports to the terms of trade and may differ between consumption and government goods.[6]

Using the home resource constraint and its analogue for the foreign economy, the difference between home and foreign GDP may be expressed:

$$y_{Dt} - y_{Dt}^* = g_y(g_t - g_t^*) + c_y(c_t - c_t^*) + (nx_t - nx_t^*)$$

$$= g_y(1 - \omega_g - \omega_g^*)(g_t - g_t^*) + \varepsilon\tau_t + c_y(1 - \omega_c - \omega_c^*)(c_t - c_t^*). \tag{15}$$

This equation says that home relative output $y_{Dt} - y_{Dt}^*$ depends on three factors—home relative government spending, the terms of trade, and home relative consumption—and is very useful for considering how a rise in foreign-government spending g_t^* (identified with higher core spending below) affects the composition of aggregate demand across the home and foreign economy. Specifically, the "direct" effect of a rise in foreign-government spending of 1 percentage point of baseline GDP $g_y g_t^*$ is to reduce home relative output by $(1 - \omega_g - \omega_g^*)$ %, with the smaller-than-unity response reflecting that some government spending may be imported. We call this the direct effect because it holds relative prices (i.e., the terms of trade) constant. The latter two terms capture the strength of the rebalancing channel, and both vary positively with the terms of trade. In particular, the term $\varepsilon\tau_t$ captures how the home country's terms of trade depreciation—which would be expected following a rise in foreign-government spending—shifts some demand toward the home country through a net exports channel. The responsiveness coefficient ε is a weighted average of the import price sensitivity of private consumption and government services (i.e., $\varepsilon = c_y(\omega_C + \omega_C^*)\varepsilon_c + g_y(\omega_G + \omega_G^*)\varepsilon_g$). Moreover, home relative consumption $c_t - c_t^*$ also varies positively with the terms of trade through the complete markets risk-sharing condition (equation [16] below), and thus also contributes to rebalancing:

$$c_t - c_t^* = \varkappa(c_{t-1} - c_{t-1}^*) + \hat{\sigma}(1 - \omega_C - \omega_C^*)\tau_t + \frac{1}{\sigma}(v_t - v_t^*). \tag{16}$$

It may seem surprising that home relative consumption rises in response to the foreign-government spending shock. To provide more intuition for why this occurs in the benchmark model, it is helpful to draw on the consumption Euler equations to link the consumption differential to the long-term real interest rate differentials in each economy:

$$c_t - c_t^* = \varkappa(c_{t-1} - c_{t-1}^*) - \hat{\sigma}(1 - \omega_C - \omega_C^*)(r_{Lt} - r_{Lt}^*) + \frac{1}{\sigma}(v_t - v_t^*), \tag{17}$$

where the long-term real interest rate differential $(r_{Lt} - r_{Lt}^*)$ may in turn be expressed either in terms of future short-term real interest rates or in terms of expected inflation differentials:

$$r_{Lt} - r_{Lt}^* = E_t \sum_{j=0}^{\infty}(r_{t+j} - r_{t+j}^*) = -E_t \sum_{j=1}^{\infty}(\pi_{Dt+j} - \pi_{Dt+j}^*). \tag{18}$$

A foreign-government spending hike initially causes foreign inflation to rise relative to home inflation, implying that the home terms of trade depreciates. But for relative prices to converge in the long run—as they must, given that the government-spending shock is stationary—long-run-expected inflation in the home country must *exceed* long-run-expected inflation abroad (i.e., $E_t\Sigma_{j=1}^{\infty}\pi_{Dt+j} > E_t\Sigma_{j=1}^{\infty}\pi_{Dt+j}^*$ in equation [18]), implying that expected long-run real interest rates fall at home relative to abroad.[7] Since it is the long-run real interest rate response that matters for consumption in the benchmark model, equation (17) implies that periphery relative consumption rises relative to foreign consumption (concurring with equation [16]).

Relative price convergence plays a key role in accounting for large output spillovers to the periphery following an expansion of foreign-government spending in a liquidity trap. It is important to point out that the implication that home relative consumption rises in response to higher foreign-government spending is somewhat model specific and, in particular, reflects the dependence of consumption on the long-term real interest rate in the New Keynesian model; as we will show in section VI, home relative consumption may decline if consumption depends more on current income due to "hand-to-mouth" consumption behavior, or if it depends more on the short-term real interest rate. Thus, the key implications about spillovers that we develop in the next section should not be regarded as hinging on the response of relative consumption; what matters instead is that foreign-government spending has a big enough effect on home inflation and real interest rates—including through the expectation that relative prices will eventually converge—that home consumption is affected significantly.

Turning to the home price-setting equation (4) and its foreign counterpart, it follows inflation differentials between the home and foreign economy depend on the difference between home and foreign marginal costs:

$$\pi_{Dt} - \pi_{Dt}^* = \beta(\pi_{Dt+1|t} - \pi_{Dt+1|t}^*) + \kappa_{mc}(mc_t - mc_t^*). \tag{19}$$

Relative marginal costs—using equation (5) and its foreign analogue—may be expressed:

$$mc_t - mc_t^* = \frac{\alpha + \chi}{1 - \alpha}(y_{Dt} - y_{Dt}^*) + \tau_t - (1 + \chi)(z_t - z_t^*). \qquad (20)$$

Relative marginal cost depends on relative output $y_{Dt} - y_{Dt}^*$, the terms of trade, and on exogenous productivity differentials between the home and foreign-economy consumption.[8] A rise in home relative demand boosts home relative marginal costs as wages rise more at home, and because of diminishing marginal returns to production; conversely, the rise in foreign-government spending we focus on below causes foreign relative marginal costs to increase. As noted above, relative demand can be expressed exclusively as a function of the terms of trade and exogenous shocks (given complete markets).[9]

Since inflation differences between the home and foreign economy vary inversely with terms of trade growth according to $\pi_{Dt} - \pi_{Dt}^* = -(\tau_t - \tau_{t-1})$ (see equation [A19] in appendix A), the solution for the inflation differential in equation (19) implies that the terms of trade evolves according to:

$$(\tau_t - \tau_{t-1}) = \beta(\tau_{t+1|t} - \tau_t) - \kappa_{mc}(mc_t - mc_t^*). \qquad (21)$$

From an intuitive perspective, a rise in foreign fiscal spending g_t^* initially increases aggregate demand by relatively more abroad (as seen in equation [15]). This boosts relative marginal production costs abroad, which causes the home terms of trade to depreciate (in equation [21], $mc_t^* > mc_t$, so that τ_t rises). The terms of trade depreciation helps rebalance some of the expansion in aggregate demand toward the home economy. As can be seen by reformulating equation (21), the home terms of trade continues to depreciate (i.e., $\Delta\tau_t > 0$) as long as the terms of trade remain below its flexible price level τ_t^{pot} (in discounted present value):

$$(\tau_t - \tau_{t-1}) = \beta(\tau_{t+1|t} - \tau_t) + \kappa_{mc}\phi_{mc}(\tau_t^{pot} - \tau_t). \qquad (22)$$

This expression abstracts from habit persistence for expositional convenience.[10]

Equation (22), which abstracts from habit persistence for expositional convenience, underscores that the terms of trade simply evolve as an autonomous difference equation. Thus, the evolution of the terms of trade does not depend on CU monetary policy, or whether the currency union is in a liquidity trap. Because relative output levels, relative inflation rates, and relative consumption levels also only depend on the terms of trade, monetary policy has no effect on these variables: it can only operate through effects that are felt uniformly across the currency union members.[11]

B. *Calibration*

We calibrate our model at quarterly frequency and assume a symmetric calibration for each country block aside from differences in trade intensities (due to different population sizes). While many aspects of our calibration are standard, two classes of parameters—including those that govern the responsiveness of inflation and those that influence trade flows—deserve particular emphasis.

The degree to which inflation responds to marginal cost is the key determinant of both the aggregate response of CU inflation and output and of the terms of trade response. Smets and Wouters (2003) reported a Phillips curve slope of $\kappa_{mc} = 0.009$ based on estimating a DSGE model using euro-area data, which implies a mean price contract duration of 10 quarters ($\xi_p = 0.9$). The estimated slope of $\kappa_{mc} = 0.0034$ that we report in section VI—when using the larger-scale model to fit the responses of empirical VARs to euro-area monetary policy and government-spending shocks—implies even more sluggish price adjustment.[12]

The response of relative prices in the euro area also seems consistent with a very flat Phillips curve. Although figure 1 shows that inflation has run noticeably lower in the periphery than in the core since the financial crisis, the difference in inflation rates—and implied adjustment in the terms of trade—seems quite modest in light of the much higher level of resource slack in periphery economies.[13] The upper panel of figure 2 considers the relationship between the periphery terms of trade and (periphery) relative marginal costs more directly. While the periphery's terms of trade have deteriorated ($\Delta\tau_t > 0$) since 2009 (the solid line) as periphery relative marginal costs $mc_t - mc_t^*$ have declined (the dotted line, where relative labor shares proxy for marginal cost differentials), the sensitivity appears quite low. As seen in the bottom panel, a simple ordinary least squares (OLS) regression of $(\tau_t - \tau_{t-1}) - \beta(\tau_{t+1|t} - \tau_t)$ (vertical axis) against $mc_t - mc_t^*$ (horizontal axis) as implied by equation (21) yields a slope estimate of $\kappa_{mc} = 0.006$.

Based on these considerations, we set $\kappa_{mc} = 0.005$ (consistent with $\xi_p = 0.93$), which implies very sluggish price adjustment. Even so, we recognize that there is considerable uncertainty about the Phillips curve slope. Most of the extensive literature estimating the Phillips curve slope for the industrial countries using prefinancial crisis data reported estimates in the range of $\kappa_{mc} = 0.009 - 0.014$, well above our benchmark setting.[14] As noted in section II, some recent research argues that the low estimated slopes may partly reflect various forms of model misspecification (Chris-

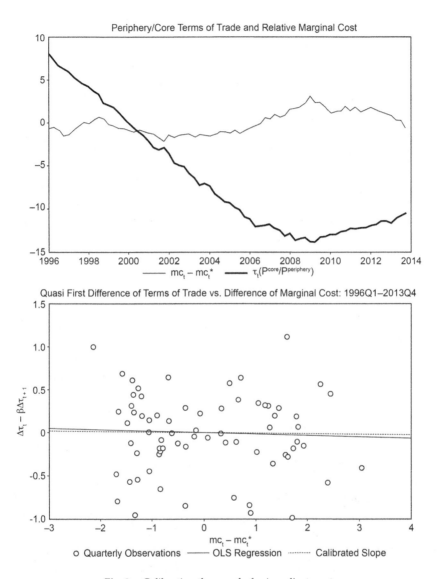

Fig. 2. Calibrating the speed of price adjustment

tiano et al. 2015; Gilchrist et al. 2015). With this in mind, we also consider the implications of a higher Phillips curve slope in our simulations below.

The second key group of parameters are those determining the responsiveness of trade flows as a share of domestic output, including the import share of private (consumption) spending ω_C, of public spending ω_G, and the trade-price elasticity of each of these components (ε_c and ε_g, respectively). Ceteris paribus, a higher trade share or higher trade-price elasticity amplifies the "leakage" associated with a core fiscal expansion to the periphery, and thus should push in the direction of more balanced effects across regions. Trade data from Eurostat for Spain and Italy indicate an average import/GDP ratio of those economies of about 22% in 2007.[15] In calibrating the trade share in our two-country framework, a notable complication involves how to treat periphery trade with non-EU members: periphery imports are closer to 14–15% of GDP if all non-EU trade is excluded from our computation. We assume an import share of 15% of GDP for the periphery in our baseline and, hence, effectively exclude non-EU trade, but recognize that the effects of a core fiscal expansion in reality would depend on how the periphery's real exchange rate varied relative to non-EU trading partners.[16] Given that periphery GDP is about half of that of the core euro-area countries, we set the country-size parameters $\zeta = 1/3$ and $\zeta^* = 2/3$; accordingly, balanced trade implies a trade share of 7.5 percent of GDP for the core.

Our model requires parsing this import share of GDP into private- and public-spending components. We set $\omega_G^* = \omega_G = 0$ under our benchmark, and then consider $\omega_G^* = 0.2$ (implying $\omega_G = 0.4$) as a high-side alternative. Under the benchmark with $\omega_G = \omega_G^* = 0$, the import share of private consumption is 20% in the periphery and 10% in the core (i.e., $\omega_C = 0.2$ and $\omega_C^* = 0.1$).[17] The trade-price elasticity for both private consumption and government spending is assumed to be slightly above unity (1.1), consistent with estimates from the macro literature on trade price elasticities.

The calibration of remaining parameters is fairly standard. The discount factor of $\beta = 0.99875$ implies a steady-state real interest rate of 0.5% (at an annualized rate). With a steady-state inflation rate of 2% (i.e., $\pi = .005$), the steady-state nominal interest rate is 2.5% (i.e., $i = .00625$ at a quarterly rate). We set the intertemporal substitution elasticity $\sigma = 1$, which is consistent with log utility over consumption.[18] The habit parameter $\varkappa$ is set to 0.8. This value is on the higher side of the range of estimates in the empirical literature, but helps our model generate a fairly plausible path for the aggregate spending multiplier, even if somewhat lower than estimated by, for example, Blanchard and Perotti (2002). The Frisch elasticity of labor supply of $1/\chi = 0.4$ and capital share of $\alpha = 0.3$ are in the typical range specified in the literature. The government share of steady state output is set to 23% ($g_y = 0.23$), which is in line with the average government-spending share of GDP in the euro area in recent years.

Our benchmark model assumes that the currency union central bank follows a Taylor rule in equation (8) that is somewhat more aggressive on inflation than a standard Taylor rule, and thus sets $\psi_\pi = 2.5$ and $\psi_x = 0.125$.

IV. Impulse Response to Higher Core Government Spending

Figure 3 examines the effects of a positive shock to core government spending that is scaled to equal 1% of CU baseline GDP (i.e., 1.5% of core GDP). The government-spending hike is assumed to last 10 quarters, after which spending returns to its baseline level; this spending path is captured by an MA(10) in our scenarios.

We begin by considering impulse responses in normal times in which monetary policy is unconstrained by the zero lower bound. These responses are shown in the left column of figure 3. From an aggregate perspective, the higher core spending boosts CU output (the solid line in panel A), CU inflation (panel C), and induces the central bank to raise the policy rate (panel E). Output rises well above potential (not shown) because the Taylor rule implies that real interest rates increase by somewhat less than the potential real rate (recalling equation [3]); the positive output gap, in turn, boosts inflation. The CU output multiplier is less than unity due to some crowding out of private consumption, though habit persistence dampens these crowding-out effects, and hence raises the spending multiplier relative to a specification abstracting from habit. As discussed above, these effects on the CU are identical to those that would be obtained in a closed economy model.

Turning to the compositional effects across core and periphery, it is evident that the stimulus to real GDP is confined exclusively to the core. While core output (dash-dotted line in panel A) rises more than 1% above baseline for the duration of the spending hike—consistent with an average spending multiplier of about 0.8—periphery output (the dashed line) contracts modestly in the short run. The relatively large increase in core GDP causes core inflation to run above periphery inflation for some time, and the implied depreciation of the periphery's terms of trade (the dashed line in panel E) boosts periphery real net exports. However, because the rise in core government spending triggers a sharp rise in real interest rates, the stimulus to periphery GDP from higher real net exports is swamped by a fall in periphery consumption.

To shed more light on why the output effects of core spending hikes are strongly tilted toward the core, it is useful to recall how relative aggregate demand $y_{Dt} - y_{Dt}^*$ is affected by core government spending (from equation [15]):

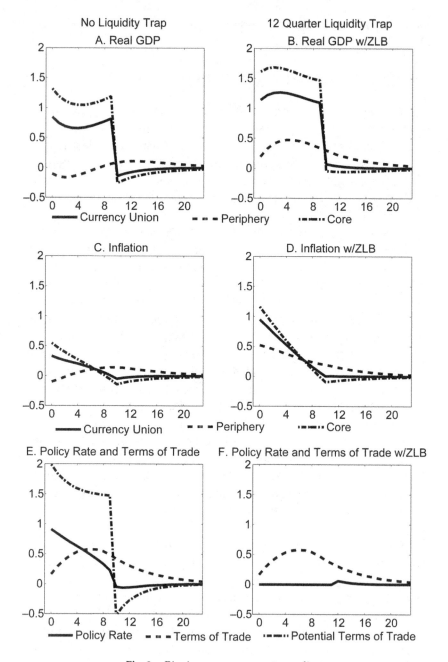

Fig. 3. Rise in core government spending

$$y_{Dt} - y_{Dt}^* = g_y(1 - \omega_g - \omega_g^*)(g_t - g_t^*) + \varepsilon\tau_t + c_y(1 - \omega_c - \omega_c^*)(c_t - c_t^*). \quad (23)$$

With the import share of government spending set to zero ($\omega_g = \omega_g^* = 0$), a 1.5% of GDP rise in core government spending (i.e., $g_y g_t^* = .015$) would cause periphery relative demand $y_{Dt} - y_{Dt}^*$ to fall by a commensurate amount if the terms of trade τ_t remained unchanged, reflecting that in this case neither relative consumption $c_t - c_t^*$ nor relative trade flows (captured by the term $\varepsilon\tau_t$) would adjust. Given sluggish price adjustment, the terms of trade in fact changes very little in the near term, which accounts for why core output in fact rises nearly 1.5% above periphery output (panel A) immediately following the shock. Subsequently, the gap between core and periphery output narrows as terms of trade depreciation (panel E) boosts periphery real net exports while causing core real net exports to contract, and also induces periphery consumption to rise relative to core consumption.[19]

Even so, the figure shows that this "rebalancing" toward the periphery is not particularly large over the period in which the fiscal expansion remains in force. The adjustment coming from relative trade flows $\varepsilon\tau_t$ is quite modest because sluggish price adjustment damps the movements in the terms of trade (panel F shows that the depreciation peaks at only 0.7%), and because the trade responsiveness parameter ε is fairly small (around 0.3) given observed trade shares and our calibration of trade price elasticities of around unity.[20] Similarly, periphery consumption rises only slightly above core consumption.[21]

We next consider the effects of core fiscal expansion in a liquidity trap. The right column of figure 3 shows the effects of the same 1.5% of GDP rise in core government spending in a liquidity trap lasting 12 quarters; the liquidity trap is generated from an adverse consumption taste shock that persistently depresses the potential real rate $r_t^{CU,pot}$.[22] At an aggregate CU level, the highly accommodative monetary policy stance in a liquidity trap makes fiscal expansion more potent in stimulating output and inflation than under the Taylor rule, which is in force in normal times. The CU output expands around 1.3% after four quarters in a 12-quarter liquidity trap (the solid line in panel B) rather than 0.7% in the case of no liquidity trap (the solid line in panel A), with the larger expansion reflecting that private consumption is "crowded in" rather than out by a fall in real interest rates. These aggregate implications are consistent with an extensive literature showing that fiscal policy has amplified effects in a liquidity trap (see Christiano, Eichenbaum, and Rebelo 2011; Woodford 2011). Consistent with this literature, the stimulus to CU output due to fiscal expansion quickly dissipates once government spending reverts to its initial level.

The more accommodative monetary policy stance in a liquidity trap relative to normal times imparts a commensurate degree of stimulus to each CU member, recalling from section II that the gap between the output responses in the core and periphery is invariant to monetary policy. Thus, as can be seen by comparing panel B with panel A, the output responses in both the periphery and core in panel B are shifted up by exactly the same amount in percent terms relative to the case of no liquidity trap (e.g., about 0.5% after four quarters). Output still expands by considerably more in the core, but the spillovers to the periphery are now positive and sizable. A liquidity trap, in effect, "lifts all boats" in tandem relative to normal times. Intuitively, both periphery and core GDP are boosted by the same degree because ECB policy rates do not rise in a liquidity trap—which provides equivalent stimulus to each member state—and due to the expansionary effect this more accommodative policy stance has on inflation in each member.

The larger GDP effects on both the periphery and core in a liquidity trap are due to a larger response of consumption relative to normal times. By contrast, given that real net exports depend only on the consumption gap $c_t - c_t^*$ and terms of trade—both of which are invariant to the stance of monetary policy—the response of real net exports turns out to be the same in a liquidity trap as in normal times. Our results showing amplified spillovers are consistent with the qualitative analysis of Farhi and Werning (2012), who also underscore how a crowding in of private consumption plays a key role in generating positive output spillovers in a liquidity trap.

Overall, changes in core government spending seem likely to exert substantial effects on periphery output in a deep liquidity trap. Under such conditions, a core government-spending hike increases periphery GDP through qualitatively similar channels as would an easing of monetary policy (if the periphery had an independent monetary policy): lower real interest rates boost periphery consumption, and terms of trade depreciation stimulates net exports. However, a key difference is that a (hypothetical) monetary easing by the periphery central bank would depress nominal interest rates and raise inflation, while the core fiscal expansion we consider relies exclusively on higher inflation to reduce real interest rates.[23] A more subtle difference—but which may have important implications for welfare, as we explore in section V—is that the stimulus to periphery GDP is very drawn out. As seen in fig-

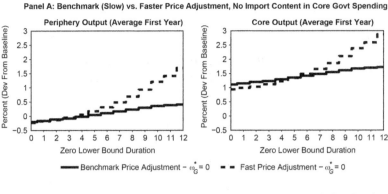

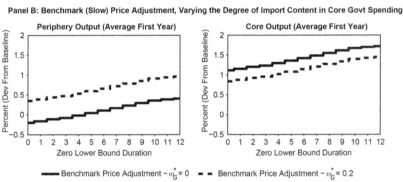

Fig. 4. Core government spending hike: Output responses in core and periphery as function of liquidity trap duration.

ure 3, periphery output (panel B) remains elevated for several years, even after the government-spending shock has died out and CU GDP returned to baseline. These longer-term expansionary effects reflect that periphery inflation must run persistently above core inflation in the medium run (panel D) to allow relative prices to converge back to their preshock level. Thus, fiscal stimulus can have longer-lived distributional effects on member states through relative price channels, even if the aggregate CU output effects dissipate quickly.

A.   The Longer the Liquidity Trap, the Stronger the Spillover Effects

A key question is how the effects of a core spending expansion vary with the expected duration of the liquidity trap. The upper panels of figure 4 show the effect of the same core government-spending expansion on both periphery output (left panel) and core output (right panel) for liquidity traps ranging in duration from zero quarters (normal times) to 12 quarters. The effects are derived as the average response over the first four quarters following the stimulus, and hence can essentially be read off the IRFs in figure 3 for both the normal times case and for the 12-quarter trap. The figure indicates that an expansion of core spending is "counterproductive" to the aim of boosting periphery output, even in a liquidity trap lasting up to about a year: periphery output falls slightly, while the GDP stimulus accrues wholly to the core.

Our result that the spillovers to the periphery are negative in a shorter-lived liquidity trap—and that the aggregate multipliers are fairly modest—may seem surprising in light of the literature suggesting a sharp disparity between the effects of fiscal expansion between a liquidity trap and normal times. There are three important reasons for why a short-lived liquidity trap does not look too different from normal times in our baseline model. The first reason is that we allow for substantial habit persistence in consumption. This allays the strong "crowding out" effects on consumption that would occur in normal times when interest rates rise in response to higher government spending, while limiting the crowding in effects due to lower real interest rates in a liquidity trap.

The second reason—explored more fully below—is that inflation is much less responsive under our calibration than often assumed in the literature.

The third reason is that government-spending shock is assumed to follow an MA(10), and hence persists well beyond the duration of the shorter-lived liquidity traps considered in the figure. As emphasized by Woodford (2011) and Christiano, Eichenbaum, and Rebelo (2011), this fiscal overhang attenuates the aggregate CU multiplier relative to an "ideally structured" fiscal intervention that dissipates before the economy exits the liquidity trap. In particular, to the extent that fiscal spending was expected to remain high even after the economy exited the liquidity trap, long-term interest rates would be pushed up, generating negative spillovers to the periphery in short-lived traps. It turns out that spillovers to the periphery would always be positive—even in a transient liquidity trap—provided that the core spending only rose during the period in which monetary policy was constrained by the ZLB. However, practical impediments would make it unlikely to achieve a rapid phase in and phase out within a few quarters; moreover, even if such a nimble fiscal response was feasible, the short duration would not translate into much stimulus to the periphery quantitatively (since inflation would not rise much).[24]

Somewhat more broadly, our results underscore that core fiscal expansion would probably only be likely to boost periphery GDP noticeably if the central bank was expected to remain accommodative for a fairly prolonged period of a couple of years or more. We should add that some caution is warranted with respect to the quantitative estimates from this simple model, as it tends to understate spillovers relative to the policy-oriented model in section VI, but this main conclusion is robust.

B.   *The Steeper the Phillips Curve, the Stronger the Spillover Effects*

While slow price adjustment seems consistent with Europe's experience since the Great Recession, it is possible that the Phillips curve slope is higher than we have assumed in our benchmark calibration. Accordingly, figure 5 shows IRFs to the core spending shock under a calibration with a steeper Phillips curve slope: specifically, we set $\xi_p = 0.88$, implying a Phillips curve slope parameter of $\kappa_{mc} = .017$, which is slightly above the median point estimates in the literature mentioned earlier.

In normal times, the faster terms of trade adjustment (panel E) generates more rebalancing toward the periphery than in the benchmark. However, monetary policy also raises interest rates (panel E) by more given the bigger increase in inflation. As a result, CU output rises by less and periphery output still contracts (as under the benchmark calibration).

The fiscal expansion under the higher Phillips curve slope does have dramatically different implications than in the benchmark in a persistent liquidity trap. With the higher Phillips curve slope, the higher inflation implies much lower real interest rates, and consequently a much larger expansion of CU GDP (comparing panel B of figure 5 with panel B of figure 3). With the larger rebalancing effect now reinforced by the bigger real interest rate decline, periphery GDP rises over 1.5% in a 12-quarter liquidity trap, over half as much as core GDP. The dashed lines in the upper panels of figure 4 show how the effects on core and periphery GDP vary with the duration of the liquidity trap under this alternative calibration.

This calibration is useful for highlighting conditions that might give rise to very large positive fiscal spillovers, and is of particular interest given that calibrations of the Phillips curve slope in this range are often used in the literature. Although the implied responsiveness of inflation seems somewhat of a stretch in light of the Great Recession experience, the scenario does underscore some upside risk to fiscal spillovers if inflation proves more responsive than assumed under the benchmark.

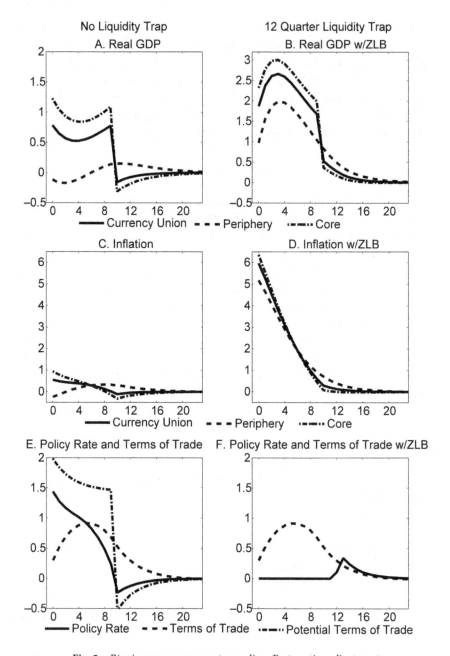

Fig. 5. Rise in core government spending: Faster price adjustment

C.   The Larger the Import Content of Spending, the Stronger the
Spillover Effects

Policymakers often draw attention to terms of trade adjustment as a key channel through which the periphery might benefit from a core fiscal expansion. But with sluggish price adjustment, the stimulus accruing through this channel is likely to be quite modest. Accordingly, we next consider how allowing for a sizable component of core spending to fall on periphery imports could facilitate rebalancing the aggregate demand stimulus more evenly across the core and periphery.

In an extreme case in which the core government spending was disbursed equally across currency union members according to population size—a "no home bias" case in which $\omega_G^* = $ one-third and $\omega_G = $ two-thirds—equation (23) indicates that the periphery and core would share equally in the stimulus. Figure 6 shows the effects in a less extreme case when the import share of core government spending ω_G^* is set to 0.20 (20% of government spending in the steady state). As this reallocation of spending has no consequences for CU aggregates, the effects of the core spending hike on CU output are identical to figure 3 (in which $\omega_G^* = 0$). However, the changes in the pattern of GDP response across core and periphery are striking: the rise in periphery GDP is more than half as large as the rise in core GDP even in normal times. Thus, core spending may provide considerable stimulus to the periphery even in a short-lived liquidity trap if it falls substantially on periphery imports. As seen in the bottom panels of figure 4, the boost to both periphery (and core) GDP is even larger in a long-lived liquidity trap.

Overall, these results underscore how direct purchases may allow core fiscal spending to have much more balanced effects on core and periphery output, even if terms of trade adjustment is quite sluggish. It is important to note, however, that the greater spillovers to periphery GDP reflect a larger boost to periphery real net exports than in the baseline without direct purchases; periphery consumption actually rises a bit less than under our baseline calibration.[25] As we will discuss in the next section, these compositional effects turn out to be consequential in evaluating the extent to which increasing the import share of government purchases affects welfare.

V.   Welfare Effects of Higher Core Government Spending

The literature analyzing the effects of fiscal expansion in a liquidity trap has largely focused on environments that abstract from differences in

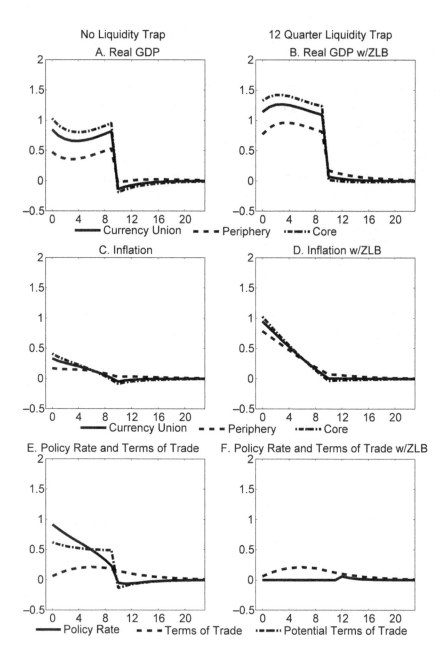

Fig. 6. Rise in core government spending: 20% imported

economic conditions across countries or states. The implicit assumption is that each member of a common currency area—whether a country or state—faces an equally severe downturn, and would get a similar boost in government spending if a stimulus package were enacted. The situation facing policymakers in Europe is different in two important respects. First, resource slack in the periphery economies is much larger than in the core, and inflation is correspondingly more subdued. Second, assuming that fiscal stimulus would have to come mainly from the core economies, the expansionary effects on CU GDP would be likely to be concentrated in the core economies.

These asymmetries across member states—both in initial business-cycle positions and in the effects of fiscal policy—have important implications for gauging the welfare effects of fiscal expansion. In this section, we illustrate some of the considerations that would seem relevant in designing a fiscal stimulus program in this environment.

To conduct our analysis, we use two alternative measures of welfare. First, we assume a standard ad hoc loss function in which the policymaker only cares about minimizing squared output gaps and inflation gaps in both the core and periphery economies:

$$L_t^{CP} = \frac{1}{4}\sum_{s=0}^{\infty} \beta^s \{\zeta[(\pi_{Dt+s}^{Per} - \pi)^2 + \lambda_y(x_{t+s}^{Per})^2] + (1-\zeta)[(\pi_{Dt+s}^{Core} - \pi)^2 + \lambda_y(x_{t+s}^{Core})^2]\}. \quad (24)$$

Thus, the welfare loss L_t^{CP} is the population-weighted average of the loss function for each CU member (core or periphery). Each region's loss function is simply a sum of the squared inflation gap and squared output gap, with the parameter λ_y determining the relative weight on the output gap set to one-third for each region. The inflation target π is set to 2%. While this loss function is admittedly simple, it helps address the interesting question of the extent to which fiscal policy can substitute for monetary policy when the latter is constrained by the ZLB by "filling in" output and inflation gaps.[26] Our second welfare measure—considered in section V.B—is based on the discounted utility of households in our model.

A. *Welfare Results under Ad Hoc Loss Function*

Fiscal Expansion in Core and Periphery (Fiscal Union)

As a useful reference point for assessing the effects of a core-only fiscal expansion, we first consider the welfare effects of fiscal expansion under the assumption that the euro-area countries were part of a fiscal union. From the perspective of the euro area as a whole, there would seem a strong rationale for fiscal expansion under current conditions: output gaps are large, inflation is below target, and monetary policy is likely to be constrained by the ZLB for a prolonged period. A fiscal union would presumably give more scope to the periphery economies to expand domestic fiscal spending than in the current environment in which concerns about debt sustainability and adverse market reactions appear to impose tight constraints. Exactly how much latitude is unclear, as it would depend on the specific features of the fiscal compact. However, it seems plausible that such a union might allow an expansion in euro-area government spending that was distributed roughly equally across member states on a per capita basis.[27] Accordingly, we assume that each member state boosts fiscal spending by a commensurate amount under fiscal union.

The welfare benefits of a fiscal stimulus program clearly depend on how output and inflation gaps in the core and periphery would evolve absent any fiscal stimulus. Our baseline assumes adverse consumption demand shocks (i.e., lower v_t) cause a prolonged recession in the euro area that is especially concentrated in the periphery.[28] The solid lines in figure 7 depict this baseline. Specifically, the output gap in the core (the solid line in panel C) is about –2% at the end of 2015 and nearly closes within three years, whereas the output gap in the periphery (panel D) is about –5% initially and slack remains sizable even after a few years. Inflation stays well below 2% in both the core (panel E) and periphery (panel F), but runs particularly low in the periphery (with some deflation on average in 2015).[29] Our calibration of the Taylor rule implies that the CU interest rate remains pinned at zero for 12 quarters (noting that the policy rate is expressed as an annualized percentage rate, or APR).

Table 1 reports the losses under the welfare measure (equation [24]) that are derived from cumulating the discounted squared output and inflation gaps from 2015:Q1 to 2020:Q4; given that the effects of the fiscal actions we consider on output and inflation gaps are small after six years, the welfare gains reported below would change very little if the horizon were extended beyond that period. Clearly, losses are heavily concentrated in the periphery.

Against this backdrop, we assume that a CU-wide fiscal stimulus is initiated that boosts government spending by 1% of baseline GDP in both the core and periphery. The stimulus begins in the same quarter

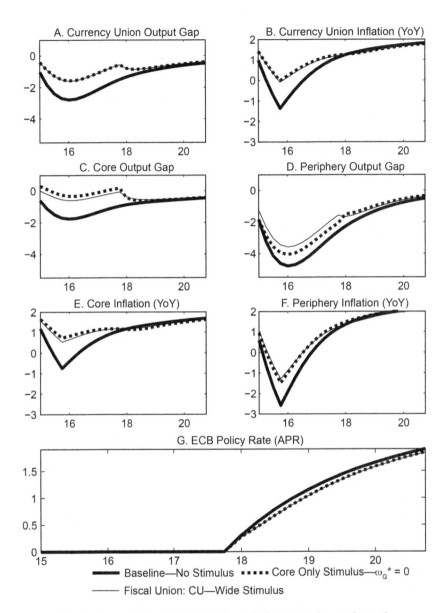

Fig. 7. Impact of fiscal stimulus when ECB keeps exit date unchanged

Table 1
Losses under Baseline: Ad Hoc Welfare Function

	Overall Loss L_t^{CP}	Core	Periphery
Discounted loss	21.5	12.5	39.5

Note: The overall loss L_t^{CP} is based on equation (24) for 2015:Q1 to 2020:Q4. The core and periphery losses are based on their respective discounted squared inflation and output gaps with $\lambda_y = 1 / 3$.

Table 2
Gains from Fiscal Expansion: Ad Hoc Welfare Function

A. Welfare Gains under Fiscal Union

	Currency Union	Core	Periphery
	11.2	7.8	18.1

B. Welfare Gains under "Core Only" Fiscal Expansion

	Currency Union	Core	Periphery
Benchmark ($\omega_G^* = 0$)	10.4	8.3	14.5
High import share ($\omega_G^* = 0.2$)	10.9	7.9	16.8

Note: The table reports absolute gains, computed as Loss^{Baseline} − Loss^{Scenario}.

as the adverse shocks and lasts 12 quarters, and thus is "well-timed" to coincide with the period in which monetary policy is constrained. We compute the model solution—both under the baseline and for the scenario with higher fiscal spending—using a nonlinear solution algorithm for solving perfect foresight models in DYNARE.[30]

The thin lines in figure 7 labeled "Fiscal Union: CU-Wide Stimulus" show the effects of this fiscal expansion. The joint fiscal expansion narrows the periphery output gap (panel D) substantially—as well as the gap between periphery inflation (panel F) and the 2% target—while nearly closing the core output gap (panel C). Panel A in table 2 reports the welfare gains from fiscal stimulus, which is measured as the difference between the welfare loss assuming no stimulus (from table 1) and the welfare loss under the stimulus program. Aggregate welfare improves substantially, with welfare losses cut by half relative to the baseline. While both the core and periphery experience welfare improvements, the periphery experiences much larger absolute gains given the large initial output and inflation gaps in that region (which are penalized heavily under the quadratic objective).

Fiscal policy in this setting is similar to monetary policy insofar as both forms of stimulus operate with equal force on each member state, and hence cannot close output (and inflation) gaps in each. Larger welfare improvements could be achieved by channeling relatively more of the fiscal stimulus to the periphery where the marginal value of additional stimulus is higher—and thus, essentially, using core and periphery spending as separate instruments to "fill gaps" in each member state.[31] Of course, political economy considerations could well preclude such targeted spending.

Fiscal Expansion Only in Core

We next assess how a fiscal expansion that was concentrated exclusively in the core would affect welfare in both the core and periphery; for comparability with the previous analysis, we continue to assume that the core spending hike equals 1% of CU GDP. As seen by the dotted lines in figure 7 labeled "Core Only Stimulus," the core spending hike provides a much larger boost to core GDP and inflation than to the periphery: the core output gap turns noticeably positive, while the periphery output gap only narrows modestly.

The first row of panel B in table 2 reports the welfare gains under the core-only fiscal expansion under our benchmark calibration in which the import content of government spending is zero ($\omega_G^* = 0$). The core fiscal expansion improves welfare by less than under the fiscal union case (reported in the upper panel), especially for the periphery. This is because the core expansion boosts aggregate demand relatively more in exactly the region (the core) in which it is "least needed" according to the ad hoc welfare criterion. The disparity in the welfare results between the core-only and fiscal union cases would be even larger if the size of the fiscal expansion under each case were chosen optimally to maximize the quadratic welfare criterion (equation [24]): this reflects that the optimal expansion turns out to be considerably larger under fiscal union because fiscal union allows more of the fiscal stimulus to be channeled to the region where its marginal value is comparatively high.[32]

Even so, it is remarkable that the core-only fiscal expansion does achieve a good portion of the welfare gains that would accrue under fiscal union. Because output and inflation gaps are very large in the periphery—and output spillovers to the periphery sizable in a long-lived liquidity trap—the periphery derives substantial benefits from core fiscal expansion. Moreover, even the core benefits from a modest-sized expansion that can help pare its own output and inflation gap.

An expansion of government spending in the core would raise welfare even more if some of the increase in core government spending was on imported periphery goods. As we have shown in section IV.C, such an approach balances the stimulus to output and inflation more evenly across the core and periphery, and thus appears more akin to fiscal union than the case in which core spending falls exclusively on domestically produced goods. For a calibration with a high core import share of 20% ($\omega_G^* = 0.2$), the effects of a core-only fiscal expansion on output and inflation gaps in each region are very similar to that achieved under fiscal union (and hence not shown in figure 7 for expositional reasons). By implication, panel B in table 2 shows that the welfare gains to the currency union approach those achieved under fiscal union, with both the core and periphery experiencing nearly commensurate welfare gains.[33]

B. Welfare Results under Utility-Based Criterion

Our previous welfare results indicate that an expansion of core government spending may improve periphery welfare considerably by shrinking the periphery's sizable output and inflation gaps, and that comparatively large welfare improvements—for both core and periphery—may be achieved to the extent that a larger share of core government spending falls on periphery imports.

We next consider the robustness of these normative results to an alternative welfare measure based on the discounted conditional expected utility of the representative household in each member state in our model:

$$
\mathbb{E}_t \sum_{j=0}^{\infty} \beta^j \left\{
\begin{array}{l}
\ln(C_{t+j} - \varkappa C_{t+j-1} - C v_{t+j}) - \chi_0 \dfrac{(N_{t+j})^{1+\chi}}{1+\chi} \\[2ex]
+ \dfrac{\vartheta_G}{1 - 1/\sigma_G} (G_{t+j} - \varkappa_G G_{t+j-1})^{1-1/\sigma_G}
\end{array}
\right\}.
\tag{25}
$$

Household utility depends positively on public and private consumption, and inversely on hours worked. Welfare in the currency union on the "utility-based" metric is simply a population-weighted average of the utility functionals of periphery and core households.[34]

Fiscal Expansion in Core and Periphery (Fiscal Union)

Panel A of table 3 reports welfare gains under fiscal union using the utility-based objective (equation [25]). Because we continue to assume

Table 3
Welfare Gains from Fiscal Expansion: Utility-Based

A. Welfare Gains under Fiscal Union

	Aggregate CU	Core	Periphery
	.015	.008	.028

B. Welfare Gains under "Core Only" Fiscal Expansion

	Aggregate CU	Core	Periphery
Benchmark ($\omega_G^* = 0$)	.010	.013	.002
High import share ($\omega_G^* = 0.2$)	.012	.027	−.018

Note: The table reports consumption equivalent compensation (CEV, henceforth), that is, the percent increase in households' consumption that makes them—in expectation—equally well off under no fiscal stimulus as when core government spending expands. Aggregate CEV is calculated as the weighted sum of CEV in the core and periphery.

that government spending in each CU member would expand by 1% of GDP under fiscal union, the impulse responses are the same as in figure 7 (the thin lines labeled "Fiscal Union"). The utility gains in the table are summarized in terms of the "consumption equivalent compensation" (CEV henceforth), which is the permanent percent increase in household private consumption—relative to the baseline with no fiscal expansion—that is required to make households equally well off as under the government-spending expansion. Following the usual approach in the literature, household welfare depends on how the fiscal expansion affects the entire infinite discounted sum of period utility. The aggregate CU CEV is a population-weighted average over the core and periphery.

As under the ad hoc loss criterion above, the equal-sized fiscal expansion in each CU member is strongly welfare improving. Fiscal expansion is beneficial because it boosts utility directly through increasing government services, and indirectly through inducing an expansion of private consumption, with the latter reflecting that the higher inflation induced by the fiscal expansion reduces real interest rates. Crucially, this increase in utility from public and private goods comes at a low cost in terms of foregone leisure because labor is underutilized and inflation suboptimally low. The low level of inflation is undesirable because it implies substantial inefficiency in goods production in our modeling framework with staggered price setting (Rotemberg and Woodford 1997), and hence acts like a tax on production; accordingly, a key benefit of fiscal expansion is that it boosts productivity by pushing inflation closer to target (assumed to be 2%). Aside from the implication—clear from panel A in table 3—that the periphery benefits more from fiscal expansion due to its relatively large degree of slack, the logic favoring fiscal expansion under fiscal union closely parallels that provided by Woodford (2011) for a closed economy. In particular, because the fiscal expansion is the same in each CU member, it has no effect on the terms of trade or net exports; accordingly, all of induced expansion in employment goes to increasing either public or private consumption.

Fiscal Expansion only in Core

The utility-based metric, in effect, poses a much more stringent test than the simple ad hoc loss function (equation [24]) for assessing whether increases in core government spending improve periphery welfare: assuming as we do that the periphery gets no direct utility benefits from the higher core government spending (e.g., from better roads in France), periphery welfare only improves if the core spending hike boosts periphery consumption enough to offset the cost of working additional hours. Thus, the composition of the rise in periphery GDP matters a great deal for welfare, as well as the timing of the rise in consumption. Even if the periphery output gap is large and the output spillovers to the periphery fairly big—conditions that lead to substantial periphery welfare improvements under the simple quadratic loss function—periphery welfare may fall under the utility-based criterion if the rise in periphery GDP is driven by net exports, or if the stimulus persists too long.

As seen in panel B in table 3 (above), the expansion of core spending in the case in which the import content is zero ($\omega_G^* = 0$) yields an improvement in core welfare. Core welfare improves because the core's sizable resource slack makes it less costly—and hence more desirable—to produce more government services. The effects on periphery welfare are more complicated. Periphery-discounted welfare improves, though by much less than core welfare. This reflects that the core fiscal expansion boosts the period utility of periphery households in the near term, but has slightly negative effects on their period utility at horizons much beyond a year.

Figure 8 is helpful for understanding these results, as it shows the "partial effects" of a rise in core government spending on key components of household welfare.[35] Focusing first on our benchmark case with $\omega_G^* = 0$—shown by the solid lines—it is evident that periphery consumption (panel B), real net exports (panel F), and employment (panel D),

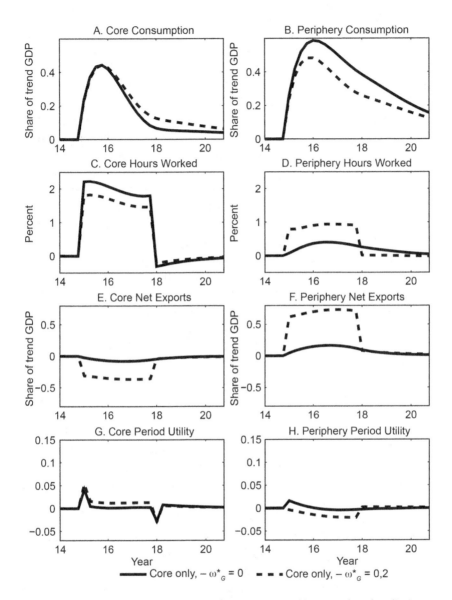

Fig. 8. Rise in core government spending in recession (deviation from baseline)

each respond positively to the core spending shock. As might be expected in a deep recession, the benefits of the rise in periphery (private) consumption outweigh the cost in terms of labor effort at least in the near term, which accounts for why the *period* utility of the representative periphery household (panel H) improves for over a year. Some of the improvement in periphery household utility reflects that the core spending hike boosts periphery inflation from a suboptimally low level, and this reduced inflation tax distortion means that less labor is required to produce any given quantity of output.

It may seem surprising that the core fiscal expansion does not provide an even more sustained boost to periphery welfare: after all, the periphery responses look very similar qualitatively to the usual effects of a favorable monetary shock under an independent monetary policy, insofar as lower periphery real interest rates crowd in consumption, and a depreciation of the periphery's terms of trade boosts real net exports. Monetary stimulus of this type might be expected to be very beneficial given the periphery's poor initial conditions. However, to achieve welfare benefits under the metric (equation [25]), it is critical that the policy action boost consumption in the near term when the gap between the marginal utility of consumption and disutility of work is especially large. From the prism of the utility-based welfare metric, there are two key problems with how the core fiscal expansion affects the periphery. First, a sizable share of the expansion in periphery output—about one-fourth under our benchmark calibration—is due to higher real net exports rather than increased periphery consumption; in effect, this diversion of employment toward net exports operates like a tax because it means that the rise in periphery employment is associated with a smaller near-term consumption boost. Second, the stimulus to periphery consumption is very spread out over time, as evident in panel B (and discussed previously in section IV.C). The protracted consumption response reflects that periphery inflation remains elevated for a long time—which holds down periphery real interest rates—to allow the terms of trade to converge back to its preshock level. This longer-term boost to periphery consumption, coming as it does after periphery consumption would have largely recovered even absent fiscal stimulus, simply is not worth the labor cost.

These considerations also help explain why an expansion of core spending causes periphery welfare to deteriorate considerably—as reported in panel B in table 3—in the case in which core imports are sizable ($\omega_G^* = 0.2$). These results differ dramatically from the implications of the ad hoc loss function in which the higher import content was a major plus for welfare in both CU members. As we have seen—and is also shown by the dashed lines in figure 8—the periphery GDP expansion under the higher import share calibration is more heavily driven by net exports, which the utility-based welfare measure views as undesirable.

Table 4
Welfare Gains of Core Fiscal Expansion under More Adverse Baseline: Utility Based

	Aggregate CU	Core	Periphery
Benchmark ($\omega_G^* = 0$)	0.021	.027	.010
High import share ($\omega_G^* = 0.2$)	0.024	.040	−0.007

Note: The table reports consumption equivalent compensation (CEV, henceforth), that is, the percent increase in households' consumption that makes them—in expectation—equally well off under no fiscal stimulus as when core government spending expands. Aggregate CEV is calculated as the weighted sum of CEV in the core and periphery.

As might be expected, a core government-spending hike yields a larger improvement in periphery household welfare if initial conditions are noticeably worse than assumed in figures 7 and 8. To illustrate this, table 4 reports the effects of the same core government-spending expansion against an alternative baseline in which output gaps in each member are much larger (slightly below –8% in the periphery, and close to –3% in the core), and inflation falls well below zero in the currency union as a whole. Periphery period utility—as well as CU welfare—improves very persistently under these conditions, leading to an improvement in the discounted welfare measure. The output spillovers to the periphery are not only larger than under the initial conditions underlying figures 7 and 8, but fueled by a bigger consumption rise; moreover, the welfare benefits of boosting both consumption and inflation are larger given the poorer initial conditions.

Taking stock of our results, each of the alternative welfare measures we have considered—ad hoc and utility based—suggests that a suitably designed fiscal stimulus program in the core can improve *near-term* welfare in both the periphery and core. The welfare improvements under each measure are clearly larger and more persistent the worse the baseline, and longer monetary policy is likely to be constrained from raising interest rates. Welfare improvements would also be larger if spillovers to periphery consumption were bigger than in our baseline (as would occur if, for example, prices were more flexible than in our benchmark). However, there is clearly some tension between how the welfare measures score policy actions which reduce the periphery output gap significantly, but do not provide much short-run stimulus to consumption. This tension can have important implications for the design of a core stimulus program, and in particular, for assessing the desirability of a higher import content of core government purchases.

Our sense is that the utility-based analysis is useful for highlighting how the welfare effects of fiscal expansion depend partly on how the stimulus affects the composition of demand—between consumption and net exports—and that fiscal policy may have long-lived effects arising through relative price channels that may possibly reduce welfare. Even so, the utility-based welfare metric probably understates some of the benefits of reducing the output gap and unemployment in economies plagued by high resource slack. Indeed, our model embeds two key assumptions—of perfect consumption risk sharing, and that all variation in labor effort occurs at the intensive margin—that tend to minimize the costs of a large output gap, and correspondingly, to understate the benefits of fiscal expansion. While these assumptions are useful for analytical tractability, household consumption in reality depends heavily on each household's employment status. These considerations suggest that policies that could markedly reduce the periphery's output gap—and, as a result, reduce both unemployment and consumption dispersion across households—would probably enhance periphery welfare. All in all, our sense is that the welfare benefits of fiscal expansion probably lie between the two measures, but tilt more in the direction suggested by the simple ad hoc loss function.

VI.   The Effects of a Core-Spending Expansion in a Larger-Scale Model

The benchmark model is useful for highlighting many of the key factors likely to shape how a core fiscal expansion would affect the periphery. However, the benchmark model likely understates both the aggregate effects of core fiscal expansion and spillovers to the periphery due to the exclusion of Keynesian multiplier and accelerator effects on household and business spending. A consequence is that the aggregate government-spending multiplier is relatively modest even in a persistent liquidity trap (unless inflation rises more than under our baseline calibration).

Accordingly, we next reconsider the effects of a core government-spending expansion in a larger-scale, two-country model with endogenous investment that closely follows Erceg and Lindé (2013). Abstracting from open economy features, the specification of each country block builds heavily on the estimated models of Christiano et al. (2005) and Smets and Wouters (2003, 2007). Thus the model includes both sticky nominal wages and prices, allowing for some intrinsic persistence in both components, habit persistence in consumption, and embeds a Q-theory investment specification modified so that changing the level of investment (rather than the capital stock) is costly. However, our model departs from this earlier literature by assuming that some fraction of households are "Keynesian," and simply consume their current after-tax income in a hand-to-mouth fashion; this contrasts with our benchmark model that assumes that all households make consumption decisions based on their permanent income. Galí, López-Salido, and Vallés (2007) show that the inclusion of non-Ricardian households helps account for structural VAR evidence, indicating that private consumption rises in response to higher government spending. Although the inclusion of hand-to-mouth agents increases the spending multiplier even in normal times, we will show that the amplification effects are considerably larger in a liquidity trap, and in particular, can help generate sizable spillovers to the periphery, even if the Phillips curve is very flat.

On the open economy dimension, the model assumes producer currency pricing as in the benchmark. Financial markets are assumed to be incomplete, meaning that there is a single "internationally traded" bond available to core and periphery households. However, given that the trade price elasticity is calibrated to be close to unity, the implications of incomplete markets are similar to those of complete markets; as we have discussed above, even complete markets may allow for sizable country-specific fluctuations in consumption given that households have different preferences over goods (see Cole and Obstfeld [1991] for a more detailed discussion).

Monetary policy is assumed to follow a Taylor-style rule, and government spending to evolve exogenously. To satisfy intertemporal fiscal balance, the distortionary tax rate on labor income is assumed to adjust to both government debt and the change in government debt. We assume that tax rates adjust inertially, so that a rise in government spending would mainly be deficit financed (at least under normal conditions). A detailed description of the model is provided in appendix B.

A. *Empirical Impulse Responses to Monetary and Fiscal Shocks in the Euro Area*

We next use a structural vector autoregression estimated on euro-area data over the 1970:1–2008:3 period to help gauge the dynamic effects of both a monetary policy shock and a shock to euro-area government spending. We will use the empirical impulse responses to each of these shocks both to estimate key parameters of our model—following the approach of Christiano et al. (2005) and Altig et al. (2011)—and to assess the model's empirical fit.[36]

Specifically, we estimate a VAR where the vector Θ_t of endogenous variables is comprised of government spending on goods and services (g_t), real GDP (y_t), real private consumption (c_t), real gross investment (inv_t), the GDP deflator inflation rate (π_{Dt}), the nominal wage (w_t), and the short-term interest rate (i_t), which we interpret as the policy rate. Following the influential analysis of Angeloni et al. (2003), which estimated monetary transmission in euro-area countries, we also include commodity prices, US output, and the federal funds rate as exogenous variables (collected in the vector Θ_t^*). We assume that the endogenous variables collected in Θ_t can be represented in reduced form as following a VAR of order p:

$$\Theta_t = \alpha + B^* (L) \Theta_t^* + B(L)\Theta_{t-1} + u_t, \tag{26}$$

$$Eu_t u_t' = V,$$

where $B(L)$ is a pth-ordered polynomial in the lag operator, L. The structural economic innovations ε_t are related to the reduced-form innovations u_t by the relation:

$$u_t = C\varepsilon_t, E\varepsilon_t\varepsilon_t' = I, \tag{27}$$

where C is a square matrix and I is the identity matrix.

We identify the monetary and fiscal spending innovations through imposing timing restrictions on the VAR. Following Christiano, Eichenbaum, and Evans (2005), we identify the monetary policy innovation by assuming that it has no contemporaneous effect on aggregate quantities and prices (i.e., all other variables are ordered before the short-term interest rate in the VAR). As in Blanchard and Perotti (2002), we identify a government-spending shock by assuming that government spending does not react contemporaneously to the remaining variables in the VAR, including output. This assumption seems reasonable over the precrisis period in light of our quarterly estimation frequency, though clearly would be problematic after the onset of the financial crisis (given that euro-area governments quickly ramped up discretionary public spending in response to current and prospective output declines). These timing restrictions are implemented by a standard Cholesky factorization of the matrix C, which orders government spending first, and the policy rate last, in the VAR.

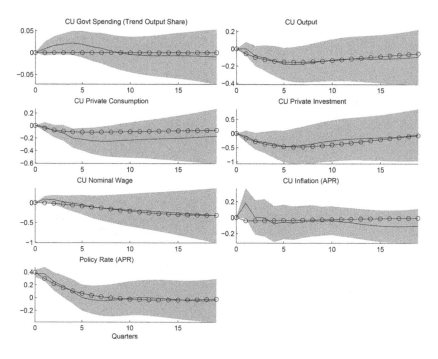

Fig. 9. Responses to monetary policy shock (–o– model, – VAR, gray area: 95% confidence interval).

The solid lines in figure 9 show the impulse responses of each variable to a one standard deviation rise in the euro-area policy rate, while 95% standard error bands (derived from Monte Carlo simulations) are shaded. A monetary policy innovation of about 40 basis points causes output to contract gradually, with the size of the decline reaching about 0.2% after two years. Private investment falls by more than GDP—presumably reflecting the high interest sensitivity of many components of investment spending—while consumption falls roughly as much as GDP. The policy tightening causes price inflation to fall about 0.1 percentage points after some delay. The initial jump in inflation is consistent with a short-lived, "price-level" puzzle typically found in VAR studies of the effects of monetary shocks (see, e.g., Christiano et al. 2005).

The responses to the euro-area government spending shock are shown by the solid lines in figure 10. To facilitate interpretation and comparison with other estimates, we scale the shock to equal 1% of euro-area GDP, which corresponds to a rise in government spending of nearly 4½%.[37] The government-spending shock boosts output persistently, and

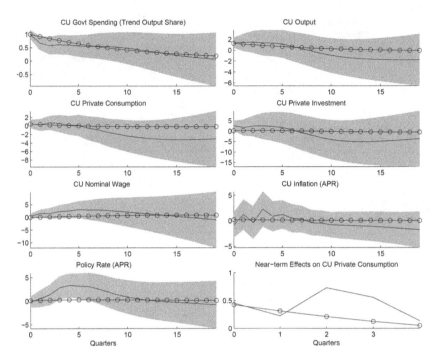

Fig. 10. Responses to CU government-spending shock (−o− model, − VAR, gray area: 95% confidence interval).

induces a substantial *crowding in* of both private consumption and total gross investment at a horizon stretching out almost two years. The actual output multiplier is about 1.5 at impact, and even somewhat higher over the next year. Thus, government-spending increases appear to have large and persistent effects on real activity, nothwithstanding a sizable rise in the policy rate. After some delay, inflation also appears to rise somewhat, though confidence intervals are wide.

The response of output to the monetary policy shock seems well in line with the evidence provided by Angeloni et al. (2003) in a similar VAR framework (as noted above), though the latter was estimated over an earlier 1965–2001 sample period. Moreover, the output responses are remarkably similar quantitatively to typical estimates of the output response to a monetary policy innovation in the United States: ACEL's VAR, for example, implies that a 40 basis-point rise in the US policy rate would cause US output to fall 0.2–0.3% after about six quarters, and Boivin, Kiley, and Mishkin (2011) report similar results.

In some contrast, our implied estimate of the euro-area government spending multiplier is substantially higher than derived by Perotti (2007) for Germany in a similar VAR-based framework, or that Guajardo, Leigh, and Pescatori (2014) found for a cross section of OECD countries—many of them European—based on a narrative approach to identifying fiscal shocks in the spirit of Romer and Romer (2010). Similarly, the US government-spending multiplier is usually estimated to be around unity—as in Blanchard and Perotti (2002)—or somewhat below, at least in normal times, in which policy rates can adjust freely. Thus, while the high government-spending multiplier we estimate in the euro area suggest the importance of Keynesian-style multiplier effects on private demand, some caution is probably warranted in light of the relatively modest variation in euro-area government spending over the past several decades, and given that evidence for other countries—and derived by alternative methods—points to somewhat lower multipliers in normal times.[38]

B.   Matching Model Responses to Empirical Responses

We follow the basic approach of Christiano et al. (2005) and Altig et al. (2011) to estimate a subset of model parameters so that the model-implied impulse responses—to both a monetary shock, and in our case, to a government-spending shock—match their empirical counterparts in figures 9 and 10 as closely as possible. We estimate an aggregate version of the model under the assumption that parameters are equal in both the core and periphery and then compare these aggregate implications to the data. Our model is formulated so that it imposes the same timing restrictions as the empirical VAR (specifically, that the monetary shock has no contemporaneous effects on other variables).

The vector of parameters Ω that we estimate play a key role in determining the interest sensitivity of domestic demand and the slopes of the price and wage Phillips curve. In particular, we estimate the vector $\Omega = \{x, \phi_I, \xi_P, \xi_W; \rho_G, \sigma_G, \sigma_M\}$ where the parameters before the semicolon are the external habit persistence parameter x, the parameter determining the costs of varying investment ϕ_I, the price contract duration parameter ξ_P, and the wage contract duration parameter ξ_W. The parameters following the semicolon characterize the persistence of the AR(1) process determining government spending (of ρ_G) and its standard deviation σ_G. The monetary innovation is assumed to be i.i.d, but exerts persistent effects given some structural persistence in the monetary policy reaction function.

Table 5
Estimated Parameters and Standard Errors

	$\varkappa$	ϕ_I	ξ_P	ξ_W	ρ_G	σ_G	σ_M
Parameter estimate	.877	1.94	.944	.871	.914	.0640	.0989
Standard error	.0494	1.580	.0121	.0660	.0253	.00518	.00735

This parameter vector is estimated conditional on calibrating all other model parameters as described in appendix B. However, a couple of features of the calibration merit some discussion. First, although we simply calibrate the share of Keynesian households, we set the population share to 0.65—and thus pin it toward the upper side of plausible empirical estimates—to help better match the crowding in of private consumption evident in the response to a government-spending shock. This choice implies that Keynesian households account for about one-third of aggregate consumption in the steady state.[39] Second, we set the parameters of the monetary policy rule according to a Taylor-style reaction function with a coefficient of 2.5 on inflation, but allow for a modest coefficient of 0.7 on the lagged interest rate in line with most empirical estimates. As we found little evidence of a response of the policy rate to the output gap (or output growth rate), we set these coefficients to zero when matching the empirical responses. Finally, the import content of government spending in each country is assumed to be the same as for private-consumption spending—13% for the periphery, and hence, 6.5% for the core.

The model impulse responses depend on the parameter vector Ω in addition to the parameters we have calibrated. We stack the first T model impulse responses to the monetary shock and the first T responses to the government-spending shock into a $2T \times 1$ vector $\Psi(\Omega)$, and denote the corresponding estimates derived from the SVAR above by $\hat{\Psi}$. Our estimator of Ω is obtained as the solution to:

$$\hat{\Omega} = \arg \min_{\Omega}(\hat{\Psi} - \Psi(\Omega))'\mathcal{F}^{-1}(\hat{\Psi} - \Psi(\Omega)), \qquad (28)$$

where $\mathcal{F}$ is a diagonal matrix based on the 95% confidence intervals for the impulse responses shown in figures 9 and 10. Thus, impulse responses that are measured with greater precision get more weight in determining the estimate of Ω. We set $T = 20$, so that impulse responses are matched for 20 quarters.

Table 5 reports the estimated parameters and standard errors (below), with the latter computed for $\hat{\Omega}$ using the delta-function method. Our estimates of habit persistence in consumption $\varkappa = 0.877$ and costs of adjusting investment ϕ_I = 1.94 indicate an important role for real rigidities in accounting for the empirical impulse responses. The estimate of habit is somewhat above typical estimates of the literature. The Calvo price contract duration parameter of ξ_P = .944 implies a very low Phillips curve slope—when expressed in terms of marginal cost—of only .0034; as indicated in section III, and as we will discuss further below, this specification is very consequential. Wage dynamics in the model depend on both the estimated wage contract duration parameter ξ_W = 0.871 and on parameters that affect strategic complementarities in wage setting (the latter include the Frisch elasticity of labor supply and the degree of substitutibility between labor types). From a reduced-form perspective that is relevant for the model simulations below, nominal wage inflation is somewhat less sensitive to the wage markup than price inflation is to the price markup.

The solid lines in figures 9 and 10 show the euro-area aggregate responses of the model to both the monetary shock and a government-spending shock, and provide insight both into the ability of the model to fit the data along these dimensions, and into key factors determining our parameter estimates. We begin with the responses to the monetary shock. As emphasized by Christiano et el. (2005), empirical responses to a monetary shock are very informative for gauging the interest sensitivity of domestic demand and its components, and also the slope of the price and wage Phillips curves: consistent with their analysis, our estimates of the structural parameters in table 5 would change little if we only fit the monetary shock (and thus can be regarded as largely "pinned down" by the monetary shock).

As seen in figure 9, the model does very well in tracking how a monetary policy tightening causes euro-area output to fall, and also performs well in accounting for the comparatively larger contraction in investment relative to consumption. The small decline in inflation in the empirical VAR is best fit with a very flat Phillips curve, which helps account for the high estimated value of the contract duration parameter ξ_P in table 5.[40] More broadly, a low implied responsiveness of inflation to resource slack seems consistent with the general resilience of euro-area inflation in the aftermath of the financial crisis. Even so, because the estimation procedure tries to make the model fit the initial rise in inflation in the empirical VAR—a "puzzle" the model cannot account for—the model impulse response understates the subsequent decline in inflation. Thus, it seems plausible that the Phillips curve slope may be at least somewhat higher than our estimate in table 5.[41]

Turning to figure 10, the model also does well in fitting the empirical responses to a rise in government spending. Notably, the model implies an initial rise in output of a little less than 1.5%, and of private consumption of almost 0.5%, both of which are very close to the empirical responses, though it does imply somewhat less persistent responses thereafter.[42] However, the model implies only a small and transient rise in investment, in contrast to the larger and more sustained response we estimate. Thus, even with a large share of rule-of-thumb households, it appears that our model may understate some of the Keynesian channels that would appear to drive the empirical responses, though the model clearly moves in the right direction relative to the simple model of section III.

C. *Core Government Spending Hike in Normal Times*

We next consider the effects of a rise in core government spending in normal times that is scaled to equal 1% of CU GDP. Given that the core and periphery are calibrated symmetrically, this rise in core government spending has exactly the same aggregate CU effects as would an equal-sized rise in both core and periphery spending. We assume core government spending is increased in a uniform fashion for 12 quarters, and then immediately cut back to zero (i.e., spending follows an MA[12] process with unit coefficients).

As seen in figure 11, the responses to a core spending hike in normal times are similar qualitatively to the benchmark model. The CU output rises a little less than 1.5% initially (panel A), then dies out as policy rates increase (panel F). The stimulus to GDP is heavily concentrated in the core (panel C). Periphery real net exports are boosted by some direct purchases of core goods/services from the core government, and from terms of trade depreciation (panel G) as the higher core government spending puts upward pressure on the relative price of core goods. However, periphery GDP (panel D) is basically flat, as this stimulus to net exports is offset by a fall in domestic demand (panel E shows consumption) that is induced by higher real interest rates. Periphery GDP would contract noticeably if the policy reaction function put even a modest weight on stabilizing the output gap (e.g., of 0.5 as under the standard Taylor rule).

The Keynesian features in this larger model—while amplifying the CU multiplier modestly—also drive a greater wedge between the response of core and periphery output. Notwithstanding the leakage

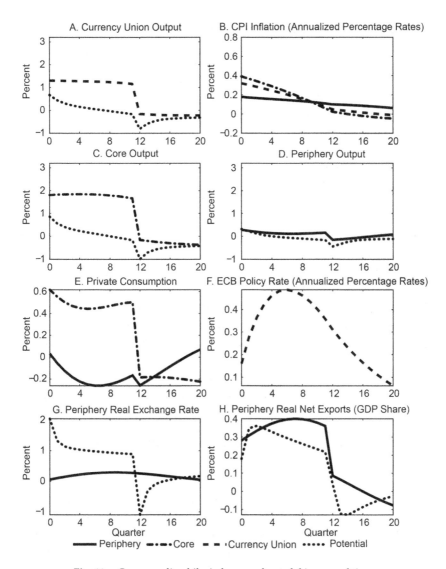

Fig. 11. Core spending hike in large-scale model in normal times

from lower core net exports, core GDP rises about 1.75% *relative* to periphery GDP in the first year following the shock. This is considerably larger than the GDP difference implied by the simple model results discussed in section IV (in which periphery private domestic demand actually rises relative to that in the core). The bigger wedge between core and periphery output responses in figure 11 seems more in line with

the literature on local multipliers, though the local multiplier implied
by our model is still only around 1.25, which is somewhat lower than
typical empirical estimates in the range of 1.5 to 2.[43] Overall, both the
estimates from the empirical VAR in figure 10 and the local multiplier
literature suggest sizable Keynesian multiplier effects that, if anything,
may be somewhat larger than captured by our model.[44]

Given our interest in spillovers, the local multiplier is important insofar as factors that raise the local multiplier tend to generate larger
negative spillovers to the periphery in normal times, at least if monetary
policy is sufficiently reactive to inflation (and/or the output gap). Intuitively, stronger Keynesian multiplier effects would imply more stimulus
to the core if monetary policy did not react. Hence, the central bank must
raise interest rates more sharply to keep CU output close to potential
and inflation from rising above target, which in turn causes a deeper
contraction in the periphery. Thus, conditions that imply a relatively
larger aggregate CU multiplier in normal times—reflecting a bigger effect on the natural real interest rate r^*—actually tend to generate bigger
negative spillovers to the periphery. Stronger multiplier (and accelerator) channels and the consequent boost in r^* have profoundly different
effects in a deep liquidity trap, as we next consider; however, it is important to keep in mind the risk that a core fiscal expansion could hurt
periphery GDP if the CU faced less extreme economic conditions (such
as a short-lived liquidity trap followed by a fast hike in policy rates).

D. Core Government Spending Hike in Liquidity Trap

We next consider the same expansion of core fiscal spending in a deep
liquidity trap that would last 12 quarters absent core fiscal stimulus. Our
baseline assumes that the adverse aggregate demand shock generating
the liquidity trap is much larger in the periphery (as in figure 7 in the
case of the simple model). In this section, we assume that the monetary
policy reaction function is very aggressive in responding to both the inflation and output gap, implying that monetary policy remains accommodative even following this sizable and persistent fiscal expansion.[45]

Aggregate CU output (solid line in panel A) rises much more in a protracted liquidity trap, and periphery GDP (panel D) also rises substantially. The rise in periphery GDP partly arises from the same channels as
emphasized in section IV. In particular, net exports rise in response to the
rise in core domestic demand and to terms of trade depreciation. Moreover, periphery real interest rates fall persistently, reflecting the expecta-

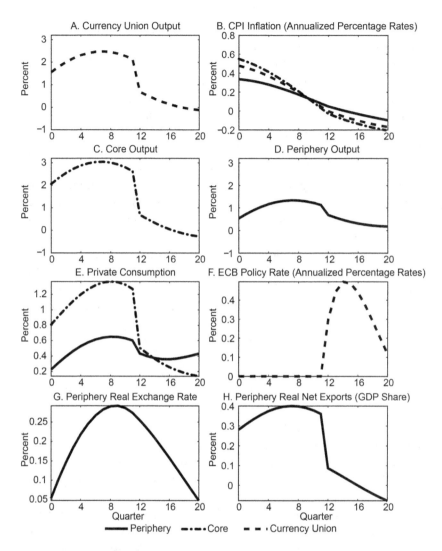

Fig. 12. Core spending hike in large-scale model in a long-lived liquidity trap

tion that periphery prices will eventually rise enough to bring the terms of trade back to its preshock level. However, Keynesian effects arising from the hand-to-mouth consumers play a substantial role in amplifying this stimulus and in contributing to periphery GDP expansion. Of course, these Keynesian effects also increase the response of core GDP.

All told, periphery GDP rises rises more than 1.25% after two years, which is almost half the expansion in core GDP. Thus, as in the benchmark model of section III, the output stimulus due to core fiscal expansion becomes more balanced in a prolonged liquidity trap. The implied CU multiplier of over 2 is in the range of estimates of the spending multiplier in a deep recession surveyed in section II.

While we view our estimates—including the aggregate government-spending multiplier and spillovers to the periphery—as quite plausible, there is clearly some uncertainty about key transmission channels. Several observations seem worthwhile in this regard. First, the model may understate the importance of multiplier/accelerator effects: as we noted, the model implies an aggregate CU government-spending multiplier lower than our empirical VAR, and a "local multiplier" modestly below empirical estimates. To allow for larger Keynesian effects, we have explored extending the model to include a financial accelerator in each country block following Christiano, Motto, and Rostagno's variant (2008) of the Bernanke, Gertler, and Gilchrist (1999) framework. In a liquidity trap, we found that both the aggregate government-spending multiplier and spillovers are enhanced by financial frictions, reflecting that the boost in nominal demand from higher core spending improves private-sector balance sheets and lowers credit spreads.

Second, the model may not adequately capture how inflation and inflation expectations evolve. As we have noted, the very flat Phillips curve slope we have imposed seems consistent with both VAR-based estimates and with the resilience of inflation during the financial crisis and its aftermath. But poor credit conditions and other adverse supply-side developments may have helped account for why inflation did not fall much, in spite of an enormous fall in output below trend (see Christiano et al. 2015; Gilchrist et al. 2015), so that the Phillips curve slope could well be higher; in this case, the multiplier and spillovers would also be larger. On the other hand, our Calvo contract specification implies an immediate jump in both inflation and inflation expectations. But it is quite plausible that inflation and inflation expectations would show a more gradual rise, perhaps more in line with the implications of Mankiw and Reis's (2002) sticky information model of price formation; or alternatively, inflation expectations could rise more gradually if expectations formation was partially adaptive. Ceteris paribus, a more gradual rise in expected inflation would tend to reduce both the aggregate multiplier and spillovers to the periphery.

Finally, it bears emphasizing that the model's implications of large spillovers depend on our assumptions that neither monetary nor fiscal policy acts to offset the stimulus. Clearly, the stimulus to the core and periphery would be much smaller if monetary policy began hiking rates more quickly as resource slack and the inflation gap closed. On the fiscal side, both the aggregate multiplier and associated spillovers would be lower if the fiscal reaction function implied a more aggressive reaction to government debt (Drautzberg and Uhlig 2015).

VII. Conclusions

Our paper has considered the implications for the euro area of a fiscal expansion in the core economies, with particular focus on how the periphery would be affected. We have shown that not only does the fiscal multiplier for the euro area as a whole become much larger in a prolonged liquidity trap, but also that the stimulative effects become relatively more balanced between the core and periphery (though still tilted in favor of the core). Periphery GDP expands as domestic demand is "crowded in" by lower real interest rates, and as net exports are boosted by terms of trade depreciation and an expansion of domestic demand in the core economies. Accordingly, fiscal policy seems a potent tool to improve welfare throughout the euro area, at least to the extent that welfare can be proxied by inflation and output gaps.

While an extensive literature has focused on the potential benefits of fiscal policy in a liquidity trap, most of this analysis has abstracted from differences in business cycle positions across member states. Our analysis suggests that fiscal spending is likely to be much more effective in boosting welfare to the extent that it can be targeted to countries or states facing relatively adverse business cycle conditions. Thus, a euro-area fiscal compact that would allow more distressed countries greater latitude to engage in deficit-financed spending could yield substantial benefits. Of course, there are many challenges of designing a fiscal union, including how to limit the moral hazard risks that such insurance might pose to other members of the compact.

From a methodological perspective, our modeling framework has abstracted from a number of features that would seem useful extensions for future research. First, our analysis is conducted under the assumption of perfect foresight, implying that the public is convinced that the economy will eventually recover absent fiscal action. The benefit of fiscal expansion would likely be greater in a stochastic environment in which fiscal expansion could help mitigate downside tail risks that likely are substantial in a prolonged liquidity trap. Second, our simple benchmark model assumes a representative agent structure with perfect risk sharing. The benefits of fiscal expansion—especially using a utility-based welfare criterion—would presumably be greater in a heterogenous agent framework in which risk sharing was much less pervasive, and each household's consumption more dependent on its particular employment opportunities.[46] Finally, it would be desirable to extend our modeling framework to allow sovereign borrowing spreads to respond endogenously to changes in fiscal policy.

Appendix A

The Benchmark Model

This appendix provides a detailed description of the benchmark model from which the log-linearized equations in section III are derived.

Households

The utility functional of household h in the home economy is given by:

$$\mathbb{E}_t \sum_{j=0}^{\infty} \beta^j s_{t+j} \left\{ \begin{array}{l} \dfrac{1}{1-1/\sigma}(C_{t+j}(h) - \varkappa C_{t+j-1} - Cv_{t+j})^{1-1/\sigma} - \chi_0 \dfrac{(N_{t+j}(h))^{1+\chi}}{1+\chi} \\[2ex] + \dfrac{\vartheta_g}{1-1/\sigma_g} G_{t+j}^{1-1/\sigma_g} + \mu_0 F\left(\dfrac{MB_{t+j+1}(h)}{P_{Ct+j}}\right) \end{array} \right\} \quad (A1)$$

The preference specification in equation (A1) implies that household h derives utility from private consumption $C_t(h)$, government spending $G_t(h)$, and real balances $MB_t(h)/P_{Ct}$, whereas utility declines in hours worked $N_t(h)$. The utility function is assumed to be separable in each of these arguments. The subutility function over consumption incorporates external habit persistence—captured by the presence of lagged aggregate consumption C_{t-1}—with the degree of habit determined by the parameter $\varkappa \in (0, 1)$. There are two types of preference shocks, including a consumption taste (demand) shock v_t, and a discount factor shock ρ_t. The latter type of shock has been widely used in the ZLB literature (see, e.g., Eggertsson 2011; Christiano et al. 2011) as a driving force of the Great Recession. Following Eggertsson and Woodford (2003), the subutility function over real balances, $F[MB_{t+j+1}(h)/P_{t+j}]$, is assumed to have a satiation point for $\overline{MB}/P$. Hence, the inclusion of money—which is a zero nominal interest asset—provides a rationale for the zero lower bound on nominal interest rates. However, we maintain the assumptions that money is additive and that μ_0 is arbitrarily small so that changes in real money balances have negligible implications for government debt and output. Finally, we assume that $0 < \beta < 1, \sigma > 0, \sigma_g > 0, \chi > 0, \chi_0 > 0$ and $\vartheta_g > 0$.

Household h faces a flow budget constraint in period t, which states that combined expenditure on goods and on the net accumulation of financial assets must equal its disposable income:

$$P_{Ct}(1 + \tau_{Ct})C_t(h) + \int_s \xi_{t,t+1}B_{t+1}(h) - B_t(h) + B_{G,t}(h)$$

$$= (1 - \tau_{N,t})W_t(h)N_t(h) - T_t + R_{Kt}K + (1 + i_{t-1}^{CU})B_{G,t-1}(h) + \Gamma_t(h). \tag{A2}$$

In equation (A2), all variables have been expressed in per capita terms. A household may spend its income either on consumption goods, which are subject to a sales tax of τ_{Ct}, or can save by investing in either government bonds $B_{G,t}(h)$ or contingent claims. The term $\xi_{t,t+1}$ denotes the price of an asset that will pay one unit of domestic currency in a particular state of nature at date $t + 1$, and $B_{t+1}(h)$ the quantity of claims purchased. Each household earns per capita labor income net of taxes $(1 - \tau_{N,t})W_t(h)N_t(h)$, earns rental income of $R_{Kt}K$ on its fixed stock of capital K, receives an aliquot share $\Gamma_t(h)$ of the firm profits, and pays lump-sum taxes of T_t to the government.[47]

Each household h maximizes the utility functional (equation [A1]) with respect to its consumption, hours worked, government bonds, and holdings of contingent claims subject to its budget constraint (equation [A2]), taking bond prices, the wage, the rental price of capital (R_{Kt}), and the price of the consumption bundle (P_{Ct}) as given. The first-order condition(s) for contingent claims both at home and abroad implies the complete markets condition that the marginal utility of a euro is equalized across home and foreign households:

$$\lambda_{ct} = \lambda_{ct}^*,$$

Because the marginal utility of consumption equals $\Lambda_{Ct} = \lambda_t P_{Ct}$ (and analogously for foreign households), the complete markets condition may be written in the familiar form:

$$\Lambda_{Ct}^* = \Lambda_{Ct}\frac{P_{Ct}^*}{P_{Ct}} = \Lambda_{Ct}Q_{Ct}. \tag{A3}$$

Thus, a depreciation of the home economy's consumption-based real exchange rate (Q_{Ct} rises) boosts the marginal utility of foreign consumption relative to the marginal utility of home consumption.

The first-order conditions with respect to C_t, N_t, and $B_{G,t}$ are given by:

$$\Lambda_{Ct} = \frac{(C_t - \varkappa C_{t-1} - Cv_t)^{-1/\sigma}}{(1 + \tau_{C,t})}, \tag{A4}$$

$$mrs_t = \frac{\chi_0 N_t^\chi}{\Lambda_{Ct}} = (1 - \tau_{N,t})\frac{W_t}{P_{Ct}},$$

$$\Lambda_{Ct} = \beta E_t \delta_t \frac{(1 + i_t^{CU})P_{Ct}}{P_{Ct+1}} \Lambda_{Ct+1}.$$

The first of these conditions indicates that the marginal utility of consumption decreases in current consumption, but increases in past consumption due to habit. The second equation is the labor supply curve, which relates the household's marginal cost of working—expressed in terms of the consumption good, that is, $mrs_t = \chi_0 N_t^\chi / \Lambda_{Ct}$—to the after-tax consumption real wage. The final expression is the consumption Euler equation, where $\delta_t = s_{t+1} / s_t$ is simply a rescaling of the time preference shock.

The problem for the foreign households h^* is isomorphic to the problem outlined above for the domestic households.

Firms and Price Setting

Below, we describe the problem for the home producers of both final and intermediate goods.

Production of Final Goods

We assume that a single final domestic output good Y_{Dt} is produced using a continuum of differentiated intermediate goods $Y_{Dt}(f)$. The technology for transforming these intermediate goods into the final output good is constant returns to scale, and is of the Dixit-Stiglitz form:

$$Y_{Dt} = [\int_0^1 Y_{Dt}(f)^{1/1+\theta_p} df]^{1+\theta_p}, \tag{A5}$$

where $\theta_p > 0$.

Firms that produce the final output good are perfectly competitive in both product and factor markets. Thus, final goods producers minimize the cost of producing a given quantity of the output index, Y_{Dt}, taking as given the price $P_{Dt}(f)$ of each intermediate good $Y_{Dt}(f)$. Moreover, final goods producers sell units of the final output good at a price P_{Dt} that can be interpreted as the aggregate domestic price index:

$$P_{Dt} = [\int_0^1 P_{Dt}(f)^{-1/\theta_p} df]^{-\theta_p}. \tag{A6}$$

Production of Domestic Intermediate Goods

Intermediate good i is produced by a monopolistically competitive firm, whose output $Y_{Dt}(i)$ is produced according to a Cobb-Douglas production function:

$$Y_{Dt}(i) = K(i)^\alpha (Z_t L_t(i))^{1-\alpha}, \tag{A7}$$

where Z_t denotes a stationary, country-specific shock to the level of technology. Intermediate goods producers face perfectly competitive factor markets for hiring capital and labor. Thus, each firm chooses $K(i)$ and $L_t(i)$, taking as given both the rental price of capital R_{Kt} and the aggregate wage rate W_t. Within a country, labor and the capital stock (albeit fixed in the aggregate) are completely mobile; thus, the standard static first-order conditions for cost minimization imply that all intermediate firms have identical marginal cost per unit of output:

$$MC_t = \left(\frac{W_t}{1-\alpha}\right)^{1-\alpha} \left(\frac{R_{Kt}}{\alpha}\right)^\alpha \frac{1}{Z_t^{1-\alpha}}, \tag{A8}$$

where the standard static cost minimization problem of the firm implies that

$$R_{Kt} = \frac{\alpha}{1-\alpha} W_t \frac{L_t}{K}. \tag{A9}$$

Intermediate goods-producing firms set prices according to Calvo-style staggered contracts, and set the same price in both the home and foreign market (i.e., the home market price $P_{Dt}(i)$ equals the price in the foreign market of $P_{Mt}^*(i)$). In particular, firm i faces a constant probability, $1 - \xi_p$, of being able to reoptimize its price, $P_{Dt}(i)$. Firms that are not allowed to reoptimize their prices in period t (which is the case with probability ξ_p), update their prices according to the following formula

$$\tilde{P}_{Dt}(i) = (1 + \pi_D)P_{Dt-1}(i), \tag{A10}$$

where π_D is the steady state (net) inflation rate and $\tilde{P}_{Dt}$ is the updated price.

Given Calvo-style pricing frictions, firm i that is allowed to reoptimize its price ($P_{Dt}^{opt}(i)$) solves the following problem

$$\max_{P_{Dt}^{opt}(i)} E_t \sum_{j=0}^{\infty} \xi_p^j \psi_{t,t+j} [(1 + \pi_D)^j P_{Dt}^{opt}(i) - MC_{t+j}] Y_{Dt+j}(i),$$

where $\psi_{t,t+j}$ is the stochastic discount factor (the conditional value of future profits in utility units, that is, $\beta^j E_t \delta_{t+j}(\lambda_{ct+j}/\lambda_{ct})$, recalling that the household is the owner of the firms), θ_p the net markup and the demand function for firm i has the following general form $Y_{Dt+j}(i) = [P_{Dt}^{opt}(i)/P_{Dt}]^{-(1+\theta_p)/\theta_p}Y_{Dt}$. The first-order condition is given by:

$$E_t\sum_{j=0}^{\infty}\xi_p^j\psi_{t,t+j}\left[\frac{(1+\pi_D)^jP_{Dt}^{opt}(i)}{1+\theta_p} - MC_{t+j}\right]Y_{Dt+j}(i) = 0. \quad (A11)$$

Given that all firms that can reoptimize set the same price, the price index for domestically produced goods evolves according to:

$$P_{Dt} = [(1-\xi_p)(P_{Dt}^{opt})^{-1/\theta_p} + \xi_p((1+\pi)P_{Dt-1})^{-1/\theta_p}]^{-\theta_p}. \quad (A12)$$

The productive structure of the foreign economy is isomorphic. Thus, the final good is comprised of a bundle of intermediate goods according to the production function $Y_{Dt}^* = [\int_0^1 Y_{Dt}^*(f)^{1/(1+\theta_p)}df]^{1+\theta_p}$, and the price of this final good is output of the final goods denoted by $P_{Dt}^* = [\int_0^1 P_{Dt}^*(f)^{-1/\theta_p}df]^{-\theta_p}$.

Traded Goods

Household consumption C_t in the home economy depends both on its consumption of the domestically produced final output good C_{Dt} and on its consumption of the foreign final output good M_{Ct} (i.e., consumer goods imports) according to the CES utility function:

$$C_t = ((1-\omega_C)^{\rho_C/(1+\rho_C)}C_{Dt}^{1/(1+\rho_C)} + \omega_C^{\rho_C/(1+\rho_C)}M_{Ct}^{1/(1+\rho_C)})^{1+\rho_C}. \quad (A13)$$

The quasi-share parameter ω_C in equation (A13) may be interpreted as determining household preferences for home relative to foreign goods, or equivalently, the degree of home bias in household consumption expenditure. The domestically produced final good is purchased at a price of P_{Dt}, while the foreign imported good is purchased at a price of P_{Mt}; given the fixed exchange rate and our assumption of producer currency pricing, the law of one price holds, so that $P_{Mt} = P_{Dt}^*$. Households choose C_{Dt} and M_{Ct} to minimize the cost of producing the consumption good C_t, taking the prices P_{Dt} and P_{Mt} as given. This familiar cost-minimization problem implies the following demand schedules for the imported and domestically produced good:

$$M_{Ct} = \omega_C\left(\frac{P_{Mt}}{P_{Ct}}\right)^{-(1+\rho_C)/\rho_C}C_t \text{ and } C_{Dt} = (1-\omega_C)\left(\frac{P_{Dt}}{P_{Ct}}\right)^{-(1+\rho_C)/\rho_C}C_t, \quad (A14)$$

while the consumer price index P_{Ct}, is given by:

$$P_{Ct} = ((1 - \omega_C)P_{Dt}^{1/(1+\rho C)} + \omega_C P_{Mt}^{1/(1+\rho C)})^{1+\rho C}. \tag{A15}$$

Similarly to households, the home government also produces final government goods (and services) G_t using both the domestically produced final good G_{Dt} and imports of the foreign final good M_{Gt} according to the CES production function:

$$G_t = ((1 - \omega_G)^{\rho G/(1+\rho G)}G_{Dt}^{1/(1+\rho G)} + \omega_G^{\rho G/(1+\rho G)}M_{Gt}^{1/(1+\rho G)})^{1+\rho G}. \tag{A16}$$

The parameter ω_G measures the import share of government consumption; thus, total home imports depend both on the demand of households, and of the government. The government's demand schedules for both the domestically produced final good and for imported goods are isomorphic to that of households:

$$M_{Gt} = \omega_G \left(\frac{P_{Mt}}{P_{Gt}}\right)^{-(1+\rho G)/\rho G} G_t \text{ and } G_{Dt} = (1 - \omega_G)\left(\frac{P_{Dt}}{P_{Gt}}\right)^{-(1+\rho G)/\rho G} G_t, \tag{A17}$$

although it is important to note that the degree of home bias in government spending ω_G may differ from that in private spending ω_C, and that the government's willingness to substitute between home and traded goods $-((1 + \rho_G)/\rho_G)$ may also differ from that of households $-((1 + \rho_C)/\rho_C)$. The price index for government purchases is given by:

$$P_{Gt} = ((1 - \omega_G)P_{Dt}^{1/(1+\rho G)} + \omega_G P_{Mt}^{1/(1+\rho G)})^{1+\rho G}. \tag{A18}$$

We define the terms-of-trade as

$$\tau_t = \frac{P_{Mt}}{P_{Dt}} = \frac{P_{Dt}^*}{P_{Dt}}, \tag{A19}$$

so that an increase in τ_t implies that the home economy can buy less imports for any given level of exports.

Fiscal Policy

The government finances its nominal spending on goods and services $P_{Gt}G_t$ through a consumption sales tax, labor tax, and lump-sum tax (we assume that seignorage revenue is de minimis). Thus, evolution of nominal government debt, $B_{G,t}$, is determined by:

$$B_{G,t} = (1 + i_{t-1})B_{G,t-1} + P_{Gt}G_t - \tau_{C,t}P_{Ct}C_t - \tau_{N,t}W_tL_t - T_t. \tag{A20}$$

We assume that the consumption sales tax $\tau_{C,t}$ and labor tax $\tau_{N,t}$ are determined exogenously, so that lump-sum taxes adjust to satisfy the government's intertemporal budget constraint. Thus, the fiscal rule has no effect on macrovariables (other than the stock of debt and the lump-sum tax level itself).

Aggregate Resource Constraints

The aggregate resource constraint for the domestic economy is given by:

$$Y_{Dt} = C_{Dt} + G_{Dt} + \frac{\zeta^*}{\zeta}[M^*_{Ct} + M^*_{Gt}], \qquad (A21)$$

where exports are weighted by the relative population size of the foreign to home country ζ^*/ζ as the variables are expressed in per capita terms. Similarly, the resource constraint for the foreign economy is given by:

$$Y^*_{Dt} = C^*_{Dt} + G^*_{Dt} + \frac{\zeta}{\zeta^*}[M_{Ct} + M_{Gt}], \qquad (A22)$$

where exports are weighted by the relative population size of the home to foreign country ζ/ζ^*. The total population is normalized to unity, that is,

$$\zeta + \zeta^* = 1. \qquad (A23)$$

We also make the assumption that trade is balanced for both private consumption and government services, which implies that:

$$\zeta\omega_C = \zeta^*\omega^*_C, \qquad (A24)$$

and

$$\zeta\omega_G = \zeta^*\omega^*_G. \qquad (A25)$$

Given complete financial markets, the current account and net foreign assets are always equal to zero. The nominal trade balance (in absolute levels) is given by

$$TB_t \equiv \frac{\zeta^*}{\zeta} P_{Dt}[M^*_{Ct} + M^*_{Gt}] - P_{Mt}[M_{Ct} + M_{Gt}]. \qquad (A26)$$

Monetary Policy

The currency union central bank is assumed to adhere to a Taylor-type policy rule subject to the ZLB. Given that we start out with a log-linearized version of the model, it is convenient to simply specify the reaction function as a linear relation (aside from the zero lower bound), expressing variables in deviation from baseline form:

$$i_t^{CU} = \max(-i, \psi_\pi \pi_t^{CU} + \psi_x x_t^{CU}). \tag{A27}$$

Here i denotes the steady-state (net) nominal interest rate (equal to $r + \pi$ where $r \equiv 1/\beta - 1$), π_t^{CU} is currency union inflation, and x_t^{CU} is the currency union output gap. Currency union inflation π_t^{CU} is itself a population-weighted average of the inflation rate π_{Ct} in both the home and foreign country:

$$\pi_t^{CU} = \zeta \pi_{Ct} + \zeta^* \pi_{Ct'}^*, \tag{A28}$$

where each country inflation rate is simply the log percentage change in the respective consumption price index (i.e., $\pi_{Ct} = \ln(P_{Ct}/P_{Ct-1})$). The CU output gap x_t^{CU} is the difference between currency union output y_t^{CU} and its potential level $y_t^{CU,pot}$, with both variables again simply population-weighted averages of the respective country variables:

$$y_t^{CU} = \zeta y_{Dt} + \zeta^* y_{Dt'}^*, \tag{A29}$$

and

$$y_t^{CU,pot} = \zeta y_{Dt}^{pot} + \zeta^* y_{Dt}^{*,pot}. \tag{A30}$$

Appendix B

The Large-Scale Open Economy Model

The large-scale model closely follows Erceg and Lindé (2013), aside from some features of the fiscal policy specification. As in the benchmark model described in appendix A, the model consists of two countries—home and foreign—that share a common currency. The larger-scale model extends the benchmark model on a number of dimensions, including allowing for endogenous investment, hand-to-mouth (HM) or "Keynesian" households, sticky wages as well as sticky prices, trade-adjustment costs, and incomplete financial markets across the two countries. Although the model we focus on in section VI abstracts from a financial accelerator, the appendix concludes with a brief description of how the model may be modified to include a financial accelerator (See Production of Capital Services).

Firms and Price Setting

Production of Domestic Intermediate Goods

As in the simple model, there is a continuum of differentiated intermediate goods (indexed by $i \in [0, 1]$) in the home country, each of which
is produced by a single monopolistically competitive firm. In the domestic market, firm i faces a demand function that varies inversely with
its output price $P_{Dt}(i)$ and directly with aggregate demand at home Y_{Dt}:

$$Y_{Dt}(i) = \left[\frac{P_{Dt}(i)}{P_{Dt}} \right]^{-(1+\theta_p)/\theta_p} Y_{Dt}, \tag{B1}$$

where $\theta_p > 0$, and P_{Dt} is an aggregate price index defined below.

Each producer utilizes capital services $K_t(i)$ and a labor index $L_t(i)$ (defined below) to produce its respective output good. The production function is assumed to have a constant elasticity of substitution (CES) form:

$$Y_{Dt}(i) = (\omega_K^{\rho/(1+\rho)} K_t(i)^{1/(1+\rho)} + \omega_L^{\rho/(1+\rho)} (Z_t L_t(i))^{1/(1+\rho)})^{1+\rho}. \tag{B2}$$

The production function exhibits constant returns to scale in both inputs,
and Z_t is a country-specific shock to the level of technology. Firms face
perfectly competitive factor markets for hiring capital and labor. Thus,
each firm chooses $K_t(i)$ and $L_t(i)$, taking as given both the rental price
of capital R_{Kt} and the aggregate wage index W_t (defined below). Firms
can costlessly adjust either factor of production, which implies that each
firm has an identical marginal cost per unit of output, MC_t. The (log-
linearized) technology shock is assumed to follow an AR(1) process:

$$z_t = \rho_z z_{t-1} + \varepsilon_{z,t}. \tag{B3}$$

We assume that purchasing power parity holds, so that each intermediate goods producer i sets the same price $P_{Dt}(i)$ in both blocks of the currency union, implying that the foreign import price $P_{Mt}^*(i) = P_{Dt}(i)$ and that
$P_{Mt}^* = P_{Dt}$. The prices of the intermediate goods are determined by Calvo-
style staggered contracts (see Calvo, 1983, and Yun, 1996). In each period, a
firm faces a constant probability, $1 - \xi_p$, of being able to reoptimize its price
($P_{Dt}(i)$). This probability of receiving a signal to reoptimize is independent across firms and time. If a firm is not allowed to optimize its prices,
we follow Christiano et al. (2005) and Smets and Wouters (2003), and
assume that the firm must reset its home price as a weighted combina-
tion of the lagged and steady state rate of inflation $P_{Dt}(i) = \widetilde{\pi_{Dt-1}} P_{Dt-1}(i) =
\pi_{Dt-1}^{\iota_p} \pi^{1-\iota_p} P_{Dt-1}(i)$ for the nonoptimizing firms. This formulation allows for
structural persistence in price setting if ι_p exceeds zero.

When a firm i is allowed to reoptimize its price in period t, the firm maximizes:

$$\max_{P_{Dt}(i)} \mathbb{E}_t \sum_{j=0}^{\infty} \psi_{t,t+j} \xi_p^j \left[\prod_{h=1}^{j} \widetilde{\pi_{Dt+h-1}}(P_{Dt}(i) - MC_{t+j}) Y_{Dt+j}(i) \right]. \tag{B4}$$

The operator $\mathbb{E}_t$ represents the conditional expectation based on the information available to agents at period t. The firm discounts profits received at date $t + j$ by the state-contingent discount factor $\psi_{t,t+j}$; for notational simplicity, we have suppressed all of the state indices.[48] The first-order condition for setting the contract price of good i is:

$$\mathbb{E}_t \sum_{j=0}^{\infty} \psi_{t,t+j} \xi_p^j \left(\frac{\prod_{h=1}^{j} \widetilde{\pi_{Dt+h-1}} P_{Dt}(i)}{(1 + \theta_p)} - MC_{t+j} \right) Y_{Dt+j}(i) = 0. \tag{B5}$$

Production of the Domestic Output Index

Because households have identical Dixit-Stiglitz preferences, it is convenient to assume that a representative aggregator combines the differentiated intermediate products into a composite home-produced good Y_{Dt}:

$$Y_{Dt} = \left[\int_0^1 Y_{Dt}(i)^{1/(1+\theta_p)} di \right]^{1+\theta_p}. \tag{B6}$$

The aggregator chooses the bundle of goods that minimizes the cost of producing Y_{Dt}, taking the price $P_{Dt}(i)$ of each intermediate good $Y_{Dt}(i)$ as given. The aggregator sells units of each sectoral output index at its unit cost P_{Dt}:

$$P_{Dt} = \left[\int_0^1 P_{Dt}(i)^{-1/\theta_p} di \right]^{-\theta_p}. \tag{B7}$$

Production of Consumption and Investment Goods

Final consumption goods are produced by a representative consumption goods distributor. This firm combines purchases of domestically produced goods with imported goods to produce a final consumption good (C_{At}) according to a constant returns to scale CES production function:

$$C_{At} = (\omega_C^{\rho_C/(1+\rho_C)} C_{Dt}^{1/(1+\rho_C)} + (1 - \omega_C)^{\rho_C/(1+\rho_C)} (\varphi_{Ct} M_{Ct})^{1/(1+\rho_C)})^{1+\rho_C}, \tag{B8}$$

where C_{Dt} denotes the consumption good distributor's demand for the index of domestically produced goods, M_{Ct} denotes the distributor's demand for the index of foreign-produced goods, and φ_{Ct} reflects costs of adjusting consumption imports. The final consumption good is used by both households and by the government.[49] The form of the production function mirrors the preferences of households and the government sector over consumption of domestically produced goods and imports. Accordingly, the quasi-share parameter ω_C may be interpreted as determining the preferences of both the private and public sector for domestic relative to foreign consumption goods, or equivalently, the degree of home bias in consumption expenditure. Finally, the adjustment cost term φ_{Ct} is assumed to take the quadratic form:

$$
\varphi_{Ct} = \left[1 - \frac{\varphi_{MC}}{2}\left(\frac{M_{Ct}/C_{Dt}}{[(M_{Ct-1})/(C_{Dt-1})]^a} - 1\right)^2\right].
\tag{B9}
$$

This specification implies that it is costly to change the proportion of domestic and foreign goods in the aggregate consumption bundle, even though the level of imports may jump costlessly in response to changes in overall consumption demand. We assume that the adjustment costs for each distributor depend on the distributor's current import ratio M_{Ct}/C_{Dt} relative to the economy-wide ratio in the previous period $(M_{Ct-1}/C_{Dt-1})^a$, so that adjustment costs are external to individual distributors.

Given the presence of adjustment costs, the representative consumption goods distributor chooses (a contingency plan for) C_{Dt} and M_{Ct} to minimize its discounted expected costs of producing the aggregate consumption good:

$$
\min_{C_{Dt+k}, M_{Ct+k}} \mathbb{E}_t \sum_{k=0}^{\infty} \Psi_{t,t+k}\{(P_{Dt+k}C_{Dt+k} + P_{Mt+k}M_{Ct+k})
$$
$$
+ P_{Ct+k}[C_{A,t+k} - (\omega_C^{\rho_C/(1+\rho_C)}C_{Dt+k}^{1/(1+\rho_C)}
\tag{B10}
$$
$$
+ (1 - \omega_C)^{\rho_C/(1+\rho_C)}(\varphi_{Ct+k}M_{Ct+k})^{1/(1+\rho_C)})^{1+\rho_C}]\}.
$$

The distributor sells the final consumption good to households and the government at a price P_{Ct}, which may be interpreted as the consumption price index (or equivalently, as the shadow cost of producing an additional unit of the consumption good).

We model the production of final investment goods in an analogous manner, although we allow the weight ω_I in the investment index to differ from that of the weight ω_C in the consumption goods index.[50]

Households and Wage Setting

We assume a continuum of monopolistically competitive households (indexed on the unit interval), each of which supplies a differentiated labor service to the intermediate goods-producing sector (the only producers demanding labor services in our framework) following Erceg, Henderson, and Levin (2000). A representative labor aggregator (or "employment agency") combines households' labor hours in the same proportions as firms would choose. Thus, the aggregator's demand for each household's labor is equal to the sum of firms' demands. The aggregate labor index L_t has the Dixit-Stiglitz form:

$$L_t = \left[\int_0^1 (\zeta N_t(h))^{1/(1+\theta_w)} dh \right]^{1+\theta_w}, \qquad (B11)$$

where $\theta_w > 0$ and $N_t(h)$ is hours worked by a typical member of household h. The parameter ζ is the size of a household of type h, and effectively determines the size of the population in the home country. The aggregator minimizes the cost of producing a given amount of the aggregate labor index, taking each household's wage rate $W_t(h)$ as given, and then sells units of the labor index to the production sector at their unit cost W_t:

$$W_t = \left[\int_0^1 W_t(h)^{-1/\theta_w} dh \right]^{-\theta_w}. \qquad (B12)$$

The aggregator's demand for the labor services of a typical member of household h is given by

$$N_t(h) = \left[\frac{W_t(h)}{W_t} \right]^{-(1+\theta_w/\theta_w)} L_t/\zeta. \qquad (B13)$$

We assume that there are two types of households: households that make intertemporal consumption, labor supply, and capital accumulation decisions in a forward-looking manner by maximizing utility subject to an intertemporal budget constraint (FL households, for "forward looking"), and the remainder that simply consume their after-tax disposable income (HM households, for "hand-to-mouth" households). The latter type receive no capital rental income or profits, and choose to set their wage to be the average wage of optimizing households. We denote the share of FL households by $1 - s$ and the share of HM households by s.

168

Blanchard, Erceg, and Lindé

We consider first the problem faced by FL households. The utility functional for an optimizing representative member of household h is

$$\mathbb{E}_t \sum_{j=0}^{\infty} \beta^j \left\{ \begin{array}{l} \dfrac{1}{1-\sigma} \left(C_{t+j}^O(h) - \varkappa C_{t+j-1}^O - C v_{ct+j} \right)^{1-\sigma} \\ + \dfrac{\chi_0 Z_{t+j}^{1-\sigma}}{1-\chi} \left(1 - N_{t+j}(h) \right)^{1-\chi} + \mu_0 F \left(\dfrac{MB_{t+j+1}(h)}{P_{Ct+j}} \right) \end{array} \right\}, \quad (B14)$$

where the discount factor β satisfies $0 < \beta < 1$. As in Smets and Wouters (2003, 2007), we allow for the possibility of external habit formation in preferences, so that each household member cares about its consumption relative to lagged aggregate consumption per capita of forward-looking agents C_{t-1}^O. The period utility function depends on an each member's current leisure $1 - N_t(h)$, his end-of-period real money balances, $MB_{t+1}(h)/P_{Ct}$, and a preference shock, v_{ct}. The subutility function $F(.)$ over real balances is assumed to have a satiation point to account for the possibility of a zero nominal interest rate (see Eggertsson and Woodford [2003] for further discussion).[51] The (log-linearized) consumption demand shock v_{ct} is assumed to follow an AR(1) process:

$$v_{ct} = \rho_v v_{ct-1} + \varepsilon_{v_c,t}. \quad (B15)$$

Forward-looking household h faces a flow budget constraint in period t, which states that its combined expenditure on goods and on the net accumulation of financial assets must equal its disposable income:

$$P_{Ct}(1 + \tau_{Ct}) C_t^O(h) + P_{It} I_t(h) + MB_{t+1}(h) - MB_t(h) + \int_s \xi_{t,t+1} B_{Dt+1}(h)$$

$$- B_{Dt}(h) + P_{Bt} B_{Gt+1} - B_{Gt} + \frac{P_{Bt}^* B_{Ft+1}(h)}{\phi_{bt}} - B_{Ft}(h) \quad (B16)$$

$$= (1 - \tau_{Nt}) W_t(h) N_t(h) + \Gamma_t(h) + TR_t(h)$$

$$+ (1 - \tau_{Kt}) R_{Kt} K_t(h) + P_{It} \tau_{Kt} \delta K_t(h) - P_{Dt} \phi_{It}(h).$$

Consumption purchases are subject to a sales tax of τ_{Ct}. Investment in physical capital augments the per capita capital stock $K_{t+1}(h)$ according to a linear transition law of the form:

$$K_{t+1}(h) = (1 - \delta) K_t(h) + I_t(h) \quad (B17)$$

where δ is the depreciation rate of capital.

Financial asset accumulation of a typical member of FL household h consists of increases in nominal money holdings $(MB_{t+1}(h) - MB_t(h))$ and the net acquisition of bonds. While the domestic financial market is complete through the existence of state-contingent bonds B_{Dt+1}, cross-border asset trade is restricted to a single nonstate contingent bond issued by the government of the foreign economy.[52]

The terms B_{Gt+1} and B_{Ft+1} represents each household member's net purchases of the government bonds issued by the home and foreign governments, respectively. Each type of bond pays one currency unit (e.g., euro) in the subsequent period and is sold at price (discount) of P_{Bt} and P^*_{Bt}, respectively. To ensure the stationarity of foreign asset positions, we follow Turnovsky (1985) by assuming that domestic households must pay a transaction cost when trading in the foreign bond. The intermediation cost depends on the ratio of economy-wide holdings of net foreign assets to nominal GDP, $P_{Dt}Y_{Dt}$, and are given by:

$$\phi_{bt} = \exp\left(-\phi_b\left(\frac{B_{Ft+1}}{P_{Dt}Y_{Dt}}\right)\right). \tag{B18}$$

If the home country is an overall net lender position internationally, then a household will earn a lower return on any holdings of foreign bonds; conversely, if the home country is a net debtor position, home households pay a higher return on their foreign liabilities. Given that the domestic government bond in the home economy and foreign bond have the same payoff, the price faced by home residents net of the transaction cost is identical, so that $P_{Bt} = P^*_{Bt}/\phi_{bt}$. The effective nominal interest rate on domestic bonds (and similarly for foreign bonds) hence equals $i_t = 1/P_{Bt} - 1$.

Each member of FL household h earns after-tax labor income, $(1 - \tau_{Nt})W_t(h)N_t(h)$, where τ_{Nt} is a stochastic tax on labor income. The household leases capital at the after-tax rental rate $(1 - \tau_{Kt})R_{Kt}$, where τ_{Kt} is a stochastic tax on capital income. The household receives a depreciation write-off of $P_{It}\tau_{Kt}\delta$ per unit of capital. Each member also receives an aliquot share $\Gamma_t(h)$ of the profits of all firms and a lump-sum government transfer, $TR_t(h)$ (which is negative in the case of a tax). Following Christiano et al. (2005), we assume that it is costly to change the level of gross investment from the previous period, so that the acceleration in the capital stock is penalized:

$$\phi_{It}(h) = \frac{1}{2}\phi_I\frac{(I_t(h) - I_{t-1})^2}{I_{t-1}}. \tag{B19}$$

In every period t, each member of FL household h maximizes the utility functional (equation [B14]) with respect to its consumption, investment, (end-of-period) capital stock, money balances, holdings of

contingent claims, and holdings of domestic and foreign bonds, subject
to its labor demand function (equation [B13]), budget constraint (equation [B46]), and transition equation for capital (equation [B17]). In doing
so, a household takes as given prices, taxes and transfers, and aggregate
quantities such as lagged aggregate consumption and the aggregate net
foreign asset position.

Forward-looking (FL) households set nominal wages in staggered
contracts that are analogous to the price contracts described above. In
particular, with probability $1 - \xi_w$, each member of a household is allowed to reoptimize its wage contract. If a household is not allowed to
optimize its wage rate, we assume each household member resets its
wage according to:

$$W_t(h) = \omega_{t-1}^{\iota_w}\omega^{1-\iota_w}W_{t-1}(h), \tag{B20}$$

where ω_{t-1} is the gross nominal wage inflation rate in period $t - 1$, that
is, W_t/W_{t-1}, and $\omega = \pi$ is the steady state rate of change in the nominal
wage (equal to gross price inflation since steady state gross productivity
growth is assumed to be unity). Dynamic indexation of this form introduces some element of structural persistence into the wage-setting process. Each member of household h chooses the value of $W_t(h)$ to maximize its utility functional (equation [B14]) subject to these constraints.

Finally, we consider the determination of consumption and labor
supply of the hand-to-mouth (HM) households. A typical member of a
HM household simply equates his nominal consumption spending,
$P_{Ct}(1 + \tau_{Ct})C_t^{HM}(h)$, to his current after-tax disposable income, which consists of labor income plus lump-sum transfers from the government:

$$P_{Ct}(1 + \tau_{Ct})C_t^{HM}(h) = (1 - \tau_{Nt})W_t(h)N_t(h) + TR_t(h). \tag{B21}$$

The HM households are assumed to set their wage equal to the average wage of the forward-looking households. Since HM households
face the same labor demand schedule as the forward-looking households, this assumption implies that each HM household works the
same number of hours as the average for forward-looking households.

Monetary Policy

As in the simple benchmark model, the currency union central bank is
assumed to adhere to a Taylor-type policy rule, although we allow here
for some inertia in the interest rate reaction function that is captured by
the term $\gamma_i i_{t-1}^{CU}$:

$$i_t^{CU} = (1 - \gamma_i)(\psi_\pi \pi_t^{CU} + \psi_x x_t^{CU} + \gamma_i i_{t-1}^{CU} + \varepsilon_{M,t}).$$ (B22)

The monetary policy shock, $\varepsilon_{M,t}$, which we use when we estimate some of the model parameters in section VI.B, is assumed to be normally and independently estimated with zero mean and standard deviation σ_M.

When monetary policy is subject to the ZLB, the policy rule is modified as follows:

$$i_t^{CU} = \max(-i, (1 - \gamma_i)(\psi_\pi \pi_t^{CU} + \psi_x x_t^{CU} + \gamma_i i_{t-1}^{CU}),$$ (B23)

where i is the steady state nominal interest rate: as before, i_t^{CU} measures the currency union policy rate as a deviation from steady state, so that $i_t^{CU} = -i$ implies that the policy rate is zero when expressed in levels.

Fiscal Policy

The government does not need to balance its budget each period, and issues nominal debt B_{Gt+1} at the end of period t to finance its deficits according to:

$$P_{Bt}B_{Gt+1} - B_{Gt} = P_{Ct}G_t + TR_t - \tau_{Nt}W_t L_t - \tau_{Ct}P_{Ct}C_t$$
$$- \tau_{Kt}(R_{Kt} - \delta P_{It})K_t - (MB_{t+1} - MB_t),$$ (B24)

where C_t is total private consumption. Equation (B24) aggregates the capital stock, money and bond holdings, and transfers and taxes over all households so that, for example, $TR_t = \int_0^1 TR_t(h)dh$. The taxes on capital τ_{Kt} and consumption τ_{Ct} are assumed to be fixed, and the ratio of real transfers to (trend) GDP, $tr_t = TR_t/P_t Y$, is also fixed.[53] Government purchases have no direct effect on the utility of households, nor do they affect the production function of the private sector.

When we estimate the model, the process for the (log of) government spending is given by an AR(1) process:

$$(g_t - g) = \rho_G(g_{t-1} - g) + \varepsilon_{g,t},$$ (B25)

where $\varepsilon_{g,t}$ is independently normally distributed with zero mean and standard deviation σ_G.[54]

We assume that policymakers in the core and periphery adjust labor income taxes to stabilize the debt/GDP ratio and the deficit. Specifically, the labor tax rate evolves according to:

$$\tau_{Nt} - \tau_N = \nu_1(\tau_{Nt-1} - \tau_N) + (1 - \nu_1)[\nu_2(b_{Gt} - b_G) + \nu_3(\Delta b_{Gt+1} - \Delta b_G)].$$ (B26)

Resource Constraint and Net Foreign Assets

The home economy's aggregate resource constraint can be written as:

$$Y_{Dt} = C_{Dt} + I_{Dt} + \phi_{It} + \frac{\zeta^*}{\zeta} M_t^*, \tag{B27}$$

where ϕ_{It} is the adjustment cost on investment aggregated across all households. The final consumption good is allocated between households and the government:

$$C_{At} = C_t + G_t, \tag{B28}$$

where C_t is (per capita) private consumption of FL (optimizing) and HM households:

$$C_t = (1 - s)C_t^O + sC_t^{HM}. \tag{B29}$$

Total exports may be allocated to either the consumption or the investment sector abroad:

$$M_t^* = M_{Ct}^* + M_{It}^*. \tag{B30}$$

The evolution of net foreign assets can be expressed as:

$$\frac{P_{B,t}^* B_{F,t+1}}{\phi_{bt}} = B_{F,t} + P_{Mt}^* \frac{\zeta^*}{\zeta} M_t^* - P_{Mt} M_t. \tag{B31}$$

This expression can be derived from the budget constraint of the FL households after imposing the government budget constraint, the consumption rule of the HM households, the definition of firm profits, and the condition that domestic state-contingent nongovernment bonds (B_{Dt+1}) are in zero net supply.

Finally, we assume that the structure of the foreign country is isomorphic to that of the home country.

Production of Capital Services

In an augmented variant of the model, we incorporated a financial accelerator mechanism into both country blocks of our benchmark model following the basic approach of Bernanke et al. (1999). Thus, the intermediate goods producers rent capital services from entrepreneurs (at the price R_{Kt}) rather than directly from households. Entrepreneurs purchase physical capital from competitive capital goods producers (and resell it back at the end of each period), with the latter employing the same technology to transform investment goods into finished capital goods as described by equations (B17) and (B19). To finance the acquisition of physical capital, each entrepreneur combines his net worth with a loan from a bank, for which the entrepreneur must pay an external finance premium (over the risk-free interest rate set by the central bank) due to an agency problem. Banks obtain funds to lend to the entrepreneurs by issuing deposits to households at the interest rate set by the central bank, with households bearing no credit risk (reflecting assumptions about free competition in banking and the ability of banks to diversify their portfolios). In equilibrium, shocks that affect entrepeneurial net worth—that is, the leverage of the corporate sector—induce fluctuations in the corporate finance premium.[55]

Solution Method and Calibration

To analyze the behavior of the model, we log-linearize the model's equations around the nonstochastic steady state. Nominal variables are rendered stationary by suitable transformations. To solve the unconstrained version of the model, we compute the reduced-form solution of the model for a given set of parameters using the numerical algorithm of Anderson and Moore (1985), which provides an efficient implementation of the solution method proposed by Blanchard and Kahn (1980). When we solve the model subject to the nonlinear monetary policy rule (B23), we use the techniques described in Hebden, Lindé, and Svensson (2009). An important feature of the Hebden, Lindé, and Svensson algorithm is that the duration of the liquidity trap is endogenously determined.[56]

The model is calibrated at a quarterly frequency. As in the simple benchmark model, the country size parameter ζ = one-third, so that the periphery (the home country) constitutes one-third of euro-area output. The trade share of the periphery is set to 15% of periphery GDP. This pins down the trade share parameters ω_C and ω_I for the home country under the additional assumption that the import intensity of consumption is equal to three-fourths that of investment. The trade share of the foreign economy is thus 7.5%. We assume that $\rho_C = \rho_I = 10$, consistent with a long-run price elasticity of demand for imported consumption and investment goods of 1.1. The adjustment cost parameters are set so that $\varphi_{M_C} = \varphi_{M_I} = 1$, which slightly damps the near-term relative price sensitivity. The financial intermediation parameter ϕ_b is set to a very small value (0.00001), which is sufficient to ensure the model has a unique steady state.

The utility functional parameter σ is set equal to 1 to ensure that the model exhibits balanced growth, while the parameter determining the degree of habit persistence in consumption is estimated to be $\varkappa = 0.877$ (as discussed in the text). The Frisch elasticity of labor supply is set to 0.4 (so $\chi = 2.5$). The utility parameter χ_0 is set so that employment comprises one-third of the household's time endowment, while the parameter μ_0 on the subutility function for real balances is set at an arbitrarily low value (so that variation in real balances do not affect equilibrium allocations). We set the share of HM agents $s = 0.65$, implying that these agents account for about one-third of aggregate private-consumption spending (the latter is much smaller than the population share of HM agents because the latter own no capital).

The parameter determining investment adjustment costs is estimated to be $\phi_I = 1.941$. The depreciation rate of capital δ is set at 0.03 (consistent with an annual depreciation rate of 12%). The parameter ρ in the CES production function of the intermediate goods producers is set to -2, implying an elasticity of substitution between capital and labor $(1 + \rho)/\rho$, of $1/2$. The quasi-capital share parameter ω_K—together with the price markup parameter of $\theta_P = 0.20$—is chosen to imply a steady state investment to output ratio of 15%. In the augmented version of the model with a financial accelerator, our calibration of parameters follows Bernanke et al. (1999). In particular, the monitoring cost, μ, expressed as a proportion of entrepreneurs' total gross revenue, is set to 0.12. The default rate of entrepreneurs is 3% per year, and the variance of the idiosyncratic productivity shocks to entrepreneurs is 0.28.

As discussed in the text, the Calvo price contract duration parameter is estimated to be $\xi_p = 0.944$, while the wage contract duration parameter is estimated to be $\xi_w = 0.871$. We set the degree of price indexation $\iota_p = 0.65$ and wage indexation indexation $\iota_w = 0.65$, while the wage markup $\theta_W =$ one-third.[57] The parameters of the monetary rule are set such that $\gamma_\pi = 2.5$, $\gamma_x = 0$, and $\gamma_i = 0.7$. With the discount factor set at $\beta = 0.99875$ and the inflation target at 2%, the steady state nominal interest rate is 2.5%.

The parameters pertaining to fiscal policy are intended to roughly capture the revenue and spending sides of euro-area government budgets. The share of government spending on goods and services is set equal to 23% of steady state output. The government debt to GDP ratio, b_G, is set to 0.75, roughly equal to the average level of debt in euro-area countries at end-2008. The ratio of transfers to GDP is set to 20%. The steady state sales (i.e., VAT) tax rate τ_C is set to 0.2, while the capital tax τ_K is set to 0.30. Given the annualized steady state real interest rate (of 0.5%), the government's intertemporal budget constraint then implies that the labor income tax rate τ_N equals 0.42 in steady state. We assume an unaggressive tax adjustment rule in equation (B26) by setting $v_1 = 0.985$ and $v_2 = v_3 = .1$.

Finally, the first-order autoregressive coefficient ρ_g on the government-spending shock is estimated to be 0.92, while the persistence of the consumption-demand shock is set to 0.9, and the technology shock 0.975 (noting that we assume that government spending follows a moving average when simulating the effects of a core government spending hike).

Endnotes

We thank Andrew Berg, Martin Eichenbaum, Emmanuel Farhi, Josef Hollmayr, Andrew Levin, Jonathan Parker, Ricardo Reis, Pedro Teles, Harald Uhlig, and Volker Wieland for helpful comments, as well as participants at the CEPR's ESSIM conference, the ECB Public Finance conference, the NBER Summer Institute, the EABCN conference in Cambridge (UK), and the 2016 NBER Macroeconomics Annual conference, and at seminars at the Federal Reserve Board, the IMF, the Bank of Portugal, the San Francisco Federal Reserve Bank, the OFCE in Paris, the JRC in Ispra, the University of Glasgow, and the Sveriges Riksbank. We especially thank Mazi Kazemi, Patrick Moran, Aaron Markiewitz, and Sher Singh for providing excellent research assistance. The views expressed in this paper are solely the responsibility of the authors and should not be interpreted as reflecting the views of the Peterson Institute of International Economics, the Riksbank, or the Board of Governors of the Federal Reserve System or of any other person associated with the Federal Reserve System. For acknowledgments, sources of research support, and disclosure of the authors' material financial relationships, if any, please see http://www.nber.org/chapters/c13784.ack.

1. While our discussion here focuses on the desirability of fiscal expansion in a prolonged liquidity trap, it bears emphasizing that a core fiscal expansion could potentially be counterproductive if monetary policy had latitude to cut interest rates sufficiently. Indeed, the analysis of Gali and Monacelli (2008) suggests that it might be desirable to respond to a contraction in periphery demand by cutting core fiscal spending—thus better aligning business cycles within the CU—and then cutting interest rates aggressively. While the implication that core consolidation is desirable is perhaps somewhat model specific, the more general message that core fiscal expansion would not be desirable if monetary policy could do the lifting seems very reasonable.

2. This decomposition depends importantly on our assumption of a symmetric structure across countries, including in the calibration of structural parameters.

3. While our model also allows for discount factor shocks, these shocks have been omitted from the description of the log-linearized equations. The discount factor shock boosts consumption demand, but has no effect on potential output or labor supply.

4. As we discuss below, government-spending shocks affect output both through influencing the potential real interest rate and potential output.

5. This expression assumes that the government spending, consumption taste, and technology shocks all follow AR(1) processes with common persistence parameter ρ.

6. In terms of the model parameters, we have $\varepsilon_c = ([(1 + \rho_C)/\rho_C](2 - \omega_C^* - \omega_C) - 1)$ and $\varepsilon_g = ([(1 + \rho_G)/\rho_G](2 - \omega_G^* - \omega_G) - 1)$, where $(1 + \rho_C)/\rho_C$ is (the absolute value of) the price elasticity of demand between domestically produced and imported private consumption goods, and $(1 + \rho_G)/\rho_G$, the corresponding price elasticity of demand for government goods and services.

7. Because the price level immediately jumps in the core when government spending increases (while rising less or falling in the periphery), the rise in the price level *going forward* (i.e., long-run-expected inflation) must be higher in the periphery.

8. While this expression abstracts from habit for convenience, relative marginal cost also depends on lagged output gaps.

9. There is also an additional role for the terms of trade to affect marginal costs—captured by the middle term of equation (20)—which reflects that a terms of trade depreciation, by increasing home relative consumption, raises home relative marginal costs through a wealth effect on wages.

10. The parameter ϕ_{mc} captures the reduced-form sensitivity of marginal cost to the terms of trade gap. Even with habit persistence, the terms of trade can be represented as a function only of the terms-of-trade gap (as a third-order difference equation).

11. Moreover, given that we have solved for both aggregate CU variables and corresponding cross-country differences, country-specific variables may be solved for by the relevant identifies. For example, given that aggregate CU output is defined as $y_t^{CU} = \zeta y_{Dt} + \zeta^* y_{Dt}^*$, output of the home country may be solved for as $y_{Dt} = y_t^{CU} + (1 - \zeta) y_t^d$, where $y_t^d = y_{Dt} - y_{Dt}^*$; foreign output is given by $y_{Dt}^* = y_t^{CU} - \zeta y_t^d$.

12. A low Phillips curve slope in the same range also helps to yield plausible inflation responses in the model following a "Great Recession-sized" shock that generates a large and persistent output gap (as shown below).

13. The unemployment rate in the periphery remained in the high teens (levels typically associated with an economic depression) through most of the 2012–2014 period, over twice the unemployment rate in core economies.

14. The median estimates of the Phillips curve slope in empirical studies by, for example, Adolfson et al. (2005), Altig et al. (2011), Galí and Gertler (1999), Galí, Gertler, and López-Salido (2001), Lindé (2005), and Smets and Wouters (2003, 2007) are in this range. As we discuss in section VI, some recent estimates based on US data point to a very flat slope closer to our benchmark calibration.

15. This computation excludes their trade with each other (so as to effectively treat them as a single country as in the model).

16. If the ECB was unconstrained by the ZLB, the ECB would tighten policy in response to higher core spending, and the euro would appreciate; however, in a deep liquidity trap, the euro (and hence periphery exchange rate) could well depreciate as real interest rates declined.

17. The sizable disparity between the import share of consumption and that of GDP reflects that nearly a quarter of output is devoted to government spending.

18. The scale parameter on the consumption taste shock ν is set to 0.01 (this parameter is set to have a negligible impact on model dynamics).

19. Our model constrains the "local currency multiplier" to be less than unity (as the 1.5% of GDP rise in core spending relative to periphery spending causes core output to rise by less than 1.5%, relative to periphery output). The model of section VI includes hand-to-mouth agents that allow the local currency multiplier to be considerably larger and closer to the empirical estimates mentioned in section II.

20. Only about one quarter of the 1.5% "autonomous" shift in demand toward the core is offset by relative price changes after 10 quarters (the final quarter of the government-spending hike).

21. Recalling the discussion in section III, periphery consumption rises more than core consumption because periphery-expected inflation exceeds core inflation (given that core prices initially rise by more and that relative prices must converge in the long run).

22. The taste shock is assumed to follow a first-order autoregression with persistence of 0.9.

23. Moreover, under an independent monetary policy in the periphery, the periphery nominal and real exchange rate would depreciate immediately.

24. As Cogan et al. (2010) have pointed out, only around a third of the increased US federal spending on goods and services authorized by the American Reconstruction and Recovery Act was earmarked to be spent within the first two years of the ARRA's passage in February 2009.

25. Because the output expansion is more balanced across regions, there is less upward pressure on the terms of trade; hence, periphery inflation does not have to rise as much to bring relative prices back to their long-run equilibrium level. This smaller

rise in periphery-expected inflation translates into a smaller rise in periphery consumption.

26. This assumption would seem most reasonable to the extent that the additional stimulus is on goods for which there was considerable scope to substitute purchases intertemporally (e.g., construction or transport equipment).

27. The large-scale expansion of US fiscal spending authorized in 2009 under the ARRA was reasonably balanced across US states in per capita terms (Orr and Sporn 2012), notwithstanding that spending on some components of these programs (such as unemployment compensation) varied with regional economic conditions.

28. The effects of fiscal stimulus on output and inflation gaps analyzed below do not hinge on the particular type of shock(s) driving the output gap in the baseline. Other shocks, such as the productivity shocks z_t and z_t^*, would yield similar results if calibrated to imply the same evolution of the core and periphery output gaps as shown in figure 7 (i.e., both the positive effects would be similar, as well as the normative implications under the quadratic criterion). This invariance reflects the tight link between output gaps and inflation in our benchmark model, and would not obtain if there were features such as wage rigidities that implied trade-offs. It is important to note that the welfare results under the utility-based criterion considered in section B do depend somewhat on the nature of the shocks driving the output and inflation gaps, reflecting that welfare depends on the evolution of consumption and other variables; however, we found that experimenting with different underlying shocks had relatively little effect on our results (provided that the alternative shocks implied similar output gap and inflation responses).

29. The output gaps in the baseline are broadly similar—albeit somewhat smaller—to those forecast by the OECD in its interim economic outlook that was released in March 2015 (for example, the OECD projects that the output gap in the euro area will be about 3% in 2015, compared with 2.5% in our baseline and almost 6% in the periphery, compared with 4% in our baseline). The large and persistent output gaps in the baseline in turn imply considerable downward pressure on inflation, notwithstanding that Phillips curve slope is very flat under our baseline calibration; under more typical calibrations of Phillips curve slope used in the literature, the decline in inflation would be even sharper.

30. We assume in our simulations below that the CU central bank does not counteract the core fiscal stimulus by raising rates any earlier than in the absence of stimulus. This limited form of commitment modestly amplifies the stimulus from the fiscal expansion. Upon exit policy rates follow the Taylor rule, and thus eventually react to the higher demand caused by the fiscal expansion.

31. As is clear from previous work by Galí and Monacelli (2008), it would not be optimal to close output or inflation gaps in each member state if there were some costs of expanding government spending (at least beyond a certain level). First, it would be essential to balance any direct fiscal costs against the benefits of reducing output (and inflation) gaps. Second, the optimal policy would also take account of how current increases in government spending affected the terms of trade and hence future output (and inflation) gaps. In particular, higher periphery government spending would boost periphery-relative prices and thus tend to hurt periphery net exports in the future. Because the optimal policy would take account of both the direct fiscal costs and the loss in future competitiveness, it would not be optimal to close the periphery output gap completely (and similarly for the core).

32. The optimal spending hike under fiscal union is 2.5% of CU GDP, while the optimal hike for the core-only case is 3.1% of core GDP, which is equal to 2.1% of CU GDP. Under an optimally sized fiscal expansion, the welfare gain to the CU is 18.0 under fiscal union, compared with 14.9 under the core-only expansion.

33. If a sizable share of the rise in core government spending fell on periphery imports, then a rise in core government spending would boost periphery GDP and welfare even in a short-lived liquidity trap, at least under this ad hoc welfare metric.

34. To perform this welfare analysis, we assume that households regard government spending on goods and services as somewhat more substitutable through time than private consumption, and that habit persistence is somewhat lower (specifically, we set $\sigma_G = 2$, so that the elasticity of substitution is 2, and the habit persistence parameter $\varkappa_G = 0.4$). Finally,

we set ϑ_G to account for a steady share of government consumption to output of .23, and χ_0 so that N (hours worked per capita) equals unity in the steady state.

35. Thus, the figure shows the deviation between the responses that include a rise in core government spending (layered onto the baseline) and the baseline.

36. Given the complications posed by the zero lower bound constraint and possible changes in the transmission of monetary and fiscal shocks following the global financial crisis, we limit the sample for our VAR analysis to the pre-crisis period.

37. The innovation to government spending is less than a tenth as large, about 0.4%.

38. The estimated impulse responses do not seem particularly sensitive to shortening the sample period (i.e., starting in the early 1980s), nor to adopting a more parsimonious specification of the VAR.

39. Because Keynesian households are assumed to own no capital in our model (and hence have much lower steady state income than forward-looking households), their share of aggregate consumption is much lower than their population share.

40. While the implied contract duration is extremely long, it is important to mention that our model does not embed firm-specific capital or other real rigidities that could help it account for the low reduced-form slope with a much shorter implied contract duration (corresponding to a significantly lower value of ξ_p).

41. On the other hand, some recent evidence based on US data also finds a very low Phillips curve slope. Brave et al. (2012) estimated the Chicago Federal Reserve's DSGE model of the United States over the 1989:1–2011:4 period, and found a Phillips curve slope of only 0.002. Lindé, Smets, and Wouters (2016) estimated a Phillips curve slope of 0.005 (identical to our estimate for the euro area), and the estimate of Del Negro, Giannoni and Schorfheide (2015) is similar.

42. The lower right panel of figure 10 shows the response of consumption in the first few quarters following the government-spending hike—and omits confidence intervals— in order to highlight the initial consumption rise.

43. Recall from section II that this literature aims to estimate how a differential rise in government spending in one region "A" versus another region "B" affects relative output levels.

44. Nakamura and Steinsson (2014) also emphasize that a simple model that embeds separable preferences as in section III generates far too low a local multiplier, and propose nonseparable preferences as a mechanism for generating a larger local multiplier (in contrast with our focus on Keynesian multiplier and accelerator channels).

45. Specifically, we assume that the ECB reaction function puts a substantial weight on the output gap of unity. This choice helps account for a protracted liquidity trap in the baseline, and also implies monetary policy "forbearance" in not reacting to the large fiscal stimulus program we consider. More broadly, it seems reasonable to characterize ECB monetary policy as putting a fairly large weight on the output gap as well as the inflation gap in the period following the intensification of the euro-area debt crisis in 2011. In particular, the ECB put more emphasis on the output gap in its communication about monetary policy, and left policy rates low in 2012–2013 even though inflation ran only modestly below 2%.

46. On the other hand, McKay, Nakamura, and Steinsson (2015) argue that taking account of borrowing constraints and uninsurable income risk may imply a somewhat lower interest elasticity of demand than implied by models that assume that financial markets are complete at the national level. A lower-interest elasticity would damp the fiscal multiplier in a liquidity trap.

47. While our description of the benchmark model allows for exogenous taxes on consumption and labor income, we abstract from these features in section III (by setting these tax rates equal to zero at all times).

48. We define $\xi_{t,t+j}$ to be the price in period t of a claim that pays one dollar if the specified state occurs in period $t + j$ (see the household problem below); then the corresponding element of $\psi_{t,t+j}$ equals $\xi_{t,t+j}$ divided by the probability that the specified state will occur.

49. Thus, the larger-scale model constrains the import share of government consumption to equal that of private consumption.

50. Government spending is assumed to fall exclusively on consumption, so that all investment is private investment.

51. For simplicity, we assume that μ_0 is sufficiently small that changes in the monetary base have a negligible impact on equilibrium allocations, at least to the first-order approximation we consider.

52. The domestic contingent claims B_{Dt+1} are in zero net supply from the standpoint of home economy as a whole.

53. Given that the central bank uses the nominal interest rate as its policy instrument, the level of seigniorage is determined by nominal money demand.

54. When we simulate the effects of higher spending in sections VI.C and VI.D, we instead assume that spending follows an MA(12) process, that is, $g_t - g = \Sigma_{s=0}^{11} \varepsilon_{g,t-s}$.

55. We follow Christiano et al. (2008) by assuming that the debt contract between entrepreneurs and banks is written in nominal terms (rather than real terms as in Bernanke et al. [1999]). For further details about the setup, see Bernanke et al. (1999) and Christiano et al. (2008). An excellent exposition is also provided in Christiano, Trabandt, and Walentin (2007).

56. In future work, it would be of interest to solve the model in a fully nonlinear form.

57. Given strategic complementarities in wage setting, the wage markup influences the slope of the wage Phillips curve.

References

Acconcia, Antonio, Giancarlo Corsetti, and Saverio Simonelli. 2014. "Mafia and Public Spending: Evidence on the Fiscal Multiplier from a Quasi-Experiment." *American Economic Review* 104 (7): 2185–209.

Adolfson, Malin, Stefan Laséen, Jesper Lindé, and Mattias Villani. 2005. "The Role of Sticky Prices in an Open Economy DSGE Model: A Bayesian Investigation." *Journal of the European Economic Association Papers and Proceedings* 3 (2-3): 444–57.

Alesina, Alberto and Silvia Ardagna. 2010. "Large Changes in Fiscal Policy: Taxes vs. Spending." In *Tax Policy in the Economy*, ed. Jeffrey Brown, 35–68. Chicago: University of Chicago Press.

Almunia, Miguel, Augustin Bénétrix, Barry Eichengreen, Kevin O'Rourke, Gisela Rua, Silvana Tenreyro, and Fabrizio Perri. 2010. "From Great Depression to Great Credit Crisis: Similarities, Differences, and Lessons," In *Economic Policy* 62, ed. G. De Ménil, R. Portes, and H.-W. Sinn. Chichester, UK: John Wiley & Sons.

Altig, David, Lawrence J. Christiano, Martin Eichenbaum, and Jesper Lindé. 2011. "Firm-Specific Capital, Nominal Rigidities and the Business Cycle." *Review of Economic Dynamics* 14 (2): 225–47.

Anderson, Gary, and George Moore. 1985. "A Linear Algebraic Procedure for Solving Linear Perfect Foresight Models." *Economics Letters* 17 (3): 247–52.

Angeloni, Ignazio, Anil K. Kashyap, Benoit Mojon, and Daniele Terlizzese. 2003. "The Output Composition Puzzle: A Difference in the Monetary Transmission Mechanism in the Euro Area and U.S." *Journal of Money, Credit, and Banking* 35:1265–306.

Auerbach, Alan J., and Yuriy Gorodnichenko. 2012. "Measuring the Output Responses to Fiscal Policy." *American Economic Journal: Economic Policy* 4 (2): 1–27.

Bernanke, Ben, Mark Gertler, and Simon Gilchrist. 1999. "The Financial Accelerator in a Quantitative Business Cycle Framework." In *Handbook of Macroeconomics*, ed. John B. Taylor and Michael Woodford. Amsterdam: North-Holland Elsevier Science.

Beetsma, Roel, Massimo Giuliodori, and Franc Klaassen. 2006. "Trade Spill-Overs of Fiscal Policy in the European Union: A Panel Analysis." *Economic Policy* 21 (48): 639–87.

Blanchard, Olivier, Eugenio Cerutti, and Lawrence Summers. 2015. "Inflation and Activity—Two Explorations and their Monetary Policy Implications." IMF Working Paper no. 15-230, November.

Blanchard, Olivier, and Charles Kahn. 1980. "The Solution of Linear Difference Models under Rational Expectations." *Econometrica* 48:1305–11.

Blanchard, Olivier, and Daniel Leigh. 2014. "Learning about Fiscal Multipliers from Growth Forecast Errors." *IMF Economic Review* 62 (2): 179–212.

Blanchard, Olivier, and Roberto Perotti. 2002. "An Empirical Characterization of the Dynamic Effects of Changes in Government Spending and Taxes on Output." *Quarterly Journal of Economics* 117 (4): 1329–68.

Brave, Scott, Jeffrey Campbell, Jonas Fisher, and Alejandro Justiniano. 2012. "The Chicago Fed DSGE Model." Federal Reserve Bank of Chicago Working Paper no. 2012-02, August.

Calvo, Guillermo. 1983. "Staggered Prices in a Utility Maximizing Framework." *Journal of Monetary Economics* 12:383–98.

Christiano, Lawrence J., Martin Eichenbaum, and Charles Evans. 2005. "Nominal Rigidities and the Dynamic Effects of a Shock to Monetary Policy." *Journal of Political Economy* 113 (1): 1–45.

Christiano, Lawrence J., Martin Eichenbaum, and Sergio Rebelo. 2011. "When is the Government Spending Multiplier Large?" *Journal of Political Economy* 119 (1): 78–121.

Christiano, Lawrence J., Martin Eichenbaum, and Mathias Trabandt. 2015. "Understanding the Great Recession." *American Economic Journal: Macroeconomics* 7 (1): 110–67.

Christiano, Lawrence J., Roberto Motto, and Massimo Rostagno. 2008. "Shocks, Structures or Monetary Policies? The Euro Area and the US after 2001." *Journal of Economic Dynamics and Control* 32 (8): 2476–506.

Christiano, Lawrence J., Mathias Trabandt, and Karl Walentin. 2007. "Introducing Financial Frictions and Unemployment into a Small Open Economy Model." Sveriges Riksbank (Central Bank of Sweden) Working Paper Series no. 214. http://www.riksbank.se/en/.

Cogan, John F., Tobias Cwik, John B. Taylor, and Volker Wieland. 2010. "New Keynesian versus Old Keynesian Government Spending Multipliers." *Journal of Economic Dynamics and Control* 34:281–95.

Cole, Harold, and Maurice Obstfeld. 1991. "Commodity Trade and International Risk Sharing: How Much Do Financial Markets Matter?" *Journal of Monetary Economics* 28 (1): 3–24.

Cook, David, and Michael B. Devereux. 2011. "Optimal Fiscal Policy in a World Liquidity Trap" *European Economic Review* 55 (2): 443–62.

Del Negro, Marco, Marc P. Giannoni, and Frank Schorfheide. 2015. "Inflation in the Great Recession and New Keynesian Models." *American Economic Journal: Macroeconomics* 7 (1): 168–96.

Drautzburg, Thorsten, and Harald Uhlig. 2015. "Fiscal Stimulus and Distortionary Taxation." *Review of Economic Dynamics* 18 (4): 894–920.

Eggertsson, Gauti. 2011. "What Fiscal Policy is Effective at Zero Interest Rates?" *NBER Macroeconomics Annual 2010*, vol. 25, ed. D. Acemoglu and M. Woodford, 59–112. Chicago: University of Chicago Press.

Eggertsson, Gauti, and Michael Woodford. 2003. "The Zero Interest-Rate Bound and Optimal Monetary Policy." *Brookings Papers on Economic Activity* 1:139–211.
Erceg, Christopher J., Dale W. Henderson, and Andrew T. Levin. 2000. "Optimal Monetary Policy with Staggered Wage and Price Contracts." *Journal of Monetary Economics* 46:281–313.
Erceg, Christopher, and Jesper Lindé. 2013. "Fiscal Consolidation in a Currency Union: Spending Cuts vs. Tax Hikes." *Journal of Economic Dynamics and Control* 37: 422–45.
———. 2014. "Is there a Fiscal Free Lunch in a Liquidity Trap?" *Journal of the European Economic Association* 12 (1): 73–107.
Farhi, Emmanuel, and Ivan Werning. 2012. "Fiscal Multipliers: Liquidity Traps and Currency Unions." Manuscript, Harvard University.
Fujiwari, Ippei, and Kozo Ueda. 2013. "The Fiscal Multiplier and Spillover in a Global Liquidity Trap." *Journal of Economic Dynamics and Control* 37:1264–83.
Galí, Jordi, and Mark Gertler. 1999. "Inflation Dynamics: A Structural Econometric Analysis." *Journal of Monetary Economics* 44:195–220.
Galí, Jordi, Mark Gertler, and David López-Salido. 2001. "European Inflation Dynamics." *European Economic Review* 45:1237–1270.
Galí, Jordi, David López-Salido, and Javier Vallés. 2007. "Understanding the Effects of Government Spending on Consumption." *Journal of the European Economic Association* 5 (1): 227–70.
Galí, Jordi, and Tommaso Monacelli. 2008. "Optimal Monetary and Fiscal Policy in a Currency Union." *Journal of International Economics* 76:116–32.
Gilchrist, Simon, Raphael Schoenle, Jae Sim, and Egon Zakrajšek. 2015. "Inflation Dynamics during the Financial Crisis." Finance and Economic Discussion Series Paper no. 2015-012, Board of Governors of the Federal Reserve System, March.
Gordon, Robert, and Robert Krenn. 2010. "The End of the Great Depression 1939–41: Policy Contributions and Fiscal Multipliers." NBER Working Paper no. 16380, Cambridge, MA.
Guajardo, Jaime, Daniel Leigh, and Andrea Pescatori. 2014. "Expansionary Austerity: International Evidence." *Journal of the European Economic Association* 12 (4): 949–68.
Hebden, James, Jesper Lindé, and Lars E. O. Svensson. 2009. "Optimal Monetary Policy in the Hybrid New Keynesian Model under the Zero Lower Bound Constraint." Photocopy, Federal Reserve Board and Sveriges Riksbank (Central Bank of Sweden).
Kollmann, Robert, Marco Ratto, Werner Roeger, and Lukas Vogel. 2014. "What Drives the German Current Account? And How Does It Affect Other EU Member States?" *Economic Policy* 30 (81): 47–93.
Lindé, Jesper. 2005. "Estimating New Keynesian Phillips Curves: A Full Information Maximum Likelihood Approach" *Journal of Monetary Economics* 52 (6): 1135–49.
Lindé, Jesper, Frank Smets, and Raf Wouters. 2016. "Challenges for Central Banks' Macro Models." Riksbank Research Paper Series no. 147, May.
Mankiw, N. Gregory, and Ricardo Reis. 2002. "Sticky Information versus Sticky Prices: A Proposal to Replace the New Keynesian Phillips Curve." *Quarterly Journal of Economics* 117 (4): 1295–328.
McKay, Alisdair, Emi Nakumura, and Jon Steinsson. 2015. "The Power of Forward Guidance Revisited." Manuscript, Columbia University.

182

Blanchard, Erceg, and Lindé

Nakamura, Emi, and Jón Steinsson. 2014. "Fiscal Stimulus in a Monetary Union: Evidence from US Regions." *American Economic Review* 104 (3): 753–92.

Orr, James, and John Sporn. 2012. "The American Recovery and Reinvestment Act of 2009: A Review of Stimulus Spending in New York and New Jersey." *Current Issues in Economics and Finance* 18 (6): 1–12.

Perotti, Roberto. 2007. "In Search of the Transmission Mechanism of Fiscal Policy." In *NBER Macroeconomics Annual*, vol. 22, ed. D. Acemoglu, K. Rogoff, and M. Woodford, 169–226. Chicago: University of Chicago Press.

Romer, Christina, and David Romer. 2010. "The Macroeconomic Effects of Tax Changes: Estimates Based on New Measures of Fiscal Shocks." *American Economic Review* 100 (3): 763–801.

Rotemberg, Julio, and Michael Woodford. 1997. "An Optimization-Based Econometric Framework for the Evaluation of Monetary Policy." In *NBER Macroeconomics Annual*, vol. 12, ed. Ben S. Bernanke and Julio Rotemberg. Cambridge, MA: MIT Press.

Smets, Frank, and Raf Wouters. 2003. "An Estimated Stochastic Dynamic General Equilibrium Model of the Euro Area." *Journal of the European Economic Association* 1 (5): 1123–75.

———. 2007. "Shocks and Frictions in US Business Cycles: A Bayesian DSGE Approach." *American Economic Review* 97 (3): 586–606.

Turnovsky, Stephen J. 1985. "Domestic and foreign disturbances in an optimizing model of exchange-rate determination." *Journal of International Money and Finance* 4 (1): 151–171.

Uhlig, Harald. 2010. "Some Fiscal Calculus." *American Economic Review Papers and Proceedings* 100 (2): 30–34.

Wieland, Volker. 1996. "Monetary Policy Targets and the Stabilization Objective: A Source of Tension within the EMS." *Journal of International Money and Finance* 15 (1): 95–116.

Woodford, Michael. 2011. "Simple Analytics of the Government Expenditure Multiplier." *American Economic Journal: Macroeconomics* 3 (1): 1–35.

Yun, Tack. 1996. "Nominal Price Rigidity, Money Supply Endogeneity, and Business Cycles." *Journal of Monetary Economics* 37:345–370.

Comment

Harald Uhlig, *University of Chicago, NBER, and CEPR*

Introduction

This paper is written as a contribution to the science of economics, and it is a beautiful contribution indeed. But let's not mince words. While the paper does not make a policy recommendation per se, it nonetheless seems to me quite plausible that readers will cite that analysis as lending strong support for the perspective that Germany ought to rescue Greece and other euro-zone countries in economic troubles, per substantially increasing its own fiscal spending. Allow me to add some additional bits of analysis of my own. While I shall not make any policy recommendation per se, either, it may then be plausible that readers of both pieces end up more sceptical regarding that rescue recommendation than if they just read the fine paper by Blanchard, Erceg, and Lindé.

Even while news has shifted to other topics, the Eurozone crisis of 2010 still lingers on. Indeed, and in many ways, we have not escaped it yet. Things are dire and far from well. Unemployment rates in Greece and Spain, say, are still ridiculously high. The Italian banking system is fragile. Good policy solutions are sorely needed. So, what to do? Are the Germany-proposed "austerity" measures the right approach? Or should one follow recommendations more in line with the views of the former Greek finance minister Varoufakis and plead for deficit spending and Keynesian multipliers? The simplest version of that route would be to have, say, Greece do lots of fiscal spending itself, bankrolled by Germany and other Eurozone members. Clearly, these proposals did not go far, politically.

This paper makes a substantial contribution to this debate, using a variety of models and analyses to shed light on the key issues. As such,

it is a sorely needed, surely welcome, thoughtful, and insightful addition. Allow me to put it that way. The policy solution considered here
is a new variant of the more-fiscal-spending approach and argues that
Germany should directly do that fiscal spending. Indeed, why reroute
those resources via Greece? Sure, the Greek government would presumably spend most of its resources on Greek goods and services,
where that spending would plausibly do the greatest amount of good
for the Greek economy, but obviously, the German government could
do just the same. In the language of the paper, and in section V.B, this
is stated as follows: "Larger welfare improvements could be achieved
by channeling relatively more of the fiscal stimulus to the periphery."
Sure, it is nice to see that the paper delivers this conclusion also formally. Perhaps the German government could choose a slightly different spending pattern. Any Germans out there in favor of free vacations
in Greece, courtesy of the German government? Perhaps that would
be easier to sell politically in Germany. But, overall, it still feels like the
conventional recipe of doing more spending in Greece, bankrolled by
the German government.

So what, exactly, does the paper do? It is a very well-crafted exercise
of examining fiscal stimulus at the zero lower bound in a two-country
version of the well-researched, much-liked, but also much-maligned
three-equation New Keynesian model. This is very mainstream these
days, and these authors provide a nice addition. The analysis is com-
plemented with a welfare analysis, with VAR evidence on monetary
and fiscal shocks, and more a complete medium-scale New Keynesian
model with capital, and so forth. I highly recommend it to any student
or researcher, who wishes to read and learn a good benchmark model
in that literature, and see how to extract results and insights. The paper
is ambitious, thoughtful, informative, lucid, and full of interesting results and detail reflecting a large amount of work. Once one buys into
the approach, one can only applaud the authors in what they deliver in
this paper.

Welfare Comparisons

The paper is also remarkably honest. It provides a welfare evaluation
of a particular policy proposal, first using an ad hoc welfare function.
With that, the advantages of the fiscal expansion are quite substantial.
Many authors might have stopped there, satisfied with the result. But
the paper also provides an evaluation based on the full calculation of

the discounted expected utility of the representative household in each member state. It provides a detailed and lucid discussion of the rather intricate channels of how the policy affects the welfare in the various countries. It finds in section V.B, for example, that "an expansion of core spending causes periphery welfare to deteriorate considerably" *and admits that* "these results differ dramatically from the implications of the ad hoc loss function in which the higher import content was a major plus for welfare in both CU members." That is not the result the authors had hoped for, I guess. After looking at these sobering results from a number of angles (some of which help to hide or ignore some of the less benign impacts of these policies), the authors remarkably conclude that "our sense is that the welfare benefits . . . probably lie between the two measures, but tilt more in the direction suggested by the simple ad hoc loss function." The authors are entitled to their assessment, of course. If you are convinced by that, wonderful. I personally feel more enamored by a model-consistent analysis including the welfare calculations. Otherwise, one has to wonder whether there is any model out there for which some ad hoc loss function would not deliver some given policy conclusion. I shall admit that theirs does not look entirely unreasonable, but still. The authors provide a careful discussion of these various measures and channels, and for readers like me, who are more inclined to trust results based on a consistent anlysis, it offers plenty of reasons to remain skeptical about the benefits of German fiscal spending to rescue Greece.

Paradigm Skepticism

Now, these skeptical conclusions are already available, conditional on the paradigm offered in the paper. Their paradigm is mainstream; it is in much use. But can one trust it enough to deliver sufficiently reliable policy advice? I believe that it is good to have it as one of the tools out there, that its conclusions and mechanisms are worth studying with sufficient care, but that any policy conclusions should be met with a considerable dose of skepticism. Allow me to elaborate my reasons.

The Phillips Cloud

At the heart of the New Keynesian approach is the Phillips curve and its relationship between inflation and the output gap, pronounced to be reliable enough as a basis for policy interventions. But how much of a Phillips curve is really there, in the data? The New Keynesian models typically use a version of

$$\pi_t = \beta E_t[\pi_{t+1}] + \kappa x_t + \varepsilon_t,$$

where π_t is inflation from $t-1$ to t, x_t is a measure of the output gap, κ is a coefficient, and ε_t is a disturbance term. The output gap is a measure of the (lack of) slack in the economy, and it may not be unreasonable to think of it as the negative of the unemployment rate, for example. The classic version of the Phillips curve is

$$\pi_t = \kappa x_t + \varepsilon_t,$$

leaving away that expectation term. There is a bit of a sleight of hand in much in that literature, in terms of deciding which term belongs on the left-hand side of the equation and which on the right-hand side. Econometricians may demand that the error term should be orthogonal to the right-hand side variable, and that may be the most benign interpretation for the reasons of writing the equations as stated. In section III.A the paper never introduces such error terms, though, which renders that reasoning mute and, in my view, a bit more honest. For example, one can rewrite the classic version of the Phillips curve equivalently as:

$$x_t = \frac{1}{\kappa}\pi_t - \frac{1}{\kappa}\varepsilon_t.$$

Now, the Phillips curve becomes the policy menu that spooks around in so many policy debates: create a bit more inflation on the right to get a bit more x_t and thus, say, a little less unemployment on the left. Conversely, the version of the equation stated previously create the monetary-fiscal interaction: a bit more x_t, say through fiscal spending, may trigger higher inflation and, in turn, through the Taylor-rule-type reaction function of the central bank, result in higher interest rates. At the zero lower bound, the central bank interest rate is too high to begin with, though, so higher inflation leaves nominal interest rates unchanged, lowering real rates instead. These lower real rates then in turn help to improve the economy, as expressed by some version of the IS equation. Put differently, fiscal stimulus may improve the economy, if one is able to ride the Phillips curve to higher inflation, lower real interest rates, and lower unemployment.

If I did not succeed in stating all this sufficiently well, I shall leave it to others to explain this reasoning in a more sensible manner (if it can

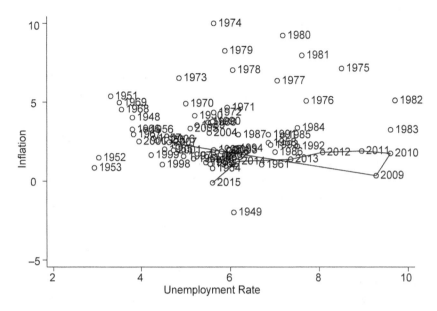

Fig. 1. The Phillips cloud

Source: The BLS and BEA.

Note: GDP deflator, annualized, average percentange change.

be done). Here, instead, I wish to ask: Is there a Phillips curve at all? Put differently, is there a clearly discernible relationship between, say, unemployment and inflation or would the search for such a relationship mainly have to point to the noise component and ε_t? If it is the latter, then the key mechanisms at the heart of the New Keynesian approach have little to do with the forces driving inflation in the data. I submit that this should lead any sensible person to question whether we are barking up the right tree here.

I fear things do not look well for the New Keynesian approach. The classic Phillips curve relationship is shown in figure 1. Let me give this relationship a more appropriate name and call it the "Phillips cloud" instead; certainly, that is what it looks to me. Fiscal stimulus ends up poking around in that cloud rather than riding a curve. Sure, there is no correction for the expectation term, as demanded by the New Keynesian version, and one can torture the data in sufficient ways to make it cough up a more visible downward sloping line. Alternatively, one may be encouraged to search for more trustworthy relationships elsewhere. I feel that this will be more productive.

Causal Interpretations of Equations

Indeed, let us talk about the causal interpretations of equations a bit more. The paper here follows the well-trodden path of many papers in that literature, so it is hard to fault the authors. As an example, consider their equation

$$y_{Dt} - y_{Dt}^* = g_y(1 - \omega_g - \omega_g^*)(g_t - g_t^*) + \varepsilon \tau_t + c_y(1 - \omega_c - \omega_c^*)(c_t - c_t^*),$$

which the authors then read as stating that "home relative output . . . depends on three factors—home relative government spending, the terms of trade, and home relative consumption." One should bear in mind, though, that one could also write this equation as:

$$c_t - c_t^* = \frac{1}{c_y(1 - \omega_c - \omega_c^*)} (g_y(1 - \omega_g - \omega_g^*)(g_t - g_t^*) + \varepsilon \tau_t - y_{Dt} - y_{Dt}^*).$$

Now, home relative consumption seems to depend on the stuff on the right-hand side. Which causal interpretation is correct? In the absence of stochastic shocks and the ability to then sort the variables in some causal way, I believe that one ought to regard these variables to simply obey a simultaneous system of equation. There is no sense in which the left-hand side of some equation "depends" on the right-hand side. Statements such as the one just cited may be helpful, on occasion, for building intuition, and I applaud the authors for trying to give the readers a helping hand here. It is important to keep in mind, though, that these are ultimately arbitrary interpretations of the equations and that they can be highly misleading.

Price and Wage Markup Shocks Are the New Keynesian Explanation for Inflation

Even if one looks at the data through a perfectly mainstream New Keynesian model, the economic forces on inflation at the center of the fiscal-spending mechanism in this paper and elsewhere in the New Keynesian literature do not really want to show up. In Fratto and Uhlig (2014), we use the standard and well-known Smets and Wouters (2007) model to account for the movements in inflation. This is meant to address the lack-of-deflation puzzle for the postcrisis years, which a number of authors have raised. It turns out that price and wage markup shocks alone account for nearly the entire movement of inflation for the entire sample period and not just postcrisis, and that these shocks account for

very little else. In essence, this benchmark New Keynesian model implies
that inflation is marching to its own drummer. If anything, the postcrisis
developments are slightly better news for the New Keynesian plumbing: there, the zero lower bound and the resulting tightness of monetary
policy has at least a small depressing effect on inflation, counteracted by
positive markup shocks to produce the slightly positive inflation that we
see. One can be happy with that reading of the data, or one can feel rather
uncomfortable with our lack of a deeper understanding of inflation and
call for a new paradigm, as Hall (2011) has done. Either way, the idea
that the relationship between fiscal spending and inflation is really crucial seems far fetched, and the New Keynesian paradigm seems to be of
little practical help here. But this relationship and the ensuing impact on
monetary policy, depending on whether it is at the zero lower bound or
not, is at much of the heart of the New Keynesian fiscal stimulus debate.

New Keynesian Models Are Discontinuous

This paper, along with much of the New Keynesian literature on fiscal
stimulus at the zero lower bound, essentially examines the following
model stated in Cochrane (2015) and building on the beautiful analysis
by Werning (2011). Werning's (2011) and then Cochrane's (2015) model
is a continuous time perfect foresight simplified New Keynesian model,
in which a liquidity trap lasts until some period T in the future. After-
ward, the Taylor rule works again and instantaneously: assuming away
shocks and output gap dynamics, $\pi_t \equiv 0$ for $t > T$. During the liquidity
trap, the dynamics are described by

$$\dot{x}_t = -\sigma^{-1}(r_t + \pi_t)$$

$$\dot{\pi}_t = \rho\pi_t - \kappa(x_t + g_t),$$

where x_t is the output gap, π_t is inflation, and g_t is government spending.
The beauty of the approach by Werning (2011) is that one can now characterize the dynamics exactly. Cochrane (2015) then shows what happens as stickiness of prices is driven to zero (see figure 2 taken from his
paper). As stickiness disappears, the reaction of the economy explodes:
in particular, the fiscal multiplier diverges to infinity. Now, clearly something is wrong here. It surely cannot be right that one can enjoy fiscal
multipliers way above 100 for a year or two, while the economy is stuck
at the zero lower bound, but prices are nearly completely flexible.
Should one then doubt the fiscal multipliers that emerge from this calcu-

lus, when price stickiness is calibrated to more conventional values? One may wish to argue that the model shown above or the model analyzed in Blanchard, Erceg, and Lindé is a local linear approximation at that point, and that there is no reason to expect this local linear approximation to work well when prices are nearly not sticky at all. As researchers analyzing a model at hand, that may be a perfectly fine defense, but as a guide to policymakers, robustness checks and understanding parameter variations are paramount. For that, it is important to understand what the model has to say, as the parameters gradually approach the frictionless limit. Let's just all agree that figure 2 may be the right answer mathematically, but cannot be the right answer for a policymaker interested in practical advice. So then, what is the right answer for the latter? If we do not have a good answer, shouldn't we then feel a bit uncomfortable with the recommendations emerging from the parameter configuration at hand? I, for one, believe we should indeed.

Real Interest Rates, Policy Uncertainty, and Price Stickiness

Let me dig a bit deeper into the economics of the New Keynesian pro-fiscal stimulus arguments, as in the paper at hand. The starting point is that real interest rates are too high due to zero lower bound considerations. Fiscal stimulus will then lower them by encouraging higher inflation. Lower real interest rates mean that households and firms get to borrow at lower real rates, stimulating the economy.

So let us pause for a moment: Does this argument sound right? It is my impression that safe real rates are really low right now in the Eurozone. Inflation is still somewhat positive, while long-term nominal interest rates on German bunds have fallen to near zero, and some short-term nominal rates are even negative. Real interest rates are negative in the Eurozone. Seriously, shouldn't safe borrowers be in heaven? Conversely, if real rates that low are not doing the trick, how much lower do they need to be? And why would anyone put an iota of confidence in the argument that additional fiscal stimulus, through its effect of inflation, can get them there? My impression, rather, is that many firms do not borrow due to the uncertainty of the policy environment, or that they can borrow only at high rates due to various risk premia charged by their banks. Or, perhaps, some version of secular stagnation makes firms not want to borrow at all.

With lots of optimism and belief in New Keynesian plumbing, fiscal stimulus may move that base rate via that cloudy inflation-output-gap trade-off discussed above. But, surely, this is second order to the bigger

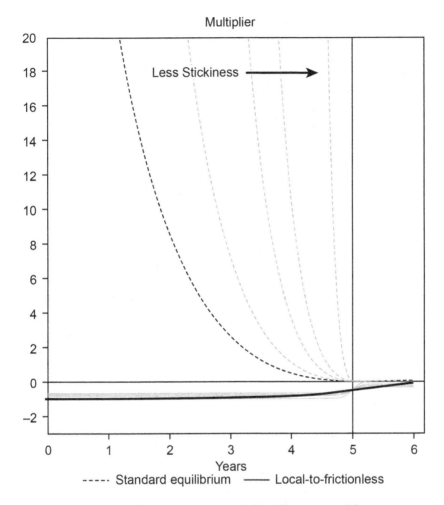

Fig. 2. Cochrane's discontinuity in New Keynesian models

problems that these firms are facing. But then why do so much heavy lifting and investment of political capital to focus on fiscal stimulus? It may be better to focus policy attention elsewhere, instead. It may help, for example, to reduce policy uncertainty. The Brexit instead created political uncertainty. Just that one decision appears to have a much larger impact on the Eurozone economy than any German fiscal stimulus possibly could. On the contrary: German fiscal stimulus debates may even create more, rather than less, harmful uncertainty. Let's start worrying about what matters!

The formulation of price stickiness is crucial. The most widely used assumption in the New Keynesian model is Calvo stickiness, where firms are allowed to change their price with some probability in any given period, or have to keep it constant (or indexed) otherwise. This results in a beautifully simple and elegant analysis. However, there is lots of evidence that price changes are state dependent instead (see, e.g., the research by Nakamura et al. [2016] or Alvarez, Lippi, and Passadore [2016], in this volume), as well as the New Keynesian skepticism by Nekarda and Ramey [2013]). Given their fine research, we ought to rely on these approaches to understand what happens in deep depressions or in the face of large fiscal interventions. With deep depressions, for example, it is a bit far fetched to believe that firms stubbornly stick to prices that they chose a long time ago, when everything was rosy. Whatever are their menu costs for changing prices, they will surely be swamped by the advantages of doing so in these situations. Now, granted, the situation in Greece, in Spain, and elsewhere is dire. We need to understand it, and we need to develop sensible policy options. I just find it hard to fathom that stubbornness to stick to prices chosen in good times long gone really is the root problem, and policy interventions that seek to remedy that particular problem may end up chasing ghosts and risk doing more harm than good.

VARs: The Inflation Response

A short remark on the empirical VAR evidence is in order. Figure 3 shows the impulse response of prices to a monetary tightening, as well as fiscal stimulus. The response to a monetary tightening exhibits a substantial price puzzle. As a consequence, I am doubtful that theirs really is a monetary policy shock. I feel there are better ways to proceed: sign restrictions as in Uhlig (2005), say, or various high-frequency approaches currently popular in the literature. I applaud the authors, though, for connecting their theory up to the time series evidence. This is not routinely done in the literature, but I feel it often should be.

Evidence on Fiscal Multipliers

This paper proposes fiscal expansion to address the challenges in Europe. How successful might that be? In any case, what is the empirical evidence? Quite a bit of current research has gone into addressing these issues, with mixed and murky results (see, e.g., Blanchard and Perotti

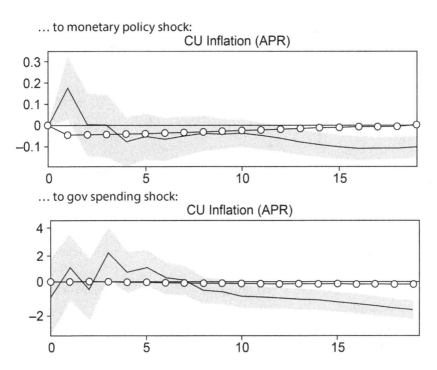

Fig. 3.   The price impulse response to a monetary tightening and a government spending shock

Note: Note the increase in the price level following a presumed surprise monetary tightening, that is, note the price puzzle arizing from the identification used by the authors.

[2002]; Mountford and Uhlig [2009]; Barro and Redlick [2011]; Ramey [2011]; Auerbach and Gorodnichenko [2012]; Namakumara and Steinsson [2014]; Ramey and Zubairy [2015]; and the discussion and survey by Whalen and Reichling [2015]). It may not be surprising that it is hard to settle these issues decisively, using time series analysis alone. For my taste, I find the analysis of Ramey (2011) and Ramey and Zubairy (2015) and therefore their results to be the most convincing. In a nutshell, they find positive but rather modest fiscal multipliers, even during episodes characterized by a version of a liquidity trap. These empirical multipliers ought to be compared to the core multipliers, calculated in the paper at hand. The zero lower bound moves these core multipliers, with the periphery multiplier staying at a practically constant distance below them (see figure 4). So, if the core multipliers are low, as the empirical evidence suggests, the periphery multipliers are even lower. These results present a further challenge in convincing a skeptic that fiscal

194

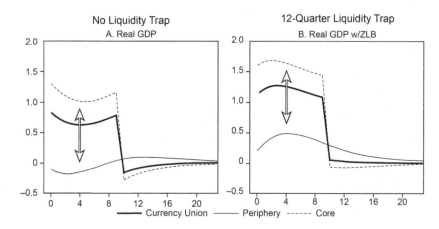

Fig. 4. Core and periphery fiscal multipliers without or with a liquidity trap

expansion in the core of the Eurozone is going to be particularly wise and helpful.

On the Approach and Interpretation

Reading this paper, one may wonder why the authors did not simply follow some social planner approach instead: formulate the objective, maximize that objective subject to feasibility and incentive constraints, and discuss how to implement the resulting mechanism. Or, more restricted, constrain the planer to use certain tax instruments. But we know from Correia et al. (2013), that such Ramsey problems easily lead to fiscal devaluations as solutions, in order to solve the relative price problems arising from regionally sticky prices. One can keep on constraining the problem until the desired policy conclusion emerges, of course. But now it has become unclear what is assumption, and what is result, and what rules one ought to follow, generally. This quickly becomes a debate about various third-best approaches. What is now a viable argument in the discussion, and what is not? I should not criticize this too much, though. This paper is far better, of course, than the beat-them-dead argument one sometimes hears from various "practical" economic advisors or economic commentators, that some approach proposed by academic economists is not politically viable, while theirs is, of course. Well, how should one know? At least, the paper writes down a coherent model and analysis, and one can then go and constructively agree or disagree on that basis.

And one can disagree on the political viability, too, of course. Germany may be the last country with some Eurozone enthusiasm, but recent opinion polls and elections show this enthusiasm to be waning. It will not be easy to convince the German voters that Germany ought to participate in costly monetary or fiscal policy measures aimed first at relieving the dire situation in Greece and elsewhere. Often, Chancellor Merkel has been criticized by the foreign press or by economists such as Krugman and others of not having assumed a bolder leadership position in Europe, of not jumping at the chance of fiscal union, after bailing out the southern states. But the truth of the matter is that Merkel and her party need to be careful themselves to not lose the support of their increasingly disillusioned German voters. Put differently, nobody really expected Great Britain to do much about the situation in Southern Europe, except for dumping the issues on the rest of Europe, per exiting from the mess. It would be good to heed that warning. While Germany is not Britain, it would be naive to count on Germany to be willing to be the residual guarantor for the rest of the Eurozone, for whatever mess arises elsewhere in the future.

Conclusions

I would not be surprised if quite a number of readers view the punchline of the Blanchard, Erceg, and Lindé paper as follows: Let Germany fiscally expand at home. This will help Greece.

As a piece of research, I admire it: it is excellent. It is ambitious, lucid, informative, and mainstream. My problem is that this New Keynesian mainstream appears to flow into the Dead Sea. Is there really much of a reliable Phillips curve? Are the inflation and real rate responses to fiscal stimulus plausible? Is the safe real rate truly too high right now? Do retailers have a problem because they are stuck with prices from better times? Is that really the first-order problem that needs solving? What about the fiscal multiplier discontinuities in these models, or the less-than-encouraging empirical evidence regarding fiscal multipliers?

I find myself in an odd place. These types of models are beautiful. And it is a good rule that only a model beats a model! I wish I had a good alternative at hand. I do not. So my critique is cheap. Mea culpa! Nonetheless, I fear that there are too many holes in this paradigm to trust it for providing robust and sensible policy advice. I agree that these authors are putting one possible version on the table, and that it is worth discussing. Nonetheless, I feel that a good degree of skepticism needs to remain. The proposal to let Germany do lots of fiscal spending at home, with the purpose of somehow thereby improving matters in Greece, would be a hard sale in Germany, in any case.

In sum: as a piece of informative and well-crafted economic analysis, thinking through one particular policy option and its mechanisms, it is truly excellent. But if you read it as providing strong support for a policy toward core fiscal stimulus in Europe, then reading my remarks may induce you to become considerably more skeptical.

Endnote

I have an ongoing consulting relationship with a Federal Reserve Bank, the Bundesbank, and the ECB. For acknowledgments, sources of research support, and disclosure of the author's material financial relationships, if any, please see http://www.nber.org/chapters/c13785.ack.

References

Alvarez, Fernando, Francesco Lippi, and Juan Passadore. 2016. "Are State and Time Dependent Models Really Different?"In *NBER Macroeconomics Annual 2016*, ed. M. Eichenbaum and J. Parker. Chicago: University of Chicago Press.
Auerbach, Alan J., and Yuriy Gorodnichenko. 2012. "Measuring the Output Responses to Fiscal Policy." *American Economic Journal: Economic Policy* 4 (2): 1–27.
Barro, Robert J., and Charles J. Redlick. 2011. "Macroeconomic Effects from Government Purchases and Taxes." *Quarterly Journal of Economics* 126 (1): 51–102.
Blanchard, Olivier, and Roberto Perotti. 2002. "An Empirical Characterization of the Dynamic Effects of Changes in Government Spending and Taxes on Output." *Quarterly Journal of Economics* 117 (4): 1329–68.
Cochrane, John H. 2015. "The New-Keynesian Liquidity Trap," Working Paper, Hoover Institution. http://faculty.chicagobooth.edu/john.cochrane/research/papers/zero_bound_2.pdf.
Correia, Isabel, Emmanuel Farhi, Juan Pablo Nicolini, and Pedro Teles. 2013. "Unconventional Fiscal Policy at the Zero Bound." *American Economic Review* 103 (4): 1172–211.
Fratto, Chiara, and Harald Uhlig. 2014. "Accounting for Post-Crisis Inflation and Employment: A Retro Analysis." NBER Working Paper no. 20707, Cambridge, MA.
Hall, Robert. 2011 "The Long Slump." *American Economic Review* 101 (2): 431–69.
Mountford, Andrew, and Harald Uhlig. 2009. "What are the Effects of Fiscal Policy Shocks?" *Journal of Applied Econometrics* 24 (April): 960–92.
Namakumara, Emi, and Jón Steinsson. 2014. "Fiscal Stimulus in a Monetary Union: Evidence from US Regions." *American Economic Review* 104 (3): 753–92.
Namakumara, Emi, Jón Steinsson, Patrick Sun, and Daniel Villar. 2016. "The Elusive Costs of Inflation: Price Dispersion During the U.S. Great Inflation." Working paper, Columbia University.
Nekarda, Christopher J., and Valerie A. Ramey. 2013. "The Cyclical Behavior of the Price-Cost Markup." NBER Working Paper no. 19099, Cambridge, MA.

Ramey, Valerie A. 2011. "Can Government Purchases Stimulate the Economy?" *Journal of Economic Literature* 49 (3): 673–85.

Ramey, Valerie A., and Sarah Zubairy. 2015. "Are Government Spending Multipliers State Dependent? Evidence from Canadian Historical Data." Working paper, University of California, San Diego.

Smets, Frank, and Raf Wouters. 2007. "Shocks and Frictions in US Business Cycles: A Bayesian DSGE Approach." *American Economic Review* 97 (3): 586–606.

Uhlig, Harald. 2005. "What are the Effects of Monetary Policy on Output? Results from an Agnostic Identification Procedure." *Journal of Monetary Economics* 52:381–419.

Werning, Iván. 2011. "Managing a Liquidity Trap: Monetary and Fiscal Policy." NBER Working Paper no. 17344, Cambridge, MA.

Whalen, Charles J., and Felix Reichling. 2015. "The Fiscal Multiplier and Economic Policy Analysis in the United States." Working Paper no. 2015-02, Macroeconomic Analysis Division, Congressional Budget Office.

Comment

Ricardo Reis, *London School of Economics*

Introduction

This paper by Blanchard, Erceg, and Linde provides a two-country model to understand the spillovers from one country's fiscal expansion on another country's macroeconomy. The authors do not want to merely provide a theoretical discussion of what determines these spillovers in abstract, but they also want to apply their framework to the euro area. After showing that spillovers from a fiscal expansion in the core to the periphery will be larger if there is a longer-lasting liquidity trap, if the Phillips curve is steeper, and if the import content of government spending is larger, they further conclude that the boost to output in the periphery is larger than the effect on consumption and welfare. Their preferred numerical estimates point to an aggregate euro-area multiplier of around 2 and a boost to welfare in both the core and the periphery.

Before thinking about what to make of their points, it helps to fix ideas by asking to which two actual euro-area regions their model might apply. The "core" country in their model has no fiscal constraint that prevents it from exogenously choosing to increase public spending. It can finance this expansion by issuing public debt, and this comes with no increase in the interest rate it pays. Moreover, it is large enough that this extra spending will make a significant material difference in the exports from the rest of the euro area. In turn, the "periphery" country is smaller, but not infinitesimal as in small open economy models, since its actions have an effect on the exchange rate and on the trade balance of the larger core economy. It has a similar structure as the core country, with the same frictions leading to inefficient production, namely monopolistic competition and price rigidities. It differs in the shocks that hit it and, therefore, in the stage of the business cycle. Both economies have nominal interest rates stuck at zero.

From this description, it seems adequate to equate the core economy with Germany in Europe. In turn, the periphery country is probably best captured by Italy, or maybe even perhaps France. This is not a model that applies easily to the peripheral countries of Greece, Ireland, or Portugal. These countries are both too small to match the periphery country in this model, and too distant from the simple new Keynesian model in this paper. Capital misallocation, fragile financial systems, bloated public sectors, or sovereign debt crises are all important features of some of these economies that would interact with fiscal expansions in a way that would have large and relevant effects on fiscal multipliers (see, e.g., Reis 2013; Gourinchas, Philippon, and Vayanos 2016, in this volume).

Focusing on Germany at the time of this conference, in 2016, the large wave of refugees into the country coming from the Middle East and Northern Africa dominated the headlines. There are a variety of public-spending programs needed to process these new immigrants and provide them with basic social services, which across the EU could be as large as 40 billion euros (Corsetti et al. 2016). While this is not the way in which the authors frame the contribution of their paper, their analysis and results can be used to answer a precise question: Will the increase in public spending in Germany to receive the refugees benefit the Italian or French economies?

The authors isolate the theoretical channels that will affect the response to this question and calibrate their model with European data to provide some estimates of how large the effects will be. In these comments, I start by discussing the channels that the authors focus on and then make three comments. First, I note a few extra channels that may be important for fiscal spillovers. Second, I discuss the difficulties with interpreting fiscal multipliers. Third, I try to complement the authors' analysis that focuses on traditional new Keynesian channels with the modern view of the euro crisis, and how they may interact with fiscal spending. Finally, I conclude by asking whether the authors' contribution and arguments are coming at the right time to gauge whether they will be effective in shaping policy choices or not.

Three Channels, Four Factors, and Two Absences

The authors focus on three channels that rely on central economic conditions, and as such are common to many modern macroeconomic models.

The first condition is the aggregate resource constraint (without investment) stating that output is equal to consumption spending, government purchases, and net exports. From this condition, applying to both core and periphery, one gets the first effect considered by the authors. An increase in core government spending will potentially raise output both in the core and in the periphery, because some of the core government spending falls on goods and services produced in the periphery.

The second condition is a negative relation between net exports and the real exchange rate. Then, an increase in core spending will lead to an appreciation of its real exchange rate, which will boost exports from the periphery, raising its output.

The third channel relies on combining the Euler equation for consumption, a no arbitrage condition between long-term real returns and one-period returns, the Fisher equation linking real rates to domestic inflation, and a common union-wide nominal interest rate that does not respond to changes in inflation. If inflation in the periphery is higher on average over the near future, then short-term and long-term real returns will be lower in the periphery. This leads to higher current consumption, and so output.

Whatever makes these three effects stronger will boost the impact of core fiscal spending on periphery's output. The authors therefore focus on four factors on which the fiscal spillover will depend. First, the longer is the expected duration of the liquidity trap then nominal interest will stay fixed for longer, so the effect of inflation on long real interests is larger. For their baseline results, countries are in a liquidity trap for three years, and the hike in government spending that generates the higher inflation and the stimulus through lower real interest rates takes place over 2.5 years. Given the history of the euro area between 2011 and 2016, these choices seem conservative.

Second, the steeper is the Phillips curve, then the more inflation will increase as a result of the fiscal stimulus, and so the larger its expansionary effect. Again, the authors are conservative, assuming a Calvo-duration of price stickiness of 3.5 years, which amounts to a very flat Phillips curve.

Third, the larger the import component of government spending in the core, then the larger the direct aggregate demand effect on periphery output. The authors calibrate this to match the average ratio of imports to GDP and a trade price elasticity of 1.1, which is line with the literature.

A fourth factor is important in assessing the fiscal spillovers to welfare. Since the periphery country runs a trade surplus in response to the fiscal expansion in the core, output in the periphery increases considerably more than its consumption. The authors argue that while the welfare of the representative agents in their model would focus on consumption, if one thinks instead of economies with considerable slack, one might want to focus on output. I would further add that the foundations in social welfare theory for equating the utility of a representative agent with a proper social welfare function in an economy with diverse people are very shaky. Therefore, arguing for an ad hoc welfare function that focuses on output instead of consumption seems defensible.

These channels and factors are all important, and the authors do well to focus on them and emphasize them. One could easily list many more that might be considered, but it is much harder to argue that any of them are as important as the ones considered by the authors. Still, two of them stand out, in my view, as being potentially as important, and so are worth mentioning.

The first is the consideration of a third region with which there is trade. Between 2010 and 2015, the current account of the Eurozone went from a surplus of 36 to 330 billion euros, while Germany's current account went from 145 to 257 billion euros. The Eurozone adjusted to the euro crisis and the fiscal austerity in the periphery in part through trade with the outside. A fiscal stimulus in the core would plausibly likewise have a significant "leakage" in its aggregate demand stimulus to outside the euro area, reducing some of the authors' estimates.

The second absent channel works through nominal wage rigidities. In new Keynesian models, wage rigidities have a large effect on how much the domestic economy expands after a fiscal stimulus, as well as on the international transmission of domestic shocks (Galí, Lopez-Salido, and Valles 2007). The slow adjustment of nominal wages in Southern Europe after 2011 suggests this is empirically relevant.

But What Do Fiscal Expansions and Multipliers Stand For?

Up to a first-order approximation, to predict how output changes after a spending stimulus (ΔY), we need to multiply the size of the stimulus (ΔG) with the partial derivative of output with respect to spending keeping everything else fixed ($\partial Y / \partial G$). The same applies to other variables rather than output. This is the spirit of most of the exercises in this paper, as well as those in the large literature that in the last few years has studied the stimulus provided by government spending.

Yet, each of the two terms that must be multiplied is problematic when trying to confront the data. Starting with ΔG, this is typically quite small in twenty-first century stimulus programs. In the days of Keynes, the bulk of government spending in developed countries indeed went to purchases of goods, for either military purposes or infrastructure. Theoretical thought experiments that involved building another bridge or highway had a clear counterpart in reality. Those days are long gone. The largest category of government spending in almost all OECD countries is nowadays transfer payments, not consumption purchases.

As a result, when one looks at the breakdown of actual fiscal stimulus programs, it jumps to the eye that most of them consisted of increases in transfers. Between 2007 and 2009, government spending shot up by 14% in the United States. Three quarters of this increase was on transfers. Looking at the increase in spending across 21 OECD countries during this period, Oh and Reis (2012) found that in 14 of them the increase in transfers exceed the increase in government consumption plus investment. Focusing on the ARRA stimulus package in the United States between 2008 and 2010, Cogan and Taylor (2012) found that almost all of it consisted of transfers to states, which in turn used it to pay down debt or fund social transfers, with little funding going to government purchases. In short, in modern stimulus packages, the ΔG seems too small for the stimulus to matter all that much.

The partial derivative term is also problematic because of what is being held fixed. The precise *ceteris paribus* experiment matters a great deal in ways that make it hard to relate these multipliers to the data. A few examples make this problem concrete. First, the authors assume that the increase in government purchases is paid off over time either using lump-sum taxes (in their simple model) or labor income taxes (in their larger model). But, in this class of models, if instead capital income taxes or consumption taxes were used, the multipliers can be quite different (Drautzburg and Uhlig 2015). Since actual fiscal stimulus packages rarely clearly specify how the deficits will be paid for in the future, this makes it hard to estimate their effect. Second, the time profile of taxes is likewise important by affecting intertemporal relative prices, and it is especially important whether the higher taxes come before or after the economy leaves the zero lower bound (Correia et al. 2013). Slight changes in the time profile of taxes can easily turn an expansionary fiscal stimulus into a contractionary policy. Third, what people know and don't know about the future size and duration of the expansion in purchases and the taxes that pay for it will likewise affect their response to the stimulus (Leeper, Walker, and Yang 2013). Again, measuring agents' expectations following a stimulus is a daunting empirical task after the fact, let alone when the policy is being discussed. Fourth, increases in purchases and their effect on real activity will affect the extent to which the fiscal automatic stabilizers act in the economy, as well as their overall effectiveness (McKay and Reis 2016).

The "all else fixed" problem with this partial derivative also applies to nonfiscal variables. One concrete example is given by the work of Feve, Matheron, and Sahuc (2013). Public and private consumption are plausibly nonseparable in the utility function of households. The standard assumption of separability makes it easier to analyze the theory of fiscal stimulus, and it is also adopted by the authors because it keeps fixed the marginal utility of consumption in response to a the stimulus. But, if there are complementarities instead, the fiscal expansion will raise this marginal utility. Because the zero lower bound equilibrium is characterized by having too low marginal utility of consumption in the present relative to the future, due to too high real interest rates, this provides another channel for the effectiveness of government purchases.

None of these caveats point to the authors' estimates being either clearly underestimated or overestimated. Moreover, most of them apply as much to this paper as they do to the large literature that in the last few years has estimate purchases multipliers. But they are still worth stating and repeating many times, as so much research energy has been spent measuring a multiplier that is hard to properly define and that multiplies something that is so small in modern fiscal expansions.

Bringing in Modern Views of the Crisis

This paper uses models and tools from the conventional macroeconomics tool kit. Brunnermeier and Reis (2016) argue that, especially when thinking about the crisis in the Eurozone, this tool kit has to be expanded in a few directions to be able to make sense of the crisis. Because this paper's policy study applies with this crisis in the background, it is likewise important to revisit the policy analysis taking these modern considerations of the crisis into account.

The first important consideration is the spread between sovereign interest rates in Germany vis-à-vis France or Italy. The sovereign debt crisis in the periphery countries started with spikes in their sovereign interest rate spreads. Given the common monetary policy, and so common exchange-rate risk, the spreads reflect primarily the differential risk of default between those countries and Germany. What would happen to this risk premia and so to the interest rate spreads following a fiscal expansion in the core?

We can think of the expansion in the core as having two effects on the chances of a default in the periphery. First, by raising domestic output in the periphery, through the channels identified by the authors, the fiscal expansion lowers the benefits of defaulting. Second, by lowering the core real interest rate, it increases the supply of capital and lowers the cost of repaying the debt. Both of these effects increase the incentives to repay the debt to foreign, and so lower the risk premia. A countervailing effect would be that if the expansion increases the risk that the core cannot repay its debt, it may raise its risk of default, thus raising interest rates for the periphery as well. This effect is likely small, given the size of the fiscal stimulus that the authors have in mind, and the level of the public debt in the core. Therefore, overall, the default channel would lower periphery real interest rates, further boosting the expansionary effects of the fiscal stimulus.

A second consideration to have is on the role of capital misallocation. The Italian economy stopped growing well before the crisis of the last few years: Italian per capita GDP barely increased between 2000 and 2010. The same applies to Portugal, and if one focuses on productivity growth, Spain, Greece, and Ireland have all gone through a slump with the creation of the financial and monetary union. The euro and the twenty-first century came with a productivity slump in the Eurozone that was followed by a crash in these countries in 2010–12.

The evidence for several countries points to misallocation of the abundant capital flows from the core to the periphery as a likely culprit for this slump (Reis 2013). In Italy, the nontradables sector grew at the expense of tradables (Benigno and Fornaro 2014). In Portugal, within nontradables, it was the least productive and competitive sectors that absorbed more of the capital flows and grew faster (Reis 2013). In Spain, even within tradable manufacturing, the dispersion of firm productivity increased as smaller and less productive firms were being kept afloat by the abundant and cheap foreign capital (Gopinath et al. 2015). How would a fiscal expansion at the core affect the allocation of capital in the periphery?

Perhaps the most important effect would come through higher exports in the periphery. Therefore, the sectors that would most benefit are those associated with exports to the core. Since more productive firms tend to export more, this would potentially promote a better allocation of resources. This channel would again potentially increase the benefits of a fiscal expansion at the core on the periphery.

Third, the crisis has shown the importance of modern banks for the transmission of macroeconomic shocks, and the need for economies to have safe assets. A fiscal expansion in the core that is funded by deficits increases the safe core public debt, alleviating some of the safe asset shortage (Caballero, Farhi, and Gourinchas 2016). At the same time, increasing the supply of national bonds when there is no euro-wide bond may accentuate the diabolic loop between banks and sovereigns at the core, making it more exposed to the possibility of sovereign debt crisis (Brunnermeier et al. 2016).

Conclusion and Would the Core Be Convinced?

This paper makes a useful contribution to a relevant and important policy question today: Would a fiscal expansion in Germany stimulate economic activity in welfare not just in Germany but in France and Italy as well? The authors isolate three important features of these economies on which the answer will depend: the import content of government purchases, the slope of the Phillips curve, and the expected duration of the zero lower bound period. Moreover, they make a persuasive case for the effects being potentially large, and for both countries being better off as a result of the fiscal expansion.

In these comments, I added three further considerations. Two other important factors on the effectiveness of fiscal stimulus are the spillover of trade with other countries outside the Eurozone and the role of nominal wage rigidity on the slope of the Phillips curve. Second, I criticized the focus on purchases multipliers because actual changes in government purchases are usually small, and the estimation of multipliers is fraught with obstacles. Third, I speculated on the effects of a fiscal stimulus on the risk premium on sovereign bonds, on misallocation of capital in the periphery, and on the supply of safe assets and the balance sheet of banks. While my hope is that these add to the understanding of the question posed by the authors, they do not detract from the relevance and significance of their contribution.

A harder question is whether a core country would be convinced by these arguments. On the positive side, this paper comes at the right time. In 2010–12, many commentators on the American side of the Atlantic frequently tried to make a case for a fiscal expansion on the European side.

That case relied on applying the same economic argument on both sides of the ocean: when nominal interest rates are zero, higher government spending does not raise real interest rates or crowd out investment, but rather lowers real interest rates because of the increase in expected inflation so that investment is crowded in and the stimulus is more powerful.

This argument went nowhere in Europe for clear and good reasons. First, to discuss a fiscal expansion for the Eurozone as a whole made little sense: there is no federal budget or government to undertake this expansion, and a program like the American Recovery and Reinvestment Act of 2009 in the United States, with a large transfer across states, is almost politically impossible to entertain in Europe. Second, the countries going through a sovereign debt crisis, like Portugal, Greece, Ireland, Italy, and Spain were not at the zero lower bound. In fact, during the two years of the crisis, even vague news that public spending would be higher than expected would lead to large run-ups in interest rates, so the extent of crowding out was very large. Third, from the perspective of the core, the German economy was booming during these years, so expansionary fiscal policy would have been procyclical. As much as American commentators were frustrated by how little influence their arguments had, European commentators were dismayed by how little relevant they were for the European situation.

In 2016, making the case for fiscal expansion makes more sense. Germany and most of the euro area seem to satisfy now the conditions for the zero lower bound, and both are projected to grow at a dismal 1.7%, so that Germany is no longer off cycle with the rest of the area. Moreover, with the refugee crisis, a modest fiscal expansion seems inevitable. It seems like a good idea to discuss now whether this fiscal expansion should be larger so that it goes beyond nonrefugee spending. The welfare benefits for the core are not very large, but they are positive. Whether the core countries will be convinced is harder to know.

Endnote

For acknowledgments, sources of research support, and disclosure of the author's material financial relationships, if any, please see http://www.nber.org/chapters/c13786.ack.

References

Benigno, Gianluca, and Luca Fornaro. 2014. "The Financial Resource Curse." *Scandinavian Journal of Economics* 116 (1): 58–86.

Brunnermeier, Markus, Luis Garicano, Philip Lane, Marco Pagano, Ricardo Reis, Tano Santos, David Thesmar, Stijn Van Nieuwerburgh, and Dimitri Vayanos. 2016. "The Sovereign-Bank Diabolic Loop and ESBies." *American Economic Review* 106 (5): 508–12.

Brunnermeier, Markus, and Ricardo Reis. 2016. "A Crash Course on the Euro Crisis." Manuscript, London School of Economics.

Caballero, Ricardo, Emmanuel Farhi, and Pierre-Olivier Gourinchas. 2016. "Safe Asset Scarcity and Aggregate Demand." *American Economic Review* 106 (5): 513–18.

Cogan, John, and John Taylor. 2012. "What the Government Purchases Multiplier Actually Multiplied in the 2009 Stimulus Package." In *Government Policies and the Delayed Economic Recovery*, ed. Lee Ohanian, John Taylor, and Ian Wright, 85–114. Stanford, CA: Hoover Institution Press.

Correia, Isabel, Emmanuel Farhi, Juan Pablo Nicolini, and Pedro Teles. 2013. "Unconventional Fiscal Policy at the Zero Bound." *American Economic Review* 103 (4): 1172–211.

Corsetti, Giancarlo, Lars Feld, Ralph Koijen, Lucrezia Reichlin, Ricardo Reis, Helene Rey, and Beatrice Weder di Mauro. 2016. *Reinforcing the Eurozone and Protecting an Open Society: Monitoring the Eurozone 2.* London: CEPR Press.

Drautzburg, Thorsten, and Harald Uhlig. 2015. "Fiscal Stimulus and Distortionary Taxation." *Review of Economic Dynamics* 18 (4): 894–920.

Feve, Patrick, Julien Matheron, and Jean-Guillaume Sahuc. 2013. "A Pitfall with Esti- mated DSGE-Based Government Spending Multipliers." *American Economic Journal: Macroeconomics* 5 (4): 141–78.

Galí, Jordi, David Lopez-Salido, and Javier Valles. 2007. "Understanding the Effects of Government Spending on Consumption." *Journal of the European Economic Association* 5 (1): 227–70.

Gopinath, Gita, Sebnem Kalemli-Ozcan, Loukas Karabarbounis, and Carolina Villegas-Sanchez. 2015. "Capital Allocation and Productivity in South Europe." NBER Working Paper no. 21453, Cambridge, MA.

Gourinchas, Pierre-Olivier, Thomas Philippon, and Dimitri Vayanos. 2016. "The Analytics of the Greek Crisis." *NBER Macroeconomics Annual 2016,* ed. M. Eichenbaum and J. Parker. Chicago: University of Chicago Press.

Leeper, Eric, Todd B. Walker, and Shu-Chun Susan Yang. 2013. "Fiscal Foresight and Information Flows." *Econometrica* 81 (3): 1115–45.

McKay, Alisdair, and Ricardo Reis. 2016. "The Role of Automatic Stabilizers in the U.S. Business Cycles." *Econometrica* 84 (1): 141–94.

Oh, Hyunseung, and Ricardo Reis. 2012. "Targeted Transfers and the Fiscal Response to the Great Recession." *Journal of Monetary Economics* 59:S50–64.

Reis, Ricardo. 2013. "The Portuguese Slump and Crash and the Euro Crisis." *Brookings Papers on Economic Activity* 46:143–93.

Discussion

Robert Hall began the discussion by raising concerns about the dependency of modern macroeconomics on the Calvo mode. He viewed the New Keynesian formulation of nominal rigidities as a mechanical and arbitrary set-up of price adjustment. He urged that more work be done on developing a workable model of inflation.

Olivier Blanchard disagreed with Robert Hall's comments about there not being a workable model of inflation. Instead, he argued that the Phillips curve is still present, but has changed over time. Specifically, he believed that the curve now has a very small slope, and there has also been a change in inflation expectation formation over time. He agreed with the general sentiment that it is important to have accurate models of inflation, and that inflation dynamics may not be fully captured by the Calvo model.

Moritz Schularick reiterated Harald Uhlig's discussion of the paper in which he raised concerns about political economy issues. Specifically, he noted that it is very difficult to increase fiscal spending in Germany. The German legislative constitution states that Germany must have a balanced budget, even at the peak of the crisis. Having a deficit to finance fiscal spending requires a declaration of national emergency, which may trigger uncertainty and undesirable political effects. He questioned whether a fiscal deficit in Germany is actually a feasible policy option.

Olivier Blanchard responded to Moritz Schularick's political economy concerns. He agreed that substantially larger fiscal spending in Germany is clearly a second- or third-best policy option, and is also politically infeasible. He believes that the first-best solution would be to have a fiscal union and institutions that would allow for a direct fiscal expansion in some other countries rather than Germany. He believes that the main issue is how to increase spending where it is needed without causing investors to become alarmed. This could be achieved via a fiscal union. However, even if it is not possible to establish a fiscal union, he believes it is still possible to do fiscal expansions in the periphery countries, in Italy and Spain for instance, without alarming investors if the expansion occurred via growth-enhancing measures rather than infrastructure investment.

Pierre-Olivier Gourinchas followed up with comments on the German constituent rule and debt brake, which was voted on in 2009 and came into effect in 2016. In the past, if a country's currency was pegged to the Germany currency, then the country would experience an appreciation in their real exchange rate if they did not meet the Germans' low inflation rates. The appreciation could eventually turn into a crisis. Therefore, the currency peg effectively forced non-German countries to adopt a low inflation regime. He believes that the constituent rule and debt brake in Germany plays a similar role, encouraging non-German countries to adopt a balanced budget or constituent rule because the debt brake effectively sends a signal that Germany will not bail out countries in the future. He believes that any deviations from this strategy by Germany would undo the signal, which he views as a real constraint on the set of feasible policies in Germany.

Christopher Erceg noted that the authors calibrate the New Keynesian model in a way that is consistent with other studies that have an extremely flat Phillips curve. As a result, the effects on inflation are muted—when the output gap rises by 1 percentage point, inflation rises by about 0.2 percentage points.

Lawrence Christiano questioned why the authors did not see a rise in welfare in their model following an increase in demand in periphery countries, since there is an inefficiently low level of output. He noted that net exports increased, which may be viewed as an investment in future consumption, and wondered if net exports are integrated into the welfare calculations.

Olivier Blanchard made the comment that welfare functions that are derived from the model itself often compound all the weaknesses of the assumptions in the model. However, he believes that there is still something to be learned from these calculations, since conceptually we care about consumption.

He noted that in the model, output and net exports rose in the short run, but consumption remained unchanged. He agreed with Lawrence

Christiano's comment that net exports may be thought of as investment in the future, and therefore affect future welfare. However, he observed that for welfare, it matters when the benefit arrives and agents' willingness to work at that moment. If higher consumption arrives when agents are very happy to work, then there may be welfare gains from shifting consumption to the future. However, if it comes at a time when the economy has nearly returned to steady state, then it is much less attractive because agents need to supply more labor at a time when they are relatively less willing to do so. The intertemporal structure of consumption, therefore, matters for welfare calculations.

Christopher Erceg further added that fiscal stimulus can have long-lasting impacts on welfare because the relative price effects on the core and periphery countries may be very long lived. Specifically, an increase in spending in core countries can result in higher prices in the core countries relative to the periphery countries. The price level in the periphery slowly converges over many years, which means that inflation remains high in the periphery for a while. High inflation results in low real interest rates in the periphery countries, which helps consumption to remain high for a while. As a result, the relative price effects can result in long-lasting welfare benefits for the periphery countries.

Paul Beaudry made the comment that the authors' model does not seem to rely on Keynesian features. He asked whether the model generates most of its results through the hand-to-mouth channel. Christopher Erceg agreed that the model relies more heavily on Keynesian multiplier effects than the response of inflation.

Mark Gertler noted that the authors' model suggests that the currency union is harmful and should be dissolved. However, as discussed already, doing so might not be politically feasible. Gertler instead suggested an intermediate policy, which might be more feasible. The idea is to have the objectives of the ECB vary over time. In normal times, the ECB would target inflation. However, in times of crises the ECB would focus on stimulating the periphery. If that policy led to overheating in the core countries, they could reduce spending.

Christopher Erceg agreed that the policy proposed by Mark Gertler may work well if it is a relatively short-lived liquidity trap. However he emphasized that in a long-run liquidity trap, it may be more complicated.

Fernando Alvarez observed that the discussions have focused on the political constraints in Germany, and wondered about the role of France. Olivier Blanchard noted that between Germany and France, it is clear that Germany is the country with the most political constraints and decision-making ability in terms of fiscal spending. Jesper Lindé agreed with Olivier Blanchard's comment that Germany has more fiscal space than France. France has no fiscal space, since they already have elevated spending levels.

3

Macrofinancial History and the New Business Cycle Facts

Òscar Jordà, *Federal Reserve Bank of San Francisco and University of California, Davis*
Moritz Schularick, *University of Bonn and CEPR*
Alan M. Taylor, *University of California, Davis, NBER, and CEPR*

"When you combine ignorance and leverage, you get some pretty interesting results."
—Warren Buffett

I. Introduction

Observation is the first step of the scientific method. This paper lays empirical groundwork for macroeconomic models that take finance seriously. The global financial crisis reminded us that financial factors play an important role in shaping the business cycle, and there is growing agreement that new and more realistic models of real financial interactions are needed. Crafting such models has become one of the top challenges for macroeconomic research. Policymakers in particular seek a better understanding of the interaction between monetary, macroprudential, and fiscal policies.

Our previous research (Schularick and Taylor 2012; Jordà, Schularick, and Taylor 2011, 2013, 2016a, 2016b) uncovered a key stylized fact of modern macroeconomic history that we may call the "financial hockey stick." The ratio of aggregate private credit to income in advanced economies has surged to unprecedented levels over the second half of the twentieth century. A central aim of this paper is to show that, alongside this great leveraging, key business cycle moments have become increasingly correlated with financial variables. Most importantly, our long-run data provide evidence that high-credit economies may not be especially volatile, but their business cycles tend to be more negatively skewed. In other words, leverage is associated with dampened business cycle volatility, but more spectacular crashes. Business cycle outcomes become more asymmetric in high-credit economies, echoing previous research on the asymmetry of cycles (McKay and Reis 2008).

A great deal of modern macroeconomic thought has relied on the small (and unrepresentative) sample of US post–World War II experience to formulate, calibrate, and test models of the business cycle; to calculate the welfare costs of fluctuations; and to analyze the benefits of stabilization policies. Yet the historical macroeconomic cross-country experience is richer. An important contribution of this paper is to introduce a new comprehensive macrofinancial historical database covering 17 advanced economies over the last 150 years.[1] This considerable data-collection effort has occupied the better part of a decade and involved a small army of research assistants.

We see two distinct advantages of using our data. First, models ostensibly based on universal economic mechanisms of the business cycle must account for patterns seen across space and time. Second, a very long-run perspective is necessary to capture enough "rare events" such as major financial dislocations and "macroeconomic disasters" to robustly analyze their impact on the volatility and persistence of real economic cycles.

We begin by deconstructing the financial hockey stick. The central development of the second half of the twentieth century is the rise of household credit, mostly of mortgages. Business credit has increased as well, but at a slower pace. Home-ownership rates have climbed in almost every industrialized economy and, with them, real house prices. Private credit has increased much faster than income. Even though households are wealthier, private credit has grown faster even than the underlying wealth. Households are more levered than at any time in history.

Next, we characterize the broad contours of the business cycle. Using a definition of turning points similar to many business cycle dating committees, such as the NBER's, we investigate features of the business cycle against the backdrop of the financial cycle. The associations we present between credit and the length of the expansion, and between deleveraging and the speed of the recovery, already hint at the deeper issues requiring further analysis. Economies grow more slowly and generally more stably post–World War II. Despite this apparent stability, financial crises since the fall of Bretton Woods still occur with devastating regularity.

These broad contours lead us to a reevaluation of conventional stylized facts on business cycles using our newer and more comprehensive data, with a particular emphasis on real financial interactions. The use of key statistical moments to describe business cycles goes back at least to the New Classical tradition that emerged in the 1970s (e.g., Kydland and Prescott 1990; Zarnowitz 1992; Backus and Kehoe 1992; Hodrick and Prescott 1997; Basu and Taylor 1999). Under this approach, the statistical properties of models are calibrated to match empirical moments in the data such as means, variances, correlations, and autocorrelations.

In the final part of the paper, we examine key business cycle moments conditional on aggregate private-credit levels. We find that rates of growth, volatility, skewness, and tail events all seem to depend on the ratio of private credit to income. Moreover, key correlations and international cross correlations appear to also depend quite importantly on this leverage measure. Business cycle properties have changed with the financialization of economies, especially in the postwar upswing of the financial hockey stick. The manner in which macroeconomic aggregates correlate with each other has evolved as leverage has risen. Credit plays a critical role in understanding aggregate economic dynamics.

II. A New Data Set for Macrofinancial Research

The data featured in this paper represent one of its main contributions. We have compiled, expanded, improved, and updated a long-run macrofinancial data set that covers 17 advanced economies since 1870 on an annual basis. The first version of the data set, unveiled in Jordà et al. (2011) and Schularick and Taylor (2012), covered core macroeconomic and financial variables for 14 countries. The latest vintage covers 17 countries and 25 real and nominal variables. Among these, there are time series that had been hitherto unavailable to researchers, especially for key financial variables such as bank credit to the nonfinancial private sector (aggregate and disaggregate) and asset prices (equities and housing). We have now brought together in one place macroeconomic data that previously had been dispersed across a variety of sources. This data set is publicly available at the NBER website.

Table 1 gives a detailed overview of the coverage of the latest vintage of the data set, which gets updated on a regular basis as more data are unearthed and as time passes. More details about the data construction appear in an extensive 100-page online appendix, which also acknowledges the support we received from colleagues all over the world.

In addition to country experts, we consulted a broad range of sources such as economic and financial history volumes and journal articles,

Table 1
A New Macrofinancial Data Set (Available Samples Per Variable and Per Country)

Country	RGDPpc	PPPGDPpc	NGDP	Population	RCons.	Inv.	Curr. Acc.	Exports	Imports	Gov. Exp.	Gov. Rev.	CPI	Nrw. Mon.
Australia	1870–2013	1870–2013	1870–2013	1870–2013	1901–2013	1870–1946 / 1949–2013	1870–2013	1870–1913 / 1915–2013	1870–1913 / 1915–2013	1902–2013	1902–2013	1870–2013	1870–2013
Belgium	1870–2013	1870–2013	1870–1913 / 1920–1939 / 1946–2013	1870–2013	1913–2013	1900–1913 / 1920–1939 / 1941 / 1943 / 1946–2013	1870–1913 / 1919–2013	1870–1913 / 1919–2013	1870–1913 / 1919–2013	1870–1912 / 1920–1939 / 1941–2013	1870–1912 / 1920–2013	1870–1914 / 1920–1939 / 1945–2013	1877–1913 / 1920–1940 / 1947–2013
Canada	1870–2013	1870–2013	1870–2013	1870–2013	1871–2013	1871–2013	1870–1945 / 1948–2013	1870–2013	1870–2013	1870–2013	1870–2013	1870–2013	1871–2013
Switzerland	1870–2013	1870–2013	1870–2013	1870–2013	1870–2013	1870–1913 / 1948–2013	1921–1939 / 1948–2013	1885–2013	1885–2013	1871–2013	1870–2013	1870–2013	1870–2013
Germany	1870–2013	1870–2013	1870–1944 / 1946–2013	1870–2013	1870–2013	1870–1913 / 1920–1939 / 1948–2013	1872–1913 / 1925–1938 / 1948–2013	1872–1913 / 1924–1943 / 1948–2013	1872–1913 / 1924–1943 / 1948–2013	1872–1913 / 1925–1938 / 1950–2013	1873–1915 / 1925–1938 / 1950–2013	1870–2013	1876–1913 / 1924–1938 / 1951–2013
Denmark	1870–2013	1870–2013	1870–2013	1870–2013	1870–2013	1870–1914 / 1922–2013	1874–1914 / 1921–2013	1870–2013	1870–2013	1870–1935 / 1937–2013	1870–1935 / 1954–2013	1870–2013	1870–1945 / 1950–2013
Spain	1870–2013	1870–2013	1870–2013	1870–2013	1870–2013	1870–2013	1870–1913 / 1931–1934 / 1940–2013	1870–1935 / 1939–2013	1870–1935 / 1939–2013	1870–1935 / 1940–2013	1870–1935 / 1940–2013	1880–2013	1874–1935 / 1941–2011
Finland	1870–2013	1870–2013	1870–2013	1870–2013	1870–2013	1870–2013	1870–2013	1870–2013	1870–2013	1882–2013	1882–2013	1870–2013	1870–2013
France	1870–2013	1870–2013	1870–1913 / 1920–1938 / 1950–2013	1870–2013	1870–2013	1870–1918 / 1920–1944 / 1946–2013	1870–1913 / 1919–1939 / 1948–2013	1870–2013	1870–2013	1870–2013	1870–2013	1870–2013	1870–1913 / 1920–2013
UK	1870–2013	1870–2013	1870–2013	1870–2013	1870–2013	1870–2013	1870–2013	1870–2013	1870–2013	1870–2013	1870–2013	1870–2013	1870–2013
Italy	1870–2013	1870–2013	1870–2013	1870–2013	1870–2013	1870–2013	1870–2013	1870–2013	1870–2013	1870–2013	1870–2013	1870–2013	1870–2013
Japan	1870–2013	1870–2013	1875–1944 / 1946–2013	1870–2013	1874–2013	1885–1944 / 1946–2013	1870–1944 / 1946–2013	1870–1943 / 1946–2013	1870–1943 / 1946–2013	1870–2013	1870–2013	1870–2013	1873–2013
Netherlands	1870–2013	1870–2013	1870–1913	1870–2013	1870–2013	1870–1913	1870–1913	1870–1943	1870–1943	1870–2013	1870–2013	1870–2013	1870–1941

Country	Broad Mon.	S.t. Rate	L.t. Rate	Stocks	Ex. Rate	Pub. Debt	Bank Lend.	Mort. Lend.	Hh. Lend.	Bus. Lend.	H. Prices	Bk. Crisis
Norway	1870–2013	1870–2013	1870–2013	1870–2013	1870–2013	1921–1939 1945–2013	1921–1939 1948–2013 1946–2013	1946–2013	1946–2013	1870–2013	1870–1943 1949–2013	1870–2013
Portugal	1870–2013	1870–2013	1870–2013	1870–2013	1910–2013	1953–2013	1870–2013	1870–2013	1870–2013	1870–2013	1870–2013	1870–2013
Sweden	1870–2013	1870–2013	1870–2013	1870–2013	1870–2013	1870–2013	1870–2013	1870–2013	1870–2013	1870–2013	1870–2013	1871–2013
USA	1870–2013	1870–2013	1870–2013	1870–2013	1870–2013	1870–2013	1870–2013	1870–2013	1870–2013	1870–2013	1870–2013	1870–2013
Australia	1870–2013	1870–1944 1948–2013	1870–2013	1870–2013	1870–2013	1870–2013	1870–1945 1948–2013	1870–1945 1952–2013	1870–1945 1952–2013	1870–1945 1952–2013	1870–2013	1870–2013
Belgium	1979–2013	1870–1914 1920–2013	1870–1912 1920–2013	1870–2013	1870–2013	1870–1913 1920–1939 1946–1979 1982–2013	1885–1913 1920–1940 1950–2013	1885–1913 1920–1939 1950–2013	1950–2013	1950–2013	1878–1913 1919–2013	1870–2013
Canada	1871–2013	1934–1944 1948–2013	1870–2013	1870–2013	1870–2013	1870–2013	1870–2013	1874–2013	1956–2013	1961–2013	1921–1949 1956–2013	1870–2013
Switzerland	1880–2013	1870–2013	1880–2013	1899–1914 1916–2013	1870–2013	1880–2013	1870–2013	1870–2013	1870–2013	1870–2013	1901–2013	1870–2013
Germany	1880–1913 1925–1938 1949–2013	1870–1914 1919–1922 1924–1944 1950–2013	1870–1921 1924–1943 1948–2013	1870–1921 1924–2013	1870–1944 1946–2013	1871–1913 1927–1943 1950–2013	1883–1920 1924–1940 1946–2013	1883–1919 1924–1940 1949–2013	1950–2013	1950–2013	1870–1922 1924–1938 1962–2013	1870–2013
Denmark	1870–1945 1950–2013	1875–2013	1870–2013	1892–2013	1870–2013	1880–1946 1953–1956 1960–1996 1998–2013	1870–2013	1875–2013	1951–2013	1951–2013	1875–2013	1870–2013
Spain	1874–1935 1941–2013	1883–1914 1920–2013	1870–1936 1940–2013	1870–2013	1870–2013	1880–1935 1940–2013	1900–1935 1946–2013	1904–1935 1946–2013	1946–2013	1946–2013	1971–2013	1870–2013
Finland	1870–2013	1870–2013	1870–1938 1948–2013	1912–2013	1870–2013	1914–2013	1870–2013	1927–2013	1948–2013	1948–2013	1905–2013	1870–2013
France	1870–1913	1870–1914	1870–2013	1870–2013	1870–2013	1880–1913	1900–1938	1870–1933	1958–2013	1958–2013	1870–2013	1870–2013

(continued)

Table 1
Continued

Country	Broad Mon.	S.t. Rate	L.t. Rate	Stocks	Ex. Rate	Pub. Debt	Bank Lend.	Mort. Lend.	Hh. Lend.	Bus. Lend.	H. Prices	Bk. Crisis
	1920–2013	1922–2013				1920–1938 1949–2013	1946–2013	1946–2013				
UK	1870–2013	1870–2013	1870–2013	1870–2013	1870–2013	1870–2013	1880–2013	1880–2013	1880–2013	1880–2013	1899–1938 1946–2012	1870–2013
Italy	1880–2013	1885–1914 1922–2013	1870–2013	1906–2013	1870–2013	1870–2013	1870–2013	1870–2013	1950–2013	1950–2013	1870–2013	1870–2013
Japan	1894–2013	1879–1938 1957–2013	1870–2013	1878–1891 1893–2013	1870 1873–2013	1875–1944 1946–2013	1874–2013	1893–1940 1946–2013	1948–2013	1948–2013	1913–1930 1936–2013	1870–2013
Netherlands	1870–1941 1945–2013	1870–1914 1919–1944 1948–2013	1870–2013	1890–1944 1946–2013	1870–2013	1870–1939 1946–2013	1900–2013	1900–2013	1990–2013	1990–2013	1870–2013	1870–2013
Norway	1870–2013	1870–1965 1967–2013	1870–2013	1914–2013	1870–2013	1880–1939 1947–2013	1870–2013	1870–2013	1978–2013	1978–2013	1870–2013	1870–2013
Portugal	1913–2013	1880–2013	1870–2013	1929–2013	1870–2013	1870–2013	1870–1903 1920–2013	1920–2013	1979–2013	1979–2013	1988–2013	1870–2013
Sweden	1871–2013	1870–2013	1870–2013	1870–2013	1870–2013	1870–2013	1871–2013	1871–2013	1871–1940 1975–2013	1975–2013	1875–2013	1870–2013
USA	1870–2013	1870–2013	1870–2013	1871–2013	1870–2013	1870–2013	1880–2013	1880–2013	1945–2013	1945–2013	1890–2013	1870–2013

Notes: See text and the online documentation (http://nber.org/data/) for more details. The abbreviations used in this table are as follows: RGDPpc: real GDP per capita; PPPGDPpc: real GDP per capita (Maddison data); NGDP: GDP, local currency; RCons: real consumption per capita; Inv: investment-to-GDP ratio; Curr. Acc.: current account-to-GDP ratio; Exports: exports, local currency; Imports: imports, local currency; Gov. Exp.: government expenditure, local currency; Gov. Rev.: government revenue, local currency; CPI: consumer price index; Nrw. mon.: narrow money, local currency; Broad mon.: broad money, local currency; S.t. rate: short-term nominal interest rate; L.t. rate: long-term nominal interest rate; Stocks: equity price index; Ex. rate: exchange rate, local currency per USD; Pub. debt: public debt-to-GDP ratio; Bank lend.: bank lending to the nonfinancial private sector; Mort. lend.: bank lending, real estate lending; Hh. lend.: bank lending, household lending; Bus. lend.: bank lending, business lending; H. Prices: housing price index; Bk. crisis: banking crisis indicator.

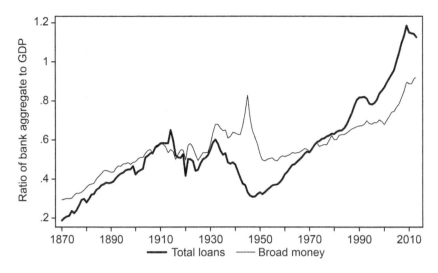

Fig. 1. The financial hockey stick

Note: *Total loans* is bank lending to the nonfinancial private sector, *broad money* is M2 or similar broad measure of money, both expressed as a ratio to GDP averaged over the 17 countries in the sample (see text).

and various publications of statistical offices and central banks. For some countries we extended existing data series from previous statistical work of financial historians or statistical offices. This was the case for Australia, Canada, Japan, and the United States. For other countries we chiefly relied on recent data collection efforts at central banks such as for Denmark, Italy, and Norway. Yet in a non-negligible number of cases we had to go back to archival sources including documents from governments, central banks, and private banks. Typically, we combined information from various sources and spliced series to create long-run data sets spanning the entire 1870–2014 period for the first time.

III.   The Financial Hockey Stick

The pivotal feature to emerge in the last 150 years of global macroeconomic history, as was first highlighted in Schularick and Taylor (2012), is the "hockey stick" pattern of private credit in advanced economies displayed in figure 1. Focusing on *private credit*, defined henceforth as bank lending to the nonfinancial private sector, we can see that this variable maintained a relatively stable relationship with gross domestic product (GDP) and broad money until the 1970s. After an initial period of financial deepening in the nineteenth century, the average level of the credit-to-GDP ratio in advanced economies reached about 50%–60% around 1900. With the exception of the deep contraction in bank lending that was seen from the crisis of the Great Depression to World War II, the ratio was stable in this range until the 1970s.

Throughout this chapter we use the term "leverage" to denote the ratio of private credit to GDP. Although leverage is often used to designate the ratio of credit to the value of the underlying asset or net worth, income leverage is equally important, as debt is serviced out of income. Net-worth-leverage is more unstable due to fluctuations in asset prices. For example, at the peak of the recent US housing boom, ratios of debt to housing wealth signaled that household leverage was declining just as ratios of debt to income were exploding (Foote, Gerardi, and Willen 2012). Similarly, corporate balance sheets based on market values may mislead: in 2006–07 overheated asset values indicated robust capital ratios in major banks that were in distress or outright failure a few months later.

In the past four decades, the volume of private credit has grown dramatically relative to both output and monetary aggregates, as shown in figure 1. The disconnect between private credit and (traditionally measured) monetary aggregates has resulted, in large part, from the shrinkage of bank reserves and the increasing reliance by financial institutions on nonmonetary means of financing, such as bond issuance and interbank lending.

Private credit in advanced economies doubled relative to GDP between 1980 and 2009, increasing from 62% in 1980 to 118% in 2010. The data also demonstrate the breathtaking surge of bank credit prior to the global financial crisis in 2008. In a little more than 10 years, between the mid-1990s and 2008–09, the average bank credit-to-GDP ratio in advanced economies rose from a little under 80% of GDP in 1995 to more than 110% of GDP in 2007. This 30 percentage points (pps) increase is likely to be a lower bound estimate as credit creation by the shadow banking system, of considerable size in the United States and to a lesser degree in the United Kingdom, is excluded from our banking-sector data.

What has been driving this great leveraging? A look at the disaggregated credit data, discussed in greater detail in Jordà, Schularick, and Taylor (2015), shows that the business of banking evolved substantially over the past 140 years. Figure 2 tracks the development of bank lending to the nonfinancial corporate sector and lending to households for our sample of 17 advanced economies. The ratio of business lending relative to GDP has remained relatively stable over the past century. On

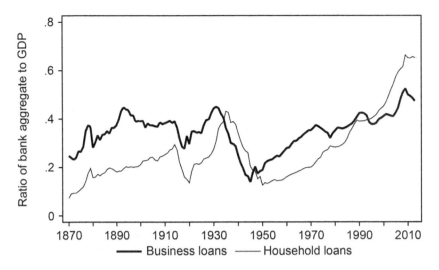

Fig. 2.   Bank lending to business and households

Note: *Business loans* and *household loans* are expressed as a ratio to GDP averaged over the 17 countries in the sample (see text).

the eve of the global financial crisis, bank credit to corporates was not meaningfully higher than on the eve of World War I.

Figure 3 tracks the evolution of mortgage and nonmortgage lending (mostly unsecured lending to businesses) relative to GDP from 1870 to the present. The graph demonstrates that mortgage borrowing has accelerated markedly in the advanced economies after World War II, a trend that is common to almost all individual economies. Mortgage lending to households accounts for the lion's share of the rise in credit-to-GDP ratios in advanced economies since 1980. To put numbers on these trends: at the turn of the nineteenth century, mortgage credit accounted for less than 20% of GDP on average. By 2010, mortgage lending represented 70% of GDP, more than three times the historical level at the beginning of the twentieth century. The main business of banks in the early 1900s consisted of making unsecured corporate loans. Today, however, the main business of banks is to extend mortgage credit, often financed with short-term borrowings. Mortgage loans now account for somewhere between one-half and two-thirds of the balance sheet of a typical advanced-country bank.

It is true that a substantial share of mortgage lending in the nineteenth century bypassed the banking system and took the form of private lending. Privately held mortgage debt likely accounted for close to 10% of

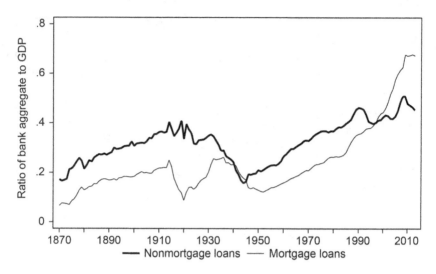

Fig. 3. The great mortgaging

Note: *Mortgage loans* and *nonmortgage loans* are expressed as a ratio to GDP averaged over the 17 countries in the sample. Mortgage lending is to households and firms. Nonmortgage lending is unsecured lending primarily to businesses (see text).

GDP at the beginning of the twentieth century. A high share of farm and nonfarm mortgages was held outside banks in the United States and Germany (Hoffman, Postel-Vinay, and Rosenthal 2000). A key development in the twentieth century was the subsequent transition of these earlier forms of "informal" real estate finance into the hands of banks and the banking system in the course of the twentieth century.

Moreover, even as we discuss the key aggregate trends, we do not mean to downplay the considerable cross-country heterogeneity in the data. Table 2 decomposes for each country the increase of total bank lending to GDP ratios over the past 50 years into growth of household debt and business debt as well as secured and unsecured lending. The percentage point change in the ratio of private credit to GDP in Spain was about three times higher than in Japan and more than twice as high as in Germany and Switzerland. However, it is equally clear from the table that the increase in the private credit-to-GDP ratio, as well as the central role played by mortgage credit to households, are both widespread phenomena.

The central question that we address in the remainder of the paper is to see if and how this secular growth of finance, the growing leverage of incomes, and the changes in the composition of bank lending have

Table 2
Change in Bank Lending-to-GDP Ratios (Multiple), 1960–2012

Country	Total Lending (1)	Mortgage (2)	Nonmortgage (3)	Households (4)	Business (5)
Netherlands	1.31	0.67	0.63	—	—
Denmark	1.18	0.98	0.19	0.75	0.43
Australia	1.12	0.72	0.40	0.78	0.34
Spain	1.11	0.78	0.33	0.70	0.41
Portugal	1.01	0.59	0.42	—	—
USA*	0.82	0.43	0.39	0.40	0.42
USA	0.21	0.17	0.04	0.13	0.07
Sweden	0.76	0.48	0.29	—	—
Great Britain	0.73	0.51	0.23	0.61	0.12
Canada	0.69	0.39	0.30	0.60	—
Finland	0.62	0.27	0.35	0.42	0.19
Switzerland	0.61	0.83	−0.21	0.60	0.01
Italy	0.55	0.49	0.07	0.39	0.16
France	0.54	0.41	0.12	0.41	0.13
Belgium	0.51	0.32	0.19	0.34	0.17
Germany	0.49	0.28	0.21	0.20	0.29
Norway	0.40	0.53	−0.13	—	—
Japan	0.38	0.41	−0.03	0.28	0.10
Average	0.72	0.52	0.20	0.48	0.20
Fraction of Average	1.00	0.72	0.28	0.71	0.29

Notes: Column (1) reports the change in the ratio of total lending to GDP between 1960 and 2012 ordered from largest to smallest change. Columns (2) and (3) report the change due to real estate versus non-real estate lending. Columns (4) and (5) instead report the change due to lending to households versus lending to businesses. The USA entry with * includes credit market debt. *Average* reports the across-country average for each column. *Fraction of average* reports the fraction of column (1) average explained by each category pair in columns (2) versus (3) and (4) versus (5). Notice that averages in columns (4) and (5) have been rescaled due to missing data so as to add up to total lending average reported in column (1). (See text.)

gone hand in hand with changes in the behavior of macroeconomic aggregates over the business cycle.

IV. Household Leverage, Home Ownership, and House Prices

A natural question to ask is whether this surge in household borrowing occurred on the intensive or extensive margin. In other words, did more households borrow or did households borrow more? Ideally, we would have long-run household-level data to address this question, but absent such figures we can nonetheless infer some broad trends from our data. If households increased debt levels, not only relative to in-

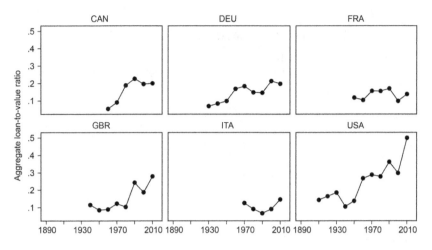

Fig. 4. Ratio of household mortgage lending to the value of the housing stock

come but also relative to asset values, this would raise greater concerns about the macroeconomic stability risks stemming from more highly leveraged household portfolios.

Historical data for the total value of the residential housing stock (structures and land) are only available for a number of benchmark years. We relate those to the total volume of outstanding mortgage debt to get an idea about long-run trends in real estate leverage ratios. Regarding sources, we combine data from Goldsmith's (1985) classic study of national balance sheets with recent estimates of wealth-to-income ratios by Piketty and Zucman (2013). Margins of error are wide, as it is generally difficult to separate the value of residential land from overall land for the historical period. We had to make various assumptions on the basis of available data for certain years.

Figure 4 shows that the ratio of household mortgage debt to the value of real estate has increased considerably in the United States and the United Kingdom in the past three decades. In the United States, mortgage debt-to-housing value climbed from 28% in 1980 to over 40% in 2013, and in the United Kingdom from slightly more than 10% to 28%. A general upward trend in the second half of the twentieth century is also clearly discernible in a number of other countries.

Figure 5 shows that this upward trend in debt-to-asset ratios coincided with a surge in global house prices, as discussed in Knoll, Schularick, and Steger (2015). Real house prices exhibit a hockey-stick pattern just like the credit aggregates. Having stayed constant for the first

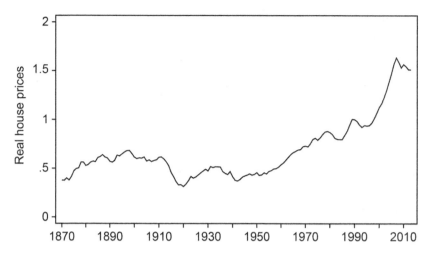

Fig. 5. Real house prices, 1870–2013

Source: Knoll, Schularick, and Steger (2015).

Note: Average CPI-deflated house price index for 14 advanced countries.

century of modern economic growth, global house prices embarked on a steep ascent in the second half of the twentieth century and tripled within three decades of the onset of large-scale financial liberalization.

A second trend is equally important: the extensive margin of mortgage borrowing also played a role. Table 3 demonstrates that the rise in economy-wide leverage has financed a substantial expansion of home ownership in many countries. The idea that home ownership is an intrinsic part of the national identity is widely accepted in many countries, but in most cases it is a relatively recent phenomenon. Before World War II, home ownership was not widespread. In the United Kingdom, for instance, home-ownership rates were in the low 20% range in the 1920s. In the United States, the home-ownership rate did not cross the 50% bar until after World War II, when generous provisions in the GI Bill helped push it up by about 10 percentage points. For the sample average, home-ownership rates were around 40% after World War II. By the first decade of the twenty-first century, they had risen to 60%—an increase of about 20 percentage points in the course of the past half century. In some countries, such as Italy, we observe that home-ownership rates doubled after World War II. In others, such as France and the United Kingdom, they went up by nearly 50%.

Quantitative evidence on the causes of such pronounced differences in home-ownership rates between advanced economies is still scarce.

Table 3
Home-Ownership Rates in the Twentieth Century (Owner-Occupied Share of Units, Percent)

	Canada	Germany	France	Italy	Switzerland	United Kingdom	United States	Average
1900							47	
1910							46	
1920						23	46	
1930							48	
1940	57					32	44	
1950	66	39	38	40	37	32	47	43
1960	66	34	41	45	34	42	62	46
1970	60	36	45	50	29	50	63	48
1980	63	39	47	59	30	58	64	51
1990	63	39	55	67	31	68	64	55
2000	66	45	56	80	35	69	67	60
2013	69	45	58	82	37	64	65	60

Source: See Jordà et al. (2016a, table 3).
Note: Owner-occupied share of units, percent.

Differences in rental regulation, tax policies, and other forms of government involvement, as well as ease of access to mortgage finance and historical path dependencies, likely all played a role. Studies in historical sociology, such as Kohl (2014), explain differences in home-ownership rates between the United States, Germany, and France, as a consequence of the dominant role played by the organization of urban housing markets. In all countries, the share of owner-occupied housing is roughly comparable in rural areas; rather, the stark differences in aggregate ownership rates are mainly a function of the differences in the organization of urban housing across countries.

Divergent trajectories in housing policy also matter. In the United States, the Great Depression was the main catalyst for new policies aimed at facilitating home ownership. Yet government interventions in the housing market remained an important part of the policy landscape after World War II, or even intensified. In the US case, the Veterans Administration (VA) was established through the GI Bill in 1944. The VA guaranteed loans with high loan-to-value ratios over 90%, with some loans passing the 100% loan-to-value mark (Fetter 2013). Forty percent of all mortgages were federally subsidized in the 1950s. The GI Bill is credited with explaining up to one-quarter of the post–World War II increase in the rate of home ownership. In many European countries, the government already took a more active role in the housing sector following World War I. But

European housing policies tended to focus on public construction and ownership of housing, whereas in the United States, the emphasis was on financial support for individual home ownership through the subsidization of mortgage interest rates or public loan guarantees.

The experience with the Great Depression was also formative with regard to the growing role of the state in regulating and ultimately backstopping the financial sector. The most prominent innovation was deposit insurance. In the United States, deposit insurance was introduced as part of the comprehensive Banking Act of 1933, commonly known as the Glass-Steagall Act. Some European countries like Switzerland and Belgium also introduced deposit insurance schemes in the 1930s. In the majority of European countries deposit insurance was introduced in the decades following World War II, albeit with considerable institutional variety (Demirgüç-Kunt, Kane, and Laeven 2013). However, different American and European approaches to the organization of deposit insurance are observable. This is because, at least in the early stages, European deposit insurance schemes relied chiefly on industry arrangements. The United States stands out as the first country that committed the tax payer to backstopping the banking system.

A common effect of the Depression, however, was that in almost all countries the role of the state as a financial player increased. After the devastating consequences of a dysfunctional financial sector had become apparent during the 1930s, the sector was kept on a short leash. Directly or indirectly, the state became more intertwined with finance. Among the major economies, Germany clearly went to one extreme by turning the financial sector into little more than a handmaiden of larger policy goals in the 1930s. In doing so, it inadvertently pioneered various instruments of financial repression (e.g., channeling deposits into government debt) that, in one form or the other, became part of the European financial policy tool kit after World War II. For instance, France ran a tight system of controls on savings flows in the postwar decades (Monnet 2014).

In this long-run context, can we say in any quantitative way the role played by debt-income and debt-wealth changes over time in the evolution of leverage? To this end, figure 6 and table 4 provide comparisons of borrowing, wealth, and GDP. The figure displays three grand ratios for the average of the United States, United Kingdom, France, and Germany over the post–World War II era in 20-year windows. Panel (a) displays total private lending to the nonfinancial sector (total lending) as a ratio to GDP (solid line), total lending as a ratio to total wealth (dashed

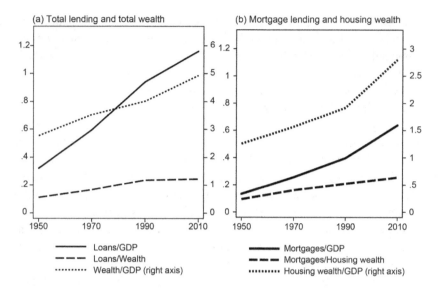

Fig. 6. Leverage—loans, wealth, and income in the United States, United Kingdom, France, and Germany, averages

Source: Data on wealth and housing wealth available online at http:piketty.pse.ens.fr/en/capitalisback from Piketty and Zucman (2013). All other data collected by the authors. Note: Variables expressed as ratios. Right-hand-side axes always refer to wealth over GDP ratios.

line), and total wealth as a ratio to GDP (dotted line). Panel (b) of the same figure presents a similar but more granular decomposition to focus on the housing market: the ratio of mortgages to GDP (solid thick line), the ratio of mortgages to housing wealth (dashed line), and the ratio of housing wealth to GDP (dotted line). Data on wealth come from Piketty and Zucman (2013) and are available only for selected countries and a limited sample.

Similarly, table 4 displays these three grand ratios, again organized by the same principles: panel (a), for all categories of lending and wealth; panel (b), for mortgages and housing wealth. The table provides data for the United States, United Kingdom, France, and Germany, as well as the average across all four, which is used to construct figure 6. It should be clear from the definition of these three grand ratios that our concept of *leverage*, defined as the ratio of lending to GDP, is mechanically linked to the ratio of lending to wealth times the ratio of wealth to GDP.

Figure 6 and panel (b) of table 4, in particular, give a compelling reason to focus on the ratio of mortgages to GDP rather than as a ratio to

Table 4
Leverage—Grand Ratios for Loans, Wealth, and GDP in the United States, United Kingdom, France, and Germany (Averages and by Country)

	(a) All Wealth, All Loans				(b) Housing Wealth, Mortgage Loans			
	1950	1970	1990	2010	1950	1970	1990	2010
Loans/GDP								
US	0.55	0.90	1.2	1.65	0.30	0.44	0.63	0.92
UK	0.23	0.30	0.88	1.07	0.09	0.15	0.38	0.65
France	0.32	0.59	0.79	0.98	0.10	0.19	0.30	0.52
Germany	0.19	0.59	0.87	0.95	0.03	0.25	0.27	0.46
Average	0.32	0.59	0.94	1.16	0.13	0.26	0.40	0.64
Loans/Wealth								
US	0.14	0.23	0.29	0.38	0.18	0.26	0.35	0.47
UK	0.11	0.09	0.19	0.20	0.08	0.11	0.19	0.21
France	0.11	0.16	0.21	0.16	0.08	0.12	0.16	0.13
Germany	0.08	0.19	0.24	0.23	0.04	0.17	0.14	0.19
Average	0.11	0.17	0.24	0.24	0.09	0.16	0.21	0.25
Wealth/GDP								
US	3.80	4.00	4.19	4.31	1.70	1.71	1.83	1.94
UK	2.08	3.33	4.62	5.23	1.11	1.44	1.99	3.03
France	2.91	3.63	3.68	6.05	1.30	1.64	1.94	3.83
Germany	2.29	3.13	3.55	4.14	0.91	1.48	1.91	2.39
Average	2.77	3.52	4.01	4.93	1.26	1.57	1.92	2.80

Sources: Piketty and Zucman (2013). Excel tables are available online (http://piketty.pse.ens.fr/en/capitalisback). Excel tables for DEU, FRA, USA, GBR, tables 6f, column (3) "national wealth" for wealth and column (4) "including housing" for national housing wealth. The 1950 data on wealth for France refers to 1954. Loans refers to total bank loans to the private, nonfinancial sector. Data on bank loans and mortgages and data on GDP collected by the authors. Ratios calculated in local currency.

housing wealth. In the span of the last 60 years, the ratio of mortgages to GDP is nearly six times larger; whereas, measured against housing wealth, mortgages have almost tripled. Of course, the reason for this divergence is the accumulation of housing wealth over the this period, which has more than doubled when measured against GDP.

Summing up, our study of the financial hockey stick has yielded three core insights. First, the sharp rise of aggregate credit-to-income ratios is linked mainly to rising mortgage borrowing by households. Bank lending to the business sector has played a subsidiary role in this process and has remained roughly constant relative to income. Second, the rise in aggregate mortgage borrowing relative to income has been driven by substantially higher aggregate loan-to-value ratios against the backdrop of house price gains that have outpaced income growth in the final decades of the twentieth century. Lastly, the extensive margin of increasing home-ownership rates mattered, too. In many countries, home-ownership rates have increased considerably. The financial hockey stick can therefore be understood as a corollary of more highly leveraged home ownership against substantially higher asset prices.

V. Expansions, Recessions, and Credit

What are the key features of business and financial cycles in advanced economies over the last 150 years? A natural way to tackle this question is to divide our annual frequency sample into periods of real GDP per capita growth or *expansions*, and years of real GDP per capita decline or *recessions*. At annual frequency, this classification is roughly equivalent to the dating of peaks and troughs routinely issued by business cycle committees, such as the NBER's for the United States. We will use the same approach to discuss cycles based on real credit per capita (measured by our private credit variable deflated with the CPI index). This will allow us to contrast the GDP and credit cycles.

This characterization of the cycle does not depend on the method chosen to detrend the data, or on how potential output and its dynamics are determined. Rather, it is based on the observation that in economies where the capital stock and population are growing, negative economic growth represents a sharp deterioration in business activity, well beyond the vagaries of random noise.[2]

In a recent paper, McKay and Reis (2008) reach back to Mitchell (1927) to discuss two features of the business cycle, "brevity" and "violence," in Mitchell's words.[3] Harding and Pagan (2002) provide more operational definitions that are roughly equivalent. In their paper, brevity refers to the *duration* of a cyclical phase, expressed in years. Violence refers to the average *rate* of change per year. It is calculated as the overall change during a cyclical phase divided by its duration and expressed as percent change per year.

These simple statistics, duration (or violence) and rate (or brevity), can be used to summarize the main features of business and credit cycles. Table 5 shows two empirical regularities: (1) the growth cycles in real GDP (per capita) and in real credit growth using turning points in GDP; and (2) the same comparison between GDP and credit, this time using turning points in credit. In both cases, the statistics are reported

Table 5
Duration and Rate of Change—GDP versus Credit Cycles

	Expansions			Recessions		
	Full	Pre-WWII	Post-WWII	Full	Pre-WWII	Post-WWII
GDP-based cycles						
Duration (years)	5.1	3.1	8.6	1.5	1.6	1.4
	(5.5)	(2.7)	(7.2)	(0.9)	(1.0)	(0.8)
Rate (% p.a)						
GDP	3.7	4.1	3.0	−2.5	−2.9	−1.7)
	(2.3)	(2.5)	(1.7)	(2.5)	(2.8)	(1.5)
Credit	4.6	4.7	4.5	2.2	3.7	0.0
	(10)	(13)	(4.3)	(8.0)	(8.9)	(5.7)
P-value H_0 : GDP = credit	0.10	0.46	0.00	0.00	0.00	0.00
Observations	315	203	112	323	209	114
Credit-based cycles						
Duration (years)	6.1	4.2	8.3	1.9	1.7	2.0
	(6.4)	(4.3)	(7.6)	(1.5)	(1.5)	(1.5)
Rate (% p.a.)						
GDP	2.1	1.6	2.8	1.2	1.5	0.8
	(3.1)	(3.7)	(2.0)	(3.3)	(3.8)	(2.4)
Credit	7.0	7.9	5.9	−5.0	−6.5	−3.3
	(5.6)	(6.8)	(3.5)	(6.7)	(8.4)	(3.1)
P-value H_0 : GDP = credit	0.00	0.00	0.00	0.00	0.00	0.00
Observations	240	130	110	254	141	113

Notes: *GDP-based cycles* refers to turning points determined by real GDP per capita. *Credit-based cycles* refers to turning points determined by real bank lending per capita. *Duration* refers to the number of years that each phase between turning points lasts. *Rate* refers to the annual rate of change between turning points in percent per year. Standard errors in parenthesis. *P-value H_0 : GDP = credit* refers to test of the null that the rate of growth for real GDP per capita and real bank lending per capita are the same (see text).

as an average for the full sample of 17 advanced economies, and for the pre– and post–World War II subsamples.

What are the features of the modern business cycle? Output expansions have almost tripled after World War II, from 3.1 to 8.6 years, whereas credit expansions have roughly doubled, from 4.2 to 8.3 years. On the other hand, recessions tend to be briefer and roughly similar before and after World War II. Moreover, there is little difference (certainly no statistically significant difference) between the duration of output and credit-based recessions. The elongation of output expansions after World War II coincides with a reduction in the rate of growth, from 4.1 to 3.0% per annum (p.a.), accompanied with a reduction in volatility. Expansions are more gradual and less volatile. A similar phenomenon is visible in recessions, where the rate of decline essentially halves from 2.9% p.a. pre–World War II to 1.7% p.a. post–World War II.

Interestingly, the behavior of credit is very similar across eras, but only during expansions. The rate of credit growth is remarkably stable through the entire period, from 4.7% pre–World War II to 4.5% post–World War II. Credit seems to grow on a par with output before World War II (the null cannot be rejected formally with a p-value of 0.46), whereas it grows nearly 1.5 percentage points faster than output post–World War II, a statistically significant difference (with a p-value below 0.01). In recessions, credit growth continues almost unabated in the pre–World War II era (it declines from 4.7% p.a. in expansion to 3.7% p.a. in recession) but it grinds to a halt post–World War II (from 4.5% p.a. in expansion to 0% p.a. in recession).

Credit cycles do not exactly align with business cycles. This can be seen via the *concordance index*, defined as the average fraction of the time two variables spend in the same cyclical phase. This index equals 1 when cycles from both variables exactly match, that is, both are in expansion and in recession at a given time. The index is 0 if one of the variables is in expansion and the other is in recession, or vice versa.

Using this definition, before World War II the concordance index is 0.61, suggesting a weak link between output and credit cycles. If output is in expansion, it is almost a coin toss whether credit is in expansion or in recession. However, post–World War II the concordance index rises to 0.79. This value is similar, for example, to the concordance index between output and investment cycles post–World War II.

Another way to see the increased synchronization between output and credit cycles is made clear in the bottom panel of table 5. The duration of credit expansions is about one year longer than the duration of GDP expansions pre–World War II, but roughly the same length post–World War II. Credit recessions are slightly longer than GDP recessions (by about three months, on average), but not dramatically different. Thus both types of cycle exhibit considerable asymmetry in duration between expansion and recession phases.

As we can also see in table 5, things are quite different when considering the average rate of growth during each expansion/recession phase. Whereas credit grew in expansion at nearly 8% p.a. pre–World War II, output grew at only 1.6% p.a. After World War II, the tables are turned. Credit grows 2 percentage points slower, but output grows almost twice as fast. On average, there is a much tighter connection between growth in the economy and growth in credit after World War II.

Table 6
Duration and Rate of Real GDP Cycles—Stratified by Credit Growth in Current Expansion

	Current Expansion			Subsequent Recession		
	Full Sample	Pre-WWII	Post-WWII	Full Sample	Pre-WWII	Post-WWII
Duration (years)						
High credit	6.3	3.4	10.2	1.6	1.5	1.7
Expansion	(6.5)	(3.2)	(7.1)	(0.9)	(0.8)	(0.9)
Low credit	3.8	2.6	7.0	1.5	1.6	1.3
Expansion	(3.6)	(1.9)	(6.6)	(0.8)	(1.0)	(0.5)
rate (% p.a.)						
High credit	3.3	3.8	3.0	−2.4	−3.0	−1.8
Expansion	(2.0)	(2.3)	(1.5)	(2.3)	(2.8)	(1.3)
Low credit	4.1	4.7	2.7	−2.7	−3.3	−1.6
Expansion	(2.5)	(2.7)	(1.4)	(2.8)	(3.2)	(1.7)
Observations	271	164	107	261	153	108

Notes: *Rate* refers to the annual rate of change between turning points. *Duration* refers to the number of years that each phase between turning points lasts. *High/low credit* refers to whether credit growth during the expansion is above/below country-specific means. Recessions sorted by behavior of credit (above/below country-specific mean) in the preceding expansion. Standard errors in parenthesis (see text).

Perhaps the more obvious takeaway is that credit turns out to be a more *violent* variable than GDP. Credit expansions and recessions exhibit wilder swings than GDP expansions and recessions.

These results raise some intriguing questions. What is behind the longer duration of expansions since World War II? What connection, if any, does this phenomenon have to do with credit? In previous research (Jordà et al. 2013), we showed that rapid growth of credit in the expansion is usually associated with deeper and longer-lasting recessions, everything else equal. But what about the opposite? Does rapid deleveraging in the recession lead to faster and brighter recoveries? And what is the relationship between credit in the expansion and its duration? Does more rapid deleveraging make the recession last longer? In order to answer some of these questions, we stratify the results by credit growth in the next two tables.

In table 6 we stratify results depending on whether credit in the current expansion is above or below country-specific means and examine how this correlates with the current expansion and subsequent recession. Consistent with the results reported in our previous work (Jordà et al. 2013), rapid credit growth during the expansion is associated with a deeper recession, especially in the post–World War II era. Compare

Table 7
Duration and Rate of Real GDP Cycles—Stratified by Credit Growth in Current Recession

	Current Recession			Subsequent Expansion		
	Full Sample	Pre-WWII	Post-WWII	Full Sample	Pre-WWII	Post-WWII
Duration (years)						
High credit	1.5	1.5	1.3	3.9	2.8	6.4
Recession	(0.9)	(0.9)	(.5)	(3.7)	(2.3)	(4.9)
Low credit	1.6	1.7	1.6	6.1	3.2	10.2
Recession	(0.9)	(1.0)	(0.9)	(6.4)	(2.9)	(8.2)
Rate (% p.a.)						
High credit	−3.2	−4.0	−1.9	4	4.8	2.7
Recession	(3.0)	(3.3)	(1.7)	(2.5)	(2.8)	(1.3)
Low credit	−1.9	−2.3	−1.4	3.4	3.8	2.9
Recession	(1.7)	(2.1)	(1.2)	(2.1)	(2.4)	(1.4)
Observations	287	173	114	269	165	104

Notes: *Duration* refers to the number of periods that each phase between turning points lasts. *Rate* refers to the annual rate of change between turning points. *High/low credit* refers to whether credit growth during the recession is above/below country-specific means. Expansions sorted by behavior of credit (above/below country-specific mean) in the preceding recession. Standard errors in parenthesis (see text).

here rates of decline per annum, −1.8% versus −1.6% with the recession lasting about five months more. However, it is also true that the expansion itself lasts about three years longer (and at a higher per annum rate of growth). Pre–World War II, expansions last about nine months longer when credit grows above average, and there is little difference in the brevity of recessions.

The shaft and the blade of our financial hockey stick thus also appear to mark a shift in the manner in which credit and the economy interact. Since World War II, rapid credit growth is associated with longer-lasting expansions (by about three years) and more rapid rates of growth (3.0% versus 2.7%). However, when the recession hits, the economic slowdown is also deeper. In terms of a crude trade-off, periods with above mean credit growth are associated with an additional 12% growth in output relative to a 1% loss during the following recession, a net gain of nearly 11% over the 12 years that the entire cycle lasts (expansion plus recession), that is, almost an extra 1% per year.

As a complement to these results, table 7 provides a similar stratification based on whether credit grows above or below country-specific means during the current *recession*, and then examines the current recession and the subsequent expansion. A *high credit* bin here means that credit grew above average during the recession (or that there was less deleveraging, in some cases). The *low credit* bin is associated with recessions in which credit grew below average or there was more deleveraging, in some cases.

On a first pass, for the post–World War II era only, low credit growth in a recession is associated with a slightly deeper recession (less violent, but longer lasting, for a total loss in output of 2.5% versus 2.25%), but with a more robust expansion thereafter (about 12% more in cumulative terms over the subsequent expansion, with the expansion lasting about four years longer). There does not seem to be as marked an effect pre–World War II.

Tables 6 and 7 reveal an interesting juxtaposition: in the post–World War II era, whereas rapid credit growth in the expansion is associated with a longer expansion, a deeper recession but an overall net gain, it is below average credit growth in the recession that results in more growth in the expansion even at a small cost of a deeper recession in the short term. It is natural to ask then the extent to which high credit growth cycles follow each other. Is rapid growth in the expansion followed by a quick deceleration in the recession? Or is there no relation? To answer these questions, one can calculate the state-transition probability matrix relating each type of cycle binned by above or below credit growth. This transition probability matrix is reported in table A1 in the appendix.

Table A1 suggests that knowing whether the state of the preceding expansion was in the *high credit* or *low credit* bins has little predictive power about the state in the current recession or the expansion that follows (the transition probabilities across all possible states are almost all 0.5). The type of recession also appears to have little influence on the type of expansion the economy is likely to experience. However, in the post–World War II era we do find that a *low credit* recession is slightly more likely ($p = 0.62$) to be followed by a *low credit* expansion. This contrasts with the pre–World War II sample where a *low credit* recession seem to affect only the likelihood ($p = 0.71$) that the following recession would also be *low credit*. By and large, it is safe to say that the type of recession or expansion experienced seems to have very little influence on future cyclical activity.

VI.   Credit and the Real Economy: A Historical and International Perspective

This section follows in the footsteps of the real business cycle literature. First, we reexamine core stylized facts about aggregate fluctuations using our richer data set. Second, we study the correlation between real and financial variables, as well the evolution of these correlations over time in greater detail. The overarching question is whether the increase in the size of the financial sector discussed in previous sections left its mark on the relation between real and financial variables over the business cycle.

We structure the discussion around three key insights. First, we confirm that the volatility of real variables has declined over time, specially since the mid-1980s. The origins of this so called Great Moderation, first discovered by McConnell and Pérez-Quirós (2000), are still a matter of lively debate. Institutional labor-market mechanisms, such as a combination of deunionization and skill-biased technological change, are a favorite of Acemoglu, Aghion, and Violante (2001). Loss of bargaining power by workers is a plausible explanation for what happened in the United States and in the United Kingdom, yet the Great Moderation transcended these Anglo-Saxon economies, and was felt in nearly every advanced economy in our sample (cf. Stock and Watson 2005). As a result, alternative explanations have naturally gravitated toward phenomena with wider reach. Among them, some have argued for the "better policy" explanation, such as Boivin and Giannoni (2006). For others, the evolving role of commodity prices in more service-oriented economies along with more stable markets are an important factor, such as for Nakov and Pescatori (2010). Of course, sheer dumb luck, a sequence of positive shocks more precisely, is Ahmed, Levin, and Wilson's (2004) explanation. The debate rages on. And yet, despite the moderation of real fluctuations, the volatility of asset prices has increased over the twentieth century.

Second, the correlation of output, consumption, and investment growth with credit has grown substantially over time and with a great deal of variation in the timing depending on the economy considered. Credit, not money, is much more closely associated with changes in GDP, investment, and consumption today than it was in earlier, less-leveraged eras of modern economic development. Third, the correlation between price-level changes (inflation) and credit has also increased substantially and has become as close as the nexus between monetary aggregates and inflation. This too marks a change with earlier times when money, not credit, exhibited the closest correlation with inflation.

We start by reporting standard deviations (volatility) and autocorrelations of variables with their first lag (persistence) of real aggregates (output, consumption, investment, current account as a ratio to GDP), as well as those of price levels and real asset prices. In keeping with standard practice in this literature, all variables have been detrended using the Hodrick-Prescott filter, which removes low-frequency movements from the data.[4]

Finally, we follow general practice and report results for the full sample, 1870–2013, and also present the results over the following subsamples: the gold standard era (1870–1913); the interwar period (1919–1938); the Bretton Woods period (1948–1971); and the era of fiat money and floating exchange rates (1972–2013). We exclude World War I and World War II. This split of the sample by time period corresponds only loosely to the rise of leverage on a country-by-country basis. The next section of the paper directly conditions the business cycle moments on credit-to-GDP levels for a more precise match on this dimension.

A. Volatility and Persistence of the Business Cycle

Two basic features of the data are reported in table 8: volatility (generally measured by the standard deviation of the log of HP-detrended annual data) and persistence (measured with the first-order serial correlation parameter). In line with previous studies, our data show that output volatility peaked in the interwar period, driven by the devastating collapse of output during the Great Depression. The Bretton Woods and free-floating eras generally exhibited lower output volatility than the gold standard period. The standard deviation of log output was about 50% higher in the pre–World War II period than after the war. The idea of declining macroeconomic fluctuations is further strengthened by the behavior of consumption and investment. Relative to gold standard times, the standard deviation of investment and consumption was 50% lower in the post–World War II years.

At the same time, persistence has also increased significantly. In the course of the twentieth century, business cycles have generally become shallower and longer, as reported earlier. A similar picture emerges with respect to price-level fluctuations. In terms of price-level stability, it is noteworthy that the free-floating era stands out from the periods of fixed exchange rates with respect to the volatility of the price level. The interwar period also stands out, but both relative to the gold standard era and the Bretton Woods period, the past four decades have been marked by a much lower variance of prices.

Table 8 reveals a surprising insight: contrary to the Great Moderation, the standard deviation of real stock prices has increased. As we have

Table 8
Properties of Macroeconomic Aggregates and Asset Prices—Moments of
Detrended Variables

	Subsample			
	Gold Standard	Interwar	Bretton Woods	Float
Volatility (s.d.)				
Log real output p.c.	0.03	0.06	0.03	0.02
Log real consumption p.c.	0.04	0.06	0.03	0.02
Log real investment p.c.	0.12	0.25	0.08	0.08
Current account/GDP	1.83	2.57	1.70	1.67
Log CPI	0.09	1.11	0.09	0.03
Log real share prices	0.13	0.22	0.20	0.25
Log real house prices	0.09	0.14	0.09	0.09
Persistence (autocorrelation)				
Log real output p.c.	0.49	0.63	0.79	0.65
Log real consumption p.c.	0.35	0.55	0.73	0.71
Log real investment p.c.	0.47	0.57	0.57	0.66
Current account/GDP	0.30	0.20	0.21	0.43
Log CPI	0.83	0.58	0.90	0.80
Log real share prices	0.42	0.61	0.63	0.57
Log real house prices	0.46	0.50	0.60	0.75

Notes: Variables detrended using the HP filter with $\lambda = 100$. *Volatility* refers to the S.D. of
the detrended series; *persistence* refers to first-order serial correlation in the detrended
series. All variables in logs and in per capita except for the current account to GDP ratio.
Output, consumption, and investment reported in real terms, per capita (p.c.), deflated by
the CPI. Share prices and house prices deflated by the CPI (see text).

seen before, both output and consumption have become less volatile
over the same period. The divergence between the declining volatility
in consumption and output on the one hand, and increasingly volatile
asset prices on the other, is also noteworthy as it seems to apply only
to stock prices. The standard deviation of detrended real house prices
has remained relatively stable over time. The interwar period stands
out with respect to volatility of house prices because real estate prices
fluctuated strongly after World War I, particularly in Europe, and then
again during the Great Depression, as discussed in Knoll, Schularick,
and Steger (2015).

What about the behavior of different expenditure components over
time? Table 9 shows that key empirical relationships established in the
earlier literature are robust to our more comprehensive data set. Consumption is about as volatile as output (in terms of relative standard deviations), although less so in the United States. However, investment is
consistently more volatile than output (more than twice as much). Table 9

Table 9
Properties of National Expenditure Components—Moments of Differenced Variables

	Full sample		Pre-WWII		Post-WWII		Float	
	United States	Pooled	United States	Pooled	United States	Pooled	United States	Pooled
Standard Deviations Relative to Output								
sd(c)/sd(y)	0.77	1.05	0.77	1.09	0.72	1.01	0.94	1.02
sd(i)/sd(y)	5.20	3.41	5.54	3.70	2.86	2.82	2.68	3.22
sd(g)/sd(y)	2.74	2.77	2.32	2.94	4.27	2.35	1.67	1.73
sd(nx)/sd(y)	0.62	1.73	0.70	2.01	0.54	1.41	0.60	1.37
Correlations with Output								
corr(c,y)	0.87	0.73	0.90	0.72	0.69	0.75	0.90	0.82
corr(i,y)	0.70	0.59	0.77	0.59	0.20	0.59	0.82	0.82
corr(g,y)	-0.10	0.00	-0.29	-0.03	0.43	0.10	-0.28	-0.06
corr(nx,y)	-0.18	-0.15	-0.14	-0.11	-0.34	-0.24	-0.62	-0.33

Notes: Variables detrended using the HP filter with $\lambda = 100$. Raw variables are log real per capita quantities, except net export share ($nx = NX/GDP$). *Standard deviations* reported as a ratio to the standard deviation of detrended output. *Correlation with output* is simple correlation coefficient with detrended output. Full sample: 1870–2013; Pre-WWII: 1870–1938; Post-WW-: 1948–1971; Float: 1972–2013 (see text).

also shows that these relationships hold for virtually all countries and across subperiods. There is some evidence that the relative volatility of investment and government spending is declining over time.

We also confirm that consumption and investment are procyclical with output. This comovement seems to increase over time, potentially reflecting better measurement. In contrast to consumption and investment, government expenditures exhibit much less of a systematic tendency to comove with output, suggesting perhaps a fiscal smoothing mechanism at work. Net export changes are also only weakly correlated with output movements.

Overall, with more and better data we confirm a number of key stylized facts from the literature. Output volatility has declined over time, consumption is less, and investment considerably more volatile than output, and both comove positively with output. Government spending and net exports generally fluctuate in a way less clearly correlated with output. Despite broad-based evidence of declining amplitudes of real fluctuations, the volatility of real asset prices has not declined— and, in the case of stock prices, actually increased in the second half of the twentieth century relative to the pre–World War II period.

B.   Credit, Money, and the Business Cycle

Evaluating the merits of alternative stabilization policies is one of the key objectives of macroeconomics. It is therefore natural to ask how the cross-correlations of real and financial variables have developed over time. In table 10, we track the correlations of credit as well as money growth rates with output, consumption, investment, and asset price growth rates. Thus, looking now at first differences, the main goal is to determine if and how these correlations have changed over time, especially with the sharp rise of credit associated with the financial hockey stick.

These correlations have become larger. Table 10 shows that before World War II the correlations of credit growth and output growth were positive but low. In the post–World War II era, the correlations between credit and real variables have increased substantially, doubling from one period to the other. This pattern not only holds for credit and output. It is even more evident for investment and consumption, which were only loosely correlated with movements in credit before World War II. Unsurprisingly, in light of the dominant role played by mortgage lending in the growth of leverage, the correlation between credit

Table 10
Real Money and Credit Growth: Cross Correlations with Real Variables

	Full Sample		Pre-WWII		Post-WWII		Float	
	United States	Pooled	United States	Pooled	United States	Pooled	United States	Pooled
Real money growth								
Δy	0.36	0.20	0.47	0.12	0.24	0.33	0.22	0.29
Δc	0.33	0.20	0.35	0.08	0.50	0.36	0.47	0.32
Δi	0.17	0.11	0.25	0.06	-0.02	0.21	0.07	0.24
Δhp	0.16	0.30	0.11	0.24	0.26	0.33	0.22	0.27
Real credit growth								
Δy	0.40	0.21	0.30	0.04	0.67	0.53	0.76	0.46
Δc	0.34	0.25	0.21	0.11	0.68	0.52	0.80	0.48
Δi	0.15	0.20	0.10	0.10	0.52	0.42	0.63	0.46
Δhp	-0.01	0.37	-0.18	0.29	0.41	0.45	0.55	0.49

Notes: All variables expressed in first differences of the log and in real per capita terms. Correlations between real money growth and real credit growth (measured with total bank lending to the nonfinancial sector) with: the growth rate of output (Δy); consumption (Δc); investment (Δi); and house prices (Δhp). Full sample: 1870–2013; Pre-WWII: 1870–1938; Post-WWII: 1948–1971; Float: 1972–2013 (see text).

Table 11
Nominal Money and Credit Growth: Cross Correlations with Inflation

Country	Broad money growth (M2 or similar)				Private credit growth (bank loans)			
	Full	Pre-WWII	Post-WWII	Float	Full	Pre-WWII	Post-WW2	Float
AUS	0.52	0.27	0.40	0.49	0.51	0.23	0.40	0.44
BEL	−0.07	—	−0.07	−0.07	0.41	0.39	0.32	0.49
CAN	0.57	0.51	0.51	0.70	0.50	0.46	0.33	0.65
CHE	0.35	0.33	0.13	0.10	0.29	0.30	0.20	0.22
DEU	0.49	0.59	0.17	0.48	0.22	0.32	0.08	0.52
DNK	0.42	0.33	0.39	0.38	0.43	0.35	0.39	0.47
ESP	0.61	0.25	0.54	0.74	0.29	−0.20	0.36	0.45
FIN	0.34	0.20	0.41	0.66	0.41	0.36	0.40	0.52
FRA	0.48	0.44	0.41	0.45	0.39	0.16	0.68	0.63
GBR	0.61	0.46	0.38	0.44	0.58	0.45	0.38	0.49
ITA	0.51	0.47	0.38	0.73	0.48	0.49	0.28	0.66
JPN	0.43	0.01	0.58	0.61	0.54	0.47	0.72	0.53
NLD	0.33	0.36	0.14	0.31	0.66	0.65	0.41	0.49
NOR	0.57	0.43	0.49	0.60	0.60	0.61	0.33	0.48
PRT	0.70	0.81	0.64	0.71	0.33	0.19	0.42	0.50
SWE	0.53	0.60	0.26	0.29	0.65	0.66	0.44	0.56
USA	0.53	0.61	0.21	0.27	0.51	0.67	−0.02	0.25
Pooled	0.51	0.43	0.46	0.55	0.43	0.34	0.44	0.54

Notes: Correlations between broad money growth and private credit growth (measured with total bank lending to the nonfinancial sector) with CPI inflation. Full sample: 1870–2013; Pre-WWII: 1870–1938; Post-WWII: 1948–1971; Float: 1972–2013 (see text).

growth and house price growth has never been higher than in the past few decades.

The comparison with the cross-correlation of monetary aggregates with real variables shown in table 10 echoes our previous research (Jordà et al. 2015). In the age of credit, monetary aggregates come a distant second when it comes to the association with macroeconomic variables. Real changes in M2 were more closely associated with cyclical fluctuations in real variables than credit before World War II. This is no longer true in the postwar era. As table 10 demonstrates, in recent times changes in real credit are generally much more tightly aligned with real fluctuations than those of money.

The growing importance of credit is also a key finding of this part of the analysis. In table 11 we study the relationship between private credit, broad money, and price inflation. Are changes in the nominal quantity of broad money or changes in credit volumes more closely associated with inflation? Before World War II, broad money is generally more closely associated with inflation than credit. Moreover, the relationship between monetary factors and inflation appears relatively stable over time. Correlation coefficients are between 0.4 and 0.55 for all subperiods.

The growing correlation between credit and inflation rates is noteworthy. In the pre–World War II data, the correlation between loan growth and inflation was positive, but relatively low. In the post–World War II era, correlation coefficients rose and are of a similar magnitude to those of money and inflation. The mean correlation increased from 0.33 in the pre–World War II era to 0.54 in the free-floating period. Clearly, both nominal aggregates exhibit a relatively tight relation with inflation, but here too the importance of credit appears to have been growing.

VII. Business Cycle Moments and Leverage

We have emphasized two important points in previous sections. First, we invoked the financial hockey stick. Advanced economies over the last 40 years have experienced an unprecedented shift in bank lending relative to GDP after a preceding century of near stability. Second, the manner in which macroeconomic aggregates correlate with each other has evolved over time. Moreover, such correlations can vary considerably from one country to another within a given era.

In this section, following up on the latter point, we focus our argument on a different set of goalposts, but with the same purpose in mind. We now show that the alternative approach of describing business cycle properties in terms of key moments has arguably missed a very important driving force in the aggregate economic dynamics by ignoring the role of credit.

In this respect, and to zoom in on key stylized facts in the results that follow, we now adopt a straightforward empirical approach to summarize the data, by looking at the correlation (or, graphically, a scatter) of any given macroeconomic statistical moment of interest ($\hat{m}$) with the credit-to-GDP ratio ($\bar{x}$). Formally, we take the panel data for all countries i and all years t, construct rolling 10-year windows of data y_{it} over the entire sample within which we compute a country-window specific moment $\hat{m}(y_{it})$, which we seek to relate to the average credit-to-GDP ratio $\bar{x}_{it}$. Finally, we present the data and correlations using a binscatter diagram. In all such diagrams that follow, the points displayed are summary data for each moment computed when the credit-to-GDP ratio is grouped into 20 bins. The full sample regression line is then also plotted. Country fixed effects and a global real GDP per capita control are also included.

A. Central Moments Are Correlated with Leverage

To start with some of the most widely employed business cycle moments, figure 7 presents the mean, s.d., skewness, and 10th percentile of the annual growth rate of real GDP per capita, real consumption per capita, and real investment per capita (in 10-year rolling windows) using binscatters plotted against the (average in-window) credit/GDP ratio for our full historical sample. Figure 8 reports the exact same binscatters, for the exact same moments, but restricting attention to the post–World War II sample. As a complement and robustness check, we report pooled binscatters without country fixed effects or the global real GDP per capita control in the appendix, and those results include variation across both time and space.

With four moments of three variables, the figure consists of twelve panels. It is immediately apparent that the assumption of stable parameters is widely rejected by the data. Nonzero slopes are clearly evident, and these slopes are statistically significantly different from zero. Moreover, in some cases the binscatter displays possible nonlinearities (e.g., the binscatter for the mean of real GDP growth in the first row, column [a] in figure 7). We now discuss the results in more detail.

In figure 7, column (a), we see first in row 1 that mean real GDP per capita growth is virtually uncorrelated with credit/GDP, but the mean does appear hump shaped, with lower mean growth at very low levels of credit/GDP and also at very high levels. This observation is consistent with an emerging notion: there can be "too much finance." This literature, which argues that the link between the size of the financial sector and economic growth may not be linear or monotonic (King and Levine 1993), with small or even negative impacts possible when an economy is highly leveraged (Philippon and Reshef 2013; Ceccheti and Kharroubi 2015; Arcand, Berkes, and Panizza 2015).

In row 2 we see that the s.d. of real GDP growth is declining in credit/GDP, suggesting a great moderation effect of sorts, whereby volatility has fallen as advanced economies have leveraged up. However, in row 3 we see that the third moment reveals a more subtle angle to this story. Although the right tail of growth appears to become subdued as credit/GDP rises, the left tail does not, as indicated by rising skewness of growth outcomes. This rising skew fits with our earlier empirical work, in this and other papers, and the work of others, showing that leveraged economies are more at risk of steeper downturns and slower recoveries, often times these taking the form of financial crisis

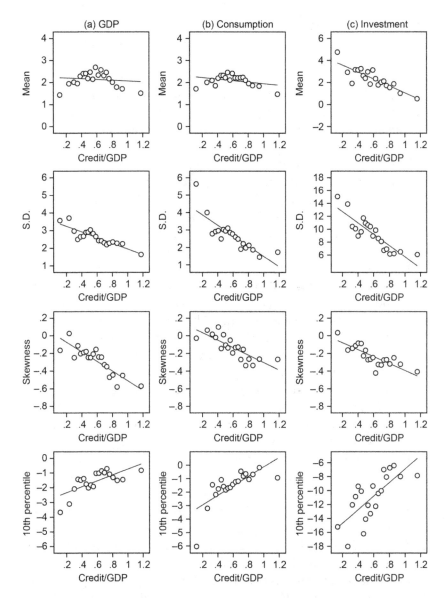

Fig. 7. Central moments: Binscatters against credit/GDP ratio for mean, s.d., skewness, and 10th percentile of annual growth rate of real GDP per capita, real consumption per capita, real investment per capita, full sample 1870–2013, controlling for country fixed effects and global growth rate.

Note: Binscatters based on 20 bins using 10-year rolling windows to calculate moments. Fitted line obtained using the full sample (see text).

recessions (Reinhart and Rogoff 2009, 2013; Schularick and Taylor 2012; Jordà et al. 2013). From a theoretical standpoint, this result argues for macroeconomic models with an allowance for banking or financial sectors whose scale can influence the shape of recession outcomes. Even so, row 4 data on the lowest decile also suggest that lower-tail outcomes are somewhat better under higher credit/GDP, so the volatility effect dominates to mitigate the "rare disasters" as credit/GDP rises in this full sample setup.

To summarize, we have shown that the key moments of real GDP per capita growth are far from stable parameters, and historically they have varied with leverage. These results were obtained exploiting the full sample, but the patterns in the post–World War II sample, the era of the financial hockey stick, may be even more interesting. In figure 8, we therefore repeat the analysis using only post-1950 data.

The post–World War II data tell an even more striking story. As before, more credit is associated with less volatility in growth, consumption, and investment, but the decline in mean growth is much sharper. In the postwar data, we are on the right side of the hump in growth rates. Output skew also becomes more extremely correlated with credit/GDP in the negative sense, even if the consumption and output correlations change less. Adding up all the effects, the row 4 results on shifts in the lowest decile now indicate that lower-tail outcomes are worse under higher credit/GDP, so the worse mean and skew effects dominate to worsen the "rare disasters" as credit/GDP rises in the post–World War II data.

To present some simple summary data, in table 12 we stratify the sample into high and low bins, using the mean credit-to-GDP ratio as the threshold. We then calculate business cycle moments with and without country fixed effects. The table shows again that central business cycle moments change with leverage levels. But the full sample and post–World War II results again reveal the dramatic shifts that took place in the era of the financial hockey stick.[5]

The table thus reinforces the principal hypothesis of the paper: high credit is associated with less volatility in growth, consumption, and investment. Equally consistently, we find that the mean drops and skewness becomes more negative at high levels of debt. Credit may be associated with a dampening of the volatility of the cycle, but is also associated with more spectacular crashes, and worse tail events. In the post–World War II period, the time of the financial hockey stick, these patterns grow more pronounced.

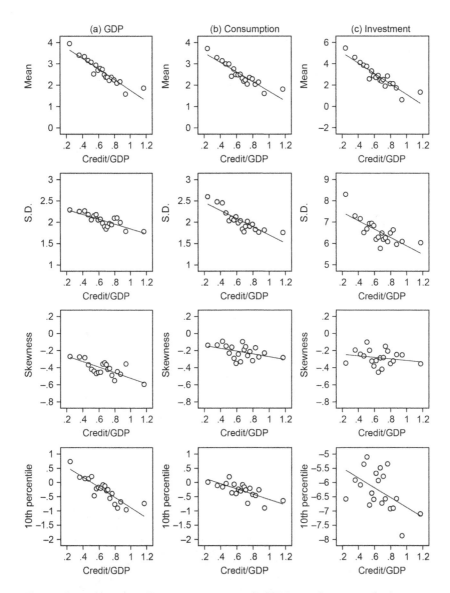

Fig. 8. Central moments: Binscatters against credit/GDP ratio for mean, s.d., skewness, and 10th percentile of annual growth rate of real GDP per capita, real consumption per capita, real investment per capita, post-WWII sample 1950–2013, controlling for country fixed effects and global growth rate.

Note: Binscatters based on 20 bins using 10-year rolling windows to calculate moments. Fitted line obtained using the full sample (see text).

Table 12
Business Cycle Moments

	Real GDP Growth Per Capita		Real Consumption Growth Per Capita		Real Investment Growth Per Capita	
	High Credit	Low Credit	High Credit	Low Credit	High Credit	Low Credit
Full Sample, 1870–2013						
Mean						
Pooled	1.5	2.2	1.5	2.2	1.2	2.9
Fixed effects	1.7	2.0	1.7	2.0	1.7	2.3
Standard deviation						
Pooled	2.9	3.7	3.3	3.9	10.4	13.9
Fixed effects	2.6	3.2	3.1	3.6	9.8	12.9
Skewness						
Pooled	−0.6	−0.7	−0.2	−0.2	−0.6	−2.8
Fixed effects	−0.7	−0.2	−0.2	0.0	−0.2	−2.3
10th percentile						
Pooled	−1.8	−2.0	−1.9	−2.3	−10.1	−9.1
Fixed effects	−1.3	−1.5	−1.6	−2.3	−8.5	−8.7
Observations	945	976	913	896	911	900
Post–WWII sample, 1950–2013						
Mean						
Pooled	1.5	3.2	1.4	3.1	1.0	3.7
Fixed effects	2.2	2.6	2.0	2.6	2.3	2.6
Standard deviation						
Pooled	2.3	2.5	2.2	2.7	7.5	7.0
Fixed effects	1.8	2.1	2.0	2.4	6.8	6.7
Skewness						
Pooled	−0.8	0.2	−0.3	0.4	−0.5	−0.1
Fixed effects	−0.8	0.1	−0.4	0.0	−0.6	−0.3
10th percentile						
Pooled	−1.2	0.3	−1.0	−0.2	−8.4	−4.6
Fixed effects	0.1	0.0	−0.3	−0.2	−6.0	−5.3
Observations	488	600	488	600	488	596

Notes: Summary table for mean, s.d., skewness, and 10th percentile at high/low levels of credit/GDP. *Pooled* refers to moments calculated with a pooled sample; *fixed effects* refers to moments calculated with controls for country fixed effects and global growth rate; *high/ low credit* refers to whether the ratio of credit to GDP is above or below country specific means (see text).

B. *Cross Moments Are Correlated with Leverage*

Our next set of results explores whether high-frequency movements in the key macrovariables cohere with movements in credit, and whether these are stable relationships over the wide span of historical experience. To summarize: yes and no. Figure 9 presents the correlation of

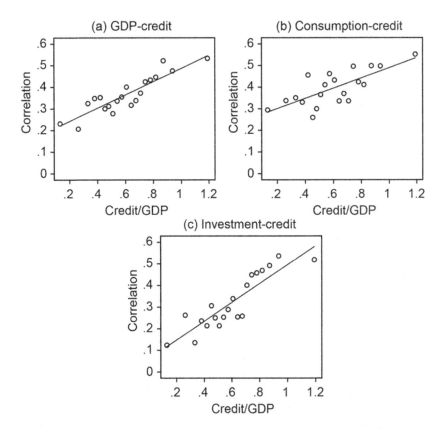

Fig. 9. Cross moments: Binscatters against credit/GDP ratio for correlation of annual growth rate of real credit per capita with real consumption per capita and real investment per capita, controlling for country fixed effects and global growth rate.

Note: Binscatters based on 20 bins using 10-year rolling windows to calculate moments. Fitted line obtained using the full sample (see text).

annual growth rate of real GDP per capita, real consumption per capita, and real investment per capita with the annual growth rate of real credit per capita using binscatters plotted against the credit/GDP ratio for our full historical sample.

Panel (a) shows that booms in real GDP per capita growth tend to be associated with booms in real credit per capita, since this correlation is positive in general. However, in low-leverage economies this correlation is about 0.2, rising to more than double or 0.5 in high-leverage economies. So this reduced-form coherence of output and credit is much amplified in more leveraged economies, an intriguing result.

The same also holds true for both of the two key components of GDP, consumption and investment. Panel (b) shows that the correlation of

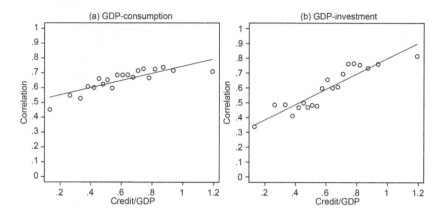

Fig. 10. Cross moments: Binscatters against credit/GDP ratio for correlation of annual growth rate of real consumption per capita, and real investment per capita with the annual growth rate of real GDP per capita, controlling for country fixed effects and global growth rate.

Note: Binscatters based on 20 bins using 10-year rolling windows to calculate moments. Fitted line obtained using the full sample (see text).

real consumption per capita growth and real credit per capita growth is positive and rising with the credit/GDP ratio. Panel (c) shows that the correlation of real investment per capita growth and real credit per capita growth is positive and rising with the credit/GDP ratio. These findings suggest that the new generation of macroeconomic models need to match macrofluctuations in such a way that both real consumption and real investment exhibit greater comovement with credit in more leveraged worlds.

Consistent with the above, our next analysis of cross moments asks if high-frequency movements in consumption and investment are correlated with GDP. This is a very common business cycle moment that models have sought to match (e.g., Backus and Kehoe 1992; Backus, Kehoe, and Kydland 1992). But again, as one might expect given the prior results, these are not fixed parameters.

Figure 10 presents the correlation of annual growth rates of real consumption per capita and real investment per capita with annual growth rates of real GDP per capita, with binscatters plotted against the credit/GDP ratio for our full historical sample. Panel (a) shows that booms in real GDP per capita growth tend to be associated with booms in real consumption per capita, since this correlation is positive in general. However, in low-leverage economies this correlation is about 0.4, rising to 0.7 in high-leverage economies. Panel (b) shows that booms in real GDP per capita growth tend to be associated with booms in real investment per capita, since this correlation is also positive. However, in low-leverage economies this correlation is about 0.4, rising to 0.8 in high-leverage economies.

Maybe this is all not so terribly surprising, since we have already seen from the previous figure that all of the growth rates of these three aggregates—output, consumption, and investment—are more closely tied to the credit cycle as leverage rises; hence, it is to be expected that they should also tend to become more closely tied to each other. Once again, this suggests that a key challenge for macroeconomic models is to develop a formulation whereby the coherence of the macroeconomic aggregates operates through a financial channel, and does so more strongly as the economy levers up.

C. International Moments Are Correlated with Leverage

Our final set of results turns to the moments of notable relevance for those interested in international business cycle models (e.g., Backus et al. 1992; Basu and Taylor 1999). Devotees of this subfield ponder what we can learn from movements in macrovariables in multiple countries, either from looking at between-country correlations in aggregate outcomes, and/or by looking at the moments of key cross-border indicators like imports, exports, and the current account. We present three figures that give an overview of our findings in this area, and that again confirm how even at the international level, the key business cycle moments of interest in the literature have not been fixed, immutable parameters, but have shifted in tandem with the size of domestic financial systems.

Using the now familiar technique of binscatters employed above, figure 11 presents three kinds of moments: volatility ratios of local annual growth rates of real consumption per capita relative to real GDP per capita, local annual growth rates of real consumption per capita relative to "world" (i.e., year sample mean) growth of real GDP per capita, and also the volatility of "world" real GDP per capita, with each of these moments plotted against the credit/GDP ratio for our full historical sample. The volatility ratio of local annual growth rates of real consumption per capita relative to real GDP per capita are fairly stable, and do not seem to depend much on leverage measured by credit/GDP; they may even be falling slightly, albeit the ratio exceeds 1 throughout the range, which indicates next to no international smoothing.

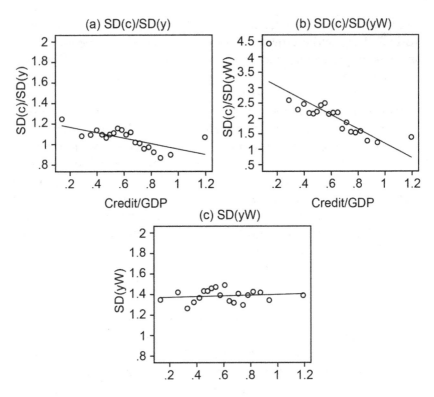

Fig. 11. International moments: Binscatters against credit/GDP ratio for volatility ratios of local annual growth rates of real consumption per capita and real GDP per capita, local annual growth rates of real consumption per capita and world real GDP per capita, and volatility of world real GDP per capita, controlling for country fixed effects and global growth rate.

Note: Binscatters based on 20 bins using 10-year rolling windows to calculate moments. Fitted line obtained using the full sample; y refers to country-specific output, and yW refers to global output (i.e., 17-country weighted mean). (See text.)

This result is consistent with Backus and Kehoe (1992) and Backus, Kehoe, and Kydland (1992). The volatility ratio of local annual growth rates of real consumption per capita relative to world real GDP per capita falls as credit/GDP rises; but, the ratio again exceeds 1 throughout the range, which indicates limited risk sharing except in cases with large financial systems. The volatility of world real GDP per capita has not tended to fall as leverage rises. It may be asked how this is consistent with the earlier result that country-level real GDP per capita growth saw its s.d. fall as leverage rose, but the answer lies in shifts in cross-country output correlations, as we shall see in a second. These findings suggest that international macromodels may need to take into account the size of domestic financial systems when trying to replicate real world moments. In worlds with larger financial systems, smoothing and risk sharing may be enhanced, but at the global level, volatility may be increased, creating some potential tradeoffs (see, e.g., Caballero, Farhi, and Gourinchas 2008).

Figure 12 presents binscatters of four moments that capture the correlation of local and world cycles. From first to last these are, respectively, the correlation of local and "world" annual growth rates of real GDP per capita, real consumption per capita, real investment per capita, and real credit per capita, with each of these shown using binscatters plotted against the credit/GDP ratio for our full historical sample.

Panel (a) shows that the correlation of local and "world" annual growth rates of real GDP per capita is highly correlated with leverage measured by credit/GDP. Thus, more leveraged economies have also tended to be economies with a local business cycle more tightly linked to the world cycle. Panel (b) shows that the correlation of local and "world" annual growth rates of real consumption per capita is also highly correlated with the leverage measure. This shows that the convergence of consumption growth to a common value, a risk-sharing feature, seems to be associated with larger financial systems. However, the prior result suggests that ceteris is not paribus, in that those same highly leveraged economies also happen to have less risk sharing to do in the first place, having stronger output correlations. This then helps to explain why, in the previous figure, the consumption-output volatility ratio is relatively flat as leverage varies.

Finally, panels (c) and (d) show that the correlation of local and "world" annual growth rates of real investment per capita and real credit per capita are also highly correlated with the leverage measure. Country-level investment and credit boom-and-bust cycles tend to move more in sync with each other in a world with more leveraged economies. In total, this set of results points to the important role that domestic and, collectively, global financial systems might play in shaping business cycles at the local and world levels. Greater commonality of cycles is apparent in output, consumption, investment, and credit as financial systems lever up, and while this could reflect a purely coincidental increase in, say, real common shocks that "just-so-happened" to arise in those periods, it is also prima facie evidence that more leveraged economies may operate under very different model parameters with greater transmission of real and or financial shocks possible in worlds with more credit.

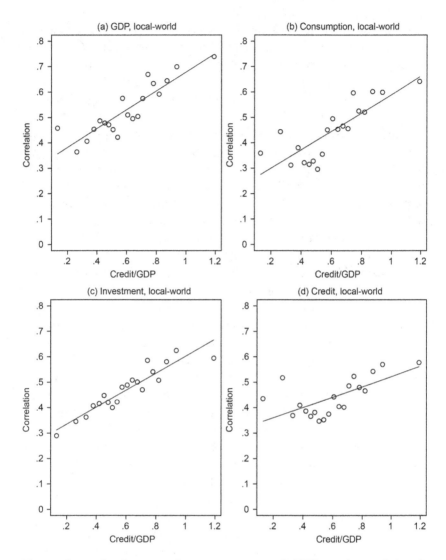

Fig. 12. International moments: Binscatters against credit/GDP ratio for correlation of local and world annual growth rates of real GDP per capita, real consumption per capita, real investment per capita, and real credit per capita, controlling for country fixed effects and global growth rate.

Note: Binscatters based on 20 bins using 10-year rolling windows to calculate moments. Fitted line obtained using the full sample (see text).

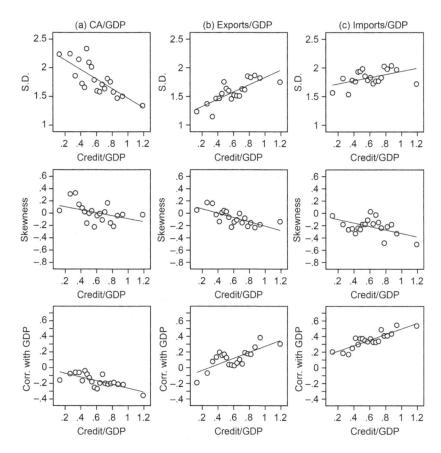

Fig. 13. International moments: Binscatters against credit/GDP ratio for s.d. and skewness of d.CA/GDP, d.exports/GDP, and d.imports/GDP, and their correlation with annual growth rates of real GDP per capita, controlling for country fixed effects and global growth rate.

Note: Binscatters based on 20 bins using 10-year rolling windows to calculate moments. Fitted line obtained using the full sample (see text).

In our very last set of results, figure 13 presents binscatters for key moments of the three principal balance-of-payments variables, the annual change in the current account, exports, and imports, all measured relative to GDP, shown in panels (a), (b), and (c) lined up in columns. The first row of the figure shows the s.d., the second row the skewness, and the final row the correlation with annual growth rate of real GDP per capita.

The first row shows that the s.d. of the the annual change in CA/GDP is falling slightly with leverage, even though the s.d. of the the annual change in exports/GDP and imports/GDP are rising slightly with leverage. Thus it seems that increased volatility of gross balance of payments flows may be more associated with leverage than is the case for a net flow like the current account.

The second row shows that all of the third moments show an amplification in the negative direction with leverage, as skewness goes more negative for the annual change in CA/GDP, exports/GDP, and imports/GDP. In the case of the net flow in the current account, these stylized facts suggest that models of reversals or "sudden-stop" phenomena may reflect some financial channels, whereby a sharper correction is more likely when the world is more leveraged. In the case of the gross flows measured by exports/GDP and imports/GDP, the results could be seen to be consistent with models where the cyclical influence of financial systems on trade flows can be particularly sharp during contractions of credit and trade flows.

The third row reveals subtle shifts in the cyclical correlations of the balance-of-payments variables. The correlations of the annual change in CA/GDP, exports/GDP, and imports/GDP with real GDP per capita are typically amplified by more leverage as seen in other results. The change in CA/GDP is countercyclical (the correlation is negative), but this effect is more negative with high leverage. The change in exports/GDP and imports/GDP are both typically procyclical (the correlation is positive), but this effect is more positive with high leverage, and for these variables imports/GDP shows greater procyclicality (rising from 0.2 to 0.6) than exports/GDP (rising from 0 to 0.4) throughout the range. This suggests that local leverage levels may hold more powerful influence on the cyclicality of the import demand side than on the export supply side, lending prima facie support for theories that emphasize the impact of financial-sector leverage on demand rather than supply channels.

VIII. Conclusion

The advanced economies have become more financialized over the last 150 years, and dramatically so since the 1970s. Never in the history of the industrial world has leverage been higher, whether measured by private credit to the nonfinancial sector relative to income as we do in much of the paper, or relative to wealth as we do for a more select subsample of economies.

A stark fact of our recent past, the "financial hockey stick," is a key feature of history that is exposed by the new data set we introduce in this paper. But beyond this, the new data can help expand the catalog of available business cycle facts to a much longer time frame, a wider range of countries, and a richer set of macroeconomic and financial variables. Derived from an arduous, multiyear collection effort, the data can help to further our progress toward a new, quantitative, macrofinancial history of the advanced economies from which we can derive new business cycle facts. The new facts seen here have significant implications for macroeconomics, probably too many to discuss individually, with many more yet to be discovered by others interested in exploring our new data.

At a basic level, our core result—that higher leverage goes hand in hand with less volatility, but more severe tail events—is compatible with the idea that expanding private credit may be safe for small shocks, but dangerous for big shocks. Put differently, leverage may expose the system to bigger, rare-event crashes, but it may help smooth more routine, small disturbances. This meshes well with two recent lines of thinking about macrofinancial interactions.

Many models with financial frictions in the tradition of the canonical Bernanke, Gertler, and Gilchrist (1999) model share a mechanism by which small shocks to net worth are amplified through financial feedback loops. The amplification channels generated by these models typically operate through the corporate sector. However, such models based on corporate leverage have had mixed results when taken to the data (e.g., Kocherlakota 2000). We offer at least two explanations for this result. First, there is the observation that the great leveraging of the second half of the twentieth century took place primarily in the household and not the corporate sector. Second, it is only with a much longer sample that enough rare disasters can be recorded to analyze the data. Thus, we are led to wonder if the less well-known extension by Bernanke et al. (1999) with an application to the household balance sheet has been unduly neglected.

In other strands of the macrofinance literature, the household balance sheet is taking center stage. Although the literature continues to build on the venerable Kiyotaki and Moore (1997) model, increasing attention has shifted to households and mortgage borrowing. Iacoviello (2005) is perhaps the most influential theoretical paper in this tradition. On the empirical side, Mian and Sufi (2013, 2014) provide microeconomic evidence on the role of housing leverage in the recent financial crisis and the pace of the recovery from the Great Recession. Our data are entirely consistent with their findings and with the dynamics generated by Iacoviello's (2005) model.

Other researchers have focused less on who does the borrowing and more on how credit markets operate. Leverage makes the financial system less stable leading to increasing systemic risks as new macrofinancial models with strong nonlinear responses to shocks show (e.g., Brunnermeier and Sannikov 2014). Adrian and Boyarchenko (2015) show that higher leverage generates higher consumption growth and lower consumption volatility in normal times at the cost of endogenous systemic financial risk. The predictions of these models are also consistent with evidence emerging from our new data.

Higher levels of debt may also trigger more pronounced deleveraging pressures in case of a sharp fall in asset prices or a tightening of borrowing limits. Following the logic laid out by Eggertsson and Krugman (2012), this may aggravate aggregate demand shortfalls—consistent with our observation of fatter left tails in high-debt regimes. Korinek and Simsek (2016) present a model where increasing household leverage gives rise to increasing aggregate demand externalities that may help explain the more severe recessions experienced in highly leveraged economies.

Along with financialization, we showed that advanced economies have become more synchronized, perhaps lessening the ability to hedge financial risk internationally. Moreover, economies have become more stable over time just as asset prices have become more volatile. In this regard, our results are in line with new research by Caballero et al. (2008) and Caballero and Krishnamurthy (2009).

New data open new horizons for exploration. Just as in any modern science, our understanding of macroeconomics and finance evolves as new evidence is introduced, whether to refute old theories or to unearth new facts.

Appendix

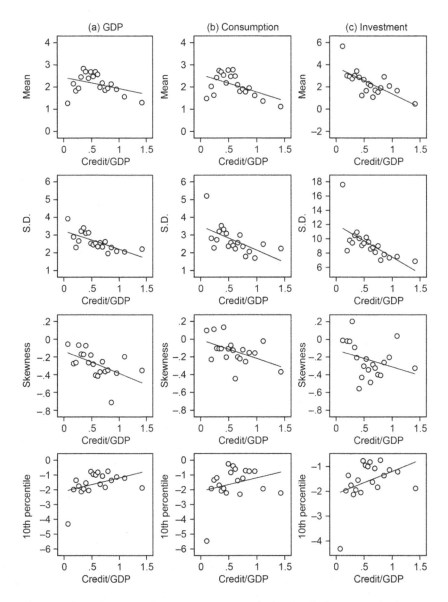

Fig. A1. Central moments: Binscatters against credit/GDP ratio for mean, s.d., skewness, and 10th percentile of annual growth rate of real GDP per capita, real consumption per capita, real investment per capita, full sample 1870–2013, no fixed effects.

Note: Binscatters based on 20 bins using 10-year rolling windows to calculate moments. Fitted line obtained using the full sample (see text).

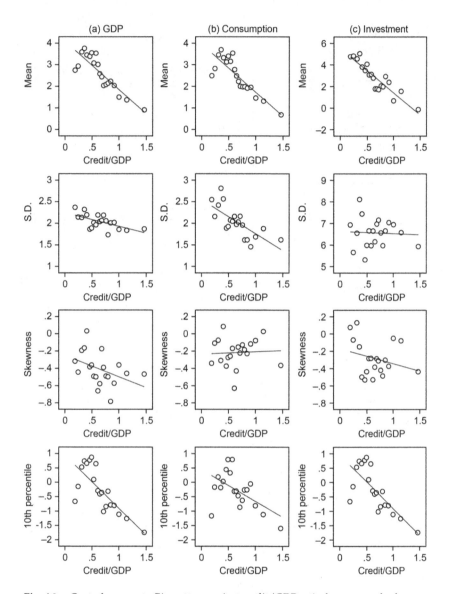

Fig. A2. Central moments: Binscatters against credit/GDP ratio for mean, s.d., skewness, and 10th percentile of annual growth rate of real GDP per capita, real consumption per capita, real investment per capita, post-WW2 sample 1950–2013, no fixed effects

Note: Binscatters based on 20 bins using 10-year rolling windows to calculate moments. Fitted line obtained using the full sample (see text).

Endnotes

We are grateful to Martin Eichenbaum and Jonathan Parker for their guidance and support. For helpful comments we thank our discussants Mark Gertler and Atif Mian, as well as the other conference participants. The scale of the data collection effort would not have been possible without the generous support of many colleagues at research institutions, national archives, central banks, and statistical offices who shared their data or directed us to potential sources. We are equally indebted to a large number of dedicated and enthusiastic research assistants in various places who chased references through many libraries and archives in various countries, in particular Katharina Knoll and Felix Ward. We are also especially grateful to Helen Irvin for outstanding assistance with the data analysis. Last, but not least, we have benefited from generous grants from the Institute for New Economic Thinking and the Volkswagen Foundation, who supported different parts of the data collection and analysis effort. The views expressed in this paper are the sole responsibility of the authors and do not necessarily reflect the views of the Federal Reserve Bank of San Francisco or the Federal Reserve System. For acknowledgments, sources of research support, and disclosure of the authors' material financial relationships, if any, please see http://www.nber.org/chapters/c13776.ack.

1. See http://www.macrohistory.net/data/.
2. We use a per capita measure of real GDP here to account for cyclical variations in economic activity across a wide range of historical epochs, which vary widely in the background rate of population growth.
3. "Business contractions appear to be briefer and more violent than business expansions" (Mitchell 1927, 333).
4. Using $\lambda = 100$ for annual data. For a more detailed discussion of the different detrending methods such as the Baxter-King band-pass filter and their impact on macroeconomic aggregates, see the discussion in Basu and Taylor (1999) as well as Canova (1998).
5. The bins in the table use the mean credit-to-GDP ratio as the threshold variable. Almost identical results are obtained if a smoothed variable, using the lagged five-year moving average of the ratio is employed instead, and are therefore not reported.

References

Acemoglu, Daron, Philippe Aghion, and Giovanni L. Violante. 2001. "Deunionization, Technical Change and Inequality." *Carnegie-Rochester Conference Series on Public Policy* 55 (1): 229–64.
Adrian, Tobias, and Nina Boyarchenko. 2015. "Intermediary Leverage Cycles and Financial Stability." Federal Reserve Bank of New York Staff Report no. 567. https://www.newyorkfed.org/medialibrary/media/research/staff_reports/sr567.pdf.
Ahmed, Shaghil, Andrew Levin, and Beth Anne Wilson. 2004. "Recent U.S. Macroeconomic Stability: Good Policies, Good Practices, or Good Luck?" *Review of Economics and Statistics* 86 (3): 824–32.
Arcand, Jean Louis, Enrico Berkes, and Ugo Panizza. 2015. "Too Much Finance?" *Journal of Economic Growth* 20 (2): 105–48.
Backus, David K., and Patrick J. Kehoe. 1992. "International Evidence on the Historical Properties of Business Cycles." *American Economic Review* 82 (4): 864–88.
Backus, David K., Patrick J. Kehoe, and Finn E. Kydland. 1992. "International Real Business Cycles." *Journal of Political Economy* 100 (4): 745–75.
Basu, Susanto, and Alan M. Taylor. 1999. "Business Cycles in International Historical Perspective." *Journal of Economics Perspectives* 13 (2): 45–68.
Bernanke, Ben S., Mark Gertler, and Simon Gilchrist. 1999. "The Financial Accelerator in a Quantitative Business Cycle Framework." In *Handbook of Macro-*

economics, vol. 1C, ed. John B. Taylor and Michael Woodford, 1341–93. Amsterdam: Elsevier.

Boivin, Jean, and Marc P. Giannoni. 2006. "Has Monetary Policy Become More Effective?" *Review of Economics and Statistics* 88 (3): 445–62.

Brunnermeier, Markus K., and Yuliy Sannikov. 2014. "A Macroeconomic Model with a Financial Sector." *American Economic Review* 104 (2): 379–421.

Caballero, Ricardo, Emmanuel Farhi, and Pierre-Olivier Gourinchas. 2008. "An Equilibrium Model of 'Global Imbalances' and Low Interest Rates." *American Economic Review* 98 (1): 358–93.

Canova, Fabio. 1998. "Detrending and Business Cycle Facts." *Journal of Monetary Economics* 41 (3): 475–512.

Cecchetti, Stephen G., and Enisse Kharroubi. 2015. "Why Does Financial Sector Growth Crowd Out Real Economic Growth?" CEPR Discussion Paper no. 10642, Center for Economic and Policy Research.

Demirgüç-Kunt, Asli, Edward Kane, and Luc Laeven. 2013. "Deposit Insurance Database." World Bank Policy Research Working Paper no. 6934, Washington, DC, World Bank.

Eggertsson, Gauti B., and Paul Krugman. 2012. "Debt, Deleveraging, and the Liquidity Trap: A Fisher-Minsky-Koo Approach." *Quarterly Journal of Economics* 127 (3): 1469–513.

Fetter, Daniel K. 2013. "How Do Mortgage Subsidies Affect Home Ownership? Evidence from the Mid-century GI Bills." *American Economic Journal* 5 (2): 111–147.

Foote, Christopher L., Kristopher S. Gerardi, and Paul S. Willen. 2012. "Why Did So Many People Make So Many *Ex Post* Bad Decisions?" NBER Working Paper no. 18082, Cambridge, MA.

Goldsmith, Raymond W. 1985. *Comparative National Balance Sheets: A Study of Twenty Countries, 1688–1979.* Chicago: University of Chicago Press.

Harding, Don, and Adrian Pagan. 2002. "Dissecting the Cycle: A Methodological Investigation." *Journal of Monetary Economics* 49 (2): 365–81.

Hodrick, Robert J., and Edward C. Prescott. 1997. "Postwar U.S. Business Cycles: An Empirical Investigation." *Journal of Money, Credit and Banking* 29 (1): 1–16.

Hoffman, Philip T., Gilles Postel-Vinay, and Jean-Laurent Rosenthal. 2000. *Priceless Markets: The Political Economy of Credit in Paris, 1660–1870.* Chicago: University of Chicago Press.

Jordà, Òscar, Moritz Schularick, and Alan M. Taylor. 2011. "Financial Crises, Credit Booms, and External Imbalances." *IMF Economic Review* 59:340–78.

———. 2013. "When Credit Bites Back." *Journal of Money, Credit, and Banking* 45 (s2): 3–28.

———. 2015. "Betting the House." *Journal of International Economics* 96 (S1): S2–18.

———. 2016a. "The Great Mortgaging: Housing Finance, Crises, and Business Cycles." *Economic Policy* 31 (85): 107–52.

———. 2016b. "Sovereigns vs. Banks: Credit, Crises and Consequences." *Journal of the European Economic Association* 14 (1): 45–79.

King, Robert G., and Ross Levine. 1993. "Finance, Entrepreneurship and Growth." *Journal of Monetary Economics* 32 (3): 513–42.

Knoll, Katharina, Moritz Schularick, and Thomas Steger. Forthcoming. "No Price Like Home: Global House Prices." *American Economic Review.*

Kocherlakota, Narayana R. 2000. "Creating Business Cycles through Credit Constraints." *Federal Reserve Bank of Minneapolis Quarterly Review* 24 (3): 2–10.

Kohl, Sebastian. 2014. "Homeowner Nations or Nations of Tenants: How Historical Institutions in Urban Politics, Housing Finance and Construction Set Germany, France, and the US on Different Housing Paths." *Studies on the Social and Political Constitution of the Economy.* Cologne: IMPRS-SPCE.

Korinek, Anton, and Alp Simsek. 2016. "Liquidity Trap and Excessive Leverage." *American Economic Review* 106 (3): 699–738.

Kydland, Finn E., and Edward C. Prescott. 1990. "Business Cycles: Real Facts and Monetary Myth." *Federal Reserve Bank of Minneapolis Quarterly Review* 14:3–18.

McConnell, Margaret, and Gabriel Pérez-Quirós. 2000. "Output Fluctuations in the United States: What Has Changed Since the Early 1980s." *American Economic Review* 90 (5): 1464–76.

McKay, Alisdair, and Ricardo Reis. 2008. "The Brevity and Violence of Contractions and Expansions." *Journal of Monetary Economics* 55:738–51.

Mian, Atif, and Amir Sufi. 2013. "Household Leverage and the Recession of 2007–09." *IMF Economic Review* 58 (1): 74–117.

———. 2014. *House of Debt: How They (and You) Caused the Great Recession, and How We Can Prevent It from Happening Again.* Chicago: University of Chicago Press.

Mitchell, Wesley C. 1913. *Business Cycles.* Berkeley, Calif.: University of California Press.

———. 1927. *Business Cycles: The Problem and Its Setting.* New York: National Bureau of Economic Research.

Monnet, Eric. 2014. "Monetary Policy without Interest Rates: Evidence from France's Golden Age (1948 to 1973) Using a Narrative Approach." *American Economic Journal: Macroeconomics* 6 (4): 137–69.

Nakov, Anton, and Andrea Pescatori. 2010. "Oil and the Great Moderation." *Economic Journal* 120 (543): 131–56.

Philippon, Thomas, and Ariell Reshef. 2013. "An International Look at the Growth of Modern Finance." *Journal of Economic Perspectives* 27 (2): 73–96.

Piketty, Thomas, and Gabriel Zucman. 2013. "Capital is Back: Wealth-Income Ratios in Rich Countries, 1700–2013." CEPR Discussion Paper no. 9588, Center for Economic Policy and Research.

Reinhart, Carmen, and Kenneth S. Rogoff. 2009. *This Time is Different: Eight Centuries of Financial Folly.* Princeton, NJ: Princeton University Press.

———. 2013. "Banking Crises: An Equal Opportunity Menace." *Journal of Banking and Finance* 37 (11): 4557–73.

Schularick, Moritz, and Alan M. Taylor. 2012. "Credit Booms Gone Bust: Monetary Policy, Leverage Cycles, and Financial Crises." *American Economic Review* 102 (2): 1029–61.

Stock, James H., and Mark W. Watson. 2005. "Understanding Changes in International Business Cycle Dynamics." *Journal of the European Economic Association* 3 (5): 968–1006.

Zarnowitz, Victor. 1992. "Facts and Factors in the Recent Evolution of Business Cycles in the United States." In *Business Cycles: Theory, History, Indicators, and Forecasting,* ed. V. Zarnowitz, 77–124. Cambridge, MA: National Bureau of Economic Research.

Comment

Mark Gertler, *New York University and NBER*

Introduction

This paper is part of an interesting and important research agenda by the authors that examines the link between financial aggregates and economic activity. This work has its roots in the classic work of Gurley and Shaw (1967) and Goldsmith (1969), which analyzed the link between financial development and growth. The authors work with a much cleaner data set than was available earlier. The data set consists of a variety of information from relatively homogenous advanced economies over a long period of time. The data further contains a very rich set of financial and real variables. In addition, they use more advanced statistical methods than were readily available to earlier researchers (witness bin scatter plots!) The net result is that the authors are able to put together a much sharper and exhaustive set of a facts than what the early literature has provided. No doubt these facts will provide an important guide for future research.

The paper lays out the facts in a very clear organized manner and makes a convincing case for robustness. Accordingly, rather than summarizing the results, I will instead focus on three sets of issues that involve identification and interpretation: The first involves the general problem of identification with aggregate credit quantities and real sector data. The second involves the need for incorporating information about credit prices (e.g., spreads), as well as quantities in order to interpret the evidence. The third involves the how to interpret the leading indicator properties of household debt for financial crises. The authors appear to suggest that it implies that financial distress was largely confined to the household sector. This, however, ignores the central role that banking distress played in the crisis. In addition, I show that it ignores evidence that the nonfinancial business sector felt significant financial distress as well.

Credit Quantities and Identification

It is not at all a criticism of the authors to point out that identification is an issue with the kind of evidence they present, but rather a note of caution to suggest that more work needs to be done before a decisive interpretation of the facts is possible. Indeed, identification issues have been front and center in this literature from the beginning. For example, both Gurley and Shaw (1967) and Goldsmith (1969) present two robust findings. First, per capita GDP is positively correlated with the ratio of credit to GDP, D/Y, and, second, it is positively correlated with the ratio of nominal output to money PY/M, otherwise known as the velocity of money. Both D/Y and PY/M measure financial development. (Velocity measures financial development since it rises with increased availability of money substitutes.) Accordingly, the results make clear a positive relation between financial and economic development.

The evidence, however, is silent on causality. Once could well imagine mutual feedback. Improved credit markets raise real activity. But at the same time, a greater level of real activity can generate more credit market activity. Ideally, one would like to know the relative causal importance of each factor. Unfortunately, it is not possible to answer this question from aggregate data alone. One possible way out is to use disaggregated data. For example, Rajan and Zingales use industry data to show that financial development can cause growth. In particular, they find that credit-dependent industries grow faster than other industries as the financial sector develops.

A similar kind of identification issue arises with several of the authors' findings. For example, the authors show that there is a negative correlation between financial deepening as measured by credit to GDP and growth. One possibility is that high credit to GDP could reflect inefficient overdevelopment of the financial sector, leading to lower growth. But causality could go in the other direction. The countries in the data set are relatively advanced. As advanced economies mature, growth rates tend to decline, implying a negative correlation between per capita output and growth. Indeed, the basic Solow models yield this prediction: capital deepening over time leads to higher per capita output and lower growth. Accordingly, what the data could be capturing is simply that financial markets tend to deepen as economies mature. The aggregate data alone is not sufficient to sort out causality. Perhaps the use of disaggregated data could be helpful in this regard, along the lines of Rajan and Zingales.

Interpreting Cyclical Comovements in Credit and Monetary Aggregates

Another set of facts involves cyclical comovements. The authors show that the correlation between output and credit aggregates has increased over time, while it has decreased for monetary aggregates. These are facts that should guide model building. But it is important to recognize that in the absence of further information, they do not provide any clear implications for the importance of either monetary policy effectiveness or credit market frictions.

Modern theory stresses that monetary policy transmits through the economy via interest rates. Central banks use short-term interest rates as the instrument of monetary policy. They adjust the money supply to hit the target rate. The correlation between output and the money supply accordingly reflects the central bank accommodating money demand. Why then might this correlation have declined over time? Increased availability of money substitutes likely introducing variation in the relation between output and various monetary aggregates. Note, however, that this variation has no implications for interest rate setting or policy transmission.

Similarly, to interpret the correlation between credit aggregates it is necessary to disentangle demand versus supply. Doing so requires information on credit prices (e.g., credit spreads) as well as credit quantities. I illustrate with the following simple framework:

Let R^b be the borrowers' gross required return, R the gross riskless rate, Y aggregate output, and L working capital loans. Then suppose that aggregate demand varies inversely with the cost of capital, as follows:

$$Y = \Psi(R^b)e^\varepsilon \tag{1}$$

with $\Psi' < 0$, and where ε is a random disturbance to demand. Next, suppose that firms need working-capital loans to finance production: The demand for working-capital loans varies positively with output, as follows:

$$L = \phi Y \tag{2}$$

with $\phi > 0$. Notice that because credit demand varies positively with output, Y and L will comove positively. However, to determine the extent to which financial factors matter for aggregate activity, information about credit prices is also necessary.

For example, suppose that financial markets are frictionless, so that $R^b = R$ (to a first order). In this case, Y and L are the following functions of ε and R:

$$Y = \Psi(R)e^{\varepsilon}$$

$$L = \phi Y \tag{3}$$

where we assume R is given by monetary policy. In this instance, output Y and credit L comove, but financial frictions are completely irrelevant to output dynamics. The strong comovement of Y and L reflects only the passive response of credit demand.

Now suppose that there are frictions in financial markets that drive a wedge between the required return on capital and the riskless rates. Let ρ denote the external finance premium that arises due to credit market frictions. Then we can express R^b to a first order as

$$R^b = \rho + R. \tag{4}$$

Combining equation (4) with equations (1) and (2) then yields solution for Y and L given ρ and R:

$$Y = \Psi(\rho + R)e^{\varepsilon}$$

$$L = \phi Y. \tag{5}$$

A financial crisis is then a disruption of intermediation that leads to an increase in the external finance premium ρ. The increase in ρ in turn leads to a contraction in both L and Y. In this instance, the comovement between credit and output reflects financial factors. The increase in the credit spread signals that financial factors are at work. In this way, credit prices help disentangle whether credit-supply or credit-demand factors underlie the comovement between credit and output.

Household Leverage as a Predictor of Financial Crises

From some (cool) bins scatter plots, the authors show that a high ratio of bank debt to GDP is associated with lower variance of GDP growth but greater tail risk. In particular, as debt to GDP increases, the distribution of output becomes skewed to the left, with the worst possible outcomes lower. A sensible interpretation of the facts is that in normal times, deep credit markets facilitate borrowing to smooth spending, which in turn smooths output, leading to reduced output volatility. At the same time, high leverage exposes the economy to infrequent financial crises that can lead to catastrophic drops in output. Indeed, the facts and story fit well postwar output dynamics for advanced economies. As credit markets deepened beginning in the early 1980s, most advanced economies entered a "Great Moderation" phase, where the volatility of output dropped. By late in the first decade of the twenty-first century, however, a housing/credit bubble paved the way for the global financial crisis that precipitated the Great Recession.

A second set of facts that the authors emphasize is that in the postwar era, it has been largely household debt that has surged prior to a financial crisis. Mortgage debt, in turn, has largely accounted for the precrisis expansion of household debt. There is no doubt that the origins of the Great Recession involve the behavior of mortgage lending. A decline in global long-term interest rates beginning early in the first decade of the twenty-first century in conjunction with a significant decline in lending standards led to a boom in house prices, housing construction, and mortgages. As the house price boom began to reverse itself, mortgage defaults began, ultimately triggering the financial crisis that led to the Great Recession.

The buildup of household leverage was unambiguously important for Great Recession. The authors do a nice job of organizing the data to make this point. However, they leap a bit overboard by drawing the conclusion that financial constraints on the household sector alone are sufficient to explain the financial and real crisis. A recent paper by Midrigan and Philippon (2016) make clear why borrowing constraints on households alone cannot provide a full accounting of the crisis. The authors develop a macroeconomic model where households can borrow to finance nondurable consumption using housing as collateral. In addition, the model economy consists of different regions that produce traded and nontraded goods. Accordingly, the framework can produce the Mian and Sufi (2013) cross-section evidence on regional credit growth and consumption and employment. Midrigan and Philippon then show that while a model with only financial constraints on households can account for the cross-sectional evidence, it cannot come close to matching the severity of the output decline during the Great Recession. The impact on consumer nondurable spending is simply too modest. While household

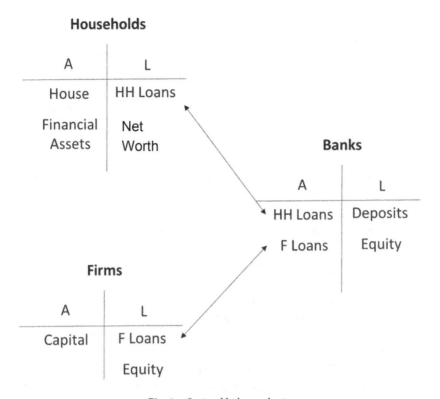

Fig. 1. Sectoral balance sheets

debt can help explain the persistence of the spending decline, other factors are needed to account for the severity of the economic contraction.

Key to any financial crisis is the exposure of the banking system. The recent financial crisis was no exception. Banks (broadly defined) are critical conduits of credit to all sectors. When banks are subject to financial distress, the flow of credit is impeded to the broad spectrum of nonfinancial borrowers, including firms as well as households.

Figure 1 illustrates the interconnection between household, firm, and bank balance sheets. (I simplify a bit for expositional purposes). For households, assets consist of housing and financial assets. Liabilities are loans from banks and net worth. Loans to households along with loans to firms are bank assets. Bank liabilities are deposits and equity. In turn, loans along with equity are on the liability side of firm balance sheets, while assets consist of capital.

The point of the figure is that it is misleading to analyze the balance sheet position of one sector of the economy independent of the others.

Unquestionably, the crisis was preceded by a rapid buildup of mortgages, which appear as household liabilities. But mortgages also appear on the asset side of bank balance sheets. Further, the lion's share of the growth in mortgages since the late 1990s was absorbed by the thinly capitalized shadow banking sector. Indeed, securitized mortgage loans, more than other type of asset, accounted for the huge expansion of shadow banking. Accordingly, while the mortgage boom increased the vulnerability of household balance sheets, it also significantly increased the fragility of the banking system. The subsequent collapse of the banking system in turn greatly impeded the flow of credit to both households and firms.

Indeed, it is not possible to accurately characterize the contraction in economic activity during the Great Recession without explicitly taking into account the financial collapse. There were two key episodes. (See Gertler, Kiyotaki, and Prestipino [2016] for details). First, starting in August 2007, the asset-backed commercial paper market began to unravel steadily. The triggering events were an initial wave of defaults on subprime mortgages that led to concerns about the quality of securities that were tied to these types of assets. The contraction in this type of intermediation raised the financing costs of loans that were typically securitized, such mortgages, autos, and credit card debt. This initial disruption contributed significantly to the slowdown in economic activity that began in the fall of 2007. (See, e.g., Benmelech, Meisenzahl, and Ramacharan 2016).

The second major event, and the most pivotal, was the unraveling of the entire investment banking system in September 2008 that followed in the wake of the Lehman Brothers bankruptcy and the run on money market funds. The collapse of the shadow banking sector also weakened commercial banks that in many cases had implicit comments to absorb investment bank assets. The net effect was a severe disruption of intermediation, reflected in skyrocketing credit costs across the board. The jump in borrowing costs lead to huge drops in economic activity in the fourth quarter of 2008 and first quarter of 2009.

Figure 2 illustrates how financial distress hit the nonfinancial business sector. Both panels plot the spread between the returns on an index of corporate bonds and similar maturity government bonds as an indicator of credit costs faced by nonfinancial firms (See Gilchrist and Zakrajšek 2012). This credit spread clearly skyrocketed during the Great Recession. The top panel shows how the spread comoves with the senior loan officer survey of the percent of banks that are tightening credit

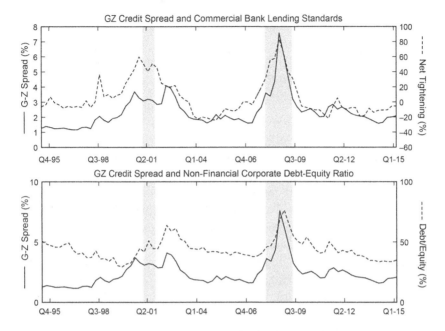

Fig. 2.   Credit spreads, terms of lending, and firms' balance sheets

terms each period. Note that during the Great Recession the survey shows an unusually high degree of tightening. The increase in the credit spread, further, mirrors the degree of tightening, suggesting the latter was a contributing factor to the former.

The bottom panel plots the debt-equity ratio of the nonfinancial business sector against the credit spread. Much of the variation in this ratio is due to fluctuations in the market value of equity. The panel shows that during the Great Recession, firm balance sheets weakened considerably: there was a sharp increase in the debt-equity ratio, which was likely another important factor contributing to the rise in the credit spread. Even though a run-up in firm debt did not lead the recession, there was a significant weakening of firms' financial positions that likely raised the cost of credit access. (For panel data evidence that the nonfinancial firms indeed face tighter borrowing constraints, see Giroud and Mueller [2016]).

In sum, even though a run-up in household debt clearly led the Great Recession, it does not follow that only financial frictions in the household sector were relevant to the crisis. Frictions in both banking and the nonfinancial business sector were relevant as well.

Is the Past Prologue?

Household leverage led the recent financial crisis. Will it lead the next? The history of financial regulation goes as follows: Design regulations to fight the last war. Markets then find their way around the regulations. This leads to a new crisis that differs in nature.

The regulatory system that predated the Great Recession was a product of the US commercial banking crisis of the late 1980s. What made the banks vulnerable was excessive investment in risky commercial real estate. The regulatory response under the Basel Accord was to tighten capital requirements on commercial banks. While the capital requirements made commercial banks safer, they also precipitated the growth of the shadow banking system. Rather than hold mortgages directly on commercial bank balance sheets, it was possible to avoid capital requirements by securitizing and then selling them to shadow banks, setting the stage for the next crisis.

The recent Dodd-Frank regulation has similarly reduced the likelihood of a crisis exactly like the last one. The question then is whether, once again, regulatory arbitrage may lead to a new kind of crisis. At least according to the BIS, this is a definite possibility. The new financial hockey stick noted by the BIS is dollar-denominated borrowing by private corporations in emerging-market economies. Though still at manageable levels, leverage in this sector has been growing rapidly. The broader point, though, is past correlations of certain types of debt with economic activity may not provide a guide to the future.

Concluding Remarks

John Gurley once said, "Money is a veil, but when the veil flutters the economy sputters." What we learn from Jordà, Moritz, and Taylor is to replace the word money with credit.

Endnote

For acknowledgments, sources of research support, and disclosure of the author's material financial relationships, if any, please see http://www.nber.org/chapters/c13777.ack.

References

Benmelech, Efraim, Ralf Meisenzahl, and Rodney Ramacharan. 2016. "The Real Effects of Liquidity during the Financial Crisis: Evidence from Automobiles." NBER Working Paper no. 22148, Cambridge, MA.

Gertler, Mark, Nobuhiro Kiyotaki, and Andrea Prestipino. 2016. "Wholesale Banking and Bank Runs in Macroeconomic Modeling of Financial Crises." NBER Working Paper no. 21892, Cambridge, MA.

Gilchrist, Simon, and Egon Zakrajšek. 2012. "Credit Spreads and Business Fluctuations." *American Economic Review* 102 (4): 1692–720.

Giroud, Xavier, and Holger Mueller. 2016. "Firm Leverage, Consumer Demand, and Unemployment During the Great Recession." *Quarterly Journal of Economics* doi: 10.1093/qje/qjw035.

Goldsmith, Raymond. 1969. *Financial Structure and Development*. New Haven, CT: Yale University Press.

Gurley, John, and Edward Shaw. 1967. "Financial Structure and Economic Development." *Economic and Cultural Change* 15 (3): 257–68.

Midrigan, Virgiliu, and Thomas Philippon. 2016. "Household Leverage and the Great Recession." Manuscript, New York University.

Mian, Atif, and Amir Sufi. 2013. "Household Balance Sheets, Consumption and the Economic Slump." *Quarterly Journal of Economics* doi: 10.1093/qje/qjt020.

Comment

Atif Mian, *Princeton University and NBER*

This paper is a continuation of an impressive line of work that the Jordà et al. team have put together in recent years. The authors have assembled an impressive historical data series on the long-term dynamics of debt, asset prices, and real outcomes. Their prior work has documented the "credit hockey stick" (Schularick and Taylor [2012]; that is, the substantial rise in private credit to GDP since 1950, with two-thirds of the increase driven by household credit [Jordà, Schularick, and Taylor 2016]).

What is new in this paper is that Jordà et al. show that many important macro moments are closely correlated with the rise in credit to GDP, or the credit hockey stick. While there are many results in the paper, I will focus on the results that are new relative to their prior work and that I find most interesting. First, GDP growth slows down, as does GDP volatility when credit to GDP rises. Moreover, negative skewness for GDP growth increases as the left tail becomes worse when credit to GDP increases. In other words, crises tend to occur more frequently.

Second, there is globalization of cycles as variables become more correlated with the rise in credit to GDP. In particular, GDP growth becomes more correlated with credit. GDP growth also becomes more correlated with investment growth, and growth at country level becomes more correlated with global growth. All of these correlations increase with credit to GDP.

The paper is careful to present these findings as basic empirical facts, and does not try to link the results strongly with any particular hypothesis. Yet the results are useful collectively in addressing the important question of why credit to GDP has increased so much around the world in the first place. I discuss possible hypotheses for this question, and how the results in this paper help us in sorting out the different hypotheses.

One possible hypothesis for the rise in credit to GDP is that it is the result of greater formalization of the economy. If firms and households move from informal and internal funding to formal external financing, then the economy will naturally record a higher level of credit to GDP even if there is no other real change in the economy. For example, firms may shift from financing their investments internally to financing these through intermediaries. Such formalization of the financing structure will lead to an increase in total credit, but will not be accompanied by any fundamental shift in the overall pattern of investment.

A related form of formalization is in the household sector, when renting households start owning homes through mortgage loans. There are two qualitatively equivalent ways households can live in a house. They can either rent the property from the landlord, or they can own the property with a small down payment and pay the landlord rent in the form of interest rate on the mortgage that the landlord holds. As more rental properties turn into mortgaged owner-occupied units, there will naturally be a higher level of household credit to GDP. However, the allocation of housing units may not materially change despite the increase in household credit to GDP.

If the increase in credit to GDP documented by Jordà et al. is primarily the result of formalization of the economy, then the rise in credit is not fundamentally important, as it does not lead to a different allocation of capital. It is likely that some of the increase in credit to GDP reflects such formalization of the economy. For example, the authors show that the home-ownership rate has increased steadily from 43% in 1950 to 60% in 2013, consistent with the view that rental homes have been converted into mortgaged owner-occupancy. However, formalization alone is unlikely to be the full story. For example, leverage conditional on owning a home has also gone up. Similarly, real house prices have increased by a factor of three since 1950, when they have been largely flat between 1870 and 1950. A reclassification of assets from rental to owner-occupied should not result in higher prices, all else equal. The independent increase in leverage on the intensive margin and the rise in house prices suggests that there are other mechanisms at play that need to be investigated.

A second hypothesis for the rise in credit to GDP is that the financial sector has developed to allow for more risk sharing at various margins. For example, financial development may enable households to borrow in order to smooth out idiosyncratic labor-income risk. Countries may be able to borrow and lend internationally in order to smooth out country-specific consumption volatility. Firms may be better able to absorb liquidity shocks and avoid having to adjust the size of their balance sheet. An improvement in risk-sharing capacity along these dimensions would reduce consumption volatility and investment volatility. This can further lead to an increased appetite for borrowing as households and firms feel more protected through the financial market. If a higher level of credit to GDP reflects better risk-sharing opportunities, then that should be welfare enhancing.

Is there evidence for the risk-sharing hypothesis in the paper? The paper does show a decline in consumption and output volatility with the rise in credit to GDP, consistent with the notion that risk sharing has improved. However, *relative* volatility of consumption with respect to output has not changed much. If there is more risk sharing for consumption smoothing purposes, then we would expect to see a decline in relative consumption volatility as well. Similarly, the authors find no evidence of increased consumption risk sharing across countries. It does not appear that the rapid increase in global credit to GDP is associated with an increased ability of countries to smooth out their idiosyncratic consumption shocks.

Finally, and this is perhaps the most damning evidence against a risk-sharing hypothesis, an increase in credit to GDP is associated with more negative skewness and a greater likelihood of large crashes. One could argue that risk sharing allows people to "drive faster" by leveraging more, and this shows up as an increase in negative skewness. However, as pointed out earlier, there is no evidence of faster growth with rising credit to GDP. Thus, increase in credit to GDP is associated with both lower GDP growth and more skewed negative returns. The most recent global financial crisis has further exposed the limited ability of the global economy to share financial risks across borrowers and creditors.

A third hypothesis for the rise in credit to GDP is that financial development has reduced the financial wedge that reflects financial frictions. A fall in financial frictions would enable entrepreneurs with high marginal product of capital to borrow and invest, leading to higher growth. However, there is little support for this hypothesis. As already mentioned, the paper shows that GDP growth slows down as credit to GDP rises. Higher levels of credit to GDP is associated with lower GDP growth, contrary to the predictions of the financial wedge hypothesis.

Moreover, there is no evidence that investment rates have gone up with the rise in credit to GDP. If the rise in credit to GDP reflects lower financial frictions and higher investment and growth, it is hard to find direct evidence for that in the data.

There is additional evidence that rise in credit to GDP is not associated with higher growth. In a recent paper (Mian, Sufi, and Verner 2015), we show in a simple VAR set up that increase in credit to GDP over a three-year period is followed by a *slowdown* in GDP across a wide range of developed economies. Moreover, not all credit is created equally. The negative predictability result is entirely driven by the change in household credit to GDP. There is no such relationship for nonfinancial corporate credit.

The unexpected negative relationship between growth in credit and subsequent output growth, and the importance of household credit in generating this result, suggests that household borrowing may be "excessive" from a macro perspective. This is an exciting area of further research, driven in part by the Jordà et al. research agenda. There is a growing theoretical literature that suggests reasons ranging from demand externalities to behavioral biases that may lead to an excessive growth in credit at the expense of subsequent economic performance (e.g., Bordalo, Gennaioli, and Shleifer 2016; Eggertsson and Krugman 2012; Farhi and Werning 2013; Korinek and Simsek 2016).

Our own analysis in Mian et al. (2016) shows that low mortgage spreads predict growth in household credit to GDP, followed by a decline in GDP. Moreover, growth in household credit to GDP predicts negative GDP forecasting errors. These results suggest that credit markets may become frothy at times, leading to excessive credit build up that in turn proves costly due to typical New Keynesian macro frictions.

What is the role of modern finance in the macro economy? The evidence put together by Jordà et al. and related literature suggests that the relationship between finance and the macro economy does not always follow traditional textbook predictions. We need more nuanced models that take into account the possibility that credit growth can be excessive, and understand what factors contribute to such possibilities. A deeper question is why the "credit hockey stick" is a phenomena of the more recent decades. Is it driven by technological changes, or some structural economic forces such as rising inequality or "savings glut"? These are fascinating questions that have been raised in part by the excellent work of Jordà and colleagues.

Endnote

For acknowledgments, sources of research support, and disclosure of the author's material financial relationships, if any, please see http://www.nber.org/chapters/c13778.ack.

References

Bordalo, P., N. Gennaioli, and A. Shleifer. 2016. "Diagnostic Expectations and Credit Cycles." NBER Working Paper no. 22266, Cambridge, MA.

Eggertsson, G. B., and P. Krugman. 2012. "Debt, Deleveraging, and the Liquidity Trap: A Fisher-Minsky-Koo Approach." *Quarterly Journal of Economics* 127 (3): 1469–1513.

Farhi, E., and I. Werning. 2013. "A Theory of Macro-Prudential Policies in the Presence of Nominal Rigidities." NBER Working Paper no. 19313, Cambridge, MA.

Jordà, Òscar, Moritz Schularick, and Alan M. Taylor. 2016. "The Great Mortgaging: Housing Finance, Crises, and Business Cycles." *Economic Policy* 31 (85): 107–52.

Korinek, A., and A. Simsek. 2016. "Liquidity Trap and Excessive Leverage." *American Economic Review* 106 (3): 699–738.

Mian, Atif, Amir Sufi, and Emil Verner. 2015. "Household Debt and Business Cycles Worldwide." NBER Working Paper no. 21581, Cambridge, MA.

Schularick, Moritz, and Alan M. Taylor. 2012. "Credit Booms Gone Bust: Monetary Policy, Leverage Cycles, and Financial Crises." *American Economic Review* 102 (2): 1029–61.

Discussion

Jeffrey Campbell began the discussion by making two comments. First, he argued that credit expansion between 1980 and 1995 was driven by regulatory regime changes. He claimed that the previous regulatory regime was extremely restrictive. The restrictive regime meant that the savings and loans institutions exploited yield curve strategies to make profit. Those strategies contributed toward their insolvency in the 1970s. He argued that the regulatory changes that occurred in the 1980s lead to a huge expansion in US household credit.

Second, Campbell claimed that the authors' finding of a negative correlation between credit growth and GDP growth is not a puzzle. He referenced earlier joint work with Zvi Hercowitz, where they were able to generate a negative correlation following credit liberalization within a New Keynesian model with borrowers and savers and balanced growth path preferences.

Martin Eichenbaum offered an alternative explanation to Jeffrey Campbell's neoclassical view for the case of Portugal. After Portugal entered the Eurozone, consumer debt increased significantly. He believes that Portuguese consumers may have been overoptimistic about their future income prospects.

Pierre-Olivier Gourinchas reiterated Martin Eichenbaum's comments for the case of Portugal, and noted that prior to the crisis, there was not a slowdown in growth. Instead, nontradable consumption, housing, and capital inflows all increased before coming to an abrupt stop during the crisis. This pattern does not seem to be consistent with the negative correlation between output growth and credit to GDP. He also noted that saying that some, but not all, findings in the relevant literature on emerging markets are consistent with the authors' results.

Òscar Jordà acknowledged Martin Eichenbaum and Pierre-Olivier Gourinchas's comments. He agreed that more work needs to be done to think about the correlation between output growth and credit-to-GDP growth during crisis periods versus noncrisis periods.

Narayana Kocherlakota next asked how much of the growth in credit-to-GDP ratio prior to the financial crisis can be attributed to monetary policy action. He also asked how much of the subsequent slow recovery after the financial crisis can be attributed to insufficiently accommodative monetary policy.

Kocherlakota also made the comment that for most standard models with private information, debt emerges as an optimal contract. However, he argues that in the real world, debt contracts are not necessarily the optimal contract to have, given large correlated losses and default rates. Therefore, he urges the authors to think about what features are missing in standard models with private information about individual debt contracts.

Moritz Schularick agreed with the general discussion in the audience that there is heterogeneity across countries in terms of credit and housing trends. However, he argued that one of the benefits of the data set that they had assembled is that it is possible to extract the country-specific trends to obtain common trends across countries that are correlated with business cycles.

Harald Uhlig expressed concern over the secular trends in growth, which may not be fully taken into account by the time dummies in the authors' regressions. He wondered whether the secular trends are driving the very linear relationship between output growth and credit-to-GDP ratios that the authors find. He suggested that the authors examine the relationship between output growth and credit to GDP at the tail ends of the observations and see if there are any asymmetries in that relationship.

Greg Mankiw followed up on Harald Uhlig's comment about the secular slowdown in growth, and referred to Robert Gordon's work on the topic. He wondered to what extent the correlations between output growth and credit-to-GDP ratios were driven by decade-to-decade fluctuations, rather than cross-country fluctuations.

Moritz Schularick expressed surprise by the amount of discussion on the secular trends. He noted that the paper focuses more on volatility and skewness of the variables, rather than average trends.

Robert Gordon urged the authors to think more about whether the fluctuations in the credit-to-GDP ratios were driven by the numerator or by the dominator of the ratio. He noted that the decline in credit/ GDP ratio after 1930s/40s was due to the enormous jump in nominal GDP that took place between the 1920s and 1950s. He believed that the economy was out of equilibrium, with real GDP and prices increasing substantially between 1929 and 1948. As a result, the credit-to-GDP ratio fell significantly to abnormally low levels because credit had not caught up with the tremendous increase in nominal GDP. He argues that only after 1970 was there a "true" movement in credit to GDP outside of the range already established in the 1920s.

Moritz Schularick noted that after World War II, credit was mostly diverted from the private sector to the government. If government credit was included in the authors' cross-county credit-to-GDP ratios, then the difference in the numerator (credit) versus the denominator (GDP) would not be as stark.

Jonathan Parker spoke next, making two comments. First, he wondered whether the authors' facts could be explained by fluctuations in beliefs about the future and an important role for credit in the consumption of durable goods. There are times when agents borrow to consume durables because of optimism about the future. Durable consumption drives house construction and other durable good purchases, which boosts GDP. However, when the economy experiences a negative shock and enters a recession, households can no longer borrow to consume durables, leading to a steeper drop in output.

Second, Parker observed that the paper focuses entirely on credit. However, there are other financial contracts, besides credit, that agents can use to obtain money and fund consumption.

Moritz Schularick responded to Jonathan Parker's comments, noting that the findings in the paper are likely to apply to other financial markets beyond the credit market. He referred to, for instance, the "financial hockey stick" in equity markets, particularly from the 1970s onward. He argued that the point of the paper is to extend the analysis of house prices and mortgage debt/GDP trends by focusing on the credit side, which is what has really changed over time. He believes that durable goods consumption, particularly home ownership, is highly correlated with house prices and mortgage debt, and all three matter for financial stability. Schularick also commented that an interesting question is why banks have effectively adopted a strategy similar to the strategy of real estate hedge funds, borrowing short from the public and investing long in real estate.

Martin Eichenbaum observed that Canada is a great example for the authors to consider when thinking about the relationship between house prices, mortgage debt-to-GDP ratios, and financial crises. In Canada, debt-to-income ratios are very high and the debt is largely held by banks. However, about 80% of the debt is insured by the Canadian government, which means that a crisis in the Canadian housing market will not be tied to a financial crisis.

Fernando Alvarez asked whether the mortgage debt is denominated in local currency or foreign currency. Moritz Schularick responded that most of the debt is in local currency.

Paul Beaudry next asked if the mix between consumption and investment changes between crisis and boom periods. If in these credit boom periods, output rises mainly due to investment, then the implications are very different from credit boom periods where output is all driven by consumption. Moritz Schularick replied that they had not looked into the consumption and investment compositions.

4

Forward Guidance and Macroeconomic Outcomes since the Financial Crisis

Jeffrey R. Campbell, *Federal Reserve Bank of Chicago, CentER, Tilburg University*
Jonas D. M. Fisher, *Federal Reserve Bank of Chicago*
Alejandro Justiniano, *Federal Reserve Bank of Chicago*
Leonardo Melosi, *Federal Reserve Bank of Chicago*

I. Introduction

Over the last thirty years the FOMC completely revised its communications policy, eventually making guidance about the future path of the funds rate a central component of those communications. Before 1994, the change in the Fed funds rate was the *only* policy action taken on a meeting date. Indeed, the FOMC typically issued no communication at a meeting's conclusion, and market participants were left to infer any policy rate change from the trading activity of the System Open Market Account desk. Since its February 1994 meeting, the FOMC has typically made a postmeeting statement. Although these began as terse announcements of anticipated tightening and loosening in money markets, the FOMC soon routinely announced its policy rate decision and justification for it within the context of the committee's macroeconomic outlook. In May 1999, the committee added forward-looking language to its statement that indicated whether the balance of risks to the achievement of its dual mandate was tilted toward undesirable inflation or output performance. As the FOMC followed the subsequent trend set by inflation-targeting central banks toward greater transparency regarding its policy goals and actions, its statement's forward-looking language expanded. Most notably, the FOMC repeatedly stated its expectation of maintaining low interest rates in the wake of the 2001 recession for a "considerable period." Once the removal of that accommodation was underway, the committee consistently forecasted that it would be removed "at a pace that is likely to be measured."

After the FOMC cut the federal funds rate to its effective lower bound (ELB) in December 2008, even more explicit forward guidance became one of the only tools available to it for providing monetary accommodation.[1] In December 2008, the committee began using language that the funds rate would remain exceptionally low for "some time." In March 2009, the FOMC replaced "some time" with "extended period." The FOMC introduced calendar-based forward guidance in August 2011, when the corresponding statement indicated that exceptionally low levels of the funds rate would remain in place "at least through mid-2013." The Evans rule, whereby the maintenance of low rates is tied to specific economic conditions, replaced the calendar-based language in the December 2012 statement.[2] While the specificity of the Evans rule was dropped in March 2014, the statement has continued to highlight that any future policy tightening will be closely tied to tangible evidence about the state of the economy.[3]

To better understand FOMC communication policy, Campbell et al. (2012) introduced the theoretical distinction between *Delphic* and *Odyssean* forward guidance. The former gets its name from the oracle of Delphi, who forecasted the future but promised nothing. Just so, central bankers routinely discuss macroeconomic fundamentals and outcomes objectively while forecasting their own likely responses to future developments. Moreover, since the May 1999 meeting the policy statement routinely includes an assessment of current conditions as well as references to how the committee expects the economy to evolve in coming months. In contrast, Odyssean forward guidance consists of central bankers' statements that bind them to future courses of action. Just as Odysseus bound himself to his ship's mast so he could enjoy the Sirens' song without succumbing to the inevitable temptation to drown himself while swimming toward them, a central banker can improve welfare by publicly committing to a time-inconsistent plan that uses expectations of suboptimal future outcomes to improve current economic conditions. The forward guidance that implements the time-inconsistent Ramsey plans in Eggertsson and Woodford (2003) is Odyssean.

This paper aims to quantify the impact of Odyssean FOMC forward guidance on macroeconomic outcomes since the financial crisis that unwound from 2007 to 2009. Before the crisis, academic interest in forward guidance primarily arose from the aforementioned changes in its communication policy. The FOMC's use of more explicit forward guidance to provide monetary stimulus after the crisis gave the topic much greater policy relevance. So motivated, Campbell et al. (2012) extended the work of the previous empirical literature on forward guidance in two directions. First, they demonstrated that data from the postcrisis period continued to conform to the patterns documented by Gürkaynak, Sack, and Swanson (2005) in which yields on long-dated securities responded significantly to changes in federal funds rate futures on days with FOMC statements. That is, the financial crisis did not permanently damage the transmission mechanism from forward-guidance shocks to asset prices. Second, they examined how private expectations of macroeconomic variables responded to forward-guidance shocks in the precrisis period. They found strong evidence that an unexpected tightening of future rates *lowered* unemployment expectations.

Campbell et al. (2012) hypothesized that this *event-study activity puzzle* arises from Delphic forward guidance. If FOMC statements reveal information about near-term economic developments that would otherwise remain out of the public's hands, then the direct effects of the fundamentals so revealed (e.g., lower unemployment and higher inflation from strong aggregate demand) will accompany the optimal policy response to those fundamentals (e.g., an increase in expected future policy rates). That is, regressions of expectation revisions on changes in expected interest rates suffer from a simultaneity problem when FOMC statements contain Delphic forward guidance.

If the event-study activity puzzle reflects that FOMC communications are limited to be mostly Delphic, then it casts doubt on the possibility that the FOMC has been able to communicate Odyssean guidance to improve macroeconomic outcomes since the financial crisis. Therefore, we begin our analysis with an examination of the Delphic hypothesis using direct measures of FOMC private information based on now-public Greenbook and Tealbook forecasts. We find that the puzzling responses of private-sector forecasts to FOMC announcements can be attributed entirely to Delphic forward guidance. However, a large fraction of the variability in federal funds futures rates on days with FOMC announcements remains unexplained by our measure of FOMC private information. Therefore, we conclude from this examination that the high-frequency event-study approach to identification leaves open the possibility that the FOMC has communicated Odyssean guidance.

Hanson and Stein (2015) present other evidence that casts doubt on the New Keynesian (NK) mechanism by which forward guidance is transmitted to the broader economy. They found that changes in the stance of monetary policy substantially influence long-dated instantaneous real forward rates. They argue that this reflects variation in term premia that is absent from log-linearized NK models in which the expectations theory of the term structure holds good and real rates should not be affected much beyond the duration of price stickiness. These findings raise questions about the use of standard NK models for identifying the effects of Odyssean forward guidance. Therefore, we reconsider the Hanson-Stein findings using our measures of forward-guidance shocks and the FOMC private information revealed on announcement days. We argue that the effects of appropriately measured forward-guidance shocks on long-dated real forward rates are actually quite small, enough so that they might be explained by Delphic guidance about the long-run course of the economy communicated on announcement days. While further empirical scrutiny of this hypothesis is warranted, at this stage the evidence does not seem to disqualify using a NK framework to analyze the effects of forward guidance.

Our ultimate goal is to assess whether the FOMC improved economic performance since the financial crisis using Odyssean guidance. Below we review a nascent literature that examines the macroeconomic effects of forward guidance using VARs. This literature uses a variety of strategies to identify forward-guidance shocks and finds that they have influenced real activity as does Odyssean forward guidance in standard NK models, at least qualitatively. Nevertheless, VARs are inadequate for addressing our question. The literature pools pre- and postcrisis data to improve power, yet there is clear evidence that the nature of forward guidance changed substantially after the crisis. Consequently, there is too little data to apply reduced-form tools in the period of our interest.

Given the generally validating (or at least not invalidating) findings of the event study and VAR literature for NK models with Odyssean guidance, we undertake our assessment with an enhanced version of the workhorse medium-scale model pioneered by Christiano, Eichenbaum, and Evans (2005) and Smets and Wouters (2007). The model's forward guidance is entirely Odyssean. It takes the form of unanticipated signals from the central bank about the future values of the interest rate rule's time-varying intercept, building on the insights of Laséen and Svensson (2011) and Campbell et al. (2012). Since our question is empirical, we estimate the forward-guidance signals' stochastic structure. To do so we develop a new methodology that allows us to integrate the information obtained from high-frequency identification of forward guidance on FOMC announcement days into an estimated model of quarterly macroeconomic fluctuations. Our approach identifies forward guidance using the term structure of overnight interest rate futures rates. As such we identify forward guidance as interpreted by market participants, which may or may not be as intended by the members of the FOMC.

In addition to introducing forward guidance to the monetary policy rule, we make two changes to the preferences of the workhorse model. First, we include an additively separable stochastic preference for holding government bonds, as in Fisher (2015). This preference generates a spread between the policy rate and the rate of return on capital because government bonds yield benefits over and above the transfer of consumption from one period to the next. As such, it is possible to simultaneously match key long-run features of aggregate quantities and prices and to set the long-run real policy rate to a realistic value. Furthermore, the presence of this spread brings discounting to the linearized intertemporal consumption Euler equation. As discussed by Campbell et al. (2016), Carlstrom, Fuerst, and Paustian (2015), Del Negro, Giannoni, and Patterson (2015), Kiley (2014), and McKay, Nakamura, and Steinsson (2015), the absence of such discounting in standard NK models explains why the effects of Odyssean guidance can be implausibly large. With the discounting that arises from an empirically plausible spread, such large effects are mitigated in our model.[4] The second change to the standard specification is to use Jaimovich and Rebelo (2009) preferences. In models with technology news shocks, these dampen the income effect on labor supply and thereby enhance business cycle comovement. We give them the opportunity to do the same for monetary news shocks.

Our model's estimation uses an unusually large number of data series: model-consistent measures of GDP, consumption and investment based on chain aggregated NIPA data, a measure of hours worked adjusted for demographic trends, multiple indicators of wage and price inflation, a survey-based measure of long-run inflation expectations, and the current policy rate along with market-based measures of its expected future values from Eurodollar and OIS markets. The estimation itself is somewhat nonstandard. We first calibrate parameters that the model has in common with the standard real business cycle framework to match long-run averages from the US economy. This "first-moments-first" approach ensures that any success in replicating second moments does not come at the cost of counterfactual long-run predictions. We estimate the remaining parameters that govern pricing frictions, real rigidities, and the model's shocks using relatively standard Bayesian methods. Because our estimation forces basic NIPA data and interest-rate futures data to coexist, we expect it to minimize any empirical "forward-guidance puzzle" of the kind highlighted by Del Negro, Giannoni, and Patterson (2015).

The sample period for our baseline estimation is 1993:Q1 to 2008:Q3. We demonstrate that over this period the model produces a credible business cycle history driven primarily by shocks to technology, the demand for government bonds, investment demand, and the representative household's discount rate. Furthermore, we verify that the model implies relatively modest effects of forward guidance, that is, it does *not* display Del Negro et al.'s (2015) forward-guidance puzzle. Hence, it appears to be a credible laboratory within which to conduct the analysis of monetary policy.

We use the estimated model to measure the effects of forward guidance from 2008:Q4 to 2014:Q4. Our measurement involves setting all the parameters to their baseline estimated values except for those governing the forward-guidance shocks. These we reestimate using futures rates extending 10 quarters ahead instead of the 4 quarters used in the first sample period. For the evaluation of recent monetary policy, we compare the empirical outcomes with counterfactual outcomes from a version of the model without forward guidance. Our model is linear, and we use data on interest rate futures both to identify the forward guidance and to enforce the ELB on expected future interest rates. This presents a technical challenge: How do we remove the guidance while enforcing the ELB? Our solution is to replace the forward-guidance shocks identified from the data with those chosen by a policymaker who wishes to minimize deviations from the baseline interest-rate rule subject to never violating the ELB and taking as given the nonmonetary shocks identified with the reestimated model. Our findings suggest that the purely rule-based policy would have delivered a shallower recession and kept inflation closer to target in the years immediately following the crisis than FOMC forward guidance did in practice. However, starting toward the end of 2011, after the Fed's introduction of "calendar-based" communications, the FOMC's Odyssean guidance appears to have boosted real activity and moved inflation closer to target.[5]

The remainder of the paper begins with our analysis of FOMC private information using high-frequency identification and a brief discussion of the VAR evidence on the effects of forward guidance. After this we describe the structural model, measurement and estimation of the model, properties of the estimated model, and our counterfactual policy analysis. The final section discusses aspects of forward guidance that are necessarily absent from a full information rational expectations framework like ours.

II. Measures of Forward Guidance and Its Effects

There is a large and growing literature that identifies the effects of forward guidance using event studies. Our review of this literature, below, affirms that it indeed solves many of identification problems associated with traditional VAR methods, but nevertheless introduces other obstacles to identification. We follow our review with a new accounting framework that precisely delineates these difficulties. One of these difficulties arises from the potential presence of Delphic forward guidance in FOMC statements. We present new empirical work that measures the impact of these Delphic communications on expected future policy rates. This allows us to purge measured forward guidance of its Delphic component. When we do so we find that it explains the event-study activity puzzle, but leaves intact the previously measured effects on prices of short- and medium-duration assets. Our accounting framework identifies a second difficulty previously examined by Rigobon and Sack (2004): even on FOMC announcement days asset prices move for reasons that have nothing to do with monetary policy. Any systematic covariances due to these day-to-day movements can contaminate event-study regression estimates. We show that this is indeed the case when employing Hanson and Stein's (2015) preferred measure of the stance of monetary policy. When we redo their analysis with a measure that is empirically immune to this critique, their finding of implausibly large effects of forward guidance on long-dated instantaneous forward rates go away. We conclude this section with a brief review of the VAR evidence on the macroeconomic effects of forward guidance.

A. Measurement with High-Frequency Data

Both policy experience and modern macroeconomic theory emphasize the influence of the private sector's expectations of future outcomes on current macroeconomic performance, so the FOMC's statments and other communications can be reasonably characterized as policy actions *additional* to any adjustments in the policy rate. However, the conditions under which such communications are *effective* remain unclear. Krugman (1998) and Eggertsson and Woodford (2003) implicitly assume that monetary policymakers can manipulate private-sector expectations to be consistent with any rational expectations equilibrium. Unsurprisingly, this assumption makes proper communication policy very effective at improving macroeconomic outcomes. In contrast, Bassetto (2016) models central bank communications as "cheap talk." When the central bank has private information about its own preferences, such cheap talk can communicate that to the public and thereby improve outcomes. However, these communications leave the equilibrium set unchanged if the public and policymaker are equally well informed. In this sense, central bank communications about future objectives and constraints are redundant policy instruments.

Although theory provides no certain identification of the efficacy of central bank communication, the high-frequency estimation strategy pioneered by Kuttner (2001) can be used to shed empirical light upon it. The FOMC's policy actions occur at discrete moments, usually during the US business day. Financial market participants trade on these actions, and the resulting changes in asset prices can be used to identify their unexpected components. Kuttner (2001) measured the unexpected change in the current policy rate with changes in the price of the futures contract that settled based on the average Fed funds rate in the month containing the FOMC meeting. Building on this work, Kohn and Sack (2004) measured the variance of asset price changes on days of FOMC meetings with and without accompanying postmeeting statements. After carefully controlling for the effects of any contemporaneous public announcements of macroeconomic news, they found that issuing a statement substantially increased the variance of Fed funds futures contracts dated three months ahead, as well as eurodollar futures contracts dated two and four quarters ahead. (See their table 3.) That is, central bank communications substantially change asset prices closely associated with policy rate changes in the near future. In this sense, FOMC communications demonstrably include forward guidance.[6]

Gürkaynak, Sack, and Swanson (2005) continued this research agenda by examining the content of FOMC forward guidance in more detail and by characterizing its effects on Treasury yields. Specifically, Gürkaynak et al. (2005) measured changes in federal funds futures and Eurodollar futures contracts with one year or less to expiration over 30-minute windows centered on FOMC announcements. They then demonstrated that these changes have a simple two-factor structure in which the factors themselves account for nearly all of the sample variance. After an appropriate rotation, they label these the *target* and *path* factors. By assumption these are orthogonal; and only the target factor influences the current policy rate. Therefore, the path factor definitionally captures the effects of forward guidance on expected future policy rates.[7] Gürkaynak et al. (2005) furthermore showed that the path factor's largest realizations coincided with historically prominent cases of forward guidance. (See their table 4.) Finally, they demonstrated that the path factor substantially influences the yields on two, five, and ten-year Treasury notes. In modern macroeconomic models, central bank forward guidance influences current economic performance only to the extent that it changes such bond rates, so this finding is necessary for us to continue entertaining the hypothesis that it can be an effective policy tool.

Campbell et al. (2012) extended the work of Gürkaynak et al. in two directions. First, they demonstrated that data from the postcrisis period continued to conform to the patterns documented by Gürkaynak et al. That is, the financial crisis did not permanently damage the transmission mechanism from forward guidance to asset prices. Second, they examined how private expectations of macroeconomic variables responded to forward-guidance shocks in the precrisis period. They found strong evidence that an unexpected tightening of future rates *lowered* unemployment expectations and weaker evidence that it *raised* inflation expectations. (See their table 3.)

The finding that private expectations' responses are the *opposite* of those we would expect from a simple NK model with shocks to expected future policy actions (i.e., forward-guidance shocks) clearly indicates that something other than such a simple story is at work. Campbell et al. (2012) hypothesized that their results arise from Delphic forward guidance. If FOMC statements reveal information about near-term economic developments that would otherwise remain out of the public's hands, then the direct effects of the fundamentals so revealed (e.g., lower unemployment and higher inflation from expected demand strength) will accompany the optimal policy response to those fundamentals (e.g., an increase in expected future policy rates). That is, regressions of expectation revisions on changes in expected interest rates suffer from a simultaneity problem when FOMC statements contain Delphic forward guidance. Although this Delphic hypothesis is reasonable, it could also be wrong. Campbell et al. (2012) did not even commence with its empirical examination. Accordingly, we take up this challenge below by using direct measures of FOMC private information based on now-public Greenbook forecasts.

Additional scrutiny of asset price responses to FOMC forward guidance has also raised questions about the content and transmission of forward guidance. In the canonical log-linear New Keynesian model, the expectations theory of the term structure holds good; changes in long-dated interest rates perfectly reflect concomitant changes in expected future spot interest rates. This applies to both real and nominal interest rates, but it is uncommon for monetary policy to influence expected real interest rates far beyond the duration of price stickiness. In contrast to this prediction, Hanson and Stein (2015) found that changes in the stance of monetary policy substantially influence long-dated instantaneous forward rates. For FOMC meeting days, they regressed two-day changes in the ten-year ahead nominal instantaneous treasury yield, real TIPS yield, and implied inflation compensation (as measured by Gürkaynak, Sack, and Wright [2006, 2008]) on the changes in the two-year, zero-coupon nominal yield (also from Gürkaynak et al. [2006]), their preferred measure of the stance of monetary policy. They find no impact of the two-year nominal rate on forward-inflation compensation, but the same rate has substantial effects on both the real and nominal forward rates.

Hanson and Stein dismiss out of hand the possibility that these estimated responses reflect changes in expected spot interest rates 10 years ahead that are driven by monetary policy actions. We find this dismissal especially justified since long-dated inflation compensation does not respond to the two-year rate. They consider two alternative explanations for their findings. Perhaps FOMC communications contain Delphic forward guidance about changes in the long-run real rate of interest (which is obviously out of the committee's control). Alternatively, investors might "reach for yield" when short rates fall by shifting their portfolios into longer-dated securities. This additional demand reduces their prices, but not the expectations of outcomes 10 years hence. That is, the observed price changes reflect changes in term premia. Although Hanson and Stein cannot conclusively dismiss the Delphic explanation for their finding, they prefer the premium-based alternative for a variety of empirical reasons. Our measures of the private information the FOMC might reveal in forward guidance allow us to examine their Delphic hypothesis more directly.

B. An Accounting Framework

To enable a more precise discussion of the measurement of forward guidance and the estimation and interpretation of its effects, we present here a simple accounting framework for asset prices. The framework characterizes the prices of two fundamental assets, a zero-duration, risk-free nominal security and a corresponding inflation-protected (hereafter "real") security. In addition to these two assets, households also trade futures

contracts with all future expiration dates on these two securities. Time
is continuous, but there is a central bank that makes policy decisions at
discrete moments (hereafter "meetings") that are one unit of time apart
from each other. The current value of the nominal security is the central
bank's policy rate, so this is fixed between the central bank's meetings.

The central bank follows a policy rule like that in Laséen and Svensson (2011) and Campbell et al. (2012). At meeting-instant t^*, the policy
rate i_{t^*} is set to

$$i_{t^*} = g_{t^*} + \sum_{j=0}^{M} \xi^{j}_{t^*-j}. \qquad (1)$$

Here, $g_{t^*} \equiv g(\Omega^{c}_{t^*-\varepsilon})$ is the systematic component of monetary policy,
with $\Omega^{c}_{t^*-\varepsilon}$ denoting the central bank's information set as of the moment
$t^* - \varepsilon$. The small time increment ε represents an implementation delay,
such as the time taken to transmit the central bank's policy rule choice
to its trading desk. The remaining terms are the monetary policy shocks.
The shock $\xi^{0}_{t^*}$ is the *current* monetary policy shock, and it is uncorrelated
with its own leads and lags. Furthermore, it is a surprise in the sense
that even an observer with knowledge of both $g(\cdot)$ and $\Omega^{c}_{t^*-\varepsilon}$ cannot predict it. That is, $\xi^{0}_{t^*} \notin \Omega^{c}_{t^*-\varepsilon}$. The remaining terms are forward-guidance
shocks that the central bank revealed after past meetings. After the
meeting at $t^* - j$, the central bank revealed $\xi^{j}_{t^*-j}$. At that moment, it became common knowledge that this would be applied to the interest-rate
rule j meetings hence (that is, at t^*). The central bank revealed shocks
that influence i_{t^*} for the last M meetings. The set of all public informa-
tion at time t is $\Omega^{p}_{t} \subset \Omega^{c}_{t}$. If $\bar{\Omega}^{p}_{t} \cap \Omega^{c}_{t}$ is not empty, then the central bank
has private information.

At exactly t^*, the central bank issues a statement to the public. This contains two components, which we label Delphic (d_{t^*}) and Odyssean (o_{t^*}).
The Delphic component reveals some of the central bank's private information. If the central bank either chooses to reveal nothing or has nothing
to reveal (when $\Omega^{c}_{t-\varepsilon} = \Omega^{p}_{t-\varepsilon}$), then d_t equals the empty set, a trivial statement. Otherwise, we assume that $g_{t^*} \in d_t$, so that the private sector can
calculate $\xi^{0}_{t^*}$ from i_{t^*} and d_{t^*}. The Odyssean component equals a vector of
forward-guidance shocks, $o_{t^*} \equiv (\xi^{1}_{t^*}, \ldots, \xi^{M}_{t^*})$. Like the current policy shock,
o_{t^*} is uncorrelated with its own leads and lags and those $\xi^{0}_{t^*}$. However, it
may be correlated with $\xi^{0}_{t^*}$ itself. Furthermore, the elements of o_{t^*} may
be correlated with each other. We also assume that and $o_{t^*} \notin \Omega^{c}_{t^*-\varepsilon}$. In
this specific sense, d_{t^*} and o_{t^*} encompass Delphic and Odyssean forward
guidance.[8]

At that same moment the central bank announces i_{t^*}, d_{t^*}, and o_{t^*}, the media also communicates news n_{t^*} to the public. Without loss of generality, we assume that $n_{t^*} \notin \Omega^c_{t^*-\varepsilon} \cup \{i_{t^*}, d_{t^*}, o_{t^*}\}$. That is, n_{t^*} is not merely a regurgitation of the central bank's policy action and statement. The public learns nothing else between $t^* - \varepsilon$ and t^*, so we have

$$\Omega^p_{t^*} = \Omega^p_{t^*-\varepsilon} \cup \{i_{t^*}\} \cup \{o_{t^*}\} \cup \{d_{t^*}\} \cup \{n_{t^*}\}. \qquad (2)$$

The real value of the nominal bond is subject to erosion (or enhancement) by inflation, which equals $\pi_t \in \Omega^p_t$ at instant t. This inflation and the returns to the real and nominal bonds satisfy the Fisher equation,

$$r_t = i_t - \pi_t,$$

always.

When two households execute a futures contract at instant t, which expires in n periods, one of them agrees to exchange a zero-duration bond with a fixed yield, $f_t(n)$, (set at instant t) for the otherwise equivalent zero-duration bond with the interest rate prevailing at instant $t + n$. We use the superscripts r and i to distinguish the forward rates on real and nominal bonds from each other, and we define the n-period forward instantaneous inflation compensation with $f_t^\pi(n) \equiv f_t^i(n) - f_t^r(n)$. Following Piazzesi and Swanson (2008), we define the realized excess returns to the buyers of the n-period futures contracts and the realized excess inflation premium with

$$x_t^i(n) \equiv f_t^i(n) - i_{t+n}, \quad x_t^r(n) \equiv f_t^r(n) - r_{t+n}, \quad \text{and} \quad x_t^\pi(n) \equiv f_t^\pi(n) - \pi_{t+n}.$$

Continuing, we define the n-period nominal, real, and inflation-compensation term premiums as the expectations of the corresponding excess returns given Ω^p_t. That is

$$\bar{x}_t^i(n) \equiv \mathbb{E}\left[x_t^i(n) \mid \Omega^p_t\right], \quad \bar{x}_t^r(n) \equiv \mathbb{E}\left[x_t^r(n) \mid \Omega^p_t\right], \quad \text{and}$$

$$\bar{x}_t^\pi(n) \equiv \mathbb{E}\left[x_t^\pi(n) \mid \Omega^p_t\right].$$

Below, we use the notation $\bar{z}_t(n)$ to denote the expectation of z_{t+n} given Ω^p_t. By construction $f_t^z(n) = \bar{z}_{t+n} + \bar{x}_t^z(n)$, for $z = i, r, c$.

Completing the framework requires us to describe the evolution of inflation and the determination of futures prices. We assume that π_t evolves stochastically, and that $\pi_\tau \in \Omega^p_t$ for all $\tau \leq t$. Otherwise, we leave inflation's stochastic process and the influence of monetary policy upon it unspecified. We make the weakest possible assumption regarding the futures prices: the rate of each contract consummated at t is a function of Ω_t^p only. Henceforth, we leave this dependence implicit in our expressions. While this imposes very little structure, it is sufficient for our accounting purposes.

With the framework's specification complete, we can proceed to consider the measurement of monetary policy disturbances using high-frequency, asset-price data. Consider first a stylized version of the Kuttner (2001) measurement strategy.[9] Given the price of a futures' contract with floating rate $i_{t^*} \equiv f_{t^*}^i(0)$ written at $t^* - \varepsilon$, this procedure proxies for $\xi_{t^*}^0$ with

$$\Delta_\varepsilon f_{t^*}^i(0) \equiv f_{t^*}^i(0) - f_{t^*-\varepsilon}^i(\varepsilon).$$

To determine the requirements for $\Delta_\varepsilon f_{t^*}^i(0) \approx \xi_{t^*}^0$, use the monetary policy rule and the term premium's definition to get

$$\Delta_\varepsilon f_{t^*}^i(0) - \xi_{t^*}^0 = -\bar{x}_{t-\varepsilon}^i(\varepsilon) + g(\Omega_{t^*-\varepsilon}^c) - \mathbb{E}[g(\Omega_{t^*-\varepsilon}^c) \mid \Omega_{t^*-\varepsilon}^p]. \tag{3}$$

The estimation error's first component is the ε-period term premium, and we label the remaining terms' sum the contribution of central bank private information. So for this stylized version of the Kuttner procedure to yield reasonably accurate sequences of contemporaneous policy shocks, the term premium should vary little across meetings and the central bank should not base its current policy-rate choices on any private information in its possession. The requirement on the term premium is consistent with the results of Piazzesi and Swanson (2008), which show that this premium's variance is concentrated at business cycle frequencies. We test the assumption on private information below.

As noted above, Gürkaynak et al. (2005) and Campbell et al. (2012) extended the Kuttner strategy to measure the surprise component of expected future policy rates with changes in nominal futures rates. For $j \in \{1, 2, \ldots, M\}$, these changes can be written as

$$\begin{aligned}
\Delta_\varepsilon f_{t^*}^i(j) &\equiv f_{t^*}^i(j) - f_{t^*-\varepsilon}^i(j + \varepsilon) \\
&= \bar{i}_{t^*}(j) - \bar{i}_{t^*-\varepsilon}(j + \varepsilon) + \bar{x}_{t^*}^i(j) - \bar{x}_{t^*-\varepsilon}^i(j + \varepsilon) \\
&= \xi_{t^*}^j + \bar{g}_{t^*}(j) - \bar{g}_{t^*-\varepsilon}(j + \varepsilon) + \bar{x}_{t^*}^i(j) - \bar{x}_{t^*-\varepsilon}^i(j + \varepsilon) \\
&= \xi_{t^*}^j + \Delta_\varepsilon \bar{g}_{t^*}(j) + \Delta_\varepsilon \bar{x}_{t^*}^i(j).
\end{aligned}$$

Analogously to the current policy rate, the futures-based surprise measure sums the forward-guidance shock, a revision to the expectation of the interest-rate rule's systematic component, and a policy-induced change in the term premium.

By definition, the shock $\xi_{t^*}^j$ is one component of Odyssean forward guidance. The revision to the expectations of g_{t^*+j} embodies other Odyssean forward guidance (the revelation of o_{t^*}), the current policy shock ($\xi^0_{t^*}$), Delphic forward guidance (the revelation of d_{t^*}), and public news (the receipt of n_{t^*}). Although the public receives these pieces of information simultaneously, it is helpful to imagine them being received sequentially in the order $n_{t^*}, d_{t^*}, \xi^0_{t^*}, o_{t^*}$. This allows us to write $\Delta_\varepsilon \bar{g}_{t^*}(j)$ as the sum of four orthogonal components, each of which reflects one of these messages:

$$\Delta_\varepsilon \bar{g}_{t^*}(j) = \iota^o_{t^*}(j) + \iota^{\xi^0}_{t^*}(j) + \iota^d_{t^*}(j) + \iota^n_{t^*}(j); \qquad \text{with}$$

$$\iota^n_{t^*}(j) \equiv \mathbb{E}[g_{t^*+j} \mid \Omega^p_{t^*-\varepsilon} \cup \{n_{t^*}\}] - \mathbb{E}[g_{t^*+j} \mid \Omega^p_{t^*-\varepsilon}]$$

$$\iota^d_{t^*}(j) \equiv \mathbb{E}[g_{t^*+j} \mid \Omega^p_{t^*-\varepsilon} \cup \{n_{t^*}\} \cup \{d_{t^*}\}] - \mathbb{E}[g_{t^*+j} \mid \Omega^p_{t^*-\varepsilon} \cup \{n_{t^*}\}]$$

$$\iota^{\xi^0}_{t^*}(j) \equiv \mathbb{E}[g_{t^*+j} \mid \Omega^p_{t^*-\varepsilon} \cup \{n_{t^*}\} \cup \{d_{t^*}\} \cup \{\xi^0_{t^*}\}]$$

$$\qquad -\mathbb{E}[g_{t^*+j} \mid \Omega^p_{t^*-\varepsilon} \cup \{n_{t^*}\} \cup \{d_{t^*}\}], \qquad \text{and}$$

$$\iota^o_{t^*}(j) \equiv \mathbb{E}[g_{t^*+j} \mid \Omega^p_{t^*-\varepsilon} \cup \{n_{t^*}\} \cup \{d_{t^*}\} \cup \{\xi^0_{t^*}\} \cup \{o_{t^*}\}]$$

$$\qquad -\mathbb{E}[g_{t^*+j} \mid \Omega^p_{t^*-\varepsilon} \cup \{n_{t^*}\} \cup \{d_{t^*}\} \cup \{\xi^0_{t^*}\}]$$

$$\qquad = \mathbb{E}[g_{t^*+j} \mid \Omega^p_{t^*}] - \mathbb{E}[g_{t^*+j} \mid \Omega^p_{t^*-\varepsilon} \cup \{n_{t^*}\} \cup \{d_{t^*}\} \cup \{\xi^0_{t^*}\}].$$

If we again appeal to Piazzesi and Swanson (2008) to justify ignoring the term premium's change, we can write the surprise change in the j-period ahead forward rate as

$$\Delta_\varepsilon f^j_{t^*}(j) \approx \xi^j_{t^*} + \iota^o_{t^*}(j) + \iota^{\xi^0}_{t^*}(j) + \iota^d_{t^*}(j) + \iota^n_{t^*}(j). \qquad (4)$$

If the public and central bank were always equally well informed and there were no Odyssean forward guidance, then the first, second, and fourth terms would identically equal zero. The change in the futures rate would equal a contribution from the propagation of the current policy shock through the economy and into the policy rule's value in $t^* + j$, $\iota^{\xi^0}_{t^*}(j)$, and a term from the arrival of news from sources other than the central bank, $\iota^n_{t^*}(j)$. The inclusion of Delphic forward guidance introduces $\iota^d_{t^*}(j)$. Finally, Odyssean forward guidance makes the first two terms nonzero. In this sense, equation (4) decomposes the surprise in the j-period ahead futures contract rate into four components: Odyssean forward guidance (the first two terms summed), Delphic forward guidance, the current policy shock's propagation, and the effects of coincident news.

The characterization of the standard monetary shock measurement scheme is now in place, so we can proceed to consider the identification of their effects. For this, consider the change in the futures' contract rate for the nominal bond at some date $t^* + h$, where $h > M$. This inequality ensures that ξ_t^j only influences i_{t^*+h} indirectly through its effects on $\Omega^c_{t^*+h^\downarrow-\varepsilon}$. (Here, $h^\downarrow$ is the greatest integer less than h.) Therefore, we can decompose the change in the forward rate into eight components.

$$\Delta_\varepsilon f_{t^*}^i(h) = \Delta_\varepsilon \bar{g}_{t^*}^i(h) + \Delta_\varepsilon \bar{x}_{t^*}^i(h)$$

$$= \iota_{t^*}^o(h) + \iota_{t^*}^{\xi^0}(h) + \iota_{t^*}^d(h) + \iota_{t^*}^n(h) \tag{5}$$

$$+\eta_{t^*}^o(h) + \eta_{t^*}^{\xi^0}(h) + \eta_{t^*}^d(h) + \eta_{t^*}^n(h)$$

The $\iota(h)$ shocks are defined analogously to those for j, but with $g_{t+h} = g_{t+h^\downarrow}$. (That is, the systematic component of monetary policy is fixed between meetings.) The $\eta(h)$ shocks give the analogous decomposition for the surprise change in the term premium. Hanson and Stein (2015) strongly suggest that these last shocks are *not* identically zero for large values of h.

We are now prepared to characterize the results of regressing $\Delta_\varepsilon f_{t^*}^i(h)$ on $\Delta_\varepsilon f_{t^*}^i(j)$. In population, this yields the coefficient

$$\beta(h, j) \equiv \frac{\mathbb{E}\left[\Delta_\varepsilon f_{t^*}^i(h)\Delta_\varepsilon f_{t^*}^i(j)\right]}{\mathbb{E}\left[\Delta_\varepsilon f_{t^*}^i(j)^2\right]}.$$

These expectations are taken by averaging over an infinite sample of meetings. Using the decompositions in (4) and (5), we can express this coefficient as a weighted average of four regression coefficients.

$$\beta(h, j) = \frac{\sigma^2(\xi_{t^*}^j + \iota_{t^*}^o(j))}{\sigma^2(\Delta_\varepsilon f_{t^*}^i(j))} \beta^o(h, j) + \frac{\sigma^2(\iota_{t^*}^{\xi^0}(j))}{\sigma^2(\Delta_\varepsilon f_{t^*}^i(j))} \beta^{\xi^0}(h, j)$$

$$+ \frac{\sigma^2(\iota_{t^*}^d(j))}{\sigma^2(\Delta_\varepsilon f_{t^*}^i(j))} \beta^d(h, j) + \frac{\sigma^2(\iota_{t^*}^n(j))}{\sigma^2(\Delta_\varepsilon f_{t^*}^i(j))} \beta^n(h, j). \tag{6}$$

The weights in equation (6) sum to one, and the regression coefficients are defined with

$$\beta^o(h, j) \equiv \frac{\mathbb{E}[(\xi_{t^*}^j + \iota_{t^*}^o(j))(\iota_{t^*}^o(h) + \eta_{t^*}^o(h))]}{\sigma^2(\xi_{t^*}^j + \iota_{t^*}^o(j))},$$

$$\beta^{\xi^0}(h, j) \equiv \frac{\mathbb{E}[\iota_{t^*}^{\xi^0}(j)(\iota_{t^*}^{\xi^0}(h) + \eta_{t^*}^{\xi^0}(h))]}{\sigma^2(\iota_{t^*}^{\xi^0}(j))},$$

$$\beta^d(h, j) \equiv \frac{\mathbb{E}[\iota_{t^*}^d(j)(\iota_{t^*}^d(h) + \eta_{t^*}^d(h))]}{\sigma^2(\iota_{t^*}^d(j))}, \text{ and}$$

$$\beta^n(h, j) \equiv \frac{\mathbb{E}[\iota_{t^*}^n(j)(\iota_{t^*}^n(h) + \eta_{t^*}^n(h))]}{\sigma^2(\iota_{t^*}^n(j))}.$$

These four regression coefficients are the "pure" measures of the effects of Odyssean forward guidance, the current policy rate, Delphic forward guidance, and public news on $f_{t^*}^i(h)$. The identifiable regression coefficient weights these with variance contributions. Of course, analogous decompositions can be derived for the responses of $f_{t^*}^r(h)$ and $f_{t^*}^\pi(h)$.

Regardless of the asset under examination, the identified responses of asset prices to short-dated nominal interest-rate futures conflate the responses that directly map into simple models' impulse-response functions for future policy shocks with responses to Delphic forward guidance and news shocks. Therefore, the interpretation of this "cleanly" identified coefficient is far from straightforward. The Hanson and Stein (2015) results cited above strongly suggest that innovations to the expected systematic component of monetary policy are correlated with innovations to term premia. That is, the covariances of the $\iota(j)$ shocks with $\eta(h)$ shocks are not zero. Furthermore, when public news shocks influence expectations of future monetary policy ($\beta^n(h, j) \neq 0$), high-frequency measurement does not by itself solve the classical simultaneous equations problem. Rigobon and Sack (2004) emphasize this obstacle and propose avoiding it by using estimates of asset price responses from days *without* FOMC policy actions to remove the influence of $\beta^n(h, j)$ from $\beta(h, j)$. Below, we undertake an effort to measure $\beta^d(h, j)$ based on measures of the information that could possibly be included within Delphic forward guidance.

C. The FOMC's Delphic Forward Guidance

Unlike some inflation-targeting central banks abroad, the FOMC publishes no consensus forecasts of macroeconomic fundamentals and interest rates. Accordingly, the committee's postmeeting statements have historically lacked much quantitative content. Our approach to measuring Delphic forward guidance therefore does nothing with the statements themselves. Rather, we measure information that was available to FOMC participants, but that was not in the public information set. Specifically, we take the forecasts for CPI inflation, GDP growth, and the unemployment rate contained in the committee's Greenbook, and subtract the analogous consensus (that is, average) forecasts from the most recent Blue Chip survey.[10]

The measured forecast differences cover the current quarter (the "nowcast") and the next four quarters. To keep our results interpretable, we reduce these 15 variables to 6 by conducting a factor analysis

Table 1
Factor Structure of Short-Term FOMC Private Information

	Factors' Shares of Variance					
	CPI-Inflation		GDP Growth		Unemployment	
	Short	Long	Short	Long	Short	Long
Current quarter	80	0	68	0	99	0
Next quarter	26	42	33	13	77	19
Two quarters hence	10	71	58	4	47	51
Three quarters hence	14	87	3	77	36	63
Four quarters hence	13	77	9	66	30	67

identical to that applied by Gürkaynak et al. (2005) to the interest-rate futures data. The factor analogous to the path factor, which by construction has no impact on the forecast of the current quarter's value, we call the "long" factor. The other one is the "short" factor. Table 1 reports the variance decompositions for these variables. With the exception of GDP growth one and two quarters into the future, these two factors account for the vast majority of observed variance.

Our next step uses these measures of FOMC private information to measure the information revealed in FOMC statements, as reflected in the concurrent changes in market expected interest rates. Table 2 reports the associated regression estimates and Wald tests for the exclusion of groups of regressors. Asymptotic standard errors are reported below each regression coefficient. For both coefficients' t-statistics and the Wald tests, we calculated critical values using 100,000 bootstrap replications that treat the meetings as independent. The significance stars that accompany the coefficient estimates and Wald test statistics come from these bootstrap calculations. Unsurprisingly, our reliance on bootstrapped critical values makes the results seem less "significant" than they otherwise would be. In that sense, our procedure is conservative. The regressions include 12 variables each, the 6 principle components from the current meeting as well as those from the *previous* meeting. These regressors might be relevant, because no theory requires the FOMC to reveal its information in a timely manner.

Table 2's first column reports the results from using changes in the current policy rate on the date of a FOMC meeting announcement as the dependent variable. The regression R^2 equals 0.13, and none of the estimated coefficients are statistically significant. More importantly, none of the Wald tests indicate that the included variables have explanatory

Table 2
The FOMC Revelation of Private Information

	Current Rate	Four Quarters Ahead
CPI short factor	−0.40	−1.25
	(0.79)	(0.99)
CPI long factor	−1.62	−4.99
	(5.37)	(6.72)
GDP short factor	−1.38	4.00
	(2.00)	(2.50)
GDP long factor	3.72	9.16**
	(2.68)	(3.36)
U short factor	−8.93	−11.13
	(5.04)	(6.31)
U long factor	−6.08	4.69
	(6.09)	(7.64)
CPI short factor lag	0.53	0.37
	(0.77)	(0.96)
CPI long factor lag	−0.73	3.48
	(5.32)	(6.66)
GDP short factor lag	0.99	1.16
	(1.86)	(2.33)
GDP long factor lag	−2.17	−11.13***
	(2.91)	(3.64)
U short factor lag	−0.17	−1.65
	(5.22)	(6.54)
U long factor lag	6.70	−3.11
	(6.02)	(7.54)
R^2	0.13	0.23
	Wald Tests	
All variables	15.76	33.33**
Current variables	8.52	11.08
Lagged variables	4.47	19.34***
CPI measures	1.01	1.78
GDP measures	6.01	19.25***
U measures	7.23	7.79

power.[11] Equation (3) identifies Delphic forward guidance as a possible complication for the identification scheme of Kuttner (2001), so this absence of evidence for short-run Delphic forward guidance influencing the current policy rate indicates that this is not a practical difficulty.

The second column reports results from using the four-quarters ahead futures contract rate as the dependent variable. Here, the R^2 is substantially higher, 0.23. Two of the GDP coefficients are statistically significant, those multiplying the long factors from the current and past meetings. The former is positive, as we would expect if high expected GDP growth leads policymakers to signal tighter future policy. The latter coefficient is, however, negative. We do not find this too disturbing though, because the analogous coefficients on the two regressors that should have high correlations with the GDP long factor, the CPI and unemployment ("U") long factors have the expected signs. They have economically significant magnitudes, but they are measured imprecisely. The Wald test rejects the null hypothesis that all of the variables can be rejected at the 5% level. So it does appear that Delphic forward guidance is associated with the statement. Perhaps more surprisingly, it appears that this guidance comes mostly from private information available in the previous meeting. The Wald test rejects the null that these variables can be excluded at the 1% level. On the other hand, the Wald test does not reject the null that the most recently obtained private information can be excluded. We interpret these results as indicating *latency* in the transmission of private information from the Federal Reserve's staff forecasters through FOMC participants and into the committee's statement. It seems that participants digest newly acquired information between meetings before incorporating it into statements.

The regression results in table 2 provide one means of measuring short-run Delphic forward guidance: decompose the four-quarters ahead futures rate into fitted values and residuals. The fitted values are our measure of short-run Delphic forward guidance. We emphasize "short run" because the information used in its identification only covers the next several quarters.[12] Although we doubt that other variables are available that substantially add to our measure of private FOMC information about the economy's near-term performance, there could be other information about longer-run outcomes. Even if those outcomes are outside of the FOMC's control (e.g., the long-run real interest rate), the FOMC's information about them might still be revealed in post-meeting statements and thereby influence asset prices. Since the regression's residuals can contain both longer-run Delphic forward guidance as well as Odyssean forward guidance, we refrain from applying any more structural interpretation to the regression's residuals.

Above, we discussed the possibility that Delphic forward guidance could be responsible for the counterintuitive effects of measured forward guidance on forecast revisions documented by Campbell et al. (2012). Table 3 provides evidence on that point. For the four forecasts of each variable available in our data, its first column reports estimated coefficients from bivariate regressions of the Blue Chip survey's revision to that forecast (from the survey prior to the meeting to the one following it) on the four-quarters ahead futures rate innovation itself. Each

Table 3
Blue Chip Forecasts' Responses to Decomposed Monetary Policy

| | Baseline Regressions | | With Delphic Decomposition | | |
	Future Policy Rate	R^2	Delphic Component	Residual	R^2
CPI Inflation					
Next quarter	−0.01	0.00	0.54	−0.18	0.01
	(0.25)		(0.52)	(0.29)	
Two quarters hence	−0.10	0.01	0.22	−0.20	0.03
	(0.11)		(0.22)	(0.12)	
Three quarters hence	−0.06	0.01	0.14	−0.12	0.02
	(0.07)		(0.15)	(0.08)	
Four quarters hence	0.00	0.00	0.23*	−0.07	0.04
	(0.06)		(0.12)	(0.07)	
GDP Growth					
Next quarter	0.66***	0.03	2.88**	−0.01	0.12
	(0.36)		(0.72)	(0.40)	
Two quarters hence	0.27	0.01	1.75***	−0.18	0.14
	(0.20)		(0.40)	(0.22)	
Three quarters hence	0.07	0.00	0.66**	−0.11	0.07
	(0.12)		(0.23)	(0.13)	
Four quarters hence	0.06	0.00	0.29	−0.01	0.02
	(0.09)		(0.19)	(0.10)	
Unemployment					
Next quarter	−0.21**	0.05	−0.88***	−0.01	0.21
	(0.05)		(0.16)	(0.09)	
Two quarters hence	−0.19	0.02	−1.08***	0.09	0.19
	(0.11)		(0.20)	(0.11)	
Three quarters hence	−0.17	0.02	−1.28***	0.16	0.20
	(0.13)		(0.24)	(0.13)	
Four quarters hence	−0.18	0.02	−1.18***	0.12	0.17
	(0.12)		(0.24)	(0.13)	

coefficient's asymptotic standard error is below it. The second column reports these regressions' R^2 measures. For the CPI forecasts, the regression coefficients and R^2's are all very close to zero. The coefficient for the forecast of next quarter's GDP growth forecast is positive and statistically significant at the 1% level.[13] A naive reading of this would suggest that tightening monetary policy raises expected GDP growth. The coefficients for the remaining GDP forecasts are positive, but not statistically significant. The forecast of next quarter's unemployment rate has a statistically significant (at the 5% level) and negative coefficient. The unemployment forecasts at other horizons have similar coefficients, but they are measured less precisely. Again, a naive interpretation of this evidence would suggest that tightening monetary policy lowers the unemployment rate.

Table 2's remaining columns report the results from the analogous regressions that use the policy rate's decomposition into its short-run Delphic component and the associated residual. The CPI-forecast regressions have positive coefficients multiplying the forward rate's Delphic component, and negative coefficients multiplying the forward rate's residual. One of the coefficients multiplying the Delphic component is statistically significant at the 10% level, but otherwise inference from the simpler regression with only the forward rate itself remains unchanged.[14] The results from the GDP and unemployment forecast regressions differ substantially from this result. The GDP forecasts for one, two, and three quarters out all have statistically significant and large coefficients multiplying the forward rate's Delphic component. The coefficients multiplying the residual component are all negative but small and not statistically significant. The same pattern is true for the unemployment forecasts. The forward rate's Delphic component has negative and statistically significant (at the 1% level) coefficients, while the residual component has coefficients that are much closer to zero and (with one exception) positive. In light of these results, it should be no surprise that the R^2 measures from these regressions are much higher than those for the CPI-forecast regressions. Nevertheless, substantial variance in the forecast revisions remains.

Overall, the results of table 3 validate the Delphic hypothesis as applied to the revisions of Blue Chip forecasts: the FOMC's statements reveal its private information (probably with a lag), and this influences expectations of short-run interest rates. The same information leads to substantial revisions of private forecasts, so we see forecasts of GDP growth and unemployment rising "in response to" increases in expected future policy rates. Of course, much remains to be uncovered because the portion of the expected future policy rate that is unexplained by FOMC private information (about 80% of its variance) has no statistically significant effect on short-term forecast revisions. We hope that better measurement of the FOMC's Delphic forward guidance that focuses more on medium-run and long-run economic outcomes combined with the inclusion of variables that are (theoretically) orthogonal to measured Delphic forward guidance, but nevertheless relevant for private forecast revisions, will yield a better understanding of how this residual's movements change expectations.

Table 4

Treasury Price Responses to Decomposed Monetary Policy

	Baseline Regressions		With Delphic Decomposition		
	Future Policy Rate	R^2	Delphic Component	Residual	R^2
Two-year instantaneous forward					
Nominal	0.86***	0.30	0.47	0.72***	0.31
	(0.14)		(0.26)	(0.18)	
Real	1.04***	0.29	0.77**	0.75***	0.40
	(0.29)		(0.25)	(0.17)	
Inflation compensation	−0.18	0.02	−0.31	−0.03	0.03
	(0.15)		(0.29)	(0.20)	
Five-year instantaneous forward					
Nominal	0.27**	0.06	0.14	0.31***	0.06
	(0.10)		(0.21)	(0.11)	
Real	0.23***	0.09	0.13	0.26***	0.09
	(0.07)		(0.15)	(0.08)	
Inflation compensation	0.04	0.00	0.01	0.04	0.00
	(0.07)		(0.15)	(0.08)	
Ten-year instantaneous forward					
Nominal	0.14*	0.03	−0.10	0.20***	0.05
	(0.08)		(0.16)	(0.09)	
Real	0.15**	0.06	0.02	0.18***	0.08
	(0.05)		(0.11)	(0.06)	
Inflation compensation	−0.01	0.00	−0.12	0.02	0.01
	(0.05)		(0.11)	(0.06)	

Our attempt to place the results of Hanson and Stein (2015) within the context of Delphic forward guidance is summarized in table 4. Its first two columns report regressions analogous to those reported by those authors. The dependent variables are the instantaneous forward nominal rates, real rates, and inflation compensation rates at the two-, five-, and ten-year horizons calculated by Gürkaynak et al. (2006, 2008).[15] The independent variable is the same four-quarters ahead nominal futures rate examined in tables 2 and 3. We comment further on the implications of this differ-ence below. For now, note that our results are comparable to theirs. The future policy rate has large, positive, and statistically significant effects on both the nominal and real rates. These effects get smaller as the securities' horizons increase, but they do not disappear, even at a ten-year horizon.

One important difference between our estimates and Hanson and Stein's is that these regressions' R^2s are much lower than those they report for their baseline case. This can be entirely attributed to our use of a different monetary policy indicator.[16] Hanson and Stein measured the stance of monetary policy with the nominal two-year, zero-coupon yield from Gürkaynak et al. (2006). We were concerned that shocks to public news relevant for Treasury yield curves, but not directly arising from monetary policy, could be unduly contributing to the measured relationship between these asset prices. To examine this hypothesis, we estimated the regressions of Hanson and Stein using data from *five days before* each FOMC meeting. For recent meetings, this places the data within the "blackout period" during which staff and policymaker commentary on monetary policy developments is prohibited. Nevertheless, the coefficient estimates we obtain from those days are similar to those reported in Hanson and Stein (2015).[17] In contrast, the estimates from the same days using changes in the forward rate we employ show no relationship between the two prices. In this specific sense, the forward rate that we employ is a "purer" measure of FOMC policy intentions than is the two-year, zero-coupon nominal treasury rate.

The remaining columns of table 4 report the results from the analogous regressions that decompose the future policy rate into its short-run Delphic and residual components. Here, the results are very striking. As one might expect, the short-run Delphic component has a large and statistically significant effect on the two-year instantaneous forward real rate. Unfortunately though, the sample is too short to precisely decompose that real effect into effects on the nominal rate and inflation compensation. However, the Delphic component has no measurable effects on any of the five-year or ten-year securities. In contrast, the residual component has large and statistically significant (at the 1% level) on the real and nominal forward rates at all three horizons. Just as in the original Hanson and Stein regressions, neither the Delphic component nor the residual has much of an effect on forward inflation compensation.

As we noted above, Hanson and Stein (2015) discussed two explanations for their findings, Delphic forward guidance (in their words, "the revelation of the Fed's private information about the future evolution of the economy."[18]) and changes in term premiums driven by yield-oriented investors. Although we cannot decisively eliminate the possibility of monetary policy impacting term premiums (nor do we wish to do so), we believe that the evidence in table 4 favors an information-based interpretation. The Delphic component of the four-quarters-ahead futures rate increases rates at the short end of the yield curve but *not* at the long end. It could be that the strong economic fundamentals that underly a Delphic increase in expected policy rates increase demand for treasuries that exactly offsets the flight of yield-oriented investors back to shorter-dated securities, but in that case we would expect the Delphic component to raise short interest rates much more than does the residual component. There is no evidence that this is the case. In an information-based story, the Delphic component only matters for short-dated securities simply because it is short-run information. The effects of the residual component on long rates can then be understood as the revelation of information about long-run outcomes. The standard deviation of this residual component is approximately 10 basis points. If we take these over eight meetings, this results in an annual standard deviation of revisions to the long-run real rate of $0.18\sqrt{8} \times 10^2 \approx 5$ basis points per year. This is hardly so large that it would be the dominant factor in long-run rates. Nevertheless, further empirical scrutiny of such an information-based hypothesis is warranted.

D. Evidence from VARs

The reduced-form empirical evidence discussed above has the advantage that it relies on relatively weak identifying assumptions, but this approach currently has little to say about the impact of Odyssean forward-guidance shocks on macroeconomic outcomes. However, there is a nascent literature that addresses this issue by making stronger assumptions. This literature builds on the traditional approach to identifying monetary policy shocks using VARs pioneered by Bernanke and Blinder (1992) and reviewed by Christiano, Eichenbaum, and Evans (1999). The traditional approach measures monetary policy shocks with changes in a policy indicator, typically the federal funds rate, that are orthogonal to a particular information set defined by a subset of the variables included in the VAR. Unlike high-frequency identification, then, this literature takes a stand on the nature of the monetary policy rule and, in particular, the information used by the Fed in making its policy choices.

The traditional approach ignores forward guidance because it implicitly assumes for $\xi^j_{t-j} = 0$ for $j > 0$ in the policy rule defined in equation (1). Ramey (2016) discusses the challenges to identifying monetary policy shocks when this assumption is violated and Campbell et al. (2012) find that a substantial fraction of the residual variation in an estimated policy rule is forecastable. So this assumption is not innocuous. The new monetary VAR literature allows that $\xi^j_{t-j} \neq 0$ and makes a variety of assumptions to extract this information from different specifications of the policy rule.

Gertler and Karadi (2015) extract this information by using changes in four quarter ahead fed funds futures on FOMC days as instruments for the policy residuals with the one year treasury yield as the policy indicator. Like most of the new literature they focus on a sample that includes observations from both before and after the funds rate attained its lower bound. Following a positive instrumented forward guidance shock real activity and prices fall. These findings are qualitatively consistent with the predictions of NK models. However Gertler and Karadi (2015) also find that the response of long-term interest rate cannot be explained by the expected path of short rates (as predicted by their VAR), which is the principle channel through which forward guidance operates in NK models. Bundick and Smith (2015) also use high-frequency data to identify forward guidance shocks in a VAR, and they also find that real activity contracts after a positive forward-guidance shock. Their results are particularly noteworthy since their sample only covers the period at the ELB.

D'Amico and King (2016) use a sign restriction methodology to extract forward-guidance shocks. They include survey expectations in VARs that include the three-month T-bill rate as the policy indicator. Forward-guidance shocks are identified as innovations in expected T-bill rates that drive them oppositely to survey expectations of output and prices. This identification strategy is attractive because it isolates shocks in which Odyssean dominates Delphic guidance. D'Amico and King (2016) also find that realized output and consumer prices decline in response to positive forward-guidance shocks.

Finally, Ben Zeev, Gunn, and Khan (2015) extract forward guidance from policy rule residuals using Barsky and Sims's (2011) method of identifying news shocks. They first construct policy residuals as the difference between the federal funds rate and a prespecified policy rule. Forward-guidance shocks are then identified from a VAR as the linear combination of reduced-form residuals that are orthogonal to the policy residuals and maximize the contribution to the policy residual's forecast error variance over a finite horizon. They find that after a positive forward-guidance shock the federal funds rate does indeed rise gradually and is accompanied by declines in output and prices.

This literature is in its early stages and is subject to many of the perceived shortcomings of the traditional approach reviewed by Ramey (2016). Nevertheless, the similarity in the findings across distinct identification strategies is striking. Taken at face value they generally support the view that forward-guidance influences output and prices much as predicted by standard NK models, at least qualitatively. However, there are limits to what can be accomplished with reduced-form analysis.

Our ultimate goal is to quantify the impact of forward guidance on macroeconomic outcomes since the financial crisis. In principle, an estimated VAR can be used to address this question, for example, by simulating it under the assumption of no forward-guidance shocks. However, conducting such an exercise does not guarantee that the lower bound on nominal rates will be respected. Furthermore the nature of forward guidance clearly changed during the ELB period, so there is a very short sample available for estimation. Therefore, we address our question within the context of a fully specified structural model. While such an approach inevitably requires even stronger assumptions than employed in the VAR literature, it does make it possible to consider a richer array of forward guidance and to impose the lower bound constraint when we consider our counterfactual exercise. The generally validating (or not invalidating) event study and VAR findings we have described above motivate us to do this within a NK setting.

III. The Model

We employ an enhanced version of the canonical medium-scale NK model pioneered by Christiano et al. (2005) and Smets and Wouters (2007). Our model incorporates many of the refinements that have been introduced since these seminal papers were written. In addition, we model forward guidance building on Laséen and Svensson (2011) and Campbell et al. (2012), introduce a preference for government bonds as suggested by Fisher (2015), and employ Jaimovich and Rebelo (2009) preferences over consumption and work. Since much of the model's specification is familiar, we emphasize the novel aspects of our framework together with a complete description of the underlying structural shocks, which is essential to understand the experiments discussed below. For a complete characterization of the model see the online appendix.

A. Households

The economy consists of a large number of identical, infinitely lived households with preferences described by the lifetime utility function

$$E_0 \sum_{t=0}^{\infty} \beta^t \varepsilon_t^b \left[U(V_t) + \varepsilon_t^s L\left(\frac{B_{t+1}}{P_t R_t}\right) \right]. \tag{7}$$

The period utility function U is specified as

$$U(V) = \frac{V^{1-\gamma_C} - 1}{1 - \gamma_C}$$

with $\gamma_C > 0$. The argument of U is given by

$$V_t = C_t - \varrho\bar{C}_{t-1} - X_t H_t^{1+\gamma_H}$$

where C_t denotes the household's date t consumption purchased in the final goods market at nominal price P_t, $\bar{C}_t$ denotes *aggregate* per capita consumption (which is equal to C_t in equilibrium), H_t denotes hours worked, and X_t evolves as

$$X_t = (C_t - \varrho\bar{C}_{t-1})^\mu X_{t-1}^{1-\mu}.$$

These are the preferences introduced in Jaimovich and Rebelo (2009), except that we have modified them to include external habit formation in consumption.[19] These preferences include the parameter $\mu \in (0, 1)$, which controls the wealth elasticity of labor supply while preserving compatibility with balanced growth. The parameter $\varrho > 0$ determines the degree of habit formation and γ_H controls the Frisch elasticity of labor supply in the special case in which $\varrho = \mu = 0$. As $\mu \to 0$, and in the absence of habit formation these preferences reduce to the specification considered by Greenwood, Hercowitz, and Huffman (1988). In this special case labor supply depends only on the current real wage faced by households and is independent of the marginal utility of wealth. So as μ and ϱ get smaller, anticipated changes in income have smaller effects on current labor supply. Conversely, as μ gets larger the wealth elasticity gets larger, and in the polar case when $\mu = 1$ preferences reduce to the standard preferences proposed by King, Plosser, and Rebelo (1988).

Jaimovich and Rebelo (2009) introduced their preferences because of their implications for the propagation of news about future production possibilities. With standard preferences news about improved production possibilities in the future raises current wealth, thereby increasing current consumption and lowering labor supply. They found that allowing for flexibility in the short run effects of wealth on labor supply, it was possible to generate business cycle comovement in response to news about future production possibilities. We similarly include these preferences because of our focus on news about future settings of monetary policy, that is, forward guidance. In NK models news about future settings of monetary policy influence current activity in part through wealth effects.

The household's subjective discount factor is decomposed into the nonstochastic component $\beta \in (0, 1)$ and the exogenous *discount factor shock* ε_t^b. This shock has been shown by Justiniano, Primiceri, and Tambalotti (2010) and others to be an important driver of consumption fluctuations. In addition it is often used, for example by Eggertsson and Woodford (2003), to motivate why monetary policy might become constrained by the ELB, and so it is particularly relevant for our analysis. We assume ε_t^b evolves according to

$$\ln \varepsilon_t^b = \rho_b \ln \varepsilon_{t-1}^b + \eta_t^b, \eta_t^b \sim N(0, \sigma_b^2),$$

The second novel feature of preferences is the inclusion of the increasing and concave period utility function L. The argument of L, $B_{t+1} / (P_t R_t)$, represents the real value of one-period government bonds purchased by the household at date t. It comprises of the nominal quantity of those assets, B_{t+1}, their return from date t to date $t + 1$, R_t, and the nominal price of consumption, P_t. Including L introduces a demand for risk-free government bonds that is absent from existing empirical NK models. Krishnamurthy and Vissing-Jorgensen (2011) used such preferences to study the market for government securities.

Including this model feature allows the interest rate controlled by the central bank, R_t, to deviate from the return to installed capital. NK models typically maintain the assumption that these two rates of return coincide. Since the level of the federal funds rate is usually included as an observable in estimation, the assumption of equality potentially influences the values of parameters and the business cycle decompositions derived from those parameters. We show below that a spread between private and government rates of return introduces discounting into the household's linearized intertemporal Euler equation for consumption, which is otherwise absent.

A second reason for introducing "liquidity preferences" is that, as demonstrated by Fisher (2015), these preferences provide a simple microfoundation for the ad hoc shock to the household's consumption Euler equation introduced by Smets and Wouters (2007). This shock plays a crucial role in empirical NK models because it is one of the few sources of comovement between consumption and investment and, therefore, in estimated models often appears as a major source of cyclical fluctuations. In our context this shock is the preference shifter ε_t^s in equation (7). We assume it evolves according to

$$\ln \varepsilon_t^s = \rho_s \ln \varepsilon_{t-1}^s + \eta_t^s, \eta_t^s \sim N(0, \sigma_s^2).$$

Since it directly impacts the utility of "safe and liquid" government bonds, we refer to ε_t^s as the *liquidity preference shock*.

Households own the installed capital stock K_t. This is assumed to evolve over time according to

$$K_t = [1 - \delta(u_t)] K_{t-1} + \varepsilon_t^i \left[1 - S\left(\frac{I_t}{q_t I_{t-1}}\right)\right] I_t.$$

where I_t denotes gross investment and S and its argument correspond to the kind of investment adjustment costs introduced by Christiano et al. (2005). We assume that S evaluated along the nonstochastic growth path satisfies $S = S' = 0$ and $S'' > 0$. The term q_t, defined below, corresponds to the growth rate of investment's stochastic trend in equilibrium. The technology for transforming investment goods into installed capital is subject to the shock ε_t^i. We assume this *investment-demand shock* evolves according to

$$\ln \varepsilon_t^i = \rho_i \ln \varepsilon_{t-1}^i + \eta_t^i, \quad \eta_t^i \sim N(0, \sigma_i^2).$$

The owners of installed capital can control the intensity with which it is utilized. Let u_t measure capacity utilization in period t. Then the effective amount of capital services supplied to firms in period t is $u_t K_t$. We assume that increasing the intensity of capacity utilization entails a cost in the form of faster depreciation, given by $\delta(u_t)$. We assume the functional form

$$\delta(u_t) = \delta_0 + \delta_1(u_t - 1) + \frac{\delta_2}{2}(u_t - 1)^2,$$

with $\delta_0, \delta_1, \delta_2 > 0$. The parameter δ_2 determines the sensitivity of capacity utilization to variation in the rental rate of capital; the parameter δ_1 governs the steady state utilization rate, which we normalize to unity; and the parameter δ_0 corresponds to the rate of depreciation along the nonstochastic growth path or steady state.

B.   Goods Markets

Households own all goods producers. Perfectly competitive firms produce the composite final good Y_t that sells for price P_t. They produce the final good using differentiated intermediate inputs purchased from a unit mass of monopolistically competitive firms, with technology

$$Y_t = \left(\int_0^1 Y_{it}^{1/(1+\lambda_t^p)} di\right)^{1+\lambda_t^p}$$

and Y_{it} denotes the quantity of inputs purchased from intermediate good producer i. Each intermediate good producer sells its product at a markup over marginal cost shocked by λ_t^p, which evolves according to

$$\ln \lambda_t^p = (1 - \rho_p) \ln \lambda_*^p + \rho_p \ln \lambda_{t-1}^p - \theta_p \eta_{t-1}^p + \eta_t^p, \ \eta_t^p \sim N(0, \sigma_p).$$

The parameter λ_*^p denotes the markup in the steady state. We refer to λ_t^p as the *price markup shock*.

Intermediate goods producer i produces Y_{it} using the technology:

$$Y_{it} = (K_{it}^e)^\alpha [A_t^Y H_{it}^d]^{1-\alpha} - A_t \Phi, \tag{8}$$

where H_{it}^d is composite labor input bought at wage W_t in a competitive market from the labor compositors described below; $K_{it}^e = U_{it} K_{it}$ is effective capital rented from households; and Φ is the fixed costs of production, paid in final goods (the value of Φ is chosen so that aggregate monopoly profits of intermediate goods producers are zero in steady state.) The term A_t^Y is the level of the neutral technology. This is a nonstationary process that evolves as

$$\nu_t = (1 - \rho_\nu) \nu_* + \rho_\nu \nu_{t-1} + \eta_t^\nu, \ \eta_t^\nu \sim N(0, \sigma_\nu^2),$$

where $\nu_t \equiv \ln (A_t^Y / A_{t-1}^Y)$. We refer to ν_t as the *neutral technology shock*. The term A_t in equation (8) is the stochastic trend of equilibrium consumption and output measured in consumption units given by $A_t = A_t^Y (A_t^I)^{\alpha/(1-\alpha)}$, where A_t^I is the level of the investment-specific technology described below. We use z_t to denote the log growth rate of A_t: $z_t = \nu_t + \alpha \omega_t / (1 - \alpha)$.

The intermediate goods producers maximize profits according to a Calvo pricing scheme. Each firm is subject to an exogenous probability of having the opportunity to adjust its price, $\zeta_p \in (0, 1)$. Absent this opportunity firms index the previously set price using the exogenous formula $\pi_{t-1}^{\iota_p} \pi_*^{1-\iota_p}$, where π_* is the the central bank's inflation target (corresponding to steady state inflation), and $\iota_p \in [0, 1]$.

Perfectly competitive firms supply investment goods to households at price P_t^I in consumption units using a linear technology that transforms final goods into investment at rate A_t^I. The investment-specific technology A_t^I is a nonstationary process that evolves as

$$\omega_t = (1 - \rho_\omega) \omega_* + \rho_\omega \omega_{t-1} + \eta_t^\omega, \ \eta_t^\omega \sim N(0, \sigma_\omega^2),$$

where $\omega_t \equiv \log (A_t^I / A_{t-1}^I)$. The parameter ω_* is the mean growth rate of the investment-specific technology. We refer to ω_t as the *investment-specific technology shock*. In equilibrium, investment has a stochastic trend with log growth rate equal to $\nu_t + \omega_t / (1 - \alpha)$.

C. Labor Markets

We adopt Smets and Wouters's (2007) strategy for introducing sticky wages into an environment that includes preferences that are nonseparable in consumption and labor. Households rent their homogenous labor in a perfectly competitive market to a unit mass of household-owned labor guilds at wage W_t^h. Each labor guild is endowed with a technology that allows it to differentiate the households' labor. They rent this differentiated labor to the labor compositors, also owned by households, as monopolistic competitors. The labor compositors repackage the differentiated labor into the homogenous factor input H_t^s supplied to intermediate goods producers. The labor repackaging technology is given by

$$H_t^s = \left(\int_0^1 H_{it}^{1/(1+\lambda_t^w)} di \right)^{1+\lambda_t^w},$$

where H_{it} is the differentiated labor of guild i and λ_t^w drives the guilds' markup over their marginal cost, W_t^h. We assume the *wage markup shock* λ_t^w follows an exogenous process similar to λ_t^p:

$$\ln \lambda_t^w = (1 - \rho_w) \ln \lambda_*^w + \rho_w \ln \lambda_{t-1}^w - \theta_w \epsilon_{t-1}^w + \eta_t^w, \quad \eta_t^w \sim N(0, \sigma_w^2).$$

The labor guilds maximize profits according to a Calvo wage-setting scheme. Each guild is subject to an exogenous probability of having the opportunity to adjust its wage, $\zeta_w \in (0, 1)$. Absent this opportunity, a guild indexes their previously set wage using the exogenous formula $(\pi_{t-1} z_{t-1})^{\iota_w} (\pi_* z_*)^{1-\iota_w}$, where $\iota_w \in [0, 1]$ and $z_t = \nu_t + \alpha \omega_t / (1 - \alpha)$ is the log growth rate of the stochastic trend A_t.

D. Central Bank and Government

The central bank sets the nominal interest rate on one-period government bonds, R_t, using a parametric specification of the monetary policy rule stated above in equation (1). Specifically,

$$\ln R_t = \rho_R \ln R_{t-1} + (1 - \rho_R) \ln R_t^n + \sum_{j=0}^{M} \xi_{t-j}^j. \tag{9}$$

The parameter $\rho_R \in [0, 1]$ governs the degree of interest-rate smoothing and R^n is the *notional* target interest rate, that is, the rate the central bank would choose in the absence of interest-rate smoothing. Recall that the first of these disturbances, ξ_t^0, is the usual contemporaneous monetary policy disturbance, while the remaining shocks are *forward guidance* shocks because they are revealed to the public before they are applied to the policy rule. Agents see ξ_t^j in quarter t, and it applies to the rule j

quarters hence. This approach to modeling forward guidance was introduced by Laséen and Svensson (2011) and studied previously by Campbell et al. (2012), Del Negro et al. (2015), and Ben Zeev et al. (2015).
Gather all monetary policy shocks into the vector ε_t^1,

$$\varepsilon_t^1 \equiv \left(\xi_t^0, \xi_t^1, \dots, \xi_t^M\right)'. \tag{10}$$

Each realization of ε_t^1 influences the expected path of interest rates. Since
we wish to map expectation revisions, which are uncorrelated over time
by construction, into realizations of ε_t^1; we assume that ε_t^1 is also uncorrelated over time.

The notional rate R^n is set according to

$$\ln R_t^n = \ln r_* + \ln \pi_t^* + \frac{\psi_1}{4} E_t \sum_{j=-2}^{1} \left(\ln \pi_{t+j} - \ln \pi_t^*\right)$$
$$+ \frac{\psi_2}{4} E_t \sum_{j=-2}^{1} (\ln Y_{t+j} - \ln y^* - \ln A_{t+j}). \tag{11}$$

The constant r_* corresponds to the steady state real interest rate and π_t^*
is an exogenous inflation drift that could be interpreted as the central
bank's intermediate target for inflation. The drift term is included to
address inflation's low-frequency movements during our sample.[20] We
call it the *inflation drift shock* and it evolves as

$$\ln \pi_t^* = (1 - \rho_\pi)\pi_* + \rho_\pi \ln \pi_{t-1}^* + +\eta_t^\pi, \eta_t^\pi \sim N(0, \sigma_\pi^2),$$

where π_* is steady state inflation. The last two terms in equation (11)
correspond to the inflation and output gaps that drive the central bank's
response to the economy's shocks, with the parameters $\psi_1, \psi_2 \geq 0$ determining the elasticity of the response to these gaps. The inflation gap
is a four-quarter moving average of the difference between twice and
once lagged, current, and expected one-period-ahead log inflation and
the contemporaneous value of the drift term. The output gap is a four-
quarter moving average of the difference between twice and once
lagged, current, and expected one-period-ahead log aggregate output
and its stochastic trend. The constant y_* denotes steady state output in
the model. Its inclusion in equation (11) guarantees that the gaps are
closed and the steady state nominal interest rate on government bonds
is $R_* = r_* \pi_*$.

Notice that our specification of the monetary policy rule and the assumption of rational expectations imply that forward guidance in the
model is all Odyssean. When forming expectations at any given date,

agents take the current and past forward guidance to be binding commitments to deviate from the policy rule. This guidance does not reveal information about the economy that is not already known to agents other than these commitments to deviate from the rule. Our empirical findings in section II clearly indicate that FOMC communications contain Delphic guidance. This evidence is based on high-frequency identification, and perhaps at the quarterly frequency Delphic guidance is not essential for understanding quarterly fluctuations. Recent work, discussed in the conclusion, suggests this may not be the case. In any event, we view our formulation as a necessary first step in assessing the quantitative impact of the FOMC's extensive use of forward guidance since the crisis.

The government issues bonds B_{t+1} and collects lump-sum taxes T_t to pay for government spending $G_t = A_t g_t$ in the final goods market. Therefore, its one-period budget constraint is

$$G_t + B_t = T_t + \frac{B_{t+1}}{R_t}.$$

We assume the government balances its budget every period, so government bonds are in zero net supply, $B_t = 0$, in equilibrium.[21] The *government-spending shock* g_t evolves as

$$\ln g_t = (1 - \rho_g) \ln s^g_* + \rho_g \ln g_{t-1} + \eta^g_t, \quad \eta^g_t \sim N(0, \sigma^2_g),$$

where s^g_* is a parameter equal to government's share of output in steady state.

E.   Equilibrium

Equilibrium is defined in the usual way. Agents optimize as described above and prices adjust to clear all markets except those for intermediate goods and differentiated labor. The constancy of the capital-labor ratio across intermediate good producers, Calvo pricing and wage setting, and our functional form assumptions for aggregating differentiated intermediate goods and labor, eliminates any heterogeneity from the log linearized equilibrium. At its core this is a real business cycle model and the first-order conditions and resource constraints of the real side of the economy are the same. In addition to these equations, the equilibrium is characterized by the wage and price Phillips curves derived from the Calvo price- and wage-setting schemes and the monetary policy rule.

In equilibrium, households are always on their labor-supply schedules and so they are willing to work at the going wage W^h_t. Guilds

charge a markup over W_t^h, but must deliver the differentiated labor demanded by the intermediate goods firms no matter the wage they have
set. This demand is derived from the fact that intermediate good firms
are contracted to deliver their goods to the final good firms no matter
the price they have set. The wedges between revenues and costs for
guilds and intermediate good firms, reflecting the absence of price adjustment to guarantee market clearing, are made up with positive or
negative dividends to the household. Otherwise profits are zero.

We study the solution to the log linearized equilibrium conditions
of the detrended economy and apply econometric techniques that rely
on linearity to estimate a subset of the parameters and to conduct our
counterfactual experiment. One may question how such an approach
can be squared with the ELB. Without forward-guidance shocks it is
possible that at some dates the model's forecast would have the ELB
violated in the future, even if it were not contemporaneously. For example, the forecasted evolution of the output and inflation gaps might
dictate a negative nominal policy rate. We use data on expected future
funds rates, which of course do not violate the ELB, in our list of observables when we estimate our model. The forward-guidance shocks give
our model the flexibility to fit these data and thereby respect the ELB.

One equilibrium condition is worth emphasizing at this stage because it illustrates some important differences between our model and
standard NK models. Consider the log-linearized intertemporal consumption Euler equation:

$$\hat{\lambda}_t = \theta_s(\hat{R}_t + E_t[(\hat{\lambda}_{t+1} - \hat{\pi}_{t+1} - \gamma_c\hat{z}_{t+1}]) + \hat{\varepsilon}_t^s + (1 - \theta_s)\hat{\varepsilon}_t^b, \quad (12)$$

where $\theta_s \equiv R_* / R_*^P$ is the ratio of the gross rate of return on government bonds to private bonds (which correspond to the return to capital)
in the steady state, λ_t is the shadow value of consumption (the detrended Lagrange multiplier on the household's budget constraint), π_t
is the gross rate of inflation in the consumption price, and "hats" denote
log deviations from steady state. With a positive steady state spread
$R_*^P > R_*$ and $\theta_s < 1$. In this case both liquidity $\hat{\varepsilon}_t^s$ and $\hat{\varepsilon}_t^b$ appear in the
Euler equation, whereas in Smets and Wouters (2007) only $\hat{\varepsilon}_t^s$ appears.[22]

When $\theta_s < 1$, discounting is introduced into the linearized consumption Euler equation that is otherwise not present. McKay et al. (2015)
and Del Negro et al. (2015) argue that the absence of such discounting
explains the large effects of forward guidance that have been emphasized in the literature. For convenience, set the shocks to zero and assume that from some finite date onward inflation and the policy rate

equal their steady state values. Then the linearized Euler equation can be solved forward to obtain

$$\hat{\lambda}_t = \sum_{j=0}^{\infty} \theta_s^{j+1}(\hat{R}_{t+j} - \hat{\pi}_{t+j}). \qquad (13)$$

In standard NK models the spread equals zero, $\theta_s = 1$, and the sum of the deviations from steady state of the real return on government bonds pins down consumption's shadow value. This has the perverse implication that, ceteris paribus, a credible commitment to change the policy rate tomorrow has the same impact as a commitment to do the same change 10 years out. With a spread, $\theta_s < 1$, the direct effects of expected future real rates on the shadow value of consumption decline with the horizon of the rate increase, with the rate of decline increasing in the size of the spread. Similar discounting is obtained by Del Negro et al. (2015) (perpetual youth), Gabaix (2016) (bounded rationality), and McKay et al. (2015) (incomplete markets). Del Negro et al. (2015) and McKay et al. (2015) find smaller effects of forward guidance with discounting.

IV. Measurement and Estimation

The model's estimation follows a somewhat nonstandard approach. We first calibrate parameters that the model has in common with standard real business cycle models to match long-run averages from the US economy calculated using data over the entire post–World War II period. This "first-moments-first" approach ensures that any success in replicating second moments does not come at the cost of counterfactual long-run predictions. The remainder of the estimation relies on relatively standard Bayesian methods and focuses on the 1993:Q1–2008:Q3 period.[23] This section briefly discusses our data and then presents our hybrid calibration-Bayesian estimation strategy with particular emphasis on how we identify the forward-guidance signals.[24]

A. Data

Our Bayesian estimation uses 18 quarterly time series variables for the 1993:Q1–2008:Q3 sample, including measures of output, consumption, investment, hours worked, the real price of investment, the real price of government consumption plus net exports, wage and consumer price inflation, average inflation expected over the next 10 years, the federal funds rate (our measure of the rate of return on government bonds in the model), and four quarters of federal funds rate futures rates. Our calibration uses data measuring the capital stock, capital's share of aggregate income and nominal expenditure shares. Finally, we use changes in federal funds rate futures on FOMC days to center the priors in our estimation of forward guidance. This section describes how all of these variables enter into our analysis.

Our measurement of macroeconomic variables derives from three simple principles that set our analysis apart from most modern business cycle studies. First, we want to perform inference with a measure of labor input that best addresses demographic and other low frequency developments in the labor market. Second, we want our measures of real quantities and prices to be consistent with the chain-weighting procedures used in the NIPA. Third, because it is implausible that any one measure of wages or prices is an adequate proxy for wages and prices in the model, we want to use multiple indicators of these objects in our estimation.

Hours

Empirical studies of medium-scale NK models typically measure labor input with hours per capita constructed directly from estimates of hours worked from the BEA and the civilian population over the age of 16 obtained from the BLS. Such measures do not correspond well with business cycle models because of underlying low-frequency variation. As a consequence, the results obtained in these studies are difficult to interpret. In our context, measures of the output gap are directly affected by the measure of hours. This in turn affects the estimate of the coefficient on the output gap in the policy rule and consequently impacts our identification of forward-guidance shocks. Clearly the measurement of hours is crucial to our analysis.

We use a simple procedure for overcoming this discrepancy between model and data.[25] Assume that hours per worker outside and inside the private-business sector are the same. Then it is straightforward to show that hours per capita for the economy as a whole, H^{pc}, can be measured as three variables multiplied together: hours per worker in the private-business sector, the employment rate, and the labor force participation rate. Measures of these objects are available from the BLS Establishment Survey (ES) and Current Population Survey (CPS). Therefore we define H^{pc} to be

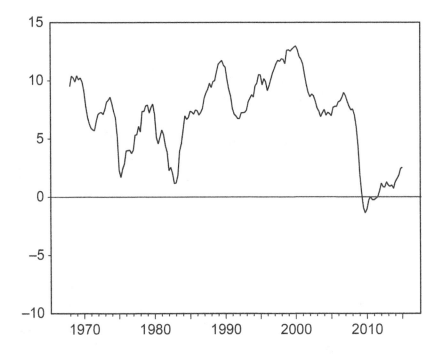

Fig. 1. Total economy-wide log per capita hours worked

$$H^{pc} \equiv \frac{H^{ES}}{E^{ES}} \frac{E^{CPS}}{LF^{CPS}} \frac{LF^{CPS}}{P^{CPS}}, \tag{14}$$

where H^{ES} and E^{ES} denote hours and employment in the private-business sector from the ES; and E^{CPS}, LF^{CPS}, and P^{CPS} denote total civilian employment, the labor force and civilian population over the age of 16 obtained from the CPS.[26] Applying the log operator we obtain a simple additive decomposition of log per capita hours.

Figure 1 displays log per capita hours calculated using the right-hand side of equation (14) over the period 1968:Q1 to 2015:Q1. One indication that this measure is problematic is that as of 2015:Q1, it is near the trough of the 1982 recession. While the labor market in 2015:Q1 arguably had some way to go to reach full employment, it seems unlikely that those conditions were representative of the trough of a major recession.

A clearer picture of the labor market is obtained by considering the three constituent parts of log hours per capita displayed in figure 2. This figure shows that per capita hours confounds low-frequency movements

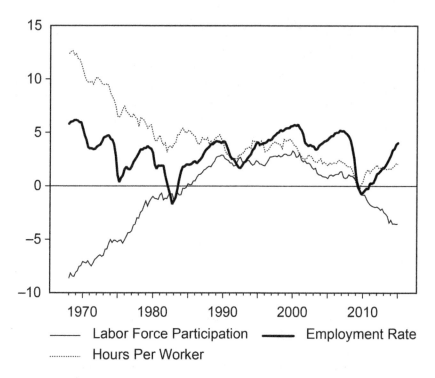

Fig. 2. The three components of per capita hours worked

in all three of its components. These movements can be attributed to a variety of demographic and social developments, as well as changes in the underlying structure of the economy related to technological change and, perhaps, the growing role of international trade.

Figure 2 strongly suggests that conventional measures of per capita hours are problematic; it is hard to argue that all variation in them is due to factors driving the business cycle. We are then presented with two main alternatives to consider. Either we incorporate the underlying trends into our models or we remove the trends prior to analysis. Developing structural models of the trends is an extremely challenging task and goes far beyond the scope of a business cycle study. Therefore, we take the latter approach.

To do so we take advantage of work done at the Federal Reserve Board to address evolving demographic effects, as well as other secular changes in the labor market described in Aaronson et al. (2014), Fleischman and Roberts (2011), and Roberts (2014). The Board estimates variables that can be used to detrend all three components of per capita

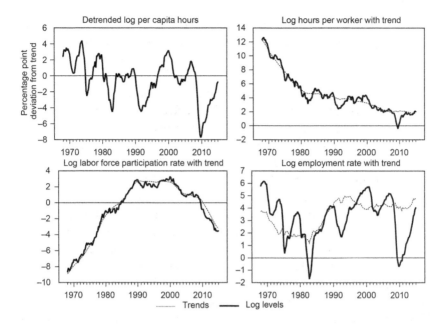

Fig. 3. Detrending per capita hours

hours.[27] We do not incorporate the estimation of these trends into our analysis. Instead, we take them as given to construct an observable for per capita hours that is then used in the estimation of our model. Figure 3 displays the three components of per capita hours along with their trends and detrended per capita hours, which is derived as the sum of the differences between each component and its trend. We use this latter variable as our observable for per capita hours, H^{obs}.

Aggregate Quantities and Prices

Our measure of capital needs to be economy-wide to be consistent with our measure of hours. Therefore, our measure of capital is the net stock of fixed assets and consumer durables from the BEA, which includes private nonresidential and residential capital, government capital, and the stock of consumer durables. Investment is measured consistently with this measure of the capital stock (I_t^{obs}). Similarly, the measure of capital income we use to calculate capital's income share augments the NIPA measure to include the service flows from government capital and the stock consumer durables. Our concept of capital is also inconsistent with the NIPA measure of real GDP, which includes the service flows from the stock of residential capital but excludes the service flows from the stocks of consumer durables and government capital. Therefore, the measure of GDP we use in estimation augments the NIPA measure to include these two service flows. Our measure of consumption (C_t^{obs}) includes the NIPA measure of consumption of nondurables and services plus the service flow from the stock of consumer durables. We measure the inverse of the real investment price as the ratio of the price deflators corresponding to our measures of consumption and investment (inflation in this variable is denoted $\pi^{i,obs}$).

In our model consumption, investment and government spending are homogenous final goods when measured in consumption units. Real GDP as measured in the NIPA is a chain-weighted aggregate of these goods measured in their own units. If the model excluded government spending, then we could calculate the growth rate of real GDP in the model using consumption and investment in their own units and inflation in the real investment price. With government consumption in the model as well, calculating real GDP growth in the model requires having on hand the real price of government consumption plus net exports. We now explain this.

The BEA measures real GDP growth using the Fisher ideal index. In our context the formula is

$$\frac{Q_t^{obs}}{Q_{t-1}^{obs}} = \left(\frac{\Sigma P_{j,t-1}^{obs} Y_{j,t}^{obs}}{\Sigma P_{j,t-1}^{obs} Y_{j,t-1}^{obs}}\right)^{1/2} \left(\frac{\Sigma P_{j,t}^{obs} Y_{j,t}^{obs}}{\Sigma P_{j,t}^{obs} Y_{j,t-1}^{obs}}\right)^{1/2}$$

where the superscript "obs" denotes "observable" according to our measurement strategy. The summations are over $j = c, i, g$; P_j denotes nominal deflator for j and Y_j denotes real expenditures on j. We can rewrite the two terms in the formula and make the translation to model variables and observable relative prices to arrive at:

$$\frac{Q_t}{Q_{t-1}} = z_t \left(\frac{c_t + e^{-\omega t} i_t + g_t / \pi_t^{g,obs}}{c_{t-1} + i_{t-1} + g_{t-1}}\right)^{1/2} \left(\frac{c_t + i_t + g_t}{c_{t-1} + e^{\omega t} i_{t-1} + \pi_t^{g,obs} g_{t-1}}\right)^{1/2} ,(15)$$

where $c_t = C_t / A_t$ and $i_t = I_t / A_t^I$. We identify Q_t / Q_{t-1} with our empirical measure of real GDP growth.[28] In deriving this formula we have used the fact that we identify the investment shock with the inverse of inflation in the real price of investment, as the model's linear investment technology suggests. The variable $\pi_t^{g,obs}$ denotes inflation in the real price of government consumption plus net exports.

Our model includes all the variables in equation (15) except for $\pi_t^{g,obs}$. To be consistent with our measurement of GDP, consumption, and investment, we measure $\pi_t^{g,obs}$ using the price deflator corresponding to the real quantity of government consumption (including the service flow from government capital) plus net exports, divided by the deflator corresponding to our measure of consumption. To measure GDP in the model, we estimate an auxiliary regression for $\pi_t^{g,obs}$ modeled as an AR(2) independent of and not feeding into the structural equations of the model. That is, this variable is only used in measurement. It affects equilibrium outcomes through the identification of shocks, but not directly through agents' decisions.[29]

Wage and Price Inflation

In most empirical studies of medium-scale NK models, variables are measured with a single empirical counterpart. We measure wage and price inflation in our model with multiple empirical analogues.[30] Specifically, in the measurement equations each observable is expressed as a linear function of its model counterpart, plus a constant to reflect discrepancies in sample averages across different wage and price inflation measures, plus idiosyncratic measurement error. In the case of price inflation, we include an additional variable in the measurement equations, discussed below. Our price measures are core CPI, core PCE, and market-based PCE. For wages we use average hourly earnings of production and nonsupervisory workers for total private industry from the payroll survey and the BEA's employment cost index for total compensation of all civilian workers.

We include an additional variable in the measurement equations for price inflation because the price of consumption goods in the model is conceptually different from the CPI and PCE measures we use in estimation. Model consumption is nondurable, yet the CPI and PCE price indices include prices of durable consumption goods. We address this incongruity by augmenting the measurement equations for price inflation to include linear functions of the consumer durable nominal price inflation as measured by the BEA ($\pi_t^{d,obs}$). The weights on model inflation and consumer durable inflation in the measurement equations are estimated. Consumer durable inflation is included in our measurement similar to how we include government plus net exports real price inflation to measure real GDP growth. It is modeled as an AR(2) independent of and not feeding into the structural equations of the model. Just as in the GDP case this inflation rate does affect equilibrium outcomes through the identification of shocks, but not directly through agents' decisions.

Including multiple wage and price series has several advantages. First, as made clear by Justiniano et al. (2013), doing so in principle reduces the role of markup shocks in explaining cyclical fluctuations. In most empirical NK models these shocks play an outsized role in explaining labor market dynamics, yet they are difficult to interpret.[31] Second, inflation that enters the monetary policy rule is identified using three inflation series that are major inputs into actual monetary policy making. This contrasts with the many studies that measure inflation using the GDP deflator, which is seldom referenced as a key input in policy formation. Third, as discussed by Barsky, Justiniano, and Melosi (2014) and Justiniano et al. (2013) it tends to reduce the trade-off between inflation and output stabilization, which shapes whether or not the ELB is binding in New Keynesian models.

Monetary Policy Variables

We measure expectations of CPI inflation over the next ten years with the Survey of Professional Forecasters' measure, $\pi_t^{40,obs}$. This variable helps us identify the inflation drift π_t^* in equation (11). The remaining variables we use to identify monetary policy are the (quarterly average) federal funds rate (R_t^{obs}) and (end-of-quarter instantaneous) federal funds futures rates 1 to 4 quarters ahead (first sample) and 1 to 10 quarters ahead (second sample) based on Eurodollar and overnight interest rate swap data ($R_t^{j,obs}$).[32] These data inform the forward-guidance signals. In our identification of these signals we use both the quarterly measures of future rates and the change in the futures rates in a day-long window around policy announcements. The changes on FOMC announcement days are used to inform the priors in our factor representation of forward guidance, described below. The quarterly data are used in the actual estimation of the model.

B. Calibration

We calibrate α, s_*^g, s_*^i (investment's steady state share of final goods), δ_0, π_*^g (the "steady state" value of inflation in the real government spending price), ω_*, z_*, and θ_s by matching the same number of targets calculated with our data to the model's steady state. Our targets include average values of capital's share of income, government and investment shares of nominal output, the capital-to-output ratio, real per capita GDP growth, inflation in the real investment good price, inflation in the

Table 5
Calibrated Parameters

Parameter	Targets	Value
α	Capital's share of income	0.4
s_*^g	Government + net exports' share of nominal GDP	0.15
s_*^i	Investment's share of nominal GDP	0.26
δ_0	Capital: Output ratio	0.016
π_*^g	Government + net exports real price inflation	1.0025
ω_*	Investment real price inflation	1.0037
z_*	Per capita real GDP growth	1.0049
θ_s	Nominal federal funds rate	0.9867
δ_1	Steady state function of Capital: Output ratio, z_* and ω_*	0.016
β	Steady state function of δ_0, δ_1, ω_*, z_* and γ_C	0.9862

real government plus net exports price, and the federal funds rate. Using steady-state conditions, δ_1 can be expressed as a function of the capital-to-output ratio, z_* and ω_*. In turn the real return on capital can be expressed as a function of δ_0, δ_1 and ω_*. Assuming a steady state inflation rate, $\pi_* = 2$, we obtain the nominal return on capital, R_*^P. The parameter θ_s is then calibrated to the ratio of the 1993:Q1–2007:Q3 average gross federal funds rate to R_*^P thereby ensuring the model is consistent with the large deviation of money market interest rates and rates of return on physical capital. In steady state β can be expressed as a function of δ_0, δ_1, ω_*, z_* and a given value of γ_C. We estimate γ_C along with the rest of the model's parameters using Bayesian methods and this yields a value for β. The calibrated parameter values and proximate targets are in table 5.

C. Bayesian Estimation

We use Bayesian methods to estimate all the parameters except those fixed by the calibration described above (and a few others such as steady state markups) using the sample period 1993:Q1–2008:Q3, where the breakpoint is the last quarter before the federal funds rate attained its ELB. For the second sample, 2008:Q4–2014:Q4, we hold fixed every calibrated parameter as well as the other parameter values we estimate using the first sample, except for those associated with the forward guidance signals and the variance of the inflation drift. We reestimate the inflation drift's variance because the standard deviation of long-run expected inflation in the second sample is many times smaller than it is in the first.[33] To implement these methods we formulate the system of log linearized equilibrium conditions in state-space form with the equilibrium implied by the parameter values characterized by the state equation and the mapping from model variables to the data summarized by the measurement equation.

The measurement equations are as follows:

$$\Delta \ln Q_t^{obs} = f(\hat{c}_t, \hat{c}_{t-1}, \hat{i}_t, \hat{i}_{t-1}, \hat{g}_t, \hat{g}_{t-1}, \hat{\omega}_t, \hat{\omega}_{t-1}, \hat{\pi}_t^{g, obs})$$

$$\Delta \ln C_t^{obs} = z_* + \Delta \hat{c}_t + \hat{z}_t$$

$$\Delta \ln I_t^{obs} = z_* + \omega_* + \Delta \hat{i}_t + \hat{z}_t + \hat{\omega}_t$$

$$\log H_t^{obs} = \hat{H}_t$$

$$\pi_t^{i, obs} = \omega_* + \hat{\omega}_t + \varepsilon_t^i$$

$$R_t^{obs} = R_* + \hat{R}_t$$

$$R_t^{j, obs} = R_* + E_t \hat{R}_{t+j}, \ j = 1, 2, 3, 4$$

$$\pi_t^{40, obs} = \pi_* + \pi_*^{40} + \frac{1}{4} \sum_{i=37}^{40} E_t \hat{\pi}_{t+i} + \varepsilon_t^{40, \pi}$$

$$\pi_t^{j, obs} = \pi_* + \pi_*^j + \beta^{\pi, j} \hat{\pi}_t + \gamma^{\pi, j} \pi_t^{d, obs} + \varepsilon_t^{j, p}, \ \text{with} \ \beta^{\pi, 1} = 1, j = 1, 2, 3$$

$$\Delta \ln w_t^{j, obs} = z_* + w_*^j + \beta^{w, j} (\hat{w}_t - \hat{w}_{t-1} + \hat{z}_t) + \varepsilon_t^{j, w}, \ \text{with} \ \beta^{w, 1} = 1, j = 1, 2$$

$$\pi_t^{d, obs} = \pi_*^d + \beta_{1,1} \pi_{t-1}^{d, obs} + \beta_{1,2} \pi_{t-2}^{d, obs} + \varepsilon_t^d$$

$$\pi_t^{g, obs} = \pi_*^g + \beta_{2,1} \pi_{t-1}^{g, obs} + \beta_{2,2} \pi_{t-2}^{g, obs} + \varepsilon_t^g$$

The first equation is the log linearized version of equation (15) with the right-hand side of that equation summarized by the linear function f. These measurement equations introduce some additional notation: $\pi_t^{j, obs}$ correspond to the three inflation indicators discussed above; $w_t^{j, obs}$ are the real counterparts to the nominal wage indicators discussed above, where these variables are measured by deflating the nominal wages by core PCE; ε_t^i, $\varepsilon_t^{40, \pi}$, $\varepsilon_t^{j, p}$ and $\varepsilon_t^{j, w}$ denote classical measurement errors; ε_t^d and ε_t^g denote regression residuals; π_*^j are constants that account for the average differences between the observable measures of inflation and inflation expectations and the model's steady state inflation; $\beta^{\pi, j}$ and $\gamma^{\pi, j}$ denote the factor loadings relating observable inflation to model inflation and observed consumer durable inflation; and $\beta_{i, j}$ denote regression coefficients.

Notice that our estimation respects the lower bound on the policy rate. This is because we measure expected future rates in the model, the

$E_t \hat{R}_{t+j}$, using the corresponding empirical futures rates, the $R_t^{j,obs}$. Because our estimation forces basic NIPA data and interest rate futures data to coexist, we expect the estimation to minimize any forward guidance puzzle.

D. Estimation of Forward Guidance

Our Bayesian estimation is similar to many other studies except that we introduce new methods to identify the forward-guidance signals. These methods involve using changes in federal funds futures rates in one-day windows surrounding FOMC announcements, following the reduced-form empirical literature, to center a prior on our structural representation of the policy signals. Since we use data on expected future federal funds rates to identify the policy signals, our methodology identifies forward guidance as interpreted by market participants. Consequently, we have no way of identifying the FOMC's true intentions. However our approach has the advantage of ensuring that despite our model being linear, our estimation of it enforces the ELB.

To explain our methodology it is helpful to introduce some notation. Using s_t to denote the model's state vector and y_t to denote the vector of observables (the left-hand-side variables in the equations listed above) the log linearized solution of our model can be represented in state-space form with the following state and measurement equations:

$$s_t = \Gamma_0 s_{t-1} + \Gamma_1 \varepsilon_t^1 + \Gamma_2 \varepsilon_t^2 \tag{16}$$

$$y_t = A + B s_t + C u_t, \tag{17}$$

where we have reordered the equations so the first $k + 1$ rows of s_t contain the quarterly average of the quarter t policy rate and the expectations of the end of quarter policy rate in quarter $t + 1, \ldots, t + k$. In the first (second) sample estimation k equals four (ten) and these expectations are given by $E_t R_{t+j}$, $j = 1, 2, \ldots, k$. We gather the current policy shocks and the k signals revealed at period t about the policy implemented in the next k quarters into ε_t^1 (see also equation [10]). Accordingly, the matrix Γ_1 has $k + 1$ columns. The remaining non-policy shocks are contained in ε_t^2. Values of the model's parameters determine the matrices Γ_0, Γ_1, Γ_2, A, B and C and variance-covariance matrix of the shock processes.

To bridge forward guidance in the structural model with the event-study literature discussed in section II.B, we rely on the high-frequency analysis of Gürkaynak, Sack, and Swanson (2005). These authors document that the (intra-) daily changes in the current and expected federal funds rate, $\Delta_\varepsilon s_t^{(0:k)}$ with Δ_ε the first-difference operator only for announcement dates, are well described by a two-factor model

$$\Delta_\varepsilon s_t^{(0:k)} = \Lambda f_t + u_t$$

$$E(\Delta_\varepsilon s_t^{(0:k)}[\Delta_\varepsilon s_t^{(0:k)}]') = \Lambda \Omega \Lambda' + \Sigma \tag{18}$$

where f_t are the two factors, u_t the idiosyncratic errors, while the matrix Λ contains the factor loadings and is of dimension $(k + 1) \times 2$. Notice that the variance-covariance matrix of the data is then parsimoniously given as a function of the loadings together with Ω and Σ, the variance-covariance matrices of the factors and idiosyncratic errors, respectively.

The high-frequency identification of forward guidance rests on the premise that signals about the future path of interest rates are communicated by the FOMC on announcement days with very little other news about the economy. While the evidence presented in section II.C suggests the FOMC reveals private information about the state of the economy on announcement days, this Delphic guidance accounts for only a fifth of the variation in futures rates on announcement days, leaving room for the possibility that Odyssean guidance explains most of it. If our structural model were observed daily as well, and only Odyssean guidance were revealed on announcement days, the nonpolicy shocks (ε_t^2) are zero and the state of the economy, s_{t-1} is unchanged, such that from equation (16) the structural model for those days would imply

$$\Delta_\varepsilon s_t^{(0:k)} = \Gamma_1 \varepsilon_t^1.$$

Hence, embedding the Gürkaynak, Sack, and Swanson factor structure within our structural model would establish a clear mapping between the structural policy shocks ε_t^1 and the reduced-form high-frequency factors and idiosyncratic errors. To see this, invert the above and plug it into equation (18) to obtain

$$\varepsilon_t^1 = [\Gamma_1^{-1}\Lambda]f_t + \Gamma_1^{-1}u_t$$

and

$$E(\varepsilon_t^1 \varepsilon_t^{1'}) = \Gamma_1^{-1}\Lambda\Omega\Lambda'\Gamma_1' + \Gamma_1^{-1}\Sigma\Gamma_1'. \tag{19}$$

Put differently, with a daily structural model augmented to include a Gürkaynak, Sack, and Swanson factor structure, we could use the reduced-form estimates of the factor loadings and covariances directly to inform their model-based counterparts. Combined with our structural parameters, which pin down Γ_1, this would inform the transmission of forward-guidance signals.

However, the structural model is cast at a quarterly frequency. Therefore, from one quarter to another nonpolicy shocks are realized as well, and most likely influence the expected path of policy through their impact on the expected path of the inflation and output gaps. It is also likely that additional forward-guidance signals are communicated outside of announcement days. Consequently, we do not expect equation (19) to hold exactly. Yet the nature of the high-frequency identification suggests that estimates of Λ, Ω and Σ using high-frequency data should still be very informative about their model counterparts (even in the presence of Delphic guidance on announcement days.)

These considerations motivate our strategy for estimating the forward-guidance signals. Specifically, in the first sample we estimate Gürkaynak, Sack, and Swanson's "target" and "path" factor model using changes in futures rates on announcement days and then use the resulting factor loadings to center a prior on Λ, Ω and Σ, which we now take to denote parameters of our business cycle model. We then estimate Λ, Ω and Σ along with the model's other noncalibrated parameters. For the second sample, we center the prior using a two-factor model based on the sample period 2009:Q1–2014:Q4. We use a different normalization of the factors for the ELB period since the funds rate target is essentially constant.[34] The online appendix describes our high-frequency estimation in detail.

Note that this strategy differs from the one implemented by Campbell et al. (2012). In that paper the factor structure is put directly on the forward-guidance signals ε_t^1. Here, the factor structure is put instead on the reduced-form signals $\Gamma_1 \varepsilon_t^1$. The current approach has two key advantages. First, we are able to tie our estimation more closely to the reduced-form empirical literature. Second, an impulse to forward guidance is much easier to interpret. For example, an idiosyncratic reduced-form signal about the funds rate h-quarters ahead does not engender an endogenous policy reaction immediately in the opposite direction to counteract the ensuing increases in the output and inflation gaps, as occurs with the analogous structural signal (see, e.g., Del Negro et al. 2015; Ben Zeev et al. 2015). Instead, it unleashes a vector of structural signals that ensures that in equilibrium only the expected policy rate h-quarters ahead changes with expected policy rates for j-quarters ahead, $j < h$, unchanged.

Table 6
Key Inferred Parameter Values

Parameter	Description	Value
δ_2	Utilization sensitivity to capital's rental rate	.026
γ_C	Coefficient of relative risk aversion	.92
κ_p	Price Phillips curve slope	.004
κ_w	Wage Phillips curve slope	.003
μ	Wealth effect in preferences	.10
ι_p	Lagged inflation's coefficient in price Phillips curve	.23
ι_p	Lagged inflation's coefficient in wage Phillips curve	.80
ϱ	Habit coefficient	.80
γ_H	Labor supply elasticity	.57
$S''(1)$	Investment adjustment costs	5.03
ψ_1	Taylor inflation gap elasticity	1.76
ψ_2	Taylor output gap elasticity	.43
ρ_R	Interest rate smoothing	.78
ρ_b	Discount rate shock serial correlation	.81
ρ_g	Government spending shock serial correlation	.90
ρ_s	Liquidity preference shock serial correlation	.86
ρ_i	Investment demand shock serial correlation	.70
ρ_ω	Investment technology growth serial correlation	.35
ρ_ν	Neutral technology growth serial correlation	.60

E.   Parameter Estimates

The resulting values of the model's key parameters (modes of the posterior distributions) are displayed in table 6. Many of the parameter estimates are similar to those found in the literature, including small price and wage Phillips curve slopes, the parameters governing the model's real rigidities, and the magnitudes of the policy reaction function coefficients. Notice that the inferred value of the JR wealth effect parameter μ is .1, much lower than the value of 1 that corresponds to the standard preference specification. Evidently the best fit of the data requires that the short-run wealth effects on labor supply be much smaller than is typically assumed.

V.   The Estimated Model

This section describes our estimated model. Our objective is to establish its plausibility as a tool for performing counterfactual policy experiments. To accomplish this we study the estimated model's implications for the sources of business cycle fluctuations, the dynamics of the inflation and output gaps, and the shocks underlying the 2001 recession and the Great Recession.

Table 7
Percent of Variation at Business Cycle Frequencies by Shock

			Shocks			
Variable	Technology	Liquidity preference	Investment demand	Discount rate	Policy	All other
GDP	.65	.15	.10	.02	.02	.06
Consumption	.24	.24	.01	.45	.04	.02
Investment	.54	.07	.23	.09	.01	.06
Hours	.37	.47	.02	.00	.07	.09
Inflation	.14	.03	.15	.10	.00	.58
Fed. funds rate	.11	.41	.15	.07	.16	.10

Note: The technology shock category includes neutral and investment-specific shocks.

A.   Source of Business Cycle Variation

The sources of business cycle variation in key aggregate variables for the sample 1993:Q1–2007:Q3 are shown in table 7. Technology shocks (neutral and investment specific) play a prominent role in explaining fluctuations in all the real variables. Liquidity preference shocks are the prime driver of hours and discount factor shocks play a similar role for consumption. The markup shocks are included in the "all other" category. They are essentially irrelevant for real activity. However, price markup shocks account for more than 50% of inflation fluctuations. Finally, forward-guidance shocks explain no more than 16% of the business cycle variation in the funds rate, and an even smaller share for real activity. This suggests our estimated model does not display an empirical forward-guidance puzzle.

Most variation in the model is explained by the four shocks to the discount factor, investment demand, liquidity preference, and neutral technology. To get a better sense of why this is so, consider figures 4 and 5. Figure 4 displays responses of GDP, consumption, investment, and hours to one standard deviation impulses to these shocks. The units of the responses are percentage point deviations from steady state at an annual rate. The figure demonstrates that business cycle comovement is induced by the technology and liquidity preference shocks only. These shocks induce relatively large responses of all the variables. The responses to the liquidity preference shock indicate that periods of unexpected high demand for government bonds coincide with contractions in real activity. The discount factor shock induces large movements in consumption and investment in opposite directions with very little impact on GDP and hours. The investment demand shock has little impact

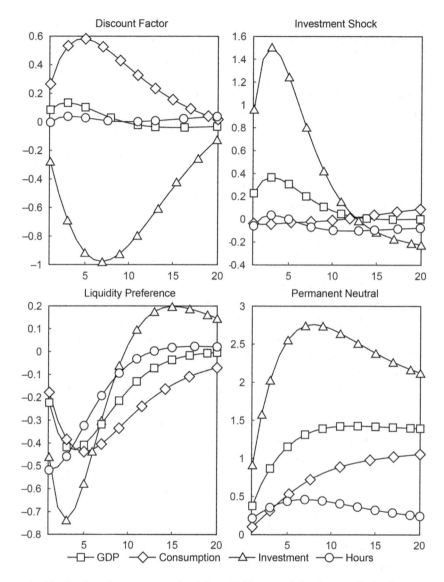

Fig. 4.   Impulse responses of activity variables to main business cycle shocks

on consumption and hours, somewhat large effects on GDP and very large effects on investment.

Figure 5 shows how inflation and the funds rate respond to the four main shocks (the funds rate is measured in percentage points so a response of .01 corresponds to 1 basis point.) The small responses of infla-

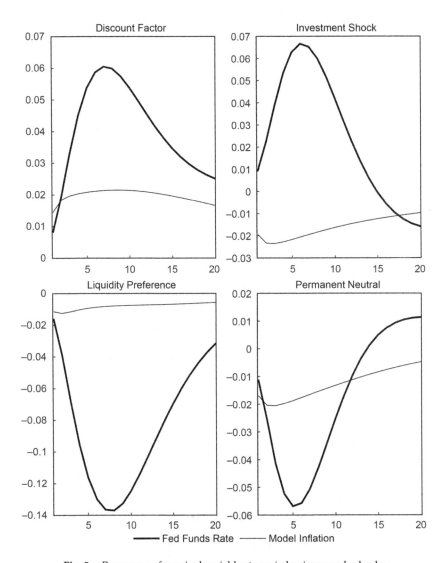

Fig. 5. Responses of nominal variables to main business cycle shocks

tion reflects the small value of the price-Phillips curve slope. Notice that
the funds rate falls in the aftermath of a positive technology shock. This
mainly reflects the fact that the output's short-run response is smaller
than its long-run one due to the model's real rigidities so that the output gap turns negative initially. The liquidity preference shock induces
the largest movements in the funds rate. The funds rate drops to accom-
modate an increase in the demand for government bonds.

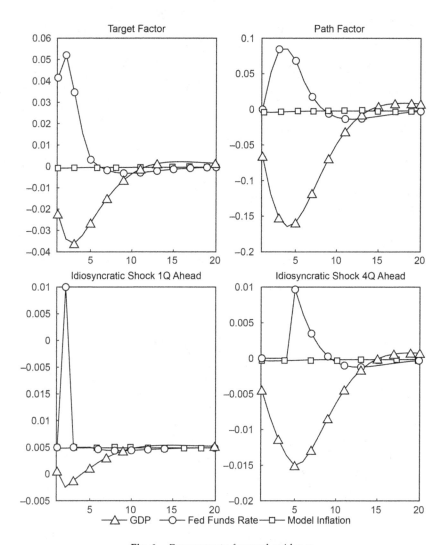

Fig. 6. Responses to forward guidance

Figure 6 shows how GDP, inflation, and the funds rate respond to one standard deviation innovations to each of the two forward-guidance factors and two idiosyncratic shocks to the one quarter-ahead and four quarters-ahead federal funds futures rates. In the first sample we normalize the factors as in Gürkaynak, Sack, and Swanson (2005): the "path" factor does not impact the current funds rate while the "target" factor does. The nature of these shocks is to unleash a sequence of forward-guidance signals such that the equilibrium path of the funds

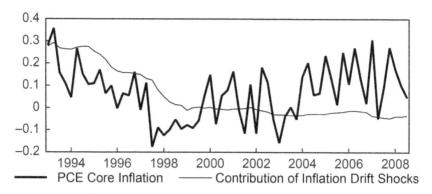

Fig. 7.   Contribution of inflation drift shocks to PCE core inflation
Note: Quarterly rates relative to steady state.

rate is as stipulated by the factor structure. At the conclusion of the guidance, the endogenous component of the rule is the sole driver of policy. The figure demonstrates that when the funds rate is expected to be above the level stipulated by the policy rule output and inflation decline, although inflation's response is very small due to the relatively flat price-Phillips curve.

The responses to the idiosyncratic forward-guidance shocks displayed in figure 6 are particularly informative. The idiosyncratic shocks correspond to a binding commitment by the central bank to not change rates for $k - 1 > 0$ quarters, then increase the policy rate in quarter k, after which rates follow the rule. Like the shocks to the factors, the idiosyncratic shocks unleash a sequence of signals that yield the funds rate paths in the plots as equilibrium outcomes. The four quarters-ahead idiosyncratic shock is roughly the same size as the one quarter-ahead shock, but it is also delayed by four quarters. As expected, this delay leads to a larger response of GDP compared to the one quarter-ahead shock, but the response is very small, reflecting the small size of the shock.

B.   The Dynamics of the Inflation and Output Gaps

Figure 7 shows core PCE inflation (thick line) and the path of core PCE inflation implied by the model's inflation drift shock alone (thin line). By constraining the drift to be close to a random walk, the model is able to account for the low-frequency trend in inflation. The difference in the two variables closely corresponds to the model's inflation gap. This

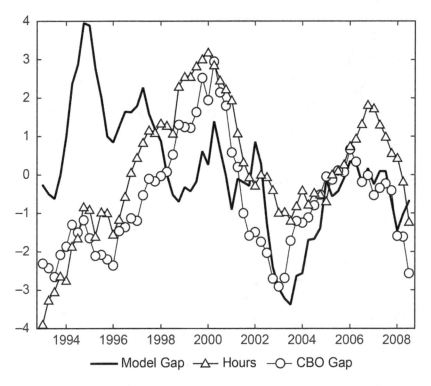

Fig. 8. Model and CBO output gaps with hours, 1993:Q1–2008:Q3
Note: Gaps are in percentage point deviations from stochastic trend and potential. Hours
is deviation from steady state.

was negative in the early part of the sample and positive later on. These
dynamics to some extent rationalize the path of the Fed funds rate over
this period. Note that the drift shock is pinned down by the long-run
inflation survey expectations and the relatively high level of the thin
line early on reflects the lag in expectations relative to realized inflation.

Figure 8 shows the model's output gap (deviation of output from its
stochastic trend) along with the CBO output gap and our measure of
hours. Hours and the CBO gap have similar dynamics. The model gap
follows the contours of hours and the CBO gap after 1999. Before 1999
the model's gap is substantially larger than both hours and the CBO
gap. The large positive model gap in 1994 is consistent with the FOMC's
concerns about inflation during that time. Notice that after the 2001 recession the CBO and model gap follow each other quite closely. In both
cases the expansion in the first decade of the twenty-first century is not

interpreted to have brought the economy much above its potential. The plausibility of the dynamics of the model gap in our view lend credibility to our estimated model.

C.   Forecast Error Decompositions of the Last Two Recessions

Figure 9 plots forecast error decompositions of GDP growth, hours, and the funds rate, conditional on the NBER business cycle peak in 2001:Q1 running through to 2002:Q1.[35] The triangles indicate the conditional forecast, the circles correspond to actual outcomes, and the bars indicate the contribution of shocks to the forecast error. The contributions do not add up to the forecast error since we only consider a subset of the model's shocks. At the business cycle peak the model forecasts GDP growth to rise above its steady state, hours to remain high, and hardly any movement in the funds rate. As realized output and hours come in lower than expected the funds rate drops sharply. Negative neutral technology shocks and an increase in the demand for government bonds drove the recession with the latter driving most of the declines in hours.

Figures 10 and 11 plot forecast error decompositions corresponding to the Great Recession. We split this decomposition into two parts because of the sample split in our estimation and the length of the recession. The decomposition in figure 10 is conditioned on the state of the economy as of the NBER business cycle peak in 2007:Q3. Interestingly, in the early part of the recession output and hours did not come in sharply below the forecast. Later on they do. The unanticipated declines in output and hours are more than explained by sharp increases in the demand for government bonds as well as negative neutral technology shocks.[36] The contribution of forward guidance is indicated by the "policy" bar. According to the model, past and present forward guidance boosted output and hours, but its effects were much too small to prevent the recession from gaining momentum.

Figure 11 is conditioned on the state of the economy as of 2008:Q4. Output growth is forecasted to drop sharply in 2009:Q1 before moving back to steady state. Interestingly, this is about as it turned out. Hours is forecast to stay below steady state, but came in much worse. An outward shift in the demand for government bonds is the major factor pulling down output and hours. With output there are offsetting shocks. The forecast decomposition suggests forward guidance is a substantial drag on the economy starting in 2009:Q2. Essentially the

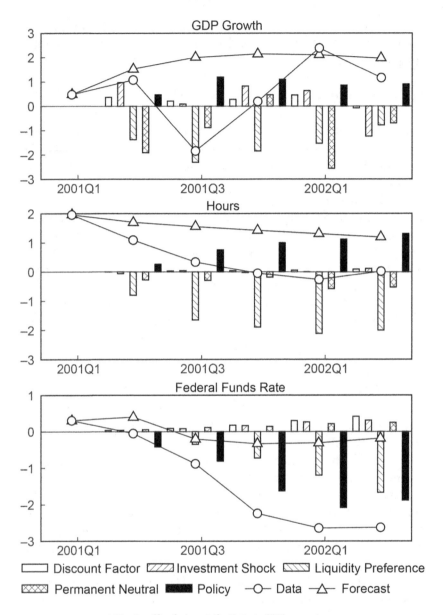

Fig. 9. Shocks' contributions to 2001 recession

Note: GDP growth is quarterly deviation from steady state at an annual percentage rate, hours is percentage point deviation from steady state, and the funds rate is displayed as deviation from its steady state at an annual rate.

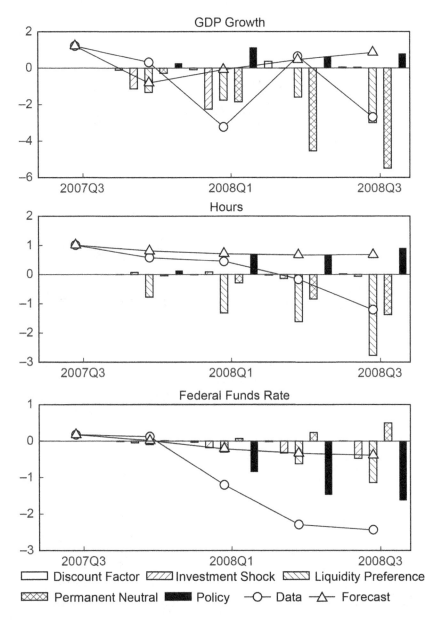

Fig. 10. Shocks' contributions to Great Recession, part I

Note: GDP growth is quarterly deviation from steady state at an annual percentage rate, hours is percentage point deviation from steady state, and the funds rate is displayed as deviation from its steady state at an annual rate.

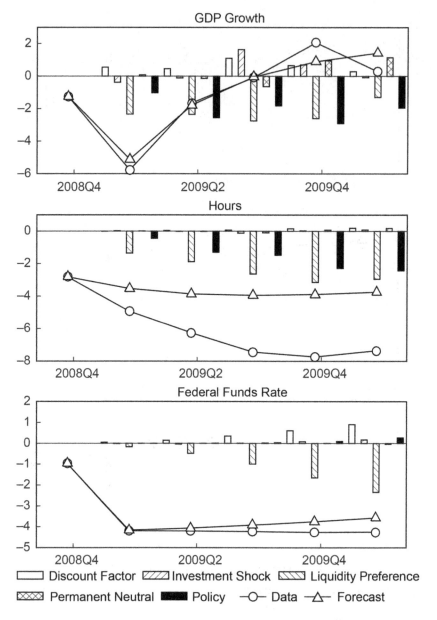

Fig. 11. Shocks' contributions to Great Recession, part II

Note: GDP growth is quarterly deviation from steady state at an annual percentage rate, hours is percentage point deviation from steady state, and the funds rate is displayed as deviation from its steady state at an annual rate.

market's expectations of future funds rates is steeper than predicted by the policy rule alone. This finding is reflected in our counterfactual analysis discussed below.

It is instructive to compare this decomposition of the Great Recession to the one calculated in Christiano, Eichenbaum, and Trabandt (2015). Their model attributes a large portion of the Great Recession to a "consumption wedge" and a "financial wedge." The consumption wedge enters their model in the same way as our liquidity preference shock. The financial wedge enters as the discount factor does in the investment Euler equation in our model. However their financial wedge, unlike our discount factor shock, does not appear in the consumption Euler equation. These differences notwithstanding, the discount and liquidity preference shocks in our framework span the same space as the two wedges in Christiano et al. (2015). Since the discount rate appears in both the consumption and investment Euler equations, our "wedges" are correlated. In the end we attribute the onset of the Great Recession mostly to the liquidity preference shock, while Christiano et al. (2015) attribute it mostly to the financial wedge. Their result derives from calibrating the financial wedge to the bond spread estimated by Gilchrist and Zakrajšek (2012). The consumption wedge is essentially a residual. Another difference in our decompositions is that Christiano et al. (2015) do not use data on federal funds rate futures to inform their analysis.

VI. Counterfactual Policy Analysis

For the evaluation of recent monetary policy, we compare outcomes from the data with counterfactual outcomes from a version of the model without forward guidance. Our model is linear, and we use shocks to expected future interest rates both to provide forward guidance and to enforce the ELB on expected future interest rates. This presents a technical challenge: How do we remove the guidance while enforcing the ELB? Our solution is to replace the policy signals identified from the data with those chosen by a policymaker who wishes to minimize deviations from the estimated interest rate rule subject to never violating the effective lower bound. We begin this section by describing how we do this and then we discuss our findings from implementing the methodology. We conclude this section by demonstrating that our findings do not reflect Del Negro et al.'s (2015) forward-guidance puzzle.

A. *Methodology*

Our model after being solved can be represented in linear state-space form summarized by equations (16) and (17). Estimated values of the economic model's structural parameters determine the matrices Γ_0, Γ_1, Γ_2, A, B and C in those equations, as well as the variance and covariance matrices of the shock processes. With these objects and the observed data in hand, we can apply the Kalman smoother to recover estimates of s_t, ε_t^1, ε_t^2, and u_t. We wish to construct a counterfactual series for the observables y_t based on the model economy being confronted with the same sequence of nonmonetary shocks, ε_t^2, but in which the monetary authority replaces ε_t^1 with those chosen to minimize deviations from the estimated interest rate rule subject to never violating the ELB. We accomplish this as follows.

To begin we normalize the starting date of our calculations to $t = 0$. In period 0 the state equations for the current and expected policy rate are

$$s_0^{(0:k)} = \Gamma_0^{(0:k)} s_{-1} + \Gamma_1^{(0:k)} \varepsilon_0^1 + \Gamma_2^{(0:k)} \varepsilon_0^2.$$

If the ELB was not a constraint, it would be feasible to replace ε_0^1 with a vector of zeros. We call this path for interest rates the *Taylor Ideal Path* (TIP) because the interest rate path would fit the policy rule exactly at all horizons. Consider the problem of choosing $\bar{\varepsilon}_0^1$ to minimize the distance between the counterfactual path of interest rates and the TIP subject to the feasibility constraint that the interest rate for the current and the k future quarters are no less than the ELB. Since the difference between the counterfactual interest rate path and the TIP equals $\Gamma_1^{(0:k)} \varepsilon_0^1$, the program can be written as

$$\min_{\varepsilon_0^1} \quad \varepsilon_0^{1\prime} \Gamma_1^{(0:k)\prime} \Gamma_1^{(0:k)} \varepsilon_0^1 \tag{20}$$

subject to the feasibility constraint: $\Gamma_0^{(0:k)} s_{-1} + \Gamma_1^{(0:k)} \varepsilon_0^1 + \Gamma_2^{(0:k)} \varepsilon_0^2 \geq .125 / 4.$[37] Here, s_{-1} and ε_0^2 come from the application of the Kalman smoother to the estimated model. Since the objective is quadratic and the constraint set is convex, this problem has a connected set of solutions and generically we expect the solution to be unique. We hypothesize that if the submatrix $\Gamma_1^{(0:k)}$ is full rank, then the solution is unique. Denote this unique solution with $\bar{\varepsilon}_0^1$. Given this we obtain $\bar{s}_0 = \Gamma_0 s_{-1} + \Gamma_1 \bar{\varepsilon}_0^1 + \Gamma_2 \varepsilon_0^2$ from the state equations.

In period 1, we choose ε_1^1 to solve the programming problem analogous to that above in equation(20) with $\bar{s}_0$ replacing s_{-1} and ε_1^2 replacing

ε_0^2 in the feasibility constraint. We denote this programming problem's solution as $\bar{\varepsilon}_1^1$, and we use it to obtain $\bar{s}_1 = \Gamma_0 \bar{s}_0 + \Gamma_1 \bar{\varepsilon}_1^1 + \Gamma_2 \varepsilon_1^2$ from the state equations (16). Continuing this recursively until the end of the sample yields $\bar{\varepsilon}_t^1$ and $\bar{s}_t$ for $t = \{0, \ldots, T\}$. We call the corresponding sequence of interest rates the *Taylor Maximum Fidelity Path* (TMFP).

We can calculate an alternative path for our observables given the TMFP using the measurement equations (17): $\bar{y}_t = A + B\bar{s}_t + Cu_t$. The difference between the actual data y_t and the *Taylor Maximum Fidelity Outcomes* $\bar{y}_t$ captures the effects of forward guidance. We study this counterfactual policy using the nonmonetary shocks identified with the Kalman smoother over the sample period 2008:Q4–2014:Q4 after reestimating forward guidance and the inflation drift variance over this period as described in Section IV.D.

B. Results

Since they underly our identification of forward guidance in the second sample, and therefore the nonmonetary shocks during that period as well, we begin by considering the empirical future funds rate term structures over the period 2009–2014.[38] Figure 12 shows the empirical futures paths quarterly and by year. Through 2009, market participants saw liftoff around the corner. Starting in 2010 the expected duration of being at the lower bound extended a bit, but liftoff was still seen as a few quarters hence at most. By the end of 2011, as the economy appeared to deteriorate, the futures path changed dramatically: the funds rate was expected to stay near zero through most of 2013. This change in expectations occurred around the time calendar-based guidance was introduced into the FOMC's postmeeting statement in August 2011. The statement language changed from the June meeting's "The Committee continues to anticipate . . . exceptionally low levels for the federal funds rate for *an extended period*" (emphasis added) to "The Committee currently anticipates . . . exceptionally low levels for the federal funds rate *at least through mid-2013*" (emphasis added).

Figure 13 shows the empirical values of the current and federal funds futures rates from 1 quarter to 10 quarters ahead along with their TMFP counterparts over the second sample. Notice that except for a small deviation in 2009, the current funds rates are almost identical under the two scenarios. Any differences in policy are reflected in the forward guidance. Before 2011 the TMFP is more accommodative than markets expected. For example, in 2010:Q4 the TMFP is at or very near the effec-

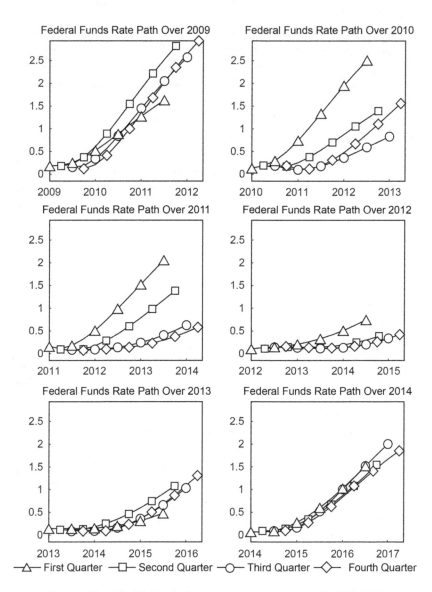

Fig. 12. Empirical fed funds futures term structure quarterly, 2009–2014

tive lower bound six quarters ahead. Only starting in mid-2011 does the market path fall below the TMFP. Substantial differences begin appearing five quarters out, with the largest differences at the longer horizons.

At a conceptual level, the forward-guidance path in the data differs from the TMFP for two reasons. First, the FOMC might have wished

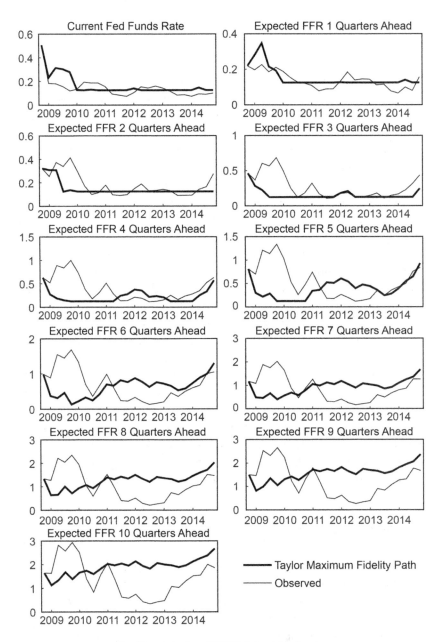

Fig. 13. Actual and TMFP federal funds rates

to differ from the TMFP. In this case, the FOMC and public were in sync. Second, the FOMC might have miscommunicated its intentions to the public. Since we only examine market data, we cannot distinguish between these two hypotheses. However, it appears that forward guidance as "heard" by market participants was tighter than that which would have arisen from a perfectly credible policy rule estimated with data from before the financial crisis subject to the ELB constraint. Interestingly, while the TMFPs are *more* accommodative than expected by market participants in 2009–2010, they are *less* accommodative than assumed by the board staff in the projections submitted to the FOMC during that period.[39] At this stage it is an open question whether the FOMC intended to communicate the market path or something in between the board staff's projection and the market path such as the TMFP path.[40]

Figure 14 shows how the differences in the two expected paths for the funds rate translate into differences in macroeconomic outcomes. By these measures the forward guidance interpreted by markets from FOMC communications lead to worse outcomes than under the TMFP through mid 2011. This is consistent with the more accommodative guidance early on in the TMFP case (and our forecast decomposition of the Great Recession discussed above). From this perspective it would have been more effective for the Fed to communicate that it would be adhering quite closely to its historical policy rule and lifting off when that rule dictated doing so.

Toward the end of 2011, the Fed seems to have found its communications legs. By communicating that its policy would be looser than dictated by the rule alone, it achieved more favorable outcomes than would have been the case otherwise. Interestingly, the divergence in the outcomes occurs around the time the FOMC began using calendar-based forward guidance in August 2011.

C. The Forward-Guidance Puzzle

In our model, extending a near zero interest rate peg for additional periods leads to initial responses of output and inflation that grow with the length of the extension and eventually become explosive. This is endemic to all NK models that follow in the tradition of Christiano et al. (2005) and Smets and Wouters (2007). Del Negro et al. (2015) show that in their estimated medium-scale NK model that an extension of a 10-quarter zero interest rate peg for just one additional quarter generates extremely large and implausible initial responses of output and inflation. They call this phenomenon the "forward-guidance puzzle."

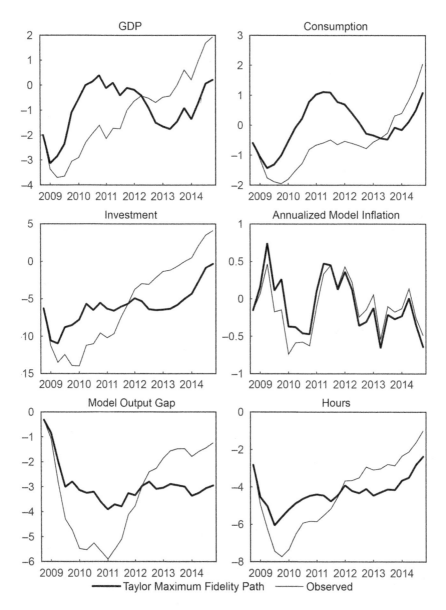

Fig. 14. Actual and Taylor Maximum Fidelity outcomes

Note: Output, consumption, and investment are displayed as percentage point deviations from their values in 2008:Q3. Inflation is depicted relative to the 2% steady state.

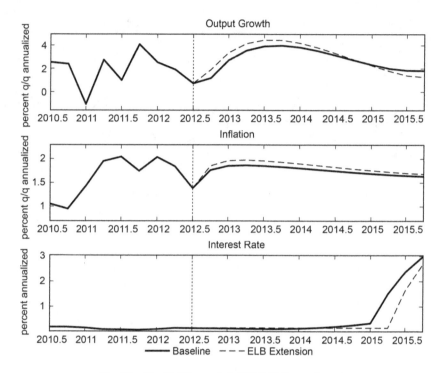

Fig. 15.   The Del Negro et al. (2015) ELB experiment

Their results suggest that the exploding responses to an extended interest rate peg in theory are actually empirically relevant. In contrast, we find relatively modest effects of forward guidance based on our counterfactual experiment. As such our estimated model seems not to exhibit an *empirical* forward-guidance puzzle, by which we mean at least for experiments founded on observed interest rate expectations.

To show that this is indeed the case, we reproduce the interest rate peg experiment Del Negro et al. (2015) use to define the forward-guidance puzzle. Figure 15 matches figure 4 from Del Negro et al. (2015) except that it is constructed using our estimated model. The experiment involves extending the ELB by just one quarter from the path expected as of 2012:Q2. The baseline forecasts are the solid lines and are conditioned on Fed funds futures rates for the next two years and a half, as observed at that point in time. The paths derived from extending the peg by an additional quarter are the dashed lines.

Del Negro et al. (2015) find that the response of output growth when the peg is extended a single quarter peaks at a large value in the first period (2012:Q3) and declines gradually thereafter. In particular, the predicted four-quarter growth rate of GDP for 2012 jumps from 1.9 in their baseline to 3.5 under the peg (see table 3 in their paper). In stark contrast the effects of extending the peg in our estimated model are very small, closely following the baseline forecast. Indeed, our comparable numbers for the four-quarter growth rate of GDP in 2012 are 1.6 under the baseline and 1.8 under the extended peg.

Figure 15 demonstrates that the forward-guidance puzzle is not a generic feature of medium-scale NK models estimated with US data. Eventually the responses of key variables will become implausibly large as an interest peg is extended, increasing the appeal of mechanisms that may counter the quantitative bite of these effects. Nonetheless, our results indicate that some medium-scale NK models estimated with US data deliver plausible responses for empirically founded pegs.

A natural question is what features of our model and estimation explain the discrepancy between our results and those of Del Negro et al. (2015). We highlight three key differences that might explain the absence of a forward-guidance puzzle in our setting: the inclusion of a spread between the interest rate controlled by the central bank and the rate of return on physical capital, JR preferences, and the data used to estimate the model.

Recall from the discussion in section III.E that the spread introduces discounting into the linearized consumption Euler equation that is otherwise not present. Just as shown by Del Negro et al. (2015) and Nakamura and Steinsson (2015), this discounting reduces the quantitative effects of forward guidance. So the spread may be one reason why our estimated model does not display a forward-guidance puzzle. To gauge this, we eliminate the effects of the spread, while holding fixed the other parameters and the state conditioning the forecast, and redo the experiment plotted in figure 15. When we eliminate the spread the predicted yearly growth rate of GDP in the first two years is roughly 0.1 and 0.2 percentage points higher than shown in figure 15. Otherwise, the general contours of the paths are unchanged. So while clearly helping to dampen the effects of forward guidance, this model feature on its own does not explain the absence of very large effects of forward guidance. Of course, including the spread could change our parameter estimates and the conditioning state and this may be important.

Now consider JR preferences. These preferences with $\mu = 1$ represent the specification often employed in empirical NK studies. While we cannot isolate the effects of having estimated $\mu = .1 \ll 1$, we have reproduced our TMFP counterfactual using estimates obtained by cali-brating μ = .99. When we do this we obtain somewhat larger effects of forward guidance as measured by the TMFP counterfactual experiment. When we redo the peg experiment we find the impact of eliminating the spread is similar to the model with μ estimated. So including JR preferences also reduces the effects of forward guidance, but this model feature on its own does not explain the absence of the puzzle either and nor does the combination of JR preferences and the spread.

The third key difference is the data that we use for inference. Del Negro et al. (2015) use just five observables to estimate their model. Our estimation is based on a much richer set of data that includes 18 observables for the first sample and 10 futures rates and survey expec-tations of inflation in the second sample. Of particular interest is that we estimate our model with data on expected federal funds rates. These data help to identify the monetary policy rule in the first sample and the forward-guidance signals in both samples. Their inclusion might have delivered a configuration of parameters, states, and shocks that imply much more plausible effects of forward guidance than had we followed Del Negro et al. (2015) by ignoring these data in estimation and using them only to identify forward guidance *after* estimating the model. Of course the other differences in the data brought to estimation, such as our measure of hours, lead to differences in inferred parameters, states, and shocks, which should influence the effects of forward guidance as well.

VII. Conclusion

When viewed through the lens of our full information, rational-expectations framework, FOMC forward guidance had mixed effects. Throughout 2009 and into mid-2010, financial market prices indicated that the FOMC would raise interest rates *sooner* than its precrisis interest rate rule would have prescribed, and from mid-2010 through mid-2011 financial market participants essentially believed that the FOMC would deviate little from this rule. Our model indicates these expectations of tighter-than-usual policy cost the US economy a decline in the output gap's trough from −4% to −6%. At its August 2011 meeting, the FOMC became more specific about its forward guidance, forecasting that the policy rate would remain at its ELB "at least through mid-2013." There-after, interest rate futures began to indicate that the FOMC's policy accommodation would last substantially longer, and we estimate that this contributed to a much more rapid recovery in the output gap than would have occurred otherwise.

The policy analysis underlying these conclusions compares the FOMC's actual performance with that of a hypothetical policymaker who deviates as little from the precrisis interest rate rule as the ELB will allow. The model allows no misunderstanding between this policymaker and the public. All actors understand the policymaker's goals and means of achieving them perfectly. The real world is not so generous to the FOMC. To achieve such perfect communications, the FOMC and public must share a language rich enough to describe policy contingencies and actions, the FOMC must state its policy choices clearly in that language, and private agents must correctly decode the FOMC's statements. Communications obstacles could have prevented any one of these three necessary conditions from being fulfilled. First, the situation in which the FOMC found itself in December 2008 was truly unprecedented, so the language needed to describe it to the public was necessarily a work in progress. Second, the FOMC speaks as a committee and not as an individual; the diplomatic process by which any such committee makes decisions sometimes sacrifices clarity for the sake of consensus. Finally, financial market participants' primary goal is profit and they only concern themselves with decoding the FOMC's "true" intentions to the extent that is serves that goal.

Given these practical communications difficulties, we should acknowledge that there are really two reasons that the FOMC's forward guidance, *as represented by futures' market prices*, could differ from the Taylor Maximum Fidelity Path of our model. First, the FOMC might have actually chosen a different policy. This seems particularly likely *after August 2011*. Second, the FOMC might have chosen the TMFP path but communication difficulties interfered with its implementation. *Possibly*, this occurred at some time between December 2008 and August 2011. Indeed, Andrade et al. (2015) find that forward guidance during this time greatly reduced dispersion of professionals' forecasts for interest rates without changing their disagreement about output growth or interest rates. They interpret this as disagreement among professional forecasters about whether the FOMC's forward guidance was Delphic or Odyssean. The contributions of disagreement and other such communications difficulties to the policy outcomes we document remain ripe for future study.

Recent advancements in developing and estimating dynamic general equilibrium models in which agents have private information can improve our understanding about the relevance of these communication obstacles. Melosi (2016) shows that, in a model in which agents have private information about the economy's fundamentals and policy actions are publicly observable, changes in the current policy rate have Delphic effects. This result suggests that Delphic effects are sizable and substantially affect the macroeconomic propagation of policy and nonpolicy shocks. We view these models as promising laboratories for further examination of monetary policy and forward guidance with communications obstacles.

Endnotes

We thank Gauti Eggertsson, Chris Gust, and Narayana Kocherkota for their helpful discussions of this paper and Theodore Bogusz for extraordinarily helpful research assistance. Thanks also to Stefania D'Amico, Spencer Krane, and Frank Smets for their very useful input. The views expressed herein are those of the authors. They do not necessarily represent those of the Federal Reserve Bank of Chicago, the Federal Reserve System, or its Board of Governors. For acknowledgments, sources of research support, and disclosure of the authors' material financial relationships, if any, please see http://www.nber.org/chapters/c13764.ack.
1. Recently, several foreign central banks have successfully lowered policy rates below zero. However, throughout the period of our interest, the FOMC has acted as if the near zero ELB has been a binding constraint.
2. The Evans rule is named after its main advocate, President Charles Evans of the Federal Reserve Bank of Chicago.
3. The other main tool of monetary policy since the financial crisis was "quantitative easing" (QE). While there is considerable debate over the importance of the various possible channels through which QE might affect real activity, it is widely viewed to, at least in part, involve influencing private-sector expectations of future short-term interest rates. See Evans et al. (2015) for references to the relevant literature. Krishnamurthy and Vissing-Jorgensen (2011) argued that signaling lower rates for longer is the main channel through which QE affects borrowing rate, so QE also can be viewed through the lens of forward guidance.
4. See Del Negro et al. (2015), Gabaix (2016), and McKay et al. (2015) for alternative approaches to introducing linearized Euler equation discounting.
5. Engen, Laubach, and Reifschneider (2015) use a very different methodology based on the Board of Governors' FRB/US macroeconometric model to argue that improved macroeconomic outcomes from unconventional monetary policy were late to appear.
6. One might object that such asset price changes reflect only movements in term premiums rather than changes in underlying expectations of future interest rates. Indeed, Piazzesi and Swanson (2008) document substantial variation in these securities' expected excess holding returns. However, this variation occurs over business cycle frequencies and so is not obviously relevant for the high-frequency changes measured by Kohn and Sack (2004).
7. This statement is subject to the terms and conditions in footnote 6.
8. Since o_{t^*} is revealed to the public, it obviously is in Ω_t^c for $t > t^*$. Thus, the past values of these forward-guidance shocks appear on the right-hand side of equation (1) redundantly. This redundancy emphasizes that they are expected deviations from the systematic part of monetary policy.
9. Kuttner used futures contracts for which the floating rate was the average Fed funds rate realized over the contract month, and so inference of the Fed funds shock from the change in this contract's price requires careful accounting of the FOMC meeting's monthly timing. This work is obviously unnecessary in our more abstract environment.

10. The Blue Chip survey collects forecasters' responses at the beginning of each calendar month and the results are published on or about the 10th of the month. We match each Greenbook with the current month's Blue Chip forecast if the Greenbook publication date was on or after the 10th. Otherwise, we use the previous month's Blue Chip forecast. Of course, public information that was not available to Blue Chip's private forecasters will be incorporated into the Greenbook forecasts. This biases our procedure *against* finding substantial effects of FOMC "private" information on innovations in interest rates and forecasts.

11. Barakchian and Crowe (2013) also fail to find any substantial effect of FOMC private information on innovations to their measure of the current policy stance. (See their table 1.)

12. Our tables omit this qualifier only because of space constraints.

13. Just as with the estimates in table 2, we tabulated statistical significance of all coefficients in this table using 100,000 bootstrap replications.

14. These regressions R^2s are very low, which is perhaps unsurprising since much more information is revealed over the month than the FOMC's forward guidance. Improving inference by including other measurable relevant variables, such as differences between data releases and their consensus expectations, is on our research agenda.

15. The estimation with the two-year rates uses a sample that starts only in 2004, when sufficiently many previously issued TIPS had aged into this maturity to enable measurement of the yield curve at this very short horizon.

16. Hanson and Stein (2015) considered the robustness of their results to using a policy indicator very similar to that we employ, the three-quarters ahead Eurodollar futures rate. Their estimated coefficients and R^2s are correspondingly similar to those we report. Please see their table 2 for more details.

17. See Nakamura and Steinsson (2015) for a related critique of the Hanson-Stein results.

18. See the third full paragraph of their page 430.

19. Schmitt-Grohé and Uribe (2012) study a real business cycle model with the same preferences, except their formulation involves internal habit.

20. See Smets and Wouters (2003) for an early example of an NK model with an inflation drift term in the monetary policy rule.

21. With the introduction of liquidity preferences, it is natural to extend the model to include a positive supply of government bonds. Doing so would be a step toward an environment where QE could be studied alongside forward guidance. We leave this avenue of inquiry to future work.

22. Equation (12) only holds for $\theta_s < 1$ since it is based on rescaling the variance of the liquidity preference shock by $(R_t^p - R_t) / R_t^p$. When $\theta_s = 1$ both shocks drop from the Euler equation, but it is otherwise unchanged.

23. While the federal funds futures market operated before 1993:Q1, it was relatively illiquid.

24. The discussion leaves out many important details. See the online appendix for these details.

25. See Francis and Ramey (2009), Galí (2005), and Ramey (2012) for related discussions of nonstationarity in per capita hours worked.

26. It is standard in the literature to measure hours per capita using a measure of hours from the ES and a measure of population obtained from the CPS. A similar decomposition of this measure of per capita hours reveals that it embeds the discrepancy in measures of employment in the two surveys. There is substantial variation in the survey discrepancy (see Aaronson, Rissman, and Sullivan 2004) that further complicates the interpretation of results based on standard measures of per capita hours. We avoid this issue because the numerator and denominator in each ratio from which we build our per capita hours series are always obtained from the same survey.

27. These variables are obtained from http://www.federalreserve.gov/econresdata/frbus/data_only_package.zip.

28. Edge, Kiley, and Laforte (2010) also measure model output using chain weighting.

29. To include this inflation rate as an exogenous shock would only have meaning if government consumption was endogenously determined, which it is not in our model. Apart from representing a major departure from standard medium-scale NK models, we

think the presence of net exports in our empirical measure of G_t justifies treating government spending in the model as exogenous.

30. See also Boivin and Giannoni (2006), Galí, Smets, and Wouters (2012), and Justiniano, Primaceri, and Tambalotti (2013).

31. This forms a major component of Chari, Kehoe, and McGrattan's (2009) critique of NK models.

32. The funds rate paths implied by these contracts include a 1 basis point-per-month adjustment for term premiums through 2011:Q2. We do not apply any adjustments after this date, when it appears that term premiums disappeared or perhaps turned negative. The unadjusted data yield very similar results.

33. Throughout we calibrate the persistence of the inflation drift to $\rho_\pi = .99$.

34. Two factors account for 99.5% of the variance in the FOMC-day changes in futures rates over the second sample period and slightly less in the first sample.

35. We do not include inflation in this figure because it varies little relative to the forecast, and most of the forecast errors are due to price markup shocks.

36. In 2008:Q3 these two shocks' contributions to the decline in GDP are very large. Had it not been for large positive contributions to GDP from government spending plus net exports and its real price, GDP would have plummeted much faster.

37. The lower bound is the midpoint of the annualized 0–25 basis point range targeted by the FOMC over the second sample expressed at a quarterly rate.

38. As emphasized in footnote 1, page I–2 of the January 22, 2009 GreenBook, the ELB complicates inference about market expectations of the federal funds rate path. With the nominal federal funds rate at its ELB, the probability distribution for future short-term interest rates is skewed to the upside. Thus, even though the market's modal forecast may be that the federal funds rate will remain close to zero for some time, its mean forecast is likely to be increasingly above zero as the forecast horizon increases because the odds of "lifting off" from the zero lower bound increase with time.

39. This conclusion is based on an examination of publicly available Greenbooks and Tealbooks. See, for example, page II-2 of Greenbook Part 1, December 9, 2009, and page 2 of 100 in Tealbook A, December 8, 2010. Documents produced by the board staff for later FOMC meetings are unavailable to us as we write due to their five-year publication lag. We thank Narayana Kocherlakota for highlighting the value of comparing board staff forecasts to the market path in his discussion of the conference draft of this paper in which we did not make such a comparison.

40. This paragraph is motivated by Narayana Kocherlakota's discussion of the conference draft of this paper. In that discussion he emphasized the distinction between the market path of interest rates and what the FOMC intended to communicate. The conference draft was silent on this issue.

References

Aaronson, D., E. Rissman, and D. Sullivan. 2004. "Assessing the Jobless Recovery." *Federal Reserve Bank of Chicago Economic Perspectives* 28: 2–20.

Aaronson, S., T. Cajner, B. Fallick, F. Galbis-Reig, C. Smith, and W. Wascher. 2014. "Labor Force Participation: Recent Developments and Future Prospects." *Brookings Papers on Economic Activity* Fall:197–275.

Andrade, P., G. Gaballo, E. Mengus, and B. Mojon. 2015. "Forward Guidance and Heterogeneous Beliefs." Working Paper no. 573, Banque de France.

Barakchian, S. M., and C. Crowe. 2013. "Monetary Policy Matters: Evidence from New Shocks Data." *Journal of Monetary Economics* 60:950–966.

Barsky, R., A. Justiniano, and L. Melosi. 2014. "The Natural Rate of Interest and Its Usefulness for Monetary Policy." *American Economic Review Papers & Proceedings* 104 (5): 37–43.

Barsky, R., and E. Sims. 2011. "News Shocks and Business Cycles." *Journal of Monetary Economics* 58 (3): 273–89.

Bassetto, M. 2016. "Forward Guidance: Communication, Committment, or Both?" Manuscript, Federal Reserve Bank of Chicago.

Ben Zeev, N., C. Gunn, and H. Khan. 2015. "Monetary News Shocks." Manuscript, Carleton University.

Bernanke, B. S., and A. S. Blinder. 1992. "The Federal Funds Rate and the Channels of Monetary Transmission." *American Economic Review* 82 (4): 901–21.

Boivin, J., and M. Giannoni. 2006. "DSGE Models in a Data-Rich Environment." NBER Working Paper no. 12772, Cambridge, MA.

Bundick, B., and A. L. Smith. 2015. "The Dynamic Effects of Forward Guidance Shocks." Manuscript, Federal Reserve Bank of Kansas City.

Campbell, J. R., C. L. Evans, J. D. Fisher, and A. Justiniano. 2012. "Macroeconomic Effects of Federal Reserve Forward Guidance." *Brookings Papers on Economic Activity* Spring:1–54.

Campbell, J., J. Fisher, A. Justiniano, and L. Melosi. 2016. "The Forward Guidance Puzzle, the Taylor Principle, and Liquidity Traps: Three Sides of the Same Coin." Manuscript, Federal Reserve Bank of Chicago.

Carlstrom, C., T. Fuerst, and M. Paustian. 2015. "Inflation and Output in New Keynesian Models with a Transient Interest Rate Peg." *Journal of Monetary Economics* 76 (C): 230–43.

Chari, V. V., P. J. Kehoe, and E. R. McGrattan. 2009. "New Keynesian Models: Not Yet Useful for Policy Analysis." *American Economic Journal: Macroeconomics* 1 (1): 242–66.

Christiano, L., M. Eichenbaum, and C. Evans. 1999. "Monetary Policy Shocks: What Have We Learned and to What End?" In *Handbook of of Macroeconomics*, vol. 1, ed. J. Taylor and M. Woodford, 65–148. Amsterdam: Elsevier.

———. 2005. "Nominal Rigidities and the Dynamic Effects of a Shock to Monetary Policy." *Journal of Political Economy* 113 (1): 1–45.

Christiano, L., M. Eichenbaum, and M. Trabandt. 2015. "Understanding the Great Recession." *American Economic Journal: Macroeconomics* 7 (1): 110–67.

D'Amico, S., and T. King. 2016. "What Does Anticipated Monetary Policy Do?" Manuscript, Federal Reserve Bank of Chicago.

Del Negro, M., M. P. Giannoni, and C. Patterson. 2015. "The Forward Guidance Puzzle." Working Paper, Federal Reserve Bank of New York.

Edge, R., M. T. Kiley, and J.-P. Laforte. 2010. "Natural Rate Measures in an Estimated DSGE Model of the US Economy." *Journal of Economic Dynamics and Control* 32 (8): 2512–35.

Eggertsson, G. B., and M. Woodford. 2003. "The Zero Bound on Interest Rates and Optimal Monetary Policy." *Brookings Papers on Economic Activity*. Spring: 139–211.

Engen, E. M., T. T. Laubach, and D. Reifschneider. 2015. "The Macroeconomic Effects of the Federal Reserve's Unconventional Monetary Policy." Finance and Ecnomics Discussion Series no. 2012-5, Board of Governors of the Federal Reserve System.

Evans, C., J. Fisher, F. Gourio, and S. Krane. 2015. "Risk Management for Monetary Policy near the Zero Lower Bound." *Brookings Papers on Economic Activity*. Spring: 141–196

Fisher, J. 2015. "On the Structural Interpretation of the Smets-Wouters 'Risk Premium' Shock." *Journal of Money, Credit and Banking* 47 (2-3): 511–16.

Fleischman, C. A., and J. M. Roberts. 2011. "From Many Series, One Cycle:

Improved Estimates of the Business Cycle from a Multivariate Unobserved Components Model." Finance and Economics Discussion Series Working Paper no. 2011-46, Board of Governors of the Federal Reserve System.

Francis, N., and V. Ramey. 2009. "Measures of Per Capita Hours and Their Implications for the Technology-Hours Debate." *Journal of Money, Credit and Banking* 41:1071–98.

Gabaix, X. 2016. "A Behavioral New Keynesian Model." Manuscript, Harvard University.

Galí, J. 2005. "Trends, Hours, Balanced Growth and the Role of Technology in the Business Cycle." Federal Reserve Bank of St. Louis *Review* 87 (4): 459–86.

Galí, J., F. Smets, and F. Wouters. 2012. "Unemployment in an Estimated New Keynesian Model. In *NBER Macroeconomics Annual 2011*, vol. 26, ed. D. Acemogulu and M. Woodford. Chicago: University of Chicago Press.

Gertler, M., and P. Karadi. 2015. "Monetary Policy Surprises, Credit Costs, and Economic Activity." *American Economic Journal: Macroeconomics* 7 (1): 44–76.

Gilchrist, S., and E. Zakrajšek. 2012. "Credit Spreads and Business Cycle Fluctuations." *American Economic Review* 102 (4): 1692–720.

Greenwood, J., Z. Hercowitz, and G. Huffman. 1988. "Investment, Capacity Utilization, and the Real Business Cycle." *American Economic Review* 78: 402–17.

Gürkaynak, R., B. Sack, and E. Swanson. 2005. "Do Actions Speak Louder than Words? The Response of Asset Prices to Monetary Policy Actions and Statements." *International Journal of Central Banking* 1 (1): 55–93.

Gürkaynak, R. S., B. Sack, and J. H. Wright. 2006. "The US Treasury Yield Curve: 1961 to the Present." Finance and Economics Discussion Series no. 2006-28, Board of Governors of the Federal Reserve System.

———. 2008. "The TIPS Yield Curve and Inflation Compensation." Finance and Economics Discussion Series no. 2008-05, Board of Governors of the Federal Reserve System.

Hanson, S. G., and J. C. Stein. 2015. "Monetary Policy and Long-Term Interest Rates." *Journal of Financial Economics* 115: 429–48.

Jaimovich, N., and S. Rebelo. 2009. "Can News about the Future Drive the Business Cycle?" *American Economic Review* 99 (4): 1097–118.

Justiniano, A., G. E. Primiceri, and A. Tambalotti. 2010. "Investment Shocks and Business Cycles." *Journal of Monetary Economics* 57 (2): 132–45.

———. 2013. "Is There a Trade-Off between Inflation and Output Stabilization?" *American Economic Journal: Macroeconomics* 5 (2): 1–31.

Kiley, M. T. 2014. "Policy Paradoxes in the New Keynesian Model." Finance and Economics Discussion Series Working Paper no. 2014-29, Board of Governors of the Federal Reserve System.

King, R. G., C. I. Plosser, and S. T. Rebelo. 1988. "Production, Growth and Business Cycles I: The Basic Neoclassical Model." *Journal of Monetary Economics* 21:195–232.

Kohn, D., and B. Sack. 2004. "Central Bank Talk: Does it Matter and Why? In *Macroeconomics, Monetary Policy, and Financial Stability*, Proceedings of a Conference held by the Bank of Canada, June, Ottawa, Ontario, 175–206.

Krishnamurthy, A., and A. Vissing-Jorgensen. 2011. "The Effects of Quantitative Easing on Interest Rates: Channels and Implications for Policy." *Brookings Papers on Economic Activity* Fall:215–65.

Krugman, P. R. 1998. "It's Baaack: Japan's Slump and the Return of the Liquidity Trap." *Brookings Papers on Economic Activity* Fall:137–87.

Kuttner, K. N. 2001. "Monetary Policy Surprises and Interest Rates: Evidence from the Federal Funds Futures Market." *Journal of Monetary Economics* 47:523–44.

Laséen, S., and L. E. Svensson. 2011. "Anticipated Alternative Policy-Rate Paths in Policy Simulations." *International Journal of Central Banking* 7 (3): 1–35.

McKay, A., E. Nakamura, and J. Steinsson. 2015. "The Power of Forward Guidance Revisited." Manuscript, Columbia University.

Melosi, L. 2016. "Signaling Effects of Monetary Policy." forthcoming in *Review of Economic Studies*.

Nakamura, E., and J. Steinsson. 2015. "High Frequency Identification of Monetary Nonneutrality." Manuscript, Columbia University.

Piazzesi, M., and E. Swanson. 2008. "Futures Prices as Risk-Adjusted Forecasts of Monetary Policy." *Journal of Monetary Economics* 55: 677–91.

Ramey, V. 2012. "The Impact of Hours Measures on the Trend and Cycle Behavior of US Labor Productivity." Manuscript, University of California, San Diego.

———. 2016. "Macroeconomic Shocks and their Propagration." NBER Working Paper no. 21978, Cambridge, MA.

Rigobon, R., and B. Sack. 2004. "The Impact of Monetary Policy on Asset Prices." *Journal of Monetary Economics* 51 (8): 1553–75.

Roberts, J. M. 2014. "Estimation of Latent Variables for the FRBUS Model." Board of Governors of the Federal Reserve System. http://www.federalreserve.gov/econresdata/frbus/files/frbus_package.zip.

Schmitt-Grohé, S., and M. Uribe. 2012. "What's News in Business Cycles." *Econometrica* 80 (6): 2733–64.

Smets, F., and R. Wouters. 2003. "An Estimated Dynamic Stochastic General Equilibrium Model of the Euro Area." *Journal of the European Economic Association* 1 (5): 1123–75.

———. 2007. "Shocks and Frictions in US Business Cycles: A Bayesian DSGE Approach." *American Economic Review* 97 (3): 586–606.

Comment

Narayana Kocherlakota, *University of Rochester and NBER*

This is an ambitious paper with many different elements. My discussion will focus on only one aspect of the authors' rich analysis. After the federal funds rate hit its effective lower bound in 2008, the Federal Open Market Committee (FOMC) actively used forward guidance—communication about the future evolution of the fed funds rate—as a way to shape the stance of monetary policy. The paper provides evidence that from late 2008 until 2011, monetary policy was too tight relative to a model benchmark. This evidence raises a key question: Was policy so tight during this time frame because the FOMC intended it to be that tight? Or were there problems in the FOMC's communications to the public about the committee's intentions?

In my discussion, I address this question using valuable information in the FOMC's Summary of Economic Projections (SEP). I conclude that the FOMC did face communication challenges in the first half of 2009. However, I argue that market-based expectations were actually largely aligned with FOMC policy intentions by the end of 2009. During the second half of 2009 and most of 2010, most policymakers foresaw stronger inflationary pressures than are embedded in the authors' model's forecasts. That led them to favor higher interest rates. As well, because of concerns about financial stability, a small number of policymakers favored using a tighter reaction function than the Taylor Rule.

(Full disclosure: I was president of the Federal Reserve Bank of Minneapolis from October 2009 to December 2015. So, I was an FOMC participant for much of the relevant period.)

The Summary of Economic Projections

In making my argument, I rely heavily on the SEP. I hope to illustrate that the SEP (which first started in 2007) will be a useful guide to Fed researchers for years to come. Let me start then by describing how the SEP works.

Four times per year, FOMC participants (all 12 presidents and the members of the Federal Reserve's Board of Governors) submit their forecasts for key macroeconomic variables. Importantly, a given participant's forecast is conditional on what he or she sees as being appropriate monetary policy. For example, a participant might be concerned that, under the likely policy path preferred by the FOMC, inflation will rise to 3% or 4%. That concern would not be reflected in that participant's submission to the SEP because that participant would see a tighter policy path as appropriate.

After the relevant meeting, the FOMC releases summary statistics from the SEP to the public. However, after the standard five-year lag, the FOMC releases the full set of submissions along with the transcript. Unfortunately, the submissions remain anonymous for another five years. As a result, it is impossible to link a participant's submissions at one meeting to his/her submissions at another until a decade after both meetings. (Somewhat amazingly, a participant's submission is actually anonymous to other participants for that full 10 years. As a consequence, within a meeting and for a decade thereafter, FOMC participants are left to guess which of their colleagues made which projection.)

Because of the five-year lag, the full (but still anonymous) SEP is currently available only through 2010. As well, the SEP only began to include quantitative forecasts for the optimal evolution of the federal funds rate beginning in 2012. So, most of my analysis will rely on participants' qualitative assessments of the appropriate stance of monetary policy.

The SEP is now conducted every other meeting. During the 2009–10 period, it was conducted during the January, April, June, and November meetings.

My Approach

In what follows, I will look at four FOMC meetings (June 2009, November 2009, June 2010, and November 2010). I will compare three distinct outlooks for the date of the first liftoff of the federal funds rate from the zero to 25 basis point range that was established in December 2008 (and lasted until December 2015).

The first is the outlook of the staff of the Board of Governors (as depicted in premeeting preparation materials called the Greenbook/Bluebook and later the Tealbook). The staff relied heavily on the Taylor Rule to formulate this outlook. They typically foresaw a later liftoff than is predicted by the authors' model.

The second is the outlook reflected in financial market prices (as described by Board staff). The last is the outlook under appropriate monetary policy as described by the various FOMC participants in their SEP submissions.

It will be useful to keep in mind the following sequence of events:

December 2008: FOMC lowers the effective federal funds rate to a target range of 0 to 0.25%. It will stay in this range for the next seven years (unemployment rate is 7.2%).

March 2009: FOMC introduces "extended period" language to characterize its expectations for the period of time that the federal funds rate will stay extraordinarily low (unemployment rate is 8.5%).

November 2009: In its postmeeting public statement, the FOMC provides "conditionality" that will trigger liftoff of the federal funds rate from the effective lower bound (unemployment rate is 10%).

April–May 2010: European debt crisis begins (unemployment rate is 9.6% in May).

August 2010: Bernanke gives speech at Jackson Hole that is widely interpreted as signaling the near-term launch of a new large-scale asset purchase program (QE2) by the FOMC (unemployment rate is 9.5%).

November 2010: FOMC launches QE2 (unemployment rate is 9.8%).

June 2009

I begin with June 2009—a few months after the FOMC initiated the use of the "extended period" language. In June 2009, the staff outlook was that the FOMC would not lift off until early 2012.[1] The June 2009 SEP reveals that a majority of FOMC participants supported this policy stance (or an easier one).[2] However, financial markets foresaw liftoff in late 2009.[3]

This differential is the kind of huge communications gap between the FOMC's intentions and market expectations that the authors stress.

What was the source of this gap? There is necessarily some speculation involved in answering this question, but here is my current explanation. The words "extended period" were widely understood to mean "about six months." By using the "extended period" language, the FOMC meant to communicate that interest rate liftoff would not take place for *at least* six months. Market participants understood the words to mean that liftoff would take place *exactly* in six months.

November 2009

In November 2009, the Board staff projected that liftoff would occur in early 2012.[4] By contrast, the market-based outlook was that liftoff would take place toward the middle of 2010.[5] This seems like a large gap. However, 11 out of 17 FOMC participants said in the November 2010 SEP that they favored a tighter policy path than the Board staff forecast. There is some judgment in this assessment—but, by my reading, over half of the participants pointed specifically to a 2010 liftoff.[6]

Why did so many FOMC participants favor a tighter path of policy than was contained in the staff outlook? Most policymakers expressed little concern about the reaction function being used by Board staff (the Taylor Rule). However, they projected that inflationary pressures would prove stronger than forecast by staff. A couple implicitly favored a different policy rule because they said that keeping rates so low for so long could lead to financial instabilities.

The November 2009 SEP suggests that, by the second half of 2009, there is at most a small communication gap between FOMC participants and markets.

March–May 2010

This section is a little bit of an aside from my main themes. However, it does illustrate that, in early 2010, the FOMC wanted to be sure that the public understood that it might raise rates *before* six months had passed.

Recall that the FOMC had introduced explicit economic conditionality in November 2009 to better describe what it meant by "extended period." Here is Chairman Ben Bernanke in the March 2010 FOMC meeting[7]: "this is clearly not a fixed time commitment. It is a conditional statement. I would just ask . . . that everybody emphasize in talking about this publicly that it is conditional and that we are tying our policy to the state of the economy." In May 2010, I gave a speech[8] in Wisconsin in which I attempted to carry out the Chair's instructions by saying that, "readers of the FOMC statement should pay very careful attention to its explicit conditionality. The statement says that the committee will raise interest rates if economic conditions change appropriately—whether that's in three weeks, three months, or three years."

June 2010

In June 2010, the Board staff outlook[9] was that liftoff would take place in the summer of 2012. Board staff reported that the market-based expectation[10] was that liftoff would take place in the first quarter of 2011. However, they noted that the distribution of the first date of liftoff imputed from market prices was highly skewed. The mode of the distribution was correspondingly much later, in late 2011.

As in November 2009, 11 out of 17 FOMC participants said in their SEP submissions[11] that they believed that, under appropriate monetary policy, liftoff would come sooner than was being forecast by Board staff. Most pointed to a liftoff date that was similar to the mode of the market-based outlook (or earlier). Again, there is little sign that the FOMC is miscommunicating its policy intentions to market participants.

November 2010

In November 2010, the FOMC launched a large-scale asset purchase program (popularly known as QE2). The staff projected[12] that liftoff would take place in the fourth quarter of 2012. The market-based expectation was that liftoff would take place in mid-2012. However, the market-based expectation for the federal funds rate was that it would be only 50 basis points by the fourth quarter of 2012. The market-based modal outlook was that liftoff would not take place until the second half of 2013.[13] At the same time, over half of FOMC participants say in their SEP submissions that their outlook for the appropriate evolution of the federal funds rate agreed with the Board staff's outlook.[14]

Thus, by the end of 2010, there is a general agreement between the Board staff's outlook, FOMC participants' assessments of appropriate monetary policy, and the outlook for the federal funds rate implied by financial market prices.

Final Thoughts

The authors use a statistical approach to model the intentions of FOMC participants. I believe that the information in the SEP is a valuable supplement to these kinds of more formal approaches. The information in the SEP will become especially useful in 2018, when the FOMC releases the first sets of projections with quantitative forecasts of the evolution of the federal funds rate.

I am left with two final questions about the FOMC's intentions in 2009–10. First, why did policymakers expect so much stronger inflationary pressures than did Board staff? Second, why did policymakers lean so heavily on the Taylor Rule as a guide to policy? I suspect that these questions are likely to be central to any analysis of US monetary policy during this period.

Endnotes

For acknowledgments, sources of research support, and disclosure of the author's material financial relationships, if any, please see http://www.nber.org/chapters/c13765.ack.

1. June 2009, Greenbook, I-17.
2. June 2009, Summary of Economic Projections, 17–18.
3. June 2009, Bluebook, 14.
4. October 2009, Greenbook, I-20.
5. October 2009, Bluebook, 2–3.
6. November 2009, Summary of Economic Projections, 18–19.
7. March 2010 FOMC transcript, 119.
8. See https://www.minneapolisfed.org/news-and-events/presidents-speeches/economic-outlook-and-economic-choices.
9. June 2010, Tealbook A, 2.
10. June 2010, Tealbook A, 49.
11. June 2010, Summary of Economic Projections, 17–18.
12. October 2010, Tealbook Part A, 3.
13. October 2010, Tealbook Part A, 46.
14. November 2010, Summary of Economic Projections, 18–19.

Comment

Gauti B. Eggertsson, Brown University and NBER

When the Federal Reserve cut the nominal interest rate down to zero in response to the crisis of 2008 it started relying to an increasing extent on what has been termed "forward guidance." Even if it could cut the interest rates no more, it could still have an effect on the market perception of *future Federal Fund Rates*.

This paper tries to answer the following questions: First, did forward guidance have any effect according to high-frequency data from financial markets? If so, what were they? Second, the authors study a medium-scale DSGE model and attempt to address the same question from the perspective of a structural model. This is an incredibly ambitious paper, a great piece of work, that is trying to answer one of the major macroeconomic questions today.

Building on previous work by a subset of the authors (Campbell et al. 2012), they define Delphic forward guidance as one that reveals something about future economic fundamentals for a given policy rule, while Odyssean forward guidance is explicit communication about the future policy rule itself, and I will try to clarify below how I believe we should think about this. As we will see, Delphic forward guidance that lowers future nominal interest rates will then tend to be contractionary, while Odyssean forward guidance will be expansionary. Forward guidance can thus, in principle, either have made the crisis worse or better: that is an empirical question the authors attempt to address. Broadly speaking, the authors find evidence that forward guidance had meaningful effects on economic variables. According to their reduced-form empirical results, Delphic forward guidance accounts for a nontrivial amount of the variation in federal funds future rates on FOMC announcement days. Moreover, their structural model suggests an intriguing result:

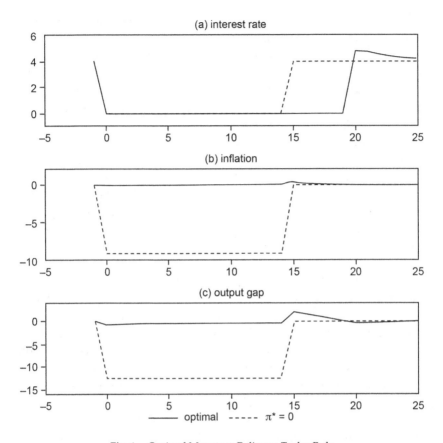

Fig. 1. Optimal Monetary Policy vs Taylor Rule

forward guidance was, on net, contractionary from 2008 to 2011, but then became expansionary thereafter. Before proceeding, I find it useful, motivated by the paper, to clarify a bit how I like to think about forward guidance in theory via a simple model. I then offer comments on the results.

Forward Guidance in Theory

Figure 1 is from Eggertsson and Woodford (2003). It shows the solution of a standard New Keynesian model under optimal monetary policy with commitment at the zero lower bound (solid line) and compares it with a policy that targets zero inflation whenever possible. The figure shows what happens under these two policy regimes in the case the natural rate of interest is negative for 15 periods for output, inflation, and the short-term nominal interest rate.

If the central bank were to target zero inflation, it would raise the nominal interest rate as soon as the shock is over and achieve zero inflation without any output gap from period 15 onward. This is the dashed line. The problems is that in this case there is no policy accommodation from period 0 to period 15, due to the ZLB, which leads to a big recession. The optimal policy commitment, instead, achieves a much better outcome by the central bank pledging to keep the nominal interest rate at zero even after the shock is over (from period 15 to 20), thus accommodating an output boom once the shock is over and modest inflation. The result of this commitment is to essentially do away with the recession in periods 0–15 by lowering the real interest rate during the time the ZLB is binding and creating expectations of higher future income.

This example is sometimes used to motivate forward guidance. Imagine we are in the zero inflation policy regime, which can, for example, be motivated by a standard Taylor rule with a zero implicit inflation target (nothing changes by having the inflation target higher in terms of the logic of the result). Then all you have to do—taking the figure literally—is to say you will keep the nominal interest rate at zero beyond the time at which the shock is over for five extra periods. This, then, should increase the demand and presumably move the economy from the dashed line closer to the sold line.

The authors have in earlier work emphasized one problem with this interpretation when applied to real world policy. Suppose forward guidance is simply an unconditional announcement of the nominal rates being lower in the future than people previously anticipated? You thought we would keep the nominal interest rate low for one more year? Guess what: It is now two years! The problem with an announcement of this kind is this: How should the public interpret it? While one interpretation would be that the central bank is moving from a low inflation-targeting regime like in the figure above to something closer to full commitment, there is another possibility. What if the public instead interprets this as signaling nothing about the monetary policy rule, but instead that the Federal Reserve is just more pessimistic about the future due to weaker fundamentals? In this case there seems little reason to expect the "forward guidance" to be expansionary. Instead one may very well expect it to be contractionary. The authors call the former type of forward guidance Odyssean—it commits the central bank to changing its policy rule—while they term the second one Delphic—nothing has changed in terms of policy, the outlook is now just darker than before.

A Simple Model

Before going further, I thought that it would be useful to firm up this insight by illustrating it in a modest variation of the New Keynesian model. Let us denote output in deviation from steady state $\hat{Y}_t$, inflation by π_t, the nominal interest rate by i_t, and the natural rate of interest by r_t^n. This is the real interest rate the central bank needs to achieve for output to be at potential. Finally, let us denote peoples' expectations about future variables by $\tilde{E}_t$ where I put the tilda on top of the expectation operator – and here I am being "loose" – to distinguish it from our typical rational expectation operator, as this belief function of the public may or may not be pinned down by the true data generating process underlying the model. The model is then summarized by

$$\hat{Y}_t = \tilde{E}_t \hat{Y}_{t+1} - \sigma(i_t - \tilde{E}_t \pi_{t+1} - r_t^n)$$

$$\pi_t = \kappa \hat{Y}_t + \beta \tilde{E}_t \pi_{t+1}$$

$$i_t = \max(0, r_t^n + \phi_\pi \pi_t + \varepsilon_t)$$

and can be easily solved by making explicit assumptions on the stochastic process r_t^n. Let us suppose that the public believes that r_t^n follows a two-state Markov process as in Eggertsson and Woodford (2003), whereby $r_t^n = r_S^n$ in period 0 and then reverts back to an absorbing steady state $r_t^n = r_L > 0$ with a perceived probability of $1 - \mu$ at each time. Let us denote the stochastic time period in which it is back to normal by τ. In addition to this, let us assume that the monetary policy follows the policy rule as specified above with $\varepsilon_t = 0$ for all time periods, except the time at which the shock reverts to steady state τ, in which case it may take on a different value denoted ε_τ^M.

   Under these assumptions it can be shown that in the long run, that is, for $t > \tau$ there is only one bounded solution at a positive interest rate given by $\pi_L = \hat{Y}_L = 0$ and $i_L = r_L$.[1] Taking this as given, the solution at time τ (the "medium run") is given by

$$\hat{Y}_M = \frac{-\sigma}{1 + \sigma \phi_\pi \kappa} \varepsilon_M$$

and

$$\pi_M = \frac{-\sigma \kappa}{1 + \sigma \phi_\pi \kappa} \varepsilon_M.$$

Using these two expressions it can finally be shown that the solution in the short run, that is, at all times $0 < t < \tau$, the solution for output is given by

$$\hat{Y}_S = -\psi(\mu)\varepsilon_M + \gamma(\mu)r_S^n \qquad (1)$$

where the coefficients $\psi > 0$ and $\gamma > 0$ are defined in the footnote and $\psi'(\mu) < 0$ and $\gamma'(\mu) < 0$.[2] We can also solve for the expected nominal interest rate in the medium term to obtain

$$E_S i_M = (1 - \mu)i_M + \mu * 0 = (1 - \mu)r_L + (1 - \mu)\frac{1}{1 + \sigma\phi_\pi\kappa}\varepsilon_M. \qquad (2)$$

Expressions (1) and (2) reveal two basic insights that put a bit of structure on the key argument the authors make about the nature of forward guidance. First, observe that output depends on the public belief about future monetary policy ε_t^M once the ZLB is no longer binding. In particular, we see that if the central bank commits to keeping the nominal rate lower in the medium run when the ZLB is no longer binding, this will unambiguously increase output in the short run. Moreover, and perhaps somewhat obviously, we see by expression (2) that this will lower peoples' expectations about medium-term interest rates. Hence, this is an example of a successful expansionary *Odyssian forward guidance*. The formulas above, however, also reveal another result. Set $\varepsilon_M = 0$ and imagine that the government makes an announcement that has an effect on the private-sector belief about the duration of the shock, that is, the public belief about μ, a variable that in principle could depend on various "fundamentals." According to formula (1) this will unambiguously lead to a contraction in output, as $\gamma'(\mu) < 0$. Moreover, we see in formula (2) that this will also lead to lower expectations of future interest rates.

The bottom line then is that in and by itself, if the public is not certain about μ or ε_M, the Federal Reserve announcement about lower future nominal interest rates could be interpreted in one of two ways, (1) it signals a more pessimistic view about the evolution of the economy (higher μ), or (2) it signals that the central bank will set interest rates in the future lower for given fundamental (lower ε_M). Importantly, while (2) is unambiguously expansionary as in Eggertsson and Woodford (2003), we see that the first type of communication is contractionary. In theory, then, if we suppose that Federal Reserve communication may not only reveal something about its own policy reaction, but also something about underlying economic fundamentals, forward guidance defined as credible communication about future nominal interest rates has an ambiguous effect on output, depending on if it is Odyssian or Delphic.

What Did the Fed Do?

What was the Federal Reserve attempting to do post-2008? Was it trying to signal something about future fundamentals or trying to convey something about policy? One interesting aspect of this period is that people inside the Fed—and outside it—did not even agree on the answer to that question at the time, and do not agree on it now, either. I have heard people inside and outside of the Fed take both sides of this argument, some claiming the communication implied no further commitment while others saying it did. I find it useful to think of the Federal Reserve communication as having, in the beginning, largely relied on time dependent commitment up until about late 2012, at which time the Federal Reserve started to adopt more explicit thresholds or state-contingent commitment. As we will see, one can well argue that these communications had different implications in theory. Indeed, one interpretation of the results presented in this paper is that the time-contingent commitments pre-2012 were Delphic, while the state-contingent commitments post-2012 were Odyssian. I would not go that far, however.

My own interpretation of this period, having been at the Federal Reserve Bank of New York at the time and observed day-to-day gyrations of the market closely, was that several of the policy announcement had strong Odyssean effects, even those that seemed purely to refer to time horizons, for example, the statement that the rates would stay low for "some time" (December 2008), for an "extended period" (March 2009), and "at least to mid-2013" (August 2013). I would even go so far to suggest that some of these announcement had a strong Odyssean effect, even when some policymakers seemed to explicitly protest to the market that they did not imply any firm commitment.

The way I rationalized this point of view at the time—and still do—may seem a bit contradictory. It is that by stating specific dates, or horizons, the Federal Reserve made keeping rates low a "default option." In this case in most peoples' minds it was made costly to deviate from this default—it required explanation. I have yet to see anyone formalize this notion, but my hunch is that this is what was going on; indeed, I suspect that the forward guidance language was helpful in achieving accommodation throughout the recovery period and thus preventing inflation from falling further. Yet, I also agree with the authors—and it was also my impression at the time—that forward guidance as practiced was sometimes a double-edged sword due the problem that the market could interpret the communication as signaling economic weakness rather than a more aggressive policy stance. Moreover, I do think there were occasions when the policy language might have had this negative effect. The FOMC announcement in August 2011 being a prime suspect (see Del Negro, Giannoni, and Patterson 2012). But before going further, it is worth asking: Can one do better in theory?

What Is Effective Forward Guidance?

As we have just seen, one problem with forward guidance, when used in terms of giving signals about lower future nominal interest rates, is that it can be contractionary if people interpret the language as signaling bad fundamentals. How can this problem be addressed? This was actually a question that Michael Woodford and I asked ourselves more than 13 years ago in Eggertsson and Woodford (2003). What we showed in that paper was that the Federal Reserve could, in fact, specify their optimal policy commitment via "thresholds" (although we did not use that name at the time). In particular, we showed in a simple New Keynesian model that if the Fed said it would keep the interest rate at zero until a particular target was achieved, which was defined as a weighted average of the price level and the output gap, it could replicate the full commitment equilibrium. Perhaps most interestingly, we showed how one could compute this criterion (which was supposed to creep upward the longer the ZLB lasted) without needing any estimate for the shock hitting the economy r_t^n or the persistence parameter of the shock μ. All one needed was information about the output gap and the "deep" structural parameters of the model.

This result implied that the Federal Reserve did not need to signal anything about how long the zero lower bound would be binding—instead—it should simply specify the criterion that had to be met for raising rates. The market could then infer by itself the implied duration of the ZLB, and the Delphic/Odyssean signaling problem would be gone altogether.

I think it is fair to say that the policy adopted by the Federal Reserve in December 2012 came a lot closer to this ideal when it adopted what the authors call the Evans rule, when the Federal Reserve said it would """keep the target range . . . at 0 to 1/4 and currently anticipates that this . . . will be appropriate at least as long as the unemployment rate remains above 6.5%, inflation between one and two years ahead is projected to be no more than half a percentage point above the Committee's 2% longer-run goal." While this was not exactly the Eggerts-son and Woodford (2003) formula, it was a lot closer in the sense that it stated conditions needed for raising rates—letting the market do the computing of the timing of the liftoff itself—and promising to hold off lifting rates even if there would be some slight overshooting of infla-tion, conditional on it not been projected to be too far off in two-years ahead forecasts of inflation.

Empirical Measures of Forward Guidance in Practice

We have just seen that forward guidance if interpreted as simply stating a forecast about future Fed Funds Rate could either be contractionary or expansionary, depending on how people interpret the reason for the forecast. We have also seen how effective forward guidance can be done in theory with thresholds. What does high-frequency data say about the effect of forward guidance? The authors' results suggest that a non-trivial part of forward guidance done by the Fed was, in fact, Delphic in nature.

One interesting idea in the paper is to look at the response of markets to Fed announcements taking into account the forecast of both the Fed and market participants. In particular, the paper looks at the forecast from the Federal Reserve Greenbook about economic fundamentals (in-flation, GDP, and unemployment) and subtract from it the analogous consensus forecast from the Blue Chip survey, which is a survey of Wall Street forecasters. The authors suggest that we should interpret this dif-ference as a measure of Delphic forward guidance, that is, the extent to which the statements of the Federal Reserve reveal something about economic fundamentals (μ in the language of the simple model above). Hence, if the Fed is forecasting a grimmer outlook than that of the private sector, this will show up in their proxy. This interesting proxy accounts for about 20% of variation in the unexpected changes in ex-pected Fed Funds Rate in the data. This, then, suggests plenty of room for Odyssean guidance, or what I term ε_M in my model above.

One problem with this interpretation is that there is another natural candidate for why the Feds' views and the private sector could differ on fundamentals as captured by this proxy. Suppose that instead Fed has knowledge about the future Federal Funds Rate policy function that is unknown to the private sector prior to the meeting, that is, knowledge about ε_M in our example above. The Federal Reserve goes into the meet-ing more optimistic than the private sector because it is aware it is just

about to reveal a plan for more expansionary policy. In some respects
this also seems like quite a natural assumption, since if the Federal Reserve has private information about anything, presumably its own actions would be high on the list. I see no particular reason for why one
could not interpret the authors' proxy in this way. One problem, however, with this interpretation is that this type of policy communication
should be expansionary, while as the authors show it works in the opposite direction. I think it is fair to say, therefore, that the empirical results presented here are still quite open to different interpretations, although I tend to agree with the authors' (but this is simply because then
the response coefficient is consistent with my own prior!).

Some additional evidence that looks to me to be quite compelling
and complimentary to the evidence presented here, are presented in
Del Negro, Giannoni, and Patterson (2012). They show, via event analysis, that time-dependent forward guidance of the form made in August 2011 likely was Delphic in nature, or contractionary, while the one
in September 2012 was Odyssian, or expansionary, when the Federal
Reserve said it anticipated that a "highly accommodative stance . . .
will remain appropriate for a considerable time after the economic recovery strengthens . . . at least through mid-2015." These authors estimate significant effects of this announcement on GDP growth and
inflation.

Time-Dependent Forward Guidance and Threshold-Based One?

One reading of this paper, especially the modeling part, is that forward
guidance was largely contractionary from 2008 to 2011 when it mainly
focused on giving guidance about future dates at which rates would
increase. It then became expansionary as the forward guidance took a
slightly different form and started becoming contingent of economic
outcomes —or thresholds—like the December announcement in 2012
that I referred to above. From a theoretical standpoint, one explanation
for this could be that forward guidance was largely interpreted as a
signal of bad fundamentals in the beginning of the period, while then
becoming expansionary once the communication was put in a more
proper "threshold" format.

As I have already suggested above, my own impressions living
through this period was that the forward guidance between 2008 and
2011 was in fact largely expansionary for the reason I stated above (by
making low rates "default"), even if on some occasions it had mixed

success such as the August FOMC announcement in 2011. My reading of Del Negro et al. (2012) confirms that prior. But this leaves me with the question of why the structural model presented here seems to suggest that forward guidance was in fact contractionary until late 2012. Let me offer some speculation on that point, which I suspect we will continue to debate in coming years.

To understand the reason for the result in the authors' model, it is useful to observe how they identify forward guidance in their structural estimation. What they do—which is a key innovation and a very clever one—is to look at what their model forecasts the nominal interest rate to be (and the model is estimated on observed ex post data), and then compare it to the market forecast at the time, which they extract from asset markets. To the extent there is a discrepancy between the two, they identify the resulting residual as deviation of the policy rule and as coming about due to forward guidance. A key observation is that the market was expecting a more rapid increase in Fed Funds Rate pre-2012 than the model, which the authors then interpret as contractionary forward guidance (i.e., a faster normalization than should be implied by the model).

But is it appropriate to identify forward guidance in this way? My guess—and this is only a guess—is that here we might be leaning a bit too hard on model consistent expectations—assuming that the model represents reality and that market participants base their forecast on this particular reality. And then estimating the model by maximizing the chance that what we observed in the data in fact represents that underlying data generating process. I am guessing that the reason the market expected faster recovery for the Fed Funds Rate than is indicated by the model was not due to forward guidance. Instead, my guess is that the market erroneously assumed at that time that the recovery would be much quicker than we have ended up seeing. I suspect that this type of market miscalculation will be incorrectly identified as contractionary forward guidance in the model. But this is just a conjecture. Finding out the right answer will be on the agenda for future research. And this is an excellent start.

Endnotes

For acknowledgments, sources of research support, and disclosure of the author's material financial relationships, if any, please see http://www.nber.org/chapters/c13766.ack.
1. Here we are deliberately ignoring the possibility that the ZLB may be binding due to self-fulfilling expectations.

2. Where we have defined

$$\psi \equiv -\frac{(1-\mu)(1-\beta\mu+\sigma\kappa)}{(1-\beta\mu)(1-\mu)-\mu\sigma\kappa}\frac{\sigma}{1+\sigma\phi_\pi\kappa},$$

$$\gamma \equiv \frac{\sigma(1-\beta\mu)}{(1-\beta\mu)(1-\mu)-\mu\sigma\kappa},$$

and assume the parameter restriction $(1-\beta\mu)(1-\mu) > \mu\sigma\kappa$ as in Eggertsson (2010).

References

Campbell, J. R., C. L. Evans, D. Fisher, and A. Justiniano. 2012. "Macroeconomic Effects of Federal Reserve Forward Guidance." *Brookings Papers on Economic Activity* Spring:2012.

Del Negro, M., M. Giannoni, and C. Patterson. 2012. "The Forward Guidance Puzzle." Staff Report no. 574, Federal Reserve Bank of New York.

Eggertsson, G. 2010. "What Fiscal Policy is Effective at Zero Interest Rates?" In *NBER Macroeconomics Annual 2010*, vol. 25, ed. D. Acemoglu and M. Woodford, 59–112. Chicago: University of Chicago Press.

Eggertsson, G., and M. Woodford. 2003. "The Zero Interest-Rate Bound and Optimal Monetary Policy." *Brookings Papers on Economic Activity* 2003:1.

Discussion

A number of participants offered comments on the strengths and limitations of attempting to decompose Federal Reserve policy into Delphic and Odyssean components. In addition, they discussed other important considerations in studying and designing monetary policy.

Frederic Mishkin opened the discussion by commenting that there is strong evidence for Odyssean guidance starting from the precrisis period without the zero lower bound. He noted that after the Fed committed to keeping rates fixed in 2004, the Federal Funds futures markets subsequently reacted less to incoming economic data. He also noted that it is important to distinguish between calendar- and noncalendar-based forms of Odyssean guidance. Calendar-based guidance, as was seen in 2011, is relatively easy to communicate to market participants. However, such guidance limits ex-post flexibility of the Fed to respond to future negative shocks, increasing their propagation in the economy.

Following up on the complexity of communicating policy intentions, Olivier Blanchard suggested it may also be useful to separate issues in communicating general policy intentions from communicating time-inconsistent policy, which he noted is much harder.

Mishkin further pondered on how the Fed can communicate its reactions to future economic news clearly, with respect to the Delphic versus Odyssean decomposition. Communicating the reaction function itself is essential to implementing responsive monetary policy. For example, if the Fed communicates that it will ease in response to bad news and that bad news arrives, the market will bring down long rates immediately, reducing propagation. Mishkin reiterated that communicating such reaction functions can be complicated and that it might be better to use calendar-based guidance in extreme circumstances.

Thomas Philippon, building on the issues raised by Blanchard and Mishkin, noted that there needs to be a clear discussion of the links between calendar-based communications, rule, or threshold-based policy, and their interactions with commitment. H first asked which type of policy is easier to communicate, and what is the comparative advantage of calendar-based communication with respect to effectively conveying policy rules to markets. By contrast, communicating the optimal policy in the model of Eggertsson and Woodford (2003), for example, would be very difficult, even ignoring the issue of commitment, because of its complicated state-contingent nature. Second, considering commitment explicitly, Philippon reiterated the point in Eggertsson's discussion that the type of communication can impact the market's view about the commitment of the Federal Reserve. He recommended the paper undertake a more thorough discussion of these issues.

Steven Strongin commented that considering how financial markets process monetary policy and ultimately incorporate it into market prices highlights the importance of time inconsistency. Time-based guidance, he argued, is hard for markets to incorporate into prices because it typically embeds time inconsistency, since the Federal Reserve Bank may change its policy depending on the actual realized outcome. In contrast, outcome-based guidance is easy to embed into market outlooks and interest rate forward markets because the market understands the conditionality that breaks the guidance.

Ricardo Reis noted that there are a range of announcements that the Federal Reserve can make beyond announcements about its interest rate policy and its assessment of the state of the economy. For instance, announcements by the Federal Reserve Bank about its purchases and unwinding of assets can affect the economy.

Reis also noted that since 1994, the Federal Reserve has made deliberate efforts to be more transparent about separating its views on the economy from its interest rate policy. Therefore, we should expect to see the effect of Delphic policy decline over time if the Fed has been doing a better job transmitting what it thinks about the economy outside of pure interest rate changes. Thus, Reis noted he was struck by the result that Delphic forward guidance still accounts for 20% of the transmission of policy into forward interest rate expectations. He suggested splitting the sample into the period before and after 1994, to examine whether the Fed has successfully increased transparency over time.

Presenter Jeffrey Campbell responded to Reis's first point by noting that the results were little changed when the analysis was done with and without major quantitative easing announcements. On Reis's second point, Campbell argued that the market does not seem to be responding to information released through secondary communications. He cited Kohn and Sack (2003), which showed that the volatility of asset prices only increased around FOMC meeting dates and the Humphrey-Hawkins testimony, but did not rise after speeches by the chairman and other participants.

Harald Uhlig noted that the most important thing he learned from the paper was that Delphic communication is large and important, but that the Fed does not do a great job in distinguishing this type of communication from its policy intentions. This made him wonder why the Fed only releases the identities behind committee member forecasts 10 years later, instead of immediately. If the identities were known, then the market could track the forecasts of individual members over time to develop a better understanding of Fed policy. Uhlig asked what political considerations govern which forecasts are delivered to the FOMC committee members versus the public. These issues, he noted, raise questions about whether the paper is correctly identifying the Delphic component of policy communication.

Mishkin responded that there is a proposal within the Fed to link the forecasts of individuals over time, but keeping the identity of the individual anonymous. Uhlig responded that releasing the identities is crucial to assuage concerns that political economy considerations are clouding the information released in the forecasts. Mishkin agreed that this is an important issue and suspects the reason it is not done is because committee members do not want to be accountable for their forecasts.

Laura Veldkamp raised the possibility that the measured gap between market expectations and the Fed's intended forward guidance could be due to mismeasurement, rather than communication failure. This could occur if the Fed is reporting median expectations, but the market measures are of means. Asymmetries in these distributions could arise from tail risk or failure to correctly risk-adjust market-based measures. Campbell acknowledged the concerns raised by Veldkamp, and noted that the paper attempts to control for risk pricing using a term premium adjustment.

Emi Nakamura raised the concern that the Greenbook forecasts used as a proxy for the Federal Reserve's private information are compiled by different individuals, rather than those on the FOMC committee. Therefore, the Greenbook forecasts may not necessarily reflect the private information set of the committee members that were deciding policy. She wondered if this affects the empirical exercises in the paper. Campbell agreed in principle that the forecasts of the Federal Reserve staff do not necessarily have to be adopted by policymakers in their decision-making process, despite their good track record of forecasting. However, he noted, in that case the regression results of the paper would look very different, as the paper documents that some of the private information in the staff forecasts does indeed leak into asset prices through policymaker statements.

Narayana Kocherlakota concluded the discussion with a few practical comments on FOMC communications. First, in response to Reis's comment, he argued that the FOMC does try to offer a collective assessment of the economy in the first few paragraphs of the statement. The language and content of these paragraphs are decided in the meeting and reflect the collective assessment of the committee as a whole and of what is going on inside the meeting. Thus Kocherlakota argued that the committee is deliberately using Delphic guidance in these first paragraphs and attempts to separate it from interest rate decisions, though how well separation works in practice is a different matter. Finally, he noted that while it may be a good idea to allow committee member forecasts to be tracked in a panel fashion, it is also a good thing that the committee's collective assessment is what drives policy.

5

Are State- and Time-Dependent Models Really Different?

Fernando Alvarez, *University of Chicago and NBER*

Francesco Lippi, *Einaudi Institute for Economics and Finance, University of Sassari, and CEPR*

Juan Passadore, *Einaudi Institute for Economics and Finance*

I. Introduction

During the last decade, the analysis of new microdata has contributed to advancing the sticky price literature by challenging existing models and fostering the development of new ones. Indeed, current frontier models are consistent with several cross-sectional facts about the size distribution as well as the timing of price changes uncovered by the microdata. An open issue in this research agenda concerns the nature of, or the appropriate underlying friction used, to model sticky prices. Two alternative assumptions to generate infrequent adjustment of prices involve either a fixed cost, as in the Golosov and Lucas (2007) menu-cost model, or a limited information-gathering and information-processing ability, as in Reis's (2006) "rational inattentiveness" setup. Following the descriptions used in the literature, we refer to these types of models as "state-dependent" models or "time-dependent" models.[1] Some scholars argue that information frictions will generate stronger real effects of monetary policy shocks (e.g., Mankiw and Reis 2002; Klenow and Kryvtsov 2008), but a systematic comparison of the consequences of each of these mechanisms for the transmission of monetary policy shocks has not been developed. Under what circumstances does the nature of the underlying friction matter for the propagation of monetary shocks? What kind of empirical evidence can be used to identify the nature of the underlying friction? This paper casts light on these questions by presenting new theoretical results and some evidence that bears upon such theories.

The first part of the paper formalizes the definition of time-dependent and state-dependent models (TD and SD, respectively), and analyzes the propagation of monetary shocks under the different frictions. The class of models we consider embeds (approximately) several classic sticky price models, such as Taylor (1980), Calvo (1983), Reis (2006), Golosov and Lucas (2007), Nakamura and Steinsson (2010), Midrigan (2011), Bonomo, Carvalho, and Garcia (2010), Bhattarai and Schoenle (2014), Carvalho and Schwartzman (2015), and several other cases that are novel in the literature. All the models considered are characterized by the presence of idiosyncratic shocks with continuous paths. We concentrate on three types of analytical results which, taken together show that what distinguishes state- and time-dependent models is their reaction to a *large* aggregate shock.

Our main finding is that for *small shocks* the nature of the friction is *irrelevant*, that is, the propagation of the nominal shock is the same in state- and time-dependent models provided that the models are fit to the same steady-state moments.[2]

More specifically, in our first result we follow the lead of Caballero and Engel (2007) and analyze the *impact* effect of a monetary shock on inflation, a statistic they refer to as the "flexibility index." This statistic corresponds to the impact effect (i.e., the initial point) of the impulse response function: the inflation reaction at the time of the shock. We show that the flexibility index is always zero in TD models. More surprisingly, we show that the shock does not have a first-order effect on the aggregate price even in SD models, so that for small shocks the impact is approximately zero provided that firms follow an Ss decision rule (possibly multidimensional) and that the shocks faced by the firms follow a diffusion.

Our second result extends this irrelevance beyond the impact effect by considering the total cumulated *output* response triggered by a small monetary shock (measured by the area under the output impulse response function). For economies with low inflation we show that the total cumulated output response is the same in TD and SD models provided the models are fit to the same steady-state moments, namely, that they have the same frequency of adjustment and the same kurtosis of the size of price changes. These results are quite robust: we show that they also apply in the presence of moderate rates of steady-state inflation. One message from these results is that, as long as one is interested in understanding the propagation of small monetary shocks, then what matters are these important moments that the models are fitted to (frequency and kurtosis), while the underlying nature of the nominal friction is irrelevant.

The third result highlights a key difference between SD and TD models, which appears when the aggregate shock is large. In TD models the impulse response function of prices at any given horizon is proportional to the size of the shock. Furthermore, as implied by our previous results, the impact effect of the shock on aggregate prices is zero for any shock size. These features imply that the shape of the impulse response does not depend on the size of the shock. Instead, the inherent nonlinear nature of decision rules of SD models implies that for aggregate shocks above a minimum size, the economy displays full price flexibility. Thus, for SD models the impact effect of the shock depends on their *size*. This prediction suggests a simple test for the nature of the friction behind sticky prices: TD models predict a proportional response in terms of the size of the shock, while SD models predict a nonlinear response with respect to the size of the shocks.

The second part of the paper presents an empirical investigation of the hypothesis, inspired by the above theoretical results, that the response of inflation to a monetary shock, particularly on impact, depends on the size of the shock. We follow the international economics literature that studies the pass-through of exchange rate shocks on to prices, as in, for example, Burstein and Gopinath (2014). In particular, we use a panel of monthly data from a large number of countries about CPI inflation and the nominal exchange rate (bilateral exchange rate versus the dollar). To keep in line with the theory, we restrict attention to countries with moderate inflation in the post–Bretton Woods period.[3]

Our empirical exploration uncovers some evidence of a nonlinear pass-through of devaluation on inflation for a sample that excludes countries in a fixed exchange rate regime as classified by Levy-Yeyati and Sturzenegger (2003) and Ilzetzki, Reinhart, and Rogoff (2008). This evidence is consistent with the prediction that the inflation response to an exchange rate shock depends on the size of the shock. For instance, in the month following the shock the elasticity of inflation with respect to a 5.5% shock is almost two times larger than the elasticity to a 1% shock. Interestingly, those differences can be noticed only in the first months after the impact and eventually disappear, consistent with the view that large shocks trigger a faster response of the economy. Our baseline results are robust to including countries in a fixed exchange rate regime in the post-1990 sample, and holds with different functional form specifications (piecewise linear, quadratic and cubic, or distributed lags), as well as different controls (e.g., for fixed versus flex exchange rate regime, GDP growth rates). We also highlight some dimensions along which these empirical patterns are not robust. The nonlinear effect is not robust to the introduction of fixed exchange rate countries into the full sample, and it is not robust to removing outliers as defined by the size of the large devaluations. In particular, removing the largest devaluation from the sample drastically increases the standard errors of the nonlinear coefficient on impact, making them statistically not significant at conventional confidence levels.[4] Nevertheless, dropping large outliers either increases or yields very similar point estimates of the nonlinear coefficient.

A. Novelty and Relation to Literature

Our analysis is inspired by the work of Klenow and Kryvtsov (2008). Like them, we also aim at investigating the nature of the frictions that underlie sticky prices. The two papers, however, have a different focus. Their pioneering paper mostly focuses on the documentation of the microfacts and on assessing the success of several classic models (encompassed by our framework) in matching the cross-sectional data. Their analysis does not investigate how the different models behave in response to an aggregate shock, which instead is the focus of our analysis. We aim to identify the implications of the different frictions for the propagation of aggregate shocks, and provide original analytic results that are useful for a systematic comparison of the two approaches. Our empirical exploration shares the objective of Gagnon, Lopez-Salido, and Vincent (2012) of identifying the extent to which pricing behavior displays state-dependent features.[5]

Our first result extends the theoretical analysis of Caballero and Engel (2007) about the aggregate flexibility of an economy, which focuses on the impact effect of a monetary shock. We analytically show that in several TD and SD models of the last generation featuring idiosyncratic shocks, a small monetary shock does not have a first-order effect on the aggregate price level. Second, this paper unifies recent results that focus on the full profile of the impulse response function, not just on the impact effect. These results build on, and extend, previous contributions in Alvarez and Lippi (2014), Alvarez, Le Bihan, and Lippi (2016), and Alvarez, Lippi, and Paciello (2016). We generalize the previous results by showing that they also hold in settings that feature both state- and time-dependent frictions as considered by Abel, Eberly, and Panageas

(2007, 2013), Alvarez, Lippi, and Paciello (2011), Bonomo et al. (2010), and Bonomo et al. (2016).

While the class of models we analyze is large, we comment next on some models that do not belong to it. For instance, in models with no idiosyncratic shocks such as Sheshinski and Weiss (1983), and the classic analysis of monetary shocks in this environment by Caplin and Spulber (1987) and Caplin and Leahy (1991), small monetary shocks have a first-order impact effect on inflation. We discuss the relation with these results in detail in section IV.A. Moreover, our setup with idiosyncratic shocks with continuous paths rules out models where firms are hit by infrequent and large idiosyncratic shocks, as considered by Gertler and Leahy (2008) or Midrigan (2011). While not all of our theoretical results hold as stated for these models, the main idea still applies. In particular, small monetary shocks have no impact effect (i.e., they are second order), but large monetary shocks have a first-order effect due to the state dependence of the decision rules.

Our paper also provides some novel empirical analysis of the nonlinear pass-through prediction. Even though most of the pass-through literature focuses on the magnitude of linear terms (e.g., Burstein and Gopinath 2014; Campa and Goldberg 2005; Martins 2005), there at least two papers that test for nonlinearities with a specification that is similar to ours. Pollard and Coughlin (2004) study the nonlinear response to exchange rate shocks of US industries using import prices and find that firms in over half the industries respond asymmetrically. Bussiere (2013) studies the nonlinear response to exchange rate shocks using import and export prices of G7 countries and finds evidence, with a specification similar to ours, of a nonlinear response in country-by-country regressions, as well as in panel regressions. A recent paper by Bonadio, Fischer, and Saure (2016) analyzes the pass-through into import and export prices using disaggregated daily data for Switzerland following the large appreciation (11%) of the Swiss franc in January 2015. This case study shows that the speed of the exchange rate pass-through is high in the case of this large shock: the half life of the shock is slightly above one week.

More broadly, we see our paper as a contribution to the burgeoning literature on nonlinear effects in macroeconomics. Examples of this literature are the macrofinance models such as Brunnermeier and Sannikov (2014), as well as the models featuring the zero lower bound such as Fernandez-Villaverde et al. (2015). In these models, shocks in different regions of the state space have differential effects, which turns out to be important for policy. Our contribution focuses on the differential effect of shocks according to their size, as in the seminal empirical analysis of fiscal policy by Giavazzi, Jappelli, and Pagano (2000), and the more recent quantitative models as in, for example, Kaplan and Violante (2014). The class of SD models we analyze, like these models, features a size asymmetry in the economy's response to small and large shocks. The application and the models are, of course, different: we focus on how prices respond to aggregate nominal shocks, they focus on the consumption response to fiscal shocks. Also, we offer some exploratory evidence of the nonlinear pass-through of nominal exchange rate changes on inflation using a large panel of countries.[6]

B.   Organization of the Paper

The next section gives a broad, nontechnical overview of the modeling setup and a summary of the main results. Section III describes the setups we use to analyze state-dependent models and time-dependent models, as well as a setting featuring both time- and state-dependent features. Section IV outlines the main theoretical results we derive for these economies concerning the propagation of monetary shocks. We first discuss the result on the equivalence between these models in the presence of small monetary shocks. Next, we discuss the differences between these models that appear with large shocks. Section V presents the empirical analysis, and section VI concludes.

II.   Overview of Main Results

We start by defining the elements for state-dependent (SD) and time-dependent (TD) setups. A *state-dependent* setup is one where price changes occur if the state, given by current profits or markups, attains a critical level. The SD models are characterized by decision rules that depend on the value of the state. In the presence of adjustment costs necessary to model sticky prices, the state space of the problem is split in two regions, one where inaction is optimal and another where the firms find it optimal to adjust prices to return the state to a point located well inside this set. Price changes occur when the state reaches the boundary of the inaction region. A *time-dependent* model is one where the times between consecutive price changes are statistically independent of the state (e.g., the current markup or profits of the firm). Instead, the time elapsed since the last price change (and potentially the duration of the previous price spell) completely determines the hazard rate of price changes. We show how the decision rules that correspond to TD or SD can be derived from an explicit profit maximization problem in the presence of fixed cost to observing the state ($\psi_o > 0$) or fixed cost to adjusting the nominal price ($\psi_m > 0$), respectively.

Our analysis focuses on the propagation of a permanent unexpected shock δ, measuring the change (in log points) of the nominal marginal cost of all firms, starting from the steady state of an economy with an inflation rate π and idiosyncratic shocks with variance σ^2. There are three theoretical results that we discuss. The first result concerns the impact effect of δ on the price level. For this result we do not need to specify the whole economy, instead we just take a continuum of firms that solve the type of problem described above and that face a common (once and for all) nominal cost shock.[7] We show that for both TD and SD models a small monetary shock δ has a second-order effect on the price level $\mathcal{P}(\delta, t)$ on impact, for any $\pi > 0$ provided that $\sigma > 0$. Formally, let $\mathcal{P}(\delta, t)$ be the price level $t \geq 0$ periods after an unexpected increase of the money supply of size δ. This implies

$$\mathcal{P}(\delta, t) = \Theta(\delta) + \int_0^t \theta(\delta, s)ds, \tag{1}$$

where $\Theta(\delta)$ denotes the impact response of the price level at the time of the shock. In particular, we show that in all TD, SD, and mixed models, we have that $\Theta'(0) = 0$, that is, that there is no first-order effect of the monetary shock on the price level. An illustration of this result can be seen in figure 1, which plots the response of output to a permanent monetary shock for three economies characterized by the same frequency of price changes per year (normalized to unity) and different kurtosis of the size distribution of price changes. It appears that as the 1% shock hits the economy, output increases by approximately 1% in all economies, since the CPI does not respond on impact.[8] This result is of interest because it clarifies previous analyses of the impact effect. For instance, Caballero and Engel (2007) propose a theoretical characterization of the impact effect, $\Theta'(0)$, which they refer to as the *flexibility index*, as a way to characterize different sticky price models. Thus in a large class of models, with $\sigma > 0$ and $\pi > 0$, the flexibility index is zero.

While monetary shocks do not have a first-order impact on the aggregate price level in neither TD nor SD models, the reason behind this

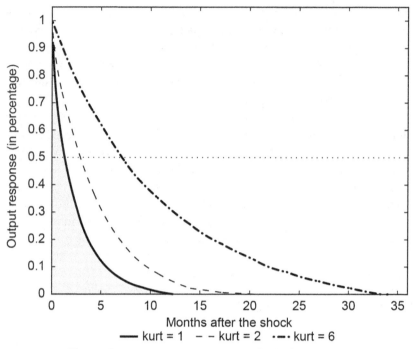

Fig. 1. Output response to a monetary shock of size $\delta = 1\%$

Note: The figure represents an economy with $\varepsilon = 1$, $N(\Delta p_i) = 1.0$, and $std(\Delta p_i) = 0.10$. The three curves correspond to economies with a steady state kurtosis of the size of price changes equal to 1, 2, and 6, respectively.

result is different. For TD models, the distribution of the number of firms adjusting at different times is independent of the aggregate shock. Thus, the aggregate price level does not jump on impact, that is, $\Theta(\delta) = 0$ for all δ. For SD models the result is due to the fact that there is no "mass" of firms close to the adjustment boundaries (literally, a zero density), which in turn is explained because the boundaries are exit points where all firms adjust.[9] Thus, in SD models $\Theta(\delta)$ is of order δ^2, so small shocks trigger extremely small jumps.

An important property of the impact effect concerns how it changes as a function of inflation, π, relative to the volatility of the idiosyncratic shocks σ. While for $\sigma > 0$ the impact effect Θ is of order δ^2, we notice that the impact effect is increasing with π and that the effect becomes first order as π / σ diverges. The menu-cost models of Sheshinski and Weiss (1983) and Caplin and Spulber (1987) illustrate this point: in both models the impact effect $\Theta(\delta)$ is of order δ, the reason is that in these models $\sigma = 0$ and $\pi > 0$, so that the ratio diverges. Thus, since the impact effect is second order but it is increasing in π, in the empirical analysis we will focus on low-inflation countries where the lack of response to small shocks should be easier to detect.

The second result goes beyond the analysis of the impact effect and considers a summary measure for the whole profile of the impulse response function. We derive this second result focusing on economies where the steady-state inflation equals (or is close to) zero.[10] Moreover, for this result we completely specify a general equilibrium effect, so the shock is interpreted as a monetary shock. Specifically, the summary statistic that we choose is the area under the output impulse response function following an increase of the money supply of size δ. We denote this magnitude by $\mathcal{M}(\delta)$, for example, the area that appears for illustrative purposes in figure 1 for three models with kurtosis equal to 1, 2, and 6, respectively. Formally, the cumulative output $\mathcal{M}$ after a shock δ is:

$$\mathcal{M}(\delta) = \frac{1}{\varepsilon} \int_0^\infty (\delta - \mathcal{P}(\delta, t))dt \qquad (2)$$

where $\mathcal{P}(\delta, t)$ is the aggregate price level t periods after the shock δ. The argument of the integral gives the aggregate real wages at time t, which are then mapped into output by $1 / \varepsilon$, a parameter related to the elasticity of the labor supply. Integrating over time gives the total cumulative real output. We find the $\mathcal{M}$ statistic convenient for two reasons. First, it combines in a single value the persistence and the size of the output response, and it is closely related to the output variance due to monetary shocks, which is sometimes used in the literature.[11] Second, for small monetary shocks (like the ones typically considered in the literature) this statistic is completely encoded by a simple formula that involves the frequency of price changes $N(\Delta p_i)$ and the kurtosis of price changes $Kur(\Delta p_i)$.

We show that in state-dependent (SD) and time-dependent (TD) models, as well as in models where both TD and SD features, the total cumulative output effect of a small unexpected monetary shock depends on the ratio between two steady-state statistics: the kurtosis of the size-distribution of price changes $Kur(\Delta p_i)$ and the average number of price changes per year $N(\Delta p_i)$. Formally, given the labor supply elasticity $1 / \varepsilon - 1$ we show that for a small monetary shock δ the cumulative output $\mathcal{M}$ is accurately approximated by the following expression:

$$\mathcal{M}(\delta) \approx \frac{\delta}{6\varepsilon} \frac{Kur(\Delta p_i)}{N(\Delta p_i)}.$$
(3)

An immediate implication of this result is that for small monetary shocks the underlying friction is irrelevant (provided the economies have the same frequency and kurtosis of price changes).

The explanation of why this result holds is involved, but its interpretation is not. The ratio in equation (3) controls for both the degree of flexibility of the economy, as measured by $N(\Delta p_i)$, as well as for the presence of "selection" effects, as measured by $Kurt(\Delta p_i)$.[12] On the one hand, that the cumulative impulse response depends on the degree of flexibility is hardly surprising. On the other hand, that the selection effect is captured completely by the steady-state kurtosis of prices is, at least to us, more surprising. Moreover, that exactly the same expression holds for state-dependent and time-dependent models is, again at least to us, revealing. In summary, the reason is that the selection effect operates equally in terms of the size distribution of price changes (which is the mechanism for state-dependent models) as well as on the distribution of times between adjustments (which is the mechanism for time-dependent models). Our result states that as long as any two models produce the same level of kurtosis (of the size of price changes) as well as the same average frequency of price changes then the total cumulated output response produced by a monetary shock is the same across these models, in spite of the fact that their underlying frictions might differ.

The third theoretical result is that TD and SD models behave differently in response to large shocks. Using the notation of equation (18) we have that $\Theta'(\delta) = 0$ for any value of the shock δ in TD models. This is intuitive since the timing of pricing decisions is by definition independent of the state. Thus TD models imply an impulse response function for the aggregate price level proportional to the size of the shock. Formally, for all shock sizes δ there is no impact effect on prices in TD models, so that $\Theta(\delta) = 0$. Moreover, TD models have a proportional flow effect $\theta(\delta, t) = \theta(1, t)\delta$ at all horizons $t \geq 0$. These two results imply that

TDmodels: $\mathcal{P}(\delta, t) = \mathcal{P}(1, t)\delta$, for all δ,

so that the function $\mathcal{P}(\cdot, t)$ is linear with a zero intercept.

Instead, in SD models we have that $\Theta'(0) = 0$ but $\Theta'(\delta) > 0$ for $\delta > 0$, and thus $\Theta''(0) > 0$. In particular, SD models imply a minimum shock size such that all shocks above this size give rise to full price flexibility (monetary neutrality). Formally, we can show that there is a shock $\bar{\delta} < \infty$ such that for all $\delta \geq \bar{\delta}$ we have $\Theta(\delta) = \delta$ and $\theta(\delta, t) = 0$ or, that the economy displays full price flexibility for sufficiently large shocks. Thus in SD models $\mathcal{P}(\cdot, t)$ has unit derivative with respect to δ for large values of δ:

$$\text{SD models: } \mathcal{P}(\delta, t) = \delta \text{ for all } t \text{ if } \delta \geq \bar{\delta},$$

$$\text{otherwise } \mathcal{P}(\delta, 0) = \frac{1}{2} \Theta''(0)\delta^2 + o(\delta^2).$$

We explore the hypothesis of a nonlinear response to nominal shocks following the ideas in Burstein and Gopinath (2014) and Campa and Goldberg (2005), as well many others in the pass-through literature, and use nominal exchange rate fluctuations as a proxy for an "orthogonal" nominal shock to the firms' nominal costs. Since we seek to identify the different behavior of the economy conditioning on the *size* of the exchange rate shocks, it is important that we have a large number of observations to be able to include as many episodes as possible of small as well as of large shocks.

We use an unbalanced panel of monthly data from the post–Bretton Woods period for about 70 countries in periods of moderate inflation. Our focus on moderate inflation countries is suggested by the theory: as inflation increases the impact effect $\Theta(\delta)$ of a small nominal shock δ becomes larger, so that the difference between a small and a large shock becomes harder to detect.[13] Since the data are monthly we cannot really estimate the impact effect $\Theta(\delta)$, but we can measure the CPI change after the shock $\mathcal{P}(\delta, t)$ where t, the time elapsed, is one month.[14] The monthly data provide yet another reason to focus on low inflation: while the frequency of price adjustment is unresponsive to inflation at low inflation rates, the frequency increases as inflation enters the two-digit range (see the evidence in Gagnon [2009] and Alvarez et al. [2015]), so that the propagation of shocks is faster and its shape becomes harder to detect.

We compute an inflation forecast at different horizons conditional on an exchange rate innovation using a simple nonlinear regression.[15] We measure the pass-through from exchange rate changes to inflation for $t = 1, 3, 6, 12$, and 24 months, allowing for the magnitude of the pass-through to depend on the size of the exchange rate shock. A key issue in estimation concerns the simultaneous interaction between inflation and the nominal exchange rate, which opens the possibility of reverse causation. We think reverse causation is especially likely for countries in a fixed exchange rate regime, where large devaluations may occur as a "realignment" after periods of above average inflation. For this reason, we also control for the type of *de facto* exchange rate regime distinguishing between flexible, managed, and fixed exchange rates (as classified by Levy-Yeyati and Sturzenegger [2003], Reinhart and Rogoff [2004], and the following update in Ilzetzki, Reinhart, and Rogoff 2008]). Also, the (near) random-walk nature of exchange rates in floating-exchange rate countries makes such a sample more appropriate to use our specification to test the hypothesis of the differential (in terms of size) impact effect of exchange rate shocks.

We test whether the short-term pass-through, namely, the conditional correlation between the nominal exchange rate innovations and inflation (at various horizons) is bigger for large exchange rate movements than for small ones. This is because the theory of SD models predicts a larger response of inflation to nominal shocks in the presence of large shocks, while TD models predict the shape of the impulse response function to be independent of the size of the shock. Various nonlinear functional forms were considered: a quadratic specification, and a cubic as well as a piecewise linear specification. In table 2 we report the estimates of the quadratic specification:

$$\pi_{i,(t,t+h)} = \alpha_i + \delta_t + \beta_h \Delta e_{i,t} + \gamma_h (\Delta e_{i,t})^2 sign(\Delta e_{i,t}) + \varepsilon_{it}^\pi, \qquad (4)$$

where $\pi_{i,(t,t+h)}$ is the inflation rate of country i in the period from month t to month $t + h$ (for $h = 1, 3, 6, 12, 24$), $\Delta e_{i,t}$ is the devaluation from month $t - 1$ to month t.[16] The sign operator is used to impose "symmetry," that is, that the inflation effect of a large devaluation equals the deflation effect of a large appreciation. All regressions use time and country dummies (fixed effects) and standard errors are computed using STATA's robust standard error options (similar results obtain by clustering errors at the period or country level).

Our empirical results, summarized in table 2, uncover some evidence of a nonlinear effect, that is, of a statistically significant γ_h coefficient, in the sample that excludes countries in a fixed exchange rate regime.[17] The top panel of the table shows that the impulse response of inflation to large shock is above the response to a small shock up to the six-month horizon. After 24 months, the two impulse responses coincide, with a pass-through of about 10%. This is consistent with the hypothesis that larger nominal shocks have a shorter half life. As mentioned in the introduction, in section V we discuss the dimensions in which this result is robust and the ones in which it is not (see tables 3–8).

III. Setup for Model Economies

In this section, we describe the class of model economies for which we characterize the effect of a once-and-for-all monetary shock. Section III.A defines the economic environment within which firms operate. In sections III.B, III.C, and III.D, we define state dependent, time dependent, and mixed-type pricing rules, and describe the pricing problem of a firm under which each one of these rules optimally emerges. In these problems the firms take a constant interest rate as well the common part of their nominal marginal cost as given. In a sense, this is an "industry analysis" as, for instance, in Eichenbaum, Jaimovich, and Rebelo (2011). In appendix A we describe a setup where the results hold and can be interpreted as the general equilibrium response to a nominal shock in a closed economy model. Our main results, in section IV, characterize the propagation of the monetary shock under these different pricing rules.

A. Firms' Price-Setting Problem

We first describe the static production function of the firms and then we define the price gaps, a concept we will use to characterize the firm's decision rules.

Production

Each firm k produces and sells a quantity y_{ki} of n goods (each indexed by i), each with a linear labor-only technology with productivity $1 / Z$:

$$y_{ki}(t) = \frac{\ell_{ki}(t)}{Z_{ki}(t)} \quad \text{where} \quad Z_{ki}(t) = \exp(\sigma \mathcal{W}_{ki}(t)),$$

where $\ell_{ki}(t)$ its the labor input. Firm k is subject to a productivity shock that is common across all its products, $\overline{\mathcal{W}}_k$, as well as to idiosyncratic productivity shocks $\tilde{\mathcal{W}}_{ki}$, independent across products. In particular, we assume the log of productivity follows a brownian motion $\mathcal{W}_{ki}(t)$ with variance σ^2, namely:

$$\mathcal{W}_{ki}(t) = \frac{\overline{\sigma}}{\sqrt{\overline{\sigma}^2 + \sigma^2}} \overline{\mathcal{W}}_k(t) + \frac{\sigma}{\sqrt{\overline{\sigma}^2 + \sigma^2}} \tilde{\mathcal{W}}_{ki}(t), \tag{5}$$

where the processes $\{\overline{\mathcal{W}}_k(t), \tilde{\mathcal{W}}_{ki}(t)\}$ are independent across k and i. In words, the process for $\{\mathcal{W}_{ki}\}$ are independent across firms, have a common component with volatility $\overline{\sigma}$, and product specific volatility σ.

Profit Function and Price Gaps

For all the model specifications that we consider we can define a "price gap," g_{ki}, namely, the log difference between the current nominal price and the static profit-maximizing price for good i sold by firm k. In particular, we let $P_{ki}(t)$ be the nominal price at time t and $W(t)Z_{ki}(t)$ be the nominal marginal cost of production for good i and firm k, where $W(t)$ is the nominal wage at time t. Each firm faces a demand with a constant elasticity η for the bundle of its n products, which has an elasticity of substitution ρ between each of its n varieties.[18] We define the price gap $g_{ki}(t)$ as the log of the difference between the current price and the static profit-maximizing price:

$$g_{ki}(t) = \log P_{ki}(t) - \log(W(t)Z_{ki}(t)) - \log(\eta / (\eta - 1))$$
$$= \log P_{ki}(t) - W_{ki}(t) - \log W(t) - \log(\eta / (\eta - 1)),$$

where we omit the firm k subindex whenever it causes no misunderstanding. Since we consider the case of constant inflation π, which induces a constant drift in the nominal wage $W(t)$, and productivity follows a brownian motion, the law of motion of the price gaps will also follow a brownian motion with drift equal to minus the inflation rate and possibly with correlation between products. Thus, absent a price adjustment, each price gap g_{ki} has continuous paths:

$$dg_{ki}(t) = -\pi dt + \sigma dW_{ki}(t). \tag{6}$$

We let $\Pi(P_{k1}(t), ..., P_{kn}(t), Z_{k1}(t), ..., Z_{kn}(t), W(t); c(t))$ denote the nominal profits of firm k, that is, its total nominal revenue minus production costs. We can approximate this profit function around the frictionless profit maximizing prices as:

$$\Pi(P_{k1}(t), ..., P_{kn}(t), Z_{k1}(t), ..., Z_{kn}(t), W(t); c(t))$$

$$= W(t)\left[\frac{\rho(\eta - 1)}{2n}\left(\sum_{i=1}^{n}g_{ki}^2(t)\right) - \frac{(\rho - \eta)(\eta - 1)}{2n^2}\left(\sum_{i=1}^{n}g_{ki}(t)\right)^2\right] \tag{7}$$

$$+ o(\|(c(t), g_{k1}(t), ..., g_{kn}(t))\|^2) + \text{terms independent of } g_k(t),$$

where $o(x)$ a function of order smaller than x. This second-order approximation is useful because it simplifies the objective function to be used in the dynamic problem. Notice that profits can be expressed as a function of price gaps. The variable $c(t)$ stands for any variable that enters in the profit function in a weakly separable way. For instance, in the general equilibrium model of section A, $c(t)$ corresponds to the aggregate consumption. In that model $c(t)$ is a shifter of the quantity demanded—due to its effect on the aggregate ideal price index—and also indirectly affects the present value of profits through its effect on the real rate. Nevertheless, up to a second order, we argue we can disregard these effects. We make this approximation precise in section A.1.

B.   State-Dependent Pricing Rules

We describe a price-setting problem where the firm's optimal decision rules are *state dependent*, that is, where price changes occur when the state, given by current profits or markups, attains a critical level. We assume that firms have to pay a fixed *menu cost* to simultaneously adjust the price charge for the n products it produces.

State-Dependent and Ss Decision Rules

We let $g = (g_1, \ldots, g_n)$ be the vector of the n price gaps for the firm, where we omit the firm index k for simplicity. A *state-dependent decision rule* is described by an inaction set $\mathcal{I} \subset \mathbb{R}^n$ and a value of the price gap $g^* \in \mathcal{I}$. Given these two elements, the optimal state-dependent decision rule is inaction if $g(t) \in \mathcal{I}$, and otherwise if $g(t) \notin \mathcal{I}$, then prices are changed so that the vector of price gaps right after the adjustment equal $g(t) = g^*$. We note that if $g^* = 0$, that is, if the n price gaps are set to zero, then it means that when prices are adjusted they are all set to a value that maximizes the static profits.

   In general, the inaction set can be described by a function $b : \mathbb{R}^n \to \mathbb{R}$:

$$(g_1, \ldots, g_n) \in \mathcal{I} \; \to \; b(g_1, \ldots, g_n) \leq 0$$

$$\text{and} \tag{8}$$

$$(g_1, \ldots, g_n) \notin \mathcal{I} \; \to \; b(g_1, \ldots, g_n) > 0.$$

We will consider the case where the n products enter symmetrically, so that b is symmetric and the n elements of g^* are identical. Symmetry provides a convenient mapping from the inaction set $\mathcal{I}$ into an Ss rule given by two (scalar) threshold functions, one for the lower bound $\underline{g} : \mathbb{R}^{n-1} \to \mathbb{R}$, and one for the upper bound $\overline{g} : \mathbb{R}^{n-1} \to \mathbb{R}$. In an Ss rule prices are changed if, given the rest of the price gaps, the price gap of any product (say product 1) reaches either a lower threshold $\underline{g}$, or an upper threshold $\bar{g}$, that is:

$$(g_1, g_2, \ldots, g_n) \in \mathcal{I} \iff \underline{g}(g_2, \ldots, g_n) \leq g_1 \leq \bar{g}(g_2, \ldots, g_n). \quad (9)$$

Summarizing, we can describe an Ss rule by the optimal return point g^* and either a function b or the pair of functions $(\underline{g}, \bar{g})$.

Microfoundation of State-Dependent Model

We can microfound the state-dependent rules described in equation (8) or equation (9) as the solution of the following problem. Consider a firm that chooses when to change prices, that is, the stopping times $\{\tau_i\}$ as well as the price changes $\Delta P_j(\tau_i)$ at those times to maximize:

$$\max_{\{\tau_i, \Delta P_j(\tau_i), j=1,\ldots,n, i=1,2,\ldots\}} \mathbb{E} \left[\begin{array}{l} \int_0^\infty e^{-rt} \Pi(\{P_1(t), \ldots, P_n(t), Z_1(t), \ldots, Z_n(t)\}, W(t)) \\ dt - \sum_{i=1}^\infty e^{-r\tau_i} \psi_m W(\tau_i) \end{array} \right] \quad (10)$$

$$P_j(t) = P_j(\tau_i) \text{ for all } t \in (\tau_i, \tau_{i+1}] \quad \text{and} \quad \Delta P_j(\tau_i) = \lim_{\varepsilon \downarrow 0} P_j(\tau_i + \varepsilon) - P_j(\tau_i).$$

The two main parameters for this class of models are the size of the menu cost ψ_m and the number of products n. The key assumption for the multiproduct specification (where $n > 1$) is that once the menu cost ψ_m is paid, the firm can adjust the prices of all goods at no extra cost. We will provide an analytic characterization of this nonconcave stochastic sequence problem by solving an approximate version that uses the quadratic profit function defined in equation (7). Several models discussed in the recent literature are nested as special cases of the state-dependent setup. We briefly recall some of them next.

Classic Menu Cost

The menu-cost problem, as in Golosov and Lucas (2007), is obtained setting $n = 1$. In this model the menu cost is constant at ψ, and with zero inflation the optimal policy is the well-known Ss rule: firms adjust their prices when the distance (in absolute value) between the actual price and the profit-maximizing price gap reaches a value $\pm\bar{g}$. This model produces a size distribution of price changes that is degenerate: when the price adjustments occur and are of size $\pm\bar{g}$.

Multiproduct Models

This model allows for $n \geq 2$ and any value of π. Different values of n map into several models studied in the literature. For example, the case with $n = 2$ and normal innovations to productivity is studied in Midrigan (2011), and the one with $n = 3$ was studied in Bhattarai and Schoenle (2014). For large values of n (technically $n \to \infty$, but in practice for $n > 10$) the model produces staggered pricing, where the time elapsed between two price adjustments is constant, as in Taylor (1980). Alvarez and Lippi (2014) show that with zero inflation $\pi = 0$, and with $\eta = \rho$ (which implies that the elasticity of substitution between bundles is the same as the elasticity between varieties in a bundle), then the function b describing the optimal Ss rule can be written as:

$$b(g_1, \ldots, g_n) = \sum_{i=1}^{n} g_i^2 - \bar{y} \quad \text{and} \quad g_i^* = 0 \quad \text{for all } i = 1, \ldots, n, \quad (11)$$

for an optimally determined value of $\bar{y}$. Equivalently, we can write b in terms of the optimal thresholds:

$$\underline{g}(g_2, \ldots, g_n) = -\left(\bar{y} - \sum_{i=2}^{n} g_i^2\right)^{1/2} \quad \text{and} \quad \overline{g}(g_2, \ldots, g_n) = \left(\bar{y} - \sum_{i=2}^{n} g_i^2\right)^{1/2}. \quad (12)$$

The key economic insight of this model is that this framework generates small price changes, since the stopping times (for price adjustments) are defined by the sum of n price gaps, which implies that an individual price gap at the time of adjustment can take any value in $(-\sqrt{\bar{y}}, \sqrt{\bar{y}})$.[19]

In the case where the elasticity of substitution $\eta \neq \rho$, and/or there is steady-state inflation, so $\pi \neq 0$, and/or there is correlation between the idiosyncratic shocks to the products, so $\bar{\sigma} > 0$, we have that the function b that defines the set of inaction $\mathcal{I}$ can be written as:

$$b(g_1, \ldots, g_n) = \sum_{i=1}^{n} g_i^2 - \bar{y}\left(\sum_{i=1}^{n} g_i\right), \quad (13)$$

where, with a slight abuse of notation, we use $\bar{y}$ to denote a function $\bar{y} : \mathbb{R} \to \mathbb{R}$. In this more general case we can define two scalars $y \equiv \sum_{i=1}^{n} g_i^2$ and $z \equiv \sum_{i=1}^{n} g_i$ which we can use to define the inaction set. Moreover, one can show that the diffusions for (y, z) follow themselves a first-order Markov process, that is, so they are sufficient to define the state of the problem.[20]

C.   Time-Dependent Pricing Rules

We now describe a price-setting problem where the firm's optimal decision rules are *time dependent*, that is, where the time between consecutive price changes is statistically independent of the current markup
or profits of the firm. Under such a rule the time elapsed since the last
price change completely determines the hazard rate of price changes.

More formally, let an observation be an event in which the firm collects and process all the information that is necessary for price setting.
Absent other frictions, observation time will coincide with the times of
a change of prices to adapt to the newly gathered information. Let τ_i be
the date of the ith observation: at this time the firm uses all available
information to adjust its price(s) and to decide the time of the next observation, τ_{i+1}. Formally, we allow for random dates in the sense that
$\tau_{i+1} - \tau_i$ is a random variable with (right) cumulative distribution func-
tion H, that is, $\Pr\{\tau_{i+1} - \tau_i \geq t|\tau_i\} = H(t|\tau_i)$. The defining characteristic of
a time-dependent model is that the realization of τ_{i+1} is independent of
the information relevant for price setting, that is, it is independent of
the price gaps $\{g_1(t), \dots, g_n(t)\}$ for $t \geq \tau_i$. Note that with this definition
price changes cannot have any selection, where we use selection in the
sense of Golosov and Lucas (2007).

A well-known example of TD models is Taylor's (1980) model of staggered price setting, where price adjustments are deterministically
spaced every T periods, or $H(t) = 1$ for $t < T$, and $H(t) = 0$ otherwise.
Another well-known example is the model by Mankiw and Reis (2002),
where the times elapsed between successive observations are exponentially distributed, or $H(t) = e^{-\lambda t}$ so that the mean time elapsed between
observations is $1 / \lambda$.[21] More general versions of these models allow the
distribution of times to follow a first-order Markov process $H(t; t_0)$ where
the distribution of times elapsed between observations t is allowed to
depend on duration of the previous spell between observations t_0.

Aggregating the behavior across firms, each described by the function H, provides a characterization of the stationary cross-sectional distribution of the "times until the next observation": $Q(t)$. That is, the
fraction of firms that, at any point in time, will wait at least t units of
time until the next observation. We denote the right CDF of such distribution by $Q(t)$, which determines the time it takes for an aggregate
shock to be incorporated into the information set of a given fraction of
firms, that is, the speed at which the monetary shock propagates into
the aggregate price level.

Microfoundation of Time-Dependent Pricing Rules

While the the distribution function H is assumed as a primitive of the analysis in several TD models, the literature following Caballero (1989) and Reis (2006) has provided an explicit profit-maximization problem subject to information frictions to rationalize the origins of H. We describe a model with explicit microfoundations, based on Alvarez, Lippi, and Paciello (2016), that rationalizes inattentive behavior as the optimal policy given the cost of collecting and processing information. The firm price-setting problem balances the costs and benefits of gathering information. We assume that to gather information about the nominal marginal cost the firm must pay an "observation cost" along the lines discussed by Caballero (1989) and Reis (2006). In particular, we assume that by paying an observation cost ψ_0, firms learn the current value of the production cost $(Z_1, \ldots, Z_n)$, which is the key variable to decide prices. We interpret the observation cost as the physical cost of acquiring the information needed to make the price decision as well as costs associated with the decision making in the firm (gathering and aggregating information; e.g., Zbaracki et al. [2004]; Reis [2006]). Alternatively, these costs represent the cognitive costs associated with gathering extra information, as found in experimental evidence on tracking problems (see Magnani, Gorry, and Oprea 2016).

The problem for the firm consists in deciding, at each observation date τ_i, the time until the new planned observation date T_i, as well the prices consistent with the available information:

$$\max_{\{T_i, P_j(t), j=1,\ldots,n, i=1,2,\ldots,t\geq 0\}} \mathbb{E} \left[\begin{array}{l} \int_0^\infty e^{-rt}\Pi(P_1(t), \ldots, P_n(t), Z_1(t), \ldots, Z_n(t), \\ \\ W(t); c(t))dt - \sum_{i=1}^\infty e^{-r\tau_i}\psi_0(\tau_i)W(\tau_i) \end{array} \right], \quad (14)$$

where $\tau_{i+1} = \min\{s_i, T_i\} + \tau_i$, where s_i is an exponential distributed r.v., and T_i and $P_j(t)$ for $t \in [\tau_i, \tau_{i+1})$ only depend on information gathered at $\tau_0, \tau_1, \ldots, \tau_i$.

The value of the state of the firm is $(Z_1, \ldots, Z_n)$, which is the information required to set the prices that maximize current profits. We assume that the state is only observed infrequently. In particular, we assume that there are two ways in which the firm can observe it. First, exogenously and at an exponentially distributed time with duration λ, the state becomes known to the firm. Second, the firm decides when it plans to observe the state. Specifically, we assume that at the time of the ith observation (planned or not), denoted by τ_i the following events take place: (a) the observation cost $\psi_o(\tau_i)$ is realized, and (b) the firm obtains a signal $\zeta(\tau_i)$ that is informative about the value of the next observation cost at different horizons. At this time, the firm decides the time elapsed T_i until then new planned observation, say $T_i + \tau_i$. Thus the next observation occurs either when the exogenous observation time, denoted by s_i arrives, or when the next planned observation occurs, that is, $\tau_{i+1} = \min\{s_i, T_i\} + \tau_i$. The decision of T_i depends only on the information available at time τ_i. This information consists on the observation costs, signals, and production cost at the current and past observation dates $\tau_0, \tau_1, \ldots, \tau_i$. Furthermore, we assume that (c) production and observation cost and exogenous observation times are all statistically independent, and that (d) nominal marginal cost for each product follows a martingale. Note that (d) implies that there are no incentives to change prices between observations, that is, there are no incentives for price plans.[22] Assumptions (a)–(d) imply that the optimally chosen time between observations, or equivalently between price adjustments, is a function of the signal obtained at the beginning of the price spell, and that the size of price adjustment is independent of the time elapsed between price adjustments, that is, these assumptions imply a *time-dependent* model.[23]

Our motivation for introducing the exogenous observation dates, that is, those triggered by s_i, is to nest the popular model of sticky information where observations (and price changes) occur with a constant probability per unit of time λdt. On the other end, by setting $\lambda = 0$, we can abstract from this feature and all the observations involve a cost-benefit analysis in setting T_i. In general, in the determination of T_i, the value of λ has the same effect as a higher interest rate in the decision of the firm for T_i.

Our choice of the processes for the observation cost and signals is general enough to nest several cases studied in the literature.

Constant time between observations. If there are no exogenous observation times, that is, $\lambda = 0$, and observation cost ψ_o are constant, then the time between observation is constant. Caballero (1989) and Reis (2006) analyze this case.

Calvo model. There are two setups for this model that give rise to the same distribution of price durations as in the Calvo model. The first one, as explained above, is obtained if all changes are exogenous, that is, when ψ_o is very large. The second obtains even if $\lambda = 0$, but there is particular distribution of ψ_o and signals so that the firm finds it optimal to observe at exponentially distributed times.[24]

Markovian times. We refer to Markovian times the case where the times between observations (and price changes) form a first-order Markov process, so times are random with the current time between observations depending statistically on the duration of the previous spell between observations. This is obtained in a very natural case where the current value of the observation cost is itself the signal for the next observation cost. This case is analyzed both in Reis (2006) (for negligibly small observation costs levels) and Alvarez, Lippi, and Paciello (2016). In particular, we assume that the observation cost follows a continuous time Markov chain, so that for each value θ_0 there is a time-invariant probability per unit of time to transit to some other values. Thus, when a state is observed by the firm, the value of the observation cost serves as a signal of future observation costs at different horizons, directly implied by the Markov chain. The firm's decision rule becomes a function $T(\theta_0)$, so that times between observations are random, each of them corresponding to a value of the realized observation cost θ_0. The economics of this choice balance the benefit of future observations with the expected cost at different horizons. The key property to understand the variability of the T is the forecastability of future observation costs, which is tightly related with the *persistence* of the Markov chain. Furthermore, the property of the Markov chain are important to construct the cross-sectional distribution of times until the next adjustment $Q(t)$, an object of interest for the impulse response of shocks.

D.   State- and Time-Dependent Models

We briefly review models that combine state- and time-dependent elements. In these models, the decision rule of the firm depends both on the time elapsed since the last price change as well as on the state (e.g., whether markups have reached a critical level). We discuss two examples: the first one is a version of the state-dependent model where at exogenously random dates the menu cost is set to zero. The second example is one where there are both observation and menu costs (in appendix D we write out both problems formally).

Multiproduct Calvo[+] Model

The first example adds to the state-dependent problem described above the arrival of free adjustment opportunities at a constant rate λ. Equivalently, one can interpret the model as one with a random menu cost that, in a period of length dt, equals ψ_m with probability $(1 - \lambda dt)$, or equal zero with probability λdt. This random menu cost introduces exogenous adjustment times in a way that is similar to the one described for the exogenous observation times in time-dependent models. This model is referred to as the Calvo[+] model, a combination with features of the Golosov and Lucas model as well as the Calvo model, and was first studied by Nakamura and Steinsson (2010). The multiproduct version of this model is studied in Alvarez, Le Bihan, and Lippi (2016).

The optimal policy for this case is a combination of state- and time-dependent policy. As in the state-dependent case, prices change the first time the boundary of the inaction set is reached. But also, as in the time-dependent case, the price changes when a free adjustment opportunity arrives. Thus, the stopping time τ_{i+1} is given by the first time (after the adjustment at τ_i) at which the state either reaches the boundary of the inaction set or that an opportunity to adjust at zero cost occurs.

Positive Menu and Observation Costs

The second example combines both observation and menu costs.[25] Observations will happen at discretely separated periods of times, and we denote the ith observation by the stopping time τ_i. Observations are subject to a constant fixed cost $\psi_o > 0$. Upon an observation the firm will decide whether to adjust prices or not, which we denote by the indicator $a(\tau_i) \in \{0, 1\}$. If a price adjustment occurs, then a menu costs $\psi_m > 0$ must be paid. The optimal decision rule combines features of the state- and time-dependent rules. Upon the current observation at time τ_i and with the relevant information gathered until that time (i.e., the value of the state) the firm decides the time until the next observation, T_i, so that the next observation occurs at $\tau_{i+1} = \tau_i + T_i$. Also upon an observation at time τ_i, the firm decides whether to adjust prices or not, that is, whether $a(\tau_i) \in \{1, 0\}$. Note that the pricing decision has a state-dependent feature, in that upon an observation the firm will keep prices constant if the state is in the inaction set, and adjust them otherwise. But, differently from the menu-cost model described above, upon an observation the firm may find its state strictly outside of the inaction region, that is, it may strictly prefer to adjust. Versions of this model are analyzed in Alvarez et al. (2011), Alvarez, Lippi, and Paciello (2016), Bonomo, Carvalho, and Garcia (2010), and Bonomo et al. (2016).

E.   Steady-State Price-Setting Statistics

For future reference, we introduce three steady-state statistics that summarize price-setting behavior and we consider a steady state with idiosyncratic shocks, no aggregate shocks, and trend inflation π. Define $N(\Delta p_i; \pi)$ as the average number of price changes per unit of time (say per year); $Var(\Delta p_i; \pi)$ as the standard deviation of the distribution of the size of (nonzero) price changes and as the $Kurt(\Delta p_i; \pi)$ the kurtosis of the distribution of the size of (nonzero) price changes. It will be useful to index each of these statistics with the steady-state inflation rate π. Notice that, in principle, these statistics are directly measurable in microdata sets. We focus on these statistics because for the three classes of models described above, the ratio $Kurt(\Delta p_i; \pi)$ / $N(\Delta p_i; \pi)$ provides a sufficient summary of statistics for the real effects of a small monetary shock. This is the object of the next section. In appendix E we show that there is an identity between $N(\Delta p_i)$ and $Std(\Delta p_i)$ for small inflation rate, uncovering the trade-off that any decision rule around zero inflation faces.

IV.   The Propagation of Monetary Shocks

In this section, we characterize the effect on the aggregate price level and on output of a monetary shock. Up to now, we focused on the firm pricing problems under different frictions and defined steady-state statistics. Turns out that, under a convenient GE structure that has been widely adopted in the literature (see, e.g., Caballero and Engel 1993; Golosov and Lucas 2007; Alvarez and Lippi 2014), the effect on prices and output of monetary shocks can be characterized by the impact of the monetary shocks on price gaps, ignoring GE effects. We start by reviewing these results. Aided with this structure, we then turn to prove the main results in the paper. First, we show in Proposition 1 that the impact effect on prices of a small monetary shock is second order in state-dependent and time-dependent models. Second, we show in Proposition 2 that the effect of a small monetary shock on output can be summarized by the kurtosis both in time- and state-dependent models. Finally, we show in Proposition 3 that impact effect on prices of large monetary shocks is first order in state-dependent models and zero in time-dependent models.[26]

Preliminaries. The GE structure that is developed in appendix A follows Golosov and Lucas (2007) and, in particular, Alvarez and Lippi

(2014). In this structure, what will determine the propagation of shocks up to first order will be price gaps; GE effects can be ignored by the firm, greatly simplifying the analysis. There are three reasons for this. First, it can be shown that after a monetary shock of size δ:

$$R(t) = r + \pi, \log \frac{W(t)}{\overline{W}(t)} = \delta \text{ for all } t \geq 0, \tag{15}$$

where $R(t)$ is the real interest rate, $\overline{W}(t)$ is the wage rate in steady state before the shock, and $W(t)$ is the wage rate after the shock. Thus, the real interest rate is unchanged by the shock and wages respond on impact. Furthermore, deviations of prices from steady state relate one-to-one to deviations on output according to:

$$\log \frac{c(t)}{\bar{c}} = \frac{1}{\varepsilon}\left(\delta - \log \frac{P(t)}{\overline{P}(t)}\right), \tag{16}$$

where $\bar{c}$ is the constant flexible price equilibrium output and where $P(t)$ is the ideal price index at time $t \geq 0$ and $\overline{P}(t)$ is the path of the price level in the steady state before the shock, with $\overline{P}(t) = e^{\pi t}\overline{P}$ for all $t \geq 0$. Second, as shown in Alvarez and Lippi (2014), the price level after a monetary shock can be approximated as a function of the price gaps. In particular, it can be shown that:

$$\log \frac{P(t)}{\overline{P}(t)} = \delta + \int_0^1 \left(\frac{1}{n}\sum_{i=1}^n (g_{ki}(t) - \tilde{g}_{ki})\right) dk$$

$$+ \int_0^1 \left(\sum_{i=1}^n o(||p_{ki}(t) - \tilde{p}_{ki}(t)||)\right) dk, \tag{17}$$

where $\tilde{g}_{ki}$ are the price gaps in the steady state *before* the shock and $o(x)$ denotes a function of order smaller than x.[27] Therefore, to understand the impact effect on prices of a monetary shock, it is sufficient to understand the effect of the monetary shock on price gaps. In addition, as we discussed in section III, in an approximation to the firms pricing problem we can ignore general equilibrium effects and focus only on price gaps. Third, it helps to reinterpret a simple cost shock, the one we will focus on, as the general equilibrium response of a closed economy to a once-and-for-all shock to the money supply. We start with a preshock path of wages $\overline{W}(t) = \overline{W}e^{\pi t}$ for $t \geq 0$ and a preshock steady-state equilibrium aggregate price level $\overline{P}(t) = \overline{P}e^{\pi t}$. Following the shock at time $t = 0$, under the simplifying assumptions discussed in appendix A, it can be shown that $W(t) = e^\delta \bar{W}(t)$ all $t \geq 0$. So, a monetary shock will imply raising wages on impact. This will imply a change in the price gaps and a reaction for some firms that will up to first order ignore general-equilbrium effects. The effect over price gaps will be aggregated into the price level up to first order. Finally, the deviations of the price level from the steady-state level will then imply deviation in output from its steady-state level.

Impulse Responses: Definitions and Some Properties. Regarding prices, the impulse response of prices can be defined as

$$\mathcal{P}(\delta, t; \pi) = \Theta(\delta; \pi) + \int_0^t \theta(\delta, s; \pi)ds. \qquad (18)$$

The impulse response is made of two parts: an instantaneous impact adjustment (a jump) of the aggregate price level, which occurs at the time of the shock, denoted by $\Theta(\delta; \pi)$, and a continuous flow of adjustments from $t > 0$ on, denoted by $\theta(\delta, t)$. In the next subsection we will study $\Theta(\delta)$. This statistic was first used by Caballero and Engel (1993, 2007), to summarize the degree of flexibility of an economy. We note a few properties of the impulse response of prices: (a) the impact effect is bounded by δ, (b) in the long term the shock is completely pass-through to prices, and (c) in the flexible price case prices jump on impact:

$$0 \leq \mathcal{P}(0, \delta; \pi) \equiv \Theta(\delta; \pi) \leq \delta, \lim_{t \to \infty} \mathcal{P}(t, \delta; \pi) = \delta, \text{ and } \mathcal{P}^{flex}(t, \delta; \pi) = \delta,$$

where we use the super-index *flex* for the flexible price case. Regarding output, in our GE version, output and prices are tightly negatively related after the shock, so we can easily compute the output effect. The negative relationship comes from the assumption that agents are on their labor supply schedule, and that nominal wages jump on impact. Thus the effect on output mirrors the one on real wages. This logic gives:

$$\mathcal{Y}(\delta, t; \pi) = \frac{1}{\varepsilon}[\delta - \mathcal{P}(\delta, t; \pi)], \qquad (19)$$

where $1/\varepsilon$ is a parameter describing the uncompensated labor supply elasticity, as described in appendix A. We define, as a summary measure of the impulse response, its cumulative version, that is, the area under equation (19)

$$\mathcal{M}(\delta; \pi) = \int_0^\infty \mathcal{Y}(\delta, t; \pi)dt. \qquad (20)$$

For the cumulative effect of output we also have

$$0 \leq \mathcal{Y}(0, \delta; \pi) \equiv \frac{1}{\varepsilon}[\delta - \Theta(\delta; \pi)] \leq \frac{\delta}{\varepsilon}, \lim_{t \to \infty} \mathcal{Y}(t, \delta; \pi) = 0 \text{ for all } \delta$$

$\mathcal{Y}^{flex}(t, \delta; \pi) = 0$ for all $t \geq 0$ and thus $\mathcal{M}^{flex}(\delta; \pi) = 0$ for all δ.

A. Small Shocks: SD and TD Models Are Identical on Impact

We now show that the impact effect of a monetary shock on prices is second order. This holds for all the models considered here, that is, those models with a general equilibrium set up as described in section A and with state-dependent decision rules as described in section III.B, and/or time-dependent decisions rules as described in section III.C, and/or those with features of both as described in section III.D.

We start by discussing the intuition of the impact effect of a monetary shock. Notice that equation (17) implies that the impact effect of a monetary shock is given by

$$\Theta(\delta; \pi) = \delta + \int_0^1 \left(\frac{1}{n} \sum_{i=1}^{n} [g_{ki}(0) - \tilde{g}_{ki}] \right) dk, \tag{21}$$

where $\tilde{g}_{ki}$ are the price gaps just before the monetary shock. Right after the monetary shocks price gaps will change to $g_{ki}(0)$. This change has two parts. First, mechanically, the log nominal wage increases by δ, so that every single price gap decreases by δ. Notice that this mechanical effect cancels with the first term δ on equation (18). Second, as a consequence of the changes in wages some firms may decide to adjust their prices right after the shock occurs (depending on the type of model), so that for those products and firms there is an extra change in the price gap $g_{ki}(0)$. To see this, notice that the price gap of firm k product i right after the shock can be decomposed as the price gap preshock $\tilde{g}_{ki}$ minus the common increase in wages δ plus the increase in prices $\log P_{ki}(0) - \log \tilde{P}_{ki}(0)$

$$g_{ki}(0) = \tilde{g}_{ki} - \delta + (\log P_{ki}(0) - \log \tilde{P}_{ki}(0)). \tag{22}$$

The first two terms are mechanical, and the third is the only one that depends on what the firms do. We introduce price gaps, instead of working directly with the price increases, due to two reasons. One is that in state-dependent models price gaps are the state, hence, it facilitates to understand what will happen. Second, in all models the contribution of a firm k product i to the output deviation from steady state can be written in terms of the price gap. The statement of the Proposition follows:

Proposition 1. *Let $\Theta(\delta; \pi)$, defined in equation (18), be the impact effect on the price level of a once-and-for-all monetary shock of size δ for an economy starting at steady-state inflation π. Fix the inflation rate π. If the decision rules are state dependent as in equation (9), and $\sigma > 0$, then:*

$$\Theta(\delta; \pi) = \Theta'(0; \pi)\delta + o(\delta) \quad \text{with} \quad \Theta'(0; \pi) \equiv \frac{\partial}{\partial \delta}\Theta(\delta; \pi)\bigg|_{\delta=0} = 0, \quad (23)$$

where $o(\delta)$ means of order smaller than δ. If the decision rules are time dependent as in equation (14), then:

$$\Theta(\delta; \pi) = 0 \text{ for all } \delta \text{ and for all } \pi. \quad (24)$$

The proposition states that there is no first-order effect of a small monetary shock in either a SD and as well as in a TD model. The result is stronger for time-dependent models in the sense that the impact effect is zero for any size of the monetary shock. We give a brief intuitive explanation of the result. Note that for both time- and state-dependent models, the aggregate shock increases wages by δ log points, and thus decreases every price gap. Firms in time- and state-dependent models react differently. In both cases, the firms that change their prices on impact will change, on average, by a discrete amount proportional to δ. Nevertheless, in both cases we will conclude that the fraction of firms that adjust on impact, denoted by $I(\delta)$ is of order smaller than δ, that is, we argue that $I'(0) = 0$. The argument why $I'(0) = 0$ is different for time- than for state-=dependent models.

In the case of state-dependent models described in section III.B, the reason why $I'(0) = 0$ is that the firm's decision to change prices depends on whether the state after the shock is outside the set of inaction $\mathcal{I}$. For instance, in the one product case $n = 1$, prices are adjusted when the price gap reaches either boundary of the range of inaction given by an interval $[\underline{g}, \overline{g}]$. A key argument in these models is that in steady state, right before the shock occurred, there is a zero density at the boundaries of the range of inaction. Then the fraction of firms that adjust is proportional to δ, for small δ. In particular, denoting by f the steady-state density of the price gaps, the fraction that adjusts equals $I(\delta) = \int_{\underline{g}}^{\underline{g}+\delta} f(g)dg = f(\underline{g})\delta + o(\delta)$. The fact that in steady state there is zero density around the boundary, that is, that $f(\underline{g}) = f(\overline{g}) = 0$, is a general feature of the state-dependent Ss decision rules with idiosyncratic shocks ($\sigma > 0$), and it is so because at the boundary of the range of inaction firms exit (i.e., prices are adjusted) when they get an idiosyncratic shock that will push them outside. Interestingly, this argument extends to multiproduct $n \geq 1$, with correlated shocks across products, and inaction sets given implicitly by ranges equation (9).

In the case of time-dependent models described in section III.C, the reason why $I'(0) = 0$ is that the firm's decision rules depend on the time elapsed since the last adjustment. Hence, even if the price gap changes, the firm will not be aware of it until the next review time (decided in the past) comes due. Finally, since the model is set in continuous time, on impact there is a negligible fraction of firms adjusting, that is, the number that adjusts in an interval of length dt equals $(1 / N(\Delta p_i; \pi))dt$. Hence, as $dt \to 0$, the fraction of firms that change prices to go zero and $I(\delta) \to 0$ for any δ! Note that we are assuming that the information about the change in the price gap due to change on wages is not observed until the time at which firms have previously scheduled their decision to learn the state, which is the key assumption of time-dependent models based on inattentiveness. The argument for models with both time- and state-dependent features, as in section III.D, is more complicated, but unsurprisingly the results still holds.

The Logic of the General Proof

The next paragraphs illustrate the logic of the proof of Proposition 1 for SD models in the general case with many goods and allows for correlated shocks across goods. The proof has two parts. The first part shows that the steady-state density f of price gaps g evaluated at the boundary of the inaction set is zero. We write this as Lemma 1 and include its proof in appendix B.

Lemma 1. *Assume $\sigma > 0$ for a SD model. Then, there is zero density at an exit point, that is, if $b(g) = 0$, then $f(g) = 0$.*

The logic of the result in Lemma 1 is easier to see in the one dimensional case ($n = 1$), which we present separately. The idea behind this result is that the boundary of the inaction set is an exit point, that is, if a firm price gap hits the boundary it will change the price, discretely changing the price gap. This behavior, where the steady-state mass "escapes" with nonnegligible probability to discretely far away regions of the state space implies that the steady-state density has to be zero (this is in contrast with the behavior everywhere else where the mass moves only to closed-by states). Specifically, consider a discrete state discrete space. We let the time periods be of length Δ and a state space for the price gap be of size $\sqrt{\Delta}\sigma$. The price gap $g(t + \Delta) - g(t) = \sqrt{\Delta}\sigma$ with probability $(1/2)[1 - \pi\sqrt{\Delta}/\sigma]$ and down to $-\sqrt{\Delta}\sigma$ with the complementary probability. Thus the expected change and expected square change of g per period are $-\pi\Delta$ and σ^Δ, respectively. The range of inaction is given by an interval $[\underline{g}, \overline{g}]$. We write the analog to the Kolmogorov forward equation in discrete time for the probability of each value g in the state space as for any $g \neq g^*$:

$$
f(g; \Delta) = \begin{cases}
f(g - \sqrt{\Delta}\sigma; \Delta)\dfrac{1}{2}\left[1 - \dfrac{\pi\sqrt{\Delta}}{\sigma}\right] & \text{for } g \leq \overline{g} \\[3ex]
\begin{aligned}
&f(g - \sqrt{\Delta}\sigma; \Delta)\dfrac{1}{2}\left[1 - \dfrac{\pi\sqrt{\Delta}}{\sigma}\right] \\[2ex]
&+ f(g + \sqrt{\Delta}\sigma; \Delta)\dfrac{1}{2}\left[1 + \dfrac{\pi\sqrt{\Delta}}{\sigma}\right]
\end{aligned} & \text{for } \underline{g} \leq g \leq \overline{g} \quad (25) \\[3ex]
f(g + \sqrt{\Delta}\sigma; \Delta)\dfrac{1}{2}\left[1 + \dfrac{\pi\sqrt{\Delta}}{\sigma}\right] & \text{for } g \geq \underline{g}.
\end{cases}
$$

At the upper bound we have:

$$
f(\overline{g}) = \lim_{\Delta\downarrow} f(\overline{g}; \Delta) = \lim_{\Delta\downarrow} f(\overline{g} - \sqrt{\Delta}\sigma; \Delta)\lim_{\Delta\downarrow}\frac{1}{2}\left[1 - \frac{\pi\sqrt{\Delta}}{\sigma}\right] = f(\overline{g})\frac{1}{2}, \quad (26)
$$

where we use that, provided that $\sigma > 0$, the density $f(\cdot)$ is continuous in the closure of the range on inaction in the first and last equalities. We obtain that the only possible solution of $f(\overline{g}) = f(\overline{g}) / 2$ is $f(\overline{g}) = 0$. An analogous argument shows that $f(\underline{g}) = 0$.

The second part shows that the impact effect on aggregate prices is of second order with respect to δ. In the general case, we define the fraction of firms (or price-gap vectors) that adjust prices in impact as $I(\delta)$ as

$$
I(\delta) = \int_{-\infty}^{\infty}\left[\cdots\int_{-\infty}^{\infty} f(g_1, g_2, \ldots, g_n)1_{\{b(g_1-\delta, g_2-\delta, \ldots, g_n-\delta)>0\}}dg_n \cdots\right]dg_1, \quad (27)
$$

where we use that $f(g) = 0$ if $b(g) < 0$. Thus $I(\delta)$ integrates using the density f the firms whose price gaps will be outside the set of inaction, that is, $b(g_1 - \delta, g_2 - \delta, \ldots, g_n - \delta) > 0$, after the aggregate shock δ. We set the second part as Lemma 2.

Lemma 2.   *Assume that there is no density on the boundary of the inaction set. Then, there is no first-order impact effect on prices, that is, $I'(0) = 0$.*

In the one dimensional case, Lemma 2 follows from direct computation of I and of its derivative, as shown in the text. The main idea is that the firms that change prices on impact for a small aggregate shock δ are those close to the lower boundary of the inaction set, since price gaps decrease all by δ. Thus if the density of price gaps are zero at the lower boundary, there is no first-order effect on the fraction of firms adjusting. The n-dimensional case is more involved, in this case the price gap for each firm is a vector for which each of its components decreases by δ with the shock. In the $n > 1$ case we also had to take into account a general (unknown) shape of the n-dimensional set of inaction and the correlation among the price gap from different products of the firm. In particular, in the $n > 1$ case there is no simple lower bound for the range on inaction as is in the one dimensional case. We prove Lemma 2 by finding a function $\bar{I}(\delta)$, which is a suitable upper bound for $I(\delta)$. The upper-bound function $\bar{I}(\delta)$, which is inspired by the one dimensional, also has zero derivative when evaluated at $\delta = 0$. While technically the proof is more involved, the logic is the same as in the one dimensional case: for a small aggregate shock δ the firm that will change its price in impact has to belong to the boundary of the set of inaction.

How the Impact Effect Varies with Inflation

We conclude the analysis of the impact effect with a discussion of the role of inflation, π, relative to the volatility of the idiosyncratic shocks σ. Let us focus on a positive monetary shock $\delta > 0$ in the reminder of this paragraph. This shock increases the desired price of all firms by an amount δ. First, we note that the impact effect is independent of the inflation rate in TD models just because, by assumption, decision rules do not depend on the state. But inflation does change the impact effect in SD models. In particular, while for finite values of the ratio π / σ the impact effect Θ is of order δ^2, as stated in equation (24) , we notice that the impact effect is increasing with π and that the effect becomes first order as $\pi / \sigma \to \infty$. This is the case, for instance, in the classic menu-cost models of Sheshinski and Weiss (1983) and Caplin and Spulber (1987): in both models the impact effect $\Theta(\delta)$ is of order δ, since in these models $\sigma = 0$ and $\pi > 0$, so that the ratio diverges. Thus, since the impact effect is second order but it is increasing in π, in the empirical analysis we will focus on low-inflation countries where the lack of response to small shocks should be easier to detect.

We briefly expand on the reason why in the case of $n = 1$, as π / σ increases, the impact effect of an aggregate monetary shock increases. As explained above, the first-order term on $\Theta(\delta, \pi)$ is given by the invariant density $f(g, \pi)$. A straightforward analysis of the Kolmogorov forward equation solved by f shows that as inflation rises relative to the variance of the idiosyncratic shock σ^2, the shape of $f(\cdot, \pi)$ changes in the segment $[\underline{g}, g^*]$ as follows. The density f is linear in g for $\pi = 0$, and it becomes concave in g for $\pi > 0$, with curvature $-f''(g, \pi) / f'(g, \pi) = 2\pi / \sigma^2$. In the limit as $\pi / \sigma^2 \to \infty$ the density $f(g)$ is strictly positive, and $f(\cdot)$ is constant, so that there is a first-order effect. Note that this is the case in the classical analysis of Sheshinski and Weiss (1983) and Caplin and Spulber (1987), because there are no idiosyncraric shocks $\sigma = 0$. The reason why the invariant distribution "piles up" more density around $\underline{g}$ as inflation rises is straightforward: the price gaps drift to $\underline{g}$ at speed π, and they only go up when they are hit by a positive idiosyncratic shock (with variance σ^2).

In appendix F we formally analyze how the impact effect varies with inflation around small inflation rates. For simplicity we focus on a model with one good $n = 1$ and assume the adjustment thresholds $\overline{g}, \underline{g}$ and optimal return point g^* are fixed at the level corresponding to zero inflation.[28] Since $f(\underline{g}; \pi) = 0$, expanding the first nonzero term of the impact effect Θ as a function of the inflation rate we can obtain that:

$$\Theta(\delta; \pi) = \frac{1}{2} f'(\underline{g}; \pi)\delta^2 + o(\delta) \approx \frac{1}{2}[f'(\underline{g}; 0) + f'_\pi(\underline{g}; 0)\pi]\delta^2$$

$$= \frac{1}{2}\left[\frac{1}{\overline{g}^2} + \frac{1}{\sigma^2\overline{g}}\pi\right]\delta^2$$

$$= \frac{1}{Std\,[\Delta p_i]}\left[\frac{2}{Std\,[\Delta p_i]} + \frac{\pi}{\sigma^2}\right]\delta^2.$$

The approximation shows that the impact effect is increasing in the ratio π / σ^2, since around zero inflation the steady-state standard deviation of price changes is given by $Std[\Delta p_i] = 2\overline{g}$.

Finally, we note that in both TD and SD models a higher inflation rate tends to increase the average number of price adjustments per unit of time $N(\Delta p_i; \pi)$, even though the elasticity of the frequency of price adjustment to the inflation rate is zero at $\pi = 0$ in models with $\sigma > 0$ (see

Alvarez et al. [2011] and Alvarez, Le Bihan, and Lippi [2016] for formal proofs). This implies that for small rates of inflation (or deflation) the frequency of price adjustments is very close to the frequency that occurs at zero inflation (see Alvarez and Lippi [2014] for a formal proof). In practice, this theoretical prediction is consistent with evidence on the small elasticity of the frequency of price changes in Gagnon (2009) and Alvarez et al. (2015), who show that the frequency is basically insensitive to inflation for rates between 5 and 10% (in absolute value).

B.   Small Shocks: SD and TD Have Identical Cumulated Propagation

The next result uses a simple GE model to characterize the cumulative output effect, $\mathcal{M}(\delta, \pi)$, of a shock δ. We focus on the cumulative output effects, namely, the area under the output impulse response function to a monetary shock because it is a measure of the real effects of monetary policy that naturally combines the duration of the output response with the depth of the response. We show that this effect is well approximated by the ratio of two steady-state statistics: $N(\Delta p_i; \pi)$, the average number of price adjustments per unit of time, and $Kurt(\Delta p_i; \pi)$, the kurtosis of the size distribution of (nonzero) price changes. These two statistics, in turn, depend on all the structural parameters of a particular model. But once the models for which the proposition applies are matched with these two statistics, then these models will have the same cumulative effect after a small monetary shock.

Proposition 2.   *Let $\mathcal{M}(\delta; \pi)$, defined in equation (20), be the cumulative impulse response of output to a once-and-for-all monetary shock of size δ for an economy starting at steady-state inflation π. Then*

$$\mathcal{M}(\delta; \pi) = \frac{Kurt(\Delta p_i; 0)}{\varepsilon 6 N(\Delta p_i; 0)}\delta + o(\|(\delta, \pi)\|^2), \qquad (28)$$

where $o(x)$ means of order smaller than x. Moreover,

$$\frac{\partial}{\partial \pi}\left(\frac{Kurt(\Delta p_i; \pi)}{N(\Delta p_i; \pi)}\right)\Bigg|_{\pi=0} = 0. \qquad (29)$$

The explanation of why this result holds is involved, but its interpretation is not. The ratio in equation (28) controls for both the selection effect, as measured by $Kurt(\Delta p_i; \pi)$, and for the degree of flexibility of the economy, as measured by $N(\Delta p_i; \pi)$. On the one hand, that the cumulative impulse response depends on the degree of flexibility is hardly surprising. On the other hand, that the selection effect is captured completely by the steady-state kurtosis of prices is, at least to us, more surprising. The role of kurtosis is more novel and embodies the extent to which "selection" in the size as well as in the timing of price changes occurs.[29] The selection effect, a terminology introduced by Golosov and Lucas (2007), indicates that firms that change prices after the monetary shock are the firms whose prices are in greatest need of adjustment, a hallmark of SD models. Selection gives rise to large price adjustments after the shock, so that the CPI response is fast.[30] Such selection is absent in TD models where the adjusting firms are chosen based on (possibly stochastic functions of) calendar time, not based on their state. In addition to selection in the *size* of price changes, recent contributions have highlighted a related selection effect in TD models that relates to the *timing* of price changes.[31] Surprisingly, the kurtosis of the steady-state distribution of the size of price changes also encodes this type of selection, which is central to TD models. For instance, in the models of Taylor and Calvo, calibrated to the same mean frequency of price changes $N(\Delta p_i)$, the *size* of the average price change across adjusting firms is constant (after a monetary shock), so there is no selection concerning the size. Yet the real cumulative output effect in Calvo is twice the effect in Taylor. This happens because in Taylor the time elapsed between adjustments is a constant $T = 1 / N(\Delta p_i)$, while in Calvo it has an exponential distribution (with mean T), with a thick right tail of firms that adjust very late.[32] This paper collects and extends previous results by showing that equation (28) also holds for models with both TD and SD components. Formally, the result is shown for SD models in Alvarez, Le Bihan, and Lippi (2016) and the result for TD models in Alvarez, Lippi, and Paciello (2016) for the case of $n = 1$ products.[33] For the multiproduct version of the Calvo$^+$ model, which showcases features of both SD and TD models, the result is also shown in Alvarez, Le Bihan, and Lippi (2016).[34] In particular, appendix G provides numerical evidence that the result also holds in models that combine those frictions. Also, in that appendix this result is illustrated by aggregating and computing the impulse response of a decisions rules for a price-setting problem with both a menu cost as well as an observation cost, based on Alvarez, Lippi, and Paciello (2011, 2015, 2016).[35]

Extending the Expression for the Area under the Impulse Response for TD Models to n Products

Here we argue that Propositions 1 and 2 in Alvarez, Lippi, and Paciello (2016) hold with no changes for the $n > 1$ case, which establishes Proposition 2 for the TD case. Consider the TD model in its multiproduct version. Alvarez, Lippi, and Paciello (2016) show that equation (28) holds for that model with $n = 1$. This result extends in a straightforward way to the multiproduct case of $n > 1$. To see why, let τ be the time elapsed between observations, noticing that since the menu cost is zero, τ, it is also the time between price changes. Recall that when an observation occurs every single product of the firm change its price, "closing" its gaps (this, instead, extends from the one to the n products, since it only requires the symmetry or exchangeability and the lack of drift). Thus the state of the economy is still the distribution of times until the next review, the same as the one dimensional object in Alvarez, Lippi, and Paciello (2016) denoted by $Q(t)$ with density $q(t)$. At the time of the adjustment (or of the observation) we can then consider each of the n products of the firms in isolation. This is because the marginal distribution of the price gaps of each of the n products is the same, and hence the result is identical. Note that this result holds even if the price gaps have an arbitrary correlation between the products of the same firm. It only requires that the marginal distribution of each price gaps be normal.

The expression in equation (28) can be regarded as a *second-order* approximation to $\mathcal{M}(\delta; \pi)$. This expression means that

$$0 = \frac{\partial \mathcal{M}(0, 0)}{\partial \pi} = \frac{\partial^2 \mathcal{M}(0, 0)}{\partial \delta^2} = \frac{\partial^2 \mathcal{M}(0, 0)}{\partial \pi^2} = \frac{\partial^2 \mathcal{M}(0, 0)}{\partial \delta \, \partial \pi}, \qquad (30)$$

that is, the approximation in equation (28) holds up to second order, and thus it is very accurate for small values of δ and π. There are two different arguments for why these derivatives are zero. First, relative to π, note that by definition $\mathcal{M}(0, \pi) = 0$ for all π, since when there is no shock there is no response. Thus, all derivatives with respect to π are zero at $\delta = 0$. The reason why the second derivatives, especially the one with respect to δ, are zero is due to the symmetry of the $\mathcal{M}$ function. In particular, $\mathcal{M}(\delta; \pi) = -\mathcal{M}(-\delta; -\pi)$. This means that the effect of prices and output when there is a negative shock in an economy with deflation is the same (in absolute) value than an economy with inflation and a positive shock. Thus taking any second derivative of this function, and evaluating at $(\delta, \pi) = (0, 0)$, we obtain the desired result. Thus, the key is to argue the symmetry of this function. This in turn depends, among other things, on the use of the second-order approximation of the profit function, as developed in equation (41), to argue for the symmetry of the optimal decision rules. Finally we explain the significance of the fact that the approximation itself has zero derivative with respect to inflation, that is, the importance of equation (29). This means that the expression for $\mathcal{M}(\delta; \pi)$ is accurate for economies with low inflation rates.

In principle, microdata on prices can be used to construct empirical measures of kurtosis. In constructing such measures, care must be taken of small measurement errors (lots of small price changes are just noise) and heterogeneity (pooling together goods with different volatility of price changes), which may mechanically contribute to generating a high value of kurtosis, as stressed in Cavallo and Rigobon (2016). Section 2 of Alvarez, Le Bihan, and Lippi (2016) uses such statistical procedures and estimated kurtosis values in the neighborhood of 4. This is useful to decide "where the data stand" between a Golosov-Lucas model (with kurtosis 1) versus a Calvo model (with kurtosis 6).

Three Examples

To illustrate the point that models with different degrees of time and state dependence can generate the same cumulative output response after a permanent shock, we describe three setups that give the same value of $\mathcal{M}$ for small δ in spite of their different nature and steady-state behavior in other dimensions than those involved by the formula in equation (28). We concentrate on describing $Kurt(\Delta p_i; 0)$, since in all these models it is easy to change other parameters, such as the fixed adjustment or observation cost, to produce the same value of $N(\Delta p_i; 0)$. We focus on three examples where $Kurt(\Delta p_i) = 3$. The first example is a state-dependent model with many products, that is, with $n \rightarrow \infty$. This model produces a size distribution of price changes that is normal (see Alvarez and Lippi [2014] for a proof), so that the kurtosis equals 3. The second example is a pure time-dependent model, with constant observation cost $\psi_o > 0$ (and zero menu cost $\psi_m = 0$). This model is analyzed by, for example, Reis (2006), and like the previous model it also produces a size distribution of price changes that is normal, so its kurtosis equals to 3. While the first two models have identical steady-state statistics in terms of distribution of adjustment times and the size distribution of price changes, the third one is different. The third example is the so-called Calvo-plus model of Nakamura and Steinsson (2010). In this model $n = 1$ and while some prices occur upon the arrival of a free adjustment opportunities, other are decided by the firm after paying the menu cost. Alvarez, Le Bihan, and Lippi (2016) show that if the fraction of price adjustment due to free adjustment opportunities is 90%, then the model produces a kurtosis of the size of price changes that is equal to 3 (although the distribution function of the size of price changes is not normal). Notice that these three models are set up to have the same mean duration between price adjustments, but other moments of the distribution of adjustment times will differ. Moreover, the models also differ in terms of the nature of the friction (menu cost versus observation). In spite of these differences, Proposition 2 states that the cumulative output effect of a small monetary shock is identical in these models.

C. Large Shocks: State and Time-Dependent Models Differ

In this section we examine the impact effect on prices of large shocks. The result differs between time- and state-dependent models. For time-dependent models, the size of the monetary shock δ is immaterial. Instead, for state-dependent models, large shocks behave differently than small shocks.

Proposition 3.   *Consider the impact effect of a once-and-for-all change in money of size δ for an economy at steady state with inflation rate π. Then in a time-dependent model as in section III.C we have:*

$$\Theta(\delta; \pi) = 0 \text{ for all } \delta \geq 0, \tag{31}$$

while in a state-dependent model, as in section III.B, with $\eta = \rho$ and no correlation between the idiosyncratic shocks across the products of the firm ($\bar{\sigma} > 0$) we have:

$$\frac{\partial \Theta(\delta; 0)}{\partial \delta} \geq 0 \text{ with } \frac{\Theta(\delta; 0)}{\delta} \to 1 \text{ as } \delta \to 2Std(\Delta p_i; 0), \tag{32}$$

and in the general state-dependent decision rules as in equation (9) with $\sigma > 0$, for each π there is a $\bar{\delta}(\pi)$ such that:

$$\Theta(\delta; \pi) = \delta \text{ for all } \delta \geq \bar{\delta}(\pi). \tag{33}$$

The explanation why the effect of monetary shocks in time-dependent models is independent of the size of the monetary shock δ, is familiar from the Calvo model, and it is the exactly the same as the one given for small shocks. The fact that for state-dependent models the impact effect is different for large versus small shocks is the hallmark of fixed cost-adjustment models. Put simply, when the shock is large enough, a large fraction of firms will pay the fixed cost and adjust. Interestingly, equation (32) gives a hint of when a shock is large enough so that all the firms will adjust immediately, namely when the shock δ is larger than the steady-state standard deviation of price changes. This result can be easily seen in the case of $n = 1$ product, since the standard deviation of price changes $Std(\Delta p_i) = \bar{g}$, since price changes are $\pm\bar{g}$ with the same probability. Recall that in this case the distribution of price gaps in the steady state right before the shock lies in the interval $[-\bar{g}, \bar{g}]$. Thus, when the shock is large enough so that $\delta > 2\bar{g}$, then every single firm will find that right after the shock has its price gap outside the range of inaction. A similar reasoning holds for any number of products, that is, for $n \geq 1$. The proof of the result in equation (32) and a characterization of this function are developed in Proposition 8(iii) and Proposition 10 of Alvarez and Lippi (2014).

In the general case, fixing all the parameters that define the set of inaction, one can find a value of δ that is large enough so that every price gap vector after the aggregate shock is outside the set of inaction, that is, $(g_1 - \delta, g_2 - \delta, \ldots, g_n - \delta) \notin \mathcal{I}$. This only requires that the set of inaction $\mathcal{I} \subset \mathbb{R}^n$ is bounded. Thus, one can take $\bar{\delta}(\pi)$ to be the difference between the largest and smallest values in $\mathcal{I}$.[36] Alvarez, Le Bihan, and Lippi (2016) characterize $\bar{\delta}(0)$, the smallest value of the aggregate shock δ for which all firms adjust their prices on impact for a multiproduct Calvo⁺ model. In this case, for each value of $n \geq 1$ the threshold $\bar{\delta}(0)$ is a function of $\ell \in [0, 1]$, the fraction of all price changes that occur due to the Calvo parameters. As ℓ increases, the value of $\bar{\delta}(0)$ also increases, and indeed as $\ell \to 1$ then $\bar{\delta} \to \infty$. This is quite intuitive: as the importance of the time dependence of the decision rules increase (i.e., as ℓ increases), then threshold for the aggregate shock $\bar{\delta}$ increases.

V. Some Exploratory Evidence

In this section we exploit the predictions of Propositions 1 and 3 to explore the nature of the friction that underlies a sticky response to shocks. As discussed above, on the one hand theory predicts that with time dependent rules the impact effect is independent of the size of the shock. On the other hand, with state dependent rules theory predicts that the impact effect is second order for small shocks and first order for large shocks. Thus, if the impact of a cost shock on prices depends on the size of the shock, the evidence will point towards state dependence. In the empirical exploration, in particular, we study whether changes on the exchange rate of different sizes imply a differential effect for inflation at different horizons after the shock. We focus on low inflation countries since the approximation of Propositions 1 and 3 is accurate, as discussed in Section 4, for low levels of inflation. In addition, we study the period post Bretton Woods, so that changes in the exchange rate better approximate an unexpected and permanent shock in costs. Overall, in our exploratory results, we find some evidence of non-linear effects. This evidence is stronger for flexible exchange countries. We will discuss the dimensions in which this result is robust, and the ones in which it is not.

A. Data

We start from the whole sample of Consumer Price Index and Exchange rate data from the International Financial Statistics database from the IMF. For the CPI index we use "CPI of all items." For the Exchange rate we use the end-of-period exchange rate in units of domestic currency per unit of US dollars.[37] With this data we construct an initial unbalanced panel $\{\pi_{i,t}, \Delta e_{i,t}\}_{i \in \mathcal{I}, t \in T_i}$ where $\mathcal{I}$ is the set of all countries and T_i is the set of dates for which observations are available for country i. To be consistent with the setups described in sections III and IV, we restrict the sample in two dimensions. First, by focusing on low-inflation countries. As discussed in section IV, the result that the impact effect is second order for state-dependent models, Proposition 1, is accurate for low levels of inflation because as inflation increases the higher-order terms also increase. Still, to identify the effects of large shocks, large devaluations/revaluations are needed in the sample and these events are sometimes associated with countries experiencing moderate and high inflation rates. With this trade-off in mind, we restrict the sample as follows: we include the inflation rate of country i in period t in the sample if the 10-year moving average of annual inflation is less than 8% (for our baseline specification).[38] Second, we further restrict the sample by focusing on the observations after Bretton Woods. The once-and-for-all monetary shock has two main features: it is unexpected and permanent. The evidence in this direction favors flexible exchange rate countries. To classify a country as a flexible exchange rate country, we follow the classifications of Reinhart and Rogoff (2004), Ilzetzki, Reinhart, and Rogoff (2008), and Levy-Yeyati and Sturzenegger (2003). With these two restrictions, we obtain a (unbalanced) panel for our main specification.[39]

Table 1 summarizes inflation, devaluations, and other main features of our panel data (see table H1 in appendix H for more information). There are 13,025 observations in the main sample. The panel is unbal-

Table 1
Descriptive Statistics

Sample	Mean(π)	SD(π)	Mean(Δe)	SD(Δe)	No. Large Innovations| Δe |		
					>7%	>10%	>15%
Post–1974 Sample, Inflation Threshold 8%							
All countries (13,025 obs.)	3.51	3.76	0.08	2.81	368	131	22
No fixed ER (6,137 obs.)	3.14	3.38	0.14	3.00	229	88	18
Post–1990 Sample, Inflation Threshold 8%							
All countries (8,488 obs.)	2.95	2.80	0.13	2.87	272	109	18
No fixed ER (5,010 obs.)	2.76	2.75	0.19	3.07	204	82	16

Note: Inflation π is the 12-month percentage change of the CPI. The innovations \| Δe \| are the percent depreciation (or appreciation) of the bilateral nominal exchange rate versus the US dollar over a one-month period. The criterion for including a country-month observation in the sample is that the 60-month moving average inflation in that month is below 8% (per year) and a per-capita GDP in that country-month of at least $5,000 (PPP).

anced because of different data availability among countries for the CPI and exchange rate data and because countries enter and exit the sample over time depending on their inflation rates. For inflation, we report the mean and volatility of annual inflation. For devaluation, we report mean and volatility of our main independent variable, monthly devaluation. Note that the mean devaluation is not zero, but the mean is usually at least an order of magnitude smaller than the volatility. The number of devaluations/revaluations that are higher than 7, 10, and 15% are 368, 131, and 22, respectively. Our preferred specification focuses on the sample of countries that are not classified as fixed exchange rate regimes by Ilzetzki, Reinhart, and Rogoff (2008). For this sample, mean and volatility of inflation is slightly higher and the number of devaluations/revaluations that are higher than 7, 10, and 15% are 229, 88, and 18, respectively.

B.   Specification

Our baseline specification is given by:

$$\pi_{i,(t,t+h)} = \alpha_i + \delta_t + \beta_h \Delta e_{i,t} + \gamma_h (\Delta e_{i,t})^2 sign(\Delta e_{i,t}) + \varepsilon_{it}^\pi, \qquad (34)$$

where $\pi_{i,(t,t+h)}$ is the inflation rate of country i on the period from date t to date $t + h$, Δe_t is the devaluation from date $t - 1$ to date t, and both variables are measured in percent, so that $\Delta e_{i,t} = 1$ is 1%.[40] The structural innovation is given by ε_{it}^π. The first term in the regression is a fixed effect for country i that captures unobserved effects that are constant over time (e.g., the average inflation rate). The second term is a time fixed effect that captures aggregate shocks that are common to the whole group of countries. The third term is the linear component of the pass-through where the coefficient β_h measures the impact of a devaluation on period t over inflation on the period that goes from t to $t + h$. The fourth term measures whether large changes in the exchange rate have a higher pass-through. If this is the case for horizon h we should expect that $\gamma_h > 0$. Note that the $sign(\cdot)$ operator is introduced for symmetry.[41]

One note of caution is due: the regression coefficient can be interpreted as a measure of the response of inflation to an exogenous nominal exchange rate innovation under the assumption that the shock is orthogonal to the other regressors and unanticipated. This assumption, which gave us a motive to focus on flexible exchange rate countries where exchange rates are close to random walks, must be taken with caution. First, the specification implies that changes in inflation do not feed back in devaluation by directly assuming that the nominal exchange rate follows a random walk with its own structural shocks. Second, it can be the case that large swings on the exchange rate are associated with some particular observable or unobservable economic conditions that are not modeled; that is, shocks to the exchange rate are not orthogonal. For example, a large devaluation might occur after a sustained appreciation of the real exchange rate. In this case, a large devaluation could imply a lower pass through (see, e.g., Burstein, Eichenbaum, and Rebelo 2005; Burstein and Gopinath 2014). In addition, devaluations might occur during bad times, as in Kehoe and Ruhl (2009), or might actually occur as the equilibrium response to real shocks as suggested in Burstein, Eichenbaum, and Rebelo (2007).

C. Main Results

The results for our main specification are in table 2. Overall, we find some evidence of nonlinear effects. In particular, we find a statistically significant correlation between large devaluations/revaluations and higher inflation transmission for the complete sample and for the sample where we restrict to countries not classified as having fixed an exchange rate regime as defined in Ilzetzki, Reinhart, and Rogoff (2008). First, in the top panel of table 2 we report the results of a panel regression of equation (34) for the sample excluding fixed exchange rate countries post-1974. As one would expect, the total pass-through

Table 2
Inflation Pass-Through: Baseline Specification

	1974–2014 Sample, Excluding Fixed ER Countries (6,811 Obs.)				
Horizon h:	1 Month	3 Months	6 Months	12 Months	24 Months
β_h (linear term)	0.009**	0.027***	0.056***	0.053***	0.098***
	(0.004)	(0.008)	(0.012)	(0.016)	(0.023)
$\gamma_h \times 100$ (quadratic term)	0.114***	0.152***	0.104	0.111	−0.060
	(0.027)	(0.054)	(0.106)	(0.133)	(0.158)
R^2	0.20	0.31	0.41	0.51	0.62

	1974–2014 Sample, All Countries (13,723 Obs.)				
Horizon h:	1 Month	3 Months	6 Months	12 Months	24 Months
β_h (linear term)	0.019***	0.039***	0.062***	0.091***	0.184***
	(0.004)	(0.010)	(0.013)	(0.021)	(0.024)
$\gamma_h \times 100$ (quadratic term)	0.058**	0.166	0.097	0.104	−0.448***
	(0.028)	(0.112)	(0.140)	(0.257)	(0.149)
R^2	0.11	0.19	0.28	0.39	0.46

	1990–2014 Sample, All Countries (9,179 Obs.)				
horizon h:	1 Month	3 Months	6 Months	12 Months	24 Months
β_h (linear term)	0.009***	0.033***	0.060***	0.074***	0.109***
	(0.003)	(0.006)	0.009)	(0.012)	(0.019)
$\gamma_h \times 100$ (quadratic term)	0.088***	0.105**	0.008	−0.088	−0.314***
	(0.021)	(0.045)	(0.066)	(0.073)	(0.107)
R^2	0.17	0.28	0.37	0.47	0.53

Note: All regressions include time and country fixed effects. Exchange rates for all countries except the United States are expressed as the bilateral exchange rate with the United States, and as the effective exchange rate for the United States. The sample excluding fixed ER countries drops countries with a preannounced or de facto peg, crawling peg, or band narrower than ±2% using the Ilzetzki, Reinhart, and Rogoff (2008) exchange rate regime classification. The criterion for including a country-month observation in the sample is that the 60-month moving average inflation in that month is below 8% (per year) and a per-capita GDP in that country-month of at least $5,000 (PPP). Robust standard errors in parenthesis. See section V for details.
***Significant at the 1% level.
**Significant at the 5% level.
*Significant at the 10% level.

of exchange rate into prices increases with the horizon; from 0.01 after one month to around 0.1 after two years for a 1% shock. The nonlinear component of the pass-through is statistically different from zero, and it is quantitatively relevant for large shocks. The estimated coefficients imply that a devaluation (revaluation) of 10% is associated with a 0.2% point of increase in the inflation rate on impact. The nonlinear component is significant at the three-month horizon. Second, in the mid-panel we report the estimates of equation (34) obtained when using all countries (i.e., not tossing those classified as fixed exchange rate regimes). In this case, the nonlinear component decreases, but it is still statistically significant. We notice that in this sample the total pass-through is higher at every horizon compared to the sample that excludes "fixed exchange rate countries," both through the linear and nonlinear component. The inclusion in the sample of countries that are on a fixed exchange rate arrangement also gives rise, across several specifications, to a significant and negative coefficient for the nonlinear term at the 24-month horizon. None of the theories that we reviewed can fit this pattern, which we find puzzling. We conjecture that this may be related to the low pass-through of large devaluations that can happen (in countries on a fixed exchange rate regime) as a response to a persistent misalignment of the real exchange rate, as documented in Burstein, Eichenbaum, and Rebelo (2005), and Burstein and Gopinath (2014). Finally, in the bottom panel of table 2 we restrict to a sample with both fixed and flexible exchange rate countries, but with observations after 1990. The nonlinear component is again significant, with a smaller overall pass-through than in the middle panel. This is consistent with the evidence of a lower pass-through post-1990 discussed in Taylor (2000).

D. Robustness

We perform six robustness checks (corresponding to table 3 to table 8) to our main specification and sample (table 2). The results are robust to a different nonlinear specification (table 3), to the definition of low inflation country (table 4), to the removal of time fixed effects (table 5), to the exclusion of countries whose exchange rate regime is unclassified (table 6), and to a different classification of exchange rate regimes (table 7). Instead, the results lose statistical significance if we remove "outliers" as identified by the largest devaluation (table 8). We next discuss each one of these robustness checks in more detail.

In table 3 we show that the results are robust to a different nonlinear specification. In particular, we estimate the following:

$$\pi_{i,(t,t+h)} = \alpha_i + \delta_t + \beta_h \Delta e_{i,t} + \gamma_h \Delta e_{i,t} \mathcal{I}(|\Delta e_{i,t}| > K) + \varepsilon_{it}^\pi, \qquad (36)$$

where the only difference with equation (34) is the introduction of $\mathcal{I}(|\Delta e_t| > K)$, as an indicator of whether the devaluation (or revaluation) in period t was higher than $K\%$ in absolute value instead of the qua-

Table 3
Inflation Pass-Through: Piecewise Linear Specification

	1974–2014 Sample, Excluding Fixed ER Countries (6,816 Obs.)				
Horizon h:	1 Month	3 Months	6 Months	12 Months	24 Months
β_h (linear term)	0.015***	0.034***	0.058***	0.058***	0.094***
	(0.004)	(0.007)	(0.009)	(0.014)	(0.020)
$\gamma_h \times 100$ (nonlinear term)	0.017**	0.027*	0.027	0.019	−0.006
	(0.008)	(0.016)	(0.023)	(0.035)	(0.049)
R^2	0.30	0.45	0.41	0.51	0.62

	1974–2014 Sample, All Countries (13,733 Obs.)				
Horizon h:	1 Month	3 Months	6 Months	12 Months	24 Months
β_h (linear term)	0.022***	0.047***	0.064***	0.092***	0.157***
	(0.004)	(0.007)	(0.010)	(0.014)	(0.022)
$\gamma_h \times 100$ (nonlinear term)	0.012*	0.027	0.029	0.033	−0.047
	(0.007)	(0.018)	(0.024)	(0.038)	(0.046)
R^2	0.16	0.26	0.28	0.39	0.46

	1990–2014 Sample, All Countries (9,184 Obs.)				
Horizon h:	1 Month	3 Months	6 Months	12 Months	24 Months
β_h (linear term)	0.014***	0.038***	0.059***	0.072***	0.100***
	(0.003)	(0.005)	(0.007)	(0.011)	(0.017)
$\gamma_h \times 100$ (nonlinear term)	0.014**	0.017	0.004	−0.020	−0.066**
	(0.006)	(0.011)	(0.014)	(0.022)	(0.032)
R^2	0.30	0.44	0.37	0.47	0.53

Note: All regressions include time and country fixed effects. Exchange rates for all countries except the United States are expressed as the bilateral exchange rate with the United States, and as the effective exchange rate for the United States. The sample excluding fixed ER countries drops countries with a preannounced or de facto peg, crawling peg, or band narrower than ±2% using the Ilzetzki, Reinhart, and Rogoff (2008) exchange rate regime classification. The piecewise linear specification uses a threshold for large devaluations equal to 10%. The criterion for including a country-month observation in the sample is that the 60-month moving average inflation in that month is below 8% (per year) and a per-capita GDP in that country-month of at least $5,000 (PPP). Robust standard errors in parenthesis. See section V for details.
***Significant at the 1% level.
**Significant at the 5% level.
*Significant at the 10% level.

dratic term. We report results for $K = 10$, but we also check robustness for $K = 5, 20$. There is evidence of nonlinearity for the sample of countries that are not classified as a fixed exchange rate regime. The evidence is weaker for the sample of all countries. The linear portion of the pass-through is in line with the one for the main specification in table 2. We also run a nonlinear specification with a cubic nonlinear term (instead of the quadratic) and the results are similar (table not displayed).

In table 4 we show that the results are robust to a different definition of low-inflation country. We run the baseline specification under different samples depending on the inflation threshold that we use for the moving average. Recall that in the main sample an observation for country i in period t is in the sample if $\pi_{i,t}^{MA} = (\sum_{k=-60}^{k=60} \pi_{i,t+k}) / 120 \le \mathcal{K} = 8$. We find that, if the threshold used is too low, for example, a $\mathcal{K} = 4$, the nonlinear term γ_h is not significant. This is also the case if the inflation

Table 4
Robustness: Inflation Pass-Through on Impact (1 Month)

	1974–2014 Sample: All Countries				
Inflation threshold below:	4%	5%	6%	8%	10%
Nonlinear effect	×	✓✓✓	✓✓	✓✓	×
No. obs.	8,263	9,774	11,030	13,723	16,157
	1974–2014 Sample: Excluding Fixed ER Countries				
Inflation threshold below:	4%	5%	6%	8%	10%
Nonlinear effect	×	✓✓✓	✓✓✓	✓✓✓	×
No. obs.	4,566	5,240	5,795	6,811	7,587
	1990–2014 Sample: All Countries				
Inflation threshold below:	4%	5%	6%	8%	10%
Nonlinear effect	×	✓✓✓	✓✓✓	✓✓✓	✓
No. obs.	6,678	7,651	8,314	9,179	9,813
	1990–2014 Sample: Excluding Fixed ER Countries				
Inflation threshold below:	4%	5%	6%	8%	10%
Nonlinear effect	×	✓✓✓	✓✓✓	✓✓✓	✓
No. obs.	4,227	4,751	5,145	5,684	5,997

Note: All regressions include time and country fixed effects. Standard errors are computed using Stata robust options to deal with minor problems about normality, heteroscedasticity, or some observations that exhibit large residuals, leverage, or influence. The sample excluding fixed ER countries drops countries with a preannounced or de facto peg, crawling peg, or band narrower than ±2% using the Ilzetzki, Reinhart, and Rogoff (2008) exchange rate regime classification. The criterion for including a country-month observation in the sample is that the 60-month moving average inflation in that month is below 8% (per year) and a per-capita GDP in that country-month of at least $5,000 (PPP).
✓✓✓ Significant at the 1% level.
✓✓ Significant at the 5% level.
✓ Significant at the 10% level.
× Not statistically different from zero at the 10% level.

threshold is set too high. For example, for a threshold of 10%, results are not significant for the post-1974 samples, and significant at 10% confidence level for the post-1990 sample. Still, the nonlinear term cannot be rejected for the thresholds of 5, 6, and 8% for the samples post-1974 and post-1990 for all countries.

In table 5 we show that the results are robust to removing time fixed

Table 5
Inflation Pass-Through: Excluding Time Fixed Effects

	1974–2014 Sample, Excluding Fixed ER Countries (6,811 Obs.)				
Horizon h:	1 Month	3 Months	6 Months	12 Months	24 Months
β_h (linear term)	−0.005	−0.000	0.008	0.000	−0.016
	(0.003)	(0.006)	(0.011)	0.015)	(0.022)
$\gamma_h \times 100$ (quadratic term)	0.119***	0.172***	0.193	0.168	0.102
	(0.027)	(0.056)	(0.123)	(0.146)	(0.177)
R^2	0.05	0.11	0.18	0.28	0.40

	1974–2014 Sample, All Countries (13,723 Obs.)				
Horizon h:	1 Month	3 Months	6 Months	12 Months	24 Months
β_h (linear term)	0.013***	0.026***	0.031***	0.058***	0.096***
	(0.004)	(0.008)	(0.012)	(0.019)	(0.022)
$\gamma_h \times 100$ (quadratic term)	0.039	0.117	0.132	0.072	−0.326*
	(0.035)	(0.101)	(0.140)	(0.258)	(0.186)
R^2	0.02	0.06	0.11	0.17	0.23

	1990–2014 Sample, All Countries (9,179 Obs.)				
Horizon h:	1 Month	3 Months	6 Months	12 Months	24 Months
β_h (linear term)	−0.005*	0.001	0.002	0.001	−0.006
	(0.002)	(0.005)	(0.008)	(0.011)	(0.016)
$\gamma_h \times 100$ (quadratic term)	0.108***	0.154***	0.165*	0.069	−0.063
	(0.021)	(0.045)	(0.090)	(0.088)	(0.112)
R^2	0.05	0.11	0.18	0.27	0.38

Note: All regressions include country fixed effects. Exchange rates for all countries except the United States are expressed as the bilateral exchange rate with the United States, and as the effective exchange rate for the United States. The sample excluding fixed ER countries drops countries with a preannounced or de facto peg, crawling peg, or band narrower than ±2% using the Ilzetzki, Reinhart, and Rogoff (2008) exchange rate regime classification. The criterion for including a country-month observation in the sample is that the 60-month moving average inflation in that month is below 8% (per year) and a per-capita GDP in that country-month of at least $5,000 (PPP). Robust standard errors in parenthesis.
***Significant at the 1% level.
**Significant at the 5% level.
*Significant at the 10% level.

effects. The idea is that adding time fixed effects would remove aggregate shock to the exchange rate common to all other countries; for example, a change in the US monetary policy. Results regarding the nonlinearity of the impact effect are robust in this specification as well.[42]

In table 6 we show that the results are robust to the exclusion of countries that are not classified by Ilzetzki, Reinhart, and Rogoff (2008). This

Table 6
Robustness: Excluding Unclassified Countries

	1974–2010 Sample, Excluding Fixed ER Countries (3,896 Obs.)				
Horizon h:	1 Month	3 Months	6 Months	12 Months	24 Months
β_h (linear term)	0.008	0.013	0.029**	0.029*	0.081***
	(0.005)	(0.009)	(0.012)	(0.017)	(0.024)
$\gamma_h \times 100$ (quadratic term)	0.096***	0.149***	0.134	0.138	−0.034
	(0.021)	(0.038)	(0.089)	(0.119)	(0.152)
R^2	0.26	0.41	0.55	0.61	0.69

	1974–2010 Sample, All Countries (10,808 Obs.)				
Horizon h:	1 Month	3 Months	6 Months	12 Months	24 Months
β_h (linear term)	0.024***	0.044***	0.062***	0.097***	0.188***
	(0.005)	(0.010)	(0.014)	(0.023)	(0.026)
$\gamma_h \times 100$ (quadratic term)	0.029	0.133	0.079	0.090	−0.434***
	(0.032)	(0.111)	(0.140)	(0.275)	(0.148)
R^2	0.11	0.19	0.29	0.40	0.47

	1990–2010 Sample, All Countries (6,436 Obs.)				
Horizon h:	1 Month	3 Months	6 Months	12 Months	24 Months
β_h (linear term)	0.011***	0.029***	0.045***	0.065***	0.100***
	(0.004)	(0.007)	(0.009)	(0.014)	(0.021)
$\gamma_h \times 100$ (quadratic term)	0.064***	0.082**	0.023	−0.074	−0.294***
	(0.023)	(0.041)	(0.061)	(0.074)	(0.100)
R^2	0.18	0.30	0.42	0.48	0.54

Note: All regressions include time and country fixed effects. Exchange rates for all countries except the United States are expressed as the bilateral exchange rate with the United States, and as the effective exchange rate for the United States. The sample excluding fixed ER countries drops countries with a preannounced or de facto peg, crawling peg, or band narrower than ±2% using the Ilzetzki, Reinhart, and Rogoff (2008) exchange rate regime classification. We exclude from the sample unclassiffied countries. The criterion for including a country-month observation in the sample is that the 60-month moving average inflation in that month is below 8% (per year) and a per-capita GDP in that country-month of at least $5,000 (PPP). Robust standard errors in parenthesis. See section V for details.
***Significant at the 1% level.
**Significant at the 5% level.
*Significant at the 10% level.

will decrease the number of total observations. In this case, the two-year linear pass-through is again in line with the the main specification. Nonlinear effects are rejected for the sample of all countries (fixed and flex), but cannot be rejected for the sample excluding the fixed exchange rate countries, as we can see from the top panel. For the sample of fixed and flexible exchange rate countries post-1990, nonlinear effects cannot be rejected.

In table 7 we show that the results are robust to a different classification of fixed exchange rate countries. In particular, we rerun the main specification for the main sample using the classification in Levy-Yeyati and Sturzenegger (2003). The linear component of the pass-through is again similar to the one in table 2. Nonlinear effects cannot be rejected on impact.

In table 8 we show that the statistical significance of the nonlinear term is not robust to dropping "outliers." In particular, in table 8 we present the results of estimating our main specification for each sample and dropping the observation (country-month pair) with the largest devaluation of the exchange rate. Thus, the size of the sample of table 2 and table 8 differ by one observation. The consequence of dropping the largest outlier is to yield a substantial increase in the standard errors of the estimated coefficients and a modest change of their values. In particular, in most cases the coefficient corresponding to the nonlinear term is no longer statistically significant at conventional confidence levels. We also tried dropping the two largest devaluations, and the results are similar (results not shown). Instead, dropping one or more observations with the highest inflation rates has no effect on the results. We conclude with one remark on large devaluations in our sample and the notion of "outliers" in our empirical analysis. Large devaluations are obviously crucial to our analysis of size-dependent propagation of shocks: absent large devaluations, we could not implement our analysis. Our quest for low-inflation countries and large devaluations makes it hard to gather a lot of observations that are useful to estimate the nonlinear effect. As shown in table 1, the sample that excludes the countries on a fixed ER regime has only 18 devaluations larger than 15%, and only 5 devaluations larger than 20% (not reported in the table). Indeed, the largest one is the 46% devaluation by South Korea (in 1996) and the second largest is around 22%. Dropping the Korean "outlier" is critical for the statistical significance of the nonlinear coefficient in our baseline regression. As mentioned, this is a single but important observation that is relevant in our sample of low-inflation countries that feature a few large devaluations.

Table 7
Inflation Pass-Through: Levy-Yeyati and Sturzenegger Classification

Horizon h:	1974–2014 Sample, Excluding Fixed ER Countries (9,570 Obs.)				
	1 Month	3 Months	6 Months	12 Months	24 Months
β_h (linear term)	0.011***	0.031***	0.065***	0.088***	0.125***
	(0.004)	(0.007)	(0.011)	(0.014)	(0.020)
$\gamma_h \times 100$ (quadratic term)	0.108***	0.160**	0.082	−0.010	−0.227*
	(0.036)	(0.076)	(0.121)	(0.133)	(0.130)
R^2	0.29	0.44	0.42	0.54	0.61

Horizon h:	1974–2014 Sample, All Countries (13,733 Obs.)				
	1 Month	3 Months	6 Months	12 Months	24 Months
β_h (linear term)	0.020***	0.040***	0.064***	0.092***	0.184***
	(0.004)	(0.010)	(0.013)	(0.021)	(0.024)
$\gamma_h \times 100$ (quadratic term)	0.057**	0.166	0.091	0.097	−0.448***
	(0.028)	(0.112)	(0.138)	(0.255)	(0.149)
R^2	0.16	0.26	0.28	0.39	0.46

Horizon h:	1990–2014 Sample, All Countries (9,184 Obs.)				
	1 Month	3 Months	6 Months	12 Months	24 Months
β_h (linear term)	0.010***	0.033***	0.060***	0.074***	0.109***
	(0.003)	(0.006)	(0.009)	(0.012)	(0.019)
$\gamma_h \times 100$ (quadratic term)	0.088***	0.109**	0.008	−0.088	−0.314***
	(0.022)	(0.046)	(0.066)	(0.073)	(0.107)
R^2	0.30	0.44	0.37	0.47	0.53

Note: All regressions include time and country fixed effects. Exchange rates for all countries except the United States are expressed as the bilateral exchange rate with the United States, and as the effective exchange rate for the United States. The sample excluding fixed ER countries drops countries with a preannounced or de facto peg, crawling peg, or band narrower than ±2% using the Levy-Yeyati and Sturzenegger (2003) exchange rate regime classification. The criterion for including a country-month observation in the sample is that the 60-month moving average inflation in that month is below 8% (per year) and a per-capita GDP in that country-month of at least $5,000 (PPP). Robust standard errors in parenthesis. See section V for details.
***Significant at the 1% level.
**Significant at the 5% level.
*Significant at the 10% level.

VI. Concluding Remarks

We showed analytically that in a broad class of models the propagation of a monetary impulse is independent of the nature of the sticky price friction when shocks are *small*. In particular, we proved that for economies with low inflation the total cumulated output response is approximately the same in TD and SD models, provided the models

Table 8
Inflation Pass-Through: Excluding Outliers

	1974–2014 Sample, Excluding Fixed ER Countries (6,810 Obs.)				
Horizon h:	1 Month	3 Months	6 Months	12 Months	24 Months
β_h (linear term)	0.006	0.021**	0.034**	0.028	0.075**
	(0.006)	(0.010)	(0.015)	(0.023)	(0.035)
$\gamma_h \times 100$ (quadratic term)	0.154*	0.251	0.443*	0.482	0.280
	(0.084)	(0.163)	(0.253)	(0.389)	(0.570)
R^2	0.20	0.31	0.41	0.51	0.62

	1974–2014 Sample, All Countries (13,722 Obs.)				
Horizon h:	1 Month	3 Months	6 Months	12 Months	24 Months
β_h (linear term)	0.020***	0.029**	0.044***	0.061**	0.186***
	(0.005)	(0.013)	(0.014)	(0.027)	(0.030)
$\gamma_h \times 100$ (quadratic term)	0.048	0.323	0.364*	0.543	–0.479
	(0.065)	(0.200)	(0.210)	(0.420)	(0.394)
R^2	0.11	0.19	0.28	0.39	0.46

	1990–2014 Sample, All Countries (9,178 Obs.)				
Horizon h:	1 Month	3 Months	6 Months	12 Months	24 Months
β_h (linear term)	0.009*	0.029***	0.048***	0.070***	0.119***
	(0.005)	(0.009)	(0.011)	(0.018)	(0.027)
$\gamma_h \times 100$ (quadratic term)	0.099	0.167	0.175	–0.026	–0.462
	(0.063)	(0.128)	(0.138)	(0.240)	(0.348)
R^2	0.17	0.28	0.37	0.47	0.53

Note: All regressions include time and country fixed effects. To examine the effect of outliers, the largest devaluation in each sample is excluded. Exchange rates for all countries except the United States are expressed as the bilateral exchange rate with the United States, and as the effective exchange rate for the United States. The sample excluding fixed ER countries drops countries with a preannounced or de facto peg, crawling peg, or band narrower than ±2% using the Ilzetzki, Reinhart, and Rogoff (2008) exchange rate regime classification. The criterion for including a country-month observation in the sample is that the 60-month moving average inflation in that month is below 8% (per year) and a per-capita GDP in that country-month of at least $5,000 (PPP). Robust standard errors in parenthesis.
***Significant at the 1% level.
**Significant at the 5% level.
*Significant at the 10% level.

are fit to the same frequency of adjustment and the same kurtosis of the size of price changes. These results are quite robust: we show that they also apply in the presence of moderate rates of steady-state inflation. The main message from these results is that, as long as one is interested in understanding the propagation of small monetary shocks, what matters are the frequency and the kurtosis that the models are fitted to. In short, the underlying nature of the nominal friction is irrelevant for the propagation of small shocks. Instead, the propagation of large shocks depends on the nature of the friction: the impulse response of inflation to monetary shocks is independent of the shock size in time-dependent models, while it is nonlinear in state-dependent models.

We devised a simple test for the presence of such nonlinear effects using data on exchange rate devaluations and inflation for a panel of countries from 1974 to 2014. We presented some evidence of a nonlinear effect of exchange rate changes on prices in a sample of flexible-exchange rate countries with low inflation. Our baseline results are robust to different functional form specifications (piecewise linear, quadratic, or distributed lags), as well as different controls (e.g., the same results appear when controlling for GDP growth rates, when no time fixed effects are used, or when a different exchange rate regime classification is used). We also highlight some dimensions along which these empirical patterns are not robust. The nonlinear effect is not robust to the introduction of fixed exchange rate countries into the full sample, and it is not robust to removing outliers as defined by the size of the large devaluations. In particular, removing the largest devaluation from the sample drastically increases the standard errors of the nonlinear coefficient on impact, making them statistically not significant at conventional confidence levels. Nevertheless, dropping large outliers either increases or yields very similar point estimates of the nonlinear coefficient.

Appendix A

General Equilibrium Setup

The general equilibrium setup is essentially the one in Golosov and Lucas (2007), adapted to multiproduct firms (see appendix B in Alvarez and Lippi [2014] for details). Households have a constant discount rate r and an instantaneous utility function that is additively separable: a CES consumption aggregate c, linear in labor hours ℓ, log in real balances M / P, with constant intertemporal elasticity of substitution $1 / \varepsilon$ for the consumption aggregate, so that the labor supply elasticity to real wages is $1 / \varepsilon - 1$.

HH Lifetime Utility: $\int_0^\infty e^{-rt} \left(\dfrac{c(t)^{1-\varepsilon} - 1}{1 - \varepsilon} - \alpha \ell(t) + \log \dfrac{M(t)}{P(t)} \right) dt$ (A1) with CES aggregate:

$$c(t) = \left(\int_0^1 \left(\sum_{i=1}^n [A_{ki}(t)c_{ki}(t)]^{(1-1/\rho)} \right)^{[\rho/(\rho-1)](1-1/\eta)} dk \right)^{\eta/(\eta-1)}. \tag{A2}$$

The specification assumes a continuum of Dixit-Stiglitz monopolistic sellers, index by k. Each seller sells n goods, indexed by the subscript i, where $\eta > 1$ is the substitution elasticity between sellers (or varieties) and ρ is the elasticity of substitution between products for each seller. If the elasticities of substitution are the same, that is, $\rho = \eta$, then we have the simpler expression:

$$c(t) = \left(\int_0^1 \sum_{i=1}^n [A_{ki}(t)c_{ki}(t)]^{1-1/\eta} dk \right)^{\eta/(\eta-1)}$$

To keep the expenditure shares stationary across goods in the face of the permanent idiosyncratic shocks, we assume offsetting preference shocks A_{ki}.[43]

The budget constraint of the representative agent is

$$M(0) + \int_0^\infty Q(t)[\bar{\Pi}(t) + \tau(t) + W(t)\ell(t) - R(t)M(t) - \int_0^1 \Sigma_{i=1} P_{k,i}(t)c_{ki}(t)dk]dt = 0,$$

where $R(t)$ is the nominal interest rates, $Q(t) = \exp(-\int_0^t R(s)ds)$ the price of a nominal bond, $W(t)$ the nominal wage, $\tau(t)$ the lump sum nominal transfers, and $\bar{\Pi}(t)$ the aggregate (net) nominal profits of firms.

A convenient implication of this setup is that nominal wages are proportional to the money supply in equilibrium, so that a monetary shock increases the firms' marginal costs proportionately. In particular, from the first-order conditions of the households' problem we obtain that

$$W(t) = \alpha(r + \pi)M(t), \tag{A3}$$

where π is coming from a steady-state growth in money supply, as we will detail below. For futher reference, we can also obtain that

$$c(t)^{-\varepsilon} = \frac{\alpha}{1 + \tau_l} \frac{P(t)}{W(t)}. \tag{A4}$$

This equation will pin down the impulse response function of output. In particular, note that the deviation of output from its steady-state level will depend on the deviation of the price level from the steady-state price level.

Optimal Firm-Decision Rules and Price Gaps

In this section we show that, in equilibrium, the nonlinear profit function of the firm can be replaced by a simple quadratic objective function
that depends exclusively on the firm's price gaps. This simplifies the
solution of the problem, first by simplifying the state space of the firm,
and second by allowing an analytical solution of the firms's decision
rules.

An Approximation to the Profit Function: We describe how the profits
of the firms, once we replace the demand from the household first-order
conditions problem, as well as using the equilibrium values of nominal
wages and nominal interest rates. From here we obtain two results: a
description of the state of the firm's problem, and a characterization (up
to second order) of the objective function of the firm. We note that the
firm's profit depend on nominal wages, nominal interest rates, but also
aggregate consumption, trough its determination of equilibrium real
rates as well as a shifter of the firm's individual demand. Thus, if we let
$V(\mathbf{p_k}, \mathbf{c}; p_k)$ be the value of the firm k gross profits (i.e., without subtract-
ing the observation and/or menu costs) as a function of initial price gap
vector p_k, and for an arbitrary stochastic process for prices $\mathbf{p_k}$, and a
path of aggregate consumption $\mathbf{c}$, we can show (see appendix B in Alvarez and Lippi [2014]) that:

$$V(\mathbf{p_k}, \mathbf{c}; p_k) = -\Upsilon\left(\frac{W(0)}{\overline{W}(0)}\right)\mathbb{E}\left[\int_0^\infty e^{-rt}B\left(\sum_{i=1}^n g_{ik}^2(t)\right)dt \,\middle|\, g_k(0) = g_k\right]$$

$$+ \mathbb{E}\left[\int_0^\infty e^{-rt}o\left(||\,(g_k(t), c(t) - \overline{c})\,||^2\right)dt \,\middle|\, g_k(0) = g_k\right] \quad (A5)$$

$$+ \iota(\delta, \mathbf{c}),$$

where $\Upsilon > 0$ is a function only on $W(0) / \overline{W}$ and where $\iota(\cdot)$ is only a
function of δ and the path of consumption and where $o(x)$ denotes a
function that is of smaller order than x. In particular, this means that
there are no interactions between $g_{ki}(t)c(t)$, and hence $c(t)$ does not impact, up to first order, the determination of the optimal prices, provided that the price gaps and the shock are both small. Moreover, if we
include the menu and observation cost, they can be measured in terms
of frictionless profits; for instance, the normalized menu cost will be
$\psi = \psi_m / \hat{\Pi}(0)$, where the normalized profit function $\hat{\Pi}$ is defined be-

low. Importantly, note that aggregate consumption does not feature on this problem, that is, it does not interact with the price gaps. Finally, the constant $B = (1 / 2)\eta(\eta - 1)$. If the elasticity of substitution η between firms and the n products produced by a firm have elasticity ρ is different, then instead of $B(\sum_{i=1}^{n} g_{ki}^2(t))$ the quadratic approximation gives:

$$\frac{\rho(\eta - 1)}{2n} \left(\sum_{i=1}^{n} g_{ki}^2(t) \right) - \frac{(\rho - \eta)(\eta - 1)}{2n^2} \left(\sum_{i=1}^{n} g_{ki}(t) \right)^2. \tag{A6}$$

Note this is a function of two scalars, the sum of the squares of the price gaps, omitting the firm's index k we have: $y \equiv \sum_{j=1}^{n} g_j^2$ as well as the sum of price gaps $z \equiv \sum_{j=1}^{n} g_j$.

Deriving the Approximation: The remainder of this section provides details to show the result in equation (A5) first, given that cost shocks follow a random walk, and that nominal interest rates are constant, wages growth at a constant rate, then current profits of the firm can be written as a function of price gaps and of exogenous process. Second, consider the discounted nominal profits of the firm k can we written as, where for simplicity we consider the case with $\eta = \rho$:

$$Q(t)W(t)A_{ki}(t)Z_{ki}(t)^{1-\eta} \ \tilde{\Pi}(c(t), g_{ki}(t))$$

$$= Q(t)W(t)A_{ki}(t)Z_{ki}(t)^{1-\eta} \ c(t)^{1-\eta\epsilon}e^{-\eta g_{ki}(t)} \left[e^{g_{ik}(t)} \frac{\eta}{\eta - 1} - 1 \right],$$

where we define the profits $\tilde{\Pi}$ depending only on price gaps and aggregate consumption. Thus we can write the expected discounted profits (not taking into account menu or observation costs) for firm k with initial price gap vector p_k as:

$$\mathbb{E} \left[\int_0^\infty Q(t) \left(\sum_{i=1}^{n} W(t)Z_{ki}(t)^{1-\eta}A_{ki}(t)\tilde{\Pi}[c(t), g_{ki}(t)] \right) dt \Big| g_k(0) = g_k \right]$$

with price gaps evolving as

$$g_{ki}(t) = g_{ki} - \log \frac{Z_{ki}(t)}{Z_{ik}(0)} - \log \frac{W(t)}{W(0)} + \sum_{\tau_j < t} \Delta g_{ki}(\tau_j)$$

for each product $i = 1, \ldots, n$.

Then

$$V(\mathbf{p}_k, \mathbf{c}; p_k) \equiv \mathbb{E}\left[\int_0^\infty e^{-(r+\pi)t}\left(\sum_{i=1}^n W(t)c(t)^{1-\varepsilon n}\hat{\Pi}(g_{ik}(t))\right)dt\,\Big|\,g(0) = g\right], \text{(A7)}$$

where we define the normalized profits as

$$\hat{\Pi}(g) \equiv e^{-ng}\left[e^g\,\frac{\eta}{\eta-1} - 1\right].$$

Conducting an expansion in equation (A7) around zero price gaps and zero aggregate shock (i.e., stead- state consumption), we obtain equation (A5).

Price Gaps, State Space, and Aggregate Shocks: Consider the case of zero inflation $\pi = 0$. The combination of the different assumptions give that: (a) idiosyncratic shocks to cost, and hence price gaps, are driftless random walks, (b) steady-state inflation is zero ($\pi = 0$), and (c) strategic complementarities of aggregate consumption do not (first order) affect optimal decision rules. In turn, (a–c) imply that, as stated above, both in state-dependent and time-dependent models, when prices are adjusted, the price gap is closed. Also, as a corollary, in state-dependent models the state for problem of the firm is given by the n-dimensional vector of the price gaps, and the inaction set have relatively simple form. For instance, for $n = 1$ product, the inaction set is an interval, and for $n > 1$ when the elasticities are the same $\rho = \eta$, and uncorrelated shocks across products ($\bar{\sigma} = 0$), it is a hypersphere. Furthermore, after a once-and-for-all shock aggregate nominal shock starting from a steady state, we have that (d) equilibrium nominal wages once and for, and (e) equilibrium nominal interest rates are constant. Thus, (a–e) imply that for an impulse response function we can assume that the decision rules of the firms stay the same before and after the aggregate shock. In particular, to compute the price level, the only effect is to instantaneously and simultaneously for all firms and products, price gaps are reduced by the same percentage, and subsequently price changes are given by the same decision rules as in steady state.

GE Version of Impulse Response Function

Note that we can use the general equilibrium model that we just specified to re-interpret the cost shock in equation (15) as a shock to money supply. In particular, the shock that we are studying is produced by a path of money $\log M(t) = \log \bar{M}(t) + \delta$ for all $t \geq 0$, where $\bar{M}(t) = \bar{M}e^{\pi t}$ is the preshock expected path of money, with level $\bar{M}$ right before the shock at time $t = 0$. Using that the labor market is frictionless, so households are in their labor supply, this implies that output can we written as function or real wages, which using a first-order approximation can we written as:

$$\log \frac{c(t)}{\bar{c}} = \frac{1}{\varepsilon}\left(\delta - \log \frac{P(t)}{\bar{P}(t)}\right),\qquad (A8)$$

where $\bar{c}$ is the constant flexible price equilibrium output and where $P(t)$ is the ideal price index at time $t \geq 0$ and $\bar{P}(t)$ is the path of the price level in the steady state before the shock, with $\bar{P}(t) = e^{\pi t}\bar{P}$ for all $t \geq 0$.

Impulse Responses and Price Gaps

Finally, note that to study the response of output and the price level to a cost shock (or a monetary shock), under the structure developed in this section, one only needs to focus on the distribution of price gaps. First, recall that it can be shown that:

$$\log \frac{P(t)}{\bar{P}(t)} = \delta + \int_0^1 \left(\frac{1}{n}\sum_{i=1}^n (g_{ki}(t) - \tilde{g}_{ki})\right) dk$$

$$+ \int_0^1 \left(\sum_{i=1}^n o(\| p_{ki}(t) - \tilde{p}_{ki}(t) \|)\right) dk.\qquad (A9)$$

So, the effect over the price level depends, up to first order, on price gaps of the firms. These price gaps in turn depend of the current price and of the frictionless optimal price. Second, in addition, equation (A5) implies that to study the optimal price setting each firm can regard its objective function to be quadratic and ignore all the other general equilibrium effects. Third, since wages adjust on impact, we can simple reset every single firm price gap to be δ smaller log points, and track its aggregate effect keeping the same optimal rules than in steady state. Finally, consumption is related to the price level by equation (A8).

Appendix B

Proofs

Proof (of Lemma 1). Here we use that the invariant density of Brownian motion is continuous on the (closure) of the inaction set, that is, on

$\{g \in \mathbb{R}^n : b(g) \le 0\}$. This continuity follows as long as $\sigma > 0$. Our proof strategy is to fix a boundary given by the function $b(\cdot; \Delta)$, and considers a discrete time, discrete state representation, with a time period of length Δ. We write $b(g; \Delta)$ so that in the discrete time version we let $b(g; \Delta) > 0$ for any point that is outside the inaction set and $b(g; \Delta) \le 0$ for those inside. In particular, we develop the discrete time version of the Kolmogorov forward equation for the density, that is, a difference equation in the probabilities evaluated finitely many values of g, denoted by $f(g; \Delta)$. We establish that for a value of g for which $b(g) = 0$, then $\lim_{\Delta \downarrow 0} f(g; \Delta) = 0$.

We will consider a discrete time, discrete state space representation of the vector of price gaps. Time periods are of length Δ and thus given by $t = s\Delta$ for nonnegative integers $s = 1, 2, \ldots$. The state space is given by an equally spaced grid with the same step size $\sigma\sqrt{\Delta}$ in each of the n dimensions. Thus in each dimension the price gap takes the values $j\sigma\sqrt{\Delta}$ for the integers $j = 0, \pm 1, \pm 2, \ldots$. To describe the law of motion of $\{g(t)\}$ we will use $n + 2$ random variables in each period. These random variables are i.i.d. trough time, and independent of each other. The first two random variables $q(t)$ is used to model the importance of the common component relative to the idiosyncratic component of the price gap. The variable $\bar{w}(t)$ is used to model the innovations on the common component of each price gap. The remaining n random variables $\{\tilde{w}_{it}\}_{i=1}^n$ are used to model the innovations on the idiosyncratic component of each of the n price gaps. The distribution of the random variables are:

$$q(t) = \begin{cases} 0 \text{ with probability } 1 - \rho \\ 1 \text{ with probability } \quad \rho. \end{cases}$$

The random variable $\bar{w}(t)$ is distributed as:

$$\bar{w}(t) = \begin{cases} +1 \text{ with probability } \dfrac{1}{2}\left[1 - \dfrac{\pi\sqrt{\Delta}}{\sigma}\right] \\ -1 \text{ with probability } \dfrac{1}{2}\left[1 + \dfrac{\pi\sqrt{\Delta}}{\sigma}\right] \end{cases}$$

and for each $i = 1, \ldots, n$ we have that each of the random variables $w_i(t)$ are distributed as:

$$\tilde{w}_i(t) = \begin{cases} +1 \text{ with probability } \dfrac{1}{2}\left[1 - \dfrac{\pi\sqrt{\Delta}}{\sigma}\right] \\[2em] -1 \text{ with probability } \dfrac{1}{2}\left[1 + \dfrac{\pi\sqrt{\Delta}}{\sigma}\right]. \end{cases}$$

Thus we have that each price gap $i = 1, \ldots, n$ has changes given by:

$$g_i(t + \Delta) - g_i(t) = \sqrt{\Delta}\sigma[q(t + \Delta)\bar{w}(t + \Delta) + (1 - q(t + \Delta))\tilde{w}_i(t + \Delta)].$$

In words: with probability ρ the price gaps of all products $i = 1, 2, \ldots,$ n move either all up or all down together. With probability $1 - \rho$ the up and down movements are independent across products. In the case of an up or a down movement the steps are always of the same size, but the probabilities of the up and down are adjusted away from $1/2$ to take the negative drift into account. With these definitions we have:

$$\mathbb{E}[g_i(t + \Delta) - g_i(t)] = -\pi\Delta \text{ for all } i = 1, 2, \ldots, n,$$

$$\mathbb{E}[(g_i(t + \Delta) - g_i(t))^2] = \sigma^2\Delta \text{ for all } i = 1, 2, \ldots, n,$$

$$\mathbb{E}[(g_i(t + \Delta) - g_i(t))(g_j(t + \Delta) - g_j(t))] = \rho\sigma^2\Delta \text{ for all } i \neq j = 1, 2, \ldots, n.$$

Take any $g' \neq g^*$, so that g' is not the optimal return point. Then the mass in g comes from adjacent points in the state space that belong to the inaction set, that is:

$$f(g'; \Delta) = \sum_{\{g : g'_i = g_i \pm \sqrt{\Delta}\sigma, i=1,\ldots,n\}} f(g; \Delta) 1_{\{b(g;\Delta) \leq 0\}}$$

$$\Pr\{g'_1 = g_1 \pm \sqrt{\Delta}\sigma, \cdots, g'_n = g_n \pm \sqrt{\Delta}\sigma\}. \tag{B1}$$

The indicator makes sure that only mass that comes from points within the range of inaction can transit from g to g'. Note that at most mass could come from 2^n different points, since in each dimension g_i could have either increase or decrease.

The same steps then for the one dimensional case apply to the general $n > 1$ dimensional case. For simplicity we concentrate first on the case of independence shocks across the products. In this case, we will take a value of g' for which $b(g'; \Delta) = 0$. For $\Delta > 0$ but small enough, there will be some state g for which $g'_i = g_i \pm \sqrt{\Delta}\sigma$ and for which $b(g) > 0$. In words, the point g' of the state space has fewer than 2^n adjacent points that belong to the range of inaction that can move to g' in exactly one time period of length Δ. We thus have that if $b(g'; \Delta) = 0$ then $\#\{g:g'_i=g_i \pm \sqrt{\Delta}\sigma\} < 2^n$.

$$f(g'; \Delta) \leq (1 - \rho)\left(\frac{1}{2}\left[1 + \frac{\pi\sqrt{\Delta}}{\sigma}\right]\right)^n \sum_{\{g:g'_i=g_i\pm\sqrt{\Delta}\sigma,i=1,...,n\}} f(g; \Delta)1_{\{b(g;\Delta)\leq0\}}$$

$$+ \rho\left[1 + \frac{\pi\sqrt{\Delta}}{\sigma}\right][f(g' - \sqrt{\Delta}\sigma; \Delta) + f(g' + \sqrt{\Delta}\sigma; \Delta)].$$

There are two reasons for the inequality. The first is that we use for all changes the one with higher probability, the down step. The second is that we disregard the possibility that $b(g) > 0$ when either all the price gaps move up or down together (so there is no indicator in the second term of the right-hand side). For small enough Δ we have:

$$\sum_{\{g:g'_i=g_i\pm\sqrt{\Delta}\sigma,i=1,...,n\}} 1_{\{b(g;\Delta)\leq0\}} \leq 2^n - 1,$$

so that there is at least one state which uncontrolled will move to g', but that it does not belong to the inaction set. Thus taking limits:

$$\lim_{\Delta\downarrow0} \sum_{\{g:g'_i=g_i\pm\sqrt{\Delta}\sigma,i=1,...,n\}} 1_{\{b(g;\Delta)\leq0\}} \leq 2^n - 1.$$

Moreover, for those g for which $g'_i = g_i \pm \sqrt{\Delta}\sigma$ for all $i = 1, \ldots, n$ we have, by the assumed continuity of the density in the closure of the range of inaction, that:

$$\lim_{\Delta\downarrow0}f(g'_1 \pm \sqrt{\Delta}\sigma,\ldots, g'_n \pm \sqrt{\Delta}\sigma; \Delta) = \lim_{\Delta\downarrow0}f(g'; \Delta) = f(g').$$

Hence we have that taking limits on equation (B1) for values of g' for which $b(g'; \Delta) = 0$:

$$f(g') = \lim_{\Delta \downarrow 0} f(g'; \Delta)$$

$$\leq (1 - \rho) \lim_{\Delta \downarrow 0} (1 - \rho) \left(\frac{1}{2} \left[1 + \frac{\pi\sqrt{\Delta}}{\sigma} \right] \right)^n \sum_{\{g : g'_i = g_i \pm \sqrt{\Delta}\sigma\}} f(g; \Delta) 1_{\{b(g;\Delta) \leq 0\}}$$

$$+ \rho \frac{1}{2} \lim_{\Delta \downarrow 0} [f(g' - \sqrt{\Delta}\sigma; \Delta) + f(g' + \sqrt{\Delta}\sigma; \Delta)]$$

$$= \rho f(g') + (1 - \rho) f(g') \left(\frac{1}{2} \right)^n (2^n - 1)$$

$$= f(g') \left[1 - (1 - \rho) \left(\frac{1}{2} \right)^n \right],$$

or $f(g') \leq f(g')[1 - (1 - \rho)(1 / 2)^n]$ which again requires that $f(g') = 0$.

Proof (of Lemma 2). To establish the desired result in the general multi-product case, we first develop an expression for an upper bound of $I(\delta)$, denoted by $\bar{I}(\delta)$. We will show that $I(0) = \bar{I}(0)$, that $I(\delta) \leq \bar{I}(\delta)$, and that $\bar{I}'(0) = 0$, which implies the desired result $I'(0) = 0$. Instead, the upper-bound function $\bar{I}(\delta)$ is given by:

$$\bar{I}(\delta) = n \int_{-\infty}^{\infty} \cdots \left[\int_{-\infty}^{\infty} \left[\int_{\underline{g}(g_1-\delta, g_2-\delta, \ldots, g_{n-1}-\delta)}^{\underline{g}(g_1-\delta, g_2-\delta, \ldots, g_{n-1}-\delta)+\delta} f(g_1, g_2, \ldots, g_n) dg_n \right] dg_{n-1} \cdots \right] dg_1,$$

where the set $\mathbb{G}_{n-1}$ and the function $\underline{g} : \mathbb{G}_{n-1} \to \mathbb{R}$ are defined as:

$$\mathbb{G}_{n-1} \equiv \{g_1, g_2, \ldots, g_{n-1} \in \mathbb{R}^{n-1} : \exists g_n \in \mathbb{R}$$

$$\text{such that} \quad (g_1, g_2, g_3, \ldots, g_n) \in \mathcal{I}\}$$

$$\underline{g}(g_1, g_2, \ldots, g_{n-1}) \equiv \min_x \{x : (g_1, g_2, \ldots, g_{n-1}, x) \in \mathcal{I}\}$$

$$\text{for} \quad (g_1, g_2, \ldots, g_{n-1}) \in \mathbb{G}_{n-1}.$$

$\bar{I}(\delta)$ as n times the number of firms that adjust its price on impact because one price has gotten below the lower sS bound (for simplicity we have taken this to be the n price gap, but given exchangeability, it does not matter which one it is). The reason why $\bar{I}(\delta)$ in an upper bound of $I(\delta)$ is that in $\bar{I}$ there is some double counting. The double counting comes from the fact that for some values of g there may have been lower boundaries corresponding to more than one price gap that are crossed after the shock δ. This establishes that $I(\delta) \leq \bar{I}(\delta)$. That $\bar{I}(0) = 0$ it follows directly from its definition, since the last intergral is performed in a degenerate interval if $\delta = 0$. Finally we have:

$$\bar{I}'(\delta) = n\int_{-\infty}^{\infty} \cdots \left[\int_{-\infty}^{\infty} \left[\frac{\partial}{\partial \delta} \int_{\underline{g}(g_1-\delta, g_2-\delta, \ldots, g_{n-1}-\delta)}^{\underline{g}(g_1-\delta, g_2-\delta, \ldots, g_{n-1}-\delta)+\delta} f(g_1, g_2, \ldots, g_n)dg_n \right] dg_{n-1} \cdots \right] dg_1$$

with

$$\frac{\partial}{\partial \delta} \int_{\underline{g}(g_1-\delta, g_2-\delta, \ldots, g_{n-1}-\delta)}^{\underline{g}(g_1-\delta, g_2-\delta, \ldots, g_{n-1}-\delta)+\delta} f(g_1, g_2, \ldots, g_n)dg_n$$

$$= f(g_1, g_2, \ldots, \underline{g}(g_1 - \delta, g_2 - \delta, \ldots, g_{n-1} - \delta))$$

which equals zero when evaluated at $\delta = 0$, since $f(g_1, g_2, \ldots, \underline{g}(g_1, g_2, \ldots, g_{n-1}))$ is the density at the boundary of the range of inaction. Thus $\bar{I}'(0) = 0$.

Appendix C

Random Observation Cost

In this appendix we describe the setup for observation cost and signals. The time line in figure C1 describes the structure of the observation cost ψ'_o, the associated signal ζ, and production cost $z = (z_1, \ldots, z_n)$ that occurs at the time τ_i and at the time of the next observation τ_{i+1}, which is $\min\{T_i, s_i\}$ periods after the current observation τ_i. In another words, T_i is decided at τ_i.

Immediately after paying the observation cost at time τ_i, the firm learns the current value of $(z_1, \ldots, z_n)$ and receives a signal ζ, which is informative about the future realizations of the observation cost ψ'_o. Recall that at time τ_i the firm decides its planned elapsed time until the next observation T_i. Recall that the firm also reviews at an exogenous exponentially distributed time s_i with parameter λ. Thus the time elapsed until next observation will occur at the earliest time between s_i, which is a random variable, or T_i, which as of time τ_i is decided, and thus known, that is, nonrandom. Summarizing the time for the $i + 1$ observation is given by $\tau_i + \min\{s_i, T_i\}$.

The signal ζ summarizes all the information about the value of the observation cost to be paid $T = \min\{s_i, T_i\}$ periods from now. Mathematically we write $F(\psi'_o; T \mid \zeta)$ to be the CDF of the observation cost ψ'_o to be paid T periods after the current observation, conditional on the signal ζ. The dependence of the distribution F on T allows the distribu-

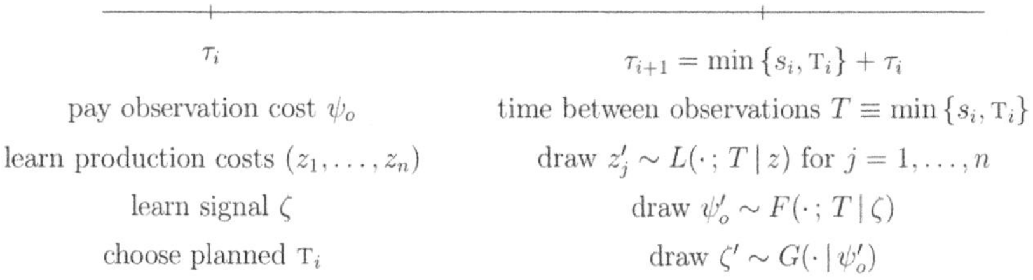

τ_i	$\tau_{i+1} = \min\{s_i, \mathrm{T}_i\} + \tau_i$
pay observation cost ψ_o	time between observations $T \equiv \min\{s_i, \mathrm{T}_i\}$
learn production costs $(z_1, \dots, z_n)$	draw $z'_j \sim L(\cdot\,; T\,|\,z)$ for $j = 1, \dots, n$
learn signal ζ	draw $\psi'_o \sim F(\cdot\,; T\,|\,\zeta)$
choose planned T_i	draw $\zeta' \sim G(\cdot \mid \psi'_o)$

Fig. C1.   Time Line

tion of the observation cost ψ_o, to vary with the time elapsed between observations. The functions F and G fully characterize the process for the observation cost, and provide enough flexibility to cover cases discussed in the literature as well as generalizations that we find useful. The expected observation cost is the key input to decide T.

Upon the next observation, when a particular cost ψ'_o is realized, a new signal ζ' is drawn from the CDF $G(\cdot|\psi_o)$. The other key input to decide T is the distribution of $z_j(\tau_{i+1})$ conditional on $z(\tau_i)$, which, given the assumption that the log of $\{z_j\}$ are random walks, we can summarize them as $L(\cdot\,;T|z)$. These distributions allows to compute the benefit of gathering information, that is, of choosing a small value of T_j.

In this setup we can obtain several of the cases analyzed in the literature. For instance, the model of deterministic observation times studied by Caballero (1989) and Reis (2006) is encompassed by our framework if the signal is uninformative about the future observation cost, which is the case if $F(\psi'_o, T_0|\zeta_0) = F(\psi'_o, T_1|\zeta_1)$ for all ψ'_o and all pairs (T_0, ζ_0). In this case, the distribution G is irrelevant because, given that the signal is uninformative, the mechanism to obtain the new signal is irrelevant.

Another case discussed in the literature is one where the firm's observation times are i.i.d., as proposed by Reis (2006). This setup provides a foundation to i.i.d. observation times: the firm has to draw a signal about the future observation cost that is both informative about the next observation cost and independent of all other shocks (including the current value of the observation cost). In this case, the particular form of the distribution G is relevant. Formally, observation times are i.i.d. in our model if and only if $G(\zeta|\tilde{\psi}_o) = G(\zeta|\bar{\psi}_o)$ for all ζ and all pairs $\tilde{\psi}_o, \bar{\psi}_o$. The distribution F shapes the precision of the signal. Finally, the more general case where $G(\zeta|\tilde{\psi}_o) \neq G(\zeta|\bar{\psi}_o)$ for at least some ζ and some pairs $\tilde{\psi}_o, \bar{\psi}_o$ allows us to extend our analysis to the case of observation times correlated over time, a case which we find more reasonable than the i.i.d. assumption.

Appendix D

Time- and State-Dependent Firms' Problem

In the multiproduct Calvo$^+$ model the firms solves:

$$\max_{\{\tau_i, \Delta P_j(\tau_i), j=1,\ldots,n, i=1,2,\ldots\}} \mathbb{E}\left[\begin{array}{l} \int_0^\infty e^{-rt}\Pi(P_1(t), \ldots, P_n(t), Z_1(t), \ldots, Z_n(t), W(t); \\[2mm] c(t))dt - \sum_{i=1}^\infty e^{-r\tau_i}\psi_m 1_{\{dU(\tau_i)=1\}}W(\tau_i) \end{array}\right] \quad (D1)$$

$P_j(t) = P_j(\tau_i)$ for all $t \in (\tau_i, \tau_{i+1}]$ and $\Delta P_j(\tau_i) = \lim_{\varepsilon\downarrow 0}P_j(\tau_i + \varepsilon) - P_j(\tau_i)$,

where $\{U(t)\}$ is a Poisson process with intensity λ.

In the problem with observation and menu cost the firm solves

$$\max_{\{t_i, a(\tau_i), \Delta P_j(\tau_i), j=1,\ldots,n, i=1,2,\ldots\}} \mathbb{E}\left[\begin{array}{l} \int_0^\infty e^{-rt}\Pi(P_1(t), \ldots, P_n(t), Z_1(t), \ldots, Z_n(t), W(t); \\[2mm] c(t))\ dt - \sum_{i=1}^\infty e^{-r\tau_i}\psi_0[1 + a(\tau_i)\psi_m]W(\tau_i) \end{array}\right], \quad (D2)$$

where $\tau_{i+1} = T_i + \tau_i$ where T_i is the time between observations, T_i and $a(\tau_i)$ $\in \{0, 1\}$ only depend on information gathered at $\tau_0, \tau_1, \ldots, \tau_i, P_j(t) = P_j(s)$ for all $s, t \in (\tau_i, \tau_{i+1})$ and

$$\Delta P_j(\tau_i) = \begin{cases} \lim_{\varepsilon\downarrow 0}P_i(\tau_i + \varepsilon) - P_i(\tau_i) & \text{if } a(\tau_i) = 1 \\ 0 & \text{if } a(\tau_i) = 0. \end{cases}$$

We simplify the problem assuming that both observation and menu costs are nonrandom.

Appendix E

Trade-Off of Sticky Price Models around Zero Inflation

In all the microfounded models, we consider the nominal price upon adjustment is reset at the optimal price maximizing level, that is, the price gap is "closed," so that the size of the price adjustment is equal to (minus) the price gap, or $\Delta g_i = -\Delta \log P_i$. In this broad class of models we have that the following property holds for any decision rules and $n \geq 1$:

$$N(\Delta p_i; 0) \ Var(\Delta p_i; 0) = \sigma^2, \text{ and } \frac{\partial}{\partial \pi} [N(\Delta p_i; \pi) Var(\Delta p_i; \pi)] \mid_{\pi=0} = 0, \quad \text{(E1)}$$

which states that the total number of price adjustments per period denoted by $N(\Delta p_i; \pi)$ times the variance of the size of price changes, $Var(\Delta p_i; \pi)$ equals the variance of the innovations to the price gaps σ^2. This equation, which holds for any policy for inflation around zero, which ends up closing the price gap upon adjustments (even nonoptimal policies) highlights the key trade-off of a sticky price problem, that between the frequency of costly adjustments, or information gathering, versus the mean deviation of nominal prices from their optimal level.

Appendix F

Sensitivity of Impact Effect to Inflation

In this section we derive the case of a state-dependent model with one good $n = 1$. We explicitly write the barriers and the optimal return point as function of inflation for a given $\sigma > 0$. At zero inflation we have: $\bar{g}(0) = -\underline{g}(0) > 0$ and $g^*(0) = 0$. We would like to obtain an expansion of $I(\delta, \pi)$. We have

$$I(\delta; \pi) = f(\underline{g}(\pi); \pi)\delta + \frac{1}{2} f'(\underline{g}(\pi); \pi)\delta^2 + \frac{1}{6} f''(\underline{g}(\pi); \pi)\delta^3 + o(\delta^3)$$

$$= \frac{1}{2} f'(\underline{g}(\pi); \pi)\delta^2 + \frac{1}{6} f''(\underline{g}(\pi); \pi)\delta^3 + o(\delta^3),$$

where f' and f'' denote the derivatives of the density with respect to g, and where f'_π and f''_π denote the (cross) derivatives with respect to π. Note that at $\pi = 0$, $f(\cdot, 0)$ is linear so that $f''(g, 0) = 0$. We thus have:

$$I(\delta; \pi) = I(\delta; 0) + \frac{1}{2} \frac{\partial}{\partial \pi} f'(\underline{g}(0); 0)\pi\delta^2 + o(\| (\delta, \pi) \|^3)$$

$$= \frac{1}{2} f'(\underline{g}(0); 0)\delta^2 + \frac{1}{2} \frac{\partial}{\partial \pi} f'(\underline{g}(0); 0)\pi\delta^2 + o(\| (\delta, \pi) \|^3)$$

$$= \frac{1}{2} \frac{1}{\underline{g}(0)^2} \delta^2 + \frac{1}{2} \frac{\partial}{\partial \pi} f'(\underline{g}(0); 0)\pi\delta^2 + o(\| (\delta, \pi) \|^3).$$

To be more precise, the density depends on inflation directly, in the dependence of the Kolmogorov forward equation on π:

$$0 = f'(g; \pi, \underline{g}, \bar{g}, g^*)\pi + f''(g; , \underline{g}, \bar{g}, g^*)\frac{\sigma^2}{2}$$

$$\text{for all } g \in [\underline{g}, \bar{g}], g \neq g^*,$$

(F1)

as well as, indirectly on $\underline{g}(\pi)$, $\bar{g}(\pi)$ and $g^*(\pi)$, which depend on π. We have:

$$\frac{\partial}{\partial \pi} f'(\underline{g}(0); 0, \underline{g}(0), \bar{g}(0), g^*(0)) = f''(\underline{g}(0); 0)\underline{g}'(0) + f'_\pi(\underline{g}(0); 0)$$

$$+ f'_{\underline{g}}(\underline{g}(0); 0, \underline{g}(0), \bar{g}(0), g^*(0))\underline{g}'(0)$$

$$+ f'_{\bar{g}}(\underline{g}(0); 0, \underline{g}(0), \bar{g}(0), g^*(0))\bar{g}'(0)$$

$$+ f'_{g^*}(\underline{g}(0); 0, \underline{g}(0), \bar{g}(0), g^*(0))g^{*'}(0),$$

where we use that at $\pi = 0$ the density is linear in g, that is,

$$f(g, 0) = \frac{g - \underline{g}(0)}{\underline{g}(0)^2} \text{ for} g \in [\underline{g}(0), 0)$$

(F2)

and hence its derivative f' does not depend on g. Thus we have:

$$I(\delta; \pi) = \frac{1}{2}\frac{1}{\underline{g}(0)^2}\delta^2 + \frac{1}{2} f'_\pi(\underline{g}(0); 0)\pi\delta^2 + o(\| (\delta, \pi) \|^3).$$

We first study the effect of inflation on f' keeping the thresholds $\underline{g}, \bar{g}$ and the optimal return point g^* fixed as we change inflation. Thus, we only study the direct effect of inflation on f'. To do this, we first determine f and its derivatives. The density f solves the Kolmogorov forward equation at all $g \neq g^* = 0$. Furthermore, we use that the density is zero at the exit points. Thus there must be two constants $\underline{B}$ and $\bar{B}$:

$$f(g, a) = \begin{cases} \underline{B}(a)(e^{ag} - e^{a\underline{g}}) & \text{if } g \in [\underline{g}, g^*] \\ \bar{B}(a)(e^{ag} - e^{a\bar{g}}) & \text{if } g \in [g^*, \bar{g}] \end{cases}$$

(F3)

where we use a to denote the nonzero root of the characteristic equation for the solution of the KF equation:

$$a = -2\pi / \sigma^2.$$

(F4)

We describe the two equations for the constants $\underline{B}(a)$ and $\bar{B}(a)$. Continuity of the density $f(\cdot, a)$ at $g^* = 0$ gives

$$\underline{B}(a)(e^{ag^*} - e^{a\underline{g}}) = \bar{B}(a)(e^{ag^*} - e^{a\bar{g}})$$

and integrates to one:

$$1 = \int_{\underline{g}}^{\bar{g}} f(g, a)dg = \int_{\underline{g}}^{g^*} \underline{B}(a)(e^{ag} - e^{a\underline{g}})dg + \int_{g^*}^{\bar{g}} \bar{B}(a)(e^{ag} - e^{a\bar{g}})dg.$$

We are interested in:

$$f'(\underline{g}(0); 0) = \lim_{a \to 0} \underline{B}(a)ae^{a\underline{g}(0)} = \frac{1}{\underline{g}(0)^2} \quad \text{and} \tag{F5}$$

$$f''_\pi(\underline{g}(0); 0) = -\frac{2}{\sigma^2} \lim_{a \to 0} \frac{\partial}{\partial a} \underline{B}(a)ae^{a\underline{g}(0)} \big|_{a=0}. \tag{F6}$$

Solving for $\underline{B}$ we have:

$$1 = \underline{B}(a)\left(\frac{e^{ag^*} - e^{a\underline{g}}}{a} - e^{a\underline{g}}(g^* - \underline{g})\right)$$

$$+ \bar{B}(a)\left(\frac{e^{a\bar{g}} - e^{ag^*}}{a} - e^{a\bar{g}}(\bar{g} - g^*)\right)$$

$$= \underline{B}(a)\left(\frac{e^{ag^*} - e^{a\underline{g}}}{a} - e^{a\underline{g}}(g^* - \underline{g})\right)$$

$$+ \underline{B}(a)\frac{(e^{ag^*} - e^{a\underline{g}})}{(e^{ag^*} - e^{a\bar{g}})}\left(\frac{e^{a\bar{g}} - e^{ag^*}}{a} - e^{a\bar{g}}(\bar{g} - g^*)\right),$$

where we use that the density integrates to one and that it is continuous at zero. Then

$$1 = \underline{B}(a)\left\{ \begin{array}{l} \dfrac{e^{ag^*} - e^{a\underline{g}}}{a} - e^{a\underline{g}}(g^* - \underline{g}) \\[2ex] + \dfrac{e^{ag^*} - e^{a\underline{g}}}{e^{ag^*} - e^{a\bar{g}}}\left(\dfrac{e^{a\bar{g}} - e^{ag^*}}{a} - e^{a\bar{g}}(\bar{g} - g^*)\right) \end{array} \right\}$$

$$= -\underline{B}(a)\left\{ e^{a\underline{g}}(g^* - \underline{g}) + \frac{e^{ag^*} - e^{a\underline{g}}}{e^{ag^*} - e^{a\bar{g}}} e^{a\bar{g}}(\bar{g} - g^*) \right\}$$

$$= -\underline{B}(a)\left\{ \frac{e^{ag^*} - e^{a\bar{g}}}{e^{ag^*} - e^{a\bar{g}}} e^{a\underline{g}}(g^* - \underline{g}) + \frac{e^{ag^*} - e^{a\underline{g}}}{e^{ag^*} - e^{a\bar{g}}} e^{a\bar{g}}(\bar{g} - g^*) \right\}$$

$$= -\frac{\underline{B}(a)}{e^{ag^*} - e^{a\bar{g}}} \{(e^{ag^*} - e^{a\bar{g}})e^{a\underline{g}}(g^* - \underline{g}) + (e^{ag^*} - e^{a\underline{g}})e^{a\bar{g}}(\bar{g} - g^*)\},$$

using that $\underline{g} = -\overline{g}$ and $g^* = 0$ at $\pi = 0$:

$$1 = -\frac{B(a)}{e^{ag^*} - e^{a\overline{g}}} (\overline{g} - g^*)\{(e^{ag^*} - e^{a\overline{g}})e^{a\underline{g}} + (e^{ag^*} - e^{a\underline{g}})e^{a\overline{g}}\}$$

$$= -\underline{B}(a)\frac{(\overline{g} - g^*)}{e^{ag^*} - e^{a\overline{g}}} \{e^{ag^*}e^{a\underline{g}} - 1 + e^{ag^*}e^{a\overline{g}} - 1\}$$

$$= -\underline{B}(a)\frac{\overline{g}}{1 - e^{a\overline{g}}} \{e^{-a\overline{g}} - 1 + e^{a\overline{g}} - 1\},$$

or

$$\underline{B}(a) = -\frac{(1 - e^{a\overline{g}})}{\overline{g}(e^{-a\overline{g}} - 1 + e^{a\overline{g}} - 1)} < 0 \text{ since } a < 0.$$

We thus have:

$$\overline{g}^2 f'(\underline{g}, a) = C(\alpha) \equiv \overline{g}^2 \underline{B}(a)ae^{-a\overline{g}} = -\frac{\alpha(e^{-\alpha} - 1)}{(e^{-\alpha} - 1 + e^{\alpha} - 1)}$$

$$= -\left(\frac{1}{2}\right)\frac{-\alpha^2 + \alpha^3 / 2 - \alpha^4 / 3! + \cdots}{\alpha^2 / 2 + \alpha^4 / 4! + \alpha^6 / 6! + \cdots}$$

$$= -\left(\frac{1}{2}\right)\frac{-1 + \alpha / 2 - \alpha^2 / 3! + \cdots}{1 / 2 + \alpha^2 / 4! + \alpha^4 / 6! + \cdots}$$

where $\alpha \equiv a\overline{g} < 0$.

Note that direct computation gives

$$C(0) = 1 \quad \text{and} \quad C'(0) = -\frac{1}{2}.$$

Thus:

$$f'(\underline{g}, \pi) = \frac{1}{\overline{g}^2} C\left(-\frac{2\pi}{\sigma^2} \overline{g}\right) \to \frac{1}{\overline{g}^2} \quad \text{and}$$

$$f'_\pi(\underline{g}, 0) = -\frac{2\overline{g}}{\sigma^2 \overline{g}^2} C'(0) = \frac{1}{\sigma^2 \overline{g}}.$$

Appendix G

Accuracy of Proposition 2 in Models with Both Menu and Observation Costs

We numerically evaluate the accuracy of the approximation in Proposition 2 in models that feature the simultaneous presence of a menu cost $\psi_m > 0$ as well as an observation cost $\psi_o > 0$. The main parameter to be specified for this analysis is the ratio between the two fixed costs: $\alpha \equiv \psi_m / \psi_o$. Notice that for the special case of the observation cost only ($\psi_m = 0$ so that $\alpha = 0$) as well as the special case of the menu cost only ($\psi_o = 0$ so that $\alpha \to \infty$), we have supplied an analytic proof of the proposition in Alvarez, Le Bihan, and Lippi (2016) for $\psi_m > 0, \psi_o = 0$ and in Alvarez, Lippi, and Paciello (2016) for $\psi_o > 0, \psi_m = 0$.

To analyze the problem with $0 < \alpha < \infty$ we use the decision rules derived in Alvarez et al. (2011), and numerically compute the invariant distribution of firms in a steady state. This is a joint density defined over the time until the next review and the value of each firm price gap. We then develop the impulse response analysis by shocking the steady state of the economy and computing the under the impulse response. There is essentially one parameter in this analysis, α, since the two fixed costs enter the problem as a ratio and the policy functions are homogenous, so that the results only depend on the ratios of particular moments (e.g., frequency of adjustment versus frequency of observation; see Alvarez et al. [2011] for details). In practice, we normalize the value of $N = 1$ in all the models we consider and vary α so that the models will generate different steady state levels of kurtosis.

Figure G1 summarizes the results of our numerical analysis. The vertical axis plots the ratio of the area under the output impulse, numerically computed, and the approximation of the same object given by the ratio of the steady-state moments $Kurt(\Delta p_i) / N(\Delta p_i)$ as suggested in Proposition 2 . We consider a set of models where $0 < \alpha < 5$. The model uses a weekly time period and a cross section of 100,000 firms, and a monetary shock equal to 1%, that is, $\delta = 0.01$. It appears that the numerical accuracy of the proposition is within ±5% of the actual cumulative effect and, more importantly, that the accuracy does not display a systematic variation with respect to α.

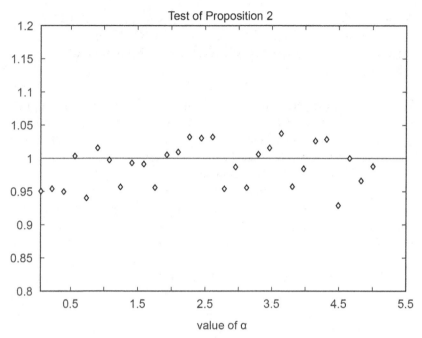

Fig. G1.   Ratio between actual and approximate cumulative output effect

Appendix H

Additional Data Documentation

Table H1 reports more summary statistics for the countries used in the analysis. The criterion for including a country-month observation in the sample is that the 60-month centered moving average inflation in that month is below 8% (per year) and a per-capita GDP in that country-month of at least $5,000 (PPP). Columns titled Mean Inf., Sd. Inf., Mean Dev., and Sd. Dev. contain the mean and standard deviation of inflation and exchange rate devaluations against the US dollar in all months for which the country is included in the sample. Columns titled Big5, Big10, Big20, Big30, and Big40 indicate the number of months with devaluations of at least X%, for X = 5, 10, 20, 30, and 40, respectively. The number of country-month observations is contained in the column titled Obs.

Table H1
Countries and Main Descriptive Statistics

Country	Inflation				Devaluation						Obs.
	Mean Inf.	Sd. Inf.	Mean Dev.	Sd. Dev.	Big5	Big10	Big20	Big30	Big40		
Algeria	0.78	2.57	0.42	1.80	5	0	0	0	0		179
Austria	0.31	0.71	-0.12	2.64	19	2	0	0	0		503
Belgium	0.33	0.38	-0.04	2.69	23	3	0	0	0		503
Bolivia	4.49	14.38	8.61	81.36	14	13	12	11	10		374
Botswana	0.78	0.69	0.68	3.79	22	8	2	0	0		299
Brazil	5.72	9.16	5.43	9.38	111	56	18	11	3		270
Bulgaria	0.27	0.66	0.24	3.43	8	2	0	0	0		101
Burkina Faso	0.52	3.98	0.10	2.64	17	3	0	0	0		374
Burundi	0.89	2.20	0.45	3.02	6	4	1	1	0		195
Cameroon	0.71	1.72	0.14	3.13	17	3	0	0	0		266
Canada	0.31	0.40	0.05	1.69	6	1	0	0	0		700
Central African Republic	0.35	2.03	0.29	3.58	10	1	0	0	0		108
Chad	0.21	3.77	-0.07	3.49	6	0	0	0	0		77
Chile	0.21	0.38	0.03	3.23	3	1	0	0	0		77
China, P.R.: Hong Kong	0.37	0.77	0.11	0.92	2	0	0	0	0		415
Colombia	1.16	1.11	1.23	5.34	16	5	3	3	2		484
Costa Rica	0.77	1.36	0.63	5.67	14	6	4	3	2		486
Cote d'Ivoire	0.60	2.55	0.11	2.69	17	3	0	0	0		363
Croatia	2.21	7.09	1.96	7.45	33	21	16	4	1		256
Czech Republic	0.28	0.59	0.02	3.69	21	3	0	0	0		245
Denmark	0.39	0.60	0.04	3.01	36	4	0	0	0		581
Dominican Republic	0.72	1.88	0.70	10.70	10	5	1	1	1		460
Egypt	0.72	1.99	0.37	4.50	5	4	2	2	1		399
El Salvador	0.71	1.20	0.25	5.00	1	1	1	1	1		400

(continued)

Table H1
Continued

Country	Inflation		Devaluation							
	Mean Inf.	Sd. Inf.	Mean Dev.	Sd. Dev.	Big5	Big10	Big20	Big30	Big40	Obs.
Ethiopia	0.53	2.36	-0.06	0.75	0	0	0	0	0	288
Finland	0.50	0.58	0.21	3.28	19	5	2	2	0	503
France	0.47	0.45	0.14	2.93	27	6	0	0	0	503
Germany	0.21	0.33	0.17	3.21	8	1	0	0	0	96
Greece	0.82	1.35	0.51	2.51	24	5	0	0	0	527
Guatemala	0.56	2.04	0.46	7.59	3	2	2	1	1	400
Haiti	0.54	2.79	0.00	0.03	0	0	0	0	0	409
Honduras	0.42	1.01	0.00	0.07	0	0	0	0	0	400
Hungary	0.60	1.21	0.16	3.58	22	8	2	0	0	353
India	0.58	1.14	0.36	3.23	4	1	1	1	1	399
Indonesia	1.07	2.32	0.88	4.89	7	5	3	3	2	269
Iran, Islamic Republic of	0.88	1.60	0.32	4.96	3	1	1	1	1	448
Iraq	0.24	0.93	-0.01	0.05	0	0	0	0	0	51
Ireland	0.14	0.36	0.54	2.63	1	0	0	0	0	24
Israel	1.75	3.44	1.55	5.14	84	32	7	4	3	700
Italy	0.60	0.59	0.22	2.47	26	2	0	0	0	503
Jamaica	0.87	1.26	0.65	4.45	12	5	2	2	2	460
Japan	0.26	0.68	-0.12	2.71	23	2	0	0	0	699
Jordan	0.62	1.95	0.36	2.09	6	1	0	0	0	197
Kazakhstan	0.65	0.56	0.33	2.99	3	2	1	0	0	113
Kenya	0.85	1.21	0.45	2.10	6	3	0	0	0	268
Korea, Republic of	0.57	0.84	0.29	3.45	21	9	3	1	1	545
Kuwait	0.32	0.89	-0.01	0.94	0	0	0	0	0	495
Latvia	1.22	3.75	0.03	3.54	11	2	0	0	0	166
Lebanon	0.30	1.04	0.00	0.00	0	0	0	0	0	81

(continued)

Libya	0.37	2.57	0.00	1.46	1	1	0	0	0	327
Lithuania	1.48	4.43	0.37	4.42	17	6	3	2	0	272
Macedonia, FYR	0.04	0.43	0.70	2.33	1	0	0	0	0	29
Madagascar	0.87	1.61	0.71	4.77	21	7	2	1	1	315
Malaysia	0.23	0.60	-0.02	1.46	3	0	0	0	0	520
Mali	0.14	1.25	0.14	3.69	4	0	0	0	0	34
Mauritania	0.59	2.64	0.10	2.11	1	0	0	4	4	54
Mexico	1.31	2.05	1.18	6.32	42	10	7	0	0	616
Montserrat	0.21	0.55	0.00	0.00	0	0	0	0	0	170
Morocco	0.46	1.03	0.26	2.34	13	3	0	1	0	399
Myanmar	1.08	2.84	0.05	2.07	4	2	1	0	0	574
Namibia	0.41	0.40	0.83	4.38	9	3	0	1	0	64
Nepal	0.69	2.00	0.44	2.54	5	4	1	0	0	322
Netherlands	0.33	0.69	-0.10	2.68	22	2	0	1	0	503
Niger	0.57	3.05	0.14	3.14	17	3	0	0	0	268
Nigeria	1.02	2.22	0.88	8.04	15	8	3	2	1	365
Norway	0.37	0.56	0.05	2.67	28	4	0	0	0	700
Oman	0.22	0.46	0.00	0.00	0	0	0	0	0	172
Pakistan	0.57	1.33	0.50	6.57	2	1	1	1	1	400
Panama	0.32	0.52	0.00	0.00	0	0	0	0	0	287
Paraguay	0.92	1.98	0.79	6.47	9	5	5	4	3	392
Peru	3.96	8.81	4.24	32.83	60	31	14	9	6	424
Philippines	0.83	1.38	0.70	5.10	11	6	4	2	2	400
Poland	2.11	8.34	2.01	10.26	22	16	7	4	3	184
Portugal	0.83	1.24	0.39	2.66	22	5	1	0	0	503
Qatar	0.15	0.65	0.00	0.00	0	0	0	0	0	94
Romania	2.96	4.67	3.17	14.27	44	19	7	6	6	295
Russian Federation	0.76	0.61	0.61	4.67	12	6	2	0	0	124
Rwanda	0.65	1.83	0.27	6.01	3	2	1	1	1	302
Saudi Arabia	0.13	0.51	0.03	0.19	0	0	0	0	0	423

Table H1
Continued

Country	Inflation		Devaluation							Obs.
	Mean Inf.	Sd. Inf.	Mean Dev.	Sd. Dev.	Big5	Big10	Big20	Big30	Big40	
Senegal	0.64	2.56	0.15	3.13	17	3	0	0	0	269
Serbia, Republic of	0.59	0.82	0.71	4.75	11	4	1	0	0	101
Sierra Leone	0.51		−0.58		0	0	0	0	0	1
Singapore	0.22	0.80	−0.12	1.51	4	0	0	0	0	652
Slovak Republic	0.50	0.86	−0.17	2.87	5	1	0	0	0	156
Slovenia	0.92	1.53	0.71	3.80	18	2	1	1	0	182
South Africa	0.64	0.65	0.45	3.68	40	11	4	0	0	519
Spain	0.70	0.72	0.30	2.98	25	8	2	0	0	503
Sri Lanka	0.57	1.07	0.62	4.80	8	3	2	1	1	399
Sudan	1.31	4.12	0.66	6.75	5	5	4	3	3	387
Sweden	0.36	0.58	0.11	2.80	30	4	0	0	0	700
Switzerland	0.21	0.40	−0.17	3.01	33	4	0	0	0	700
Tanzania	1.04	0.48	1.21	1.47	0	0	0	0	0	3
Thailand	0.44	0.77	0.10	1.33	2	1	0	0	0	353
Togo	0.58	2.52	0.10	3.21	16	2	0	0	0	244
Tunisia	0.53	0.43	0.54	2.28	0	0	0	0	0	47
Turkey	1.91	2.48	1.78	7.07	47	9	5	3	2	389
United Arab Emirates	0.23	0.84	0.00	0.00	0	0	0	0	0	101
United Kingdom	0.22	0.43	0.10	2.80	17	4	0	0	0	329
United States	0.28	0.37	−0.27	1.51	0	0	0	0	0	431
Uruguay	2.72	2.91	2.61	10.17	56	19	7	5	4	532

Endnotes

We benefited from the comments of our discussants John Leahy and Greg Kaplan, and of other conference participants. Part of the research for this paper was sponsored by the ERC advanced grant 324008. Joaquin Saldain and Jean Flemming provided excellent research assistance. For acknowledgments, sources of research support, and disclosure of the authors' material financial relationships, if any, please see http://www.nber.org/chapters/c13768.ack.

1. In the first class of models the firm's decision to adjust prices depends on the state, while in the latter class it depends only on the time elapsed since the last price change.

2. Small shocks are indeed central to several previous analyses both because they naturally emerge as the residuals in a regression, as typical in the empirical VAR literature (e.g., Christiano, Eichenbaum, and Evans 1999; Christiano, Eichenbaum, and Evans 2005), or because they provide convenient conditions for analytical approximations (e.g., Caballero and Engel 2007; Alvarez and Lippi 2014).

3. As in previous studies, one note of caution is due: the regression coefficient can be interpreted as a measure of the response of inflation to an exogenous nominal exchange rate innovation under the assumption that the shock is orthogonal to the other regressors and unanticipated. This assumption, which we discuss in the empirical analysis, is not appropriate whenever the exchange rate innovations occur in response to shocks that also affect other domestic variables, including inflation itself.

4. We are thankful to our discussant Greg Kaplan for pointing this out.

5. Gagnon et al. (2012) use disaggregated firm-level data and analyze how exchange rate devaluations impact on the timing of price adjustments, a feature that is consistent with state-dependent models. Their findings are consistent with the presence of state-dependent pricing rules.

6. It is worth noting that other papers in the literature of sticky prices have suggested nonlinear response to shocks. For example, Burstein (2006) studies the nonlinear response of inflation and output to monetary shock when firms choose price plans.

7. The approach is standard and has been used in, for example, Caballero and Engel (2007).

8. This example assumes a unit elasticity of output to real wages.

9. Technically, this last result depends on the continuous-time and continuous-path nature of the shocks, but its qualitative implications also apply to discrete-time discrete-state versions of this model.

10. Theoretically the result extends to small inflation since in the presence of idiosyncratic shocks the drift has a second-order impact on decision rules, such as the frequency of price adjustments (see Alvarez et al. [2011] for a proof in a model with both TD and SD components). For evidence supporting this claim see Gagnon (2009) and Alvarez et al. (2015), who show that decision rules are quite insensitive to the inflation for rates that are below 10%.

11. For more discussion and evidence on the equivalence between the area under the impulse response function and the variance due to monetary shocks, see footnote 21 of Nakamura and Steinsson (2010).

12. The selection effect, a terminology introduced by Golosov and Lucas (2007), indicates that firms that change prices after the monetary shock are the firms whose prices are in greatest need of adjustment, a hallmark of SD models.

13. Alternative definitions of moderate inflation are used: our baseline requires that the mean inflation rate is below $X\%$ in a 10-year time window centered on the observation date. Our baseline results use $X = 8$ but results are robust to using a threshold of $X = 6$. Smaller thresholds reduce the number of large devaluations observed in sample. The mean unconditional annual inflation in our baseline sample is below 4% (see the summary statistics reported in table 1).

14. This is a marginal improvement of the early analysis of Caballero and Engel (1993), who measured the inflation response during the year after the shock.

15. Our baseline specification uses simple nonlinear projections as suggested in Jorda (2005), but results are robust to the distributed lag specification commonly used in the international economics literature.

16. To be precise, devaluation is computed as $\Delta e_{i,t} = (e_{i,t} / e_{i,t-1} - 1) \times 100$ where $e_{i,t}$ is the end of the period bilateral exchange rate of country i against the United States, and inflation is computed as $\pi_{i,(t,t+h)} = (p_{i,t+h} / p_{i,t} - 1) \times 100$ where $h = 1, 3, 6, 12, 24$ months and $p_{i,t}$ is the price level reported for period t. Note that the CPI $p_{i,t}$ is constructed using prices that are sampled *during* period t; that is, between the end of period $t - 1$ and the end of period t.

17. This result is robust to alternative classifications of the de facto ER regime, such as Ilzetzki, Reinhart, and Rogoff (2008)] used in the table versus the one by Levy-Yeyati and Sturzenegger (2003), which includes fewer countries and was used by us for a robustness check.

18. See equations (A1) and (A2) in appendix A for a model where price gaps are derived from primitives.

19. See Alvarez and Lippi (2014) for an analytical characterization of the optimal stopping barrier $\bar{y}$, as well as the implication for the size distribution of price changes $f(\Delta p_i)$.

20. See section VI and appendix E of Alvarez and Lippi (2014) for a proof.

21. To be more precise, in the Mankiw and Reis (2002) model prices will change every period to keep up with the mean expected marginal cost. This gives rise to a very high frequency of price changes that diverges as the model moves to continuous time. This feature is a common element in models of rational inattentiveness that lack a physical cost of price adjustment. A robust pattern in the data is, however, that prices change infrequently. A simple way to obtain infrequent price changes in this class of models is to assume that the level of the nominal marginal cost is a martingale. As a result, price changes only occur when new information arrives, so that the frequency of price changes coincide with the frequency of observations. Moreover, in Alvarez et al. (2011) we show that price plans would not be optimal even in the presence of a drift in the nominal marginal cost, when a price adjustment cost is added to a similar model and calibrated to match the frequency of price changes in the US economy.

22. We do this for two reasons. First, when we introduce menu as well as observation costs, price plans will not be optimal for small departures of a martingale–see Proposition 1 in Alvarez et al. (2011). Second, if costs are not martingale and there are no menu costs, then price changes will occur as frequently as the model time periods, which will be highly counterfactual.

23. In appendix C we give more details on the structure of the cost and signals.

24. In Alvarez, Lippi, and Paciello (2016), Propositions 7 and 11 show that for any distribution of times, a distribution of signals and cost on future observation costs can be found that provides a foundation to it. This can be used to rationalize the work of researchers that start their analysis directly with the assumption that times between observations (and price changes) are i.i.d. through time with a given distribution, and study their implications for monetary policy (e.g., Bonomo et al. 2010).

25. For simplicity, and because its effects are mainly covered by the Calvo[+], we abstract from the exogenous observation times featured in equation (14) for the time-dependent case.

26. The first result in Proposition 1 concerns the impact effect on prices and output of a once-and-for-all monetary shock. The second result is for the GE version of our model, where we use the cumulative output response of an once-and-for-all monetary shock, that is, the area under the impulse response for output, as defined in equation (20). The result for the impact effect is more general in scope: for instance, it holds for all levels of the inflation rate $\pi = 0$ and holds if $\eta \neq \rho$, and/or if there is correlation between the idiosyncratic shocks across the products of the firm, that is, if $\bar{\sigma} > 0$. Indeed, for the first result we only use the form of the decision rules, either they be state-dependent Ss rules as in equation (9), or time-dependent rules as in equation (14). The second result in Proposition 2 is obtained analytically for a smaller class of economies, and with the GE interpretation of this shock. In particular, it is obtained around a zero inflation rate, and we also restrict the analysis to the case of same elasticity of substitution $\rho = \eta$, and no correlation between idiosyncratic shocks, that is, $\bar{\sigma} = 0$.

27. To understand this equation notice that the monetary shock increases the desired prices of all firms by the same amount δ. This implies a decrease by an amount δ of all

price gaps g_{ki} that are not adjusted on impact (the gaps $\tilde{g}_{ki}$ are unaffected by definition). This explains the presence of the term δ in the equation.

28. In Proposition 3 of Alvarez et al. (2015), we show analytically for the same model that at around zero inflation only 10% of the changes in inflation are accounted for changes in the thresholds, and instead 9/10 are accounted for by changes in the frequency of price increases versus price decreases. This means that ignoring the changes in thresholds, as in the approximation above, makes a very small difference.

29. For a symmetric distribution kurtosis is a scale-free statistic describing its peakedness: the extent to which "large" and "small" observations (in absolute value) appear relative to intermediate values.

30. Intuitively, a lot of selection gives rise to small kurtosis. For example, in the Golosov-Lucas model, price changes are concentrated around two values: very large and very small, which imply the smallest value of kurtosis (equal to one). In contrast, the size distribution of price adjustments in a multiproduct model with a large number of goods is normally distributed, that is, it features a large mass of small as well as very large price changes. This results in less selection, fully captured by the higher kurtosis of the size distribution.

31. See Kiley (2002), Sheedy (2010), Carvalho and Schwartzman (2015), and Alvarez, Lippi, and Paciello (2016).

32. Notice how these features are captured by kurtosis: in Taylor the constant time between adjustments T implies that price changes are drawn from a normal distribution, hence kurtosis is three. In Calvo, instead, the exponential distribution of adjustment times implies that price changes are drawn from a mixture of normals with different variances, and hence a higher kurtosis (equal to six).

33. To be precise for SD models, it follows by setting $\lambda = 0$, or equivalently $\ell = 0$, in the model in Alvarez, Le Bihan, and Lippi (2016), and the results correspond to Proposition 6 of that paper.

34. Again, this corresponds to Proposition 6 of that paper, for the case where $\lambda > 0$ and $\psi > 0$, or equivalently the case where $\ell \in (0, 1]$.

35. These computations take advantage that we have a characterization of the decision rules that allows to compute a simple problem for each ratio of the menu-to-observation cost, free of any other parameters.

36. We can take $\bar{\delta}(\pi) = g(\pi)_{max} - g(\pi)_{min}$ where $g(\pi)_{max} = \{\inf x : (x, \dots, x) \geq (g_1, \dots, g_n)$ for all $g \in \mathcal{I}(\pi)\}$ and $g(\pi)_{min} = \{\sup x : (x, \dots, x) \leq (g_1, \dots, g_n)$ for all $g \in \mathcal{I}(\pi)\}$.

37. In terms of the data by choosing CPI and Exchange rate against the United States and working at a monthly frequency we take an alternative route from the literature that studies the exchange rate pass through; see, for example, Campa and Goldberg (2005), Bussiere (2013), and the Handbook Chapter in Burstein and Gopinath (2014). The reasons for studying CPI and the exchange rate against the US dollar are to obtain as many observations as possible (monthly time series for import prices and effective exchange rate are available only for a subset of countries), and because the model outlined in section III is better suited for the pricing decisions of retailers. In addition, we work at a monthly frequency to better approximate impact effects. It is worth noting that by using Import prices and effective exchange rates we still find some weak evidence of nonlinearity. This evidence is in line with Bussiere (2013).

38. With monthly data this amounts to the following restriction: An observation for country i in period t is in the sample if $\pi_{i,t}^{MA} = (\sum_{k=-60}^{k=60} \pi_{i,t+k}) / 120 \leq \mathcal{K} = 0.08$. We check robustness of our findings for different windows (24, 36, 48 months) and inflation values (4, 6, 8, and 10%).

39. We also focus on countries that have a GDP per capita higher than 5,000 USD whenever the value of GDP per capita is available. We use the World Bank National Accounts Data, with data available after 1990 on a monthly basis. Also, we focus on countries that have populations that are higher than two million inhabitants.

40. To be precise, devaluation is computed as $\Delta e_{i,t} = (e_{i,t} / e_{i,t-1} - 1) \times 100$ where $e_{i,t}$ is the end-of-the-period bilateral exchange rate of country i against the United States and inflation is computed as $\pi_{i,(t,t+h)} = (p_{i,t+h} / p_{i,t} - 1) \times 100$ where $h = 1, 3, 6, 12, 24$ months and $p_{i,t}$ is the price level reported for period t. Note that the CPI $p_{i,t}$ is constructed using

prices that are sampled *during* period t; that is, between the end of period $t-1$ and the end of period t.

41. This specification differs from the ones usually estimated in the literature that studies exchange rate pass-through (see, e.g., Campa and Goldberg [2005], and the Handbook Chapter by Burstein and Gopinath [2014]) in two dimensions. First, instead of estimating equation (36) without a nonlinear term (i.e., $\gamma_h = 0$), several papers estimate a distributed lag regression.

$$\pi_{i,t} = \alpha_i + \delta_t + \sum_{s=0}^{T}\beta_s\Delta e_{i,t-s} + \varepsilon_{it}^\pi. \tag{35}$$

It can be shown that under the identifying assumption that the exchange rate follows a random walk the two specifications, distributed lags versus linear projections, are analogous. Second, our specification in equation (34) introduces a nonlinear term. An exception is Bussiere (2013). This paper runs cross country and country-by-country nonlinear specifications and finds nonlinearities in the pass-through of the effective exchange rate into import and export prices.

42. We thank our discussant Greg Kaplan for suggesting this alternative specification.

43. We assume that the preference shocks satisfy $A_{ki}(t) = Z_{ki}(t)^{\eta-1}$ so that the share of expenditure on different goods are constant in the frictionless case. This convenient assumption was used by Woodford (2009), Bonomo et al. (2010) Midrigan (2011), and Alvarez and Lippi (2014).

References

Abel, Andrew B., Janice C. Eberly, and Stavros Panageas. 2007. "Optimal Inattention to the Stock Market." *American Economic Review* 97 (2): 244–49.
———. 2013. "Optimal Inattention to the Stock Market with Information Costs and Transactions Costs." *Econometrica* 81 (4): 1455–81.
Alvarez, Fernando, Martin Gonzalez-Rozada, Andres Neumeyer, and Martin Beraja. 2015. "From Hyperinflation to Stable Prices: Argentina's Evidence on Menu Cost Models." Manuscript, University of Chicago.
Alvarez, Fernando, Herve Le Bihan, and Francesco Lippi. 2016. "The Real Effects of Monetary Shocks in Sticky Price Models: A Sufficient Statistic Approach." *American Economic Review* 106 (10): 2817–51.
Alvarez, Fernando, and Francesco Lippi. 2014. "Price Setting with Menu Cost for Multiproduct Firms." *Econometrica* 82 (1): 89–135.
Alvarez, Fernando, Francesco Lippi, and Luigi Paciello. 2011. "Optimal Price Setting with Observation and Menu Costs." *Quarterly Journal of Economics* 126 (4): 1909–60.
———. 2015. "Phillips Curves with Observation and Menu Costs." EIEF Working Paper Series no. 1508, Einaudi Institute for Economics and Finance.
———. 2016. "Monetary Shocks in Models with Inattentive Producers." *Review of Economic Studies* 83:421–59.
Bhattarai, Saroj, and Raphael Schoenle. 2014. "Multiproduct Firms and Price-Setting: Theory and Evidence from U.S. Producer Prices." *Journal of Monetary Economics* 66 (C): 178–92.
Bonadio, Barthelemy, Andreas M. Fischer, and Philip Saure. 2016. "The Speed of Exchange Rate Pass-Through." Working paper, Swiss National Bank.
Bonomo, Marco, Carlos Carvalho, and René Garcia. 2010. "State-Dependent Pricing under Infrequent Information: A Unified Framework." FRB Staff Report no. 455, Federal Reserve Bank of New York.
Bonomo, Marco, Carlos Carvalho, René Garcia, and Vivian Malta. 2016. "Persis-

tent Monetary Non-neutrality in an Estimated Model with Menu Costs and Partially Costly Information." Meeting Paper no. 1339, Society for Economic Dynamics.

Brunnermeier, Markus K., and Yuliy Sannikov. 2014. "A Macroeconomic Model with a Financial Sector." *American Economic Review* 104 (2) :379–421.

Burstein, Ariel T. 2006. "Inflation and Output Dynamics with State-Dependent Pricing Decisions." *Journal of Monetary Economics* 53 (7): 1235–57.

Burstein, Ariel, Martin Eichenbaum, and Sergio Rebelo. 2005. "Large Devaluations and the Real Exchange Rate." *Journal of Political Economy* 113 (4): 742–84.

———. 2007. "Modeling Exchange Rate Passthrough after Large Devaluations." *Journal of Monetary Economics* 54 (2): 346–68.

Burstein, Ariel, and Gita Gopinath. 2014. "International Prices and Exchange Rates. In *Handbook of International Economics*, vol. 4, ed. G. Gopinath, E. Helpman, and K. Rogoff, 391–451. Amsterdam: Elsevier.

Bussiere, Matthieu. 2013. "Exchange Rate Pass-Through to Trade Prices: The Role of Nonlinearities and Asymmetries." *Oxford Bulletin of Economics and Statistics* 75 (5): 731–58.

Caballero, Ricardo J. 1989. "Time Dependent Rules, Aggregate Stickiness and Information Externalities." Discussion Paper no. 198911, Columbia University.

Caballero, Ricardo J., and Eduardo M. R. A. Engel. 1993. "Microeconomic Rigidities and Aggregate Price Dynamics." *European Economic Review* 37 (4): 697–711.

———. 2007. "Price Stickiness in Ss Models: New Interpretations of Old Results." *Journal of Monetary Economics* 54 (Supplement): 100–21.

Calvo, Guillermo A. 1983. "Staggered Prices in a Utility-Maximizing Framework." *Journal of Monetary Economics* 12 (3): 383–98.

Campa, Jose Manuel, and Linda S. Goldberg. 2005. "Exchange Rate Pass-Through into Import Prices." *Review of Economics and Statistics* 87 (4): 679–90.

Caplin, Andrew, and John Leahy. 1991. "State-Dependent Pricing and the Dynamics of Money and Output." *Quarterly Journal of Economics* 106 (3): 683–708.

Caplin, Andrew S., and Daniel F. Spulber. 1987. "Menu Costs and the Neutrality of Money." *Quarterly Journal of Economics* 102 (4): 703–25.

Carvalho, Carlos, and Felipe Schwartzman. 2015. "Selection and Monetary Non-Neutrality in Time-Dependent Pricing Models." *Journal of Monetary Economics* 76 (C): 141–56.

Cavallo, Alberto, and Roberto Rigobon. 2016. "The Billion Prices Project: Using Online Prices for Measurement and Research." NBER Working Paper no. 22111, Cambridge, MA.

Christiano, Lawrence J., Martin Eichenbaum, and Charles L. Evans. 1999. "Monetary Policy Shocks: What Have We Learned and to What End?", vol. 1, part A, ed. J. Taylor and M. Woodford, 65–158. Amsterdam: Elsevier.

———. 2005. "Nominal Rigidities and the Dynamic Effects of a Shock to Monetary Policy." *Journal of Political Economy* 113 (1): 1–45.

Eichenbaum, Martin, Nir Jaimovich, and Sergio Rebelo. 2011. "Reference Prices, Costs, and Nominal Rigidities." *American Economic Review* 101 (1): 234–62.

Fernandez-Villaverde, Jesus, Pablo Guerron-Quintana, Keith Kuester, and Juan Rubio-Ramirez. 2015. "Fiscal Volatility Shocks and Economic Activity." *American Economic Review* 105 (11): 3352–84.

Gagnon, E. 2009. "Price Setting during Low and High Inflation: Evidence from Mexico*." *Quarterly Journal of Economics* 124 (3): 1221–63.

Gagnon, Etienne, David Lopez-Salido, and Nicolas Vincent. 2012. "Individual Price Adjustment along the Extensive Margin." In *NBER Macroeconomic Annual 2012*, vol. 27, ed. D. Acemoglu, J. Parker, and M. Woodford, 235–81. Chicago: University of Chicago Press.

Gertler, Mark, and John Leahy. 2008. "A Phillips Curve with an Ss Foundation." *Journal of Political Economy* 116 (3): 533–72.

Giavazzi, Francesco, Tullio Jappelli, and Marco Pagano. 2000. "Searching for Nonlinear Effects of Fiscal Policy: Evidence from Industrial and Developing Countries." *European Economic Review* 44 (7): 1259–89.

Golosov, Mikhail, and Robert E. Lucas Jr. 2007. "Menu Costs and Phillips Curves." *Journal of Political Economy* 115:171–99.

Ilzetzki, Ethan, Carmen Reinhart, and Kenneth Rogoff. 2008. "Exchange Rate Arrangements Entering the 21st Century: Which Anchor Will Hold?" Manuscript, University of Maryland and Harvard University.

Jorda, Oscar. 2005. "Estimation and Inference of Impulse Responses by Local Projections." *American Economic Review* 95 (1): 161–82.

Kaplan, Greg, and Gianluca Violante. 2014. "A Model of the Consumption Response to Fiscal Stimulus Payments." *Econometrica* 82:1199–239.

Kehoe, Timothy J., and Kim J. Ruhl. 2009. "Sudden Stops, Sectoral Reallocations, and the Real Exchange Rate." *Journal of Development Economics* 89 (2): 235–49.

Kiley, Michael. 2002. "Partial Adjustment and Staggered Price Setting." *Journal of Money, Credit and Banking* 34 (2): 283–98.

Klenow, Peter J., and Oleksiy Kryvtsov. 2008. "State-Dependent or Time-Dependent Pricing: Does It Matter for Recent U.S. Inflation?" *Quarterly Journal of Economics* 123 (3): 863–904.

Levy-Yeyati, Eduardo, and Federico Sturzenegger. 2003. "To Float or to Fix: Evidence on the Impact of Exchange Rate Regimes on Growth." *American Economic Review* 93 (4): 1173–93.

Magnani, Jacopo, Aspen Gorry, and Ryan Oprea. 2016. "Time and State Dependence in an Ss Decision Experiment." *American Economic Journal: Macroeconomics* 8 (1): 285–310.

Mankiw, N. Gregory, and Ricardo Reis. 2002. "Sticky Information versus Sticky Prices: A Proposal to Replace the New Keynesian Phillips Curve." *Quarterly Journal of Economics* 117 (4): 1295–328.

Martins, Fernando. 2005. "The Price Setting Behaviour of Portuguese Firms—Evidence from Survey Data." Working Paper Series no. 562, European Central Bank.

Midrigan, Virgiliu. 2011. "Menu Costs, Multi-Product Firms, and Aggregate Fluctuations." *Econometrica* 79 (4): 1139–80.

Nakamura, Emi, and Jon Steinsson. 2010. "Monetary Non-Neutrality in a Multisector Menu Cost Model." *Quarterly Journal of Economics* 125 (3): 961–1013.

Pollard, Patricia S., and Cletus C. Coughlin. 2004. "Size Matters: Asymmetric Exchange Rate Pass-Through at the Industry Level." Federal Reserve Bank Working Paper Series no. 2003-029C, Federal Reserve Bank of St. Louis.

Reinhart, Carmen M., and Kenneth S. Rogoff. 2004. "The Modern History of Exchange Rate Arrangements: A Reinterpretation." *Quarterly Journal of Economics* 119 (1): 1–48.

Reis, Ricardo. 2006. "Inattentive Producers." *Review of Economic Studies* 73 (3): 793–821.

Sheedy, Kevin D. 2010. "Intrinsic Inflation Persistence." *Journal of Monetary Economics* 57 (8): 1049–61.
Sheshinski, Eytan, and Yoram Weiss. 1983. "Optimum Pricing Policy under Stochastic Inflation." *Review of Economic Studies* 50 (3): 513–29.
Taylor, John B. 1980. "Aggregate Dynamics and Staggered Contracts." *Journal of Political Economy* 88 (1): 1–23.
———. 2000. "Low Inflation, Pass-Through, and the Pricing Power of Firms." *European Economic Review* 44 (7): 1389–408.
Woodford, Michael. 2009. "Information-Constrained State-Dependent Pricing." *Journal of Monetary Economics* 56:s100–24.
Zbaracki, Mark J., Mark Ritson, Daniel Levy, Shantanu Dutta, and Mark Bergen. 2004. "Managerial and Customer Costs of Price Adjustment: Direct Evidence from Industrial Markets." *Review of Economics and Statistics* 86 (2): 514–33.

Comment

John Leahy, University of Michigan and NBER

Introduction

In this paper, Alvarez, Lippi, and Passadore ask if it matters whether we model price inertia with a time-dependent rule, as in the Calvo or Taylor models, or a state-dependent rule, as in the Ss menu-cost model. They give two answers to this question, one for small shocks to the money supply and one for large shocks. For large shocks the answer is an unambiguous "yes." State dependence leads to greater price flexibility, which mutes the response of real output. This is the familiar selection effect that plays such a large role in the papers by Caplin and Spulber (1987) and Golosov and Lucas (2007). For small shocks, the answer is a more surprising "no." The authors show that it is not so much the distinction between state and time dependence that matters for the macroeconomics of price inertia, but rather the moments of distribution of price changes, in particular the kurtosis of the steady-state distribution of price changes and the expected time between price changes. Under fairly general conditions (more on this later), these moments are sufficient to characterize the cumulative response of output to a small, permanent shock to the money supply. State and time dependence work through these moments and have no independent effects.

I will focus my comments on the small shock analysis, since this is the most innovative and surprising part of the paper. I will begin with a quick literature review, then discuss the authors' sufficient statistic approach, and conclude by assessing the limitations of the result and providing suggestions for future research.

In the search for microfoundations of price rigidity, the literature has tended to focus on two prototypical models of price inertia: models with time-dependent pricing rules and models with state-dependent rules. Time-dependent rules are rules in which the timing of adjustment depends only on the time since the last price change. The motivating examples are fixed-length contracts and corporate decision cycles, both of which tend to give precedence to the calendar in determining which prices are changed and when.[1] Time dependence is usually modeled as either a fixed schedule of price changes (Taylor pricing) or Poisson price changes (Calvo pricing). On the other side are state-dependent rules. These rules tend to include some cost of changing prices. The price-adjustment decision then balances this cost of adjustment against the cost of mispricing. Prices may change or not change depending on the current state of the economy. Menu-cost models are the most prominent examples.

State- and time-dependent models have long been thought to be different. Since the focus of this paper is on the differences between these models, I list a few of the main differences discussed in the literature.

- *State dependence dampens the real effects of a money shock* (Caplin and Spulber 1987; Dotsey, King, and Wolman 1999; Golosov and Lucas 2007). In time-dependent models, the set of firms that adjust their prices at any point in time are exogenously determined. In state-dependent models, the firms that adjust their prices tend to be the firms with the most to gain from price adjustment, and these firms tend to be the firms whose prices are most out of line. The average amount of mispricing is therefore less in state-dependent models. Golosov and Lucas label this the selection effect.

- *With state dependence the response of the economy to a money shock should depend on the state of the economy* (Caplin and Leahy 1991, 1997; Caballero and Engel 2007). Aggregate shocks tend to alter the number of firms contemplating price increases and price decreases. The greater the number of firms that are contemplating price increases, the greater the effect of a positive money supply shock on inflation and the lesser the effect on output. An increase in the money supply should therefore have a greater effect on inflation in a boom than in a bust. Caballero and Engel codify this in their aggregate flexibility index. Aggregate shocks do not affect the incentive to adjust in time-dependent models because the adjustment decision is exogenous. The state dependence of money shocks is correspondingly reduced.

- *Time dependence leads to frontloading of price changes* (Ball 1994; Ascari 2004; Midrigan 2011). The future matters a lot in time-dependent models since the adjusting firm may not have another opportunity to adjust its prices for some time. If the firm expects inflation at some future date, it will have an incentive to raise its prices immediately. Ball shows that this may cause the economy to expand should firms expect deflation. Firms that expect the price level to fall in the future will cut their prices today, thereby raising output. The incentive to frontload is greatly reduced in state-dependent models since a firm can simply choose to adjust when it makes sense to adjust.

• *State dependence and strategic complementarity can lead to complex outcomes* (Ball and Romer 1990; Dotsey and King 2005). Ball and Romer point out the possibility of multiple equilibria: If firms care sufficiently about relative prices, then the incentive to adjust prices may be increasing in the prices set by others. Dotsey and King show that these strategic complementarities can cause inflation to respond with a delay to a money shock as firms wait for enough other firms to contemplate price adjustment before adjusting their prices themselves.

• *The modeling of price adjustment may affect the welfare costs of inflation* (Kiley 2002; Blanco 2015). Kiley shows that Calvo pricing can lead to some very stale prices and that this can greatly increase the welfare costs of inflation. Blanco studies the welfare costs of inflation at low inflation and finds inflation less costly in menu cost models.

The current paper takes a different view of what is important about the microeconomics of price adjustment. Rather than focusing on the distinction between state and time dependence, the authors focus on the resulting moments of the price-change distribution. They provide conditions under which the cumulative effect of a money shock on output is completely characterized by the frequency of price adjustment, the kurtosis of the price-change distribution, and a utility parameter that represents the elasticity of output with respect to the real wage. State- and time-dependent rules matter because they influence these statistics.

Their key result may be summarized in a single equation. Let $\mathcal{M}$ denote the cumulative response of output to a shock to the money supply, $\mathcal{M} = \int_0^\infty y(t)dt$ where $y(t)$ is the percent deviation of output from its steady state. Then, under certain conditions, a permanent $\delta\%$ shock to the money supply leads to a cumulative output response equal to:

$$\mathcal{M} = \frac{\delta}{6\varepsilon} \, \text{kurtosis}(\Delta p)E(T).$$

An example will help illustrate the use of the equation. Consider a world with Taylor pricing and suppose that prices change every four periods. It follows immediately that $E(T) = 4$. Suppose that the optimal price for each product follows an independent, driftless Brownian motion with infinitesimal variance σ^2, then the steady-state distribution of price changes is a normal density with variance $4\sigma^2$. The kurtosis of a normal distribution is equal to 3. Putting this all together, the formula predicts $\mathcal{M} = 2\delta/\varepsilon$. Figure 1 illustrates the output response. Time is continuous and price adjustment is uniformly distributed over the interval [0, 4]. The money shock hits at date zero. Since only a small fraction of firms adjust their prices every instant, the impact effect is equal to the size of the money shock times the elasticity of output with respect to mispricing, δ/ε. When a firm gets a chance to adjust, it adjusts one-for-one with the money shock. Since price changes are distributed uniformly over [0, 4], output returns linearly to trend, and since every firm adjusts by date 4, output reaches trend at date 4; $\mathcal{M}$ is the area under the curve that is easily seen to be equal to $2\delta/\varepsilon$, the value predicted by the formula.

This is a very surprising equation. Note all of the things that do not appear in their equation: the variance of the idiosyncratic shocks to firms' desired prices; the number of prices that the firm is setting; anything about the form of the decision making process; if this were a menu-cost model, the size of the menu cost or the size of the Ss bands. The output response depends on only four things. The first three are fairly straightforward: $\mathcal{M}$ naturally scales with the the size of the money shock δ, the expected time between price changes $E(T)$, and the elasticity of output with respect to mispricing $1/\varepsilon$. The final element is more mysterious. Magically, the kurtosis of the price-change distribution controls for all of the effects of selection and heterogeneity. I have no intu-

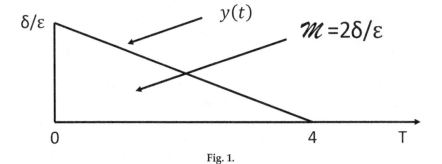

Fig. 1.

ition for this beyond the observation that larger kurtosis is associated with greater mispricing and a larger effect of money on output.

The equation is an approximation that holds under certain conditions. There are technical limitations, some of which are serious. The variance of marginal cost must be the same across products within a firm, but may differ across firms. They can handle heterogeneity in the time-dependent rules used by firms, but all firms must follow the same state-dependent rules.[2] There needs to be zero drift in marginal cost at the product level. This last requirement is in some sense the most troubling, as it would appear to be violated in the data; marginal cost is declining in some manufacturing sectors and rising in some service sectors.

Still the assumptions are no more stringent than those made in many macromodels, and the characterization of the output effects of a money shock in terms of only a few statistics is very neat and compact. I was therefore left wanting to see if their sufficient statistics worked at all in practice. Given the technical limitations, I would not expect this equation to fit the data perfectly, but it would be very nice to know if these statistics are at all informative. What is the correlation between these statistics and the real effect of a monetary policy shock? Do countries with greater kurtosis also have more potent monetary policy? What about industries? Given the large number of micropricing data sets that have been collected over the past few decades, it would be relatively simple to calculate the necessary moments. Calculating a measure of monetary policy would be more challenging, but not impossible. One could assume that ε is constant across countries. To the extent that the theory did not work one might want to begin controlling for violations of the technical assumptions, but before doing so it would be nice to know if the equation held any information in its simplest form. Simpler empirical relationships have been successfully taken to the data. I would find such an exercise much more interesting than what they actually do in the paper, which is to attempt to show that large shocks have different effects than small shocks. I see empirical work along these lines as the logical next step in their research program.

In closing, I would like to discuss the results of the paper in light of the differences between state and time dependence that are prominent in the literature discussed above. The theme of these comments is that while the assumptions that the authors make lead to very pretty results such as the equation above, these assumptions also rule out some of the potential differences between the two types of models.

First, their experiments always begin with the steady-state density.

The authors consider small shocks so that they may employ first-order approximations. Since the initial state never changes and since their approximation is linear, they can't get at the state dependence of the response of output to shocks that figures prominently in Caplin and Leahy (1991) or Caballero and Engel (2007).

Second, they can allow for lots of different types of heterogeneity, especially heterogeneity in time-dependent rules. They need this heterogeneity to be thoroughly mixed, in the sense that each type must be in their own steady state. This rules out heterogeneity that depends on the state of the economy. They cannot have time-dependent rules that depend on the aggregate state as in Ball, Mankiw, and Romer (1988), where higher inflation leads to shorter intervals between price adjustment. They cannot have the variance of idiosyncratic shocks depend on the state of the economy as in Vavra (2013). Nor can they have the time-dependent policy depend on the calendar as in Olivei and Tenreyro (2007).

Third, they make a series of assumptions so that the marginal cost of each firm is an independent Brownian motion without drift. This is a very convenient outcome since it transforms an equilibrium problem into a collection of isolated decision problems; they can solve for the pricing decisions at one firm independently from the pricing decisions of all other firms. The cost of the zero drift assumption, however, is that they do not get frontloading as in Ball (1994) or Midrigan (2011), and the strategic independence across firms means that they will not find any role for strategic complementarity as in Dotsey and King (2005).

Finally, their sufficient statistic approach does not pin down welfare. This is easy to see because the statistics are independent of so many things, in particular the variance of the idiosyncratic shocks.

In sum, this is very interesting research. The authors have made great progress on a very technically difficult problem. The simple characterization that they find is at once surprising and provocative. I look forward to seeing where they go in the future.

Endnotes

For acknowledgments, sources of research support, and disclosure of the author's material financial relationships, if any, please see http://www.nber.org/chapters/c13769.ack.

1. The authors also appeal to imperfect information, but there are problems with this interpretation. Imperfect information itself does not lead to the type of fixed prices we see in the data. Instead, firms change their prices in every period in response to their imperfect perception of how the world is changing. One needs to add auxiliary assump-

tions such as assuming the optimal price is a martingale or adding a fixed cost of price adjustment on top of the imperfect information. The former is unrealistic. The latter might as well be called a state dependence (unless one locks managers in a box so that they have no ability to see and respond to current news).

2. To see why heterogeneity in state dependence is a problem, consider an economy that is really the sum of two completely separate economies. Suppose that each has an Ss pricing policy but that the size of the Ss bands are different. Each economy separately would have kurtosis of 1 since the price-change density is a two-point density. The combined economy, however, would have a kurtosis of greater than one, since the price-change density would be a four-point density. The equation would predict that the two sectors individually were less rigid than the combined economy, even though there is no connection between the sectors.

References

Ascari, Guido. 2004. "Staggered Prices and Trend Inflation: Some Nuisances." *Review of Economic Dynamics* 7:642–67.

Ball, Laurence. 1994. "Credible Disinflation with Staggered Price-Setting." *American Economic Review* 84:282–89.

Ball, Laurence, Gregory Mankiw, and David Romer. 1988. "The New Keynesian Economics and the Output-Inflation Trade-Off." *Brookings Papers on Economic Activity* 1988 (1): 1–82.

Ball, Laurence, and David Romer. 1990. "Real Rigidities and the Non-Neutrality of Money." *Review of Economic Studies* 57:183–203.

Blanco, Julio Andres. 2015. "Optimal Inflation Target in an Economy with Menu Costs and an Occasionally Binding Zero Lower Bound." Working paper, University of Michigan.

Caballero, Ricardo, and Eduardo Engel. 2007. "Price Stickiness in Ss models: New Interpretations of Old Results." *Journal of Monetary Economics* 54:100–21.

Caplin, Andrew, and John Leahy. 1991. "State-Dependent Pricing and the Dynamics of Money and Output." *Quarterly Journal of Economics* 106:683–708.

———. 1997. "Aggregation and Optimization with State-Dependent Pricing." *Econometrica* 65:601–25.

Caplin, Andrew, and Daniel Spulber. 1987. "Menu Costs and the Neutrality of Money." *Quarterly Journal of Economics* 102:703–25.

Dotsey, Michael, and Robert King. 2005. "Implications of State-Dependent Pricing for Dynamic Macroeconomic Models." *Journal of Monetary Economics* 52:213–42.

Dotsey, Michael, Robert King, and Alexander Wolman. 1999. "State-Dependent Pricing and the General Equilibrium Dynamics of Money and Output." *Quarterly Journal of Economics* 114:655–90.

Golosov, Mikhail, and Robert Lucas. 2007. "Menu Costs and Phillips Curves." *Journal of Political Economy* 115:171–200.

Kiley, Michael. 2002. "Partial Adjustment and Staggered Price Setting." *Journal of Money Credit and Banking* 34:283–98.

Midrigan, Virgiliu. 2011. "Menu Costs, Multi-Product Firms, and Aggregate Fluctuations." *Econometrica* 79:1139–80.

Olivei, Giovanni, and Silvana Tenreyro. 2007. "The Timing of Monetary Policy Shocks." *American Economic Review* 97:636–63.

Vavra, Joseph. 2013. "Inflation Dynamics and Time-Varying Volatility: New Evidence and an Ss Interpretation." *Quarterly Journal of Economics* 129:215–58.

Comment

Greg Kaplan, University of Chicago and NBER

Introduction

Alvarez, Lippi, and Passadore undertake a novel theoretical and empirical investigation into the nature of pricing frictions, focusing on the similarities and differences between state-dependent and time-dependent pricing models. Among other results, their theoretical investigation establishes two useful comparisons of these different classes of models. First, they show that in a small period of time following the impact of a small nominal shock, the response of the aggregate price level is equally small in both state-dependent and time-dependent models, and approaches zero as the size of the shock approaches zero. Second, they show that for larger shocks, the aggregate price-level response increases linearly in the size of the shock in time-dependent models, while the aggregate price-level response is convex in the size of the shock in state-dependent models. For large enough shocks, state-dependent models feature full pass-through of nominal shocks on impact, and hence displays monetary neutrality.

Assumptions that guarantee continuity of relevant distributions drive these theoretical results. For time-dependent models, the results rely on continuity of the cross-sectional distribution of times until the next price adjustment, ruling out, for example, Calvo-style models with correlated times of price adjustment. For state-dependent models, the results rely on continuity of the cross-sectional distribution of gaps between firms' current prices and their unconstrained profit-maximizing prices, ruling out, for example, models with discrete distributions of idiosyncratic shocks. However, the underlying economic intuition that drives these two results is sufficiently strong that these predictions are likely to hold, at least approximately, even in models where the relevant assumptions do not hold exactly.

The sharpness and robustness of these theoretical predictions suggest a simple test for the nature of pricing frictions: if state-dependent pricing is quantitatively important, then one should expect to see proportionately larger price changes in response to large nominal shocks than in response to small shocks. In the empirical part of their paper, the authors test this prediction by looking for evidence of nonlinearities in the degree of exchange rate pass-through, using a monthly country-level panel of exchange rates and inflation rates.

My comments are focused on this empirical investigation. I will first summarize their empirical strategy and main results. Next, I will discuss the sources of exchange rate variation that the pass-through regressions exploit, and the extent to which this variation is a good testing ground for the theory. After that I will investigate the importance of outliers in generating this variation. I will finish with some thoughts on what we could, or should, hope to learn from an exercise such as this one. I will suggest that rather than *testing* for state dependence versus time dependence, we should simply recognize that both elements of behavior exist, and focus instead on *measuring* the circumstances under which one dominates the other. In the context of nonlinear exchange rate pass-through, this translates into asking how big is a big exchange rate shock. The answer suggested by the authors' empirical findings is "very big."[1]

Summary of Empirical Results

The authors' theoretical predictions suggest that in order to distinguish between state-dependent versus time-dependent pricing, one should look at how prices respond to small versus large exogenous nominal shocks. If the aggregate price response is proportionately larger for large shocks than for small shocks, then this speaks in favor of state-dependent pricing. If the aggregate price response is similar, then this speaks in favor of time-dependent pricing. So state-dependent models predict a convex relationship between nominal shocks and aggregate price changes, while time-dependent models predict a linear relationship.

Of course, this is only a useful strategy if one can identify and measure an exogenous nominal shock for which there is observed variation in its size. Building on insights from the literature on exchange rate pass-through (e.g., Goldberg and Knetter 1997; Campa and Goldberg 2005; Burstein and Gopinath 2014), the authors propose to use nominal exchange rate fluctuations as such exogenous shocks. The idea is that for many domestic firms, imported goods make up a significant component of their input costs and so when exchange rates depreciate, their nominal input costs increase (measured in domestic currency).

To examine the pattern of exchange rate pass-through to consumer prices, the authors construct a country-level monthly panel of bilateral USD exchange rates and consumer price indexes. They regress monthly inflation rates $\pi_{i,t}$ on a full set of country and month fixed effects, the change in the nominal exchange rate vis-à-vis the US dollar $\Delta e_{i,t}$, and a sign-adjusted quadratic function of the nominal exchange rate $|\Delta e_{it}| \Delta e_{it}$. The coefficient on the exchange rate depreciation term is the estimated measure of overall pass-through, and the coefficient on the quadratic term measures the extent to which large exchange rate movements yield proportionately larger movements in inflation.

The authors' baseline empirical specification restricts attention to 6,811 country/months from 197 countries over the period 1974–2014. The selected country/month observations are those which are classified as "flexible" according to Ilzetzki, Reinhart, and Rogoff (2008). Their sample also excludes high-inflation countries and periods, as well as country/month observations with low output per capita and/or low population. The baseline estimates in their table 2 are consistent with the predictions of the state-dependent pricing model. Over a one-month period, the estimated linear exchange rate pass-through is around 1% with a standard error of 0.4%, and there is a large and strongly significant coefficient on the quadratic term. The authors conduct a series of additional analyses that impose alternative sample-selection criteria and use different functional forms to capture the nonlinearity, and find that the evidence for nonlinear exchange rate pass-through is robust to these choices.

To better understand what drives these findings, I find it useful to look directly at scatter plots of the 6,811 monthly inflation rates and exchange rate depreciations in the estimation sample. The raw data are displayed in figure 1, panel (a), and the residuals after removing time fixed effects are displayed in figure 1, panel (b). Both figures include linear regression lines and a flexible nonlinear fitted line, together with 95% confidence intervals.[2] The scatter plot in figure 1, panel (b) reflects exactly the variation that is captured by the authors' baseline regressions. The significant linear and nonlinear effects that the authors find are both clearly evident in these scatter plots.

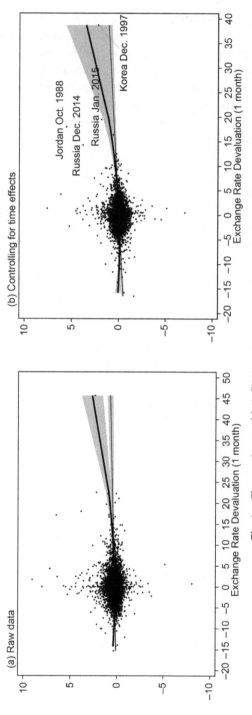

Fig. 1. Changes in monthly inflation rates versus exchange rate depreciation

(a) Raw data

(b) Controlling for time effects

Jordan Oct. 1988
Russia Dec. 2014
Russia Jan. 2015
Korea Dec. 1997

Exchange Rate Devaluation (1 month)

Sources of Exchange Rate Variation

Before discussing the sources of the estimated nonlinearity in pass-through, I want to comment briefly on the precisely estimated linear pass-through of 1% that the authors obtain. In light of the existing literature, a precisely estimated exchange rate pass-through to monthly CPI inflation of this magnitude is somewhat surprising. For example, Goldberg and Campa (2010) report quarterly estimates of exchange rate pass-through for 21 high-income countries in their table 7 that vary widely across countries, from a minimum of –11% to a maximum of +60%. The average across these countries is 1.5%, but given the variation in the estimates, a pooled regression would yield a very imprecisely estimated pass-through coefficient that is statistically indistinguishable from zero.

So why do Alvarez, Lippi, and Passadore obtain precise estimates of pass-through coefficients? The main reason is that their regressions control for time effects. Most of the existing literature, including Campa and Goldberg (2005), do not control for time effects in their regressions. The difference between controlling for time effects and not controlling for time effects on the estimated pass-through coefficients can be visualized by comparing the slopes of the linear fitted lines in figure 1, panels (a) and (b). Without controlling for time effects, the fitted line is essentially flat and the estimated coefficient is statistically indistinguishable from zero. With country fixed effects included, the pass-through coefficient falls from 1% with a standard error of 0.4% to –0.3% with a standard error of 0.3% when time effects are excluded from the regression.

The reason that whether or not one controls for time effects has such a large impact on the pass-through coefficient is because of the different sources of exchange rate variation that the two empirical approaches exploit. Intuitively, movements in bilateral USD exchange rates can originate either from a domestic shock or a US shock. Controlling for time effects removes all of the variation in these bilateral exchange rates that is common across countries, including variation that is due to disturbances that originate in the United States. Hence the only exchange rate variation that remains is variation that is specific to a given country in a given month, and so must be driven by domestic shocks. Such variation accounts for about 58% of the total monthly variation in exchange rate depreciation, and it is perhaps less surprising that this country/month-specific component of exchange rate variation is more tightly correlated with domestic CPI inflation.

However, it is not clear that for the purpose of testing for state-dependent versus time-dependent pricing, this is the variation that the authors should be exploiting. Recall that ideally the authors would like to examine the response of domestic prices to a plausibly exogenous nominal shock. If a country's bilateral USD exchange rate changed because of a shock that originated in the United States, then one could reasonably argue that this change is orthogonal to domestic economic conditions, particularly for smaller countries. This argument would suggest extracting the common component of the changes in all countries' bilateral USD exchange rates (which reflects US-sourced shocks), and to regress domestic inflation on exchange rates, instrumenting with this common component. But by controlling for time effects, the authors are doing exactly the opposite of this—they use only exchange rate variation that is due to country-specific disturbances, rather than exchange rate variation that is due to foreign disturbances.

Now, perhaps controlling for time effects is okay for studying the effects of small exchange rate movements, since one might make the argument that country-month-specific fluctuations in bilateral USD exchange rates are truly random and do not, in fact, reflect fundamental economic shocks. However, it is difficult to make this argument for large exchange rate movements, which are the key observations for detecting nonlinearity in pass-through and hence are the focus of the authors' analysis. One might reasonably suspect that a large monthly USD exchange rate depreciation that is unique to a single country might have been driven by a real economic shock that caused both the exchange rate movement and any corresponding change in inflation. If the estimated nonlinearity in pass-through is driven by large observations where orthogonality is suspect, then this poses a threat to the whole identification strategy.

Importance of Outliers

With this concern in mind, I decided to look more closely at which country-month observations are important for driving the significant estimated nonlinearity in pass-through. It turns out that the nonlinearity is being driven by four monthly exchange rate movements in three countries (South Korea, December 1997; Jordan, October 1988; Russia, December 2014 and January 2015). These observations are highlighted in figure 1, panel (b). When these four monthly observations out of the

6,811 are excluded from the estimation sample, all evidence of nonlinear exchange rate pass-through disappears. The authors mention that the December 1997 observation for Korea is important for the statistical significance of the coefficient on the nonlinear term, but these outliers drive more than just statistical significance; rather, they are entirely responsible for the conclusion of convexity in exchange rate pass-through.

Whether we interpret the authors' empirical analysis as providing evidence for state dependence in pricing thus depends on whether we believe these four monthly exchange rate movements can be safely considered to be exogenous nominal shocks. In other words, we must be convinced that in these four months the only relevant domestic shocks that might have affected CPI inflation were these exchange rate movements. Let us consider each of these observations in turn.

South Korea, December 1997

For South Korea, November–December 1997 was the peak of the 1997 Asian Financial Crisis. During these two months, their credit rating was downgraded twice, their stock market collapsed, and a massive restructuring of the financially troubled auto industry was initiated. Between November and December the Korean won depreciated by nearly 40%, and CPI inflation was around 2.5%. Put simply, there was a lot going on in South Korea at this time, much of it predictable, and the large exchange rate movement was anything but a nominal shock.

Jordan, October 1988

Since its introduction in 1950, the Jordanian dinar has almost always been pegged to various currencies. In September 1988, Jordan abandoned its peg and was floating to some degree until 1995, since when it has again been fixed. The observed exchange rate depreciation between September and October 1988 is the effect of the regime change from a fixed to floating exchange rate. For these months, the Jordanian dinar is classified by Ilzetzki, Reinhart, and Rogoff (2008) as "freely falling." I have been unable to find out more information about the circumstances in Jordan that prompted the change in exchange rate regimes, but in general, regime changes are not exogenous events. This is almost certainly not the type of exchange rate variation that we would want to use to test the predictions of the pricing models being considered here.

Russia, December 2014–January 2015

The western sanctions imposed on Russia after the start of the war with Ukraine in February 2014 led to large capital outflows. This, combined with the collapse in global oil prices in the second half of 2014, led to increasing difficulties for Russian energy companies, which culminated in a transfer of currency from the Central Bank of Russia to Rosneft, Russia's largest oil company. The bailout was accompanied by a 30% drop in the value of the ruble over two days in December 2014. At the end of December, Russian interest rates were raised to 17% and the ruble stabilized. Since then, the ruble's value has mostly followed the price of oil. This is all to say that there was a lot going on in Russia during this time. Moreover, given the importance of energy prices, it may be more appropriate to study CPI inflation excluding energy.

The importance of outliers in driving the estimated nonlinearity in pass-through highlights an element of catch-22 in this empirical strategy. In order to detect nonlinearities, we need to observe large exchange rate movements. But large exchange rate movements are almost never going to be exogenous (nor completely nominal). I think this reflects the downside of using CPI inflation as a proxy for pricing outcomes, rather than using microdata on firm-level or product-level prices. In addition to the fact that CPI inflation includes price changes for many nontradable goods and the nontradable components of tradable goods, it is much easier to argue for exogeneity of exchange rate movements with respect to individual firm-level pricing decisions than it is for movements in the aggregate consumer price index. With microdata on prices it is also possible to develop tests for pass-through that are robust to endogeneity of exchange rates (e.g., Gopinath, Itskhoki, and Rigobon 2010).

Sign Asymmetry

Before concluding, I would like to point out the evidence (or lack thereof) for a symmetric response of prices to large exchange rate movements. It is clear from the scatter plots in figure 1 that there is no evidence for large price declines in response to large exchange rate appreciations, yet the theory is unambiguously symmetric in its prediction of convexity. This is what leads the authors to include a sign-adjusted quadratic term in their regression specification. One might react to this observation by saying that we simply do not observe any large enough

monthly exchange rate appreciations in our sample to be able to evaluate whether there is a convex response in this direction. But I see this as
just highlighting the fragility of an econometric approach that is so reliant on individual outliers for identification. Moreover, the fact that all
large outliers in the sample are depreciaitons, not appreciations, further
adds to the suspicion that these are not exogenous random episodes.

Final Thoughts

Clearly, there are aspects of time-dependent pricing and state-dependent
pricing in all firms' pricing decisions (see, e.g., Nakamura and Steinsson
2008). So what exactly is it that we are after when we test for the presence of state-dependent pricing by looking for evidence of convexity
of the aggregate price-level response to nominal shocks? Is the goal to
figure out whether for a sufficiently large shock a firm will change their
prices even if they are not scheduled to do so for another few quarters?
It seems natural that they will—nothing is set in stone. Or is the goal to
figure out whether there is also an element of state dependence even for
moderately sized shocks? I prefer to ask the question of approximately
how large does a shock need to be before state dependence strongly
kicks. If there is anything to take away from the empirical analysis in
this paper, I would suggest that the answer one gets from looking at
exchange rate pass-through into CPI inflation, is that the predictions of
state dependence seem only to be evident for extremely large exchange
rate depreciations—well outside the typical range of fluctuations experienced in most developed flexible exchange rate economies. But much
more work is needed to know how much to make of this finding.

Endnotes

For acknowledgments, sources of research support, and disclosure of the author's material financial relationships, if any, please see http://www.nber.org/chapters/c13770.ack.
    1. These comments are largely based on an earlier draft of the paper. Some of them are
mentioned and recognized by the authors in the main text.
    2. I use a fractional polynomial regression to fit the nonlinearities, but other methods
give similar results (including kernel regression and local linear regression).

References

Burstein, Ariel, and Gita Gopinath. 2014. "International Prices and Exchange
    Rates." In *Handbook of International Economics*, vol. 4, ed. G. Gopinath, E.
    Helpman, and K. Rogoff, 391–451. Amsterdam: Elsevier.
Campa, Jose Manuel, and Linda S. Goldberg. 2005. "Exchange Rate Pass-
    Through into Import Prices." *Review of Economics and Statistics* 87 (4): 679–90.

Goldberg, Linds S., and José Manuel Campa. 2010. "The Sensitivity of the CPI to exchange rates: Distribution margins, imported inputs, and trade exposure." *The Review of Economics and Statistics* 92 (2): 392–407.

Goldberg, Pinelopi Koujianou, and Michael M. Knetter. 1997. "Goods Prices and Exchange Rates: What Have We Learned?" *Journal of Economic Literature* 35 (3): 1243–72.

Gopinath, Gita, Oleg Itskhoki, and Roberto Rigobon. 2010. "Currency Choice and Exchange Rate Pass-Through." *American Economic Review* 100 (1): 304–36.

Ilzetzki, Ethan, Carmen Reinhart, and Kenneth Rogoff. 2008. "Exchange Rate Arrangements Entering the 21st Century: Which Anchor Will Hold?" Manuscript, University of Maryland and Harvard University.

Nakamura, Emi, and Jón Steinsson. 2008. "Five Facts about Prices: A Reevaluation of Menu Cost Models." *Quarterly Journal of Economics* 123 (4): 1415–64.

Discussion

Robert Hall began the discussion by reiterating Greg Kaplan's concern about the results being affected by a small number of outliers. He referred to Young (2016), which showed that White robust standard errors are potentially biased toward zero in regressions that have a small number of influential observations. Hall raised concerns that the downward bias in the standard errors might be driving the authors' findings of statistically significant nonlinear effects of exchange rate changes on prices.

Michael Klein was concerned that changes in exchange rates are correlated with macroeconomic shocks that can differ across countries. He expressed surprise that the authors were able to get precise estimates of the effects of exchange rate shocks on price adjustments, given that the reduced-form regressions do not control for differences in production chains or demand across countries.

Thomas Philippon, however, was not as concerned about the extreme observations in the authors' sample. He argued that the point of the exercise was to see if prices adjusted more after big shocks than after small shocks, regardless of the type of the shock. He believed that the issue of extreme observations would be more relevant if the authors had been trying to estimate the response to a specific type of shock, such as a monetary policy shock.

Mark Gertler referred the authors to Peter Karadi's thesis for an example of a large and exogenous shock in Hungary to study price adjustment behavior.

Fernando Alvarez replied that while he had not looked at the shock in Hungary, he does have a companion paper (Alvarez et al. 2016) that uses microdata to study price adjustments in Argentina. The sample that he studied spanned three years of hyperinflation and five years of nearly zero inflation. He noted, however, that the issue with his companion paper, and with using the shock in Peter Karadi's thesis, is that there are only a small number of shocks available. For this paper, the authors instead wanted to look at a large number of big and small shocks, which is what motivated them to examine a panel data set.

Thomas Philippon also asked if the implications of financial frictions differed in state-dependent models versus time-dependent models. He referred to Gilchrist et al. (2015), which showed that financial frictions create an incentive for firms to raise prices in response to financial or demand shocks.

Fernando Alvarez acknowledged Philippon's comment, and said that more work needs to be done to understand the interaction of financial frictions and price adjustments.

Francisco Lippi spoke next, making the comment that besides the regressions, the authors also considered experimental evidence about decision making. He referred to experiments that have been run by others where undergraduate students were tasked with solving a menu-cost problem that incorporated a transaction cost for adjusting prices. In one experiment, the students were told the optimal price-adjustment rule. However, he noted that even when the students were told the optimal price-adjustment rule, there was still evidence of inattention in the distribution of adjustments. He thus thought that it might be worthwhile to take an experimental approach to distinguish between different pricing models, beyond what the authors have done with the microdata.

Ricardo Reis noted that the authors try to distinguish between state- and time-dependent models by examining the price responses to different-sized shocks. He suggested that the authors also consider if price adjustments differ depending on the timing of when the shocks is known. He argued that the timing of news about the shock would not affect the price-adjustment response in state-dependent models, but would make a difference in time-dependent models. He also referred to Klenow and Willis (2007), who take a similar approach to test different pricing models.

Laura Veldkamp spoke next, questioning how much can be learned from trying to distinguish between state-dependent and time-dependent models, which are two extreme models of price adjustments. In reality, the world is a mix of the two models.

Fernando Alvarez responded to Laura Veldkamp's comment by referring to his broader research agenda and past work. He argued that it is possible to learn about price-adjustment behavior, even in a world with a mix of both time and state dependency in price adjustment. For instance, Alvarez et al. (2016) models both state and time dependence. The authors provide a sufficient statistic for the real effects of monetary policy, which informs about the ratio of the observation cost and the menu cost. The sufficient statistic is therefore informative about the relative importance of time versus state dependency for explaining patterns of price adjustment that are observed in the data. He also referred to Alvarez et al. (2012), which provides household microevidence on observation and transaction costs of durable consumption.

Narayana Kocherlakota asked whether the trade-offs between inflation and employment for a policymaker differs under a time-dependent versus state-dependent model.

Fernando Alvarez replied that there may be differences in the trade-offs between inflation and employment if there are communication issues for the policymaker to consider. He noted that they needed to think more about the trade-offs involved.

Emi Nakamura followed up on John Leahy's discussion about strategic complementarities. She asked the authors whether strategic complementarities may amplify the price-adjustment response following large shocks. She hypothesized that since many agents adjust following large shocks, coordination frictions would be lower, which could in turn reinforce the propensity to adjust. She also referred to Boivin et al. (2008), who show that prices respond more to idiosyncratic shocks than to aggregate shocks. Idiosyncratic shocks are also larger than aggregate shocks, and therefore the larger response to the idiosyncratic shocks may be a related piece of evidence.

Fernando Alvarez noted that he and his coauthors need to think more about strategic complementarities. The strategic complementarities are difficult to include in the time- and state-dependent models, and it is not clear if they necessarily interact with time and state dependence. So far, they have nt yet thought of a way to incorporate strategic complementarities that give generalizable expressions.

Lawrence Christiano asked whether the comovement between prices and quantities differed across the two sticky price models. He referred to prior work that he had done with DSGE New Keynesian models that gave a negative covariance. The reason for the negative covariance is that agents respond to past shocks of demand and supply, and therefore when they adjust, they move along a given demand curve. He wondered if state-dependent models also robustly generate a negative covariance between prices and quantities. He suspected the answer is "no" because agents are more likely to respond immediately after a shock. Therefore, the model is more likely to produce a zero or positive covariance.

Fernando Alvarez agreed that it would be interesting to examine the covariance between prices and quantities, and the composition of demand and supply shocks. He agreed that in theory, the correlation between prices and quantities might be positive in state-dependent models. For instance, the authors examined some state-dependent models with multidimensional products, where the agent only paid a single cost to adjust any of the dimensions. The single adjustment cost meant that price adjustments, following a shock, might be positively correlated across the products, as Lawrence Christiano suggests. However, in practice, he found the correlation to be quantitatively small because agents had already adjusted many times before the shock occurred.

Fernando Alvarez also responded to general discussion about the variation in state and time dependency of price adjustments with inflation expectations. Looking at price changes during periods with extreme fluctuations in the aggregate data, such as in Argentina, he found that state-dependent models are able to generate elasticities of the frequency of price adjustments with respect to inflation that are consistent with the microevidence. For instance, the state-dependent models generate zero elasticity around zero inflation, and a high elasticity of about two-thirds during periods of high inflation because idiosyncratic shocks are also high during periods of high inflation.

Francesco Lippi reiterated that the theoretical results depend on the level of inflation. He noted that state-dependent models with idiosyncratic shocks are consistent with Gagnon (2009). The work by Gagnon (2009), based on a data set of Mexican consumer prices, show that the frequency of price changes comoves weakly with inflation when inflation is low (less than 10–15%). However, for high levels of inflation, the frequency of price changes is an important determinant of inflation.

6

Is the Macroeconomy Locally Unstable and Why Should We Care?

Paul Beaudry, *Vancouver School of Economics, University of British Columbia, and NBER*
Dana Galizia, *Carleton University*
Franck Portier, *Toulouse School of Economics and CEPR*

I. Introduction

There are two polar views about the functioning of a market economy. On the one hand, there is the view that such a system is inherently stable, with market forces tending to direct the economy toward a smooth growth path. According to this belief, most of the fluctuations in the macroeconomy result either from individually optimal adjustments to changes in the environment or from improper government interventions, with market forces acting to prevent the economy from being unstable. On the other hand, there is the view that the market economy is inherently unstable, and that left to itself it will repeatedly go through periods of socially costly booms and busts. According to this view, macroeconomic policy is needed to help stabilize an unruly system.

Most modern macroeconomic models, such as those used by large central banks and governments, are somewhere in between these two extremes. However, they are by design generally much closer to the first view than the second. In fact, most commonly used macroeconomic models have the feature that, in the absence of outside disturbances, the economy is expected to converge to a stable path. In this sense, these models are based on the premise that a decentralized economy is both a globally and locally stable system, and that market forces, in and of themselves, do not tend to produce booms and busts. The only reason why we see economic cycles in most mainstream macroeconomic models is due to outside forces that perturb an otherwise stable system. While such a framework is very tractable and flexible, the ubiquitous and recurrent feature of cycles in most market economies requires one to question whether the market economy may, by its very nature, be inherently unstable and feature recurrent booms and busts, with a bust sowing the seeds of the next boom.[1]

There are at least two reasons why much of the macroeconomic profession adheres to the idea that the market economy is best described as a system with a unique stable steady state, where fluctuations are generated only by exogenous shocks. First, the majority of modern macroeconomic models based on optimizing behavior support the view of such a stable economic system. Second, when looking at the time series behavior of many labor market variables (such as the employment rate, the unemployment rate, or the job-finding rate), the estimated impulse response functions indicate that these variables respond to shocks in a manner suggestive of a stable system. For example, if one estimates a simple AR model for labor market variables, the roots of the system are generally well below one, which is consistent with the view that the system is stable.[2]

In this paper, we question this consensus. We begin by arguing that the local stability of the macroeconomic system should not be evaluated using linear time series methods, even if nonlinearities are thought to be very minor and only relevant rather far away from the steady state. Instead, we show why it is essential to allow for the possibility of nonlinearities (even if these may be very small) when exploring whether a dynamic system is locally stable. We then derive a simple class of time series models that we use to explore the stability properties of a number of macroeconomic aggregates. Using the results, we discuss why local instability should be treated as a relevant theoretical possibility when thinking about macroeconomic dynamics.[3] The main body of the text focuses on estimating the inherent dynamics of labor market variables and other macroeconomic aggregates. As we show, when we allow for simple nonlinearities in estimation, we generally find that this significantly changes the local properties of the system; in particular, it often switches from being locally stable when the nonlinear terms are excluded to being locally unstable when they are included.

After establishing that the macroeconomic system may be locally unstable, we then turn to examining the nature of the implied dynamics. This can be done by looking at how the system, with its stochastic elements turned off, evolves when it starts away from the steady state. If the steady state is unique and locally unstable, the system will not converge to a point.[4] Instead, in such a case there are three possible outcomes. One is that the system is globally unstable; that is, that the system will explode outward until it hits the economy's underlying capacity or nonnegativity constraints. This is very unlikely to be the case for labor market variables, since it would imply, for example, that we should see the unemployment rate approaching either 100% or 0%. This leaves two remaining possibilities, both involving endogenous fluctuations. The first of these is that the system may converge to a limit cycle; that is, the system settles into a recurrent pattern of booms and busts. The second possibility is that the system exhibits chaotic dynamics; that is, the system exhibits seemingly random nonrecurrent fluctuations (despite being fully deterministic) and is sensitive to initial conditions.[5] As we shall show, when we find that the system exhibits local instability, we generally find that there is a unique steady state and that the (nonstochastic) dynamics converge to a limit cycle. In this sense, our results suggest that a significant part of macroeconomic fluctuations may reflect forces that create endogenous boom-and-bust phenomena. Further, we find no evidence of chaotic behavior; that is, we do not find evidence that the deterministic part of the system exhibits sensitivity to initial conditions, a property that would render forecasting particularly difficult.

In the last section of the paper we discuss why our findings may be relevant for policy. In particular, we explore how the effects of stabilization policy may change in the presence of local instability and limit cycles. For example, we show that reducing the impact of shocks on the economy may not always help stabilize the system in such cases, and in particular, it may only change the frequency of fluctuations without necessarily decreasing their overall amplitude.

II. A Framework for Exploring Local Stability and Endogenous Cycles

In order to discuss the issue of local stability, it is helpful to focus on a variable that reflects cyclical fluctuations, but does not exhibit secular growth. Simple examples in macroeconomics are some labor market variables, such as the unemployment rate. Let us denote such a variable, in deviation from its mean, by x_t. One generally views x_t as being locally stable if there are endogenous forces present that tend to push it back toward its steady state when slightly perturbed. Suppose we believe that the process for x_t is approximately linear near its steady state. Then one may explore the local stability properties for x by first estimating an ARMA model for x, as given by

$$x_t = \tilde{A}(L)x_{t-1} + B(L)\varepsilon_t, \qquad (1)$$

where $\tilde{A}(L)$ and $B(L)$ are polynomials in the lag operator and where ε_t is an i.i.d. process.[6] Let us denote by A the companion matrix associated with $\tilde{A}(L)$.[7] If we find that the largest eigenvalue of A is less than 1,[8] then the steady state is stable. However, even if we believe that this system may be close to linear near the steady state, and that the variance of ε may be small, such an approach can provide a misleading answer regarding whether the steady state is locally stable or unstable. This can be shown with the following example:

Suppose the data-generating process (DGP) is actually

$$x_t = \tilde{A}(L)x_{t-1} + F(x_{t-1}) + \varepsilon_t, \tag{2}$$

where $F(\cdot)$ is a nonlinear function with $F(0) = F'(0) = 0$, which would be the case, for example, if $F(\cdot)$ is a polynomial function with no constant or linear terms. In this case, whether the system is locally stable at the zero steady state depends only on the eigenvalues of the companion matrix A, and not on the function $F(\cdot)$. However, this does not necessarily mean that one can disregard $F(x_{t-1})$ in the estimation of equation (2). If the eigenvalues of A are all less than 1, and if the variance of ε is small, then omitting $F(x_{t-1})$ in the estimation of equation (2) is unlikely to alter any conclusions drawn about the local stability of the system. However, if the largest eigenvalue of A is greater than 1, then omitting $F(x_{t-1})$ can easily lead one to conclude that the system is locally stable when it is in fact locally unstable.[9] To see this most clearly, consider the situation where $\tilde{A}(L) = -\alpha$ and $F(x_{t-1}) = \beta x_{t-1}^3$, with $\alpha, \beta > 0$. Since the covariance between x_{t-1} and x_{t-1}^3 is positive but these terms enter equation (2) with opposite signs, omitting x_{t-1}^3 from the econometric specification will tend to bias the estimate of α toward zero. If the system is locally unstable ($\alpha > 1$), but β is large enough relative to $\alpha - 1$,[10] then one would nonetheless incorrectly infer that the system was locally stable. Note also in this case that the closer α is to 1, the more likely it is that even a small value of β will be enough to arrive at the wrong conclusion about the stability of the system.

We have explored the behavior of such biases in various model specifications using Monte Carlo methods. A typical example is the following: We simulated 5,000 1,000-period samples of the DGP

$$x_t = \alpha x_{t-1} - 0.6x_{t-2} - 0.3x_{t-3} - 0.01x_{t-1}^3 + .25\varepsilon_t, \tag{3}$$

where ε_t is i.i.d. $\mathcal{N}(0, 1)$, and where α takes values in $[0.5,1.5]$. For this DGP, local stability depends on whether $\mid \lambda \mid_{max}$ is greater or smaller than 1, where $\mid \lambda \mid_{max}$ is the maximum modulus of the eigenvalues of the companion matrix to $\tilde{A}(L) = \alpha - 0.6L - 0.3L^2$. When $\alpha \in [0.5, 1.5]$, this process implies that $| \lambda |_{\max} \in [0.94, 1.4]$. When $| \lambda |_{\max} \in [0.94, 1)$, the steady state $\bar{x} = 0$ is locally (and globally) stable, while when $| \lambda |_{\max} > 1$ it is locally unstable. In this latter case, the DGP is such that, in the absence of any shocks, x_t would be attracted toward a limit cycle (as long as $x_0 \neq 0$). Figure 1 plots, as a function of the DGP $| \lambda |_{\max}$ (which is in turn a function of α), the average estimated $| \lambda |_{\max}$ for both the well-specified model and a misspecified model in which the nonlinear term is dropped. The first thing to notice is that the estimate of $| \lambda |_{\max}$ for the well-specified model is unbiased, as indicated by the fact that it lies directly on the 45° line. Next, note that the difference between the estimated values of $| \lambda |_{\max}$ for the well-specified and misspecified models provides an indication of the importance of including the nonlinear term. As one can see in the figure, the bias in estimating the misspecified model is very small when $| \lambda |_{\max} < 1$ in the DGP. Thus, in this case, whether or not one includes the nonlinear term is virtually irrelevant for determining whether the steady state is locally stable. However, the same degree of nonlinearity becomes much more important when the $| \lambda |_{\max}$ in the DGP becomes greater than 1, as evidenced by the fact that the misspecified model continues to indicate that the zero steady state is stable (i.e., $| \lambda |_{\max} < 1$ for this model), when it is in fact locally unstable in the DGP. One inference that can be drawn from this exercise is that, when estimates from a linear model yield a maximum eigenvalue that is close to 1 in modulus, this may be an indication that omitting nonlinear terms has made the steady state appear to be locally stable when in fact it is not. Moreover, the degree of nonlinearity in the DGP may be very modest, but may nevertheless be important for assessing local stability. We return to this issue below in the context of our empirical results.

The above discussion suggests a simple protocol for exploring local stability. One can start by estimating a linear model for the variable of interest and examine its local stability properties. Then one can add nonlinear terms (e.g., higher-order polynomial terms) to the specification, estimate it, and check the local stability properties of the resulting nonlinear model. If the addition of the nonlinear terms causes the largest eigenvalue of the linear approximation of the system to go from below 1 to above 1, this is an indication that the system may in fact be locally unstable. This is the procedure we will follow. In following such a procedure, it is generally important to include in the nonlinear specification terms that are at least of order three, since such terms are more

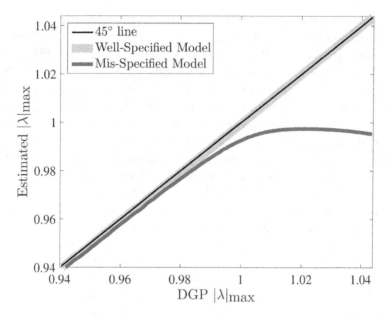

Fig. 1. Potential pitfall in assessing local stability when the DGP is nonlinear

Notes: For each of 100 values of α evenly distributed in the interval [0.5,1.5], we simulated 5,000 times a 1,000-period sample of the DGP in equation (3). From the resulting simulated data, we estimated by OLS either the well-specified equation (3) or a misspecified equation that omits the cubic term in equation (3). For each model and each α, we then computed the average maximum modulus of the eigenvalues of the companion matrix to $\tilde{A}(L) = \alpha - 0.6L - 0.3L^2$, which we denote $|\lambda|_{max}$. Figure plots, as a function of the DGP $|\lambda|_{max}$, the average estimated $|\lambda|_{max}$ for the well- and misspecified models.

likely to capture distant forces that may favor stability and whose omission would be more likely to bias in favor of inferring local stability.

A.   How to Interpret Local Instability

A common property of most modern macromodels is that fluctuations reflect the effects of exogenous shocks around a stable steady state. Macroeconomic models with unstable steady states are more of a rarity. While it is true that a Walrasian equilibrium model is unlikely to have an unstable steady state, models with strategic complementarities across agents can easily give rise to such configurations, even when the complementarities are not large enough to generate multiple equilibria. To see this, consider the following extremely simple environment describing the determination of an aggregate outcome. We have a collection of n agents indexed by i who make a decision x_{it} at each date t, with the average outcome being $x_t = n^{-1}\sum_i x_{it}$. Suppose that in the absence of any interactions across agents, their actions could be described by a stable decision rule of the form $x_{it} = \tilde{A}(L)x_{it-1} + \varepsilon_t$, where the largest eigenvalue of A (where A is the companion matrix to $\tilde{A}(L)$ as defined above) is less than one. In this case, the dynamics for x_t are given by the stable system $x_t = \tilde{A}(L)x_{t-1} + \varepsilon_t$. Now suppose we modify this environment slightly to allow for strategic complements across agents, such that the decision rule of agent i now includes a term that reflects their beliefs about the average behavior of others. In particular, suppose

$$x_{it} = \tilde{A}(L)x_{it-1} + \gamma E_{it}(x_t) + \varepsilon_t, \qquad 0 < \gamma < 1$$

where $E_{it}(x_t)$ reflects agent i's expectation of others' behavior,[11] and the parameter γ governs the degree of strategic complementarity. The dynamics of x_{it} now reflect the effects of both the stable individual-level behavior, captured by $\tilde{A}(L)$, and the strategic complementarities across agents, captured by having $0 < \gamma < 1$. Assuming a rational expectations, symmetric Nash equilibrium outcome, the dynamics for x_t are then given by

$$x_t = \frac{\tilde{A}(L)}{1 - \gamma} x_{t-1} + \varepsilon_t.$$

What are the stability properties of x_t in this case? If γ is sufficient small, then x_t will remain stable. However, if γ is sufficiently large (while remaining below 1), then one may verify that the largest eigenvalue of the companion matrix for $\tilde{A}(L) / (1 - \gamma)$ will be greater than 1, in which case the system will be unstable. Note also that if the largest eigenvalue of A is below but close to 1, then only a very small degree of strategic complementarity will be enough to produce instability in the system. The above example illustrates that in environments where agents interact, and where these interactions take the form of strategic complementarities, then the appearance of a nonstable steady state can arise quite easily. This gives rise to three possibilities: (1) the economy has more than one steady state and one or more of these other steady states is an attractor, (2) the economy has more than one steady state and all are unstable, or (3) the economy has only one steady state and therefore the economy cannot converge to a steady state. While we explore all three possibilities in our empirical work, we show that the data favor the third one, so let us focus on this possibility here. If the economy has only one steady state and it is unstable, what will the dynamics of the system look like?

If the system is globally linear, then the economy must necessarily explode. However, it is unlikely that the assumption of linearity, which may be appropriate near the steady state, remains so as one moves far away from the steady state. For example, complementarity between individuals' actions, which may be present near the steady state, is likely to give way to forces of strategic substitutability when one moves far away from the steady state. This is likely to arise since, if the economy is on an exploding path, eventually resource or nonnegativity constraints will become binding. Hence, when one considers global behavior in such environments, it is necessary to recognize that some countervailing forces are likely to appear and stop the system from exploding. Such alternative forces will be manifested as some sort of nonlinearity. If this is the case, then the local instability of the steady state will create dynamics that endogenously favor economic fluctuations, as the system will neither explode nor converge to its only steady state. This outcome can take the form of a limit cycle, wherein in the absence of shocks the economy would undergo a regular and predictable boom-and-bust pattern. Alternatively, it can produce chaotic behavior, in which the economy will fluctuate in an irregular and seemingly unpredictable fashion even in the absence of shocks, and in which the deterministic dynamics would exhibit sensitivity to initial conditions, making forecasting very difficult. Note that, while chaos is an interesting theoretical possibility, as documented below and in contrast to the limit-cycle case, we do not find any evidence to suggest that it may be empirically relevant.

Our goal in this paper will be to examine the time series behavior of several cyclical indicators of macroeconomic activity while allowing for nonlinearities. We will examine (a) whether these systems exhibit unique or multiple steady states, (b) whether the implied steady states are locally stable, and (c) if the dynamics exhibit limit cycles or chaotic behavior. In principle, the empirical exercise we perform is straightforward. We begin by estimating univariate processes allowing for nonlinear forces. We then examine whether the implied dynamics are stable or explosive near the steady state(s) by looking at the root structure of the local linear approximation. Finally, we examine the behavior of the variable if we start it away from the steady state, while shutting down the effects of any stochastic terms. In particular, if we find that a variable exhibits a unique steady state and local instability, we want to examine whether it then converges to cyclical behavior. The main difficulty with this procedure is determining the class of nonlinear models to consider, as nonlinearities can take on many forms.

B.   Baseline Univariate Model

Our approach to exploring local stability and possible endogenous cyclical behavior will be to estimate univariate models of the form

$$x_t = a_0 + \tilde{A}(L)x_{t-1} + F(x_{t-1}, x_{t-2}, \dots) + \varepsilon_t, \tag{4}$$

where x_t is a cyclical variable of interest, and $F(\cdot)$ is a multivariate polynomial function with no constant or linear terms.[13] In general, we would like to allow all the lags of x that appear in $\tilde{A}(L)x_{t-1}$ to potentially enter nonlinearly through $F(\cdot)$. As we have discussed, we also wish to allow F to be of at least order three in order to avoid potentially important biases in the estimation of $\tilde{A}(L)$. When $F(\cdot)$ is of minimum order three, however, the number of terms it contains grows very fast with the number of lags of x. For example, if F is a third-order polynomial in three lags of x, then with no further restrictions the resulting regression will feature 16 nonlinear terms, while adding a fourth lag would add another 15 terms on top of this, and so on. Since we would like to allow more distant lags to enter the regression without simultaneously having an explosion of coefficients to estimate, we impose the following two restrictions: (a) F is a polynomial of order three, and (b) lags of x beyond the second enter (4) only through an accumulation term $X_{t-1} \equiv \delta \sum_{j=0}^{\infty} (1 - \delta)^j x_{t-1-j}$. Under these restrictions, we can equivalently write (4) as

$$x_t = a_0 + a_1 x_{t-1} + a_2 x_{t-2} + a_3 X_t + F(x_{t-1}, x_{t-2}, X_{t-1}) + \varepsilon_t \tag{5}$$

where $F(\cdot)$ is a multivariate polynomial containing second- and third-order terms in its arguments.[14] There are two important things to note about the econometric specification (5). First, it embeds the standard $AR(2)$ process, which is known to be able to capture well many of the dynamics of macroeconomic variables. Second, it allows for more distant lags to play a role (through X_{t-1}) without requiring the estimation of too many extra parameters. We should emphasize that our inclusion of an accumulation term of this form is motivated by the class of models presented in Beaudry et al. (2015b), where the emergence of limit cycles is shown to be a possibility. See appendix for more details.

Handling Low-Frequency Movements

The specification we laid out in equation (5) is hopefully a sufficiently flexible way to allow us to offer new insight regarding the stability and cyclical properties of major macro aggregates. One remaining question is how to treat very low-frequency movements in the variable x_t. It is well known that most macroeconomic aggregates (even labor market variables) exhibit important low-frequency movements that are not generally thought to be related to the business cycle. For example, a variable such as total hours worked per capita, which according to many macro models should be stationary, often exhibits important low-frequency movements that are most often attributed to demographics and social change. We would like to remove such movements from our data, as they are likely to confound the cyclical properties we are interested in. In particular, in what follows we will interpret the framework we laid out above as modeling the cyclical element of a cyclical-trend unobserved component model. That is, we want to interpret the observed data as having been generated by a process of the form

$$x_t^O = x_t + x_t^T,$$

where x_t^O is the observed variable, x_t is the unobserved cyclical component of interest, x_t^T is a latent low-frequency trend, x_t and x_t^T are orthogonal series, and the process for x_t^T can be written

$$x_t^T = \int_{-\bar{\omega}}^{\bar{\omega}} [a(\omega)\cos(\omega t) + b(\omega)\sin(\omega t)]d\omega, \qquad \bar{\omega} \leq \pi. \qquad (6)$$

Here, $a(\omega)$ and $b(\omega)$ together determine the phase and amplitude associated with trend fluctuations of frequency ω, and $\bar{\omega}$ is the maximum frequency associated with trend fluctuations.

Within this framework, in order to implement our estimation of an equation such as (5) on the cyclical component of an observed macroeconomic aggregate x_t^O, it is necessary for us to take a stance on how to remove any low-frequency movements in the data that we believe are unrelated to business-cycle behavior; that is, on how to remove x_t^T. In most of our exploration, we will do this simply using a high-pass filter that removes fluctuations with periods longer than 20 years. With quarterly data, this corresponds to setting $\bar{\omega} = 2\pi / 80$ in equation (6), and making the additional identifying assumption that, not only are trend fluctuations made up entirely of frequencies below $\bar{\omega}$ (as imposed by equation [6]), but these low frequencies are *only* associated with the trend component; that is, we also assume that the cyclical component x_t is associated only with frequencies *above* $\bar{\omega}$.[15] We will include in our analysis a Monte Carlo evaluation of the potential biases in this approach to detect local instability and limit cycles in the extracted cyclical component. For robustness, we will also report results obtained using other detrending methods.

C. *Three Embedded Models*

Expanding equation (5), we get the following expression for the evolution of x_t, which we refer to as the "full" model:

$$
\begin{aligned}
x_t = \beta_0 &+ \beta_x x_{t-1} + \beta_{x'} x_{t-2} + \beta_X X_{t-1} \\
&+ \beta_{x^2} x_{t-1}^2 + \beta_{x'^2} x_{t-2}^2 + \beta_{X^2} X_{t-1}^2 \\
&+ \beta_{xx'} x_{t-1} x_{t-2} + \beta_{xX} x_{t-1} X_{t-1} + \beta_{x'X} x_{t-2} X_{t-1} \\
&+ \beta_{x^3} x_{t-1}^3 + \beta_{x'^3} x_{t-2}^3 + \beta_{X^3} X_{t-1}^3 \\
&+ \beta_{x^2 x'} x_{t-1}^2 x_{t-2} + \beta_{x^2 X} x_{t-1}^2 X_{t-1} \\
&+ \beta_{x'^2 X} x_{t-2}^2 X_{t-1} + \beta_{x'x^2} x_{t-1} x_{t-2}^2 \\
&+ \beta_{xX^2} x_{t-1} X_{t-1}^2 + \beta_{x'X^2} x_{t-2} X_{t-1}^2 \\
&+ \beta_{xx'X} x_{t-1} x_{t-2} X_{t-1} + \varepsilon_t.
\end{aligned}
\tag{7}
$$

This full model (7) allows for a rich nonlinear departure from the linear model. However, the drawback of such a specification is that it involves 20 parameters, making some properties hard to illustrate. For this reason, we will consider at the other extreme a very parsimonious version of equation (5), which consists of the inclusion of only one nonlinear term. We choose this one nonlinear term to be a cubic term in x_{t-1}. This choice, while somewhat arbitrary, is made for two reasons. First, from an intuitive standpoint, including odd-order nonlinear terms—of which the third is the lowest order—allows for a symmetric treatment of large positive and negative deviations from the steady state. Second, if there is only to be a single nonlinear term, having that term be solely in x_{t-1} seems to us to be the simplest choice. Our "minimal" model is therefore given by

$$
x_t = \beta_0 + \beta_x x_{t-1} + \beta_{x'} x_{t-2} + \beta_X X_{t-1} + \beta_{x^3} x_{t-1}^3 + \varepsilon_t.
\tag{8}
$$

As we shall see, we get very similar results based on either the minimal model or the full model, but the minimal model allows for simpler illustrations.

Finally, we will also consider an "intermediate" model that lies be-

tween these two extremes. One possibility in order to find the best intermediate specification is, for each variable under study, to start from
the full model and sequentially remove insignificant variables. As this
procedure is somewhat arbitrary, we instead choose as our intermediate model the case where we keep most third-order terms from the full
model, while eliminating all second-order terms. This has the feature of
significantly reducing the number of parameters, while still allowing for
relatively rich nonlinearities. In particular, of the seven third-order terms
in equation (7), we keep the three cubic terms and the two cross-terms
involving x_{t-1} and X_{t-1}, so that our intermediate model becomes

$$x_t = \beta_0 + \beta_x x_{t-1} + \beta_{x'} x_{t-2} + \beta_X X_{t-1}$$

$$+ \beta_{x^3} x_{t-1}^3 + \beta_{x'^3} x_{t-2}^3 + \beta_{X^3} X_{t-1}^3 \qquad (9)$$

$$+ \beta_{x^2 X} x_{t-1}^2 X_{t-1} + \beta_{xX^2} x_{t-1} X_{t-1}^2 + \varepsilon_t.$$

Our three models—full, intermediate, and minimal—together offer a
tractable nonlinear framework for examining whether certain macroeconomic variables may exhibit local instability and limit cycles. We
will also compare the behavior of these nonlinear models with two
specifications that do not feature any nonlinear terms: the "linear"
model, given by

$$x_t = \beta_0 + \beta_x x_{t-1} + \beta_{x'} x_{t-2} + \beta_X X_{t-1} + \varepsilon_t, \qquad (10)$$

and a simple $AR(2)$ model,

$$x_t = \beta_0 + \beta_x x_{t-1} + \beta_{x'} x_{t-2} + \varepsilon_t. \qquad (11)$$

D.   Estimation with Total Hours

Data Treatment and Estimation Results

The motivation we used to derive our reduced-form model is one based
on a cyclical indicator, such as hours worked per capita. Accordingly,
the first measure we examine is the (log of) BLS total hours worked,
deflated by total population. The mechanisms behind our motivating
model were not meant to explain low-frequency fluctuations such as
those related to demographic and sociological change (e.g., aging, fe-
male labor market participation, etc.). As can be seen in panel (a) of
figure 2, total hours (gray line) has exhibited important low-frequency

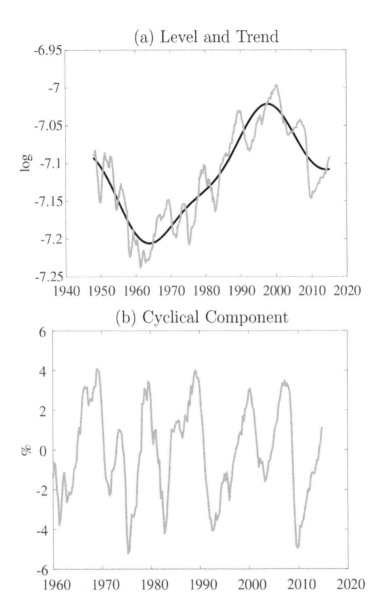

Fig. 2. Trend and cycle (high-pass filter, 80 quarters), total hours

Notes: Total hours are measured as the log of BLS total economy hours worked, deflated by total population. The trend of that series is obtained by removing from the level series its filtered component, where the filter is an 80-quarter high-pass filter, over the sample 1948:Q1–2015:Q2. The cyclical component is expressed in percentage deviation from the level series.

movements over the last 50 years. For this reason, we begin by filtering the data in order to remove these movements. We do this by using a (linear) high-pass filter that retains only fluctuations associated with periods of less than 20 years.[16] The trend (black line) and its filtered component are displayed in panels (a) and (b), respectively, of figure 2.

Once we have a series for $x = h$ (filtered hours), we then need to construct the accumulated hours series analogous to X_t to above, denoted H_t. To construct this series, we truncate the accumulation at N quarters, so that $H_t = \delta \sum_{j=0}^{N-1}(1 - \delta)^j h_{t-j}$. We set $N = 40$ so that, for example, observations of h from 1950:Q2 to 1960:Q1 are used to compute H_{1960Q1}. We assume for now that $\delta = 0.05$. Later we show that our results are robust to different values of δ.

For each of our two linear and three nonlinear models, OLS parameter estimates obtained using our total hours series are displayed in table 1, with t-statistics in parentheses. One can verify that in the nonlinear models there is always at least one significant nonlinear term. More informative are the Wald tests (see table 2) that compare the fit of the different models. For example, when testing the $AR(2)$ model against the full model, we test the joint nullity of all the coefficients except β_h and $\beta_{h'}$ (the coefficients on h_{t-1} and h_{t-2}, respectively) in the full model. The first row of table 2 shows that we reject the simple linear $AR(2)$ model against all alternatives. The second row reaches the same conclusion for the linear model. The third row shows that, at a 1% level of confidence, the minimal model is not rejected against any of the nonlinear alternatives. We first discuss the results obtained with this minimal model, since it is easiest to understand and illustrate. We will show later that results are mostly the same with the intermediate and full models.

Model Selection Using LASSO

An alternative way of selecting the model specification is to use statistical methods developed in the data-mining literature. One particular method, the LASSO (Least Absolute Shrinkage and Selection Operator), allows for both model selection and shrinkage. The method, proposed by Tibshirani (1996), consists of minimizing the residual sum of squares of the full model subject to the restriction that the sum of the absolute values of the coefficients be less than a constant. Because of the nature of this constraint, it tends to produce some coefficients that are exactly

Table 1
Estimates of Various Models, Total Hours

Variable	Value				
	$AR(2)$	Linear	Minimal	Intermediate	Full
Constant	−0.00	−0.01	−0.02	−0.01	−0.07
	(−0.02)	(−0.24)	(−0.53)	(−0.29)	(−0.85)
h_{t-1}	1.42	1.31	1.39	1.28	1.49
	(23.75)	(20.80)	(19.73)	(12.70)	(10.02)
h_{t-1}^2	—	—	—	—	−0.10
	(—)	(—)	(—)	(—)	(−1.51)
h_{t-1}^3	—	—	−0.01	−3e-03	−0.09
	(—)	(—)	(−2.39)	(−0.76)	(−1.85)
h_{t-2}	−0.48	−0.34	−0.34	−0.24	−0.44
	(−8.05)	(−4.98)	(−2.43)	(−5.12)	(−2.75)
h_{t-2}^2	—	—	—	—	−0.06
	(—)	(—)	(—)	(—)	(−0.76)
h_{t-2}^3	—	—	—	−4e-03	0.11
	(—)	(—)	(—)	(−0.83)	(1.38)
H_{t-1}	—	−0.25	−0.27	−0.03	S0.23
	(—)	(−4.11)	(−4.38)	(−0.20)	(1.09)
H_{t-1}^2	—	—	—	—	0.25
	(—)	(—)	(—)	(—)	(2.03)
H_{t-1}^3	—	—	—	−0.27	−0.40
	(—)	(—)	(—)	(−2.45)	(−2.10)
$h_{t-1}h_{t-2}$	—	—	—	—	0.17
	(—)	(—)	(—)	(—)	(1.15)
$h_{t-1}H_{t-1}$	—	—	—	—	0.25
	(—)	(—)	(—)	(—)	(1.89)
$h_{t-2}H_{t-1}$	—	—	—	—	−0.28
	(—)	(—)	(—)	(—)	(−1.88)
$h_{t-1}^2 h_{t-2}$	—	—	—	—	0.27
	(—)	(—)	(—)	(—)	(1.57)
$h_{t-1}^2 H_{t-1}$	—	—	—	6e-03	−0.32
	(—)	(—)	(—)	(0.42)	(−2.08)
$h_{t-2}^2 H_{t-1}$	—	—	—	—	−0.30
	(—)	(—)	(—)	(—)	(−1.46)
$h_{t-1}h_{t-2}^2$	—	—	—	—	−0.48
	(—)	(—)	(—)	(—)	(−2.40)
$h_{t-1}H_{t-1}^2$	—	—	—	0.04	−0.37
	(—)	(—)	(—)	(0.87)	(−1.64)
$h_{t-2}H_{t-1}^2$	—	—	—	—	0.47
	(—)	(—)	(—)	(—)	(1.79)
$h_{t-1}h_{t-2}H_{t-1}$	—	—	—	—	0.77
	(—)	(—)	(—)	(—)	(2.25)

Note: The total hours series has been filtered with an 80-quarter, high-pass filter over the sample 1948:Q1–2015:Q2. Estimation is then done over the sample 1960:Q1–2014:Q4.

Table 2
Wald Test for the Different Models, Total Hours

	H_1			
H_0	Linear (%)	Minimal (%)	Intermediate (%)	Full (%)
AR(2)	0.006	0.002	0.004	0.003
Linear	—	1.788	1.544	0.343
Minimal	—	—	7.63	1.20
Intermediate	—	—	—	2.81

Notes: The five models correspond to equations (11), (10), (8), (9), and (7). Wald test corresponds to the test of joint nullity of the coefficients of those variables that are in H_1 and not in H_0.

zero, and hence act as a model-selection device. The value of the constant in the constraint is chosen to minimize the Akaike Information Criterion. The estimated equation is given by

$$
\begin{aligned}
x_t = {}&-0.07 + 1.3x_{t-1} - 0.23x_{t-2} - 0.03x_{t-1}^2 + 0.21X_{t-1}^2 \\
&+ 0.04x_{t-1}x_{t-2} + 0.29x_{t-1}X_{t-1} - 0.30x_{t-2}X_{t-1} \\
&- 0.01x_{t-1}^3 - 0.21X_{t-1}^3 - 0.06x_{t-2}^2 X_{t-1} + 0.03x_{t-1}X_{t-1}^2 \\
&+ 0.05x_{t-1}x_{t-2}X_{t-1} + \varepsilon_t.
\end{aligned}
\tag{12}
$$

One can check that only 12 of the 18 variables of the full model are present in equation (12), the others being assigned a coefficient of zero. We will explore the robustness of the results by comparing results obtained with minimal, intermediate, full, and LASSO models.

Local Instability and Limit Cycles

For the sake of clarity, let us write down the estimated $AR(2)$, linear, and minimal models after shutting down the stochastic component:

$$
\begin{cases}
h_t = -0.00 + 1.42h_{t-1} - 0.48h_{t-2}, \\
h_t = -0.01 + 1.31h_{t-1} - 0.34h_{t-2} - 0.25H_{t-1}, \\
h_t = -0.02 + 1.39h_{t-1} - 0.34h_{t-2} - 0.27H_{t-1} - 0.01h_{t-1}^3.
\end{cases}
$$

Note that, even though our minimal model is nonlinear, it is easy to check that it has only one steady state at $h = -0.09$. In order to examine the local stability of each of these three equations, we compute the larg-

Table 3
Some Statistics for the Different Models, Total Hours

	AR(2)	Linear	Minimal	Intermediate	Full
R^2	0.94	0.94	0.94	0.94	0.95
Adj. R^2	0.94	0.94	0.94	0.94	0.95
DW	2.22	2.09	2.12	2.09	2.09
Max eig. modulus	0.86	0.96	1.01	1.01	{1.02,1.2,1.03}

Notes: The five models correspond to equations (11), (10), (8), (9), and (7). Adj. R^2 is the adjusted R^2. DW stands for the Durbin-Watson statistics for the test of autocorrelation of the residuals. $DW = 2$ corresponds to no autocorrelation. The last line gives the value of the maximum eigenvalue for the local dynamics of each model in the neighborhood of the existing steady states.

est eigenvalue of each system when linearized around its steady state. For the minimal model, this linear approximation is simply[17]

$$h_t = 1.39h_{t-1} - 0.34h_{t-2} - 0.27H_{t-1}.$$

Maximum eigenvalues are displayed in table 3.

For the $AR(2)$ model, the maximum eigenvalue is 0.86.[18] For the linear model, it is higher (0.96), but still less than 1. The steady states implied by the point estimates of the $AR(2)$ and linear models therefore indicate local stability, which is not surprising. For the nonlinear minimal model, on the other hand, the maximum eigenvalue is 1.01, so that the steady state is locally unstable. This may seem to conflict with the visual impression given by the data (figure 2, panel [b]) that the economy does not explode. In fact, it is precisely the third-order term h_{t-1}^3 that prevents explosion, since it enters negatively in the estimated equation. The steady state is thus locally unstable, but as h moves away from the steady state, the term h^3 acts as a centripetal force that pushes the economy back toward the steady state if it strays too far. As a result, the economy will oscillate without explosion and without convergence to a fixed point. This can be seen by using the minimal model to construct a deterministic forecasted path for h, conditional on information at date T_0. Formally, this deterministic forecast is computed as:

$$
\begin{cases}
\tilde{h}_{T_0} = h_{T_0}, \\
\tilde{h}_{T_0-1} = h_{T_0-1}, \\
\tilde{H}_{T_0-1} = H_{T_0-1}, \\
\tilde{h}_t = \hat{\beta}_0 + \hat{\beta}_h \tilde{h}_{t-1} + \hat{\beta}_{h'} \tilde{h}_{t-2} + \hat{\beta}_H \tilde{H}_{t-1} + \hat{\beta}_{h3} \tilde{h}_{t-1}^3 \quad \forall\, t > T_0, \\
\tilde{H}_t = (1-\delta)\tilde{H}_{t-1} + \delta \tilde{h}_t \quad \forall\, t \geq T_0.
\end{cases}
$$

We forecast h over 1,000 periods with the estimated model. We start (arbitrarily) from the first trough of the sample (i.e., 1961:Q3) and plot the forecasted path in the model state space (h_t, h_{t-1}, H_t). As we can see in panel (a) of figure 3, the trajectory is quickly attracted to a limit cycle. Figure 4 shows that this convergence holds more generally: starting from two initial conditions—one inside the limit cycle and one outside—the system converges to the limit cycle, suggesting that it is indeed attractive. Note that, as h is highly autocorrelated, there is little loss of information if one projects the limit cycle onto the (h_t, H_t) plane (panel [b] of figure 3) instead, and we will often use that representation of the limit cycle in what follows.

It is quite interesting that such a simple specification, which was motivated from our previous theoretical analysis (see Beaudry et al. 2015b), displays a limit cycle. We will document later using Monte Carlo methods that this result is unlikely to be an artifact of our data treatment. Before exploring further the properties of the minimal model, it is useful to show that we obtain similar results with the other nonlinear models. Table 3 shows that the largest eigenvalue is also greater than 1 for the intermediate and full models. As shown in figure 5, these two models (as well as the LASSO model) also generate limit cycles, with all specifications producing cycles of similar amplitudes for total hours.[19]

Let us now focus on the minimal model and look at the size and frequency of the limit cycle. As illustrated in figure 6, the deterministic forecast for the minimal model displays a cycle whose frequency and amplitude is close to the ones observed in the data. Figure 6 also displays 95% confidence bands around the deterministic forecast, and shows that after 60 quarters, the confidence bands have the same amplitude as the deterministic cycle. Panel (a) of figure 7 compares the deterministic forecast of the minimal model to the $AR(2)$ and linear model, while panel (b) compares the deterministic forecast of the intermediate, full, and LASSO models.

Other Labor Market Variables

We now explore the robustness of the results we obtained using total hours to using other labor market variables instead. In particular, we examine the behavior implied by estimating our minimal model using, sequentially, nonfarm business hours, the job-finding rate, and the rate of unemployment. For each of these variables, we report in figure 8 the deterministic forecast path in (x_t, X_t)-space, as well as x_t over time,

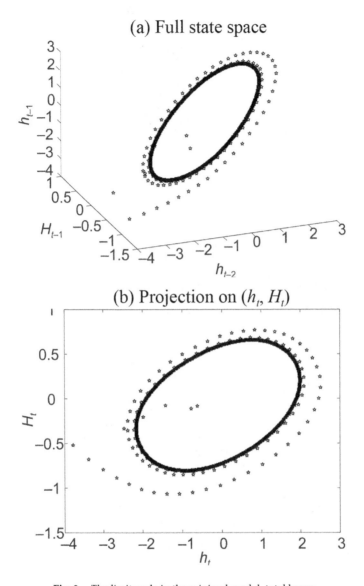

Fig. 3. The limit cycle in the minimal model, total hours

Note: This corresponds to the deterministic simulation of the minimal model (8), starting in 1961:Q3. The model has been estimated from 1960 to 2014 using 80-quarter, high-pass-filtered total hours.

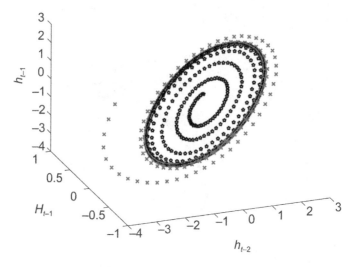

Fig. 4. Convergence to the limit cycle in the minimal model, total hours

Notes: This corresponds to the deterministic simulation of the minimal model (8), starting from two points arbitrarily chosen inside and outside the limit cycle. Those two points are, respectively, $(h_0, h_{-1}, H_{-1}) = (0.1, 0.1, 0.1)$ and $(h_0, h_{-1}, H_{-1}) = (6, 4, 10)$. The models have been estimated from 1960 to 2014 using 80-quarter, high-pass-filtered total hours. For graphical reasons, the first 13 points of each path are not shown.

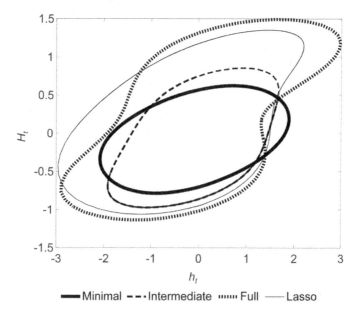

Fig. 5. The limit cycle in the four models in (h_t, H_t)-space, total hours

Note: This corresponds to the deterministic simulation of the minimal (8), intermediate (9), LASSO (12), and full (7) models, starting (arbitrarily) in 1961:Q3. The model has been estimated from 1960 to 2014 using 80-quarter, high-pass-filtered total hours.

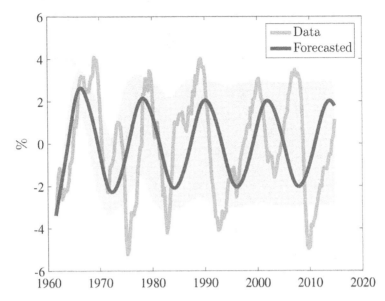

Fig. 6. Forecasted path as of 1961:Q3 with the minimal model, total hours

Notes: The dark gray line labeled "Forecasted" is the deterministic simulation of the minimal (8) model, starting (arbitrarily) in 1961:Q3, and the light gray line represents observed filtered hours. The gray area represents the 95% confidence band for the deterministic forecast, as obtained from 10,000 Monte Carlo simulations using draws from the posterior distribution over the model parameters.

where x is the variable under consideration and X its accumulated level (defined as before by $X_t \equiv \delta\sum_{i=0}^{\infty}(1 - \delta)^i x_{t-i}$). Panels (a) and (b) of figure 8 correspond to the forecasted paths for nonfarm business hours, panels (c) and (d) are those associated with the job-finding rate, and finally panels (e) and (f) correspond to the rate of unemployment. In all three cases, we start the forecast from 1961:Q3. As is clear from these figures, a limit cycle appears in all three cases, and these cycles have durations close to nine years, with amplitudes similar to the actual data.

How Significant Are Limit Cycles?

Up to now, we have checked for the existence of limit cycles using only the models' point estimates. Beyond the either/or results implied by these point estimates, it is of interest to use the sampling variability to quantify how strongly the data support the presence of instability and limit cycles. To do so, we derive estimated parameter distribu-

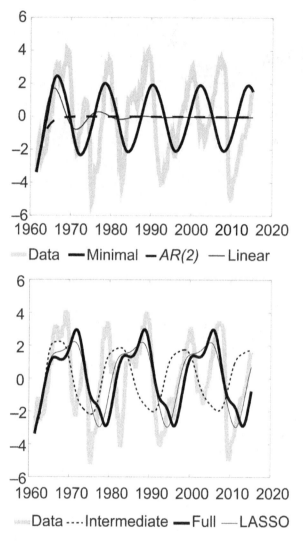

Fig. 7. The limit cycle in the four models, time series of h_t, total hours

Notes: This corresponds to the deterministic simulation of the minimal (8), intermediate (9), LASSO (12), and full (7) models, starting (arbitrarily) in 1961:Q3. The model has been estimated from 1960 to 2014 using 80-quarter, high-pass-filtered total hours.

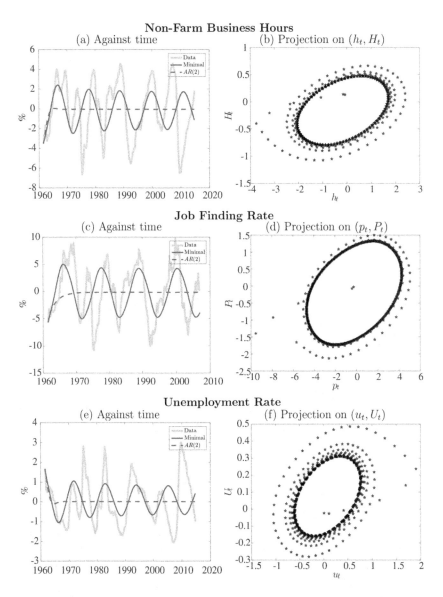

Fig. 8. The limit cycle in the minimal model, other labor market variables

Notes: Figure plots deterministic simulation of minimal model (8) starting in 1961:Q3. Model was estimated from 1960 to 2014 (–2007 for job-finding rate) using 80-quarter, high-pass-filtered series of nonfarm business hours, job-finding rate (from Shimer 2012), and unemployment rate. P and U stand for "cumulated" rates, constructed in the same way as X_t above.

Table 4
Frequency of Limit Cycles for Labor Market Variables

	Minimal (%)	Intermediate (%)	Full (%)
Total hours	74	73	78
Nonfarm bus. hours	70	55	70
Job-finding rate	76	69	59
Unemployment rate	60	32	50*

Notes: Bootstrap method used to generate 1,000 replications of the minimal, intermediate, and full model estimates for each labor market variable. For example, first cell indicates that a limit cycle was found in 74% of replications of minimal model. Data are always detrended with 80-quarter, high-pass filter before estimation. See appendix for details of samples and variable definitions. A * indicates that in more than half of replications, simulation was explosive. In such cases, we redrew bootstrap innovations until we obtained 1,000 nonexplosive replications.

tions for the minimal, intermediate, and full models using a bootstrap procedure. For each bootstrapped data set, we check for the existence of a limit cycle, which we define as meeting the following conditions: (a) starting in the simulation period corresponding to 1961:Q3,[20] the deterministic simulation of the nonlinear model estimated on this data set converges to a limit cycle; and (b) the Wald test rejects the linear model against the nonlinear one at 5%. Results are displayed in table 4. As can be seen from the table, the detection of limit cycles ranges mainly between 50 and 78%. This indicates that the null hypothesis of the absence of limit cycles in the data cannot be rejected at conventional levels of significance. Nonetheless, a person with a diffuse prior would in most cases infer that limit cycles are more likely than not.

Next, rather than focusing on our holistic definition of a limit cycle, we consider how strong the results are with regard specifically to the local instability that we have identified. To this end, we have computed— for the linear and minimal models estimated on total hours—the bootstrap distribution of the maximum eigenvalue. For the minimal model, this eigenvalue is computed for the linear approximation at the steady state.[21] Figure 9 plots the PDF for the bootstrap distributions. As can be seen, the distribution is almost entirely below one for the linear model. In contrast, allowing for a single cubic term in the estimation shifts this distribution significantly to the right, with 79% of the mass now being concentrated above 1. Again, this pattern is insufficient to reject the null hypothesis of stability at conventional levels of significance. Nonethe-

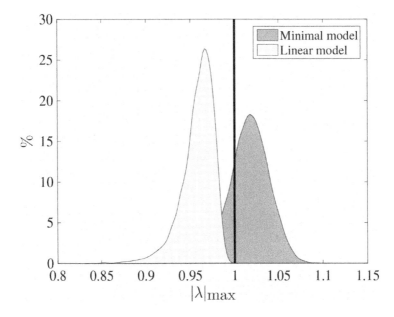

Fig. 9. Maximum eigenvalue in the linear and minimal model, total hours

Notes: Figure plots the estimated distribution of maximum eigenvalue for the linear and minimal model estimated on total hours. The densities are estimated using 1,000 bootstrap replications of each model. The models have been estimated from 1960 to 2014 using 80-quarter, high-pass-filtered series of total hours.

less, the results do clearly suggest that local instability is a relevant possibility.

Finally, as one further check on the strength of our results, we attempt to answer the following question. Suppose the DGP is indeed stable and linear. Accounting for parameter uncertainty, how likely are we to erroneously conclude that the steady state is unstable simply by allowing for nonlinearities in the estimation? To answer this question, for total hours we have computed a bootstrap distribution for the maximum eigenvalue of each nonlinear model estimated on data generated by either the $AR(2)$ or linear model, where we account for uncertainty in the parameters of the latter models. Table 5 reports instability p-values from these bootstrap distributions associated with the actual observed maximum eigenvalues (i.e., those reported in table 3). The results suggest that, accounting for sampling variability, we are unlikely to see the magnitude of instability we have observed in the data for the nonlinear models if the true DGP is one of the linear models. For example, if the true DGP were the linear model, we would obtain maximum eigenvalues

Table 5
p-Values for Maximum Eigenvalues When DGP Is
Linear/Stable, Total Hours

	Estimated Model		
DGP	Minimal (%)	Intermediate (%)	Full (%)
$AR(2)$	0.08	4.63	9.06
Linear	1.91	14.13	13.91

Notes: In this table, the DGP is either the (stable) $AR(2)$ or linear model, with parameters drawn from a bootstrapped distribution. For each of 10,000 parameter draws, a new data set was generated (again via bootstrap), and the nonlinear models were estimated on this data, yielding a distribution for the maximum eigenvalue for each nonlinear model when the DGP is linear and stable. Table reports instability p-values— that is, the probability for maximum eigenvalues of nonlinear models estimated on actual data (see table 3) to be larger than one in modulus.

for the intermediate and full models at least as great as the ones we observed in the data less than 15% of the time, and less than 2% of the time for the minimal model.

Multiplicity of Steady States

Since we are examining dynamics in a nonlinear framework, we need to recognize the potential for a multiplicity of attractors in the system. First, let us note that all the estimated equations are backward looking, so that there is (trivially) never indeterminacy in the solution to our equations.[22] In contrast, we do need to check for the existence of multiple steady states or multiple limit cycles for our estimated models. Consider first the case of multiple steady states, and focus on the minimal model when shocks are turned off:

$$h_t = \beta_0 + \beta_h h_{t-1} + \beta_{h'} h_{t-2} + \beta_H H_{t-1} + \beta_{h^3} h_{t-1}^3,$$
$$H_t = (1 - \delta)H_{t-1} + \delta h_t.$$

Estimation typically gives β_0 very close to zero, β_h larger than one, $\beta_{h'}$ and β_H negative, and β_{h^3} negative and small. Assume for simplicity that β_0 is exactly zero, such that $h = 0$ is a steady state. Nonzero steady states of the minimal model, if they exist, are the two opposite real numbers $\bar{h}$ and $-\bar{h}$, with[23]

$$\bar{h} = \sqrt{\frac{1 - \beta_h - \beta_{h'} - \beta_H}{\beta_{h3}}},$$

Restricting to the case where $\beta_{h3} < 0$, we have multiplicity of steady states if and only if

$$\beta_h + \beta_{h'} + \beta_H > 1. \tag{13}$$

Therefore, although the model is nonlinear, it can generically be in a parameter configuration with a unique steady state.

Note that, as β_H approaches zero, the condition for local instability of the zero steady state is,

$$\beta_h + \beta_{h'} > 1. \tag{14}$$

Thus, for β_H close to zero, equations (13) and (14) coincide: the occurrence of limit cycles, which requires local instability, necessarily implies multiplicity of steady states. However, when the economy has a longer memory (i.e., β_H is negative but not arbitrarily close to zero), the two conditions no longer coincide, and in particular it is possible for the steady state to be both unique and locally unstable. This is typically what the data will suggest in the minimal model.

In the case of multiplicity, the question is whether the nonzero steady states are stable or unstable when the zero steady state is unstable. Taking a first-order Taylor expansion of equation (8) around , we have the following dynamics (omitting constant terms):

$$h_t = \underbrace{(\beta_h + 3\bar{h}^2\beta_{h3})h_{t-1}}_{\tilde{\beta}_h} + \beta_{h'}h_{t-2} + \beta_H H_{t-1}. \tag{15}$$

Note that the same equation holds for the local dynamics around $-\bar{h}$. As we are looking at situations where $\beta_{h3} < 0$, we will have $\tilde{\beta}_h < \beta_{h'}$, such that it is possible that the two nonzero steady states are stable when the zero steady state is unstable. In such a case, although there exists a limit cycle in the neighborhood of zero, it would be possible to have trajectories that would start close (but not arbitrarily close) to zero and converge to $\bar{h}$ or $-\bar{h}$. The same argument can also be made for the intermediate and full models. The occurrence of additional, attractive steady states depends ultimately on the parameters of the model. Our findings suggest, however, that such a situation is unlikely to be relevant. In particular, given the coefficients as estimated on total hours, the minimal and intermediate models both feature unique steady states. Moreover, while there are three steady states for the full model (located at $h = -0.77, 0.22,$ and 1.23), all three of these steady states are locally unstable, which implies that the system cannot converge to a steady state in any of our models estimated on total hours.

Note that, for the full model, it is in principle possible that two or even all three of the steady states could be surrounded by distinct attractive limit cycles. It is not possible to prove analytically that this is not the case, but it can be checked numerically. Figure 10 displays (in (h_t, H_t)-space) four deterministic forecasts from the full model: two starting near the intermediate ($h = 0.22$) steady state, and one each starting near the high and low steady states. Steady states are indicated by stars in the figure. One observes that all trajectories apparently converge to the same closed orbit, suggesting that the existence of multiple attractive limit cycles is unlikely.

The Power of Our Limit-Cycle-Detection Procedure

One may worry that our procedure, especially our detrending procedure, might generate spurious limit cycles even if the DGP is actually

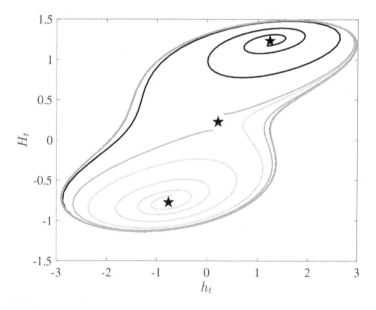

Fig. 10. Convergence to the limit cycle from the neighborhood of each of the three steady states, full model, total hours.

Notes: Figure shows deterministic forecasts starting from the neighborhoods of each of the three steady states (represented by stars). All four trajectories converge to the same limit cycle. The models have been estimated from 1960 to 2014 using 80-quarter, high-pass-filtered total hours.

locally stable, or alternatively that it may fail to detect a limit cycle when there is indeed one. We investigate these issues here using Monte Carlo analysis. First, we check that we do not spuriously find limit cycles when there are none present. To do so, we first filter (logs of) total hours with an 80-quarter, high-pass filter, so that

$$h_t^L = h_t^T + h_t$$

where h_t^L stands for levels, h_t^T for the trend and where h_t is the cyclical component. We then estimate an $AR(2)$ on the filtered data. This $AR(2)$, which is the one displayed in table 1, will serve as the DGP. We then simulate the estimated (stable) $AR(2)$ to obtain an artificial cyclical series $\hat{h}_t$, then add it to the actual trend series h_t^T to generate an artificial level series

$$\hat{h}_t^L = h_t^T + \hat{h}_t$$

By construction, these simulated level series do not feature limit cycles. We may then apply our limit-cycle-detection procedure to these simulated series in order to verify that it does not spuriously detect limit cycles where there are none. That is, we treat each simulated level series in the same way we have treated the actual level series: first filter, then estimate the minimal, intermediate, and full models, then check for the existence of a limit cycle. For each model and simulation, we check for the existence of a significant limit cycle, which we define as meeting the following conditions: (a) starting in 1961:Q3,[24] the deterministic simulation of the model converges to a limit cycle; and (b) the Wald test rejects the linear model against the nonlinear one at 5%. We perform 10,000 simulations, and report the results in the first row of table 6. The three models spuriously detect limit cycles less than 5% of the time, suggesting that our procedure is highly unlikely to detect a limit cycle if one does not exist in the DGP. The second row of table 6 shows similar results for the case where the DGP is the estimated linear model instead of the $AR(2)$.[25]

Next, we test for the possibility of missing a limit cycle with our procedure when it *does* exist in the data. In order to do so, we take the estimated minimal, intermediate, or full model as the DGP and follow the same procedure as above. The results are displayed in the bottom three rows of table 6, and show that limit cycles are relatively hard to detect using our procedure. Typically, when the estimated model is well specified (meaning that it has the same form as the DGP), our procedure detects limit cycles about half of the time.

Table 6
Percentage of Limit Cycle Detection in Monte-Carlo Simulations Simulated Hours

	Estimated Model		
DGP	Minimal (%)	Intermediate (%)	Full (%)
AR(2)	1.9	2.5	2.3
Linear	5.8	4.5	3.3
Minimal	54	34	20
Intermediate	43	51	40
Full	57	43	58

Note: In this table, the DGP is alternatively the estimated *AR*(2), linear, minimal, intermediate, or full model. The models have been estimated from 1960 to 2014 using 80-quarter, high-pass-filtered total hours, and are then simulated 10,000 times.

From these Monte Carlo simulations, we conclude that it is unlikely that we will spuriously detect limit cycles, and that correctly detecting a limit cycle when one is present occurs at best 58% of the time.

Robustness

Here we briefly discuss the robustness of our main results. We maintain focus on the case where our measure of activity is total hours per capita. We begin by examining the robustness of our results with respect to our choice of δ in the computation of H and to our detrending procedure. Recall that, in order to construct the cumulated series H, we need to make a choice for the value of δ. Table 7 shows that a limit cycle is detected generically for the minimal model, as long as δ is not too large for the intermediate and full models, and as long as δ is also not too small in the Intermediate model.

Next, table 8 considers filters other than the 80-quarter, high-pass one used so far, and also considers the model estimated with the LASSO method. Let us first note that the high-pass filter is a linear filter and therefore should not be spuriously introducing nonlinearities, so that in general we should not expect to find cycles where there are none simply by choosing a particular parameter for the filter. On the other hand, if there exists a limit cycle in the data but the filter parameter we choose removes the frequencies associated with that cycle, our procedure would in general fail to identify this cycle. Further, given the

Table 7
Robustness to δ, Total Hours

	Minimal (%)	Intermediate (%)	Full (%)
δ = .001	LC (58)	–(31)	LC (89)
δ = .01	LC (59)	–(40)	LC (85)
δ = .1	LC (76)	LC (67)	LC (66)
δ = .2	LC (40)	–(40)	–(40)

Notes: In this table, we estimate the minimal, intermediate, and full models under various values of δ. "LC" means that the estimated model displays a limit cycle. The number in parenthesis indicates the fraction of the 1,000 bootstrap replications for which we found a limit cycle with the linear model being rejected at 5% against the nonlinear one. All the models have been estimated from 1960–2014 using 80-quarter, high-pass-filtered total hours.

Table 8
Robustness to Detrending, Total Hours

	Minimal (%)	Intermediate (%)	Full (%)
High-pass 100	LC (58)	LC (35)	LC (72)
High-pass 90	LC (78)	LC (72)	LC (68)
High-pass 70	LC (80)	LC (80)	LC (80)
High-pass 60	LC (57)	LC (51)	LC (82)
High-pass 50	–(41)	LC (38)	–(67)
Band-pass(6,3,2)	–(12)	–(41)	–(37)
Hodrick-Prescott (λ = 1600)	–(28)	–(30)	–(20)
Polynomial trend (3rd-order)	–(18)	LC (29)	LC (75)
Polynomial trend (4th-order)	–(19)	LC (30)	LC (76)
Polynomial trend (5th-order)	–(53)	LC (49)	LC (76)
No detrending	–(.1)	–(21)	–(40)

Notes: In this table, we estimate the minimal (8), intermediate (9), and full (7) models using various detrending methods. "LC" means that the estimated model displays a limit cycle. The number in parenthesis indicates the fraction of the 1,000 bootstrap replications for which we found a limit cycle with the linear model being rejected at 5% against the nonlinear one. All the models have been estimated from 1960 to 2014 using total hours.

strong implicit restrictions imposed on the data when estimating our three models—which are strongest in the minimal model and weakest in the full model—we should in general expect to find that our choice of filter affects our ability to identify limit cycles even if they exist in the data, and that this sensitivity to the filter should be strongest in the minimal model and weakest in the full model. The results presented in table 8 largely support these predictions. In particular, we report results using different high-pass filters from 100 to 50 quarters, as well as for commonly used band-pass (6,32) and Hodrick-Prescott ($\lambda = 1600$) filters. We also report results for when we detrend using polynomial time trends of order three, four, and five.

Three conclusions emerge from the table. First, the detrending procedures that remove only the lowest frequencies (i.e., the 60 quarters or more high-pass filters and the polynomial time trends) are generally associated with limit cycles, while the procedures that also remove the middle range of frequencies (i.e., the band-pass [6,32] and Hodrick-Prescott [$\lambda = 1600$] filters) are not. Given the considerations discussed above, this is consistent with the view that the data features a medium-frequency limit cycle, and that two of the most commonly used filters in the business-cycle literature remove those frequencies by design. This in turn suggests the need to focus on fluctuations that are longer than traditionally thought to be associated with business cycles.

Second, the minimal model is quite sensitive to the choice of filter, with no clear pattern to this sensitivity, while the intermediate and full models are relatively insensitive. This is consistent with the view that it may be the strong model restrictions underlying the minimal model that drive much of its observed sensitivity to the filter (as opposed to spurious patterns generated by the filter itself). In particular, the fact that the more flexible specifications typically support the existence of a medium-frequency limit cycle, while the very restrictive specification may or may not depending on the filter used, is supportive of the hypothesis that a medium-frequency limit cycle is present in the data but the minimal model is too restrictive to detect it consistently. Finally, note that limit cycles are at best only found 40% of the time when we do not filter the data.

E.   Behavior in Other Countries

Here we extend our exploration of macroeconomic dynamics using data on the unemployment rate in other countries.[26] These results are

Table 9
Limit Cycles in Other Countries

Unemployment rate	Minimal (%)	Intermediate (%)	Full (%)
Australia	–(.7)	–(2)	–(11)*
Austria	LC (98)	–(38)	LC (76)
Canada	–(11)	–(22)	–(11)
Denmark	–(12)	LC (45)	LC (88)
France	–(3)	–(26)	LC (52)*
Germany	LC (79)	–(49)	LC (88)
Japan	–(7)	–(33)	–(50)
Netherlands	LC (62)	LC (78)	–(94)
Sweden	LC (65)	–(64)	LC (66)
Switzerland	–(16)*	–(52)	–(27)
United Kingdom	–(4)	–(3)	LC (78)

Notes: In this table, we estimate the minimal (8), intermediate (9), and full (7) models, considering various labor market variables. "LC" means that the estimated model displays a limit cycle. The number in parenthesis indicates the fraction of the 1,000 bootstrap replications for which we found a limit cycle with the linear model being rejected at 5% against the nonlinear one. Data are always detrended with an 80-quarter, high-pass filter before estimation. See appendix for details of samples and variable definitions. A star (*) indicates that in more than half of the replications, the simulation with bootstrap innovations was explosive, so that the pseudodata sample could not be used for estimation. In this case, we have drawn again bootstrap innovations until we obtained 1,000 nonexplosive replications.

presented in table 9. We estimate our three models for 11 countries. As can be seen in the table, we find some evidence of limit cycles in about half of the countries. Although this is somewhat low, interestingly this ratio is similar to the detection rate we have found in our Monte Carlo exercise. Looking closely at each country makes it clear why we do find limit cycles in some and not in others. As an example, let us consider Switzerland and the Netherlands. Data and deterministic forecasts for these two countries are displayed in figure 11.

Switzerland and the Netherlands both have marked low-frequency dynamics. In the case of Switzerland (figure 11, panels [a] and [c]), there appears to have been a change of regime around 1990; there was almost zero unemployment in the 1970s and 1980s, but a 3.5% average since 1990. Besides this low-frequency variation, what emerges from figure 11, panel (c), is the big recession of 1991–1993, and the progressive recovery from 1993 to 2000. Instead of a relatively regular cycle, as we have observed in the United States, we see one big cycle and four smaller ones, which is a pattern that cannot be easily captured by our reduced-form models. Hence, the minimal model estimated on this data does not exhibit a limit cycle, and the dynamics of forecasted

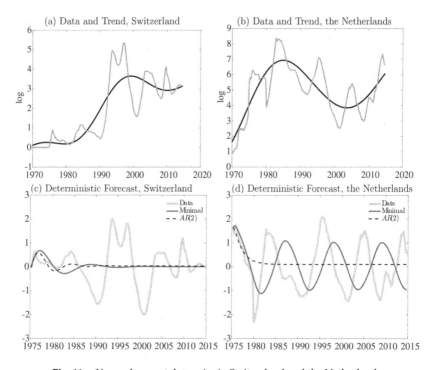

Fig. 11.   Unemployment dynamics in Switzerland and the Netherlands

Notes: Unemployment rate is observed over the sample 1970:Q1–2014:Q4. Unemployment rate is measured as "Registered Unemployment Rate" for Switzerland and as "Harmonized Unemployment Rate: All Persons" for the Netherlands. The H series is constructed assuming $N = 20$, so that estimation starts in 1975:Q2. The trend of these series is obtained by removing from the level series its filtered component, where the filter is an 80-quarter, high-pass filter. The cyclical component is expressed in percentage deviation from the level series. Deterministic forecasts are done starting from 1975:Q1, with the estimated $AR(2)$ (11) and minimal (8) models.

unemployment as of 1975 are not very different from the ones obtained with an $AR(2)$ model.[27] Things are very different for the Netherlands (figure 11, panels [b] and [d]). The low-frequency dynamics feature a marked increase from the early 1970s to the late 1980s, followed by a prolonged decline through to early in the first decade of the twenty-first century. The key determinants of those trend movements are the first and second oil shocks, followed by important labor market reforms in the 1990s. Fluctuations around this trend, however, have been very regular—and in particular we do not observe one big cycle dwarfing the others, as was the case for Switzerland—and thus the estimated minimal model features a limit cycle.

F. Quantity Variables

Difficulties

We now turn to the estimation of our nonlinear reduced-form equation using quantity variables. Before performing this exercise, we want to highlight the added difficulties associated with quantity variables. To this end, consider the simple case in which output is given by $y_t = \theta_t + h_t$, where θ is TFP, and in which hours follows as before a process of the type

$$h_t = a_0 + a_1 h_{t-1} + a_2 h_{t-2} + a_3 H_t + F(h_{t-1}, h_{t-2}, H_{t-1}) + \varepsilon_t. \quad (16)$$

In such a case, the dynamic equation for output y is given by

$$y_t = a_0 + a_1 y_{t-1} + a_2 y_{t-1} + a_3 \sum_{j=1}^{\infty} (1 - \delta)^{j-1}(y_{t-j} - \theta_{t-j}) + \varepsilon_t$$

$$+ F(y_{t-1} - \theta_{t-1}, y_{t-2} - \theta_{t-2}, \sum_{j=1}^{\infty} (1 - \delta)^{j-1}(y_{t-j} - \theta_{t-j})) \quad (17)$$

$$+ \theta_t - a_1 \theta_{t-1} - a_2 \theta_{t-2} - a_3 + \varepsilon_t.$$

If we had a good measure of θ_t, then the estimation of equation (17) would not be any more difficult than our estimation of equation (16) using hours worked. However, in the absence of a good measure of θ, the estimation of equation (17) becomes difficult. Simply using a filtered measure of y_t as a representation of $y_t - \theta_t$ is unlikely to perform well. This can be seen in practice by running a Monte Carlo experiment as follows. We take our estimates of the minimal, intermediate, or full model obtained when run on the 80-quarter, high-pass-filtered total hours series. As shown previously, all three of these estimated models feature a limit cycle. We then use this estimated model to create an artificial cyclical series of hours, to which we add the log of labor productivity taken from the data. This gives us a log-level series for artificial output. We then treat this level series in the same way we will treat the actual level series of output: filter, estimate the minimal, intermediate, and full models, then check for the occurrence of a significant limit cycle. We perform 10,000 simulations, and report in table 10 the percentage of simulations for which a limit cycle is (correctly) detected. The three models hardly detect limit cycles in these simulated output series, even if by construction they contain limit cycle forces. Detection rates are around 15% when the estimated model embeds these DGP specifications. Despite this low detection rate, we nonetheless proceed

Table 10

Percentage of Limit-Cycle Detection in Monte Carlo Simulations, Simulated Output

	Estimated Model		
DGP	Minimal (%)	Intermediate (%)	Full (%)
Minimal	14	13	5
Intermediate	12	15	6
Full	12	11	11

Note: In this table, the DGP is alternatively the estimated minimal, intermediate, and full models. The models have been estimated from 1960 to 2014 using 80-quarter, high-pass-filtered total hours, and are then simulated 10,000 times.

and examine whether our procedure detects limit cycle in the actual quantity data. As we will see, the detection rate is much lower when using quantity variables than when using labor market variables—as could be expected given the Monte Carlo exercise.

Estimation Results

We estimate the three models (7), (8), and (9) on output, total consumption, durable goods expenditures, fixed investment, various components of investment, and the capacity utilization rate. Each of these variables is again first detrended using an 80-quarter, high-pass filter. Estimation results are summarized in table 11. While we do not find much evidence of limit cycles using the minimal model, interestingly, we find in the full model limit cycles detected at a frequency of over 50% using all variables except equipment investment.

III.   Should We Care?

The previous section explored whether cyclical movements in macroeconomic variables exhibited characteristics suggestive of local instability and limit cycles. In this section, we examine whether one should care about identifying/differentiating such a possibility. There are at least two potential reasons why one might care. First, it is possible that it could lead to improved forecasting ability. Second, it is possible that policy changes could have differing effects on stable and locally unstable limit-cycle models. Our explorations suggest that, for forecasting purposes, differentiating between the two cases is likely of

Table 11

Existence of a Limit Cycle for Quantity Variables

	Minimal (%)	Intermediate (%)	Full (%)
Output	–(11)	LC (60)	–(53)
Nonfarm bus. output	—	(20) LC (64)	–(54)
Consumption	–(3)	LC (84)	LC (85)
Fixed investment	–(28)	–(12)	LC (54)*
Structures	LC (80)	LC (84)	LC (75)
Durables	–(32)	LC (75)	LC (85)
Residential	–(15)	LC (34)	–(62)*
Equipment	–(19)	–(14)	–(27)
Utilization	LC (86)	LC (80)	LC (53)*

Notes: In this table, we estimate the minimal, intermediate, and full models, considering various goods market variables. "LC" means that the estimated model displays a limit cycle. The number in parenthesis indicates the fraction of the 1,000 bootstrap replications for which we found a limit cycle with the linear model being rejected at 5% against the nonlinear one. Data are always detrended with an 80-quarter, high-pass filter before estimation. See appendix for details of samples and variable definitions. A star (*) indicates that in more than half of the replications the simulation with bootstrap innovations was explosive, so that the pseudo-data sample could not be used for estimation. In this case, we have drawn again bootstrap innovations until we obtained 1,000 nonexplosive replications.

second-order importance. This is most easily observed by recognizing that the variance of the one-step-ahead forecast error for the linear model is almost identical to that for any of the nonlinear models. However, as we argue in this section, we believe that, for policy purposes, identifying whether macroeconomic dynamics may contain limit cycles forces can be of first-order importance. In particular, we discuss how a policy aimed at countering the effects of shocks can lead to very different outcomes depending on whether the model exhibits limit cycles, even though the two models are similar in terms of standard forecast performance.

A. Theoretical Results

The goal of stabilization policy is to reduce inefficient macroeconomic volatility. In practice, this is often equated to the goal of reducing the cyclical volatility of output and employment. One stabilization approach is to direct policy toward countering or nullifying the impact of certain exogenous forces hitting the economy. In linear models, such a strategy will generally be effective, as a reduction in the variance of exogenous shocks translates directly in to a reduction in the variance of endogenous variables. However, in an environment where limit-cycle forces may be present, this strategy may no longer be effective. In particular, in this section we will show that when limit-cycle forces are present, (a) a reduction in the variance of shocks may actually increase the variance of endogenous variables; (b) even if reducing the variance of shocks reduces the variance of the outcomes, the relationship between the shock variance and outcome variance is likely to be quite weak; and (c) the principal effect of reducing the shock variance is likely to dampen higher-frequency movements while accentuating longer cyclical movements (whereas such a change in the shape of the spectrum would not arise in a linear model).

In order to look at these issues, we will focus again on a univariate setup.[28] For example, consider an environment where the dynamics of a state variable of interest x_t may we written as

$$x_t = F(x_{t-1}, x_{t-2}, \ldots) + \varepsilon_t,$$

where ε_t is an exogenous shock with variance σ_ε^2. If the function $F(\cdot)$ is linear and is such that x is stationary,[29] then the variance of x will be strictly increasing in the variance of ε. However, if the function $F(\cdot)$ is nonlinear, then the link between the variance of x,[30] denoted σ_x^2, and the variance of ε may be much more complicated. In particular, even in the case where $F(\cdot)$ is such that σ_x^2 exists and is finite, σ_x^2 will not necessarily be an increasing function of σ_ε^2. More to the point, when $F(\cdot)$ is such that the deterministic system $x_t = F(x_{t-1}, x_{t-2}, \ldots)$ admits a limit cycle, then σ_x^2 will often be decreasing in σ_ε^2 over some range. To illustrate this point, consider an order three data-generating process similar to those we have estimated in section II, but in which we remove both the accumulation and the second autoregressive terms for analytical tractability:

$$x_t = -\beta_x x_{t-1} + \beta_{x3} x_{t-1}^3 + \varepsilon_t, \tag{18}$$

Under the restrictions

$$1 < \beta_x < 2, \tag{$\mathcal{R}_1$}$$

and

$$\beta_{x3} = 1 + \beta_x, \tag{$\mathcal{R}_2$}$$

one may verify that when $\sigma_\varepsilon^2 = 0$ the system (18) possesses a limit cycle of period two[31] in which x alternates between $\bar{x}$ and $-\bar{x}$, where

$\bar{x} \equiv \sqrt{\beta_x - 1 / \beta_{x^3}}$. Moreover, this two-cycle attracts all orbits for which $0 < |x_0| < 1$. Now consider an increase in σ_ε^2. How does this affect the variance of x? Proposition 1 indicates that an increase in σ_ε^2 can lead to a decrease in σ_x^2.

Proposition 1.   *If the random variable x_t evolves according to equation (18) with restrictions $\mathfrak{R}_1$ and $\mathfrak{R}_2$, then the variance of x_t will be decreasing in σ_ε^2 when σ_ε^2 is sufficiently small.*

Proof.   See appendix.

The intuition for Proposition 1 reflects the nature of the nonlinear forces generating the limit cycle. Near the limit cycle, a shock that moves x outside of the cycle (i.e., so that $|x_t| > \bar{x}$) is countered by stronger forces pushing it back toward the cycle than is a shock that moves x *inside* the cycle (i.e., so that $|x_t| < \bar{x}$). Hence, shocks that move x inward are more persistent, and therefore, on average, for σ_ε^2 sufficiently small the system spends more time inside the cycle than outside of it. This effect causes the overall variance of x to be decreasing in σ_ε^2. Although the scope of Proposition 1 is quite limited, since it covers only a small class of data-generating processes that support limit cycles, it nevertheless makes clear that the relationship between shock variance and output variance can be negative when the underlying data-generating process admits a limit cycle.

B.   Illustrating the Effects of Changes in Shock Variance

Proposition 1 suggests that, in models featuring limit cycles, there may be a more complicated relationship between shock variance and outcome variance than the simple positive one usually encountered in stable models. To follow up on this, we have explored numerically whether this feature may arise in the richer environments of the previous section. In all cases we found that, for small values of σ_ε^2, an increase in the shock variance has either a small but noticeable negative effect or no discernible effect at all on the variance of h, while for larger values the effect is positive but substantially weaker than in a linear environment. In this sense, a robust take-away appears to be that, in environments that support limit cycles of the size we believe may be in macroeconomic data, the link between shock variance and outcome variance is likely to be very muted relative to its linear counterpart. To illustrate this, in panel (a) of figure 12 we plot the relationship between σ_ε and σ_h for the intermediate and the linear models as estimated on

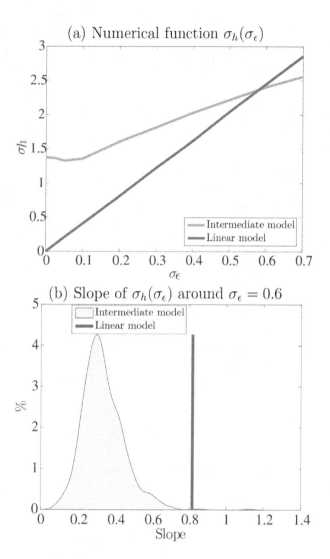

Fig. 12. Relationship between σ_h and σ_ε

Notes: For each model, we derive parameter distributions by bootstrapping with 1,000 replications. Then, for each value of σ_ε, we simulate $T_{tot} = T_{brn} + T$ periods of data, with T_{brn} = 1,000 and T = 100,000. After discarding the first T_{brn} periods of data, we compute σ_h^2 as the time average $T^{-1} \sum(h_t - \mu_h)^2$, where $\mu_h = T^{-1}\sum h_t$. For the sake of clarity, we report only the point estimates in panel (a). In panel (b), we report the bootstrap distribution of the slope of $\sigma_h(\sigma_\varepsilon)$, evaluated for the observed level $\sigma_\varepsilon \approx 0.6$, for the intermediate model. For the linear one, we report the slope at the point estimates for the parameters. For both models, the slope is computed as $[\sigma_h(0.7) - \sigma_h(0.5)] / 0.2$.

total hours worked per capita.[32] As was shown in the previous section, in the absence of shocks the intermediate model exhibits limit cycles. On the contrary, the estimated linear model has a stable steady state, so that when $\sigma_\varepsilon = 0$ we have $\sigma_h = 0$.

The are two notable features that emerge from panel (a) of figure 12. The first is that, as in the simple example of Proposition 1, the relationship between σ_ε and σ_h is actually negative for low values of σ_ε. Let us stress again, however, that this is not the pattern we think is most relevant. The second—and, we believe, more important—feature that emerges from the figure is the extent to which the relationship between σ_ε and σ_h is much weaker in the case of the nonlinear model as compared to the linear model. For example, increasing σ_ε from 0.1 to 0.5 causes σ_h to increase by 400% in the linear model, while it increases by only 62% in the intermediate model. The fact that the plotted relationship has a nonzero intercept for the limit-cycle model is not surprising, but the fact that the slope of this relationship is so much weaker on average is telling. This result is further documented in panel (b) of the same figure. Taking into account sample uncertainty, we plot the bootstrap distribution of the slope of $\sigma_h(\sigma_\varepsilon)$, evaluated for the observed level $\sigma_\varepsilon \approx 0.6$, together with the slope-point estimate for the linear model. This panel shows that the slope is lower in the intermediate model at any level of significance. This pattern suggests that stabilization policy aimed at mitigating the effects of shocks may be of more limited value than suggested by estimation of the linear model. The goal of stabilization policy in such a case may instead be to focus on identifying and mitigating the underlying forces that generate and sustain limit cycles.[33]

To further emphasize how changes in input volatility affect outcome behavior in models with or without limit cycles, in Figure 13 we plot the spectrum of the outcome variable h for several different values of σ_ε. Panel (a) shows spectra for the intermediate nonlinear specification, while panel (b) shows spectra for the linear one.

For the linear model, panel (b) illustrates that the effect of changing the volatility of ε is very simple: a fall (rise) in σ_ε decreases (increases) the spectrum substantially and uniformly. In contrast, as shown in panel (a), the effect of changing σ_ε in the model that features a limit cycle is primarily to change the shape of the spectrum. In particular, a fall in σ_ε decreases the importance of higher frequencies and accentuates the importance of lower frequencies, while a rise in σ_ε does the reverse. For example, as we can see in the figure, when we reduce σ_ε by

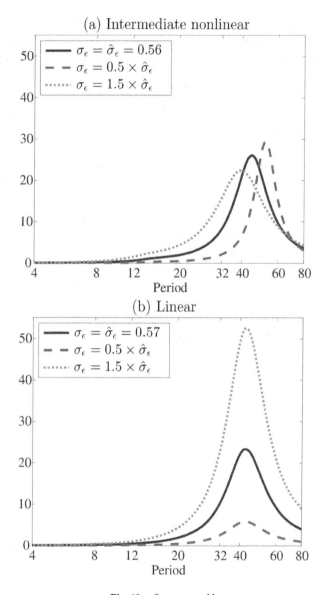

Fig. 13. Spectrum of h

Notes: For each model and each value of σ_ϵ, we simulate 100,000 data sets, each of length $T_{tot} = T_{brn} + T$ quarters, with $T_{brn} = 50,000$ and $T = 1,000$. For each simulated data set, we obtain the spectrum of h after discarding the first T_{brn} periods, then average the result across all data sets.

a third, from 0.84 (dotted line) to 0.56 (solid line)—where the latter is the value estimated for the data—the spectrum at periodicities below 40 quarters decreases substantially, while the importance of periodicities above 40 quarters increases substantially. Such observations are interesting, as they provide a potentially different perspective on how a reduction in shock volatility—such as is often thought to have arisen during the period of the great moderation—can affect the economy. If the underlying system exhibits limit cycles, a great moderation in input volatility would result in a less volatile economy in the short term, but would tend to *increase* the importance of the lower-frequency movements associated with cycles lasting around 10 years.

In summary, much of the focus of traditional macroeconomic stabilization policy is based on the view that fluctuations are primarily driven by shocks. If instead limit-cycle forces play an important part in generating fluctuations, this warrants a rethinking of how best to conduct policy. In particular, in this section we have emphasized that aiming to counter or to nullify shocks to the macroeconomy is likely to be much less effective at reducing economic volatility if limit cycles are present.[34] Such policies may somewhat reduce volatility, but the main effect may be to simply change the frequency at which fluctuations arise, with higher-frequency movements being dampened by the policy at the cost of amplifying lower-frequency movements. As a consequence, in such a case it could be best to de-emphasize a framework focused on countering shocks and move toward a stabilization framework that aims to reduce the forces that may be causing the limit cycles. For example, in our previous work (Beaudry et al. 2015b), we have emphasized the role of strategic complements in producing limit cycles. An effective stabilization policy in such a situation is one that reduces these complementarities. If the complementarity is related to precautionary saving associated with unemployment risk as in Beaudry et al. (2015a, 2015b), then policy should focus on mitigating the effect of unemployment risk on individuals by offering better unemployment insurance. Policies aimed at countering shocks in such an environment will not, in general, be hitting the important margins.

IV. Conclusion

The first aim of this paper has been to examine whether fluctuations in macroeconomic aggregates may be best described as reflecting the effects of shocks to an otherwise stable system, or whether such fluctuations may instead—to a large extent—reflect an underlying instability in the macroeconomy that repeatedly gives rise to sustained boom and bust phenomena. To examine this question, we have proposed a simple nonlinear time-series framework that has the potential to capture instability and limit-cycle behavior if it is present in the data. The framework we adopted was motivated by previous work that emphasized the role of strategic complementarities in creating local instability in environments with accumulated goods. We first focused on the behavior of labor market variables, and especially the behavior of total hours worked per capita, and found intriguing evidence in favor of the view that the macroeconomy may be locally unstable and produce limit-cycle forces. For example, we found that aggregate labor market variables often indicate the presence of forces that favor recurrent business cycles with a duration of close to nine years and an amplitude of 4–5%. When looking at aggregate output measures, we found less robust evidence.

One of the main challenges in this endeavor was to find a powerful tool for identifying local instability if it is present. As we showed using Monte Carlo methods, the approach we adopted is not very powerful, and this is especially true when looking at output measures. This suggests that it would be fruitful in future work to develop a more powerful method. Given this difficulty, it is interesting that we have been able to find as much evidence supporting the notion of local instability and limit cycles as we have. Moreover, even when we have not found local instability, we have almost always found that the system is very close to being unstable.[35] This suggests to us that the macroeconomy should be viewed as either locally unstable or very close to being locally unstable.

In the second section of the paper, we have briefly examined what the presence of local instability and limit-cycle forces could imply in terms of stabilization policy. Our main observation on this front is that stabilization policy aimed at countering the shocks hitting the economy may turn out to be very ineffective at stabilizing the economy. In particular, we have shown that a reduction in shock variances may have little effect on overall macroeconomic volatility if the economy is locally unstable. Since this analysis was performed using a reduced-form model, more structural analysis is necessary before coming to clear policy implications, but we nevertheless believe that these insights are highly suggestive of why the presence of local instability may matter for policy.

Appendix

Motivation for Baseline Specification

Consider the following demand-driven macroeconomic environment with two aggregate variables: per capita output denoted y_t, and per capita capital denoted k_t. These variables are the result of individual-level decisions by agents $i = 1$ to n, with n large. The capital stock of each agent i accumulates according to a standard accumulation equation, with depreciation rate δ, where we assume that a fixed fraction γ of agent i's purchases today, denoted y_{it}, contributes to his capital stock tomorrow as follows:

$$k_{it+1} = (1 - \delta)k_{it} + \gamma y_{it}, \qquad 0 < \gamma < 1 - \delta.$$

For ease of discussion, we want to think of agent i's capital stock as his holding of durable goods (including possibly housing) for which he receives utility directly. Output in this economy is assumed to be demand-determined, so that per capita output is simply the average of the individual-level purchases, that is, $y_t = n^{-1}\Sigma_i y_{it}$. This implies that the per capita capital stock, $k_t \equiv n^{-1}\Sigma_i k_{it}$, accumulates according to

$$k_{t+1} = (1 - \delta)k_t + \gamma y_t. \tag{A1}$$

To begin, consider the case where individual output demands are allowed to be affected by only three forces as follows:

$$y_{it} = \alpha_0 - \alpha_1 k_{it} + \alpha_2 y_{it-1} + \varepsilon_{it}. \tag{A2}$$

In equation (A2), output demand is allowed to be affected by the agent's holding of consumer capital. In particular, let us focus on the case where $\alpha_1 > 0$, which implies that more consumer capital leads to less desire for new purchases, as would be the case, for example, in the presence of diminishing marginal utility. Output demand is also allowed to exhibit inertia through $\alpha_2 \geq 0$, where this force may reflect, for example, habit or adjustment costs. Finally, we allow a random idiosyncratic term ε_{it}, which may be correlated across agents but is i.i.d. across time. A decision rule of the form given in equation (A2) can be derived from individual-level optimization, in which case the coefficients α_1 and α_2 will typically be smaller than 1. Aggregating equation (A2), we may obtain

$$y_t = \alpha_0 - \alpha_1 k_t + \alpha_2 y_{t-1} + \varepsilon_t, \tag{A3}$$

where $\varepsilon_t \equiv n^{-1}\Sigma_i \varepsilon_{it}$. Under the assumption that α_1 and α_2 are smaller than 1, equations (A1) and (A3) form a simple stable linear dynamic system. It is interesting to recognize that in this case if α_2 and $1 - \delta$ are close to 1, then the roots of this system can be very close to 1, while nonetheless staying stable. We take equations (A1) and (A3) as a simple representation of basic forces that could be driving macroeconomic fluctuations.

Now let us slightly extend the above system by introducing an additional term in the determination of individual-level demand. Here we want to add the possibility that agents' expectations about other agents' decisions may affect their own behavior. Such interaction effects can arise for many reasons. It is not our goal to take a stand on one particular reason here, but instead to argue that such interactions can drastically change the dynamics of the system, even if the effects remain small and close to linear. To capture such an effect, let us generalize the individual decision rule as follows:

$$y_{it} = \alpha_0 - \alpha_1 k_{it} + \alpha_2 y_{it-1} + G(y_{it}^e) + \varepsilon_{it}, \tag{A4}$$

where y_{it}^e is agent i's expectation about aggregate economic activity, and the function $G(\cdot)$ captures how this expectation affects his behavior. If G' is positive, agents' individual-level demands play the role of strategic complements, while if it is negative they play the role of strategic substitutes. Let us start with the extreme case where all agents base their expectations only on the past realization of y_t, and that this expectation is simply backward looking with $y_{it}^e = y_{t-1}$. In this case, the aggregate determination of output is given by

$$y_t = \alpha_0 - \alpha_1 k_t + \alpha_2 y_{t-1} + G(y_{t-1}) + \varepsilon_t. \tag{A5}$$

How does the introduction of the strategic interaction term $G(y_{t-1})$ affect the dynamic system? This depends on whether, near the steady state of the system, actions are strategic substitutes or complements. If they are strategic substitutes, then the system will tend to maintain stability and nothing very interesting is likely to happen. However, if they are strategic complements, then the dynamics may change considerably. In particular, consider the case where α_2 and $1 - \delta$ are close to 1. Then one may show that even a small degree of strategic complementarity near the steady state can render the system locally unstable.[36] In such a case, the global properties will depend on the nature of the nonlinearities in $G(\cdot)$. If the complementarities grow as the system moves away from its steady state, then it will tend to exhibit global instability, in which case the system will explode. In contrast, if the complementarities die out as the system moves away from the steady state, then the system will tend to produce either a limit cycle or chaotic behavior. Again, all this can arise even if the system remains close to linear and complementarities are rather weak. For example, suppose that G takes the form $G(y) = \mu_0 + \mu_1 y + \mu_2 y^3$. Then equation (A5) can be rewritten in univariate form using equation (A1) to eliminate k_t. Moreover, if we close the model by assuming that $y_t = h_t$, where h_t is hours worked per capita, then we can write the determination of hours as a univariate process in h_t as

$$h_t = a_0 + \mu_0 - a_1 \gamma \sum_{j=1}^{\infty} (1 - \delta)^{j-1} h_{t-j}$$
$$+ (a_2 + \mu_1) h_{t-1} + \mu_2 h_{t-1}^3 + \varepsilon_t. \tag{A6}$$

Equation (A6) is a special case of the type of univariate time-series model we estimate in section II. We emphasize here the possibility of interpreting this model as one determining hours worked as opposed to determining output, as the formulation in terms of hours worked can be shown to be more robust allowing for fluctuations in productivity (see section II.F). Note also that equation (A6) features the presence of an accumulation term, which motivates our inclusion of such a term in our econometric specification.

Data

• US Population: Total Population: all ages including Armed Forces Overseas, obtained from the FRED database (POP) from 1952:Q1 to 2015:Q2. Quarters from 1947:Q1 to 1952:Q1 are obtained from linear interpolation of the annual series of National Population obtained from US Census, where the levels have been adjusted so that the two series match in 1952:Q1.
• US total output, consumption, and the various investment types are obtained from the Bureau of Economic Analysis National Income and Product Accounts. Real quantities are computed as nominal quantities (table 1.1.5) over prices (table 1.1.4.). Sample is 1947:Q1–2015:Q2, and we do not use the observations of 2015.
• US nonfarm business output, nonfarm business hours, total hours and unemployment rate (16 years and over) are obtained from the Bureau of Labor Statistics. Sample is 1947:Q1–2015:Q2 (1948:Q1–2015:Q2 for total hours), and we do not use the observations of 2015.
• Capacity utilization: manufacturing (SIC), percent of capacity, quarterly, seasonally adjusted, obtained from the FRED database, (CUMFNS). Sample is 1948:Q1–2015Q3 and we do not use the observations of 2015.

- The series of job-finding rate was constructed by Robert Shimer. For additional details, please see Shimer (2012). The data from June 1967 and December 1975 were tabulated by Joe Ritter and made available by Hoyt Bleakley. Sample is 1948:Q1–2007:Q4.
- The various unemployment rates are obtained from the FRED database, except for France:
  - Australia: Unemployment Rate: ages 15 and over: all persons for Australia (LRUNTTTTAUQ156S), 1966:Q3–2014:Q4.
  - Austria: Registered unemployment rate for Austria (LMUNRRTTATQ156S), 1955:Q1–2014:Q4.
  - Canada: Harmonized unemployment rate: all persons for Canada (CANURHARMQDSMEI), 1956:Q1–2012:Q1.
  - Denmark: Registered unemployment rate for Denmark (LMUNRRTTDKQ156S), 1970:Q1–2014:Q4.
  - France: ILO unemployment rate, total, metropolitan France and overseas departments (001688527), Inséé Macro-economic database (BDM), 1975:Q1–2015:Q1.
  - Germany: Registered unemployment rate for Germany (LMUNRRTTDEQ156S), 1969:Q1–2014:Q1.
  - Japan: Harmonized unemployment rate: all persons for Japan (JPNURHARMQDSMEI), 1955:Q1–2012:Q1.
  - Netherlands: Harmonized unemployment rate: all persons for Netherlands (NLDURHARMQDSMEI until 2012:Q1 and harmonized unemployment: total: all persons for the Netherlands LRHUTTTTNLQ156S) after 2012:Q1 (the second-series level has been adjusted to match the first one in 2012:Q1), 1970:Q1–2014:Q4.
  - Sweden: Harmonized unemployment rate: all persons for Sweden (SWEURHARMQDSMEI), 1970:Q1–2012:Q1.
  - Switzerland: Registered unemployment rate for Switzerland (LMUNRRTTCHQ156S), 1970:Q1–2014:Q4.
  - United Kingdom: Registered unemployment rate for the United Kingdom (LMUNRRTTGBQ156S), 1956:Q1–2012:Q1.

Proof of Proposition 1

Assume that σ_ε^2 is small, so that $|x_0|$ is close to $\bar{x}$. Without loss of generality, take x_0 close to $\bar{x}$,[37] and define

$$y_t \equiv (-1)^t x_t - \bar{x}.$$

To understand y_t, note that, since x_0 is close to $\bar{x}$ and σ_ε^2 is small, we should have $x_t > 0$ for t even and $x_t < 0$ for t odd, that is, the sign of x_t

should switch every period.[38] Thus, $|y_t|$ captures the absolute deviation of x_t from the nonstochastic sequence $\bar{x}_t \equiv (-1)^t\bar{x}$ (the two-cycle), while $\text{sgn}(y_t)$ captures the direction of that deviation relative to zero: if $y_t < 0$ then x_t is "inside" the two-cycle (i.e., $|x_t| < \bar{x}$), while if $y_t > 0$ then x_t is "outside" the two-cycle (i.e., $|x_t| > \bar{x}$).

Next, it is straightforward to verify that

$$y_t = (3 - 2\beta_x)y_{t-1} - 3\sqrt{(\beta_x + 1)(\beta_x - 1)}y_{t-1}^2 - (\beta_x + 1)y_{t-1}^3 + v_t$$

where $v_t \equiv (-1)^t\varepsilon_t \sim \text{i.i.d.}N(0, \sigma_\varepsilon^2)$. Since $(3 - 2\beta_x) \in (-1, 1)$, the fixed point of this system at $y_t = 0$ is stable, and thus for σ_ε^2 small we may restrict attention to the second-order approximation to this system,

$$y_t \approx (3 - 2\beta_x)y_{t-1} - 3\sqrt{(\beta_x + 1)(\beta_x - 1)}y_{t-1}^2 + v_t \qquad \text{(A7)}$$

y_t is clearly stationary, so that we have

$$\mathbb{E}[y_t] \approx (3 - 2\beta_x)\mathbb{E}[y_t] - 3\sqrt{(\beta_x + 1)(\beta_x - 1)}\mathbb{E}[y_t^2]$$

$$= -\frac{3}{2\bar{x}}\mathbb{E}[y_t^2].$$

For $\sigma_\varepsilon^2 > 0$, we will have $\mathbb{E}[y_t^2] > 0$, and thus $\mathbb{E}[y_t] < 0$. Since $x_t = (-1)^t(y_t + \bar{x})$, we may obtain

$$\sigma_x^2 = \mathbb{E}[y_t^2] + 2\bar{x}\mathbb{E}[y_t] + \bar{x}^2$$

$$\approx \bar{x}^2 - 2\mathbb{E}[y_t^2]$$

where we have used the approximation from above to replace $\mathbb{E}[y_t]$. Thus, as σ_ε^2 increases from zero, x_t becomes less volatile, which completes the proof.

Endnotes

The authors thank the two discussants Laura Veldkamp and Ivan Werning, as well as Jonathan Parker for useful comments. For acknowledgments, sources of research support, and disclosure of the authors' material financial relationships, if any, please see http://www.nber.org/chapters/c13772.ack.

1. Although the idea of endogenous boom-and-bust cycles has a long tradition in the economics literature (Kalecki 1937; Kaldor 1940; Hicks 1950; Goodwin 1951), it is not present in most modern macromodels. Recent exceptions are Myerson (2012), Matsuyama (2013), Gu et al. (2013), and Beaudry, Galizia, and Portier (2015b).

2. In the 1980s, following Blanchard and Summers (1986), a branch of the literature explored the case of an exact unit root in unemployment series as an indication of hys-

teresis. However, in practice, estimations gave persistent but stable dynamics, as pointed out by Blanchard and Summers (1986, p. 17, fn. 1): "We shall instead use 'hysteresis' more loosely to refer to the case where the degree of dependence on the past is very high, where the sum of coefficients is close but not necessarily equal to 1."

3. A reader mainly interested in the theoretical rationale for local instability in macroeconomic models may want to consult Beaudry, Galizia, and Portier (2015b).

4. We discuss in section II.D the possibility of multiple steady states and its implications.

5. A deterministic dynamic system is considered sensitive to initial conditions when arbitrarily small differences in initial conditions can lead to significant differences in outcomes over time. In such a case, forecasting long-run outcomes is considered problematic.

6. For ease of exposition, we consider here processes without a constant term, which amounts to assuming that the steady state of the process is at zero. In our empirical exercise below, we relax this assumption.

7. If $\tilde{A}(L) = a_1 + a_2 L + \cdots + a_n L^{n-1}$, then we define the associated $n \times n$ companion matrix as follows: the first row is given by $[a_1, a_2, \ldots, a_n]$, the lower-left $(n-1) \times (n-1)$ block is given by I_{n-1}, and the remaining entries are zero.

8. Throughout this paper, for the sake of brevity the term "largest eigenvalue" will be used to refer to the eigenvalue that has the largest modulus, and when we say that an eigenvalue is greater (less) than 1, unless otherwise indicated we mean that its *modulus* is greater (less) than 1.

9. Fundamentally, if the largest eigenvalue of A is greater than 1, then the system will tend to move away from the steady state (even if the variance of ε is very small), which causes higher-order terms to become more relevant in the DGP. It is for precisely this reason that using an econometric specification containing only first-order terms is more likely to yield misleading results in such a case than in the case where the largest eigenvalue of A is less than 1.

10. In particular, if $\beta > (\mathbb{E}[x_{t-1}^2] / \mathbb{E}[x_{t-1}^4])(\alpha - 1)$.

11. We assume for simplicity that n is large enough that agents ignore the effect of their own choice x_i on x.

12. Since we will be examining behavior within a limited class of nonlinear models, one must be careful about which inferences can be made. For example, if we do not find evidence of local instability in this class, this does not imply that the macroeconomic environment is necessarily stable. However, if we do find that local instability and limit cycles appear in this limited class, it will provide some reason to question the consensus view that macroeconomic fluctuations reflect mainly the effects of shocks within an otherwise stable system.

13. Even if the cyclical variables we consider generally have a zero mean, we nevertheless allow for a nonzero intercept in our baseline specifications. Results are robust to omitting the intercept.

14. Note that the F in equation (4) and the F in equation (5) are not technically the same functions.

15. This identification assumption is quite strong, but allows for a simple two-step approach to the data: first detrend, then estimate. We leave for future research the exploration of decomposition methods that do not require this assumption.

16. We discuss the robustness of our result to the filter below. The quarterly series is filtered (80-quarter, high-pass filter) over the sample 1948:Q1–2015:Q2.

17. Note that the coefficient on h_{t-1} in this approximation is in fact different from the one reported above, though the two are equal to two decimal places.

18. Note that the maximum eigenvalue is not the autocorrelation coefficient because the process is an $AR(2)$ not an $AR(1)$.

19. Note that, except under very special circumstances that are unlikely to be encountered in our case, existence of and convergence to a limit cycle cannot be proven mathematically. As a result, throughout this paper we rely on numerical simulations to check for these properties.

20. One could repeat the deterministic simulation starting from all dates of the sample. This would make the convergence to a limit cycle unchanged or more frequent.

21. We checked that this steady state was unique in each of our bootstrap replications.

22. This does not mean that microfounded models capable of generating limit cycles never feature indeterminacy.

23. This analysis can be extended to the intermediate model when $\beta_0 = 0$. Nonzero steady states, if they exist, are the two opposite real numbers $\pm\bar{h}$ with

$$\bar{h} = \sqrt{\frac{1 - \beta_h - \beta_{h'} - \beta_H}{\beta_{h3} + \beta_{h'3} + \beta_{H3} + \beta_{h^2H} + \beta_{hH^2}}}.$$

24. One could repeat the deterministic simulation starting from all dates of the sample. This would make the convergence to a limit cycle unchanged or more frequent.

25. When we set the threshold level to 1% in the Wald tests (instead of the estimated p-value), the test fails to reject the (spurious) existence of a limit cycle 0.9% (resp. 1.5%) of the time for the minimal model when the DGP is the $AR(2)$ model (resp. the linear model), and 0.7% (resp. 1.3%) and 0.6% (reps. 8%) for the intermediate and full models.

26. See appendix for details about the source and time span of each of the series.

27. A similar pattern is found using the intermediate and full models (not shown in the figure).

28. In this section we will be discussing the effects of changes in shock variances on the variances of endogenous variables. Accordingly, results from this section need to be interpreted cautiously, given the potential for the Lucas Critique to apply.

29. That is, the roots of the polynomial $1 - F(\lambda, \lambda^2, \ldots)$ lie outside the unit circle.

30. With some abuse of terminology, we define the mean and variance of x by time averages rather than ensemble averages, that is, by $\mu_x \equiv plim_{T \to \infty}(1 / T)\sum_{t=1}^{T}x_t$ and $\sigma_x^2 \equiv plim_{T \to \infty}(1 / T)\sum_{t=1}^{T}(x_t - \mu_x)^2$, respectively, assuming these probability limits exist and are independent of the initial state x_0. Thus, according to our definition, we will have $\sigma_x^2 > 0$ even in a nonstochastic environment as long as the system does not converge to a single point.

31. See May (1979).

32. Estimated parameters are given in table 1.

33. In our previous work (Beaudry et al. 2015b) we presented a structural model where limit cycles arose as the result of a complementarity in consumption decisions generated by imperfect unemployment insurance. In that framework, the policy prescription to help stabilize the economy would therefore be to reduce the complementarity in agents' decisions by improving consumption insurance through, for example, automatic stabilizers.

34. More precisely, a reduction in input volatility may have very little impact on the overall volatility of the system when the deterministic version of the system exhibits limit cycles.

35. For most cases we found the modulus of the largest eigenvalue of the estimated system to be very close to 1.

36. See Beaudry et al. (2015b) for details. One of the insights from this example is to show that the presence of strategic complementarities in demand is likely to create local instability.

37. It is straightforward to extend the following reasoning to the case where x_0 is close to $-\bar{x}$.

38. This stems from the fact that, with x_0 close to $\bar{x}$ and σ_ε^2 small, the dynamic behavior of x_t is dominated by the same forces that generate the two-cycle.

References

Beaudry, P., D. Galizia, and F. Portier. 2015a. "Reconciling Hayek's and Keynes' Views of Recessions." NBER working paper w20101, 2014, forthcoming in the *Review of Economic Studies*.

———. 2015b. "Reviving the Limit Cycle View of Macroeconomic Fluctuations." NBER working paper w21241, 2015.

Blanchard, O. J., and L. H. Summers. 1986. "Hysteresis and the European Un-
    employment Problem." In *NBER Macroeconomics Annual 1986*, vol. 1, ed.
    S. Fischer, 15–90. Chicago: University of Chicago Press.
Goodwin, R. 1951. "The Nonlinear Accelerator and the Persistence of Business
    Cycles." *Econometrica* 19 (1): 1–17.
Gu, C., F. Mattesini, C. Monnet, and R. Wright. 2013. "Endogenous Credit
    Cycles." *Journal of Political Economy* 121 (5): 940–65.
Hicks, J. 1950. *A Contribution to the Theory of the Trade Cycle*. Oxford: Clarendon
    Press.
Kaldor, N. 1940. "A Model of the Trade Cycle." *Economic Journal* 50 (197): 78–92.
Kalecki, M. 1937. "A Theory of the Business Cycle." *Review of Economic Studies*
    4 (2): 77–97.
Matsuyama, K. 2013. "The Good, the Bad, and the Ugly: An Inquiry into the
    Causes and Nature of Credit Cycles." *Theoretical Economics* 8 (3): 623–51.
May, R. M. 1979. "Bifurcations and Dynamic Complexity in Ecological Sys-
    tems." *Annals of the New York Academy of Sciences* 357:267–81.
Myerson, R. B. 2012. "A Model of Moral-Hazard Credit Cycles." *Journal of Po-
    litical Economy* 120 (5): 847–78.
Shimer, R. 2012. "Reassessing the Ins and Outs of Unemployment. *Review of
    Economic Dynamics* 15 (2): 127–48.
Tibshirani, R. 1996. "Regression Shrinkage and Selection via the Lasso." *Journal
    of the Royal Statistical Society, Series B* 58 (1): 267–88.

Comment

Roxana Mihet, *New York University*
Laura Veldkamp, *New York University, NBER, and CEPR*

What Are the Origins of Economic Fluctuations?

Most macroeconomic models exhibit local stability. Their fluctuations come from exogenous shocks that disturb an otherwise stable system. The effects of small shocks dissipate over time, as the model returns to its steady state or to a stable growth path. The reason why this assumption seems plausible is that macroeconomic data shows a stable-growth trajectory in many developed economies. However, another possibility that fits the data is a system that is locally unstable, but globally stable, and which exhibits endogenous oscillations. Limit cycles are one possible outcome in such a system.

A (stable) limit cycle is a trajectory that attracts all neighboring trajectories, as shown in Figure 1. A system with a stable limit cycle exhibits self-sustained oscillations, as all the neighboring trajectories spiral toward the limit cycle. Thus, limit cycles can only occur in nonlinear systems.[1] Perturbations of the system away from the limit cycle do not impact its global stability. The system returns to the limit cycle, which is an attractor for the system.

A handful of economic theories can explain why economic interactions give rise to locally unstable feedbacks and oscillations. One example is the effect of trend-following expectations among market speculators, which tends to amplify price asymmetries away from fundamentals in asset markets. In Grandmont (1985), an OLG model without bequests exhibits limit cycles when there is a conflict between the wealth effect and the intertemporal elasticity of substitution effect associated with interest rate movements and sufficiently high concavity. Beaudry, Galizia, and Portier (2015) demonstrate that a DSGE model with demand complementarities related to an accumulable good

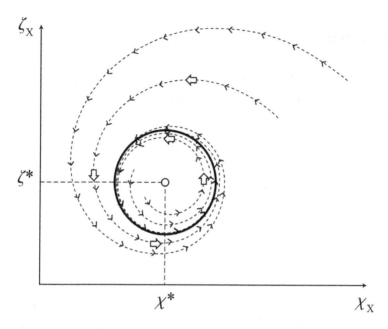

Fig. 1. Visual representation of a limit cycle

Source: Authors' representation.
Note: Independent of the starting point, the system always converges to the stable limit cycle.

can generate nonmonotonic optimal policy functions and limit cycles. Externalities in production or money can create convexities and limit cycles as in Farmer (1986) or Benhabib and Farmer (1994). Models with imperfect financial markets and heterogeneously infinitely-lived agents as in Woodford (1986, 1989), and models with three sectors and Cobb-Douglas technology as in Benhabib and Rustichini (1990) can also generate deterministic limit cycles.

While economic systems may exhibit local instability, we rarely see examples of global economic instability. The supply of physical goods is bounded by physical matter on earth. With a fixed money supply, prices are also bounded. Labor is bounded by the time in a day. Such limiting forces rule out explosive economic systems. Modeling an economic system as locally unstable, but globally stable, is an appealing way to reconcile these forces.

The theoretical possibility of limit cycles is interesting, but lacks much empirical support. Beaudry, Galizia, and Portier set out to fill that gap. The fact that there is a cycle does not reveal whether it is a limit cycle or not. The authors instead estimate time-series models on macro-economic data to determine whether the estimated stochastic processes have the properties needed for limit cycles to emerge. By examining the properties of several macroeconomic variables, they find some evidence of the existence of limit cycles.

The Economy as a Water Wheel

Limit cycles arise frequently in science. A classic example of this is a machine called a Lorenz water wheel. Imagine a bicycle wheel with cups tied to its rim. Each cup has a small hole in the bottom. Water is poured into a fixed position just to one side of the top of the wheel. When a cup catches some of the water, the wheel begins to spin around its axle. The system is locally unstable because it does not stay still as long as the water continues to flow. The state of the system (position of the wheel) fluctuates, even though the forces acting on it are constant. Fluctuations arise without shocks. Yet, the system is globally stable because the machine rotates around a fixed axle and never spins infinitely fast. If the wheel were pushed to spin faster, friction would eventually slow it back down to its original rate of rotation. The Lorenz wheel is a metaphor for business cycles in this model. The water that sets the wheel in motion is like the model's data generating process.

Two crucial ingredients create cycles in both the wheel and the business-cycle model. These two features are what this paper is testing for. First, there are nonlinear forces. The fact that the cups are tied to the rim of the wheel means that the wheel itself exerts force on the cups, changing their direction as they rotate around the axis. Without this nonlinear force, the cups might move, but they would not cycle. The second key ingredient is history dependence. On the wheel, the cups drain slowly. Thus, the level of water in any cup is an indicator of its past (as is the momentum of the wheel). If that cup has passed under the water source frequently, the cup will be fuller. If not, it will be less full. If the cups had no bottoms, they would have no history dependence. With bottomless cups and no momentum, the cycles would cease.

But nonlinearity and history dependence are not sufficient to create limit cycles. If the water is poured directly at the top of the wheel, the wheel might spin either way and switch direction from time to time in an aperiodic fashion. This is an example of chaotic dynamics, a possibility we return to at the end of this discussion. Furthermore, if we were to tie a heavy weight to one point on the wheel, the weight would fall to the bottom and stay there. Rotation would cease. Even though the nonlinear force and history dependence were still present in the system, cycles would not arise. Therefore, finding nonlinearity and history dependence in a dynamic system is a necessary but not a sufficient condition as it only creates the possibility of limit cycles. After finding evidence of these two features in macroeconomic systems, the authors then simulate the estimated stochastic processes to see whether limit cycles do indeed arise.

Is the Macroeconomy Locally Unstable?

"Physicists like to think that all you have to do is say, these are the conditions, now what happens next?"
—Richard Feynman (1965)

There are two necessary conditions for the existence of limit cycles: first, limit cycles require a nonlinear system (higher-order terms); second, they require history dependence. Nonlinear systems can give rise to a remarkable set of spatial-temporal phenomena, including periodic or chaotic system dynamics. Contrasting with the much simpler linear systems often used in macroeconomics because of the easiness of their computation, nonlinear systems may appear chaotic, unpredictable, and often even counterintuitive. Beaudry, Galizia, and Portier argue that the local stability of the macroeconomic system should not be evaluated using linear time-series methods, even if the nonlinearities are minor, or away from the steady state. Doing so could result in wrongly classifying the system as locally stable, when in fact the system is endogenously unstable.

In their paper, Beaudry, Galizia and Portier carry three different exercises. They first test for nonlinearities, and second for history dependence. Finally, they perform various simulations to assess whether the estimated coefficients induce limit cycles.

Testing for Nonlinearities and History Dependence

First, Beaudry, Galizia and Portier test for nonlinearities and history dependence by comparing the performance of a standard linear autoregressive model to various extended AR models that include nonlinear terms. The hypothesis is that including nonlinear terms causes the system to switch from local stability to local instability. The aim is to look for values on the coefficients of the nonlinear terms that can support limit cycles. Practically, the authors estimate the univariate process below with ordinary least squares and then test whether the coefficients on the nonlinear terms are different from zero. They also compute the largest eigenvalue of each univariate process when linearized around its steady state and check whether it is larger than one, which suggests local instability.

The authors allow for different nonlinear forces of the following general form:

$$x_t = a_0 + a_1 x_{t-1} + a_2 x_{t-2} + a_3 X_t + F(x_{t-1}, x_{t-2}, X_{t-1}) + \varepsilon_t \qquad (1)$$

where X_{t-1} is an accumulation term of lags of discounted infinite lags of x_t and $F(...)$ is a multivariate polynomial containing second- and third-order terms in all its arguments, including the accumulation term. The authors posit that this formulation allows more distant lags to play a role without having to estimate too many parameters. More specifically, they estimate a minimal model that includes only a third-order term x_{t-1}^3 an intermediate model that includes all the third-order terms without any second-order terms, and a full model including all third- and second-order terms.

The estimation uses detrended quarterly US data from 1950 to 2014 on labor market variables (log hours worked per capita, nonfarm business hours, the job-finding rate, and the unemployment rate) and goods market variables (output, consumption, durable goods, fixed investment, and capacity utilization). All data is detrended using a high-pass filter that removes fluctuations with periods longer than 20 years.

The results are mixed; sometimes they work, other times they do not. Nonlinearity and history dependence appear for most of the labor market variables. There is evidence from three particular time-series specifications, which seem thoughtfully chosen. For other macroeconomic variables, there is limited evidence for limit cycles. Now, whether other models would deliver the same results, or which other models the authors have tried, is unknown. Overall, these estimation results are suggestive of limit cycles.

However, testing for nonzero coefficients is a weak test. The paper claims success for limit cycles if the t-statistics on nonlinear or history-dependent terms are sufficiently high. But these statistics are for tests whose null hypothesis is that the coefficients are zero. The objective of the paper is to test for local instability. Even with nonlinear and history-dependent terms, a system can still be locally stable (recall the water wheel with the heavy weight). The null hypothesis that should be tested instead is local stability. This would amount to checking whether the coefficients of a group of nonlinear parameters are jointly not too large and positive.

These results do speak more clearly about nonlinearity. Most of the models used in macroeconomics are linear or near-linear, typically locally stable, and converge to a point. Beaudry, Galizia, and Portier reject such linear models for most of the series they examine. Standard DSGE models are usually linearized around the steady state. Standard growth models with utility over consumption and concave technology also do not exhibit limit cycles. Limit cycles are inconsistent with a representative infinitely lived agent, maximizing a concave, time-separable utility function in consumption only. But they need not be inconsistent with optimal growth models where the utility function has a more complicated form, for example, if it includes the capital stock as an additional argument (see Grandmont, 1985).

Simulating to Check for Limit Cycles

Finally, to quantify how strongly the data supports the presence of limit cycles, the authors use a bootstrap method. By estimating a model on subsets of the data, they produce a set of parameters whose frequency approximates the parameter distribution conditional on the data. Then for each combination of estimated parameters in this bootstrap set, they simulate the stochastic process described by those parameters and check to see if it exhibits cycles. They do this exercise for the three different model specifications. For the labor market variables, between 50% and 78% of the parameter estimates in the bootstrap set generate limit cycles. The interpretation of this finding is that limit cycles are a robust feature of the data.

To explore whether their detecting procedure or their detrending might generate spurious limit cycles when the data-generating process is actually locally stable, the authors use Monte Carlo analysis. They construct an artificial series that surely cannot have limit cycles, such as a linear $AR(2)$. They detrend the series, estimate the minimal, intermediate, and full models, and then check for limit cycles. They spuriously detect limit cycles less than 5% of the time. Based on this finding, the authors argue that they are unlikely to detect limit cycles that are not present. However, demonstrating that the procedure does not incorrectly detect limit cycles on an $AR(2)$ series, which cannot exhibit a limit cycle by construction, does not imply that the procedure never produces false positives for other types of processes. It does suggest that macroeconomic data is unlikely to be an $AR(2)$.

Results for a broader class of macroeconomic variables are mixed. After estimating processes for detrended output, total hours, total consumption, durable goods, investment, and the capacity-utilization rate, and simulating those processes, limit cycles emerge in a few cases. For most variables, limit cycles appear for one or two of the three econometric specifications. For structures, all three models generate cycles. No limit cycles are detected for equipment investment.

Cycles or Chaos?

"The basic idea of Western science is that you don't have to take into account the falling of a leaf on some planet in another galaxy when you're trying to account for the motion of a billiard ball on a pool table on earth. Very small influences can be neglected. There's a convergence in the way things work, and arbitrarily small influences don't blow up to have arbitrarily large effects."

—Gleick (2001)

An important future test for this research agenda is to determine whether macroeconomic data can rule out chaotic behavior, or distinguish between chaos and limit cycles. Chaos theory generalizes the properties of local instability and global stability of limit cycles. Chaotic systems exhibit oscillations in a neighborhood of an unstable equilibrium (or shift between neighborhoods of different unstable equilibria). Similar to limit cycles, chaotic systems also have an attracting set of orbits. However, in contrast to limit cycles, this attracting set of orbits is aperiodic. In other words, the variable never returns to exactly the same state.

This distinction is important because forecasting in a chaotic system is nearly impossible. Forecasting is premised on the idea of local stability: Small differences in states will diminish over time. If differences diminish, then if we see a state today that is similar, but not exactly identical, to an economic state observed in the past, we can infer that the future path of the economy will be similar to the path observed in the past. Thus, the past is a reasonable forecast of the future, even though no state is exactly the same.

In contrast, in a chaotic system, the uncertainty in a forecast increases exponentially with elapsed time. Tiny differences in initial conditions can lead to hugely different forecast results. For example, starting from nearly the same initial point, Edward Lorenz, an MIT mathematician and meteorologist, tried to use a computer to simulate the basic dynamics of weather patters. Then he resimulated the same system from what, up to machine accuracy, was the same starting point. He was surprised to find that his forecasts grew farther and farther apart until all resemblance disappeared (figure 2). If every run of a simulation can produce an entirely different dynamic, stemming only from the most minute differences in starting conditions or rounding error, then none are reliable forecasts.

Furthermore, inferring the nature of a chaotic system from data is virtually impossible. There is no existing procedure for taking chaotic data patterns and working backward to the underlying mathematical relationship. So, if chaotic patterns appear in macroeconomic data, finding the underlying equation that predicts future prices may not be possible for now.

These inference and forecasting problems pose a severe challenge for macroeconomics. If forecasting is hopeless and deducing models or mechanisms is impossible, is macroeconomics useful? The authors do not argue that the economy is chaotic. But much of their evidence of nonlinearity and history dependence supports chaos, as well as

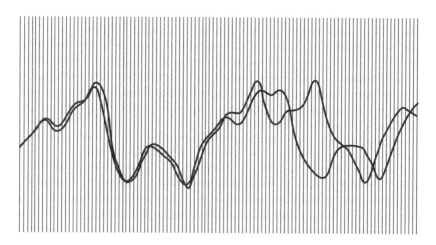

Fig. 2. Visual representation of chaotic behavior. Starting from a very similar initial point, the chaotic systems diverge.
Source: Gleick (2001).

limit cycles. Distinguishing the two can be difficult. But the challenges raised by chaotic nonlinear systems are much greater than those raised by their periodic cousins, limit cycles. Because of these important differences, more evidence should eventually be brought to bear on this question, perhaps disciplined by a quantitative structural model.

In conclusion Beaudry, Galizia, and Portier study the time-series behavior of some macroeconomic aggregates, primarily labor series, and find some evidence consistent with limit cycles. This is an important topic that taps into one of the most fundamental questions in macroeconomics: Why does the macroeconomy exhibit recurrent fluctuations? The authors bring new evidence to bear on the possibility of limit cycles. Although the evidence for many macroeconomic series is mixed, the paper offers a new approach, and hopefully opens up a new research area that tackles a timeless question.

Endnotes

For acknowledgments, sources of research support, and disclosure of the authors' material financial relationships, if any, please see http://www.nber.org/chapters/c13773.ack.
    1. Interested readers should check the Levinson-Smith and the Poincare-Bendixson theorems.

References

Beaudry Paul, Dana Galizia, and Franck Portier. 2015. "Reviving the Limit Cycle View of Macroeconomic Fluctuations." NBER Working Paper no. 21241, Cambridge, MA.
Benhabib, Jess, and R. Farmer. 1994. "Indeterminacy and Increasing Returns." *Journal of Economic Theory* 63:19–41.
Benhabib, Jess, and A. Rustichini. 1990. "Equilibrium Cycling with Small Discounting." *Journal of Economic Theory* 52:423–32.
Farmer, Roger. 1986. "Deficits and Cycles." *Journal of Economic Theory* 40:77–89.
Feynman, Richard. 1965. *The Character of Physical Law*, Modern Library ed. (1994). New York: Random House.
Gleick, James. 2001. *Chaos: Making A New Science.* New York: Penguin.
Grandmont, Jean-Michel. 1985. "On Endogenous Competitive Business Cycles." *Econometrica* 53:995–1046.
Woodford, Michael. 1986. "Stationary Sunspot Equilibria in a Finance Constrained Economy." *Journal of Economic Theory* 40:128–37.
———. 1989. "Imperfect Financial Intermediation and Complex Dynamics." In *Economic Complexity: Chaos, Sunspots, Bubbles and Nonlinearities*, ed. W. Barnett, J. Geweke, and K. Shell. Cambridge: Cambridge University Press.

Comment

Iván Werning, MIT and NBER

This is a nice paper on a fascinating topic. Early theorizing on business cycles sought to generate self-sustaining fluctuations. However, Slutzky (1937) showed the way down a different path with linear systems continuously buffered by shocks. Subsequent modeling, the Wold decomposition and its empirical implementations, elevated these ideas to a dominant methodological tradition.[1] Most of the macroeconomic canon today simply assumes business cycles are due to shocks, with stable dynamics otherwise. More generally, the role played by nonlinearities is also secondary. The present paper is an invitation to question these assumptions. It complements an interesting agenda by the same authors seeking to revive the self-sustaining view of cycles. More generally, their agenda fits in a greater theme exploring nonlinearities in macroeconomic dynamics.

The current paper does two concrete things. In the first and main part of the paper, it presents reduced-form time-series evidence that it interprets as supportive of a limit-cycle view for business cycles. In the second part, these same reduced-form relationships are used to argue that we should care whether or not a limit cycle drives the business cycle because it affects the workings of countercyclical policy. Since I believe the importance of telling apart a limit-cycle view of business cycles from a purely shock-drive view should be evident, for a variety of reasons, I will focus on the first part of the paper. This part of the paper is also relatively ambitious and breaks with the mostly theoretical tradition in the literature on limit cycles.

My main comments will raise some fundamental questions on the knowability of the issues this paper addresses. The ambition of the paper is to present reduced-form time-series evidence without theory. This is a very ingenious and creative thing to attempt and I am surprised nobody has undertaken it before. Indeed, it would be very convincing if a case could be made for limit cycles based on aggregate data alone. Unfortunately, I will argue that there are reasons why this may be a nearly impossible goal. Independently of these more fundamental issues, my reading is that the empirical evidence presented in the paper is weak and sensitive to specification. Understandably, the authors see this as a glass half full, but through the lens of standard econometric practice most readers may feel disappointed and see a glass half empty.

Overall, my take is that the evidence presented in favor of limit cycles is too weak to be persuasive. On the other hand, I believe the case for ignoring nonlinearities in macroeconomic dynamics is equally weak, and probably based on customs or convenience, rather than hard evidence. This belief was reinforced by reading this paper.

Learning about Instability and Limit Cycles from an Uncertain World?

The authors present regressions of the form

$$x_t = \mu(x_{t-1}, x_{t-2}, X_{t-1}) + \varepsilon_t, \tag{1}$$

where μ is a polynomial function and $X_{t-1} \equiv \delta \sum_{s=0}^{\infty} (1 - \delta)^s x_{t-1-s}$. They use the estimated μ to test for the presence of instability and limit cycles.

Before discussing the empirical evidence, let me step back and ask a few basic questions about this sort of strategy. To what extent can we learn about a world without uncertainty from our world with uncertainty? I will argue that one cannot do so without adopting some assumptions and that it is not entirely obvious which assumptions to adopt.

To approach this more fundamental question, let us assume ideal conditions, casting aside all econometric issues. Thus, suppose we are handed a complete description of a Markov process $\{Y_t\}$, where Y_t is a finite dimensional vector. For example, the paper works with $Y_t = (x_t, x_{t-1}, X_t)$.[2] A Markov process can be described in two ways. Perhaps the most natural representation specifies the distribution of Y_t conditional on Y_{t-1}

$$Y_t \sim G(Y_t \mid Y_{t-1}).$$

Note that no other variable or "shock" is introduced in this representation. In a discrete Markov chain case, when Y_t takes on only finite set of values then G can summarized by a $N \times N$ transition matrix $G = (g_{ij})$ where g_{ij} denotes the probability of transitioning from state i to state j.

An alternative representation is given by

$$Y_t = F(Y_{t-1}, u_t),$$

for some function F and some i.i.d. shock u_t with some given distribution. This form of representation is not unique. In particular, one can always normalize so that $F(Y_{t-1}, u_t)$ is nondecreasing in u_t for all Y_{t-1}.[3]

Now suppose we are handed a complete description of a Markov process, so we are given G or F, along with some initial condition Y_0. We are asked to come up with a deterministic path $\{Y_t\}$ that represents what would occur if "uncertainty is removed." Of course, such a deterministic world has never been observed, so this is a counterfactual exercise. We hope that the knowledge of the stochastic process will guide us.

Before focusing on the particular challenges I will highlight, it is worth noting that one obvious concern at this point is the Lucas critique, which cautions us by noting that behavior may change when uncertainty is removed. This is a valid, well-understood concern. However, I want to argue that even if we are willing to shrug off the Lucas critique, thus taking a more mechanical stance, there may still be no obvious way to proceed.

To make things more concrete, imagine we are talking about a discrete Markov chain and are given its transition matrix G. How exactly should we turn off uncertainty? We must convert the transition matrix we are given, with real numbers between 0 and 1, into a new transition matrix containing only 0s and 1s. But how? Row by row, should we take the mean, the median, or the mode? Should we use the same rule in all rows? Why are any of these appropriate?[4] How do we know which realization of Y_t corresponds to "no shock"? A moments reflection reveals that there is no single obvious answer and any choice one makes appears somewhat arbitrary.

Although the discrete case makes this point in a stark manner, the same issues arise with any process, continuous or discrete.

The authors make a choice, adopting a particular certainty equivalence notion. To see this, let us interpret their regressions as recovering the conditional expectation of Y_t conditional on Y_{t-1},[5]

$$\mu(\hat{Y}_{t-1}) \equiv \mathbb{E}[Y_t \mid Y_{t-1} = \hat{Y}_{t-1}].$$

Starting from any $\hat{Y}_0$, the authors then construct a deterministic path $\{\hat{Y}_t\}$ solving

$$\hat{Y}_t = \mu(\hat{Y}_{t-1}). \tag{2}$$

I will call the path solving equation (2) the one-step conditional expectation selection. This seems like a very natural step to take. After all, the error ε_t in the regression (1) can be interpreted as noise, and setting it to zero may then capture a situation without uncertainty. Upon reflection, however, one realizes that this is only one choice of many. Let me spell out a few alternatives.

One simple alternative also adopts a certainty equivalence, but of a different nature. We compute the entire deterministic sequence using the current conditional expectation:

$$\hat{Y}_t = \mathbb{E}[Y_t \mid Y_0 = \hat{Y}_0]. \tag{3}$$

In this alternative, the counterfactual without uncertainty takes the future variables to follow the current forecasted path. With uncertainty, future variables are random and distributed around the forecast. The counterfactual deterministic path given by equation (3) simply removes the error around this forecast.

The sequence given by equation (3) is in general different from the one constructed in the paper using equation (2). This may seem unusual for someone accustomed to working with linear autoregressive models. Indeed, the two paths are equivalent when F is linear in both Y_{t-1} and u_t. However, the entire point of the paper is to reexamine the importance of nonlinearities in dynamics, so we must now confront the difference between these two paths.

Figure 1 shows the two paths for the estimated minimal model from the paper. The thin solid line plots the limit cycle computed using equation (2) as in the paper. The thick solid line starting at $t = 0$ shows the alternative conditional expectation (3). To make the two sequences comparable, the expectation is conditioned on the value $\hat{Y}_0 = (x_0, x_{-1}, X_0)$ from the limit cycle at $t = 0$. The thick solid line shows no limit cycle, with the dynamics converging by dampening oscillations to the steady state.[6]

Is any certainty equivalent notion more natural than the other? It is hard to take a strong stance without a theoretical framework in mind. If one believes the recursive relations underlying the Markov process are primitives and invariant, then this may favor the one-step-ahead formulation (2). In practice, one caution is that such a relation may be sensitive to the length of the period chosen, for example, monthly versus quarterly. The same is not true for the conditional-expectations forecast (3).

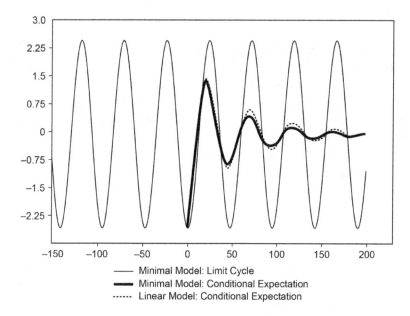

Fig. 1. The figure shows three counterfactual deterministic paths based on model estimates.

Note: The first two use the estimated minimal model: the thin line reproduces the limit cycle as in the paper, by iterating on equation (2); the solid black line is initiated with the limit-cycle path for $t \leq 0$, but computes the conditional expectation using equation (3) for $t \geq 0$ (by way of a Monte Carlo simulation). The dotted line computes the same for the estimated linear model in the paper (in this case using equation [2] coincides with equation [3]).

Another alternative to construct a shock-free counterfactual is to use the F representation and take the shock $u_t = \bar{u}$ to be constant, computing a deterministic path solving

$$\hat{Y}_t = F(\hat{Y}_{t-1}, \bar{u}). \tag{4}$$

The constant $\bar{u}$ may be set at the median or some other value, so that assuming F is increasing, this effectively selects $\hat{Y}_t$ to be the median realization of Y_t given Y_{t-1}, or any other percentile. Thus, we can call this the "percentile selection."

How does the percentile selection (4) compare to the one-step conditional expectation selection (2) used in the paper? If F is additively separable, so that $F(Y_-, u) = \mu(Y_-) + u$, then the percentile selection (4) with $\bar{u} = 0$ is equivalent to the conditional expectations selection (2).[7] However, the paper discusses no evidence for this additively separable assumption. If, instead, F is not additively separable between x and u, then selecting using (4) with a constant $\bar{u}$ is typically not the same as using the conditional expectation (2). Conversely, using the conditional expectations (2) as in the paper is equivalent to (4) but selecting a shock $\bar{u}(Y_{t-1})$ as a function of Y_{t-1}, and this function is not constant unless F is linear. If one views the F representation as a primitive and the u shock as capturing shocks, then this does not capture removing uncertainty in the sense of holding the shock constant, as the percentile selection does.

To take a very simple example, suppose

$$F(Y_{t-1}, u_t) = u_t^2 \mu(Y_{t-1})$$

with u_t i.i.d. distributed symmetrically around 0 and so that $\mathbb{E}[u_t] = 0$ and normalized to $Var[u_t] = 1$. Then $\mathbb{E}[Y_t \mid Y_{t-1}] = \mu(Y_{t-1})$ and using (2) may produce a sequence with limit cycles; however, since $F(Y_{t-1}, 0) = 0$ using (4) with $\bar{u} = 0$ gives $X_t = 0$, which is globally stable![8] Thus, in this case, if we take F and u as our primitives, using the conditional expectation is misleading: turning off shocks requires setting $u_t = 0$ using the F representation, not using the conditional expectation.

This may suggest that the right approach is always the percentile selection, but I next want to argue that this is also arbitrary and not necessarily warranted. Let me provide one example. Suppose we have two fundamental primitive shocks u_{1t} and u_{2t} that are independently distributed, symmetrically distributed around zero. Now suppose

$$Y_t = H(Y_{t-1}, u_{1t}, u_{2t}).$$

for some given function H, increasing in both u_{1t} and u_{2t}. Imagine turning off shocks and uncertainty by setting $u_{1t} = u_{2t} = 0$. If we assume H is an invariant primitive then we compute a deterministic path solving $\hat{Y}_t = H(\hat{Y}_{t-1}, 0, 0)$. However, this is generally *not* equivalent to the percentile selection using the single-shock representation F. In particular, defined the function $\bar{u}(\hat{Y}_{t-1})$ by

$$H(\hat{Y}_{t-1}, 0, 0) \equiv F(\hat{Y}_{t-1}, \bar{u}(Y_{t-1})).$$

Then $\bar{u}(\hat{Y}_{t-1})$ is not constant except in special cases. We conclude that here any fixed percentile selection with a fixed $\bar{u}$, such as the median, is inappropriate. Unfortunately, while the F representation can be identified from knowledge of the process $\{Y_t\}$ alone, H cannot.

The F representation may give one a false sense of security. After all, we have a description of the evolution of Y_t in terms of the past and a shock, u_t. The problem is that the shock u_t in the F representation lacks interpretation, it is not an economic fundamental, but purely a statistical tool, to parameterize the variation in Y_t given Y_{t-1}.

To summarize this entire discussion, the more general point is that a "no shock" world may not be adequately portrayed by the conditional expectation, the conditional median, or any other simple selection device. Moreover, as I have illustrated, different choices produce different conclusions regarding the local stability of steady states or existence of limit cycles. At the end of the day, only the $\{Y_t\}$ process with uncertainty is observed, and we are left guessing how this process would behave in the absence of shocks. Without further knowledge about the structure of uncertainty, any guess appears somewhat arbitrary.

These observations sound a pessimistic note, highlighting potential problems with attempting a reduced-form data-driven approach, as in the paper. However, to end on a more optimistic note, I believe this is precisely where theories may be helpful. Within a certain class of models, the ambiguity I have pointed out may be reduced or removed. In addition, theory may suggest looking at microeconomic evidence that underlie the mechanisms generating nonlinear dynamics or limit cycles.

Empirical Evidence and Econometrics

To explore the evidence for limit cycles, the paper takes a reduced-form univariate time-series approach. The procedure is as follows: (a) choose a series of interest, for example, quarterly total hours in the United States; (b) filter the series using a band-pass filter of 80 quarters; and (c) estimate linear and nonlinear autoregressions, using two lags plus a memory-moving average of the entire history. Specifically, they consider linear models against some nonlinear models. The crucial nonlinearity is that of a cubic term in the first lag.

Their diagnosis is then to check whether the coefficient on the nonlinear term is significant *and* whether the steady state is locally unstable in the absence of shocks, that is, at least one eigenvalue is greater than unity. Strictly speaking, this diagnostic is neither necessary nor sufficient for limit cycles. However, the authors often find that when this diagnostic is met, the implied deterministic dynamics do feature self-sustaining cycles. When applied to total labor hours in the United States this diagnosis is passed, and a limit cycle is found.

Econometrically, the outcome of this diagnosis appears somewhat sensitive to various specification choices. The authors are up front about some of the weaknesses. They show that using quantities, instead of

employment, affects their results. Similarly, their results are weakened
or disappear when using a band-pass filter to isolate business-cycle frequencies of 8–32 quarters. Their results are also somewhat sensitive
to the parametrization of the depreciation rate for the moving-average
term (see their table 7). Finally, the diagnostic is not met across all countries.

I have run a few other robustness checks and confirmed this sensitivity. Filtering total US hours with the Baxter-King filter instead of
the Christiano-Fitzgerald filter changes the conclusions. Figure 2 shows
that the two resulting filtered series look similar. Yet, as table 1 shows,
the cubic term in the minimal model specification is no longer significant. The results are also not significant when using the employment
rate of primary-age men instead of total hours, a series that arguably
has less low-frequency movements to be concerned about.

Second, econometrically the "test" procedure is to estimate the linear and nonlinear models and run the diagnosis mentioned above,
check if the coefficient on the nonlinear term is significant—which I
have noted seems quite sensitive to the specification—and check for
local instability of the steady state. The paper provides some suggestive Monte Carlo exercises showing that data generated from
the estimated linear regressions passes the diagnosis only 5% of the
time, while data generated from the estimated nonlinear regressions
passes the diagnosis 50% of the time. This is taken to be suggestive
that the diagnosis is informative. The question is what it is informative about. The linear model is a particular point in the null hypothesis set. Other points in the null (e.g., a nonlinear model that is constrained to be stable) may perform better. We may be able to reject

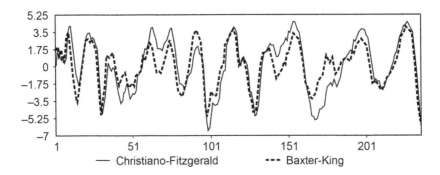

Fig. 2.   Baxter-King filter versus Christiano-Fitzgerald for total hours
Note: The *p*-values are in parentheses.

Table 1
Christiano-Fitzgerald Filter versus Baxter-King

	(1) Christiano- Fitzgerald	(2) Baxter-King
h_{t-1}	1.55	1.43
	(<0.01)	(<0.01)
h_{t-2}	-0.53	-0.45
	(<0.01)	(<0.01)
H_{t-1}	-0.21	-0.54
	(<0.01)	(<0.01)
h_{t-1}^3	-0.0032	-0.0032
	(0.14)	(0.20)
Obs.	218	209
R-squared	0.9587	0.931

the null of a linear model with confidence, but not reject the stability of the steady state with great confidence. A more standard approach performs a standard statistical test with the null hypothesis set to either: (a) the steady state is locally stable, or (b) there are no limit cycles. For a given specification, describing the number of lags and the allowed polynomial expansions, such hypotheses amount to a set of parameters, not a single coefficient, and the test should be performed on this entire set.

I suspect more rigorous tests would have low power, not unlike the unit-root literature. Testing eigenvalues less than one is similar, but even more challenging due to the attempt to capture nonlinear effects. The bootstrap simulations presented are much closer to providing the right kind of tests, especially in the case of the test for local stability (for the one for limit cycles the null is specified somewhat differently). Based on figure 9, the sampling error would allow us to reject the null using a p-value greater than 20%. One may say that this is still somewhat informative, even if not at standard levels of confidence. Seen within the greater context of the sensitivity of the results to specification, however, more caution is probably called for.

An additional problem is that a hypothesis such as local stability should be cast within a nonparametric framework. The minimal model, in particular, is heavily constrained parametrically. Thus, we are relying on a specific degree of parameterized smoothness to test a local property (e.g., the eigenvalues around the steady state). The power of such a test is probably very low.[9] The bootstrap simulations (figure 9 of the paper) provide an estimate of the sampling uncertainty, but only within the model specification allowed. In other words, the test for local stability may be compromised by the functional forms allowed. The model may be trying to fit other aspects of the data and is not flexible enough to do so while having a stable-steady state.[10]

Third, for a question as delicate as the one addressed in this paper, concerns of misspecification have to be first order. The authors adopt a parsimonious approach, but consider by necessity a restricted class of models. I am worried that the model may end up having implications that the data was not screaming out for. That the estimation procedure was fitting aspects of the data that do not speak directly to limit cycles, except for the added structure imposed in the estimation. For example, loosely speaking, perhaps the data wants a nonlinearity such as higher growth rate at peaks, but not a limit cycle. However, the specifications considered may favor one coming with the other. This concern is heightened when one realizes that limit cycles are a global property, while the identification of the parameters is based on one-step-ahead forecasts. The estimation might thus be fitting some local nonlinearities, rather than an actual limit cycles. What feature of the data is really speaking to the existence of limit cycles? It is hard to tell eyeballing the series.

Nonlinearities without Instability nor Cycles: An Example

This paper contributes to an important agenda taking nonlinearities in macro dynamics more seriously. The focus of this paper is on limit cycles, that is, that absent shocks the economy would not converge to a steady state, but instead cycle. However, while the notion that "booms sow the seeds for recessions" probably does require nonlinear dynamics, it is not necessarily exclusive to limit cycles. Let me present a simple example.

Suppose there are two possible states for x_t: booms, $x = H$, and recessions, $x = L$. Suppose the boom slowly generates weaknesses in the economy, perhaps due to excessive accumulation of debt, risk-taking investments, satiation from consumption, fatigue from labor, and so forth. Conversely, a recession slowly heals the economy, perhaps by a deleveraging process, Schumpeterian creative destruction, and so forth. We capture all this implicitly by a variable W_t that evolves according to

$$W_t = \Phi(W_{t-1}, x_{t-1}).$$

with

$$\Phi(W_{t-1}, H) > \Phi(W_{t-1}, L).$$

Assume Φ is increasing in W_{t-1} with a unique interior and globally stable steady state for each $x \in \{H, L\}$, denoted $W_L < W_H$, respectively. We assume $W_{-1} \in [W_L, W_H]$ implying that $W_t \in [W_L, W_H]$. We assume the state transitions from a boom $x_{t-1} = H$ to recession $x_t = L$ if, and only if, the economy gets a bad enough shock

$$u_t \le W_t.$$

Likewise, the economy transitions from a recession $x_{t-1} = L$ to boom $x_t = H$ if the shock is good enough, satisfying

$$u_t \ge \rho(W_t)$$

for some increasing function ρ satisfying $\rho(W_t) \ge W_t$. Suppose u_t is an i.i.d random variable drawn each period. Allowing $\rho(W) > W$ makes recovering from a recession more difficult than falling into a recession; for a given W_t it implies an inaction region for u_t given by $[W_t, \rho(W_t)]$ where the state x remains unchanged; for a given u_t is implies an inaction interval for W_t given by $[\rho^{-1}(u_t), u_t]$. This induces persistence.

Provided the shock u_t has mass below W_H and mass above $\rho(W_L)$, the economy will fall into recessions and recover from them, perpetually.[11] Thus, the state of the economy x_t will continue to fluctuate stochastically. Clearly, this economy features some nonlinearities that may be ill approximated by linearized stable dynamics. These dynamics capture the idea that a long boom makes the economy increasingly vulnerable to a recession, or that "the seeds for the recession are sown in the boom."

Yet there is little or no connection between this property and the existence of limit cycles. To see this, let us remove uncertainty by setting $u_t = \bar{u}$ for some constant $\bar{u}$, perhaps at the median. Will the economy cycle or settle down? That depends on the value of $\bar{u}$, $\rho(W_L)$ and W_H. Indeed, if

$$\rho(W_L) < \bar{u} < W_H,$$

then the determintic economy with $u_t = \bar{u}$ will go perpetually through cycles, fluctuating between $x = H$ and $x = L$.[12] Otherwise, the economy eventually converges to either L or H, depending on parameters and in some cases initial conditions. For example, if $\bar{u} > \max\{\rho(W_L), W_H\}$, then the deterministic economy converges to H eventually.

Of course, this simple model is overly simplified and special. But it is meant to drive home the point that models where "booms sowing the seeds of recessions" need not be associated with limit cycles.

Taking Stock

The authors are right to say that the study of nonlinear macroeconomic dynamics, and limit cycles in particular, is unfairly part of the backwater of macroeconomic thinking. This is a shame. This paper provides a thought-provoking look at the evidence and discusses some implications of the alternative view. As such, it is a great introduction to an important rebel line of work.

While my reading of the empirical case for limit cycles in the paper is rather weak, including some fundamental problems of knowability, I have also become convinced that the alternative hypothesis, absence of limit cycles, would have similar difficulties. Mainstream DSGE models with shocks featuring stable dynamics dominate, but is that a good reason to put them in the alternative hypothesis H_1 instead of in the null H_0? For the most part I agree with the authors that a view based on shock-driven cycles continues to be an act of faith and that the profession would do well to explore beyond these confines.

Endnotes

I am indebted to Andrés Sarto and Nathan Zorzi, who provided excellent research assistance and helpful comments in preparing this discussion. Without implicating them, I also wish to thank Isaiah Andrews, Anna Mikusheva, and Jonathan Parker for helpful discussions. For acknowledgments, sources of research support, and disclosure of the author's material financial relationships, if any, please see http://www.nber.org/chapters/c13774.ack.

1. The Wold decomposition states that a covariance-stationary process admits a representation as an infinite sum of uncorrelated shocks, not necessarily independent nor identically distributed. The result allows one to use a linear econometric model representation, even in cases where the true data-generating model is nonlinear. However, if the true model is nonlinear, then the nonlinear model provides a more accurate description of the data and can be used to make better predictions.

2. When the lags of some underlying series x_t are included in the vector $Y_t = (x_t, x_{t-1}, X_t)$ it should be understood that the second and third components are updated deterministically. Thus, the example F provided below should be interpreted as applying only to the first component, the nonlagged x_t in Y_t.

3. One could further normalize so that u_t is distributed uniformly on [0,1].

4. Note that with the discrete case, the expectation for Y_t conditional on Y_{t-1} may not even lie in the support.

5. That is, the regression is the best linear predictor given the linear and nonlinear terms that are included. But if the true conditional expectation is a polynomial, then the regression should recover it.

6. The figure also shows (dotted line) the conditional expectation using the estimated linear model. Note that since this model is linear it does not matter if we use equation (2)

or (3). We observe that the conditional expectation for the minimal model (thick solid line) is not far from that for the linear model (dotted line). Thus, the estimating nonlinearities for the minimal model are not affecting the forecast significantly.

7. This is consistent with the regression (1) and situations where $\mu(\hat{Y}_{t-1}) \equiv \mathbb{E}[Y_t \mid Y_{t-1} = \hat{Y}_{t-1}]$ so that $\mathbb{E}[\varepsilon_t \mid Y_{t-1}] = 0$, since ε_t may not be i.i.d. and $u_t = \varepsilon_t$ in general.

8. One can build more sophisticated versions such as

$$F(Y_{t-1}, u_t) = P(u_t)\mu(Y_{t-1}) + Q(u_t)$$

where P and Q are polynomials. Or even more generally, just posit that $F(Y_{t-1}, u_t)$ is a polynomial in the pair (Y_{t-1}, u_t). If desired, one can choose these polynomials to ensure that F is increasing in u_t in the relevant ranges.

9. As Fan and Jiang (2007) explain: "In general, a larger choice of bandwidth is more powerful for testing smoother alternatives, and a smaller choice of bandwidth is more powerful for testing less smooth alternatives."

10. Strictly speaking, testing local instability is not a well-posed problem without auxiliary smoothness assumptions. Indeed, one can always change the data-generating process to introduce a small amount of local stability or instability in a small neighborhood of the steady state, only imperceptibly affecting the fit to the data. Thus, the detection of local stability requires the imposition of auxiliary smoothness assumptions. However, these should be explicitly borne in mind when designing a test. Relatedly, one could also change the null to test instability of some economically meaningful magnitude in some economically meaningful region, rather than testing a strictly local property.

11. Note that $W_L < W_H$ but both $\rho(W_L) \geq W_H$ and $\rho(W_L) < W_H$ can be considered. If $\rho(W_L) < W_H$, it is more likely to reach a boom when the economy has been in a recession for a very long time than when the economy has been in a boom for a very long time.

12. The cycles are not necessarily of period 1. No steady state exists in this case, so we cannot discuss its stability/instability.

References

Fan, Jianqing, and Jiancheng Jiang. 2007. "Nonparametric Inference with Generalized Likelihood Ratio Tests." *TEST* 16 (3): 409–44.

Slutzky, Eugen. 1937. "The Summation of Random Causes as the Source of Cyclic Processes." *Econometrica* 5 (2): 105–46.

Discussion

James Stock opened the discussion by noting that filtering data that comes from a unit root process will induce cyclicality in the filtered data. Thus, it would not be surprising if the filtering process mechanically generated dynamics that look like those of a typical limit cycle. He also noted there is a large literature in testing for unit roots under nonlinearity. The distribution theory around these problems is very difficult, but might be worth looking at when developing statistical tests to formalize the exercises of the paper.

Stock also mentioned that the most interesting and provocative implications of limit-cycle dynamics would arise in multivariate settings rather than univariate settings. He therefore encouraged the authors to expand their analysis to a multivariate environment.

The presenter, Paul Beaudry, responded to Stock's concern that filtering mechanically induces limit cycles. He explained that the authors had checked for exactly this issue by examining the filtered data from a near unit root linear model. They found that the process almost never generates limit cycles.

Harald Uhlig followed up on this discussion with a suggestion to apply the procedure to data generated from an AR(2) process with two complex roots, which would necessarily have cyclicality. Filtering out the low-frequency components of that process will bound the cycle, but no longer have a unit root. The filtered process may therefore look very similar to the limit cycles the authors are finding in the data.

Robert Hall provided a pessimistic view about the outcome of aggregate approaches to exploring the question of endogenous cyclicality in macroeconomics. He summarized the latter as the notion that there are complementarities strong enough to generate locally explosive endogenous cycles, but with amplitude limited by countervailing nonlinearities. In this vein, he jokingly raised the possibility that the economy was imploding in 2009 but was saved by a cubic term. However, Hall stressed that the important question is not if this was indeed a cubic term as opposed to some other nonlinear form, but rather what was the economic mechanism that gave rise to it. Hall then expressed concern about using filtered data in these exercises because a model that can explain economic dynamics at this level needs to govern behavior at all frequencies.

Jonathan Parker framed the broader literature behind this paper as the attempt to find a parsimonious view that is most helpful for explaining the aggregate macroeconomic dynamic stochastic process. The problem with linear models, according to Parker, is that they attribute most of the variation in the data to shocks that we do not fully understand. He did note that some progress has been made in thinking about these shocks as arising from fat-tailed microeconomic shocks. In contrast, this paper uses nonlinearities to explain the variation in the data. That said, he thought the procedures under consideration had very little power to assess the importance of nonlinearities. Parker suggested that a potentially fruitful way to make progress in understanding nonlinearities might be to look at specific historical instances that cannot be explained by linear models.

Second, Parker noted that it might be worth looking at higher-order moments in the distribution, besides the mean. For instance, in some stochastic processes the variance, skewness, and kurtosis in the data may be informative about model nonlinearities.

Narayana Kocherlakota offered two comments. First, he posited that the stability of a macroeconomic system is likely to depend on both the real economy and monetary policy. He suggested exploring this further empirically by, for instance, taking the approach of previous research in identifying periods of active versus passive monetary policy in the United States.

Second, Kocherlakota questioned whether the paper was tackling the first-order issues in macroeconomic dynamics and forecasting. In his view, the important questions are related to why macroeconomic forecasting fails to predict large dramatic fluctuations.

Emi Nakamura also questioned how much there is to gain from this line of research given the poor performance of nonlinear models in macroeconomic forecasting. Beaudry agreed with Kocherlakota and Nakamura's comments that the nonlinear model has very little benefit

for forecasting purposes. However, he argued that studying local instability and limit-cycle behavior is important, because if they are present,
they suggest a limited role for policy intervention. For example, Beaudry notes that in the case of limit cycles policy would have to address
the structural cause of fluctuations, because otherwise it would only
change the frequency of cycles.

As a closing comment, Ricardo Reis suggested that the theory of limit
cycles actually lays out a clear path for formalizing statistical tests of
limit-cycle behavior. He recalled that if a bivariate stochastic process in
continuous time has a Hopf bifurcation, then it necessarily admits an
exact third-order Taylor expansion, thus providing a necessary condition for the presence of limit cycles. Further, Reis noted that the theory
also implies a particular restriction on the coefficients of the second-
and third-order terms that can potentially be used to cleanly formulate,
estimate, and test the relevant null hypothesis.

7

Crises in Economic Thought, Secular Stagnation, and Future Economic Research

Lawrence Summers, *Harvard Kennedy School and NBER*

I am very flattered by the invitation to be the dinner speaker at this conference—now celebrating its 30th anniversary. I was proud to coauthor the lead article in the inaugural volume of this series on hysteresis and European unemployment with Olivier Blanchard (Blanchard and Summers 1986). Less successful in its original incarnation was a paper I presented a couple of years later on "The Scientific Illusion in Empirical Macroeconomics" that did not get published in this forum, but was published a few years later as Summers (1991). In ways I certainly did not expect, both these papers contain ideas that I believe are relevant to current policy dilemmas.

More generally as someone who has held policy-making positions, I can attest to the influence of academic research of the kind presented and debated at these conferences. Over the years, the effect of research on policy has greatly increased. How could it be otherwise when the vast majority of the world's central bankers are now economics PhDs with experience carrying out macroeconomic research?

I have always believed that academics are most useful when they reconsider existing paradigms and least useful when they make recommendations on current policy where they often lack specific context. So, I have decided that I will try to behave in character and offer a few provocations regarding current macroeconomic thinking that come out of my work on secular stagnation and hysteresis. My hope is to make a case that analytical approaches quite different from those employed over the years at the NBER Macro Annual Conferences and by the world's central banks are necessary to make sense of current events. I will explain why I believe that current inflation-targeting regimes will not survive the next decade in most countries. Finally, I suggest a vari-

ety of issues that I believe should preoccupy macroeconomic researchers in the years ahead.

I. Crises and Macro Thought

A. *Financial Crisis and Recovery in Historical Context*

Figure 1 points out what I believe should be a (if not *the*) principal pre-
occupation of contemporary macroeconomics. We know that the Great
Depression started in the fall of 1929 and is normally thought of as
having persisted for approximately 12 years, until the onset of World
War II. We also know that the financial crisis started in 2007, and can
project 12 years forward with a mixture of eight years of actuals and
four years of CBO forecasts. The comparison is very sobering. Taking
a 12-year view, and comparing 1929 to 1941 and 2007 to 2019 periods,
US GDP will do no better over the entirety of the financial crisis and its
aftermath than it did during the Great Depression. To be sure, things
went down much faster during the Depression and they came back
much faster, but overall the financial crisis decade is comparable to the

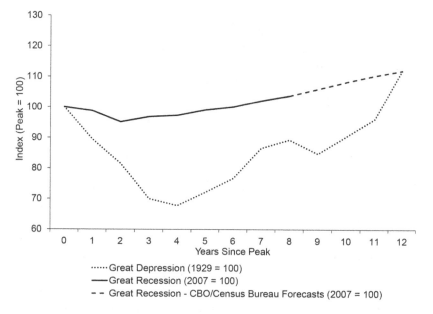

Fig. 1. US real GDP per 18-to-64-year-olds, Great Depression and Great Recession
Source: Bureau of Economic Analysis, NBER, CBO, and Census.

decade of the 1930s. The rest of the industrial world had a somewhat better Depression and has performed relatively worse in recent years. So, if these comparisons were made on a global basis, the current episode would appear even worse compared to the Great Depression.

B.   *The Depression and Economic Thought: Keynesian Fiscal Stabilization as Growth Enhancer*

In the wake of the Depression, economists came to accept that business fluctuations were more than a cyclical phenomenon. While there was much debate about the causes of the Depression and debate about how policy shaped its course, there was consensus that it did not have to happen. So, with better policy, the output and employment gaps associated with the Depression could have been mitigated, leading to higher levels of cumulative output and employment. It was the aspiration of Keynesian economics in the 1950s, 1960s, and 1970s to make societies richer over time by preventing costly downturns.

The Keynesian aspiration was not to merely reduce the amplitude of cyclical fluctuations, but also to increase overall growth. For instance, President Kennedy's 1963 Economic Report of the President argued that fiscal stimulus would boost long-run potential output: "among the costs of prolonged slack is slow growth. An economy that fails to use its productive potential fully feels no need to increase it rapidly. The incentive to invest is bent beneath the weight of excess capacity. Lack of employment opportunities slows the growth of the labor force. Defensive restrictive practices—from featherbedding to market sharing—flourish when limited markets, jobs, and incentives shrink the scope for effort and ingenuity. But when the economy breaks out of the lethargy of the past five or six years, the end to economic slack will by itself mean faster growth" (Kennedy 1963). Even those like Milton Friedman, who opposed discretionary stabilization policy, argued that appropriate policy rules would prevent or at least limit downturns in ways that raised average levels of output.

C.   *Stagflation and Economic Thought: Inflation Targeting as Output Stabilizer*

Thinking radically changed in the 1970s shortly after Milton Friedman (Friedman 1968) and Edmund Phelps (Phelps 1968) forcefully argued that there was no reason why a permanent increase in inflation should lead to a permanent reduction in unemployment. The prediction was dramatically confirmed. Some combination of reduced monetary discipline when the global monetary system became completely untethered to gold, adverse supply shocks, and policy misjudgments led to the emergence in the 1970s of high rates of inflation. Inflation coincided with what, at the time, seemed abnormally elevated unemployment and low rates of GDP growth.

What followed was a new consensus that held that demand management policy could not affect the average level of output over long periods of time. It could only effect output for limited intervals, primarily due to expectational errors and temporary wage and price rigidities. Inflation targeting became the monetary policy approach of choice around the world since policy could not affect average unemployment, but could affect average inflation. Central bank economists relied almost without exception on models that saw policy as impacting the second moment (variability) but not the first moment (level) of output and employment. Fiscal policy was discarded as a stabilization policy tool. Little wonder that Robert Lucas (Lucas 2003) was famously able to dismiss the importance of macroeconomic fluctuations.

D. *Financial Crises and Economic Thought: Primacy of the First Moment*

All of this appeared reasonable until 2008. Cyclical fluctuations were sufficiently mild and downturns sufficiently brief that one could reasonably believe that whatever was lost on the downswings was made up on the upswings. It was the era of the "Great Moderation." Even after the sharp downturn of 2008–2009, by far the most serious of the post–World War II period, it was possible to suppose that the economy had been taken down by a kind of "financial interconnection failure." This view stipulated that a breakdown in the financial intermediation system might be expected to cause a sharp, but transitory, fall in output, much as would be experienced during a telephone outage or pervasive power failure and normality would return when the connections were repaired.

Unfortunately, as figure 1 makes clear, despite the fact that the credit system was stabilized by the end of 2009, levels of output remain very depressed more than seven years after the trough of the recession. Another way to make the point is to observe that if the economy had performed as it was expected to before the financial crisis, US real GDP would be $2 trillion higher today, translating to nearly $25,000.00 of

Table 1
Projected Versus Actual Growth, 2007–2015

	Real GDP in Year 2007 (billions)	14,74
×	CBO Expected Growth in Real GDP 2007 to 2015*	24.2%
=	Expected 2015 Real GDP	18,477
–	Actual 2015 Real GDP	16,397
=	2015 GDP Shortfall	2,080
%	US Population (Billions)	0.321
=	Per Capita Real GDP Shortfall	6,479
×	Personal Income Share of GDO	86.2%
=	Shortfall Per Capita (2009 Dollars)	5,587
×	2015 Value of a 20009 Dollar (PCE Deflator)	$1.10
=	Per Capita Shortfall in Current Dollars	$6,120

*CBO Budget and Economic Outlook: FIscal Years 2008 to 2018, released
Jan 2008, Table E-1, line 3
Sources: CBO, Bureau of Economic Analysis, Census

personal income for the average family of four. As shown in table 1, the CBO economic forecast completed immediately prior to the Great Recession projected that real GDP would grow 24% by 2015. It actually managed only around 10%. This disappointment is less than what has happened in Japan over the last generation or what has happened over the same interval in Europe.

Recent events are as severe a challenge to current orthodoxy as the Depression was to the orthodoxy of John Maynard Keynes' times or the inflation of the 1970s was to the orthodoxy of its time. I submit that our current experience cannot be seriously contemplated using orthodox models that assume that macroeconomic policy choices affect the second, but not the first, moment of output.

If I am right, there are large implications for contemporary macroeconomics. There is the necessary reorientation from the study of the amplitude of fluctuations in output to the presence and persistence of output gaps between what economies produce and their potential. At the methodological level, for three decades graduate students have been taught that their goal as macroeconomists was to understand the time-series properties of key variables like output, inflation, and interest rates. The universal tool of choice has been some kind of DSGE (dynamic stochastic general equilibrium) model. If instead most of what is macroeconomically important involves occasional events that have

profound effects over long periods of time, linear time-series modeling
may be of limited relevance. The desire for microfoundations, linearity, and simplicity leads the vast majority of DSGEs to build in the assumption that monetary policies do not affect average output levels
over time. More fundamentally, theories that posit that economies are
naturally self-equilibrating without policy intervention likely assume
away the most important issues. It may well be that in 1933 or 2008,
the economy would not have found a bottom if policy had not reacted
dramatically to events.

In what follows I shall try to suggest some ideas that lie outside the
prevailing orthodoxy and may be helpful in making sense of recent developments. My position is in some sense intermediate between that
of Blanchard (2016), who critiques existing macroeconomic approaches
centered on DSGEs but comes down in favor of eclectic modification
rather than revolution, and advocates of a new heterodox macroeconomics, who often bring a negative attitude toward existing approaches without fleshing out any alternatives.

II.   Secular Stagnation

A.   Symptoms

Even at the depths of the financial crisis, no one remotely expected
that in 2016 interest rates would be close to zero, expected inflation
would be far below target, and GDP would be at current levels. As
evidenced by the rapid improvement in the stock market, shrinking
of credit spreads, and increases in the prices of real estate and housing
wealth, financial conditions improved much more rapidly than market
participants expected. Yet, table 2 shows that over the next 10 years, the
financial markets expect real interest rates in the industrial world to be
negative and inflation rates to be substantially below central banks' 2%
targets.

Figure 2 shows that current real interest rates are the culmination
of a trend that has been underway for quite a long time. Notice that
the current rate is roughly what would be expected from fitting a linear trend to the precrisis (1999–2007) period. This invites the question:
are real interest rates so low right now because of the crisis or because
there were already a set of forces underway that were depressing rates
substantially?

My judgement is that there is substantial merit to the latter view. In-

Table 2
Ten Year Interest Rates and Expected Inflation

	USA*	Japan	Euro
Nominal Swap Rate	1.05	0.08	0.02
Inflation Swaps	1.39	0.21	1.06
Real Swap Rate	–0.34	–0.13	–1.04

*Adjusted for the 0.35 percentage point avg. difference between cpi and pce.
Source: Bloomberg, Updated August 28, 2016

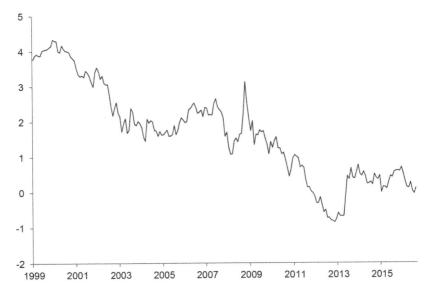

Fig. 2. US TIPS 10-year real yield

Source: Bloomberg.

deed, one simplified but largely valid interpretation of the US macro-economic history of the last several decades follows. The "recovery" has been a period of very slow growth and abnormally low real interest rates. This period was preceded by a financial crisis. That was, in turn, preceded by a period of normal growth, in which the unexciting growth in aggregate demand was accomplished only through the erosion of credit standards and a mammoth housing bubble. That, in turn, was preceded by the 2001 to 2003 recession, which, in turn, was preceded by the Internet bubble. So the last time that the economy grew satisfactory with financially normal and sustainable conditions was probably the mid- or late 1990s.

B. Causes

The essence of the secular stagnation hypothesis is that there has been a substantial backward shift in the IS curve, which explains much of what we have observed over the last two decades (Summers 2014, 2015, 2016). As is demonstrated by Rachel and Smith (2015), the shift to the IS curve can be convincingly explained by demographic changes, the impact of inequality on savings propensities, events in the developing world, changes to the relative price of capital goods, a sludging up of financial intermediation, and an increase in risk aversion and concomitant risk premiums.

The market expects the shift in the IS curve to persist for a long time. This can be seen in figure 3, which depicts expectations for Federal Reserve policy as manifested in the OIS (overnight indexed swap) forward curve. The market is saying that the long-run normal rate will be something like 2% indefinitely. There are questions about how one should adjust this for a variety of technical factors such as convexity. But there is not a plausible set of adjustments that would get the number to the 350 basis points that would have been considered on the low side of normal nine years ago, or even to the 300 basis points that the Fed is currently projecting.

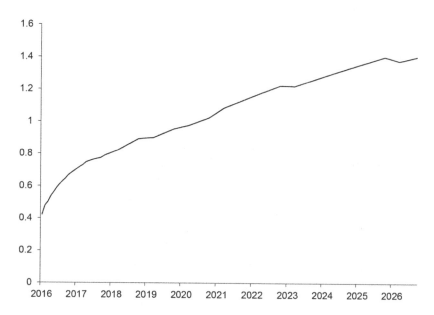

Fig. 3. Overnight indexed swap forward curve
Source: Bloomberg (updated August 2016).

From this perspective, much of what happened leading up to the financial crisis was not exogenous monetary and regulatory policy errors. It was authorities supporting a set of policies that were necessary to maintain something approaching full employment and reasonable growth given this large-scale leftward movement in the IS curve. In the face of reductions in demand, policymakers accepted the lower real rates necessary to assure full employment. These rates in turn had consequences for financial stability and set the stage for the crisis.

C. Objections and Responses

The most common argument against the secular stagnation hypothesis is that the United States is at or near full employment, so cannot be afflicted with secular stagnation. Though the unemployment rate and most other labor market indicators do not suggest large amounts of slack, I nevertheless am more convinced of the validity of the secular stagnation thesis today than I was when I first put it forward in 2013. Growth has been much lower than was expected in 2013, despite interest rates being much more stimulative than market or central bank expectations. Central banks have been unable to raise even 10-year inflation expectations to target levels. Whether or not full employment is being supported by unsustainable financial conditions remains an open question. As I discuss below, the effective lower bound on interest rates will likely inhibit an appropriate monetary policy response when the next recession arrives. I do not see how anyone can prudently be confident that the demand side will not constrain economic growth in the years to come.

Another common argument associated with Gordon (Gordon 2015) is that stagnation is a problem on the supply rather than demand side. I do not view this as a critique of, or mutually exclusive with, the idea of demand-side secular stagnation, and agree that the apparent collapse of productivity growth is a highly troubling phenomenon. Economists have a standard way of distinguishing changes in quantity that come from supply and demand shocks—looking at prices. Whereas the view that slow growth was coming from the supply side would suggest that prices should be higher than was anticipated in 2013, they are in fact substantially lower, as shown in table 3.

On the basis of the evidence laid out in Blanchard, Cerutti, and Summers (2015), I believe there is a substantial chance that productivity growth has been reduced by the shortfall in demand that we have already suffered. A corollary of this view is that if demand is increased,

Table 3
Expected 2012–2018 Inflation*

	2013	Now
Canada	1.8%	1.2%
France	1.6%	0.9%
Germany	1.3%	1.7%
Italy	1.4%	0.9%
Japan	1.1%	1.0%
United Kingdom	2.0%	1.5%
United States	1.9%	1.4%

*GDP deflator, annual rate
Sources: IMF WEO, Oct 2013 and April 2016

the result will be more rapid productivity growth. If weak demand inhibits the development of the economy's supply potential, then the possibility of a low-growth trap caused by insufficient demand emerges.

III.   Over-Optimism and the Precrisis Paradigm

The failure of precrisis modes of thought, and concomitant necessity for a paradigmatic shift, is apparent from the economics profession's repeated failure to predict what have turned out to be persistently disappointing outcomes. Experts, be they in the private sector, at central banks, or in the financial markets, have been consistently over-optimistic.

A.   Forecasts

Professional forecasters have been consistently wrong, as shown in figure 4, which depicts repeated downward revision to the IMF's world growth forecasts. Nordhaus (1987) observed many years ago a tendency for revisions in economic forecasts to be serially correlated. That has been substantially borne out for both the world as a whole and for the United States. Table 4 shows the same pattern for the US economy, with continual negative revisions.

This over-optimism is quite broad. A similar pattern is present in figure 5, which shows analysts' forecasts for companies, even though corporate profits on the whole have been a relatively bright spot; every two years analysts have been too optimistic about the next two years, and the moment when that has been truest is 2016.

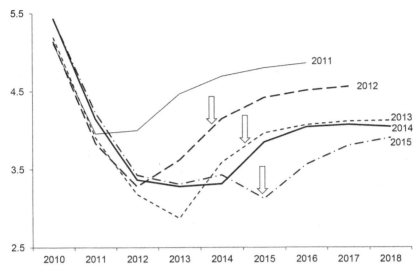

Fig. 4.   World GDP growth forecasts

Source: IMF.

Table 4
U.S. Year Ahead GDP Forecasts

	Prior June	Actual	Diff
2011	4.0	1.6	−2.4
2012	3.5	2.2	−1.3
2013	2.5	1.5	−1.0
2014	3.3	2.4	−0.9
2015	3.1	2.4	−0.7
2016	2.6	?	

Source: Federal Reserve Summary Economic
Projections

B.   Markets and Central Banks

Perhaps what is most striking is how wrong the market has been about
monetary policy. The market has consistently thought that normalization was coming. Each one of the dashed lines in figure 6 is the Fed
Funds Futures, as of a particular moment in the past. And the market
has very consistently been wrong. The only group that has been more
wrong than the market has been the central banks. At every moment the
Fed has seemed perplexed that the market did not believe its forecasts
and did not recognize the degree and strength of their commitment

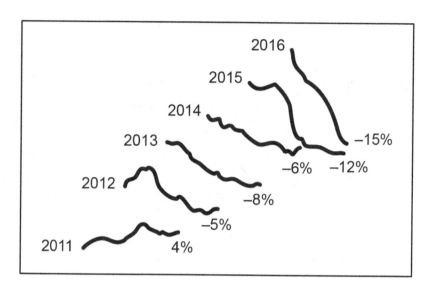

Fig. 5. Concensus bottom-up EPS estimates

Source: *Financial Times*, April 15, 2016; First Cell I/B/E/S, Goldman Sachs Global Investment Research

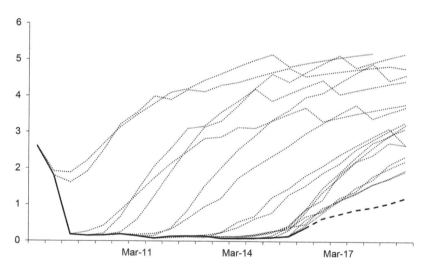

Fig. 6. Forward OIS curve

Source: Bloomberg.

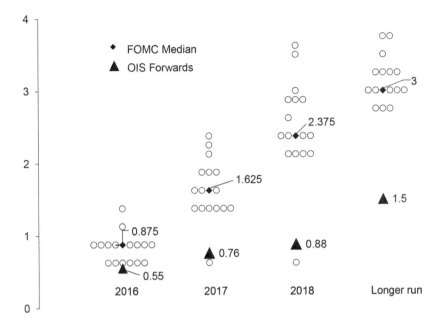

Fig. 7. FOMC versus market expectations
Source: Federal Reserve; Bloomberg (updated to August 28, 2016 data).

to normalization. That continues to be the case today. Figure 7 depicts what Fed officials predict will happen and what the market expects. There are 19 dots, one for each Federal Reserve Governor and bank president. None of them are anywhere near what the market is saying.[1]

If the Fed was determined to keep interest rates low and announcing that interest rates were going to stay low, and the markets were convinced that the Fed was well behind the curve and would have to raise interest rates much more rapidly, there would be an outcry from the markets and the economics community. But the current situation is largely passing without comment, despite the magnitude of the divergence and its persistence.

IV. Policy Options

Judging by the history of cyclical fluctuations in the United States and abroad as reflected in table 5, the odds that there will be a recession within the next three years are significantly better than 50%. Conventional monetary policy, which as discussed above has been dominant in the demand-stabilization role since the stagflation of the 1970s, is

Table 5
Three+ Year Old Expansions Percent of Time
Recession Within

	2 years	3 Years	5 Years
Japan	30%	40%	54%
Germany	53%	74%	98%
UK	28%	40%	63%
US	43%	63%	88%

*1970–present
Sources: NBER, Economic Cycle Research Institute

challenged by extremely low interest rates. Conversely, low rates make government debt less costly. For both these reasons—the limitations on monetary policy and the relaxation of the intertemporal budget constraint implicit in low rates—I expect fiscal policy to play an enhanced role in the future.

A.   *Monetary Ingenuity and Its Limits*

There is a substantial aggregate demand problem that is manifest in below-target inflation everywhere, in substantial slack in Europe and Japan, and in the prospect that the United States will, at some point in the not-too-distant-future, have slack that is not readily solvable. To counteract postwar recessions, the Fed has generally cut interest rates by at least 400 basis points. The prospect that there will be 400 basis points worth of monetary fuel to provide to the economy has to look quite remote, even considering that rates can be taken somewhat negative and risk premiums reduced through quantitative easing.

   How might monetary policy respond to all of this? One view taken by some central bankers is that if equilibrium interest rates are low, then we have to find a way to get interest rates down to equilibrium levels, and, so, you need monetary ingenuity. I think that is a reasonable point of view. It is constrained by real questions as to how much incremental monetary expansion is possible through available tools. Whether there is any political openness to the institutional reforms that would make substantially negative interest rates possible is a question that is very much in doubt. Forward guidance is another possible tool. But how effective can forward guidance really be when the futures markets are already judging that rates are going to be very close to zero? And even if low enough interest rates could be achieved, other concerns remain. It seems to me highly plausible, on the basis of all sorts of behavior that we observe, that abnormally low interest rates and extensive liquidity promote leveraging, promote reaching for yield, make bubbles more likely, and therefore run substantial risks of subsequent financial instability. Even if that is not the case, the investments that were not worthwhile at a 0% 10-year real yield, that suddenly become worthwhile at a significantly negative yield, are likely to be of low quality.

Another possibility is quantitative easing policy, or in Fed parlance, "large-scale asset purchases" (LSAP). Here, too, there are reasons to doubt efficacy. Whatever one thought about the impact of LSAP on interest rates a few years ago, the observation that long rates have fallen sharply and yield spreads between short and long rates have fallen even more rapidly since QE was suspended in 2013 has to give pause. There is also the question of whether policies that work through putting price pressure on long-term Treasury bonds impact the longer-term rates that are most important for investment decisions. Finally, advocates of LSAPs have to contend with the observation made by Greenwood et al. (2014) about the complexities posed by the distinct role of the Federal Reserve and Treasury in these markets. The period when QE was thought to have been effective, the stock of long-term public debt that markets had to absorb increased sharply because of government deficits and the Treasury's shift toward issuing more long-term debt.

I am not sure what the future will bring with respect to monetary policy. The current paradigm of independent central banks politically accountable for the attainment of inflation targets follows naturally from New Keynesian models in which monetary policy does not have long-run effects on output and in which the dynamic consistency problem leads to a bias toward excessive inflation. In today's world, where markets are indicating that insufficient rather than excessive inflation is likely to be the problem for the next decade, and where chronic output shortfalls are a real risk, I see no compelling argument for the current paradigm. Ideas that focus on credibly signaling a commitment to enough inflation to allow monetary policy flexibility, that involve taking more responsibility for avoiding output shortfalls, and that are more sensitive to financial conditions should, I predict, supersede inflation targeting over the next decade.

B. Fiscal Policy and Lower Rates

I believe that doubts about the efficacy of very low interest rates in stimulating demand, along with concerns about the possible adverse side effects, will eventually lead to substantially increased reliance on fiscal policy as a stabilization tool. Fiscal policy operates more directly and responds to the current market signals that bonds are extraordinarily high-priced, which suggests that more of them should be sold. Put differently, the nature of the government budget constraint is fundamentally different in an environment of zero real interest rates that can be locked in for long periods of time. And there are strong microeconomic arguments for believing that infrastructure investments will have a high social rate of return, at least in the United States.

Many who might otherwise be in favor of fiscal activism worry that given current high levels of government debt, it may be infeasible or imprudent to rely on fiscal expansion as a stabilization tool. This is a legitimate concern and those who think it can be avoided by relying on helicopter money (and money financed fiscal expansion) are confused. Base money is now paid interest, so is best thought of as a form of floating-rate government debt. Moreover, because there exists today no preset path for monetary policy going forward, there is no way of meaningfully committing that a given fiscal expansion will be indefinitely financed with money.

However, there are three other compelling responses to concerns about excessive borrowing. First, much incremental borrowing can be for outlays that would otherwise take place with a delay. There is a phenomenon in many countries that I term "repressed deficits," which is analogous to "repressed inflation." Repressed inflation is when a country would have inflation, but has imposed a price control. Repressed deficits take place when a government would have a budget deficit but instead defers maintenance, underpays the civil service leading to higher turnover, or does not make adequate contributions to pension plans. These actions all have the effect of pushing a liability into the future that will likely compound at a rate substantially greater than the zero real interest rate available on government debt. Increasing deficits in order to pull forward necessary investments would likely improve the government's long-run financial position.

Second, as Delong and I (DeLong and Summers 2012) demonstrate, in the current low-interest rate environment, fiscal stimulus in the form of public investment does not have to be hugely productive to pay for itself. This finding has been corroborated by the IMF (2014). Imagine a project with only a 5% return taking account of both any stimulative aspects and the output benefits of increased public capital. For each $100 invested, GDP will rise by $5 leading to about $1.50 in increased revenue collections. Leaving aside any hysteresis considerations that would just strengthen the case, this $1.50 is more than enough to cover the debt service on long-term inflation-linked bonds.

Third, it is possible for fiscal policy to be expansionary and raise demand and neutral interest rates without increasing the deficit at all. Consider the possibility that the government expands pay-as-you-go social security—that is, a system where each year the young generation pay for the old age benefits of their parents' generation. Such a system by the definition of pay-as-you-go does not impact the federal deficit. Yet its effect is to raise demand by obviating the need for as much private retirement saving as would otherwise take place. A similar impact can be achieved by deciding at present to rely more on tax finance and less on benefit cuts in dealing with funding gaps in existing entitlement programs.

V. Future Research

A.   Limiting the Incidence and Damage from Fluctuations

What does all this suggest economists should be researching? First, it is counterproductive to use models that only address the amplitude of fluctuations and not the level of output. Rather, the central macroeconomic question is likely to be how to have more output and more employment, rather than simply how to limit the amplitude of fluctuations. Lucas (Lucas 1987) was right when he said nearly 30 years ago that the welfare costs of variability were really remarkably low compared to the welfare costs of lost output. He was, however, wrong in my judgment to conclude that research should therefore focus exclusively on supply-side growth theory to the exclusion of demand-induced fluctuations. The 2008 recession was a profound demand-induced fluctuation that seems to be associated with a very large output consequence. Determining which policies will make a recurrence less likely and less damaging should be at the top of research agendas.

This focus will require openness to models in which there are multiple equilibria, continua of equilibria, and that allow a role for policy in affecting over time the first moment of output and employment. It will require much more extensive efforts to understand hysteresis phenomena. Much of this work will likely have to depend on information at the microeconomic level. It will also be important to integrate ideas relating to hysteresis with ideas stressing that pessimistic expectations can be self-fulfilling.

B. Low Rates: Causes

There is much to be done to understand why real interest rates and market expectations of future real interest rates have fallen. The main reason I put forth the idea of secular stagnation four years ago was that with the downward trend in real rates I found the then prevalent "temporary headwinds" theory implausible. I have stressed in my work the array of factors discussed in section II.B that have borne on the supply of saving and the demand for investment. Elaboration and expansion of this list seems to me the most fruitful avenue for thinking about real interest rates. It will be necessary to take account of the dynamics more than is done in most current discussions. To some extent, low rates work to stimulate demand by pulling investment forward. So today's reduction in interest rates reduces tomorrow 's neutral rate by pulling forward investment.

An alternative mode of thought associated with Ricardo Caballero and colleagues (Caballero, Farhi, and Gourinchas 2016) sees the level of interest rates as reflecting asset-allocation decisions between safe and risky assets. On this theory, interest rates may have fallen because of a "shortage" of safe assets. From this perspective variables like volatility, the risk aversion of investors, and capital requirements should determine interest rates. Accordingly, real rates on Treasury instruments may move without there being a large impact on expected returns on other assets. Indeed, Treasury yields may fall precisely because of increases in risk aversion that make ex ante returns on other assets higher.

Distinguishing between these views, as well as maintaining a focus on world interest rates, must be a continuing priority for future research.

C. Low Rates: Effects

Economists have not thought through the broad implications of a world with far lower than accustomed to normal real interest rates. To take one example, if it made sense for Harvard University to pay out 5% of its endowment in 1999, when the real interest rate was 4%, it is really quite unlikely that it makes sense to pay out 5% of its endowment in 2016 when the real interest rate is zero. It may be that they should have paid out more in 1999, but it is hard to believe that the real rate has

moved by 4% and there should be no change in the spending rules under which people operate. A more important manifestation of this phenomena is the funding of pension obligations or the long-run liabilities
of insurance companies. Whatever the right funding ratios were when
interest rates were 400 basis points, they surely should be much higher
today.

I am increasingly convinced that declining neutral real rates are the
key to understanding other phenomena that are traditionally analyzed
in different terms. Take, for example, the observations that ratios of
debt to GDP and the size of the financial sector relative to GDP have
increased. Both are widely seen as symptomatic of problems in the financial system. Here is an alternative view. Lower interest rates mean
higher multiples on all assets—that is, higher price-earnings ratios on
stocks, higher price-rent ratios on real estate, and so forth. If the total
value of assets increases, it is natural to expect that the total value of
borrowing should rise, especially when its cost—the real interest rate—
is declining. Much of what the financial sector does is involved with
managing assets and, indeed, recent research (Greenwood and Scharfstein 2013) suggests that asset-management activity is the main reason
for the growth of the financial sector. If assets systematically become
more valuable, would one not naturally expect that the costs of managing them would rise proportionally and therefore in relation to GDP?

More speculatively, there are likely other links as well. A reduction
in discount rates should systematically benefit long-horizon, high-
duration assets relative to low-duration assets. Perhaps the rise of
unicorns—highly valued technology start-up companies—is less surprising in this light as is the intermittent emergence of real estate and,
particularly, land-price bubbles.

At this point, these are all speculative hypotheses. But they are in service of a broad point in which I have high confidence. Just as a world
with high-priced energy is different in many respects from a world with
low-priced energy, so too a world with much lower real interest rates
is likely to be very different than our past experience. These differences
will require extensive exploration.

D.   *International Dimensions*

There is a huge international dimension to all of this taken up in my
recent work with Gauti Eggertsson and others (Eggertsson et al. 2016).
We argue that since global capital markets are at least substantially in-

tegrated, secular stagnation is likely to be a contagious malady. This idea is closely related to Ben Bernanke's "savings glut" hypothesis (Bernanke 2005). While I do not think it is reasonable to attribute a 25-year downward trend in real interest rates to the emergence of a few current account surplus countries, it surely is the case that real interest rates are determined on a global scale, and that there have been in recent years sharp changes in saving-investment imbalances in developing countries.

The relationship between secular stagnation and the functioning of the international monetary system requires extensive consideration. Does the current system force asymmetric adjustment with deficit countries contracting spending, but surplus countries not expanding it? How do exchange rates move when interest rate movements currently and prospectively are constrained by the zero lower bound? To what extent is an international lender of last resort necessary for global financial stability? In a world where fiscal monetary coordination within countries is difficult, how can cooperation across instruments and countries be achieved?

E.   In Demand-Short World, Should Macro Spillovers Be Ignored?

Finally, the neoclassical synthesis under which many economists have operated holds that since stabilization policy can achieve full employment, microeconomic questions can be thought of in microeconomic terms without reference to any aggregate demand spillovers. But in a world where a significant part of the time economies are demand constrained, as implied by the belief that central banks are going to fail to attain their inflation target for the next 10 years, it is hard to be this serene. What effects of microeconomic policies should be assumed to "count" and which should be assumed to be offset by macropolicies? This is now a very live question.

Endnotes

For acknowledgments, sources of research support, and disclosure of the author's material financial relationships, if any, please see http://www.nber.org/chapters/c13788.ack.

1. One can raise technical quibbles about comparing FOMC policy rate forecasts with the markets, such as that the Fed forecasts are conditional, while the market is the unconditional mean. Or that the only one of the 19 different dots that matters is Chair Yellen's dot. But no matter how one massages the dots, the point that the Federal Reserve's interest rate forecasts are not credible to the market will remain.

References

Bernanke, B. S. 2005. "The Global Saving Glut and the US Current Account Deficit." FRS Speech no. 77, Board of Governors of the Federal Reserve System.

Blanchard, O. 2016. "Do DSGE Models Have a Future?" PIIE Policy Brief, Peterson Institute for International Economics, August.

Blanchard, O., E. Cerutti, and L. Summers. 2015. "Inflation and Activity—Two Explorations and Their Monetary Policy Implications." IMF Working Paper.

Blanchard, O., and L. Summers. 1986. "Hysteresis and the European Unemployment Problem." In *NBER Macroeconomic Annual*, vol. 1, ed. S. Fischer, 15–78. Cambridge, MA: MIT Press.

Caballero, R. J., E. Farhi, and P.-O. Gourinchas. 2016. "Safe Asset Scarcity and Aggregate Demand." NBER Working Paper no. 22044, Cambridge, MA.

DeLong, J. B., and L. Summers. 2012. "Fiscal Policy in a Depressed Economy." Brookings Papers on Economic Activity, Spring. https://www.brookings.edu/bpea-articles/fiscal-policy-in-a-depressed-economy/.

Eggertsson, G., N. Mehrotra, S. Singh, and L. Summers. 2016. "A Contagious Malady? Open Economy Dimensions of Secular Stagnation." NBER Working Paper no. 22299, Cambridge, MA.

Friedman, M. 1968. "The Role of Monetary Policy." *American Economic Review* 58 (1): 1–17.

Gordon, R. J. 2015. "Secular Stagnation: A Supply-Side View." *American Economic Review* 105 (5): 54–59.

Greenwood, R., S. Hanson, J. Rudolph, and L. Summers. 2014. "Government Debt Management at the Zero Lower Bound." Working Paper no. 5, Hutchins Center on Fiscal and Monetary Policy at Brookings, September 30.

Greenwood, R., and D. Scharfstein. 2013. "The Growth of Finance." *Journal of Economic Perspectives* 27 (2): 3–28.

IMF. 2014. "Is It Time for an Infrastructure Push? The Macroeconomic Effects of Public Investment." In *World Economic Outlook*, ch. 3. International Monetary Fund. http://www.imf.org/external/pubs/ft/weo/2014/02/.

Kennedy, J. F. 1963. *Economic Report of the President*. Washington, DC: United States Government Printing Office.

Lucas, R. E. 1987. *Models of Business Cycles*. New York: Basil Blackwell.

———. 2003. "Macroeconomic Priorities." *American Economic Review* March: 1–14.

Nordhaus, W. D. 1987. "Forecasting Efficiency: Concepts and Applications." *Review of Economics and Statistics* 69 (4): 667–74.

Phelps, E. S. 1968. "Money-Wage Dynamics and Labor-Market Equilibrium." *Journal of Political Economy* 76 (4): 678–711.

Rachel, L., and T. D. Smith. 2015. "Secular Drivers of the Global Real Interest Rate." Staff Working Paper no. 571, Bank of England, December.

Summers, L. H. 1991. "The Scientific Illusion in Empirical Macroeconomics." In *New Approaches to Empirical Macroeconomics*, ed. S. Hylleberg and M. Paldam, 1–20. Oxford: Blackwell.

———. 2014. "US Economic Prospects, Secular Stagnation, Hysteresis, and the Zero Lower Bound." *Business Economics* 49 (2): 65–73.

———. 2015. "Demand Side Secular Stagnation." *American Economic Review* 105 (5): 60–65.

———. 2016. "Secular Stagnation and Monetary Policy." Federal Reserve Bank of St. Louis *Review* 98 (2): 93–110.